SPORTS

IN

NORTH

AMERICA

Volumes in This Series

SPORTS
IN
NORTH AMERICA

A DOCUMENTARY HISTORY

EDITED BY
GERALD R. GEMS

VOLUME 5

SPORTS ORGANIZED

1880–1900

Academic International Press
1996

SPORTS IN NORTH AMERICA. A DOCUMENTARY HISTORY
VOLUME 5. SPORTS ORGANIZED, 1880–1900
Edited by Gerald R. Gems

Copyright © 1996 by Academic International Press

ISBN: 0-87569-148-X

Composition by Diana Little

Printed in the United States of America

By direct subscription with the publisher

*A list of Academic International Press publications
is found at the end of this volume*

ACADEMIC INTERNATIONAL PRESS
POB 1111 • Gulf Breeze FL 32562–1111 • USA

CONTENTS

PREFACE

This volume intends to show the growth and development of sports in North America from 1880 to 1900 by utilizing the actual words of the participants. Therefore, only primary sources, complete with spelling, typographical and perhaps an occasional factual error, have been incorporated in the selections. The accounts include descriptive reports of actual events as witnessed by newspaper journalists, rules and regulations of sports governing agencies, philosophic criticisms, defenses, and rationales of sporting practices by academics, literary figures, and analytical observers, and personal expressions by the participants. Admittedly, such sources present a markedly middle class perception of sport during the period. A concerted effort was made to include the experiences of women, as well as minority racial and ethnic groups. Except for documents pertinent to the athletic experiences of middle class women, materials proved sparse, reflecting both the Anglo dominance of sport and the greater proliferation of the ethnic and African-American press after 1900.

For ease of reference chapters have been organized alphabetically. Editorial commentary introduces each chapter. Within chapters, topics, such as organization, commercialization, issues, etc. have been arranged chronologically to provide a context and background for subsequent developments. The Introduction and Chapter 1 provide a setting for the rapid expansion of sport during the period as new sport forms and new governing bodies were organized and formalized. The issues that accompanied such propagation and the social environment in which they occurred are also addressed. The following chapters treat each sport individually. Certain editorial decisions and restrictions limited the scope of the project. Only organized competitive activities requiring a greater measure of physical activity were included as sports; hence, chess was excluded. The lack of organized activity also limited references to working class activities, though particular sport forms such as boxing, and to some degree, baseball are indicative of such experiences. While newspapers, such as The Sporting Life, The Sporting and Theatrical Journal, or the National Police Gazette catered to male working class tastes and sporting interests, few copies survive, or have proved inaccessible or cost prohibitive.

Ethnic accounts, save that of American Indian tribes or African-Americans, were slightly more abundant, but in their native language form. Where they appear, I have relied on the English translations completed by the Works Progress Administration Foreign Language Press Survey in 1942.

Despite the vast preponderance of material on and influence of eastern groups in the United States, and residents of Montreal or Toronto in Canada, an effort has also been made to achieve greater balance in the regional development of sport throughout the continent.

Gerald Gems

North Central College

ACKNOWLEDGEMENTS

In a work of this scope one inevitably incurs many debts. Jill Herbig acquired the bulk of the selections through the inter-library loan services of Oesterle Library at North Central College. Carolyn Sheehy, the library director, assisted in copyright procurements. Numerous others contributed articles and supplementary materials: Lisa Pratt of the Bentley Historical Library at the University of Michigan; Ann Nelson of the Wyoming Department of Commerce; William Roberts of the Bancroft Library at the University of California, Berkeley; Sarah Blume of the Amateur Athletic Union; Jack Kelso at the University of British Columbia; Steve Gietschier of the Sporting News; Maida Goodwin, archivist at Smith College; John Duvall of the League of American Wheelmen; Jerry Schneider of the American Bowling Congress; Bill Stetson of the Babson Library at Springfield College; Philip Pines of the Trotting Horse Museum and Hall of Fame; Edward Andrus of the National Rifle Association; Kent Stephens of the College Football Hall of Fame; James Cuthbertson at Johnson C. Smith University; Karen Bednarski, curator at the United States Golf Association; Forrest Steinlage, historian of the American Turners; Susan Elliott of the National Hockey League; Donald Fritz of the Lacrosse Foundation; Sam Foulds, historian of the United States Soccer Federation; John Lutman of the D.B. Weldon Library at the University of Western Ontario; E. John B. Allen of Plymouth State College; Chas Ingles of the Canadian Ski Museum; Mary Lou LeCompte and William Richter at the University of Texas at Austin; Marie Baboyant, of the Montreal Municipal Library; and Jennifer Thomas, Colleen Dempsey, and Paul Lemieux of the National Archives of Canada. Numerous librarians at the Library of Congress, the Special Collections of the Regenstein Library at the University of Chicago, the Chicago Historical Society, and the Chicago Public Library were particularly helpful in fulfilling my innumerable requests. Don Morrow reviewed portions of the manuscript. The biggest thanks to Barbara Anderson, Rosemarie Schwantes and Becky Botos whose word processing skills proved invaluable. Their diligence and good cheer in meeting deadlines despite other myriad duties are most sincerely appreciated.

I dedicate this book to my family; for my father, who was my first and still my best coach; my mother and siblings, who cheered my efforts; and my wife and children, who give me the incentive to carry on.

INTRODUCTION

As North America moved toward greater urbanization in the latter decades of the nineteenth century, so too, did its sporting pastimes undergo rapid transformation. The largely recreational pastimes of rural folk became more formalized as people moved to the cities and urban centers expanded their geographic boundaries and their economic, political and social influence. As larger numbers of people came together in the growing towns and cities, and the sons and daughters of the upper classes met in educational institutions, they found common interests in their leisure activities. As early as the 1820s New Yorkers had organized a club for the purposes of harness racing. Horseracing associations and baseball teams proliferated by mid-century. Such groups brought formal organization to sport by codifying and standardizing rules and regulations for play. Emanating from eastern cities in the United States and from Montreal and Toronto in Canada, the regulating agencies intended to become national governing bodies by the 1880s. Between 1880 and 1900 Canadians formed at least ten national sports organizations; and more than a dozen similar associations established themselves in the United States. In Canada middle class Anglophones dominated the governance groups, while white, Anglo-Saxon Protestant males held power in the United States. Both adhered to the class based amateur ideology established by the British. Inevitably, that ideology clashed with American principles of democracy and the parallel system of professional athletic leagues already established in the 1870s. Administrative bodies brought order and structure to sporting activities and in the process new sport forms emerged. Between 1880-1900 ice hockey, golf, and Canadian football assumed modern forms, while handball, basketball, volleyball, and auto racing appeared in the United States. Previously recreational leisure activities such as bicycling, bowling, swimming, gymnastics, tennis and field sports like archery, fishing, and riflery were incorporated within the formal competitive framework.

Industrialization accompanied urbanization and fueled the growth of cities, particularly in northeastern and midwestern America. As factories and commercial businesses replaced open land they limited playing spaces. Upper and middle class participants banned together in athletic clubs and acquired their own sporting facilities, while professional teams built their own specialized sites. The working class was left with a diminishing number of vacant lots and a growing need for the burgeoning parks and playground movement.

The industrial clock seemingly regulated leisure time, particularly for the largely immigrant working class that flooded American cities after 1880. Historians have too often assumed that a six day work week left little time for leisure. However, ongoing studies continue to unravel a rich sporting and leisure life, often centered in churches, ethnic athletic clubs, labor unions, saloons and the streets. The uneven nature of employment, labor strikes, and economic declines left ample time for leisure and engendered issues over its use. The largely native Protestant upper classes often favored a strict adherence to Sabbatarianism, while a growing immigrant, non-Protestant labor force engaged in drinking, gambling, and active sporting ventures. Such active leisure pursuits of the popular culture clashed with upper class attempts to instill a passive high culture based on European models and divergent perceptions of morality.

The formal organization of sport within the urban-industrial complex followed a particular process that brought the various factions together; albeit under the dominant commercial interests. Under the guidance of capitalists and middle class managers, sporting practices assumed values congruent with those of work. They became more structured and regulated; and in the interest of time management, more efficient in form as rule changes and administrative practices reconstructed games to fit commercial needs. Training became more scientific, efficient, and specialized, which fostered greater production as measured by quantitative scores, records, and wins.

Sport assumed an even greater proportion of the entertainment for urban residents during the latter part of the nineteenth century. Urbanization provided a substantial and growing clientele of spectators willing to pay for their pleasure. Entrepreneurial opportunities abounded for promoters and players alike. Highly skilled players sold their services as professionals, drawing crowds to watch them perform. For many, sport symbolized the American dream of socioeconomic mobility. Athletes and teams were advertised as commercial products and drew considerable media coverage as promoters pushed toward the mass leisure culture of the twentieth century. Winning teams boosted civic pride and reinforced already existent commercial rivalries, so businessmen became ardent supporters of local contingents. By the 1880's the growing regulation of sport and its practitioners by governing agencies and employers, in the case of professional athletes, spawned questions and issues relevant to the nature of its administration.

Professional baseball players openly revolted, forming their own league to gain a greater share of the profits and end employer impositions. The governing bodies of amateur sport in both Canada and the United States struggled with the issues of professionalism throughout the 1880-1900 period as they tried to extend their control and authority.

The growth of sport and the purposes of the governing bodies were aided by the rapid development of technology. Widespread transport and communication networks stimulated expansion and influence beyond the eastern enclaves as the sports network began to assume the dimensions of a truly national sporting culture in both the United States and Canada. Electricity allowed for new instrumentation for more accurate measurement and lighting of arenas. Motorized vehicles spawned whole new sport forms, while technological advances in equipment prompted change in less incremental fashion in numerous sports, such as baseball, cycling, hockey, and harness racing. Photography allowed for the improvement of technique and performance, and visual images enhanced fans' interests.

As sporting interests grew during the period, cultural leaders found it necessary to rationalize the need for sport. Scientists viewed the body as a machine that could be made to run more efficiently and effectively and sports performance served as the measuring stick of human capabilities. Prestigious universities, such as Yale, initiated nutritional studies to determine the best fuels for the engine; while Harvard and the newly founded University of Chicago hired professional coaches to elicit the utmost in training methods. Psychologists believed that physical fitness held a correlation to moral development and human evolutionary progress; therefore sport served as an essential component in the training of youth. The Young Men's Christian Association assumed prominence as a promoter of wholesome sports and Christian values. Interscholastic athletics, in particular, served the utilitarian purposes of leadership training and character development among young males. Sports participation might counteract the perceived effeminate tendencies of the modern world by producing rugged, virile young men who had learned the value of both competition and cooperation in team play.

Not all shared in that idealized view. Middle class women eschewed the competitive male model and began organizing their own athletic efforts as social affairs in colleges and bicycle clubs around the country. Only a handful of women challenged Victorian strictures or the male power structures to become professional athletes.

For both men and women sport served a regenerative function, as a healthful antidote to the modern sedentary lifestyle and as a wholesome moral alternative to wanton leisure activities. Sport held various meanings and served several other functions to its multitude of practioners as well. Particular sport forms, such as yachting or horseracing, distinguished social elites from their inferiors and allowed for ostentatious displays of wealth. Golf and tennis, also popular among the rich, but financially accessible to the growing middle class, spawned country clubs and exclusive associations that distanced both groups from the laboring masses. Ethnic groups set themselves apart from the mainstream native society by their sporting organizations. Gymnastic clubs, like the German turners, Bohemian sokols, and Polish falcons, crossed class lines in an attempt to reinforce European traditions and an Old World culture. They persisted over generations but eventually succumbed to assimilation as Americanized immigrant offspring adopted native sport forms. African-Americans readily adopted the dominant sporting modes but faced exclusionary practices. Organized baseball enforced a surreptitious ban on black players by the 1880s, and John L. Sullivan, the heavyweight champion, refused the challenges of black boxers. In the 1890s Isaac Murphy enjoyed great success as a top jockey and Major Taylor won the national cycling championship; but both were forced out of competition. The white media provided almost no coverage of African-American athletes, for their success threatened the dominant precepts of white superiority inherent in Social Darwinism. For the most part, African-Americans were forced to develop their own parallel sporting structures; and they did so after 1900 when increasing numbers of black migrants moved to the relative freedom of northern cities. Newly established black newspapers duly chronicled such developments thereafter.

Nationalism also played a significant role in the growth of sport. While both Canada and the United States derived much of their sporting heritage from Great Britain, sport allowed for some cultural distinction. Sports such as ice hockey and lacrosse in Canada pointed to geographic as well as cultural differences. But whereas Canadians sought to maintain formal ties to the mother country, United States citizens opted for greater disengagement. As the United States economic growth began to challenge the British empire and the European powers for world leadership, competitive sport served a symbolic function for nationalists. International tours, athletic rivalries, and outright challenges transpired with the connotation of cultural superiority at stake. Such nationalistic sentiments doomed the idealism of the modern Olympic movement from its inception in 1896. Numerous factors contributed to the growth and development of sport over the course of the nineteenth century, but most current sport forms took on their modern appearance between 1880-1900. Governing bodies structured organizational frameworks and instituted rules and regulations that remain largely intact. The following chapters provide narrative accounts of that process.

Chapter 1

THE ORGANIZATION AND RATIONALIZATION OF SPORT

By 1880 American society had, for the most part, overcome the traditional religious opposition to sport. Although Sabbatarian issues persisted into the twentieth century, sport
assumed utilitarian social functions in the latter part of the nineteenth century. For cultural leaders who perceived a cultural and physical decline in the more sedentary modern world, sport served as a robust antidote. For upper and middle class males who perceived a growing effeminacy due to maternal influences, sport symbolized masculine
virility, strength, and power. Religious leaders who had previously shunned sport came
to realize that it might be utilized to promote wholesome moral values rather than the
gambling and drinking bouts often associated with its practice. Psychologists reasoned
that physical training might produce a strong neuromuscular system, and hence, will-
power capable of overcoming evil temptations. The Young Men's Christian Association rose to prominence during the latter part of the century as a strong proponent of
such salvation through "muscular Christianity."

Social reformers found in sport a means to assimilate the tide of European immigrants that flooded American cities after 1880. Boston, New York, and Chicago structured city parks and playgrounds to provide leisure spaces. Other towns and cities soon
followed. Trained instructors provided initiation to American sports and games, and instilled their inherent values of competition and team cooperation in immigrant offspring. Settlement houses sprung up in immigrant neighborhoods to foster similar
ventures in "Americanization."

Town and city teams fostered a sense of community and civic pride; but ethnic social athletic clubs also allowed immigrants to retain traditional customs and a separate
identity outside of the mainstream culture. Nationalists who feared such ethnic influences as a threat to their own cultural dominance, also found usefulness in sport. By
organizing and regulating sport associations and governance bodies they might eventually subsume such groups. International competitions allowed the nationalists to
challenge British and European pretensions of cultural superiority. The modern Olympic Games, despite more idealistic intentions, proved a convenient venue for such
objectives.

Sport also accommodated the rising feminist movement and rebellious youth. Males
rationalized that the growing numbers of female athletes might produce healthy native
offspring to counteract the low-born immigrants. In the cities organized sport programs
could attract delinquent youth and rehabilitate them as a means of social control. Such
objectives proved elusive as youth organized their own athletic enterprises, adapting
others to fit their own needs, and pursued the professional models that promised ce-
lebrity and greater socioeconomic status. In short, sport held diverse meanings and

values for various groups between 1880 and 1900; but the roots of a national sporting culture, that took hold in the following decades, are clearly evident.

THE RATIONALE FOR SPORT

The following brief editorial, adopted from Outing, (September 1884), p. 461, provides a sense of the burgeoning nationalism, an apologia for defeat, and the perception of sports as healthful.

AMERICAN ATHLETICS

It is rather significant of the growth and importance of athletic life in America that her representatives, who have been contesting this summer with the best specimens of physical culture to be found in England,-the mothercountry of outdoor life,-should have made a record not only much better than was expected, but one which is also a surprise to our friends over the ocean, and to meet which they were put on their mettle. The American Lacrosse team is undoubtedly the best collection of individual players that could be got together in this country. It was, perhaps to be expected that their record of victories would be a good one, for lacrosse is essentially an American game, and American men would naturally be supposed to have imbibed the facility and alertness which the native Indians display in its graceful and yet vigorous and exciting manoeuvres. It was some-what different with the Philadelphia cricketers; but in their case results have been very satisfactory. America is not a cricketing country, and it is not likely that there will ever be developed much national enthusiasm here for a game which takes a superabundance of leisure, on the part of spectators and players for the completion of each game. It is not often that Americans can devote two days to an outdoor contest of this kind. Englishmen, however, have the time, the means, and the inclination to make cricket a finished and skilful sport. At this writing the Philadelphians have not only beaten amateur clubs of the same relative standing in England that they hold here themselves, but have also vanquished and played creditable games with some of the more famous and powerful county elevens. Some of our runners and walkers, too, who have been trying their feet on English soil at the largest of English athletic games, have covered themselves with athletic glory, more than once breaking the records.

All this points in the direction of a state of things which we are most glad to see. Every one knows that English out-door life has done great things for that nation. It has made its men manly and robust, and its women healthy and physically capable. It is just as well-known that too many American men are flat-chested, and too many American women are chronic invalids. We want to see the time come when our out-door life shall be as genuine and as wholesome as that in the British Isles. The work that these

Americans have been doing this summer cannot fail to help us towards that time. It will create an interest, will spur on those who have already begun, and will help us to see how gentlemen, without neglecting the serious duties of social, intellectual, and business life, may at the same time do their duty by their physiques,-a duty which is really just as serious and necessary as that of any other phase of life, although we have been very slow in coming to believe it.

Professor Eugene Richards of Yale championed the benefits of athletic participation in several articles by employing scientific rationalizations comparing the physiological capacities of athletes to non-athletes. The following excerpts are derived from an article in The Popular Science Monthly, (April 1888), pp. 721-732.

COLLEGE ATHLETICS AND PHYSICAL DEVELOPMENT

...Now I say that, by their various athletic organizations, young men are doing this very thing for themselves that children do in play. They establish in the colleges a system of training for their various sports which affects not only the members of the higher institutions of learning, but which reaches almost every young man in the land. To express the idea in Dr. Sargent's words, "the college clubs look to the academies, the academies to the schools, the schools to the homes and firesides, to furnish candidates for athletic honors." Dr. Sargent proposes this as one of his objections to making "excellence in achievement the primary object of athletic exercise." But it is the reward which this same "excellence in achievement" receives that brings forward good material and stimulates an increasing number of men to exercise, who would never think of doing so without this stimulus. One is at a loss to understand how this fact should account (as Dr. Sargent says it does account) for the "lack of active interest in athletics." On the contrary, it is one of the principal causes of that active interest; it keeps young men in training, holds them to regular, systematic exercise, in season and out of season, through an important and critical period of their growth; it sends them into the gymnasium when the season forbids practice in the field; it restrains them from excesses, from smoking and drinking, and from late hours; it brings the whole force of college opinion to bear in favor of a healthy, moral life. To be sure, the desire to defeat a rival club or team is not the highest motive of the human mind; the honor of winning a medal in a race is not the greatest honor which earth can afford. The glory of being champions at any game seems puerile to serious-minded people; but we must take young people as we find them. If we can not induce them to exercise by the "deep moral significance" of "the beauty of symmetry of form," we must lay hold of the motives, not wrong, which do influence them. The majority of them not being open to the highest motives, we take the next best motives which appeal to them. That is the principle on which all education is conducted. Competitions, prizes, medals, honors, appeal to students, move them, and hold them to efforts which higher and worthier objects fail to call forth. By these we educate them to habits which fit them to receive the higher motives. They are their schoolmasters to train them for a better life. So it is in athletic sports. By habits of exercise from earliest youth young men are educated to appreciate the value of it. Accustomed to feel the good effects of it in themselves, or to see the good of it in the person of some upholder of the honor of their club, they learn to admire the cause of this good. The prominent athletes present examples of beauty of form and vigorous health. The sight of them stimulates many a man to try on his own person the effect of the training which he sees embodied in the winners of prizes or championships. More than this, having once learned the value of exercise to health, he forever associates together health and exercise in a necessary companionship. So the athletes preach to all men by example...

The objections of expense and time I have considered elsewhere, (Popular Science Monthly, March, 1884) but will assert here that, in these respects, athletics merely keep pace with other undertakings of modern times. More money is spent upon education than formerly. More money goes to gymnasiums. There is more money in the land. Success as well as failure costs more. But we are getting better results. We are inducing more people to exercise. The increased cost is due to the better results. Like every other good, exercise costs something. The real question is, whether the results are worth the cost. I think they are. I maintain that the saving to the health and morals of our young men all over the land is worth the whole cost of their athletic organizations.

As to time, it is undoubtedly true that some young men spend too much time in athletic exercises, but the majority of them do not do so. They spend no more time than is good for them, at a period of their lives when they are laying up physical capital. And the fact that, to be well prepared for contests, successful athletes have to keep in training the greater portion of the year, instead of during a small part of it, as formerly, is one the best features of the present system of athletics. It gives them healthy occupation for their leisure moments, and enforces habits of good living all the year, instead of for a few months...

"President Garfield said: 'There is no way in which you can get so much out of a man as by training; not in pieces, but the whole of him; and the trained men, other things being equal, are to be the masters of the world.'"

At no college in the land is more careful attention given to physical development by means of gymnastic exercises than at Amherst...

Notice Dr. Hitchcock's (Amherst Physical Director) conclusion, that "athletism does not seem to depend so much on physical gifts, accidents, or circumstances, as in the energy of will which is put into the muscles... It is the intelligent training, and not the big measures, which determine the standard of excellence in our athletic feats and sports." This will-power, guided by intelligence, makes not only successful athletes, but successful men. The training which young men receive in their sports possesses its highest value by virtue of the fact that it brings forth some of the best powers of mind and character, not because it develops mere bone and muscle.

It must not be forgotten that the conditions of American life have changed so greatly in the last century that, in order to view education aright, it is necessary to take counsel of new considerations. To be sure, the material to be worked on seems to be the same. The youthful mind and character are unchanged. Yet there are influences at work in these modern times which are destined to sap the physical strength of our young men, and thus impair the vigor of their minds and emasculate their characters, unless these influences be clearly recognized and continually counteracted. We will mention two of these influences:

1. CONCENTRATION OF POPULATION INTO CITIES.-According to the last census report, of every one hundred inhabitants in the United States, there were dwelling in towns of eight thousand inhabitants and above-

| In 1790.............3.3 | In 1850............12.5 |
| In 1820.............4.9 | In 1880............22.5 |

But these figures do not tell the whole story. Towns have grown into cities, and cities have added to their population enormously in the thirty years from 1850 to 1880, as will be seen from the following figures, showing the number of cities of various grades:

Number of Cities having Inhabitants of

IN	20,000 - 40,000	40,000 - 75,000	75,000 - 125,000	125,000 - 250,000	250,000 - 500,000	500,000 - 1,000,000	Over 1,000,000
1850...	14	7	3	3	1	1	1
1880...	55	21	9	7	4	3	1

At the last census fifty cities held 15 4/10 per cent of the aggregate population of the country. Whatever may be said in favor of city life for adults, nothing can be said in favor of its influence upon the vigor or morals of young men. Life in the cities is faster than in the country. The incentives to excess in mental work are greater. The wear and tear of the nervous system is more intense. At the same time the opportunity or necessity of physical effort for the young men of the well-to-do classes is reduced to a minimum.

2. INCREASING KNOWLEDGE DEMANDING MORE BRAIN-CULTURE.- Thus increasing demands are made upon the brain and nerves by the faster life of the cities, and by the need of a better culture to meet the competitions of that life, while the opportunities are lessened for strengthening the body against these demands. When the population was extensively engaged in rural or mechanical pursuits, without the division of labor which now obtains, the bodies of our young men were hardened by toil and invigorated by life in the open air.

That the concentration of population is reflected in the attendance at our colleges can be established by an examination of catalogues. The fact is certainly evident at Yale Univeristy, as will be seen from the accompanying figures. Of every one hundred students in the catalogue, there were registered as coming from cities of thirty thousand inhabitants and upward-

IN CATALOGUE OF	Academic Department	Sheffield Scientific School
1856 - '57...............	21 1/3	18
1871 - '72...............	44	39
1886 - '87...............	55	58

Anything that will help to counteract the disintegrating forces of city life, that will help to strengthen our city young men against the insidious forces of ill-health, against the forces of low-living, that will tend to keep young men out of disorders, out of crimes against self and society, is to be welcomed as an ally of the best education. I maintain that the system of athletics existing at our colleges and in our athletic clubs in all the cities of the land does this. It does more. Its work is not only to save but to form men. It helps our schools and colleges to send out into the world not merely scholarly ascetics, but men full of force and energy, men of strong fiber, physical and moral.

The modern gymnasium is a necessary auxiliary to every well equipped college, but it owes much of its increasing usefulness and importance to the fact that it is a training-place for athletes. There is no real antagonism between the athletic field and the gymnasium. It is not necessary to depreciate one in order to exalt the other. Existing side by side, and both rightly used, they will best contribute to the evolution of the "typical man."

E.L. Godkin established himself as one of the nation's foremost social critics. In the following piece, adopted in its entirety from the Nation, (20 December 1894), pp. 457-458, he provides a counterpoint, critiquing the argument of sport as preparation for war and finding fault with the rising spectatorsip that precluded active participation. Large crowds of spectators characterized the movement toward a commercialized leisure culture that featured sporting events as entertainment.

ATHLETICS AND HEALTH

In the recent discussion of football and of athletics in colleges the relation of athletics to health and to the sedentary lives which most college graduates have to lead, has been strangely overlooked. The football champions have, as a rule, destroyed their influence by their extravagance. For instance, Prof. Richards of Yale, in Walter Camp's learned work on 'Football Facts and Figures,' says: "Personal encounters of some sort seem absolutely necessary to the education of young men, especially men of the strongest character. Such young men, judiciously trained, constitute the best citizens of the state, and a state full of such citizens becomes thereby safest to live in, for such men are its best defence." Dr. Shattuck of Boston, in like manner, defends football as providing us with national defenders on the battle-field in case the European Powers should attack us. These deliverances have also received a very solemn endorsement from "a captain, a most valuable player," in a class prayer-meeting, who is reported by Prof. Richards to have declared on that occasion "that the great success of the team the previous season was in his opinion due to the fact that among the team and substitutes there were so many praying men." So that not only is the game good as a preparation for war, but the Almighty takes a hand in it and sees that "the praying men" get most touchdowns and goals.

These gentlemen who regard football as a good preparation for service on the battle-field are apparently under the impression that war is still conducted in the old Homeric fashion; that is, that the combatants are ranged in line a few yards apart, and, after an exchange of bad language, "clinch" and "slug" each other as they roll over in the mud, each trying to stab the other with a spear or short sword, or hold him down till another man on the same side can break his back with a club. It is extraordinary that such ideas should prevail; that, within thirty years of our own civil conflict, people should think that a battle consists of personal encounters. Battles in our day, and more and more every year as weapons improve, are nearly all carried on and decided at long range. Assaults on the front of a well-armed enemy grow rarer and rarer, because the modern rifle fire sweeps everything away and gets within a thousand yards. In the Franco-German war whole regiments perished under fire from an enemy they never saw, and with smokeless powder this result is likely to be more and more frequent. What a soldier most needs in our day, therefore, is not agility or strength of muscle, but what we may call greatness of soul, a heroic spirit, a capacity to meet death and wounds calmly, and to see them all around him without flinching. The notion that a "centre rush" or a "half-back" is any better off under such conditions than a quiet student who had drunk deep "at the fountain of heavenly radiance," is too absurd for discussion. Let any one read the account of Prince Andre's adventures at the battle of Borodino in Tolstoi's 'War and Peace,' and he will understand what we mean.

But even if war were now Homeric, or even Greek or Roman-that is carried on by means of personal collision, as it was down to the invention of gunpowder-the superiority of athletes for purposes of national defence would still be open to serious question. Pugilists are notoriously, in our time, not good soldiers. We believe no officer who cared to make a figure in a campaign would like to command a regiment of them. That any set of men can occupy themselves intently and continuously with the strengthening of their muscles and the improvement of their wind, as a preparation for extraordinary physical exertion, without damage to their mental and moral parts, is a chimera, and the people who are training up our young men in this belief have a good deal to answer for. What we need in our youths is the capacity for high resolve, and noble aims and firm courage which does not need to be stimulated by bets or gate-money.

Are we, then, opposed to athletes? By no means. We note with regret Dr. Sargent's complaint that, while football is all the rage, but little use is made of the fine gymnasium of Harvard College. This probably means that the rest of the college takes exercise in watching the football and other teams. College students, almost to a man, are intended to follow sedentary callings. They are not meant to punt, or tackle, or buck, or close with sword and shield, but to sit in counting rooms or studies, or plead in courts. Their training at college, therefore, should in all respects fit them for these pursuits and daily exercise is as necessary for the full and efficient discharge of these sedentary duties as for football, or baseball, or rowing. The men are rare indeed who can meet the demands of modern life in the pulpit, at the bar, or in the counting-room or editorial office, without a certain amount of physical exertion in the open air. Now and then there is a man who can do without this, or with very little of it, like Mr.

Evarts, or Mr. Choate, or the late Mr. David Dudley Field; and such a man has a distinct advantage over his rivals in the same field. For most men, it is an absolute necessity, if they mean to do their work well, to be what the athletes call "fit," and able to stand the competition which is the law of modern life. But then the man who takes more than he needs, or who accustoms himself to conditions which are not general among his contemporaries also, weights himself in the race as much as the man who takes less than he needs. The young fellow who comes from college requiring three hours' daily exercise with dumbbells, clubs, big stones and weights, of course, other things being equal, goes down befoe the young fellow who keeps in condition with an hour's walk or other exercise. If, too, he is so used to fresh air that one hour in a court-room muddles his brain or makes him feel faint, the other man who can stand three hours of it without damage has a distinct advantage over him, and will use it remorselessly.

No one can dip into the literature of football without seeing that it is treated throughout with an extravagance that borders on insanity. This is sure to pass: all crazes run their course. But it has done and is doing a great mischief in turning away the minds of the youth of the country from the value and necessity of moderate exercise. It has begot and is spreading the fallacy that if you are not a member of a team, and have no coach, it is not worth while doing anything to keep up your bodily vigor. It leads men to suppose that bodily vigor is of no great use unless you are going to play in a match, or to fetch and carry under the stern eye of a "captain." But the truth is that every lad in college is preparing for that greatest of all matches, the battle of life, in which he has to meet antagonists about whose strength and prowess he has no "tip," and who will surely "down" him unless he downs them. This is a battle, too, in which sound health and good spirits are of infinitely more importance than muscular strength, and in which ninety-nine men out a hundred can make a respectable figure only by maintaining their physical vigor.

In the following article, Mary Taylor Bissell, a female physician, addressed the rapidly changing lifestyles of women. Sport and exercise served to alleviate the ills of urbanization; scientists even proposed a correlation between systematic physical training and increased intelligence or morality. Bissell invoked the anthropometric measurements then popular as supporting evidence for her claims, which appeared in The Popular Science Monthly, (December 1894), pp. 145-153.

ATHLETICS FOR CITY GIRLS .

If any of my readers should chance to belong to a hardy boat crew or to a college ball team, or if in days past they have ever been numbered in such a muscular community, they will doubtless feel that the title of my paper is its own executioner. For so long as baseball and football and the boat race stand for the national expression of athletics, the experiences of girls in any similar department will seem like comparing moonlight unto sunlight, and water unto wine. In speaking of athletics for city girls, however, we shall use the phrase in a liberal sense, including not only out-of-door sports but also the general feats and training of the gymnasium. The spirit for physical recreation has invaded the atmosphere of the girl's life as well as that of the boy, and demands consideration from her standpoint.

Before we consider the influence of athletics, we may well inquire into the physical status of the girl. What is the type of the city girl, and is there any reason to believe that she is in need of any new influence to further her development? In age she is presumably under twenty; at all events, she has not yet reached that period of stable womanly development which physiology places at about the age of twenty-five. She is presumably well housed, well fed, and more or less well clothed, according to the intelligence of her guardians. She spends at least half of her young life in the schoolroom, most of that time at a desk in more or less cramped and unfavorable positions. The average city schoolgirl spends from two to four hours daily in study, according to her ambition, takes a music, drawing, or dancing lesson in addition twice or thrice weekly, and ends her day with her books or in society, depending upon her environment.

These engagements leave her about one hour's time for outdoor life and exercise, and this consists for the most part in a walk on the avenue, or a shopping expedition which often ends in a crowded, ill-ventilated store. Riding and driving are recreations, as a rule, only indulged in by the favored few. Her summer may be a season for physical freedom, but is often one of social dissipation spent in the atmosphere of a fashionable resort.

The product of these various influences is intellectually more or less successful; certainly the American girl, clever, versatile, accomplished, is an interesting type of our civilization. If we analyze her physically we shall find that she possesses the first qualification of a fine physique-viz., height. Bowditch's measurements of ten thousand public-school children in and about Boston show that in stature they surpass their English neighbors, who are popularly supposed to be superior in that respect. The writer has measured between eight and nine hundred New York city girls and women, and has found the average stature with them equal to Bowditch's measurements, sometimes surpassing them, many exhibiting unusual height. In breadth of shoulders, waist, and hips the measurements show them to be fairly well developed, although the American type appears to be less generous in this respect than the English or the German. Happily, the tendency of the day to out-of-door sports has thrown the slim-waisted girl into the shadow of unfashionableness, so that this species of deformity does not necessarily constitute part of the type. In these and certain other respects Nature has evidently intended by her original drawing to give the girls what we may call a fair chance.

But the average city girl of our experience has two or three marked physical deficiencies that are worth considering. The first of these is a shallow chest, the second is a lack of symmetry in the body, and the third is a deficiency in muscular development. The relation of the depth of the chest to the development of the vital organs is a highly important one. The "deep-chested Juno" is given us as a type of noble physical development, and we rightly associate such a conformation with what is known as the staying power. A deep chest offers a generous cage for a robust heart and expanded lungs, and is almost invariably found in athletes, who must have endurance, as well as in singers, whose efforts likewise must be long sustained. It has been found that persons most susceptible in the infection of phthisis commonly have a conformation which has been called the *phthisical habitus*-viz., a long, rather narrow, and especially a shallow chest, flattened from before backward. Whether Americans exhibit this conformation oftener than those of other nations is not precisely proved, but we are inclined to think that such is the fact. Certainly the shallow chest is present in the case of many girls examined by the writer.

The second noticeable feature, the lack of bodily symmetry, is a patent fact to all physicians who have been called upon to make physical examinations of the bodies of children, and the art of the dressmaker is continually required to conceal defects of this nature. They arise partly from habits of faulty postures in school or at home during the plastic period of growth, and largely from the coincident lack of muscular vigor which is due to the absence of proper training. From twenty-five to thirty per cent of all cases examined by the writer exhibit some degree of unsymmetrical development of the body, many of these cases showing a degree to lateral curvature of the spine, more or less marked, according to the influences which have been at work. It is a noteworthy fact that children are not born deformed, and therefore most of these minor asymmetries assume special importance as being acquired mainly through faulty hygienic conditions of environment which obviously call for every counteracting influence at our command.

The third deficiency we noted in the development of our city girl is the lack of muscle. With this we are also concerned-first, because a girl who has small muscular strength is continually living below her capacity for usefulness as well as pleasure; and second, because the external muscles of the body are the natural outlets for excessive nervous energy, as well as the great stimulators of the functions of circulation, digestion, and respiration, while the internal muscles are so widely distributed in the great organs of the body that their vigorous condition is absolutely necessary for its health. We have physiological reasons for believing that internal muscular structures often partake of the same flaccidity and nervelessness as is sometimes exhibited by the external muscles; the softened heart muscle following certain diseases or a relaxed condition of the muscular coats of the stomach is capable of working serious ill, as every practioner can testify.

That the muscle of girls is weaker than it need be we have ample proof in the statistics of our gymnasiums, which record the physical tests of strength taken at the beginning and the end of a course of physical exercise. These tests are taken with various dynamometers, and with these we find that a short course of two or three hours weekly, extending over six months, will often double the strength of the principal muscles of the body in girls from fifteen to twenty-five years of age.

Such improvement indicates that these girls were previously much below their own possibilities of development, and suggests what might have been done for them in this respect years before, had similar advantages been offered them earlier in life. The tests taken of "lung capacity" on the spirometer before and after the course, as well as measurements of the chest circumference, tell by their marked improvement the same story.

Apropos of the lack of muscular vigor in city-bred subjects we may note that oculists believe that the very marked increase in myopia among Americans during the past few years, which is especially noticeable in city life, is partly due to muscular relaxation, which deprives the tissues of the eye of their proper support and permits the degree of bulging of the globe which is an essential condition of this disease.

But granting the fact that her physical development is not perfect, what can we say of her general health? Passing by serious diseases, it is evident that our city girl has a variety of functional complaints which should have no place in the physical history of young people. Headaches, backache, dyspepsias, neuralgias are far more common than they should be. Nervously she is not stable, as the increasing number of nervous difficulties, neurasthenias, etc., would indicate. The emotional strain of conventional city life, which is felt more by the society girl than by the schoolgirl, is not an ideal atmosphere in which to cultivate the perfect flower of a stable character, and those who apparently bear it well do so at some expense of strength and nerve...

Given the limitations of a town environment, where and how shall she gain these things?...

First of all, every out-of-door sport that she can suitably undertake should be open to her, both in the sense of opportunity and also in that of consenting public opinion. The only two sports that are practicable during any considerable part of the city season are tennis and bicycling, for rowing is limited to too short a season to be considered, and riding is by reason of expense not open to the general public. As regards tennis, she is already possessor of the game so far as knowledge and public opinion are concerned, and, although objections have been raised to it on the score of its being too violent exercise, there appears to be nothing essential to the game which a healthy young woman may not engage in, if she is properly dressed. A girl who is delicate or who has any organic disorder should certainly consult her medical adviser before playing any very active game, but these exceptions should not be allowed to rule the game out for the large class of girls who are physcially qualified to enjoy and profit by it. The old rule of moderation in all things must obtain in this exercise as elsewhere.

The mention of the bicycle for women opens a field of mild controversy which is only important because some of the objections to its use are taken from the hygienic standpoint as well as from the social. Many objectors contend that the wheel is as undesirable for women as the sewing macine, while the majority of parents seriously object to what they feel to be the unpleasant publicity of the exercise. As a matter of health, which is of the first importance, the writer has made many inquiries among women who use the wheel regarding the effects of the exercise upon them, and has failed to discover a single case of injury or poor health resulting from its use. On the contrary, the testimony to its exhilarating and healthful effect is universal. Several other American physicians, qualified to speak from experience in their practice among women, have warmly commended its use. From the standpoint of a symmetrical exercise, the position is preferable to that on a horse...

The bicycle is one of the few out-of-door sports open to the average woman by reason of its convenience, comparative inexpensiveness, and pleasure; and if it need not be ruled out from hygienic reasons, I believe that we owe it to our girls to allow no others to interfere with its introduction. It is already used extensively in some of our largest cities, while in England it is popular with many whose word is fashion's law.

It can not be contended that it is essentially unwomanly. It is only at present, in cities like New York, unusual, peculiar, and therefore unfashionable. In the interests of sound health and physical recreation for the city girl the social objection may well be set aside, with the expectation that the introduction of the wheel for women will be followed by the best of results.

But with tennis practicable only in the spring and autumn, and cycling still a matter of the future, athletics for our city girls would seem to be narrowed to slender resources. What means can they employ during the long winter months for keeping muscle, nerve, and brain in good physical order? The well-ordered, properly equipped gymnasium would appear to be the only practicable substitute in the winter months for the invigorating sports possible only to the favored few, or necessarily limited to the summer season. In such a gymnasium some definite system is important. Whether it shall be Swedish or German, class work or individual practice, will be a question to be decided separately for each place. A good teacher can arouse interest with or without apparatus, in classes or individualizing her work, as required. The requirements for the building itself are abundance of fresh air and sunshine, space, and exacting cleanliness. A physician should direct the work of each pupil, endeavoring by special prescription to overcome existing deficiencies, to stimulate the will and energy in the sluggish, and to limit nervous expenditure in those of a nervous temperament.

A young girl entering such an institution will have every safeguard against harm thrown around her. Her age, strength, previous and present health will be inquired into, and heart and lungs tested to ascertain their soundness of exertion. Any lack of symmetry, as shown in the condition of the spine, shoulders, or chest, will be noted. Her inspiratory power and muscular strength will be recorded, and the individual equation will have due weight. She will be placed in a class where the general average of strength is equal to hers, but she will be advised to avoid or increase certain exercises, according to her personal needs, and to report to the director at certain intervals for further advise.

Is there any place where the quantity and quality of a girl's exercise is as carefully supervised as in this ideal gymnasium? In such an institution the system is a progressive one, and in the hands of a good instructor always remains interesting. By easy steps the pupils are led from simple to intricate exercises, reaching the most advanced work in the course of two years' training, always provided that by preliminary exercises they have gained sufficient strength and skill.

Our young pupil at the close of her hour's exercise takes a sponge or a spray bath or none at all, according to her prescription; always a brisk rub and a complete change of underclothing are advised. The general benefits to her of such training lie in the fact, first, that it exercises the entire body in a systematic, practicable manner, as no other city exercise can do. A horse, the bicycle, or a long walk, all admirable, require fair weather for their enjoyment. The gymnasium, dry, clean, cheerful, invigorating, offers variety, companionship, and physical recreation equally in storm or shine, and this is no small consideration in arranging a programme for the physical improvement of the city girl during the winter months. The regularity of the exercise is not the least of its benefits. When one has made a financial sacrifice for the pleasure of keeping a regular engagement, she has an excellent guarantee that the engagement will be met. We are all creatures of habit, and advantage should be taken of the fact in the physical as well as in the intellectual realm, and Nature's rewards are most generous to the child of system...

It is not unusual for girls to gain in six months' time several pounds in weight, two inches in chest circumference, and from twenty to fifty cubic inches in inspiratory power, while the dynamometers may show an increase in muscular strength of from fifty to one hundred per cent over the original tests...

The training of the nervous system, which is the immediate result of a systematic practice of gymnastics, is recognized as one of the greatest benefits of such exercise. It is known to physiologists that every group of muscles is controlled by certain nerve centers in the brain, and it is believed that in cases where the life and habits of the individual do not call out the activity of all the muscles, the brain areas which govern those muscles to that extent fail of development...

As illustrating the value of physical training in stimulating brain function, we have a series of observations made by Dr. Wey, Medical Director of the Elmira Reformatory, showing how dullards who took the lowest standard in scholarship, and in morals as well, became by simple but regular physical drill first more attentive, then more intelligent as to orders, less awkward (i.e., with better co-ordination of the body), and gradually, as the stimulation of the will and energy proceeded, actually better scholars, rising in some cases from the third to the first grade, and improving not only in physical appearance but in moral character. These results were entirely attributed to the awakening of mental energy through the reflex stimulation of muscular exercise.

To these benefits we may oppose the only objections we have known. The first is on the score of danger. As a matter of fact, there is little or no testimony to put upon this side that does not equally apply to many forms of exercise practiced by women, walking included. The theory that girls should not run or climb is long since exploded. Sick girls should not run or climb until they are well, but every physician knows that there would be fewer sick girls if running and climbing had always been part of a girl's early life.

Girls who have organic disease are not fit subjects for a gymnasium-there being a very few exceptions to this rule. Girls with serious spinal curvature require special exercises in the physician's office. Almost all other girls can only be benefited in a well-ordered gymnasium if they obey the rules and follow the advice offered...

A more valid objection to the gymnasium is that the exercise must be taken indoors, but this is largely overbalanced by the advantages of system and purpose in the course, and is reduced to its minimum by the fact that a well-ordered gymnasium is cool, clean, and well ventilated. The suggestion often proffered that domestic work offers as good a field for exercise for girls is not, in the writer's opinion, tenable. An atmosphere of dust is not an ideal one for physical training, and the elements of system as well as of physical recreation are lost in this scheme, for few households could arrange their economy so as to combine the schoolgirl's leisure with their own convenience, while the drudgery of the employment would cause it to be abandoned whenever possible.

It is not our intention to claim that the gymnasium is the permanently ideal place for every sort of physical training or athletic sport for girls, but only that it does at present offer the greatest good to the greatest number of our city girls in the direction of their physical development and recreation. An out-of-door inclosure for games and sports in pleasant weather would prove a great addition to its advantages. It does not

seem an impossible plan for the private schools of our city to co-operate in establishing such an out-of-door playground as this, with an instructor in games and sports, and
hours arranged for each school department. Such a ground would prove a practical and
useful extension of our too limited park life.

THE GROWTH OF SPORT

Both athletic participation, as a means of health, and athletic spectatorship, as entertainment, experienced phenomenal growth between 1880 and 1900. Spurred by urbanization, commercialization, and technological development, sporting activities assumed
greater importance in American culture. Electricity allowed for more night time events,
the telegraph provided instantaneous communication of results, and the print media
gave greater coverage to athletics, spawning the sports page. Richard Kyle Fox's National Police Gazette catered to the lurid and sporting interests of the bachelor subculture, while Alfred H. Spinks' Sporting News focused on a wider clientele. Both pub-
lishers recognized and greatly profited from the growing interest in sport.

Ethnic games, such as handball and lacrosse, became part of the American sport
fabric, while the British influence on developments in North America remained substantial, as evidenced by the introduction of golf and tennis from abroad. The games
of baseball and football continued to evolve during the period, and entirely new sports,
such as basketball, volleyball, and water polo appeared on the scene. In some cases,
the organization of such activities brought divergent groups closer to the mainstream
culture. In others, particularly the ethnic gymnastic clubs, practitioners remained tied
to European parent organizations and their sporting practices allowed them to resist
enculturation.

The growing interest in sport coupled with the normal socialization processes engendered several fads that facilitated the courting rituals of youth as well as commercial opportunities for entrepreneurs. The following details such events, as chronicled
by the Boston Globe, 4 July 1883, n.p.

SKATING BY THE SEA
SUCCESSFUL OPENING OF THE NANTASKET RINK-
NEARLY 30,000 SQUARE FEET OF SURFACE

The carrying capacity of the Nantasket steamboats making trips at 6:30 and 7
o'clock last evening was taxed to the utmost to carry the crowd which went from this
city to attend the opening of the Nantasket Roller Skating Rink. The doors were not
opened till 8 o'clock, but by 7:30 a large number of people had collected about the
main entrance.

A few minutes after 8 o'clock the band commenced to play, and the floor was
quickly crowded with skaters. There was a great rush for skates, but plenty were on

hand, and excellent arrangements for distributing them had been made. Shortly after 9 o'clock the floor was cleared, and Professor William H. Field gave an exhibition of fancy skating. Fancy bicycling by Professors Harry W. Tufts and Fred J. Sewall followed and their performance richly deserved the generous applause bestowed upon it. Miss Jennie Houghton performed some very remarkable fancy skating, and was followed by Professor J.R. Mayer, who also did some good work. After Professor Mayer had finished the guests were again admitted to the floor.

The opening was a great success, and much praise was bestowed upon the building and its management. The rink is a very large one being 220x128 feet, and it will be fitted up in the best possible style. The skating surface will accommodate nearly 1000 persons, and great care has been take to make the floor all that it should be. It was somewhat rough last night, but no doubt will shortly be put in perfect condition. Strict order will be preserved at all times at the rink, and to make this an easier task intoxicating liquors are forbidden on the premises. A cafe, 125x24 feet will be found a very pleasing feature of the establishment.

∽∞

The New York Times, 17 June 1890, p. 5, detailed the opening of the new Madison Square Garden, one of several specialized sites throughout North America that hosted high culture as well as sporting events.

OPENING OF THE NEW MADISON SQUARE GARDEN
TEN THOUSAND PEOPLE ASSEMBLE TO LISTEN
TO STRAUSS'S ORCHESTRA - A NOTABLE MUSICAL EVENT

A new and uncommon place of amusement was thrown open to the public last night. For months past there have been busy times around the site of the historic old Madison Square Garden, sacred to the memories of John L. Sullivan and P.T. Barnum, two men of widely different distinction. The old place, dirty, rickety, even dangerous, was razed to the ground, and in its place arose, with the strange celerity of contemporaneous building, the new Madison Square Garden, which was opened last night. The scene within the yellow walls was one of the most brilliant ever witnessed within an auditorium in this city. Much has been written about this great amphitheatre, but it must be seen to be appreciated. Every one should go and take a look at it, because it is one of the sights of the city.

As seen last night, the amphitheatre was a semi-elliptical structure, not to reality as large as the old Hippodrome, but in appearance larger. The easterly end is taken up with the proscenium arch and stage. The westerly end is a perfect network of boxes. If one can imagine one side of the auditorium of Covent Garden, London, put right on top of the other side, he will have a fair idea of the appearance of the west end of the new Madison Square Garden. Those who never saw Covent Garden must content themselves with picturing it as the front of a gigantic doll's house, filled with little rooms draped with red curtains and containing small animated dolls in evening dress. Stretching away from this array of boxes on either side are the galleries, and on the main floor are the parquet and orchestra chairs. Seats run up in an inclined plane under the first gallery, and just in front of these, raised a few feet above the parquet floor, are open boxes, like those of the dress circle in the Academy of Music, as it used to be.

Before going into any consideration of the merits of the entertainment something must be said as to the value of the amphitheatre for such performances as were given there last evening. The acoustics of this big auditorium are sufficiently good, but such a house requires a bigger band than that of Edward Strauss...

The immense auditorium was packed with people. There are said to be 8,000 seats and 200 boxes. Those who are fond of addition may amuse themselves with computing the number of persons in the house. The appearance of the audience was extremely brilliant. About everyone who is known to fame to have his name printed as a visitor at a summer resort was in the house, with the exception, of course, of those who have gone to the country or sailed abroad to enlighten the effete monarchies of Europe. A large part of the audience was in evening dress. The auditorium itself, as it appeared last night, was an imposing sight.

All the boxes and seats were filled, and there was an army of spectators standing. It was an assemblage that embraced representatives of almost every class and condition...

Walter Camp, writing for Harper's Weekly, 25 February 1893, p. 191, witnessed the growth of a national sporting culture as eastern influences spread westward.

CALIFORNIA ATHLETICS

Eastern athletes have already had opportunities for measuring their strength against rivals from the Middle States-but similar chances have not been offered of determining by Eastern standards what is the calibre of the athlete of the Pacific slope. It is not unnatural, therefore, that little trust has been placed in stories of performances made under Californian eyes and watches. But I can say, from recent experience, that the average Eastern man sets his standard of the performances of athletes across the continent at far too low a mark, and when contests come about, as they are sure to sooner or later, there will be surprises in store for us all. Primarily, in the climate itself lies a great advantage for the athlete of the Western coast. He can, if his training be not of so severe a nature as to make it unwise, keep in condition from one year's end to the other, and with only occasional exceptions, be sure of weather that will admit of almost daily exercise. An Eastern man at first misses that snap of cold in the air, that crispness and life, which seem to inspire our football men in November, but it is a decided question as to the value of that crispness in actual performances, and many believe-with good warrant, too-that not only a horse, but a man as well, can do more when there is no tingle of cold in the air. The stock that, in the horse line, is being bred at the Palo Alto farms, many believe, owes much to the climatic influences; and if this be true, the athlete on the Pacific slope will enjoy a similar advantage.

In making a journey through the charming ranches of the Santa Clara Valley one comes upon some fine specimens of physical development among not only the laborers but the proprietors of these favored farms. Perhaps the training of these robust fellows in the matter of food and drink would hardly accord with our notions of strictness, and certainly would not be advisable with men not accustomed to it, but it seemed to have no detrimental effect upon their physical condition. They drink the wines of the country with too great freedom. There were several instances where we had the opportunity of closely observing, and found the men of remarkable muscular development; nor were our observations of picked men only, but merely of the average. The boys brought up under such favoring conditions of out-door exercise not only for half the year, but really every day of the three hundred and sixty-five, will offer material for athletic development such as cannot be found in the East.

And the sports are by no means in their infancy. Track athletics, baseball, football, and boating are all receiving a fair share of attention, and records are being approached that will make the holders men well talked of when they journey East for competition. Henry, of the University of California, is a hurdler who will make our best flyers keep close to the timber; while Hunt and Clemans, the former from Berkeley and the latter from Palo Alto, would give Lake and Bliss plenty to do to keep them out of the halfback lines at either Cambridge or New Haven. Walton, of the Leland Stanford team, is a college catcher whose backstop work and throwing to second we do not see bettered on any of our crack college nines. There is one man now taking part in athletics on the West coast whom we are likely to see in the East in the fall at some one of the colleges. His name is Porter, and he enjoyed some early football experiences at Lehigh, but is now playing upon the Olympic Club team of San Francisco. He will probably go to Yale or Princeton, and we shall have a chance to see whether a Western player can make a place for himself. His present position is that of tackle, but he might make a good bid as a running half-back. These two universities, the University of California and the Leland Stanford, Jun., University, are the two great college rivals on the coast, but the athletic clubs, such as the Olympic of San Francisco, the Multonomah of Portland, and the Field Club of Seattle have made themselves pioneers in the work of establishing a foothold for all branches of sport. Felton Taylor, of the Olympic Club of San Francisco, is one of the most remarkably developed muscular types I have ever seen, while Captain Wood, of the Presidio, is one of those men whose unlimited powers of endurance we seldom meet with outside the ranks of professional teachers. Tobin, another Olympic Club man, is a beautiful drop-kicker, scoring from the 35 or 40 yard line.

Through the medium of graduates of the Eastern colleges an interest in the intercollegiate football game was first stimulated for the Englishmen had already introduced

Rugby along the coast. Mr. Howard, who played half-back on Billy Manning's famous Harvard team, was one of the first to stir the enthusiastic ones to take up the intercollegiate rules, and as he was a clever player both at Rugby and the American game, found little difficulty in teaching the new methods. Since that time the fact that there has been more or less steady connection between Eastern and Western football through the medium of Western men who were in the Eastern schools and colleges, and whose perennial returns from the scene of activity brought with it the newest ideas, has kept Western football fairly abreast of the times. This is true, however, in the matter of the tricks and strategy of the game rather than in the individual detail of position playing. The Western football player understands the crisscross, the tandem, the wedge direct, the flying wedge, the wedges along the line, and, in fact, is thoroughly posted upon the lastest Eastern plays, but his execution of them lacks the precision that comes from making a study of what the duty of each man in the play should be. There is a rather confused idea of what the tackle should do, where the end should stand, what the quarter's play is after passing the ball, and no definite understanding upon a dozen other points of a similar nature. The tackling is not so clean and certain as in the final games of an Eastern season, but more like what is seen in the first days of practice upon the scrub side. All this comes from the fact that the development of trick plays has come too rapidly after the first introduction of the game, and the detail of individual position, which Eastern teams have spent years in acquiring, has had but little attention paid to it in the West. Such rapid progress has been forgotten. On the other hand, the running is good, and the dodging and warding well brought out. Interference is not yet thorough, and the tendency to unfair use of the hand and arm altogether too marked. There are a few excellent kickers, but like all our American teams, the number of men able to punt or drop-kick is a great deal less than it should be.

The University Club of San Francisco is the patron of all college sports, and has already established a series of annual contests between the two rival universities of the coast by the presentation of a trophy in the shape of a silver football of exactly regulation size. The Bohemian and Pacific Union clubs, although social rather than athletic, indulge for sweet charity's sake in an annual baseball match, and there is also a yearly feature in the shape of a Yale-Harvard baseball contest, which brings out not only the old graduates of these Eastern institutions, but an enthusiastic following. W. Greer Harrison, as president of the Olympic Club, has probably done more than any other individual toward furthering the interests and development of all legitimate sport, and he is today as great an enthusiast as one can meet.

As for the material one finds out of which to make athletes and players, it is fully up to the Eastern standard-in fact, in proportion to the population, a little above it. The men are willing, and, as a rule, "good stayers." They do not like cold weather, and are not at their best when an occasional cold day comes. For this reason it would be unfortunate for them if, upon the occasion of their meeting Eastern athletes, the weather should be like our autumn days. They would not be at their best. They stand long training well, and instances of men "going fine" are rare. They have not enjoyed the coaching that has been given our Eastern athletes, because their schools of training are not yet old enough to have warranted this, and their best men have drifted out of the interest too speedily to have been of great value. But there is a time coming, and that not far off, when the athlete of the Pacific slope will want to try his mettle in contests of all kinds with his Eastern brother, and whatever the result, the winner will, as the expression has it, "know that there has been a contest."

Walter Camp

THE ORGANIZATION OF SPORT

Competition forced athletic teams to reach some consensus on rules and regulations for play. While baseball teams had already formed a national association for such purposes by 1858, most sports were organized in the years following the American Civil War. The National League of professional baseball players stimulated intercity play in the 1870s; but status conscious urban athletic clubs adhered to an amateur ideology. Disputes between such clubs over the issue of amateurism led to the formation of the Amateur Athletic Union in 1888, a governing body that subsumed most of its rivals, and imposed order, control, and its own morality on sporting practices through most of the next century.

Initially organized and administered by students, interscholastic sport came under greater scrutiny and control as school administrators sought to alleviate perceived abuses. In the process public sport became regulated by private agencies and powerful individuals who restricted participation, selected sites, and scheduled events that promoted a particular ideology, insured wholesome leisure, and often afforded commercial gain. The following notice of such intervention appeared in the Chicago Tribune, 14 October 1884, p.7.

A PRINCETON EDICT

Trenton, N.J., Oct. 13.-[Special.]-The Princeton Faculty has declared that after Jan. 1, 1885, no game shall be played with any college by any Princeton team on grounds other than those of the contesting colleges. This order will probably encounter considerable opposition among the alumni students, who regard the Thanksgiving and Decoration-Day games in New York as time-honored and legitimate institutions.

The following story, which appeared in the New York Times, 4 February 1893, p. 6, indicates that students did not suffer administrators' incursions gladly. In this case Yale authorities tried to prohibit the use of players that they deemed ineligible. In some schools, professors, graduate students, and "special" students who took only one or two courses competed freely. In the worst cases, some players had no affiliation with the institution. Such "tramp athletes," who were often compensated for their "expenses," and lionized for their deeds, persisted in offering their services until formal athletic grants in aid became a reality in the twentieth century.

THE FIGHT FOR THE UNDERGRADUATE RULE NOT OVER AT YALE

New-Haven, Conn. Feb. 3.- Unless some further influence is brought to bear on the Captains and managers of the Yale athletic teams they will not resign as they threatened to do, owing to the vote at Wednesday night's meeting rejecting a rule to which they had pledged themselves. At present Capt. McCormick and Manager Maffitt of the football association are the only ones who are eager to give up their offices, and they have promised not to do so unless all their colleagues do likewise. They retain their positions for two reasons-they think cowardice would be exhibited in resigning and they firmly believe they are in the right and bound not to give up the fight.

One of them said today: "We feel that we had the precedent of decades in making the rejected rule. In 1889 the Captains and managers of the crew made a five years' agreement to row Harvard, stipulating just what men should row, and no mass meeting of the university was called to ratify their action. In 1891 the track athletic association entered into a nine years' agreement to hold annual games with Harvard, framing its own rules as to the composition of its teams for the whole nine years, and the univeristy did not hold a mass meeting to ratify it. In 1891 the Captains and managers of the football elevens made a four years' agreement to play Harvard, also stipulating the men who were to be allowed to play on their teams. Precedent is all on our side, and we had no reason to suppose that our power would be questioned."

The "repudiated" Captains decline to say what action they will take. The Law School students who were really the power which defeated the proposed rule, are considering the feasibility of securing another mass meeting and presenting another code of rules, looking toward the purification of Yale athletics. The proposed code is not yet fully compiled but will make four years the limit of membership to all Yale leagues and establish a Faculty investigation into the records of all athletes whose amateur standing is questioned.

Schools that competed against each other necessarily had to agree to the same regulations regarding eligibility, etc. if contests were to be conducted equitably. Charges, recriminations, and ill will eventually subsided when faculty committees from the various colleges formed associations to regulate athletics. A Chicago Tribune article, 9 February 1896, provides an account of the meeting between midwestern colleges that eventually became the Big 10 Conference.

FACULTY CHAIRMEN RECOMMEND STRICTER RULES FOR ATHLETES.
REAFFIRM THE AGREEMENT OF COLLEGE PRESIDENTS MADE LAST YEAR WITH
ADDITIONAL RULES-AGREEMENT AMONG FACULTY COMMITTEES
RATIFIED WITH PLEDGE TO WORK FOR PURITY IN ATHLETICS.

Chairmen of the Faculty committees of Western universities who met at the Palmer House yesterday afternoon reaffirmed the agreement of college Presidents of last year and recommended the adoption of several new rules, drawing the line closer in the definition of an amateur in athletics and in the qualifications for eligibility to membership on teams entered in intercollegiate contests. It is probable these recommendations will be accepted by the faculties of nearly all the schools represented. The most radical change was in the substitution of the following rules for the ones which had been adopted last year:

No student shall participate in any intercollegiate contest who has ever used or is using his knowledge of athletics or athletic skill for gain.

This rule shall not apply to any student now in college at this date, Feb. 8, for what he has done in the past. This rule to be operative after Oct. 1, 1897.

No person who receives any compensation from the university for his services rendered by way of regular instruction shall be allowed to play on any team. This shall take effect Dec. 1, 1896.

No student shall participate in any intercollegiate contest after any year who shall not have been in residence at least six months of the preceding year in his course.

The first two provisions were passed by a vote of five, two of the representatives not voting. Another provision was presented providing that no person appointed a fellowship or scholarship should be eligible to university teams, but this was lost.

In addition to the provision that the proper authorities should certify to the standing of the candidates for the team a provision was recommended that each candidate should sign a statement of his eligibility.

A move towards the coordination of Faculty committees was made and the following rules were suggested:

It shall be competent for the Chairman of any athletic committee, if he believes that any university is violating the letter or spirit of their rules, definitions, or agreements, to communicate with the Chairman of the Athletic committee of the university under suspicion and make specific charges against said institution. If this is done it shall be the duty of the Athletic committee of the institution under suspicion to investigate at once the charges and report through the Chairman as to their truth or falsity, and this report shall be accepted in good faith by the committee which has brought the charges. If the charges are found to be true, it shall be the duty of the university concerned to suspend from further athletic connection with athletics the person or persons guilty of irregular conduct.

It shall be competent for the Chairman of any athletic committee to say before his own committee any charges of irregularity against the athletic committee of another college and a full investigation in which both sides are represented may be made and the results shall then be laid before the faculty of each institution concerned.

An agreement was drawn up in regard to the legitimate expenses of athletic teams and a further agreement was adopted as follows:

It is further agreed the athletic committees of the institutions here represented will do all in their power, both official and personal to keep the inter-collegiate athletics contests within their proper institutions making them incidental and not the principal features of university and intercollegiate life. All that is dishonorable, unsportsman-like, or unnecessarily rough in any branch of athletics is particularly and expressly condemned.

Prof. Conway MacMillan was chosen Chairman and called the conference to order at 9 o'clock and the session was held behind closed doors, the final adjournment being taken at 5:30 in the afternoon. The matter of the purification of athletics was thoroughly discussed before the adoption of the rules and agreement. Those present were A. Alonzo Stagg, Chicago University; J. Scott Clark, Northwestern; C.B. Nancrede, Michigan; H. H. Everett, Illinois; W.E. Stone, Purdue; C. R. Barnes, Wisconsin: and Conway MacMillan, Minnesota.

Caspar Whitney, (a prominent sportswriter) at the invitation of several of the delegates, called at the Palmer House after the session and was invited to visit several of the universities represented. The feeling of hostility seemed to have decreased, and a desire was manifested to discuss the charges he had made in a more critical manner. Mr. Whitney expressed himself as disgusted by the reports of his interference with the meeting, saying he had known nothing of the meeting when he started West, learning of it in Ann Arbor. He said he had given no invitation to dinner to the delegates Friday night, but had extended them an invitation to luncheon yesterday from a desire to meet them personally and unite in a campaign for the purification of athletics. The limited time between sessions rendered it impossible for his invitation to be accepted, and Secretary Barnes was instructed to return thanks to Mr. Whitney for the courtesy extended, and to say that the time at the disposal of the conference was so limited they were compelled to decline the invitation.

High school athletes modeled the activities of their collegiate counterparts, including their excesses and abuses. Likewise, faculty sought to control such matters. By 1898 adults in the Chicago area high schools interceded in the flourishing athletic league, which students had initiated in 1885. New York authorities followed by organizing the Public Schools Athletic League in 1903. The original constitution of the Chicago league is reprinted from the Medill High School Echo, February 1898, pp. 14-15, at the Chicago Historical Society.

THE CONSTITUTION OF THE NEW HIGH SCHOOL
LEAGUE IS AS FOLLOWS:

ARTICLE I.
Name.
This Association shall be known as the Cook County High School Athletic League.

ARTICLE II.
Object
The object of this league shall be the protection of the mutual athletic interests of the schools belonging, and the promotion in said schools of pure amateur sport.

ARTICLE III.
Control
The management of this league shall be vested in one Board of Control and in a separate Board of Managers for each branch of Athletics.

ARTICLE IV.
Section 1. The League shall consist of the following school......

Sec. 2. Any other school of High School Grade in Cook County, may secure membership in this League by a majority vote of the Board of Control upon the payment of an initiation fee of $5.00 and signing the Constitution.

ARTICLE V.
Board of Contol
Section 1. The Board of Control shall consist of one delegate from the faculty of each school, to be elected by the Athletic Association.

Sec. 2. Active members shall have a term of two years.

Sec. 3. If a substitute is sent to represent any school at a meeting of the board, he must also be a member of the faculty of that school.

Sec. 4. This Board of Control shall adopt rules governing all contests, shall hear and decide all protests, and shall have charge of all funds belonging to the League.

Sec. 5. The regular annual meeting of this Board shall be held on the second Saturday of each June.

Sec. 6. Special meetings may be called by the President of this Board, whenever necessary, and must be called if a request is made in writing by the representatives of three schools or by the request of a Board of Managers.

Sec. 7. The officers of this Board shall be a President, a Vice-President and a Secretary-Treasurer. The annual election of officers shall be held at the annual meeting of the Board in June.

ARTICLE VI.
Boards Of Managers.
Section 1. The Board of Managers for each branch of athletics shall consist of the managers of the various teams competing. These managers must be undergraduates in their respective schools and shall be subject to the same rules of eligibility as players.

Sec. 2. These Boards of Managers shall have complete charge of all affairs relating to their respective branches of athletics, except in the case of matters expressly stated by this Constitution to be under the jurisdiction of the Board of Control.

ARTICLE VII.
Sports Recognized.
The branches of athletics recognized by this league shall be football, baseball, track and field athletics, indoor baseball, basket-ball and tennis.

ARTICLE VIII.
Violation Of Rules
Any violation of these rules of this League shall render the school offending liable to expulsion by a majority vote of the Board of Control.

ARTICLE IX.
Money.
Section 1. The annual dues shall be three dollars for each branch of athletics in which a school competes.
Sec. 2. The Board of Control can levy a special fee if money is needed.
Sec. 3. The team which shall each year be declared by the Board of Control the champion team for that year in the branch of athletics which it represents shall receive in recognition thereof a pennant, which shall be paid for out of the League treasury and presented by the Board. No money shall be paid to any team from the League treasury.

ARTICLE X.
Amendments.
This Constitution may be amended at the annual meeting of the Board of Control in June, by a two-thirds vote of all the schools belonging to the League, provided that written notice of the nature of said amendments shall have been furnished each member not later than the first of June preceding.

Another way in which schools sought to provide guidance, gain control, and win victories was through the employment of professional coaches. Originally hired by students and viewed as an evil by many school authorities, the value of such expertise proved evident in the 1880s. Yale rose to prominence as an athletic power, superceding its rival, Harvard, under the guidance of Walter Camp, who continued to manage the football team for years after his graduation. William Rainey Harper, the young, energetic president of the newly-opened University of Chicago, sought Amos Alonzo Stagg, one of Camp's proteges, as a coach for its teams in 1891. As a well-known athlete, and an adherent to the doctrine of muscular Christianity, Stagg was to serve as a role model and utilize sport to publicize the school. He was the first professional coach awarded faculty status. The following letter, from the Stagg Papers at the University of Chicago, is representative of his many offers. Other academic institutions followed suit, as in the New York Times account, 25 February 1900, p. 21.

A.A. STAGG LETTER TO OLIVER C. MORSE

April 17, 1891

Mr. Oliver C. Morse,
Dear Sir;-
Your communication of April 11th received. In inviting me to become a Special Instructor in the Physical Department for the school year of 1891 & 92 at a salary of

$1200, I understand that my duties will consist of (a) training in football & baseball (b) the delivery of a lecture not more than thirty times (c) giving a short course of class room work on the "Theory of Training."

Further, I understand that the specified time of my obligation to the School shall be two hours each day.

Respectfully,

A. Alonzo Stagg

LATHAM TO TRAIN PENN MEN.
FORMER SPRINTER AND BALL PLAYER SELECTED
FROM MANY APPLICANTS.

Walter A. Latham, the former professional sprinter and ballplayer, has been engaged to succeed "Mike" Murphy as trainer of the track athletic team at the University of Pennsylvania. There were about forty applicants for the position, and the capabilities of all were carefully considered before the selection was made.

Latham was recommended for the position by Arthur Irvin, who is coaching the baseball squad at the University of Pennsylvania. "Mike" Sweeney, the world's champion high jumper, was a strong candidate for the position. "Arlie" Latham, as the new trainer is known to every baseball enthusiast throughout the country, has made a splendid record in athletics. In 1882 he won the championship of America in the professional handicap 100-yard dash, and in the following year he won the all-around championship at the Caledonian games. He has also been successful as a trainer of athletes, having handled Flynn, the world's champion sprinter.

Latham's career as a professional baseball player is familiar. He was known as the clown of the diamond, because of his humor while playing in a game. He always had some original remarks for players and the umpire, and often kept the spectators in roars of laughter. He was first heard of as a ball player in 1880, with the Buffalo team. The two following seasons he played in Philadelphia. From 1883 to 1889 he was with the famous St. Louis Browns, being then considered the star third baseman of the country. He played in Chicago in 1890, and then returned to St. Louis. He played in Cincnnati from 1893 to 1895, and then again returned to St. Louis, and was Captain of the team until the close of the season in 1897. This practically ended his career in professional baseball. He had an engagement with the Washington Club in 1899, but although he appeared in uniform, he did very little playing, being engaged to "jolly" the players and umpires, as Manager Irwin once remarked. Like many another player, he had become "shoulder-bound," and was unable to throw with his old-time speed and accuracy. During his seventeen years as a player, he always played at third base, and in his prime was regarded as the fastest player on any American team.

Latham will begin his duties as a trainer in September, Murphy having consented to remain and prepare the team for its tour in Europe this summer. Latham will have charge of all the football candidates, and next Spring he will also coach the baseball squad.

AMATEUR ATHLETIC UNION

Ethnic athletic clubs and wealthy individuals promoted particular competitions throughout the middle decades of the nineteenth century; but by the 1870s the social athletic clubs of New York, New Jersey, and Chicago vied for prominence as sponsors. In 1879 several clubs formed the National Association of Amateur Athletes of America (N4A); but the members, particularly the Manhattan A.C., and the New York A.C. fell to bickering when its star athletes were accused of professionalism. Dissension led to the withdrawal of the New York A.C. and its allies from the organization in 1886. Two years later they formed the Amateur Athletic Union and held a series of "national" championships in several sports. The Intercollegiate Amateur Athletic Association of America, founded in 1876, joined the AAU in 1889, and the governing agency extended its jurisdiction over amateur athletics thereafter. The AAU national office supplied the following.

1899
CONSTITUTION AND BY-LAWS OF THE METROPOLITAN ASSOCIATION
OF THE AMATEUR ATHLETIC UNION OF THE UNITED STATES.

CONSTITUTION

ARTICLE I.
Name.
This organization shall be known as the METROPOLITAN ASSOCIATION OF THE AMATEUR ATHLETIC UNION OF THE UNITED STATES.

ARTICLE II.
Objects.
The objects of this Association are:

1. To foster and improve amateur athletics throughout its territory, in accordance with the standards and under the rules prescribed by the Amateur Athletic Union.

2. To protect and promote the mutual interests of its members.

3. To institute, regulate and award the amateur athletic championships of this Association.

ARTICLE III.
Territory.

Until (1) the members of this Association shall fall below four in number; or (2) until the Amateur Athletic Union, under the provisions of its Constitution, shall allot a portion or portions of said territory to a new association or to new associations formed therein and admitted to active membership in said Amateur Athletic Union, the territory under the jurisdiction of this Association shall be New York State and New Jersey, north of Trenton.

ARTICLE IV.
Membership.

1. The members of this Association shall be limited to amateur organizations promoting some branch or branches of amateur athletic sports.

2. This Association, through its Board of Managers, shall be the sole judge of the qualifications of applicants for membership herein, and of the qualification of members to continue herein.

3. Each member of this Association shall be sole judge of the qualifications of individuals to become and continue members of such organization.

4. Applications for membership shall be in the form prescribed by the By-Laws of this Association, and acceptance of membership shall bind such organization to abide by the Constitution, By-Laws and Rules of the Amateur Athletic Union and of this Association, and to accept and enforce all decisions affecting or relating to such organization that may be made pursuant thereto by the Board of Governors of the A.A.U., or by the Board of Managers of this Association.

5. Any violation by any member of this Association of the Constitution, By-Laws or Rules of this Association, or order of its Board of Managers made in conformity therewith shall render such member liable to suspension by the Board of Managers, until the next Annual or Special Meeting of this Association, and to expulsion by a two-thirds vote of all the members represented at such meeting.

ARTICLE V.
Representation of Members.

1. Every member of this Association must appoint three delegates to represent it at meetings of this Association, and such delegates must be amateur members in good standing of such organization and may also appoint three alternates of such delegates, who must be amateur members of such organization or of some other member in this Association, except that no member of the Board of Managers shall be appointed an alternate. All the representatives of one member shall collectively have one vote. All delegates and alternates shall represent their respective organizations until withdrawn.

2. The appointment of every delegate and alternate shall be in writing, duly certified by the chief executive officer or secretary of the appointing member.

3. All members of the Board of Managers shall be elected from the duly appointed delegates. No alternate shall be elected a member of the Board.

4. Election of members of the Board of Managers shall only occur at the annual meeting and by a majority vote of organizations represented and entitled to vote, ex-

cept that the Board of Managers shall have power to fill vacancies, arising from any cause, from among the delegates to the Association.

5. Any member may at any time, by written notice, addressed to the Secretary-Treasurer of the Association and signed by the chief executive officer or secretary of such member, withdraw any or all of its delegates, provided a like number of newly appointed delegates be at the same time substituted for those withdrawn; and if any delegate thus withdrawn be at the time a member of the Board of Managers, the Board shall fill the vacancy as provided in Section 4 of this Article.

ARTICLE VI.
Management.

The management of the affairs of this Association shall be delegated to a Board of Managers, consisting of not more than fifteen members.

The Board of Managers so chosen, shall, from among their number, elect a President, Vice-President and a Secretary-Treasurer, each of whom shall serve for a term of one year or until his successor is chosen, and each of whom shall perform the duties prescribed by the By-Laws.

ARTICLE VII.
Duties And Powers Of The Board Of Managers.

The Board of Managers shall, in addition to the duties and powers elsewhere in this Constitution prescribed, have power and it shall be their duty:

1. To admit to membership any organization eligible under this Constitution applying therefor, if they deem proper.

2. To impose and enforce penalties for any violation of the Constitution or By-Laws of this Association.

3. To reject any entries (if deemed objectionable) at any Association Championship meeting; and to delegate this power to its committees.

4. To remove from office, by a two-thirds vote, any member of the Board of Managers who, by neglect of duty, or by conduct tending to impair his usefulness as a member of such Board, shall be deemed to have forfeited his position.

5. To fill all vacancies in the Board of Managers occurring from any cause.

6. To collect the dues and funds of the Association and to expend the same.

7. To call regular and special meetings of this Association, and to fix the time and place for holding all meetings not fixed by this Constitution.

8. To institute, locate, conduct and manage all Association championship meetings.

9. To explain, define and interpret any provision of the Constitution or By-Laws of this Association, upon request of a member.

ARTICLE VIII.
Jurisdiction.

This Association shall have jurisdiction throughout its territory over the athletic sports and exercises enumerated in the Constitution of the Amateur Athletic Union, and subject to the provisions of such Constitution, By-Laws and Rules relating thereto.

ARTICLE IX.
Conditions Of Competition.

1. The conditions of competition in and the rules governing any athletic meeting, game or entertainment given or sanctioned by this Association or its members, shall be those prescribed in the Constitution, By-Laws and Rules of the Amateur Athletic Union; provided, however, that any member may reject from its games any entry deemed objectionable.

No person shall be eligible to compete in any Association Championships, except by unanimous vote of the Board of Managers, unless he is a member of one of the members of the Association.

ARTICLE X.
Dues And Expenses.

1. Every club member shall annually pay to the Secretary-Treasurer, at least ten days before the annual meeting, $7.50 as annual dues; provided, that every applicant for membership shall remit with its application to the Secretary-Treasurer the amount of its annual dues.

2. A failure to pay said dues within the time prescribed shall operate to prevent a representation of and a vote by the delinquent member at any meeting of the Association; and a continued indebtedness for dues or other charges for a period of three months, shall operate as a loss of membership by the delinquent member.

3. The receipts from all sources shall be devoted to defraying the cost of Association championship medals or other tokens, annual dues to the Amateur Athletic Union, and for printing and other necessary expenses incurred by the Board for this Association. All expenses incurred by delegates in attending meetings of this Association and by members of the Board of Managers in attending meetings of the Board, may be paid by their respective clubs from which such delegates or managers were appointed or chosen.

ARTICLE XI.
Meetings Of The Association.

1. The annual meeting of this Association shall be held on the third Monday in September in each year.

2. Special meetings of this Association may be called by a majority vote of the Board of Managers and upon the written request of at least one-third of all members of this Association must be called, the notice to contain the date and location of such meeting, and a statement of the object thereof.

2. Fifteen days' notice of every meeting of this Association shall be mailed by the Secretary-Treasurer at the time fixed by this Article to the Secretary every member of this Association, and every such member shall promptly notify the Secretary-Treasurer of this Association of any change in office or address of its Secretary; and a notice mailed by the Secretary-Treasurer of this Association to the address last given by such member shall be deemed a full compliance on his part with the requirements of this Consitution and of the By-Laws hereunder, as to sending such notices.

4. At the meetings of this Association the following shall be the order of business:
  (1) Roll Call of Delegates.
  (2) Reading of Minutes.
  (3) Report of Board of Managers.
  (4) Secretary-Treasurer's Report.
  (5) Reports of Committees.
  (6) Resolutions, Orders and General Business.
  (7) Election of Board of Managers (if annual meeting).
  (8) Adjournment.

5. In the interval between two annual meetings of the Association, any action that might be lawfully taken at a special meeting may be so taken by mail or telegraph vote, provided that where this Constitution requires a majority vote, the vote so taken must, to be effective, be a majority vote of all members of the Association voting, and where this Constitution requires a two-thirds vote, the vote so taken must, to be effective, be a two-thirds vote of all members of the Association voting, and provided, further, that in every instance such mail or telegraph vote shall be taken by the Secretary-Treasurer, and the ballots of each member must be preserved in his files.

ARTICLE XII.
Proceedings Of Board Of Managers.

1. The annual meeting of the Board of Managers shall be convened as soon as possible after the adjournment of the annual meeting of this Association.

2. Special meetings may be called by the President upon not less than ten days' notice being given by the Secretary-Treasurer to each member of the Board of such meeting and of the object thereof. At any such meeting the members of the Board answering roll call shall constitute a quorum.

3. In the interval between two meetings of the Board, any action that might be lawfully taken at a special meeting of the Board may be so taken by mail vote, provided that where this constitution requires a majority vote, the vote so taken must, to be effective, be a majority vote of all members of the Board voting; and where this Constitution requires a two-thirds vote, the vote so taken must, to be effective, be a two-thirds vote of all members of the Board voting; and provided, that in cases where the President may deem it necessary, a vote may be taken by telegraph instead of mail; in such cases the vote to close within forty-eight hours, and provided, further, that in every instance, such mail or telegraph vote shall be taken by the Secretary-Treasurer, and the ballots of each member of the Board must be preserved in his files.

ARTICLE XIII.
Amendments.

1. No amendment shall be made to this Constitution at any meeting except by a two-thirds vote of the members repesented; or by a mail vote except by a two-thirds vote of all the members of the Association. And before a vote is taken on any proposed amendment, by mail vote or at a meeting, the said proposed amendment must have been submitted to the Board of Managers, and at least thirty days' notice thereof given by the Board to all members of the Association.

2. No amendment shall take effect until approved by a majority of the Board of Governors of the Amateur Athletic Union.

BY-LAWS.

ARTICLE I.
Managers.

1. The Board of Managers of the Association shall consist of members.

2. Said Board of Managers shall be elected by ballot at each annual meeting of this Association by a majority vote of the clubs legally represented, and shall hold office for one year, or until their successors are elected.

3. Vacancies in the Board of Managers shall be filled by the Board until the next annual meeting.

ARTICLE II.
Officers.

1. The officers of this Association, viz., President, Vice-President, Secretary-Treasurer, shall be elected by ballot by a majority vote at the annual meeting of the Board of Managers.

2. The President may order meetings of the Board of Managers where and when he shall deem necessary; shall preside at all meetings of said Board and of the Association, and generally shall perform such other duties as appertain to the office of President.

3. The Vice-President shall have the power and perform the duties of the President in the absence or inability to act of the latter.

4. The Secretary-Treasurer shall keep the records of the Association and the Board of Managers, conduct all official correspondence; issue notice of all meetings of this Association and said Board, keep a complete record of all athletic events held under the auspices of this Association, and perform such other duties as may be prescribed by the Constitution and By-Laws of said Association.

The Secretary-Treasurer shall receive all the moneys of this Association and shall pay all bills approved by the Finance Committee or by the Board of Managers, provided that necessry minor expenses, which may be paid by any committee, may be turned in to the Secretary-Treasurer as cash if recorded in detail, duly attested by the Committee and approved by the Board.

He shall, whenever required by the Board or its Finance Committee, submit and turn over to said Committee or the Board, all moneys, accounts, books, papers, vouchers and records, including bank and check books, appertaining to his office, and shall turn over the same to his successor when elected. He shall be bonded (at the expense of the Association), for an amount to be designated by the Board of Managers, not less than $1,000.

ARTICLE III.
Committees And Handicappers.

1. There shall be appointed by the President, with the approval of the Board, a Finance Committee, which shall, within two weeks next preceding the date of the annual

meeting each year, audit and examine the accounts of the Secretary-Treasurer, and make its report to the Board of Managers prior to the annual meeting next ensuing.

Said Committee shall also at other times, when requested by the Board, make an examination of the accounts of the Secretary-Treasurer, and report to the Board thereon, and may in such case require the Secretary-Treasurer to turn over to it all moneys, accounts, books, papers, vouchers and records appertaining to his office.

2. The Board of Managers shall elect from among its members a Registration Committee of three, which committee shall have the powers and duties as defined in Article XI. of the Constitution of the A.A.U.

3. The President shall also appoint a Committee on Records, a Committee on Legislation, a Committee on Membership and Investigation, and such other committees as shall be designated by the Board of Managers; the number constituting each of said committees to be fixed by the President, with the approval of the Board.

4. There shall be elected by ballot at each annual meeting one or more handicappers, who shall hold office for one year, or until their successor shall be elected.

ARTICLE IV.
Membership In The Association.

Any organization eligible under the Constitution of the Union and of this Association desiring to become a member of the Association shall make application in writing to the Secretary-Treasurer declaring:

(a) Its name, location, the number of its members and the names of its officers.

(b) Date of its organization and its purposes.

(c) That it will, if elected a member of the Association, abide by the Constitution, By-Laws and Rules of the Union and Association, and will respect, abide by and enforce all decisions of the Union and Board of Managers of this Association and the Decisions of the Registration Committees of the Union.

It shall transmit at same time the dues required by the Constitution of this Association, and a copy of its Constitution and By-Laws. Such application shall be immediately referred by the Secretary-Treasurer to the proper committee to investigate and report.

ARTICLE V.
Order Of Business.

Order of business at all meetings of the Board of Managers shall be as follows:

(a) Roll Call.

(b) Reading of Minutes.

(c) Reports of Officers and Committees.

(d) Unfinished Business.

(e) Election to fill Vacancies.

(f) New Business.

ARTICLE VI.
Championship Meetings.

1. This Association must hold annually on the Saturday preceding the third Monday in September, a field and track championship meeting, at such place and includ-

ing such events as they may determine, unless otherwise sanctioned by the Registration Committee.

They may hold such other indoor and outdoor championship meetings as they may deem best.

At least thirty days' notice of all such championship games shall be given to all members of this Association.

2. Such championship meetings shall be in charge of a Committee appointed by the Board of Managers, which Committee shall not be restricted to members of said Board, except that the Chairman of said Committee shall be a member of said Board,

3. All entries shall be sent to the Chairman of said Committee, which Committee may reject any entries which it may deem objectionable. Said Committee shall receive all protests and transmit them to the Registration Committee for final action at once, with such report or recommendation as it may deem proper.

4. Said Committee shall, subject to the approval of the Board of Managers, choose the officers at all championship meetings.

ARTICLE VII.
Amendments.

These By-Laws may be amended at any meeting of the Board by a two-thirds vote of the members present, or by a mail vote, by a two-thirds vote of the members voting, provided that at least ten days' notice shall be given to every member of the Board of the proposed amendment; but no amendment shall be operative until approved by the Board of Governors of the A.A.U. The number of the Board of Managers, however, shall be changed only by a meeting of this Association.

ATHLETIC ISSUES

The pervasive influence of sport during the latter nineteenth century caused many to question its values. Among the issues, doctors debated its healthful benefits, moralists questioned ethical practices, while others bemoaned the commercialization of sport and its effect on character development. Such concerns are evident in C.L. Dana's editorial, which appeared in Outing, June 1885, p. 362; and Dudley Sargent's piece from the American Journal of Social Science, 20 (1884), pp. 87-90.

PATHOLOGY OF SPORTS.

Mr. Charles Richards Dodge, in the February Outing, refers to the subject of the "pathology of Recreative Sports," ... based evidently upon articles which I contributed to the *Medical Record* and to *Science* of November last,...

The "lawn-tennis arm" and "lawn-tennis leg" are accidents peculiar to tennis, and having a special train of symptoms. Therefore, we give them special names for purposes of convenience. We physicians do not create the disease, but simply name it, in which there certainly can be no harm. I must add, that, since my articles have been written, another tennis injury has been noted. It is called "lawn-tennis back." In boys who begin to play tennis early, and keep up the game continuously, there is sometimes observed a peculiar overgrowth of the muscles of the back on the right side. This causes loss of straightness and symmetry to the spinal column, amounting almost to deformity. It is, I believe, a rare condition. Mr. Dodge suggests a medical nomenclature with which to portray the injuries and idiosyncrasies of bicycle-riders. There has already been one cycle-disease noted. In boys who ride much upon bicycles the continual pressure of the saddle upon the perinaeum sometimes causes irritation of the urinary passage and neighboring organs. Even a stricture may be developed, in this way, it is alleged. I believe this injury to be extremely rare, and am so far from being an alarmist, that I would freely permit young patients to ride bicycles as much, perhaps, as they wished. But it is always wise to know about possible dangers.

Locomotive-engineers who have ridden for years on springless engines, and have thus been subjected to a constant vibration, sometimes develop a peculiar state, known by the brief and expressive title of "sideromorphophobia." They are nervous, tremulous, weak and full of morbid fears and worries. I should very much like to know from some of your readers whether the jar of excessive bicycling ever ends in causing a similar condition of nervous exhaustion.

C.L. Dana, M.D.

New York City, March 12, 1885.

THE EVILS OF THE PROFESSIONAL TENDENCY OF MODERN ATHLETICS.

To many persons who are only superficially familiar with life at our fashionable shore and mountain resorts during the summer months, there would seem to be no ground for the assertion that we are an overworked people; but such superficial impression is misleading. In his days of recreation, the American does not lay aside the anxiety of his business. The mail and the telegraph are as indispensable at Newport as on Wall street. The business man's vacation is little more than a feverish combination of business and pleasure. In very recent years, however, the demands of our physical well-being have assumed a new importance. Bodily health is the basis of almost all success, and the recognition of this fact has been followed by an increased respect for the claims of a systematic physical training. Every well-equipped college is now supplied with a gymnasium. College sports are commended and encouraged by parents, and approved by college faculties. But, as in most good things, this popular encouragement may be carried too far, and be followed by pernicious results. Today we are face to face with one of these harmful results, the deplorable tendency to professionalism in our college sports. The love of competitive sport is inherent in man. Every tribe, town and city in history has its swift-footed Achilles, its Samson and its Hercules. Organized efforts for amusement come with accumulated wealth. Clubs are formed in friendly local rivalry; then prizes furnish the incentive to effort; then the object being no longer sport, but victory at any cost, specialists are hired to play at large salaries. Friendly rivalry has gone, and the bitter and unscrupulous contests of professional sportsmen have taken its place. The growth of the professional spirit in our college sports is a most serious evil. Today college clubs, like professional clubs, play to win, and to win by any possible means. The old spirit of courtesy and generous competition is disappearing, and some of our college contests now are little more than exhibitions of brutal violence. The old motto of "fair play and no favor," or "let the best man win," has lost is significance, and contests are now conducted in great part with an eye to pecuniary results. College clubs play and college crews row where they are offered the best inducements. In this way they may be said to form a business partnership with the hotel proprietors and transportation companies. Then the demoralizing work begins. The contestants are in the hands of their trainers, and the trainers are too often in the hands of the betting rings. Betting will ever be the bane of competitive contests. Sporting men bet to win. To make betting a paying business, "tips," "points," and "understandings" must be obtained, or, in other words, bets must be made frequently on a "sure thing." Many of our fashionable pool rooms are run on this principle.

Still another evil connected with our athletic sports is the mania for excitement. In this age of electricity the demand is for stimulating food, stimulating drinks, and stimulating amusements. Evenly matched games are the most exciting; if the contest be one-sided, the crowd goes away dissatisfied. To insure good financial results, therefore, a preliminary arrangement must be made whereby, whatever may be the relative skill of the contestants, the contest shall be a close one. Most of our glove contests and wrestling matches are "arranged" in this manner. The result is a degradation of the popular taste and a general distrust of athletic contests.

Another evil which is working incalculable harm to our popular sports is the notoriety given to them by the public press. When a newspaper devotes three columns of its valuable space to the detailed report of a "fistic encounter," and a few editorial lines to moralizing upon it, a hundred will read the report where one will read the homily. So great is the demand for sporting news that many large daily papers have their sporting columns and their sporting editor. The most insignificant details are published concerning the participants in college contests, and all their sayings and doings before and after the events are given to the public. The paper that publishes the most gossip of this sort sells the most copies. When it comes to a question of the moral aspect of the sports, and the eradication of certain evils connected with their practice, we have the anomalous spectacle of some of the most conservative of the great metropolitan dailies coming out in support of acknowledged evils, while the sporting papers, hitherto looked upon by some people as the representatives of professional chicanery, protest against these evils, and unite with the religious press in favor of moral principles, manly dealing and fair play in amateur sports.

The next danger that threatens our athletic sports is the attitude of educators and men of prominence with regard to them. It is only within recent years that college faculties have acknowledged that the body was worthy of any systematic training. Now there is a danger that they may go too far in the acknowledgement. They may be willing to encourage sports played according to the present vicious principles. They may not see or understand the professional spirit that has crept in, and the degradation which college sports are consequently undergoing. Gymnasiums are built, only to become the training school for specialists. In too many institutions faculties permit themselves to be influenced by the unwise, though perfectly natural, demands of the students in athletic matters. They close their eyes to the degrading influence of the professional spirit that is beginning to control college sports. But many of our leading presidents have awakened to the serious evils of our present tendency. In their addresses and reports they show great disagreement in their way of viewing the subject, but it can be safely predicted that they will all come eventually to the ground occupied by President Eliot, of Harvard, who said, in a recent report, that "college clubs and crews should be forbidden to employ trainers, to play or row with professionals, or to compete with clubs or crews who adopt either of these practices; that they should be forbidden to give exhibitions in large cities for the purpose of money making; and to receive subsidies from railroads and hotels in furtherance of this object."

Finally, the influence which the growth of the spirit of professionalism exerts upon the students themselves is dangerous. It gives them a false idea of the place and purpose of college sports; it weakens their principles of honor and fair play; it develops the skill and physique of a few students, but does not benefit the mass of students; it is maintained only at great expense, which bears heavily upon the poorer men in college; it fosters an unhealthy excitement, and seriously interferes with the proper intellectual work of college life. While the measures for reform proposed at the Intercollegiate Athletic Conference, held in New York last year, may be capable of improvement in detail, they certainly mark out, in their general tread, the line along which future progress must be made in the regeneration of college athletics.

E.L. Godkin's work from the Nation, 7 December 1893, pp. 422-423 provides a flavor of the spirit of the times as well as pointing to the sense of sport as a spectacle.

THE ATHLETIC CRAZE

We are glad that the Harvard Overseers have appointed a committee to investigate the game of football in its various aspects. We are also glad to learn that there is to be this winter a convention of the deities of the football world, to revise the rules, and probably abolish the "flying wedge" and other dangerous features of the present game. So far so good. But we would respectfully ask the college faculties whether they propose this winter to take any action looking to the reform of the game and indeed all college games on the moral side. We refer them to some paragraphs in *Harper's Weekly* on Phillips Exeter Academy, which show the effect that the inordinate attention given to athletics in colleges is having on the young boys in the preparatory schools. How many of them who have the size and weight qualifying to row or play football now think of the college to which they are going as a seat of learning? The practice, on the part of the athletic element in the colleges, of seeking them out, and bribing them by offers of a free education to come to one college rather than another, has become unhappily common, and has ceased to seem discreditable, that is, very young boys are invited to become professionals and to take what is in reality a salary for acting as football players in the guise of students. That the faculties play into the hands of these debauchers of youth by being easy with these young professionals in the examinations and recitations is at least generally believed. Can nothing be done to suppress or make disgraceful this abuse of allowing professional athletes to haunt the college buildings as sham students? Is not the presence of such men at all in colleges highly demoralizing, and likely to confuse the minds of freshmen as to the ends for which colleges exist?

Is it possible again, that the faculties, say of Yale and Princeton, look with equanimity on the enormous sums of money now received as gate-money every year in athletics by these young men in *statu pupillari*, and on the very large sums which change hands by betting in what may be called the collegiate world, beginning with the children who are preparing for college in the schools? We are informed on good authority that Yale spent last year about $47,000 on athletics, and the team went to Springfield the other day with three drawing room cars and fifty men as substitutes, doctors, trainers, rubbers, and cooks. The receipts on Thursday from the gate-money in New York cannot have fallen far short of $50,000. It was earned by exhibiting feats of strength and agility by scholars and gentlemen before an enormous city crowd, in which the gambling fraternity and the prostitutes were very prominent. Here is the *Tribune's* account of the appearance of the defeated team when the game was over:

"About the entrance to the hotel were perhaps five hundred people waiting to see what a defeated Yale team looked like. And they saw. But they never saw a more woebegone, used-up, pale-faced, bruised, and bloodied lot of respectable, healthy, sane young men before. One by one the players crawled down off the coach and passed into the hotel through the alley made by the police through the crowd. Two of the players had to be helped, half carried by substitutes. The men had come directly from the field and were in their battle clothes. Their faces were muddy and marked with bloody streaks: their sweaters were stained and reddened, their heads a mass of tangled hair. In their dilapidated condition, marked with defeat, they did not look the strong, powerful young giants that had driven away from the hotel so full of confidence and sure of victory earlier in the day."

Is this an exhibition before a waiting hotel crowd in which any man who has sense enough and money enough to send his son to college would care to have him figure?

We are not inveighing against athletic games. If the colleges were tomorrow to make football compulsory for every man in them, we should not say a word in objection. We are simply asking for moderation and decency. It seems to be the weakness of the American people to take nearly everything in "crazes." There was the greenback craze, and the silver craze, and the granger craze, and the cholera craze, and now there is the athletic craze, and the leading colleges are becoming huge training grounds for young gladiators, around whom nearly as many spectators roar as roared in the Flavian amphitheatre.

As far as can be ascertained, the thing which produces most of the evils of football and other games is the effort to improve them as a spectacle for the multitude. All the good which the amateurs of the game say results from training for it and playing it could be obtained just as well by playing on the college grounds without any spectators at all. By carrying it to the neighborhood of populous towns and cities, it takes on promptly the character of the horse-race. It furnished to the gambling fraternity something of which they are constantly in search-an interesting event of uncertain result-and sets free from the restraints of home and friends a large body of youths in a state of great excitement. One of its worst results is, however, that it frightens "the plain people" away from the colleges. The modest father who is willing to pinch himself and wife and daughters in order to give a son a college education is appalled by what he hears and sees of the results of a football match. Debt, drink, debauchery rise up before his mind's eye as a probable concomitant of "college training," and he decides to keep his pet lamb at home. The colleges are not drawing as they ought on this class. The wealthy men are going to them in greater and greater numbers, but it is not they who keep alive the traditions of American scholarship, or show the world what a college education can do by way of preparation for life. Of the effect on the members of the various teams of the conspicuousness in which they pass some months of every year, of the interviews, the newspaper gossip, and portraits, we will not speak, as nothing definite can be known about it. But if much remains of "the modest stillness and humility" which is, the poet says, so becoming in time of peace, after training for two or three matches, they must be almost more than human.

CANADA

The organization of sport in Canada preceded that of the United States. Given their closer relationship to the British crown, English speaking Canadians, both male and female, looked to the mother country as an athletic model. The Montreal Curling Club organized as early as 1807. Women had their own archery club by 1858 and the Ladies Prince of Wales Snowshoe Club originated in 1861.

While urbanization, industrialization, and technology played a similar role in the development of sport in both Canada and the United States, geography and social relations in the former created some distinct differences. French-Canadians had socialized more freely with the native Indian tribes and adapted their utilitarian practices, such as toboganning, snowshoeing, and canoeing as leisure pastimes. The Indian game of baggataway evolved into the widely practiced lacrosse by the 1860s. The climate engendered a greater interest in winter sports than in the United States, particularly in ice skating and hockey; while Canadians pursued their own version of football.

Urbanites in Montreal and Toronto were largely responsible for the organization and regulation of Canadian sport. Between 1880 and 1900 middle class organizers founded nearly a dozen governing bodies to regulate amateur sport in Canada. Spearheaded by the Montreal Amateur Athletic Association, which was established in 1881, the Amateur Athletic Association of Canada (1884) sought to govern all amateur sports, similar to its counterpart (AAU) in the United States. The Montreal Gazette, 15 December 1883, p. 8, provided an account of its founding.

AMATEUR ATHLETICS

FORMATION OF AMATEUR ATHLETIC ASSOCIATION OF CANADA.

A preliminary meeting of the delegates from the various athletic associations of the Dominion was held last evening in the Montreal Gymnasium, Mansfield street, to take steps for the organization of a Canadian Amateur Athletic Association.

The following delegates were present:-

Montreal Amateur Athletic Association - Messrs. W.L. Maltby, H.W. Becket, T.L. Paton.

Montreal Snowshoe Club- Messrs. G.R. Starke, Angus Grant and J.K. Whyte.

St. George's Snowshoe Club-Messrs. W.K. Mathews, R. Adams and W.B. Bulling.

Emerald Snowshoe Club-Messrs. T. McKenna, J.G. Tumity.

Toronto Lacrosse Club-Mr. R.R. Hamilton.

On motion Mr. W.L. Maltby was elected chairman and Mr. H.W. Becket was appointed secretary.

The secretary read the replies that had been received to the circular sent to athletic associations throughout the Dominion, which were most encouraging to the formation of such an association as proposed.

Mr. P.D. Ross, sporting editor of the *Mail*, wrote that he had been very glad to receive news of the proposed formation of a Canadian Amateur Athletic Association, and he thought the proposition would be well received in Ontario. He enclosed letters from the Toronto University, Queen's College (Kingston), Upper Canada College (Toronto), Trinity Medical School (Toronto), Toronto Fencing Club, Toronto Bankers' Athletic Associaton, Queen's Own Athletic Association, Brantford Lacrosse Club, Peterboro' Lacrosse Club, Cornwall Lacrosse Club, Branford Excelsiors; also London and Ottawa Football Clubs. Mr. Ross stated that he hoped that one of the principles of any Canadian athletic association that might be formed would be the recognition of fiats issued by such other associations as the Wheelmen's League, the Association of Amateur Oarsmen, etc.

Mr. W. Von Iffland, Secretary of the Kingston Club, wrote that they were very glad that the movement was on foot. The formation of such an association could not but be beneficial to Canadian athletes. They, however, would make the following suggestions:-That the association be governed by a general committee composed of representatives from all subordinate clubs; each club to be represented on the general committee by a certain fixed proportion of its subscribing members, say one or two per cent, thus giving the bowling clubs the best representation on the general committee; city clubs to form their own sub-committees, subservient to the general committee. A small annual subscription to the association might be imposed, to be devoted to annual competitions; these latter to be held yearly both by individual clubs and by the association. It would be advisable that some city, as Montreal, be considered as the headquarters of the association, to which all urgent references might be made.

Mr. E.S. Wigle, Secretary of the Toronto College Athletic Association, stated that he did not think their club could assist in carrying out such a scheme, except to express their hearty approval of it. They would, however, like to see the proposed association formed, and would do what they could individually to carry it through.

Mr. G.M. Harrington, Secretary of the Toronto Press Club, wrote that the club had resolved that the Toronto Press Lacrosse Club heartily approved of the proposition to form a Canadian Amateur Athletic Association.

Mr. L. Bolster, Secretary of the Toronto Fencing Club, wrote that the club heartily approved of the proposal to form a Canadian National Amateur Athletic Association, and would join but would like their fencing rules recognized and an amateur championship for fencing established.

Mr. R.M. Orchard, captain of the Brantford Lacrosse Club, stated that his club would be only too happy to help to forward in any way the objects in view, as there was no doubt that there was a pressing need for a National Amateur Association, and that it would encourage amateur sports to a much greater extent.

Mr. G. Silverhorn, Secretary of the Upper Canada College Association, stated that the club was glad to hear of the possible formation of a C.A.A.A., and so far as the club could would be glad to work under any rules laid down by the association as formed.

Mr. J.M. Clemenson, of the Trinity Medical College Athletic Club, wrote that they heartily co-operated with the M.A.A.A. in their efforts to establish a Dominion Association, and wished them every possible amount of success. That in the opinion of this club, in the regulation of the new association some provision be made for the reinstating of those athletes who have unwittingly lost their position as amateurs through some ignorance of what constituted an amateur.

Mr. A.D. Stewart, of the Police Head Quarters, Hamilton, wrote that for years he had been advocating the formation of such an association. The want had long been felt, and it would do much, if formed, to foster, encourage, and consolidate manly and legitimate sports throughout the Dominion. He looked forward with delight to the association and would aid it in every way. It was needed and should not be delayed. It would purify our sports, give confidence alike to spectator and competitor, and render athletic exercises the useful pastime they ought to be.

Letters were also read from Mr. LeBrun, Secretary of the Peterboro Lacrosse Club, Mr. H.J. Wyatt of the Toronto Bank Athletic Association, and Mr. C.W. Martin, of Ottawa, all expressing sympathy with the movement.

The chairman in opening the meeting expressed the opinion that the association in Canada had been long enough in leading strings to the American association and that a time had come for a change. Long before the American association they had had such in Montreal. There were several important questions to be considered in the formation of such an association. He expressed the opinion that Canadian amateurs were the only pure amateurs in the world, for such men as George and Myers were little less than professionals. He therefore considered that he was right in saying that Canadian amateurs were the only real ones.

Mr. Hamilton - And some of these even are a little tainted. As a rule, however, it is true.

The Chairman, continuing, said that the championship meeting would be one of the most important points, but this would be a matter for after consideration.

Mr. B.B. Hamilton, of Toronto, said he quite agreed with the chairman's remarks in regard to semi-professionals like George and Myers. Those amateurs who had unwittingly transgressed against the conditions were a source of great trouble, and such an association was much needed. If they were going to have amateur sports in Canada conducted on a proper basis, they must have a Dominion Association. The Toronto Club, he assured them, was very much interested in the matter, and he assured them that they would do all they could to help forward the movement.

Mr. Angus Grant also spoke strongly in favor of the formation of such an association as supplying a great need.

Mr. H.W. Becket then moved, seconded by Mr. Hamilton.

That the name of this association be the Amateur Athletic Association of Canada"- Carried.

Mr. Starke said the next point to be considered was who was to be admitted to the association.

Mr. McKenna asked whether it was the intention to allow lacrosse clubs to join.

Mr. Whyte thought that they should only allow those clubs to enter that held athletic meetings.

The chairman also concurred in this opinion, as otherwise they might be flooded with all kinds of amateurs.

Mr. Starke thought that the best way to get over the difficulty would be for each lacrosse club not having an athletic associaton to form one in connection with the club.

Mr. Hamilton said that the Toronto Lacrosse Club, though not so in name, was to all intents and purposes an athletic association. He considered that the membership could be made as broad as possible.

After some further discussion,

Mr. G.R. Starke moved, seconded by Mr. Angus Grant,

"That the membership of the association shall be limited to amateur athletic clubs, and to such clubs as shall hold during each year one outdoor athletic meeting, containing at least three events open to amateurs.

They shall also have embodied in their by-laws the definition of an amateur, as adopted by this association."

The motion was carried unanimously.

Mr. J.K. Whyte then moved, seconded by Mr. Tumity,

"That a committee of nine be appointed to draft a constitution and by-laws, and to report at a meeting to be called by said committee, with the understanding that the meeting be held, if possible, on the occasion of the lacrosse convention in Toronto next year." Carried.

Mr. Grant moved, seconded by Mr. Bulling, that the following be the committee, namely, Messrs. R.B. Hamilton, Massey, P.D. Ross, Toronto; C.W. Martin, Ottawa; W. Maltby, H.W. Becket, J. McKennan and F.C. Henshaw, Montreal. Carried.

On Motion Mr. Maltby was appointed chairman of the committee, and the meeting then adjourned.

The Canadian National Archives provided the following document.

THE FIRST ANNUAL REPORT
THE AMATEUR ATHLETIC ASSOCIATION
OF CANADA

Presented at Annual Meeting, Sept. 27th, 1884,

Gentlemen,

In presenting the First Annual Report of the Association, we think it well, before going into the business performed during the season, to give a brief history of the organization of the Association.

On the 3rd of December, 1883, the Montreal Amateur Athletic Association issued the following circular addressed to the Athletic Clubs of the Dominion:

MONTREAL AMATEUR ATHLETIC ASSOCIATION.

To the Secretary of the Club: Montreal, Dec. 3rd, 1883

Dear Sir,

I beg to inform you that at a meeting of the Association held in the Club Rooms, Mansfield Street, last Monday evening, 26th November, it was unanimously agreed "that we seek the co-operation of the Amateur Athletic Clubs in the Dominion, with a view to the forming of a Canadian National Amateur Athletic Association."

This Association feels that the Clubs are numerous enough to establish such an Association, and would respectfully ask your hearty co operation as well as the presence of three delegates at a meeting to be held in our Club House, Mansfield Street, at 8 o'clock on the evening of the 14th December, 1883. Your early attention is requested, and should you be unable to send a delegate or delegates write us your Club's views as fully as possible.

W.L. Maltby, President
H.W. Becket, Vice-Pres.
T.L. Paton, Hon. Sec.

In response to this Circular, your Secretary received some 25 or [?] letters from different Athletic Clubs, all heartily endorsing the scheme, and on the 14th Dec., 1883, the first meeting to form the new Association took place in the Montreal Gymnasium, Mansfield Street. There were present the following representatives:

Montreal Amateur Athletic Association, W.L. Maltby, T.L. Paton and H.W. Becket.
Montreal Snow-Shoe Club, G.R. Starke, A. Grant and J.K. Whyte.

St. George Snow-Shoe Club, W.B. Bulling, W.L. Mathews, R.P. Adams.
Toronto Lacrosse Club, R.B. Hamilton.
Emerald Snow-Shoe Club, T.E. McKenna and J.G Tumity.
Twelve in all.
The Metropolitan Athletic Association, Ottawa, wired the appointment of Messrs.
G.R. Starke, J.K. Whyte and H.W. Becket as their delegates at the meeting.
At this meeting the letters received were read and the present name of the Association adopted.
A Committee consisting of Messrs. R.B. Hamilton, John Massey and P.D. Ross, of
Toronto: C.W. Martin, Ottawa; W.L. Maltby, Thos. McKenna, F.C. Henshaw and H.W.
Becket, Montreal, was appointed to draft a Constitution and By-Laws to report at a
meeting to be called by said Committee.
This meeting took place on 24th March, 1884, in the Montreal Gymnasium, Mr.
W.L. Maltby in the Chair, Messrs. T.L. Paton, Thos. McKenna, J. McKenna, J.G.
Tumity, W.L. Mathews, Angus Grant, G.R. Starke, J.G. Ross, A.J. Corriveau and H.W.
Becket, who acted as Secretary, were also present.
A draft of the Constitution and By-Laws was read and discussed, alterations and
amendments were made, and copies ordered to be printed for distribution at meeting
of Clubs, which was called by the following Circular:

Montreal, March 26th, 1884.

Dear Sir,

Pursuant to steps taken at the Convention held in Montreal in December last, at
which it was determined to form a *Canadian Amateur Athletic Association*, a meeting
of representatives of Amateur Athletic Clubs will be held in Toronto on Friday, the 11th
April next, to adopt a Constitution and By-Laws for the Association, and elect Officers for the first year.

It is requested that your Club will send *three Delegates* to the Meeting, which will
be held in the Rooms of the *Toronto Fencing Club*, south-west corner of *King and
Church Streets*, at 2 p.m.

In connection therewith, we beg to draw your attention to the enclosed draft of Constitution and By-Laws submitted at a meeting held in Montreal, March 24, 1884.

Respectfully,

Wm.L. Maltby, Chairman

H.W. Becket, Hon. Sec.

In response to this the following Clubs were represented at the meeting in Toronto:

TORONTO.

Roger Lambe, Edward Currie,	Toronto Fencing Club.
Harry Suckling,	" Lacrosse Club.
Jas. Pearson, L.H. Whittemore, J. McLaren,	" S. Shoe Club.
W.B. Campbell, H. Burrows, P.D. Ross,	" Press L. Club.
Capt. McGee, L'ts. Bennett and Brock,	Queen's Own Rifles.
D.C. Little, R.E. Brown, J.N. McKendrick,	Toronto University.

MONTREAL.

W.L. Maltby, H.W. Becket, T.L. Paton,	Amateur Ath. Assn.
G.R. Starke, Angus Grant, J.K. Whyte,	Montreal S.S. Club.
F.C. Henshaw, W.L. Mathews, T. Gilmour,	St. George "
T.E. McKenna, J. McKenna, J.G. Tumity,	Emerald "
D.J. Fraser, Wm. Cuthbert, Chas. McWood,	Argyle "
W.S. Weldon,	Athletic "
Arthur Staveley,	Maple Leaf "
A. Lefebvre, G. Quimet,	LeCanadien "
E. Tremblay,	LeTrappeur "

HAMILTON.

A.E. Jarvis,	Leander Rowing Club.
P.D. Ross,	Fencing and Athletic Clubs.

OTTAWA.

W.C. Cousens, Douglas Stewart,	Metropolitan Ath. Assn.

BRANTFORD.

J.J. Macintosh,	Brantford Lacrosse Club.

KINGSTON.

A. McLachlan and Wm. Morris,	Queen's College

Mr. Maltby was called to the chair and Mr. H.W. Becket requested to act as Secretary. The Chairman opened the meeting with a few remarks, when the Constitution and By-Laws were read, discussed, and, with a few alterations, were accepted.

The following were elected office bearers for the year 1884:

> President - Wm.L. Maltby.
> 1st Vice-President - Jas. Pearson.
> 2nd Vice-President - W.C. Cousens, M.D.
> Treasurer - W.L. Mathews.
> Hon. Sec. - H.W. Becket.

Committee-R.B. Hamilton, Roger Lambe, A.J. Corriveau, A.D. Stewart, Lieut. Henry Brock, F.C. Henshaw, J. McKenna, J.J. Mackintosh, T.A. Bertram.

After these officers were elected the President stated that the object of the Association was to regulate such athletic sports as are not now under the control of other Associations. The Canadian Cricket, Lacrosse, Rowing, Foot-ball, and Wheelmen's Associations cover these various branches of athletic sports already. The aim of our Association is mainly to regulate amateur competitions on the cinder path.

It was decided to hold the first annual Championship Meeting in Montreal on 27th Sept., 1884.

It was also decided to accept, with a few alterations the "Laws of Athletics" as published by the National Association of Amateur Athletes of America. After which the meeting adjourned.

With these few remarks we will proceed with the report of the season's work:

It is with a great deal of pleasure that your Executive presents this, the first Annual Report of the Association to the Clubs forming the same. While regretting the fact, that comparatively few of the Amateur Athletic Clubs of the Dominion availed themselves of the privileges of membership this year, we hope that next year will double the number of names on the roll.

During the season about 150 letters were answered by your secretary.

The following applications for re-instatement as amateurs were received and investigated during the season:

D.C. Little,	Toronto, Ont.,	reinstated.
J.N. McNamara,	"	"
N.H. Bethune,	Brockville, Ont.,	rejected.
C.J. Noble,	Parkhill, Ont.	still with Committee.
C.W. Kerr,	Cobourg, Ont.,	reinstated.
H.A. Dancy,	Toronto, Ont.,	rejected.
W.F. Winslow,	Paris, Ont.,	"
R.A. Kennedy,	Stratford, Ont.,	reinstated.
Frank Wheeler,	Montreal, Que.,	"

The Annual Fall Championship Meeting of the Association took place in Montreal on Sept. 27th, 1884. Notwithstanding a steady downpour of rain, most of the sports were well contested. We annex a detailed report of the same:

FIRST ANNUAL CHAMPIONSHIP MEETING OF THE ASSOCIATION.

The first Annual Championship Meeting of the Amateur Athletic Association of Canada was held on the Montreal Lacrosse Grounds on Saturday, Sept. 27th, 1884. The wretched state of the weather interfered seriously with what otherwise would have been a brilliantly successful meeting, as with few exceptions large fields were entered for the events, including some of the best men in the country. As it was, only some two hundred spectators assembled, and several good men failed to face the starter. No records were broken, but the running time was generally good, the fine cinder path not being materially injured by the rain, but jumping was almost impossible.

The Field Officers were:

Referee-F.C. Henshaw.

Time-Keepers-H.S. Tibbs, Angus Grant and James A. Taylor.

Judges at Finish-Wm.L. Maltby, James Pearson and W.C. Cousens, M.D.

Starter-Thos. L. Paton.

Clerk and Assistant Clerks of Course-W.L. Mathews, J.G. Monk, and J.L. Gardner.

Measurers-J.W. Davis, W. McNab and S. Howard.

Scorers-A.J. Corriveau and J. McKenna.

THREE MILE WALK.

J.T. McDonald, Westside Athletic Club, New York 1

Time 24 min. 53 1/2 sec.

McDonald walked over.

THROWING HAMMER.

Geo.W. Woods, Shamrock Lacrosse Club 1

C.W. Trenholme, Montreal   "   " 2

John Hughes, Shamrock   "   " 0

Distance, 78 ft. 3in.

POLE LEAP.

D.C. Little, Toronto University 1
W. Kerr, Montreal Amateur Athletic Association 2
Jas. Elliott,   "   "   "   "... 0

Height, 9ft.

100 YARD RUN.

John T. Belcher, Kingston.. 1
C.H. Low, Montreal Amateur Athletic Association 2
A.W. Waldron, Britannia Foot-Ball Club 0
John Kermode, Shamrock Lacrosse Club 0

Time, final heat, 10 1/2 sec. 6 competitors

880 YARD RUN.

T. Moffatt, Shamrock Lacrosse Club 1
J.E. Sullivan, Pastime Athletic Club, N.Y 2
W.G. Robertson, Montreal Amateur Athletic Assn. 0
A.J. McDonald, Shamrock Lacrosse Club 0
C.E. Gault, Montreal Amateur Athletic Association 0

Time, 2 min. 5 4-5 sec. 6 competitors.

PUTTING THE SHOT.

Geo.H. Woods, Shamrock Lacrosse Club 1
W.R. Thompson,   "   "   ".. 2
John Hughes   "   "   ".. 0

Distance 33 ft. 10 in. 3 competitors.

TWO MILE RUN.

D.D. McTaggart, Montreal Amateur Athletic Assn. 1
S.D. Jones, Shamrock Lacrosse Club 2
R. Wynn, Athletic Snow-Shoe Club 0

Time, 10 min. 25 3/5 sec. 3 competitors

RUNNING HIGH JUMP.

D.C. Little, Toronto University 1
J.C. Austin, Williamsburg Athletic Club, Brooklyn 2
J. Skaife, Montreal Amateur Athletic Association 0

Height, 4 ft. 9 in. 3 competitors.

220 YARD RUN.

John T. Belcher, Kingston.. 1
F. Sabourin, Rouses Point 2
C.H. Low, Montreal Amateur Athletic Association 0
A.W. Waldron, Britannia Foot-Ball Club 0

Time, 24 1/4 sec. 5 competitors.

In the first trial heat, Low and Belcher walked over. The second trial brought out Waldron, Sabourin, and Barnheart, of Ottawa, the former leading all the way. In the final, Low took the lead, with Belcher third, but the latter on the turn ran past the leaders winning handily. A protest was entered against Sabourin on the ground of his being a professional.

RUNNING BROAD JUMP.

H. Phillips, Montreal 1

D.C. Little, Toronto University 2

J.C. Austin, Williamsburg Athletic Club 0

Distance, 19 ft. 9 1/2 in. 4 competitors.

The men literally jumped in mud a foot deep. Phillips improved each attempt and won handily, Little covering 18 ft. 7 in.

ONE MILE RUN.

N. Dewar, Toronto Lacrosse Club 1

J.W .Moffatt, Montreal Junior Lacrosse Club 2

Jas. Baird, Montreal Amateur Athletic Association 0

Time 4.46 3/4.

400 YARD RUN.

T. Moffatt, Shamrock Lacrosse Club 1

A. Barnheart, Ottawa 2

Jno. Kermode, Shamrock Lacrosse Club 0

A.W. Waldron, Britannia Foot-Ball Club 0

Time, 52 1/2 sec.

120 YARD HURDLE RACE.

L. Skaife, Montreal Amateur Athletic Association 1

J.C. Austin, Williamsburg Athletic Club 2

D.C. Little, Toronto University 0

Time, 21 sec.

The prizes were presented at the Montreal Gymnasium in the evening.

It is to be hoped that the incoming Officers will persevere in the good work begun, and that the Athletic Clubs will rally to the support of the Association, for without their aid our efforts to elevate the tone of Amateur Athletics will prove almost useless and render the Championship Meeting anything but a success.

On Behalf of the Committee,

WM.L. MALTBY, Pres.

H.W. BECKET, Hon-Sec.

Montreal, 27th Sept., 1884.

The second Annual Meeting of the Association took place on the evening of the 27th Sept. (date of Championship Games), when were present the following delegates:

Montreal Amateur Athletic Association, W.L. Maltby, T.L. Paton and M. Freeman.

Montreal Snow-Shoe Club, D.D. McTaggart, H.S. Tibbs, and J.A. Taylor.

St. George Snow-Shoe Club, F.C. Henshaw, W.L. Mathews, and T. Gilmour.

Emerald Snow-Shoe Club, J. McKenna and J.G. Tumity.

Le Trappeur Snow-Shoe Club, A.J. Corriveau.

Queen's Own Rifles Club, Capt's. McGee and Murray and Lieut Lee.

Toronto Lacrosse Club, R.B. Hamilton, W.C.Bonnell.

Toronto Snow-Shoe Club, J. Pearson and J. McLaren.

19 delegates in all.

The President, Mr. Maltby, occupied the chair. In the absence of the Secretary, the Treasurer Mr. Mathews, read minutes, which were confirmed.

The President stated that, owing to the absence from the city of the Secretary, a full report could not be submitted to the meeting, but he proceeded to give an epitome' of the season's work.

The Treasurer's Report shewed a probable deficit of $190.

After some discussion *re* the ways and means of clearing off the deficit, Messrs. Henshaw, Hamilton and Maltby spoke in favor of assessing Clubs, when it was

Moved by Mr. Jas. Pearson, seconded by Capt. McGee, "that date of paying fees this year be extended one month." Carried.

The election of Officers for ensuing year was then proceeded with, when the following gentlemen were elected to serve:

JAMES PEARSON, Toronto Lacrosse Club, President.

F.C. HENSHAW, St. George S.S. Club, Montreal. 1st Vice-Pres.

A.D. STEWART, Hamilton, 2nd Vice-Pres.

HENRY BROCK, Queen's Own Rifles, Toronto, Hon.-Secretary.

J. MCLAREN, Toronto Snow-Shoe Club, Treasurer.

Council-W.L. Maltby, H.W. Becket, R.B. Hamilton, Jas. McKenna, W. Cuthbert, A.J. Corriveau, W.C. Cousens, R. Lambe and McGregor.

After which the meeting was dismissed.

W.L. Mathews, Hon.-Treas, in Account with The Amateur Athletic Association of Canada.

DR.

April	24	Subscription Montreal Amateur Athletic Association .... $	15.00
	25	" Montreal Snow-Shoe Club	15.00
	28	" St. George Snow-Shoe Club	15.00
June	24	" Toronto " " Toronto	15.00
Aug.	5	" Brantford Lacrosse Club, Brantford	5.00
	11	" Metropolitan Athletic Assn., Ottawa	10.00
	15	" Toronto Fencing Club, Montreal	10.00
	22	" Emerald Snow-Shoe Club, Montreal	15.00
Sept.	22	" Athletic Snow-Shoe Club, Montreal	5.00
		" Le Trappeur " "	15.00
	27	" Argyle " "	10.00
		" Queen's Own Rifles Association, Toronto	15.00
		" Toronto Lacrosse Club, Toronto	15.00
		" Montreal Amateur Ath. Assn., Montreal	15.00
		" Montreal Snow-Shoe Club, Montreal	15.00
		" St. George " "	15.00
		Fees for Investigation into Amateur Standing	8.00
		Entry Fees Annual Games	34.00
		Gate Receipts	44.75
			$ 286.75

CR.

1884.

May	7	By Becket Bros., Printing, & c	$ 35.25
		Cash Book	0.40
		Postages (Treasurer)	2.00
October.		Cab Hire	0.50
		Becket Bros. (Printing By-Laws, & c.)	101.00
		John Murray (distributing Dodgers)	1.90
		Postage (Secretary)	4.71
		Witness (advertising Races)	9.00
		Canadian District Tel. Co. (distributing Dodgers)	5.00
		Star (advetising Races)	9.53
		Quinn & Co. (Bill Posting)	4.50
		J.R. Harper, on account of Medals	50.00
		T.A. Adkins, " "	39.00
		Police (Races)	8.00
		Boys selling Programmes	2.50
		Gate-keepers (five men)	7.50
		Cash in hand	5.96
			$ 286.75

Association still owes J.R. Harper 69.00

   "   "   T.A. Adkins.............................. .... 75.00

                                                                                           $ 144.00

Chapter 2

AQUATICS

Among the first to be organized, aquatic sports had a long history of informal competition. In the American South slaves rowed against one another along the Gulf Coast for the amusement of their masters. As early as 1811 barges raced on New York's Hudson River. By the 1820's rowing clubs proliferated in both the northern and southern states. In 1836 John Cox Stevens engaged Robert B. Forbes in a yacht race off the Massachusetts coast, and Stevens joined friends in establishing the New York Yacht Club in 1844. When the United States yacht, America, defeated the English Royal Yacht Squadron for a trophy in 1851 it initiated the America's Cup series with several challenges issued and immense interest generated after 1870.

Students formed college rowing clubs at prestigious institutions, such as Harvard and Yale,in the 1840's. In 1852 both schools competed in a race on Lake Winnepesaukee in New Hampshire that marked the advent of intercollegiate athletic competitions. In 1872 Philadelphia's Schulkill Navy Rowing Club proved integral in forming the National Association of Amateur Oarsmen, which organized national championships and international events.

While amateurs generally competed for health or honor among middle class colleagues, and only the wealthy could afford yachts, professional,often working class oarsmen contended for money prizes in single and double sculls. Such contests held prominence throughout much of the nineteenth century; but the popularity of rowing diminished by the 1890's as the interest and opportunities grew in other sports, particularly baseball.

ROWING

The following article, reprinted from the Boston Globe, 5 July 1883, provides a detailed account of typical rowing competitions during the latter nineteenth century.

ON THE CHARLES
THE ANNUAL ROWING REGATTA GIVEN BY THE CITY
SIX VERY EXCITING EVENTS WITNESSED BY A LARGE AND INTERESTED CROWD
LEE, THE GOOKIN BROTHERS AND THE WEST-END CREW AMONG THE WINNERS

For many years one of the principal features of the Fourth of July celebration in this city has been the rowing regatta on the Charles river. In years gone, from 30,000 to

50,000 people were drawn to the river bank by the many attractions, but yesterday—owing probably to the absence of Hanlan, Rosmer and other celebrities in the rowing world—scarcely 15,000 people witnessed the races. What the crowd lacked in numbers, however, it made up in enthusiasm, and each oarsman and crew was loudly applauded and cheered as the boats crossed the line either a winner or further back in the procession. The larger portion of the crowd was along the wall, and there, unprotected from the sun's rays—and they were terribly hot—men, women and children suffered nearly four hours without complaining of the weather or anything else. It was a good-natured crowd, and no accident or mishap occurred to mar the pleasure of the day. The well-sheltered roof of the Union boat-house provided accommodations for a large number, and innumerable small boats and a few tugs carried the balance of the crowd. The referee and the members of the press followed the races in a tug. Councilman James A. Murphy of the committee on rowing regatta was painstaking to a degree, and most of the credit for the success of the day is due to him. He was everywhere and prevented many vexatious delays that so frequently occur on an occasion of this kind.

The wind was southwest and the water was rough—almost too rough for good rowing. This accounts in part for the slow time made in all the races, excepting the professional single sculls. One or two of the oarsmen barely escaped being swamped, and many of them were obliged in the midst of a race to stop and bail out their boats.

There were six events on the programme, all exciting and full of interest. Lee had an easy time of it in the scullers' race after the first mile and a half, but before that it looked as if it belonged to anybody. The double scull race was the most interesting of the day, and Lee and McKay only won by a half a length. The Gookin brothers led from the start, but they allowed the other crew to catch them just before the finish.

The Professional Scullers' Race

The first race, the professional scullers, was started at 10.53.39, and out of the following six entries, Fred A. Plaisted, George Galsel, George W. Lee, George H. Hosmer, William Elliot and John McKay, only Plaisted, Lee, Elliot and McKay took the word. At the outset Elliot appeared to be the better man. He took a strong hold of the water with a stroke of thirty-six, and for a dozen or more strokes kept well in advance, when Plaisted who, owing to being thoughtless at the time of the send off, lost several strokes, picked up somewhat, and for between twenty-five and thirty strokes, made the work for all four quite rapid. He easily caught McKay, passed Lee and gave Elliot his wash. The effort was of too vigorous a character for Fred and he gradually fell astern and Elliot once more cut out the pace, with McKay a good second and Lee third. The latter was evidently not overworking himself as he was going along at no better then thirty strokes to the minute. These positions did not alter for three-quarters of a mile when Elliot, McKay and Lee were even, with Plaisted several lengths astern. Lee satisfied of his ability to outrow McKay, the only competitor in the race that he feared, struck a thirty-four gait and went nimbly by the Hallgonian and with an additional effort passed the ex-champion of England, McKay's effort to stay with Lee brought him upon even terms with Elliot and the latter's staying qualities having been taxed to their utmost, he went gradually astern, and from this point out the contest was a procession. Lee won as he pleased, although at the finish McKay was but a few lengths behind. Lee's time was 20 minutes 50 seconds; McKay's 21 minutes 18 seconds. Plaisted and Elliot were almost distanced.

Single-Scull Working Boat Race.

The second event was the single-scull working-boat race, generally a purse presented by the city of Boston to the Gookin brothers. For this contest there were nine entries as follows: Charles Hooper, J. Casey, J. Flannery, Fred A. Plaisted, Richard J. Gookin, M. Argey, M. Ahearn, Sylvester Gookin and P.J. Cleary. Of the above list only Casey, Flannery, Richard Gookin, M. Argey, and Sylvester Gookin appeared upon the line. At the outset the contest was of the evenest character. All five of the oarsmen were about to take the word, and for half a mile it was anybody's race. At this point the effort to keep up with the procession proved too much for Casey and he ceased rowing. Flannery an eighth of a mile further along owing to the rough water and the rapidity with which Rich Gookin was cutting the pace, dropped out. At the mile only Rich Gookin leading by several lengths, Sylvie his brother, and Argey of Chelsea were engaged. They all had slopped more or less water. Sylvie Gookin was troubled in this respect more than any of the others, as he stopped every now and then to bail out his boat. When passing the mile point Argey closed upon him, taking a lead of several lengths for the second place. At the turn Richard Gookin led by fifteen lengths over Argey, who led Sylvester Gookin half a dozen times the length of his boat. The race home was an easy one for Richard, while Sylvester Gookin and Argey had a close contest. The latter's boat however proved the most seaworthy, and at the finish he was but 30 seconds behind Richard Gookin who completed the distance in 23 minutes and 4 seconds. Sylvester Gookin's time was 24 minutes 10 seconds.

Amateur Scullers' Race.

The third event on the programme was the amateur scullers' race for which the following representatives of the local clubs had entered: James O'Neil, John J. Murphy, James G. Moffitt, John Francis, D.J. Murphy, Joseph E. Lewis, Gundie K. Dodd, George Clapp. Of the above only O'Neill, John J. Murphy, Daniel J. Murphy, Lewis and Dodd went away at the word. John J. Murphy cut the pace for half of the first mile, with Daniel Murphy crowding him hard. It was the Crescents against the paternal Shawmuts with paternity ahead. The Crescent representative made a brilliant effort after the half-mile was passed, and went to the front and for nearly a mile kept several lengths ahead. O'Neill, Lewis and Dodd rowing well astern. Nearing the turning buoy and just before the house of the Crescent Boat Club was reached, the Shawmut man let himself out to his fullest capacity, and the cheers which were ready to be bestowed upon Daniel J. Murphy were hushed into stillness when John J., the Shawmut representative, took a lead of several lengths. From this point out the Shawmut man maintained his supremacy, although at times hardly pressed by the Crescent sculler. The race for the last mile was one of the best ever seen upon the river. The distance was covered in very rough water by John J. Murphy in 22 minutes 31 1/2 seconds, and by Daniel J. Murphy in 22 minutes 33 seconds. Both men gave evidence of the labor they had performed. James H. O'Neill was third in 24 minutes 54 1/2 seconds.

The Double Scull Races.

The fourth contest was for double-scull shells, and had the following entries: Hooper and mate, J.F. Kilby and mate, Plaisted and mate, Hosmer and mate, Gookin brothers, McKay and mate, Lee and mate, Casey and mate, Elliot and mate. When the start was made, only McKay and Lee, the Gookin boys and Hooper and Barker staffed with the Gookins to the fore. For half a mile the race was quite an even one. At this point, however, the water proved too rough for Hooper and mate, and they ceased rowing. Lee and McKay had a Noah's ark of a boat and it required considerable labor to keep up its headway. On the other hand the boat of the Gookins was of modern build, and during the next mile they rowed so quickly that when they were headed for home, after having made the turn, they were at least fifteen lengths ahead of the Newark and Hallgonian delegation. The race was at this time concerned to be with the Shawmut men, and they as well as the on-lookers deemed victory a certainty. They stopped frequently to remove some of the water they were continually shipping and while they were so doing McKay and Lee kept gradually closing upon the men. Half a mile from home the lead of the Gookins had been reduced to two lengths and one of the hottest races ever witnessed on the Charles ensued. The Gookins put every ounce of muscle they possessed into their work and opened up another length. In the other boat Lee had not been doing much of any work. He was disheartened at the outset by the age of the draft in which he was rowing, but upon noticing the dilemma of the Gookins he took new courage, and with a will answered McKay's stroke. Stroke after stroke, thirty-six to the minute was the order in both boats and a quarter of a mile from home McKay and Lee were but a few feet astern. An eighth of a mile from the finish the positions of the crews had not changed. The Gookins were still ahead, going at a forty gait, Lee and his partner holding them to the task with thirty-six. Twelve lengths from the finish the struggle of the day began. The Gookins were making superhuman efforts to hold their own and McKay and Lee were encouraged by the shouts of the enthusiastic spectators. They were driving their old craft at a 44 pace, and their work was telling, but gradually. They did not gain but a foot at a time, but gain they did, and with one of the most desperate spurts ever put forth by oarsmen in the world they went across the line winning by less than ten feet in the very good time of 35 minutes. The Gookins being only 1 second later. Both crews were cheered loudly and it was conceded upon all sides one of the grandest races for the last half ever witnessed.

The Amateur Four-Oared Race

The fifth race, for amateur four-oared shells or working boats had for entries the Columbian, Bradford and Middlesex crews. At the start the Bradford four easily went to the front, but the disturbed condition of the water prevented their scull from making much headway, and the working beat of the Columbian crew soon displaced both them and the Middlesex crew, who were also rowing in a shell. The latter crew were however, soon sent well forward by the wonderful rapidity of their stroke, which rarely fell below fifty to the minute, and at times reached fifty-six. As might be supposed, with such a speedy stroke, well kept up, they quickly opened a gap of a dozen or more lengths. The Bradford's boat also rode the water well, and they soon left the Columbians well in their wake. At the turn the Middlesex crew had retained their lead, but unfortunately turned contrary to the rules of the National Association of Amateur Oarsmen. The Bradford and Columbian crews both noticed the mistake, made the correct turn, and rowed home at their pleasure, taking respectively first and second places. The time on the Middlesex crew, which finished first, was 20 minutes 48 1/2 seconds; of the Bradford crew, 22 minutes, 22 seconds; and of the Columbian boat 27 minutes 3 seconds.

The Professional Four-Oared Race.

The last event of the day, and the sixth race upon the programme, was the four-oared working boat race. Unlike the other contests of the day, which all had been of a distance of three miles, this was one of four miles with two turns. Twenty-one crews had signified their intention of contesting as follows: South End crew, Lafayette crew, Troy crew, Forest River crew #1, Enterprise crew #2, Enterprise crew #1, North End crew, Middlesex crew, #1, Shawmut crew, Middlesex crew #2; Bunker Hill crew, Leverett crew #1, Everett crew, We-row-come-at-us crew, West End crew #1, Forest River crew #2, Leverett crew #2, West End crew #2, Salem crew #1, Columbian crew. Of these, however, only South End, Lafayette, Troy, Forest River #1, North End, Middlesex #1, Shawmut, Bunker Hill, Leverett, Everett, We-row-come-at-us and the West End crew #1 joined the fight. The twelve crews presented a very handsome picture as they were sent away, with the West End boys, in answer to Danny Breen's stroke, marking out the course. Plaisted in the We-row-come-at-us hardly a dozen lengths away made a strenuous effort to hamper the West Enders, but Hill was just as clever as he with the rudder, and a collision was happily avoided. Fifty lengths from the start the race between the West End, Forest River, Leverett, Shawmut, Middlesex, We-row-come-at-us, North End, South End and Everett crews was quite interesting. The West Ends gradually drew away, and half a mile from the start the Middlesex and Shawmut crews fouled, and whatever race there was to the finish was between the Forest River and Leverett crews for second place. The West End crew had at the end of the first mile a dozen lengths the best of it, and made the turn at the second mile in 14 minutes and 45 seconds, more than thirty seconds ahead of the Forest River, their heaviest competitors. Twelve crews originally started in the contest, but upon opening up the last two miles it was found that this number had dwindled to six, and in the end of the third mile but five crews rounded the flag and remained in the race, which was finished in the following order. West End crew in 31 minutes and 29 seconds, Forest River in 31 minutes and 52 seconds, Leverett crew in 32 minutes and 22 1/2 seconds, North End crew in 33 minutes and 5 seconds, South End crew in 34 minutes and 20 seconds.

The interest in rowing subsided as track and cycling races gained in popularity. Unsavory incidents, such as the following one obtained from the Chicago Tribune, 14 September 1889, p. 6., featured some of the top professionals, and cast a pallor over the sport.

TEEMER'S CLAIM OF FOUL.
UNSATISFACTORY RESULT OF HIS RACE WITH JAKE GAUDAUR.

McKeesport, Pa., Sept. 13—The Race in single skulls between John Teemer of this city and Jacob G. Gaudaur of St. Louis came off here this evening, but instead of being the fine exhibition it was expected to be it turned out a miserable farce. Early in the afternoon Teemer went alone, and Gaudaur, accompanied by Al Hamm, his trainer, proceeded to Barnardis grove, about a quarter of a mile from the starting point of the race. At 5 o'clock six steam boats and a variety of smaller craft sailed down the river and all but the referee's boat took positions along the course utterly regardless of the rights of the contestants. The referee's boat rounded to the starting point at 5:30 and at 5:35 Teemer got into his boat and came down to the end of the course amid the cheers of hundreds of admirers on all the boats in sight. Numerous bets of $100 to $75 and $100 to $60 were offered, but none of them were taken. Teemer's friends then offered two to one on their favorite and several small bets were taken. St. John, who was on the referee's boat and had furnished the stake money for Gaudaur, declined to take any of the bets offered.

At 5:45 Gaudaur came to the starting point, and Al Hamm at the same time was seen to enter his boat a quarter of a mile further up the course and take a position well out from the shore. Gaudaur won the toss for position and took the north side of the river.

J.D. Pringle, sporting editor of the Pittsburgh, *Dispatch*, who had been chosen referee, gave the word "go" at 5:47, and away the two sculls sped, Teemer taking the lead almost at the first stroke. By the time they had reached the point where Hamm set out Teemer was nearly two boat lengths ahead, and soon took the inside track. The referee's boat was slow in starting, but was near enough to the oarsmen before a mile had been made to see Hamm get directly in Teemer's way and collide with his boat. Soon Teemer was seen to fall behind both Gaudaur and Hamm, who rowed leisurely away from him, followed closely by all the river craft carrying spectators except the referee's boat.

They reached the end of the course at 6:06, Teemer being at the time, although apparently pulling with all his might, nearly half a mile behind. Two of Teemer's brothers and Bill Nickerson of Boston, Teemer's friend, made a claim of foul when Hamm was seen to get in Teemer's way. Teemer continued on over the course, although the waves from the numerous steamers which had passed him were running four feet high.

A FIGHT

At 7 o'clock the referee, Gaudaur, Hamm, Teemer and a few of their friends met at a room in the National hotel. Teemer claimed the race on a foul. He said that Hamm came out on the course and ran into his boat, knocking a hole in it and causing it to fill with water. Hamm denied the allegation and intimated that Teemer was telling a falsehood, whereupon the latter rushed at him and struck him a blow in the face. The two men clinched and rolled on the floor, but were separated and Hamm was induced to leave the room.

By this time a crowd was at the door clamoring for admission and demanding a decision by the referee, while several hundred were in the street in front of the hotel all eager to know the result of the race. In order to avoid violence being done the referee said he would not announce his decision until tomorrow afternoon.

The crowd in attendance along the river banks and on the boats numbered at least 25,000, and as Hamm rowed in a length or two ahead of Gaudaur, while Teemer was out of sight, the crowd mistook Hamm for Teemer and the shouts which went up from the multitude for Teemer lasted for several minutes, before the mistake was discovered.

Up to the time Teemer passed Gaudaur within the first half mile or so he was rowing forty two strokes a minute, and Gaudaur two or three strokes less. It is generally believed that Pringle will decide that Teemer was fouled by Gaudaur's trainer, as all the press representatives claim they saw Hamm get in Teemer's way, though they could not say whether the boats collided or not. The time occupied by Gaudaur in passing over the course which was little if any over three miles was twenty-three minutes.

Rowing retained its popularity on college campuses, particularly in the Northeast, where seven schools forged the Intercollegiate Rowing Association in 1883. Relatively wealthy college men were considered to be above the needs or machinations of the working class professionals. The following articles, from Harper's Weekly, 27 June 1891, pp. 485-486, and Outing Magazine, October 1888, pp. 57-59, respectively chronicle the history of intercollegiate crew racing and its scientific selection and training of athletes by the latter nineteenth century.

COLLEGE BOAT-RACING IN
AMERICA
By Casper W. Whitney

The earliest recorded college boating in this country goes back to 1833, when Yale was spreading consternation among the erst-while local heroes of the fairs and Fourth of July festivities in the rural districts of Connecticut, Massachusetts, and New York. College archives fail to deal very specifically with these first aquatic conquests, but time and the collegians' fanciful conception have jointly cast a glamour of romance about these primitive athletic days which has more than supplied the deficiency. Even the townsfolk have fallen victims (and not unwilling ones) to the blandishments of the picturesque and prolific undergraduate memory, and the visitor to New Haven today may, without great search find many an "oldest inhabitant" who will wax garrulous on the prowess of Yale oarsmen in those ancient days. For ten years there was no boat racing at Yale other than the annual descents on the country bumpkins' especial field of activity. Boating, in fact, was neither a recognized nor organized college sport, training was an unexplored mystery, and desultory work was the order of the day. Harvard, in the mean time, with all the glorious facilities presented by the Charles River, was beginning likewise to take on a boating spirit.

Intercollegiate history does not enlighten us on the first days of rowing at Cambridge, but a certain dear old boy, for whose memory I have too much respect to permit a single doubt to darken even one of his deliciously impossible yarns, has poured into my ear by the hour wondrous tales of their prowess. Who shall say that even in those early days there was no rivalry between these, our two greatest seats of learning? If Yale humbled the pride of the country lads in carrying away the prizes at their

Fourth of July regatta, Harvard, so my ancient mariner informs me, was no less victorious in stealing away the hearts of the lasses who lined the bank of the Charles whenever the college boys went out for a pull.

The organization of the sport was, of course, a natural sequence, and in 1843 seven members of the Yale class of '44 formed, under the name of the Yale Boat Club, the first rowing club in America. They had a four-oared Whitehall boat, 19 feet long about 4 wide, and used 12 feet oars. In that same year three other boats were purchased by the students, one of them being a lap-streak gig for 8 oars. This, for the time being, was the pride of the university to say nothing of New Haven. It was long, narrow, and so fast that the remarkable tales of the earlier boats were in great danger of being effaced altogether from collegiate recollection.

In the following year the Harvard class of '46 had the distinction of forming the first boat club in that university. They purchased an eight-oared boat, called Oneida, that had been built for a race between Boston mechanics, and many a contest it won for them. It was a heavy lap-streak, 87 feet long, 3 1/2 feet in its widest part and tapered gradually to bow and stern. It sat low in the water, had no shear, was floored half-way up to the gunwale with wooden strips, and had hardwood gratings at either end that were the crew's absolute delight. On every state occasion these gratings were rubbed, oiled, and polished until they shone again. Plain flat wooden tholepins fitted into the gunwale; she had six whiteash oars. The Oneida stands out prominently and gallantly in the first days of college boating. She was a good boat, and won the first race with Yale in '52; she was never beaten, in fact, until '56, when race-boats were introduced; and in '57 she was sold in order to purchase a craft better adapted to excursions and less to racing. The only boat in those days that approached Oneida was Shawmut at New Haven, which in its turn became famous. It had room for six passengers, the captain's elevated seat being at the extreme end, from where he could look over the heads of the crew. In those days college boats were constructed more for pleasuring than racing, and accommodations were invariably made for guests.

But those were good old days, sure enough—at least so my ancient mariner tells me. The drudgery of training was unknown. No such discipline as we are accustomed to nowadays would have been permitted. Rowing was a recreation first, last, and always. The crews were chosen on account of their popularity as well as strength and general fitness and when they rowed half the university turned out to watch and cheer. Rowing days were veritable carnivals of aquatic sport, and not an available boat in college or town rode at anchor on such an occasion. About the only system observed was that the best oarsmen—the ones likely to fill the varsity—had absolute control of the boats in the evening, while the beginners were permitted to take their work in the morning. Beginning with the establishment of rowing clubs in '43 at Yale, followed by Harvard in '44, the sport took on a boom that carried it along with a splurge for a few years, but rather left it to shift for itself in about '49. The college faculties all this time had by no means encouraged boating, though they had tolerated it; but in '51 the students at Cambridge had a town row; and forthwith an order went out from the Harvard faculty prohibiting the construction of any new boats; consequently, in '51 and '53, Harvard depended for success upon but one boat, the trustworthy Oneida, and right well did she serve them.

In '52 Yale and Harvard contested their first race. August 3d, at Centre Harbor, Lake Winnipiseogee, in eight-oared barges, over a two-mile course. The prize was a pair of black walnut oars, and Harvard won in the *Oneida* by four lengths, a curious feature being that the stroke oar in both boats rowed upon the starboard side. Boating at this time, and in the one or two years immediately following, was not in a particularly flourishing condition at Harvard. Yale's defeat naturally gave her a bit of a set down, and consequently there was no race again until '55, when Yale again challenged. This time it was rowed at Springfield, a mile and a half—and return, and was again won by Harvard in an eight-oared barge. Yale rowing a six-oared barge. Yale had a superior boat in this year, with wooden outriggers, but pulled a short, jerky stroke, 60 to the minute, and were soon out of it. After this year the boating spirit at Harvard took on a great boom.

The first varsity boat was constructed—a 51 foot lap-streak, with no rudder—new models were made, and for the first time outriggers and spruce oars were seen at Cambridge. There was no race in '57 with Yale, but that year marked a turning-point in intercollegiate racing. Harvard built a six-oared shell—the first one in America—40 feet long (made short in order to turn a stake easily), 26 inches wide amidships, and weighing 150 pounds. The shell was made of white pine, and fitted with iron outriggers similar to those in use now, with the exception that the oars were not fastened in. Add to this outfit spoon oars, and it is hardly necessary to say that the Harvard crew of '58 were so elated that visions of aquatic victory chased everything else out of their heads. It was a great stride in rowing in those days.

In May, '58 the *Harvard Magazine* proposed the establishment of an annual intercollegiate regatta. Forthwith circulars were sent to Brown, Yale, and Trinity. At a meeting called at New Haven, May 26th, arrangements were made for a three-mile race that year at Springfield, July 23d. Considerable preparation was made by both Yale and Harvard for this event, it seeming to be filled with more importance than those which had gone before it. The drowning of the Yale stroke a few days previous to the day set for the race put an end to the regatta for that year, however. The impetus that had been given rowing by its further recognition in the establishment of an intercollegiate regatta, went merrily along and in '59 the crews settled to their work more earnestly. For the first time they began to train, restricting themselves to meat, dry bread, oatmeal, and fruit occasionally. They ran four miles before breakfast, finishing up in good speed; pulled weights in the gymnasium; rowed the full course every evening; and paid more attention to the stroke. Brown succeeded also in mustering a crew. The race was rowed on Lake Quinsigamond, mile and a half and return, in six-oared shells, and won by Harvard. The following year, '60 was a repetition in entries and results of '59, Harvard rowing in a new shell, longer and narrower than any she had used. This year also saw the first of Freshman and Sophomore races between Harvard and Yale.

From this year ('60) until '64 there were no races between Yale and Harvard; both crews, however, did some training every year, and were continually seeking improvements on their methods. During this period of intercollegiate lethargy some good at least was accomplished in the accurate surveying of the course at Springfield and on Lake Quinsigamond, with the result of showing that the time made previously was not at all to be relied upon, the starting and finishing flags having been moved from time to time without any especial regard for accuracy. In '64 came Yale's first victory, and wonderful traditions concerning Mr. Wilbur Bacon and that redoubtable crew yet hover about the halls at New Haven. Looking back from our present athletic vantage ground upon the work done by this crew, we wonder the men accomplished what they did; probably no crew in the history of American boating ever went through severer training. It may interest oarsmen of today to read a leaf from the daily work of those men: "They arose at six, walked and ran before breakfast, on an absolutely empty stomach, between three and five miles, running in heavy flannels more than half the distance, and part of that at full speed. After breakfast and recitation they rowed about four miles at speed, and again in the afternoon the same distance...much of their rowing being "on time." Beef, mutton, occasionally chicken, toasted bread, boiled rice, and weak tea was the bill of fare. No wine or beer, and but few vegetables."

One of the curiosities of this age of athletic ignorance was the report in a daily paper of the race, in which the Harvard men, who had been training without shirts, and appeared consequently with browned backs, were declared to have anointed themselves with some kind of coloring preparation warranted to strike terror to the hearts of their rivals. The costumes of the crew in this the greatest race up to that time were: for Yale, "blue handkerchiefs, flesh-colored shirts, and white trousers;" for Harvard, "red handkerchiefs, white shirts, and blue trousers." Mr. Bacon's effective work continued through '65, and again Yale won in 17 minutes 41 1/2 seconds, the fastest time ever made in this country for a three-mile race with a turn. Yale's work in both these years was the direct result of indefatigable effort ably directed. The form was not good, the men rowing a quick, jerky stroke, but their time was excellent, and they had the great advantage of long practice together. In '66 Yale began a series of experiments that lasted, with more or less disaster, for about ten years. Not content with the good material (of its kind), Mr. Bacon had succeeded, after his several years of hard work, in developing, some new men got hold of the reins, and a stroke rowed principally with the arms was introduced.

How curiously throughout the history of college rowing we find every now and again the substance being forsaken for the shadow! First Yale, then Harvard, then Yale again; and Harvard even to this day is only just beginning, after a long succession of defeats, to see through the glass darkly. Well, the Yale crew of '66 was defeated, and so also were those of '67,'68,'69. In these years, by-the-way, the oars used by both crews were shorter than they are now, while those of '65 were longer. The defeats administered to Harvard by Yale in '64 and '65 carried with them severe but masterly lessons that were learned silently and thoroughly. Harvard took warning of the "fine" trained crew from New Haven, and kept her men in sufficient flesh to permit of working off a few pounds on the day of the great struggle. In these three years Harvard made considerable progress, and began to look about for new fields of conquest. As early as '67 a desire to visit Europe and try conclusions with the English universities became manifest, and the International Regatta thrown open to the world in connection with the Paris Exposition afforded the desired opportunity. A great effort was made, but as she could muster only seven men worthy of a seat in the shell, Harvard was compelled to be content that year with a victory over Yale only.

Again, in '68 the trip to England was agitated, and a challenge sent Oxford. This was accepted, and all Harvard was beside itself with elation. From that day on the barometer of Harvard's athletic esteem climbed steadily upward. The crew was well received abroad, and made an extremely favorable impression. Space does not permit of going more into detail; Harvard was defeated by six seconds in a four mile race with Oxford, though it is not improbably that had Harvard pursued the same policy as the English crew, and taken Oxford's water, giving the back-wash she was afterward compelled to take, the time would certainly have been less. Harvard's coxswain was too sportsman-like for the Englishmen.

As though to add insult to injury, Yale in the following year,'70 defeated her, but having fouled on the turn, the race was awarded to Harvard. Yale introduced sliding seats in this year, and they were immediately taken up by all the rowing colleges. The sliding seats of those days, however, were primitive affairs. They consisted of a pine board about 4 by 12, with grooved boxwood runner sliding on steel bars; nothing to regulate the slide, or keep if from jumping off the runners. Harvard was the first crew in this year to sit "hard up," instead of in the centre of the shell. No race was arranged between Harvard and Yale in '71, though the latter sent a challenge, and an Association of American Colleges was formed, to which belonged Amherst, Bowdoin, Brown, Harvard, and Agricultural College of Massachusetts. The race of that year was won by the last named with Harvard second. In '72 Yale followed the rest, and joined the Association; and in that year produced the worst crew in her history. The race was at Springfield—three miles straightaway, with six colleges entered. Amherst won, Yale finished last. And yet in that boat sat R.J. Cook, who was receiving his first lessons in a bitter school, and was afterward to do so much for Yale boating.

The consultation of Yale workers that followed this gloomy event, concluded that they were working on the wrong basis; they had tried short jerky strokes and long slow ones; professional coaching had been followed since '64 and the foundation of a strong winning stroke seemed as far off as ever. It was resolved, therefore, to carry the war into Africa; so in the spring of '73 Mr. Cook made his trip to England. He spent many months on the Thames, closely watching the Oxford and Cambridge oarsmen, and when he returned he brought with him the fundamental principles of rowing, upon which and through which he has developed such excellent results. He brought to America "the long sweep and slow recover of the Englishmen, and he left behind the short slide," in which he had been instructed. It was by no means the English stroke as seen in England that he produced, but a stroke founded upon the rudiments of that which for years had given us the most finished oarsmen. That year, at Springfield in a three-mile straightaway, saw the first practical test of the new stroke, and Yale turned out the best crew she had in years. The newspapers had poked a great deal of fun at the Cook or English stroke, but the crew rowed in excellent form, nevertheless, and won in a field that included Harvard, which finished third to Wesleyan's second, Amherst, Massachusetts Agricultural College, Williams, Dartmouth, Trinity, Columbia, Bowdoin, and Cornell. In '74, at Saratoga, single-oar races were first introduced between Yale, Harvard and Cornell. In the varsity race of three miles straightaway, there were nine crews entered, including Trinity and Princeton. Yale and Harvard became entangled in a foul, and Columbia which had a good crew won. Thirteen crews contested at Saratoga in '75. Cornell won that year, with Yale sixth, notwithstanding her crew being captained and stroked by Mr. Cook.

In the winter of this year Yale withdrew from the rowing association of colleges, and challenged Harvard to an eight-oared four-mile race, which was promptly accepted, and thus began the Yale-Harvard annual contests as we find them today. Though Harvard had accepted Yale's challenge, yet she remained in the general association and in '76 sent a six-oared crew to Saratoga, which was defeated by Cornell, and the eight-oared varsity, stroked by Bancroft, suffered similarly in the race with Yale, stroked by Cook. In September of the same year Yale sent a four-oared crew to the Centennial, which defeated both the English crew from Cambridge and Columbia. After the Saratoga regatta of this year, Harvard withdrew from the association, and in '77 made arrangements with Yale for a race at Springfield. It was very freely predicted, by those who knew nothing of the subject, that interest would continue in the Saratoga regatta, and the Yale-Harvard race prove stupid and unattended, but the result was the opposite. Saratoga died, and Springfield, or New London, as it became next year, boomed. In '77, '78, and '79 Harvard, stroked by Bancroft, defeated Yale with increasing ease, the race of '77 by seven seconds, and that of '79 by one minute and forty-three seconds. Mr. Cook having left college, some disastrous experiments were made in the stroke during the last two years. Two years later, in June '81, Columbia sent a four-oared crew abroad to participate in the Henley regatta, which after many trials and tribulations, finally secured the Henley cup, the only English aquatic trophy, I believe, that has ever been brought to this country.

In '81 Cornell sent a four-oared crew, which had won the intercollegiate race at the Lake George regatta in '80, to England for the Henley event. Of the misfortunes that befell this unlucky crew a column could be written did space permit. After endless discussion and a great display of snobbery by the English oarsmen, their entry was finally accepted. They pulled many a discouraging race in England, but the luckless crew were never victorious. They went over to the Continent and rowed on the Danube against a Vienna crew, and here they also lost, one of the men being accused by the others of selling the race.

In '80 Yale continued following the will-o'-wisp in permitting a professional directorship of its rowing. By some very sophistical theories, Davis, the professional, had entrenched himself in the consideration of some of the powers, and there he remained. Yale won in '80 and '81 from Harvard under this regime, and the unfortunate result was to strengthen the hold of a man and system that should have been sent on their way rejoicing. They failed to look more closely into the cause. Had they done so, it would have been discovered that in those years Harvard had been particularly unfortunate, and a warning should have been accepted in the fact that notwithstanding this, Yale won by a few seconds in '81. However, Davis ruled and Yale in '82 began a series of experiments in rigging and stroke that were absurd. The result was a "donkey-engine stroke," that gave all loyal friends of Yale the horrors, and froze Bob Cook's blood in his veins. The training the men underwent was enough to have killed them; they were over-trained, and completely demoralized. Of course Harvard won. In '84 Mr. Cook came to the rescue, and out of chaos brought forth the best crew Yale had turned out up to that time. It lowered the record to 20.31, and raised a great hope in the breasts of all Yale men.

Meanwhile Harvard was taking a turn at making fatal experiments. In the winter of '84 Bancroft, Harvard's ablest adviser, ceased coaching the crew. Instead of getting some graduate who had been taught in the Bancroft school to aid him in coaching, the captain secretly employed a professional sculler, totally without experience in long-distance eight-oared rowing to counsel and advise. Yale during this time was likewise experiencing internal dissensions. The captain of the crew and Cook were not able to agree, the crew was disorganized, and the men badly trained. The result was an easy victory for Harvard, and the most costly one she had ever gained. Good sense at Yale predominated and Mr. Cook was persuaded to take the crew in hand again. At Harvard unsystematized work continued. The history of college boating from that day to this is easily told. Yale has continued under one able guidance, gone on improving her stroke, and turning out the most finished crews. Harvard has had dissension following dissension, one coach this year, another with his own pet theories the next. While Yale has been turning out fast and remarkably finished crews, that have won since '86, Harvard has slowly been struggling back to sound rowing principles. Last year especially there were hopeful signs that augur well for the near future. I could say much on the coaching methods and underlying basis of the two crews, but there is no space for comments or criticism in this article, which deals only with the history of facts, as briefly as possible. Since the dissolution of the old association, Columbia, Cornell, and the University of Pennsylvania have maintained crews, and in the past two years had an annual race, but their form is greatly inferior to either Yale or Harvard. Yale's greatest crew was that of '88 which gave the finest exhibition of rowing ever seen in America. It lowered the record to 20.10, and was undoubtedly the fastest crew that ever sat a boat. It is too bad the men were not sent abroad. Last year the Yale accepted a challenge from the Atlanta crew, probably the fastest non-collegiate eight in the country, and on May 23d, after the stroke, when a mile and a quarter out had broken his oar and jumped overboard, won the four-mile race with utmost ease, seven men sending an eight-oared shell over the water at a rate of which an eight would be proud. Such, then, is the bare history of college boat-racing in this country. The most interesting bits of reminiscence I have been compelled to leave for another time, the object in this article being to put a more or less complete resume in print.

THE TRAINING OF A UNIVERSITY CREW
By Frederick A. Stevenson,
Captain of the Yale Crew, '88

...Let us see if we cannot come right down to hard facts concerning training and ascertain what it really means in the case of a university crew.

One race is but just over when the work for the next begins. The summer's work, however, is mainly confined to the captain, for he must during that time make a careful study of the manner of coaching, of the theory of the stroke, and of the styles of rigging a shell, in preparation for the year's work. Then, too, the truly enthusiastic oarsman endeavors as much as possible to improve during the summer, mainly in getting thoroughly acquainted with the feeling and motion of the water.

But now autumn is with us again, the university is open, and once more another college athletic year is begun. The first event in the rowing department is the fall regatta. In this only the class crews take part, and the training is short and not so severe as in the spring. But these fall regattas, unimportant as they may seem to an outsider, are really a great factor in the university crew work, and should never be neglected.

The class crews are the main feeders of the university crews, and it is all-important that they should get as much practice as possible, so that they be taught the regular university crew stroke. The members of the past year's crew act as coaches. This is doubly advantageous for it both instills the right principles into the crew, and teaches the coach not only to think about the stoke and to see faults, but also to learn how they may be corrected, which is of immense advantage to him when his own work begins.

After the class races the men start work for the university crew. The captain selects from the class crews the men whom he considers fitted to train. To this number are added some who, though they may never have rowed, yet seem to have in them suitable material, and the old crew men who are not playing football. The work is light, consisting of a daily short row, and lasts only so long as the water is open.

After the Christmas recess, the real work begins. All through the fall the "weeding-out" process has been in operation. Now the ranks are once more filled, mainly with those who have been playing football during the fall, so that the number of candidates who begin the real training will be between twenty-five and thirty. Now is the time, therefore, to ask the questions of what does the training actually consist? what are the requirements for a crew man? and how are the standards of excellence to be applied?

We will consider first the training itself. The work will take from two to three hours a day. During the winter, the men assemble at the gymnasium at some fixed hour, their clothes are quickly changed, knicker-bockers, running shoes and "sweaters" being substituted, and the work of the afternoon begins. After a few moments' work in the gymnasium, a short run is taken, outside if the weather permits; if not, inside on the canvas-covered track. A distance of five or six miles is covered at a pace varying from a fast walk to a sharp trot, according to the fancy of the captain. On the return to the gymnasium after cooling off somewhat after the run, the men in a body go through a series of exercises designed to limber up the rowing muscles. Then the men are taken in squads of eight and set to work on the rowing-machines, or, what is far better, in a tank. A well-built tank is as much superior to the ordinary rowing-machine as the modern racing shell is to the old-style racing boat.

A few words will describe a tank. The only one that I know of is at Yale, and is used by the university crew in their winter work. A wall a little over three feet in height encloses a space about fifty feet in length to thirty feet in width in the basement of the gymnasium. The bottom and sides are cemented and it contains water to the depth of about two feet. A barge, securely fastened at both ends, lies in the water. This is of full size and regularly rigged to suit the men. The blades of the oar have to be either of less width or have a hole cut in the centre of the blade to diminish the great pressure. The tank is arranged so as to accelerate the current of water as much as possible as it is driven by the oars. This current is guided by means of the curved corners of the tank and by partitions running parallel to the barge over which the shank of the oar passes. By the stroke, the water is driven toward the stern outside the partition, i.e., in the channel farthest from the boat and flows back toward the bow on the inside. These side partitions come just above the surface of the water, while a partition about two-thirds as high as those at the sides runs beneath the boat and practically divides the tank in half, giving two distinct and separate circular currents. The theory is that the oarsman's strength is expended in driving the water round where ordinarily it is used in sending the boat ahead.

The crew is now seated in the boat, oars in hand, ready for the real work of the afternoon. The captain or the "coach" stands on the edge of the tank. At the command "Get ready!" off come the "sweaters," and the men come up into position ready for the catch. The coach runs his eye quickly along the boat, straightens up the men, and satisfies himself that everything is right. The rowing is now begun and lasts from a half to three-quarters of an hour. The coach goes completely round the boat on the edge of the tank, correcting faults, explaining points, often stopping the crew, and making individual men practice certain difficult points. At the close of this work the men take a shower-bath, and after being rubbed down are ready, with hearty appetites, for the supper at the training table.

Such is the general afternoon's gymnasium work during the winter. When spring comes, the tank gives way to the harbor and the gymnasium to the boat-house. Then the entire time is spent on the water, and the men are carefully watched by the coach from a steam launch.

The question of the selection of the men is the most difficult point that the captain and coach have to decide. Of course, certain physical traits are essential for a crew man, and he must have perfectly sound heart and lungs. This must be decided by a doctor's examination. He must be tough, strong and enduring, and this is shown by the work he can stand.

But more is required for the modern university crew man. The day of "beef and mere strength is past; for rowing has kept up with the times and it is now the era of skill in rowing. Brain-work is just as necessary in crew-rowing as muscular exertion. Neither is of use without the other, the two carefully combined give the winning crew. So nowadays the crew candidate has to undergo a mental as well as a physical examination. In passing judgment on these qualifications the greatest care must be used. Only those men can be selected in whom not only the captain and the coach, but every man in the boat has full confidence. This man may not always be the most skillful individual oarsman, but, the fact that the ideal is a *crew* and that eight must be chosen who will work as one man, must constantly be kept in mind. How can a crew row a hard race when there is a feeling that there is one man, in the boat whose "sand" will give out when the final test comes? Every good crew man must be an enthusiast, a hard and faithful worker, a conscientious trainer, and a man who feels at all times that the honor and glory of his university are entrusted to his care.

Too much stress cannot be laid on the subject of harmony in a crew. All must work with the same will, with the same ideal in view. Often a man must take the coach's word for what seems to him in his inexperience like a fatal blunder. Where this is mutual confidence between crew and coach, a strict adherence to what is believed to be the right principles, and honest, faithful work, defeat will come, but seldom, disgraceful defeat never.

Such are the men who make up the university crews of today. How these men are regarded in college may be judged by a remark made this year by the Dean of Yale. He said, "The rowing men are the best class of men in college, the men with whom the faculty have the least trouble."

In conclusion, I would like to say a word in reply to the oft-repeated question, whether it is beneficial to take part in college athletics. If I may be permitted to express an opinion after four years of rowing, I will most certainly answer, yes for that branch of college athletics builds a man up physically as every one admits. It does not prevent a man from standing well in his studies. The men who are most relied on in a crew are, as a rule, those who make a good showing in the recitation room. The training a man undergoes as a member of the university crew sends him out into the world not only with a sound, healthy body, but also with the habits of regularity, promptness, obedience, self-control and self-restraint thoroughly ground into him; in short, with all the personal characteristics that combine to make a successful man fully developed, I have never found a crew man who regrets the time and labor he gave to it. Every one loves it with an affection that only a crew man can understand, and looks back upon it as one of the most pleasant as well as most profitable parts of his college course.

YACHTING

Sailors adhered to the letter of the law if not the spirit by utilizing new designs, advancing technology, and smaller craft to gain victories, resulting in increasing regulation by governing bodies and the evolution of racing classes based on boat size.

Outing Magazine, November 1886, p. 171, listed rules for competitors.

CONDITIONS GOVERNING THE RACES FOR THE N.Y. C.C. CHALLENGE CUP

1. The canoes competing must come within the limits defined by the N.Y.C.C. rules.
2. The cup is to be held as a perpetual challenge trophy.
3. The competition is open to not more than three authorized representatives of any canoe club sailing under foreign colors, as many canoes representing the club holding the cup as the challenging club.
4. Two victories to be necessary to either win or hold the cup, the same canoes competing in each.
5. The races to be sailed on the waters of the club holding the cup.
6. Races sailed in the United States to be contested on waters in the vicinity of New York city under the auspices of the N.Y.C.C.
7. The distance sailed over in each race must not be less than eight nor more than ten miles, and within a time limit of three hours. The course to be mutually agreed upon.
8. The races must be sailed at a time mutually agreeable to the challengers and the holders of the cup; but one series of races to be sailed in any one year.
9. The N.Y.C.C. rules to govern the races.
10. The club holding the cup to be responsible to the N.Y.C.C. for its safe keeping. Should it dissolve its organization, the cup will then revert to the N.Y.C.C.

CONDITIONS GOVERNING AMERICAN CONTESTANTS.

11. The representatives of the holders of the cup must be selected after a series of trial races open to all members of canoe clubs in the United States. The regatta committee of the club holding the cup shall have the right to select the competitors for the international races irrespective of the result of the trial races.

12. Should the cup be won by the American contestants in the international race: First, an active member of the club holding the cup must score one victory to entitle that club to retain it. Second, if a member (or members) of any other club wins two races, his club will hold the cup. Third, should the two races be won by members of two clubs, neither being the holder of the cup, the tie will be sailed off subsequently to determine which club shall take the cup.

The Outing issue of May, 1888, pp. 160-164, voiced the concerns of participants.

THE DEATH-BLOW TO INTERNATIONAL YACHT RACING
THE PROSPECTS OF THE PRESENT SEASON — AN OBJECTIONABLE FEATURE OF
THE PRESENT DEED OF GIFT OF THE "AMERICA'S" CUP.
By Captain R.F. Coffin.

There being no prospect of an International race during the present season, the local club events may naturally be expected to attract an attention far greater than they have received for the past three years. It is true that the seasons following the early contests for the *America's* cup, the *Cambria* and *Livonia* races, and even those of the *Countess of Dufferin* and *Atlanta*, were dull, and largely from the reaction of the yachting excitements of the previous years; but since those periods yachting organizations have multiplied to a great extent, and the number of yachting men has correspondingly increased. Yacht designing has become better understood; many improvements in rig and canvas and ballast have been made, and there is a far healthier tone, in a yachting sense, among club members than formerly, and much more interest taken in the sport; and all this will, I think, check, if it does not altogether prevent, the dullness consequent upon the reaction from the excitements of the past three years; and the events of the local clubs will be numerous, well attended and interesting.

In the larger classes of yachts the schooner rig will, I think, regain during the present season some of its old-time importance. The New York, and some of the other important clubs, have anticipated this, by changing the classification of the schooners and adding to the number of classes for that rig. In the New York Club the classes for schooners have been increased from three to five. The first class, including all over one hundred feet on the water-line, is retained; but in place of the second class, which included yachts from eighty to one hundred feet, there is a class made from ninety to one hundred feet, the third class being from eighty to ninety feet, and there is a new fifth class, which includes all under seventy feet on the water-line.

The four classes of sloops have also been increased to six;, but practically the large vessels built for the International races have always formed a distinct class, and there has always seemed to be a necessity for a class to be sandwiched in between fifty-five and seventy feet. By the new rule there is a rating from fifty-three to sixty-one feet, and another from sixty-one to seventy feet.

As a rule, I have always thought this multiplying of classes unnecessary and objectionable and it has proved so over and over again, in the races for the Bennett challenge cups, over the inside course, where all schooners sailed in one class, and all sloops in another, and on several occasions the cups have been won by small yachts, and on all occasions the margin of correct time between the largest and the smallest boats has been very trifling. It will be remembered also, that in the first race for the *America's* cup, the *Magic*, one of the smallest vessels of the numerous fleet, was the victor. Still it has come to pass that length is so universally acknowledged to be the most potent factor of speed, and that the allowance of time does not compensate for difference in length, that owners will not enter their yachts when there is any considerable amount of length against them. If, therefore, clubs would have entries, they must encourage owners by multiplying the classes. Eleven classes, should they all fill, involve considerable outlay for prizes, each class receiving $250 in cash or its equivalent, and I think it would be much better to adopt the British plan and make it cash in all cases, and permit the winner to purchase a piece of silverware or other prize with it if he desires a lasting memento of his triumph,....

There is little utility now in retaining the sloop rig on any of the large yachts, as by the terms of the new Deed of Gift, they are legislated out of all chance of competition for the *America's* Cup, after having been built for the sole purpose of defending it. The only reason now for retaining the sloop rig on these yachts is that they may go across the Atlantic and bring back the Cape May and Brenton's Reef cups, which the cutter *Genesta* carried away from us, and also to bring to this country the Queen's Cup, held by the owner of the cutter *Arrow*, and offered last year as a perpetual International Challenge Cup. Mr. Chamberlayne, owner of the *Arrow* had at that time a stupid prejudice against centreboards, which it is to be presumed the numerous opinions published in the British journals since the *Thistle* race have dissipated, so that if one of the big sloops went over now he would give her a chance for this cup; something just at present very desirable as a stimulus to International yachting, since the *America's* Cup has been laid away in perpetuity at Tiffany's...

It is much to be regretted that the deed of gift of the *America's* Cup was meddled with. There was not the least necessity for it. Three races had been sailed under it, with entirely satisfactory results to the public, to the New York Yacht Club, and, as far as the deed was concerned, to the challengers, and there did not exist a single valid reason for changing it. I remember a conversation with a prominent member of the committee of revision while yet the subject was under consideration, and he said "the discussion that grew out of the extra length of the *Thistle*, as to the meaning of what that word 'dimensions' in the present deed, convinced us of the necessity of making the deed more explicit. Then, too, we think six months is too short a time to build and properly try a new yacht, now that it has been made clear that all future defenders of the cup must be of steel. The challenger can take all the time he wants to build and get his yacht in racing fettle — two or three seasons, if necessary; and we feel that is it not too much for us to have at least ten months in which to build and get our craft in racing form. But there is another reason," he continued, "more important than either of these, and that is the insertion of a clause preventing the barring out of the centreboard. You will notice a clause in the present deed, 'In case the parties cannot mutually agree upon the terms of a match, then the challenging party shall have the right to contest for the cup, subject to its rules and sailing regulations,' etc. Now," he continued, "in case a British club has the cup — and we may expect them to capture it at some time— it could refuse a challenge from a centreboard and we think that, as the cup has been successfully defended by centreboard vessels ever since the club has held it in trust, we ought now to prevent the possibility of centerboards being barred out."

These, then, I suppose, may be accepted as the reasons for the change in the second deed of gift, under which had been successfully sailed the *Genesta, Galatea* and *Thistle* matches. Not one of the reasons was of sufficient importance to excuse any tinkering with this important document. It had already been, changed once, and the legality of that action of the club had been seriously questioned; but, as the change only made plainer what was evidently the intent of the donors of the cup, the deed was not in reality altered and the action of the club was acquiesced in. Everybody realized that the owners of the old *America* never intended the cup to be contended for by a craft brought to this country in sections, on the deck of a steamer, and put together in this country after being landed; nor did they dream of a challenger being dragged through canals toward this city by mule power; nor did they desire the cup to be contended for by a steam yacht, for such a vessel was unknown at that time; and so in presenting these contingencies the club was simply giving effect to the donor's wishes, and everybody said "Amen."

The present deed, however, is a direct and radical change, and by its unfortunate phraseology confines the contests to yachts which do not now, and never have, existed. Both challenger and defended must be built, with the chances to manifestly in favor of the challenger that I marvel that the British yachting men did not seize the opportunity and get a challenge here before January 1st of this year.

As to the first reason alleged for the change, that it was necessary to specify exactly what was meant by "dimensions," that had been abundantly explained in the discussion of the *Thistle's* extra foot and a half of water-line, and this did not form a sufficient reason. There was some force in the reason given for the extension of time from six to ten months, but not enough to justify a change in the deed; while the idea that any club would think of doing anything so unsportsmanlike as to exclude the centreboard craft from competition was absurd.

In the absence, then, of any sufficient alleged reason for this change of the deed, I venture to hint that the real reason may have been Mr. Sweet's notification that he intended to challenge with a sixty-nine foot cutter; and it may have been thought wise, in view of this, to lay an anchor to windward, as it were, and provide for its recapture in case Mr. Sweet took the cup to England.

I don't believe that there was ever an intent to oblige him to relinquish his avowed intention to challenge, or a thought of putting one of the big sloops against Mr. Sweet's yacht. Public opinion would be so strong in favor of fair play that this would have been impossible; but the great success of the *Clara* under Mr. Sweet's management, was remembered, and there was a general opinion prevalent, growing out of the successes of the *Madge* and *Clara*, that the small cutter in contest with the centreboard sloop stood a better chance of winning than the large cutter did, and that Mr. Sweet's challenge was likely to be a dangerous one; and to offset his probable success, and insure an almost certain speedy recapture of the cup in case it was lost, the only seriously objectionable clause in the present deed of gift was inserted. This consists simply in the words "but without any time allowance whatever."

The limit of size for sloops having been fixed at from 60 to 90 feet water-line, and of schooners from 80 to 115 feet water-line, and the course in the event of a disagreement having been fixed over an "ocean course free from headlands," it followed, as surely as night follows day, that in the event of the cup being held by a British club an American challenger could go for it with a 115 foot schooner, with almost entire certainty of success, for either a schooner must be named to sail against her, or a 90 foot cutter must give her her tonnage allowance for rig, and then sail against her over a channel course, " without any time allowances whatever."

I do not say that it was for this reason that this clause was inserted, but I do say that this would have been a stronger and more powerful reason for changing the deed than any that has been alleged.

It is my belief that had the capture of the cup taken place, the capturing club, seeing the position to which this clause would reduce them -viz., an entire exclusion of their real racing yacht, e.i., the cutter — would have quietly taken the ground that all changes of the original deed had been illegal, and would have insisted that this very clause, which practically excluded the cutter, was inconsistent with the declaration in the original deed, that any club should always be entitled "to claim the right of sailing a match for this cup with any yacht;" and that, of course, implies that the club holding the cup could defend it "with any yacht."

There were, however, other effects from the insertion of these words which the gentlemen of the committee did not foresee. With these words in the deed it follows that any challenger, except a 90 foot cutter, must agree to whatever terms were proposed by the New York Yacht Club, or go outside and sail without allowance against a larger yacht, and with almost absolute certainty of defeat. I presume that Mr. Sweet could have trusted the club not to put the *Volunteer* or either of her big sisters against his proposed yacht, but he could not be sure of not having a yacht a couple of feet longer than his named as her competitor, and in that event he must be prepared to yield all points demanded or forfeit the allowance from such a yacht. As against the *Volunteer*, with allowance of time, there would be some chance of winning; but to sail against a yacht two or three feet longer than his own, and without any time allowance, meant certain defeat, and so Mr. Sweet withdrew his notice of intention to challenge; and so, for the same reason, several of the foreign yacht clubs have notified the New York Yacht Club that they did not care to challenge under this deed. This was another result that followed, which this committee did not anticipate.

There are others: It is vain for them to say, as members of the committee do say that the new deed permits any mutual agreement, and that these words "without time allowance" are only operative in case of disagreement. These words effectually prevent any mutual agreement, save one. If any owner of a 90 foot cutter challenges, and sends with his challenge an expressed desire to sail the outside races, without allowance of time, and if the New York Yacht Club agrees to this, that will be a mutual agreement; but no other is possible and it will be wise for the New York Yacht club to agree to this, since it has no option in the matter at all. If it refuses, it must sail these races as the result of its refusal, and this is an unexpected result to this committee, which certainly never contemplated putting its own club in a position where it would have not liberty of action whatever...

There is another result not contemplated by these wise gentlemen, and which is most serious of all, and that is that not only is the challenging yacht of necessity a 90 foot cutter, but such a challenger has much the advantage, and the odds are at least ten to eight that she takes the cup. She will challenge while yet upon the stocks, and the club must at once begin to build a yacht to meet her, as our present yachts are all too small. She comes, as I have shown, to sail the outside races, without allowance of time, and there is not alternative save to build. The challenger launches his yacht, and she sails, in all the spring events, as the *Thistle* did last year. She proves a failure, and she does not come; she proves a success, leading the *Thistle* with all ease, and leaves England after a series of triumphant races. The 90 foot sloop of the club proves a flat failure; what then? Why the *Volunteer* must sail best two out of three, outside, and without allowance of time, handicapped 4 1/2 feet of water-line length. Did this possibility strike the committee when it inserted these words in order to catch John Bull napping with a 115 foot schooner?

The British, in their objections to the new deed, have said next to nothing as to this provision, but they complain of the ten months' limit and of the requirements as to exact measurements; but I see nothing very objectionable in these. Certainly, if six months was not too long a time to build a wooden yacht in 1857, when this cup was first placed in trust, ten months is not too long now to build a steel yacht of the required size; and as to the dimensions, while the conditions of the new deed are, it must be confessed, onerous, they can be complied with without serious injustice to the challenger, and it is well to prevent future yachts which may come here from spreading out as the *Thistle* did. If the 90 foot cutter challenges, we shall find that sufficiently serious, without being obliged to ascertain afterwards that she is 92 feet. Really, the word "dimension" in the old deed was intended to mean all that is expressed in detail in the new deed...

It is not too much to say that the terms of the present deed have been condemned by the most competent and impartial judges on both sides of the Atlantic. In the foregoing article I have stated the exact facts, and I do not think that they can be controverted.

Though not as well organized, yachting had spread to the Pacific Coast with the organization of San Francisco yacht clubs shortly after the Civil War. The following article from Outing, April 1886, pp. 16-21, reports on developments of that time; but mistakenly printed the clubs' sites in Sancelito, rather than Sausalito.

YACHTS AND YACHT CLUBS OF SAN FRANCISCO
By Edwards Roberts

...There are but two yacht clubs in San Francisco, properly speaking, the Pacific and the San Francisco. The former is the more aristocratic body, the latter the more completely devoted to marine sports. The fleet of the San Francisco club outnumbers that of the Pacific, and all the owners of the best yachts connected with the latter club also belong to the other. If a better distinction than any were to be established, it would be that the San Francisco is the working club. It has on its list a great many young men who are enthusiastic sailors, it has no honorary or life members, and all, in short, who enjoy the benefits of the organization are continually contributing to its support.

The headquarters of both are at Sancelito, a little town composed of a score or more villas, that overlooks a secluded bay lying north of the passage leading to the Golden Gate. Behind the town rises Mount Tamalpais, a high and rounded hill extending westward to the ocean, while before it stretches a harbor opening into the bay and across which one may see San Francisco, three miles away. Ferry-boats run at intervals of half an hour between the city and Sancelito, and the trip across the bay affords one a surprisingly beautiful view of the island of Alcatraz, quaint as a bit of Genoa, with its fort and barracks, and of the Gate, with its blue waters and vari-colored cliffs. The San Francisco club-house is near the ferry landing, under the rugged bluff which commands the lovely scenery of short and wave, for which Sancelito is so famous. It is built on piles over the yellow beach, and is a plain, rectangular structure of redwood, one story and a half high, with square terrace surmounted by a flag-staff. The club was incorporated in September, 1875, and the house was then opened for the use of the club members. The interior is very conveniently but simply planned, and is decorated with great taste. A broad veranda extends around the outside of the house, and is prolonged at the southeastern corner as a wharf, on the extreme end of which stand a couple of saluting cannon closely bonded in heavy canvas... The principal room in the house is the assembly or dancing hall, a large, spacious chamber which has a springy and highly polished floor, and a grand piano on which gifted members delight to exhibit their accomplishments to admiring visitors. The windows command most charming prospects of bay and mountains, islands and distant cities, while the walls are ornamented with choice models of yacht hulls, among them being those of the *Cambria* and *Livonia*, probably the two finest specimens of English yacht-building that ever were launched, not even excepting the *Genesta* with her straighter and less graceful lines. The ladies' parlor is a comfortable little nook, containing some interesting marine pictures, and on the centre-table the silver-plate trophy once won by the *Emerald* in a brilliant contest. A kitchen, lunch-room, card-room, toilet-rooms and bed-chambers for the servants comprise the remainder of the establishment.

There is a broad, well-macadamized drive along the shore in Sancelito, and it leads to the Pacific club-house, half a mile farther distant from the ferry-wharf and to the southward. It is a much more ambitious structure than the other, and from the deck of the steamer, which puffs its way across from San Francisco, it looks very much like the mansion of a Central American planter. It is nearly, if not quite square, with a terrace at the summit of the broad roof, and a flag-staff from which the colors of the club depend on gala occasions. The club-house stands at the base of a high bluff, which forms the southern confine of a small, pocket-like valley, and also of a pretty cove that affords a placid anchorage ground for the smallest of sail-boats. The white walls of the club-house are relieved by masses of dark foliage behind and around it. The hills are crowned with dwarf live-oaks, which grow there in sturdy luxuriance. Two or three acres of steep, sloping land are enclosed at the waters edge around the building, within a high fence and hedge, and are beautifully laid out with winding gravel-walks, and shrubbery and flowers. Immediately in front of the grand entrance, and almost overhanging the beach, is a small esplanade, paved with marbles, and on which a formidable battery of four brass Dahlgren, twelve pounder boat-howitzers are posted for saluting. A very lofty flag-pole rises from the center of the pavement, and is reserved for the national colors. It reaches at least fifty feet nearer the zenith than the one on the roof. Farther to the south, there is a stout wharf reaching out sixty feet from the beach, and two iron saluting canon are kept there for ordinary service.

The interior of the Pacific club-house is rich and imposing. The veranda is a spacious dimensions, and the visitor ascends to it by a tall and sweeping flight of steps. Like an old-fashioned English manor-house, the first chamber entered is of immense size, and the lofty chimney-place suggests the one in the banqueting hall of Frances I., at Saint-Germain-en-Laye. It is high enough and wide enough to drive a donkey and cart into, and is furnished with gigantic fire-dogs, with shining brass knobs and an enormous iron crane. Over the mantle is a piece of curious wood-carving and some Japanese plaster statuary. The architrave above the fireplace is faced with painted tiles, all excepting three illustrating the flag-signals of the club. The three others bear inscriptions of time-worn sailors' axioms...

This club must surely be of a warlike temper, for on the red-bricked hearth, in the front of the grim fire-dogs, are arrayed three shining cannon of small caliber, like those that are usually seen on the forecastle of a yacht...

The great hall is about 50 by 40 feet. The ceiling is hung with strips of colored bunting, canopy-fashion, and four enormous albatrosses are also suspended from it, while on various ledges, over doors, windows, etc, are elks heads, stuffed eagles, cranes, storks, herons, and other objects suggestive of an adventurous, out-door existence. A magnificent model of the clipper-ship *Pacific*, with all sails spread, occupies a large space in one corner. A valuable collection of yachting views is hung upon the walls of both this and the dining hall. The latter is entered by a small vestibule,leading off the grand veranda. It is as large as the main hall, has a high wainscot, and contains a score of tables. A banqueting board was spread here after the last regatta of the club, when the prizes were delivered. The hall is splendidly adapted to such a celebration. Adjoining are the wine-room and the kitchen. Opening from the main-hall are a sitting or card room, and a ladies' parlor and toilet-rooms. There are comfortable sleeping chambers upstairs for the servants of the club. The Pacific Yacht Club was incorporated in August, 1878.

On the shore-road at Sancelito, opposite the San Francisco club-house, is a small cottage which belongs to what is known as the Bohemian Yacht Club. This is a private body, which never exceeded five members, and now has but two. It was also called the "Owl club," and five stuffed owls, representative of the five original members are still among the peculiar ornaments of the interior, perched upon a mossy branch which is fastened to the wall. There are four or five rooms, cozily fitted up, and adorned with grotesque and slightly humorous caricatures. The present two members also belong to the San Francisco Yacht Club.

Among the principal members of the Pacific and San Francisco yacht clubs are James L. Flood, John W. MacKay, J.P. Jones, George Crocker, Peter J. Donahue, Cornelius O'Connor, Philip Caduc, Isadore Gutte and C.H. Harrison. Mr. Caduc is the commodore of the Pacific, and C.H. Harrison of the San Francisco. Mr. Harrison is probably the most experienced yachtsman on the coast, having been, before coming to the United States, an officer of the Royal Thames Yacht Club. The Pacific and San Francisco yacht clubs have together about two hundred active members...

Few of the yachts on the Pacific coast have as great excellences of build and of rig as may be readily discovered in any second-rate yachting fleet in the East. The most of them were put together in ignorance of the more refined principles of marine architecture, and are tub-like and slow. Fortunately, the more prominent patrons of yachting are getting rid of their primitive and clumsy craft....

The fastest boat of the Pacific coast fleet, all things considered, is the *Lurline*. She draws 8 1/4 feet of water; her breadth of beam is 21.05 feet; length over all, 80 feet. As an old yachtsman remarked to the writer; "It is nip and tuck between her and the *Halcyon*; but the *Halcyon* has shown that she is afraid of her. In the last Pacific club regatta the *Halcyon* would not race. She is 72.03 feet long at the water-line, 83 feet over all, 21.12 beam, and drawn 10.50 of water. She carries a lug jib and a leg-of-mutton mainsail, flying staysail, water-sail and ring-sail, and some times sets a balloon-sail. The *Lurline* gives the same inventory of sails and so does the *Chispa*, except that her job is very large and is rigged with a boom...

The *Chispa*, when she was launched, and for some time afterward, was the fastest yacht on the Pacific. She was built in 1879, to beat the *Consuelo*, and did so...

The interior fittings of the most of the Pacific Coast yachts are unpretentious, and of some of them, they are exceedingly plain. The prettiest and most expensive cabin is that of the *Lurline*. She cost $20,000, and every known kind of rare wood from the four quarters of the earth was used in decorating her, from ebony to bird's-eye maple. The *Annie*, which like the *Ariel*, is of Eastern build, has a very cozy cabin, and the panels are decorated with oil paintings, representing marine scenes. The *Chispa's* cabin is lined with Lincrusta-Walton, and the beds and cushions are all adorned with a profusion of lace.

The *Lolita* yawl is employed in every hunting season as a movable shooting station. She is first run up a river or creek, and then, after being moored, is housed over with lumber, and the party on board occupy the temporary structure as a lodging place. When thus metamorphosed she presents a curious and picturesque appearance, surrounded by the tall, waving tule.

There are several favorite places to which the San Francisco yachtsmen go during the proper seasons. One is Santa Barbara, where there is a good harbor and a picturesque town, and the other is Honolulu, capital of the Hawaiian Islands. The journey to the latter is over a warm, calm sea, and the islands, with their volcanoes and tropical vegetation, are wonderfully attractive. There is not the variety of places to visit that is offered to Eastern yachtsmen, however, and the majority of boats do not venture beyond the limits of the Bay.

SWIMMING

Swimming had a long history as a recreational pastime in the United States. Educators advocated and taught swimming during the colonial and antebellum periods; but swimming for the most part, meant bathing. Organized competition did not take place until after the American Civil War. Canadians organized a swimming club in Montreal in 1850, and that city offered a $20 prize for an 1867 match. In May, 1875, residents of Toronto founded the Dolphins Swim Club, which held annual competitions starting in 1877. In 1883 the New York Athletic Club offered the first national championship in the United States. An Amateur Swimming Association was established in 1886 and the Amateur Athletic Union began conducting national championships in 1888. The Montreal Swimming Club sponsored the first Canadian championships a year later, with the first official national championship occurring at Ottawa in 1898.

Women faced particular restrictions when trying to swim. Victorian precepts of morality dictated that they wear cumbersome apparel to shield their bodies from view. The weight of such clothing proved a greater detriment than any inherent fear of the water as the following article suggests. It appeared in Outing, August 1888, pp. 431-432.

HINTS ON SWIMMING FOR WOMEN

There is one event in every canoe regatta that amuses the lay spectator—the "upset" race...

It is, to begin with, a short race, of about two hundred feet. The canoes are started just as in paddling races, and when well under way, a signal is given from shore, at which every paddler must immediately capsize his canoe, turn it completely over, regain his seat, and paddle to the finish. The overturning of the whole fleet of canoes at the same instant is a novel and ludicrous sight, and the struggles of the paddlers to crawl over the sides of the canoes, without again upsetting them, are very funny to watch...

If it was possible for girls to get such training as this, the number of drowning accidents reported in the newspapers would decrease, and the cases where expert swimmers going to the rescue of drowning maidens also lose their lives would be a record of the past, for such fatal results are mainly due to abject fear on the part of the women and their ill-directed struggles to save themselves.

A large majority of the men who indulge in aquatic sports know how to swim; only a small minority of the women who trust themselves on or in the water can swim. Few men can float, even in salt water, without some motion of the hands, or feet, or a life preserver, but almost every woman *can* if she knows how.

Floating means keeping the mouth and nose out of the water, without any muscular effort of the body or limbs, so that breathing can go on naturally. A body that floats must displace its weight of water. Men's bodies are a little heavier than a like bulk of water, unless the lungs are kept full of air, which is impossible, when breathing is continued.

Fat men and women can float, thin and muscular men cannot, for bone and muscle are heavier than water, while fat is lighter. If a man attempts to breathe under water, he simply fills his lungs with water instead of air, and then his body sinks. The same thing happens to women. To keep the mouth and nose out of water, it is necessary that every other part of the body, even to the back of the head, should be immersed to displace the greatest possible amount of water. When a women falls overboard she quite naturally wants to get out again. If a good swimmer goes to her rescue, she seizes him and attempts to lift herself out of the water, head, body, and all; which simply results in drowning her would-be rescuer, unless he is skillful, and either pinions her arms, or renders her unconscious by a partial drowning. If women were trained to have no fear of the water, even if unable to swim, not ten percent of the accidents that now happen would result fatally. It is the loss of presence of mind and coolness that does the mischief.

Thousands of women get surf and sea bathing in summer. Half an hour's practice with a swimmer who knows the first principles is enough to teach any woman (who is not too much afraid to go into the water) that she has but to lie on her back, head thrown far back and mouth and nose in the air, to float without effort for any length of time, and breathe naturally the while — unless the water is rough with breaking waves.

The whole head is raised out of water when swimming, and therefore, some effort of the arms and legs is necessary to keep if there. The more of the body that can be kept under water the easier it is to swim, as all the power can then be applied to producing motion; and none of it wasted in floating the body. The frog is a good swimming master. The whole art can be learned by watching him, and imitating his performances. Once overcome the fear of getting the head under water, and it is easy to learn to swim.

Swimming, however, is violent exercise, and, combined with the chill of the water, very tiring. Therefore, the struggles of those who cannot float, and thereby husband their strength, soon exhaust them. Thin-blooded and weak persons get exhausted and chilled must sooner, of course, than those having vigorous circulations, and stout people can remain in the water for a long time without feeling seriously inconvenienced. The learning to swim takes time, practice and some force of will. One lesson will teach any but the most nervous how to float, and that accomplished a great step is gained...

A little thought and some practice will fit sensible women to save themselves, and may teach them how to be of very great use to less intelligent people in case of an accident to a steamer or yacht....

From good lady swimmers let others take example, and with their help, learn to swim a little, even if it is ever so little, for every little helps...

The following report, which appeared in the Chicago Tribune, 28 January 1894, p. 6, gives an indication of the embryonic nature of swimming competitions during the period.

EXCITING SWIMMING TOURNAMENT
SMITH WINS THE EIGHTY YARDS HANDICAP

The Chicago Athletic Association gave a swimming tournament last evening at its club house. The events were well contested and were witnessed by several hundred persons. The first event was an eighty yards handicap race. To accommodate the eight contestants, the race was divided into two trial heats and a final. The first heat was between G.A. Thorpe (scratch), E.F. Siexas (2 seconds), J.W. Sullivan (8 seconds), and F.W. Wentworth (10 seconds). The heat was won by Thorne in 1 minute, actual time. The contestants in the second heat were: J.A. Smith (scratch), J.G. Hately (2 seconds), J.Ailing Jr. (16 seconds), and A. Cunningham (18 seconds). Smith won in 1:02 actual time. The final heat was won by Smith in one minute, with Thorne second and Cunningham third.

The next event was a contest between a man on the edge of the tank representing a fisherman and a man in the water representing a fish. A line from the fisherman's rod was attached to a harness about the swimmer's neck and shoulders. The object of the swimmer was to break the line in twenty minutes and the fisherman's to prevent it. John Robinson, the swimming instructor, was the swimmer, and J.M. Sellers held the rod. Robinson won at the end of twelve minutes.

The final event was a game of water polo. The reds were: F.W. Wentworth, W.H. Thompson, G.A. Thorne, J.F. Hately, Samuel Dexter, G.J. Williams and H.O. Matile. The blacks were: H.A. Cronin, J.A. Smith, E.F. Seixas, W.R. Crawford, V.H. Harding. Herbert Alward, and J.H. Patrick. The reds made two goals and five fouls, the blacks one goal and one foul. As two fouls count one goal for the other side the blacks won by one goal.

WATER POLO

The English Amateur Swimming Association sanctioned water polo as a sport in 1885. The Boston Athletic Association introduced the game to the United States in 1889. Water polo was included in the Olympic Games of 1900 held in Paris.

Casper Whitney, writing for Harper's Weekly, 28 February 1891, p. 157, provided a brief history and a set of rules.

WATER POLO

About two hundred years ago those of our English forefathers who loved sport, and were unable to indulge their fancies in the extravagance of polo pony and outfit, determined upon transporting the game to the water, a field that would be common property, and where the carrier required was not so expensive. In place of ponies they produced kegs, which the dear old boys straddled; for mallets they had a kind of paddle like a shinny stick, about six to eight feet long; and the ball was the prototype of that we now use. What rare good sport they must have had! Tub-racing is insipid and safe compared to sitting astride a bobbing, rolling cask, managing an unwieldy wooden paddle. Evidently, however, there was genuine merit in the sport, for it held full sway, so far as aquatic polo is concerned, and, indeed, is played abroad today, until about ten years ago, when in England our present game of water polo came first into being.

I have often wondered why, with all its mirth-provoking possibilities, none of our clubs has introduced the tub game in the summer programme, and I am glad to learn that such an attempt will be made the coming season off Travers Island by the New York Athletic Club. I predict the largest number of spectators the island has ever held if the effort is made. The game was first played in this country by the Boston Athletic Association in the fall of '89, and owes its development and success to the unceasing efforts of Mr. F.J. Wells, who is a member of the Boston and likewise of the New York Athletic clubs. Messrs. P.E. Morgan and Arnold Heilborn, of the Providence Swimming Club, were likewise pioneers in the sport over here, introducing the game at Providence, and doing much for its prosperous advance.

In this country, the game is practically football in the water, but the English method of play is quite different from ours, being, in fact, to our water polo what the old Association football is to our college game of today. In the English style of water polo the ball is struck with the hands or pushed forward, and cannot be carried, nor is one player permitted to interfere with an opponent unless he is actually in contact with the ball. Our rules allow a player to throw or carry the ball in any direction, and permit of interference anywhere within three feet of the ball. The English game undoubtedly requires more speed and skill in swimming, but loses all opportunity for expert teamwork that is possible in carrying and passing the ball. The English goal also differs from ours, for instead of a board, they have posts four feet apart, and with a crossbar, under which the ball must be driven between the uprights. Our distance between goals, from sixty to seventy feet, remains the same as abroad, though the Manhattan Athletic club has a swimming tank 100 feet long, the full length of which its team uses.

To a very large extent, the formation of our rules has been governed by the size of our tanks. In England, where such tanks are possible as the Lambeth Baths in London, that present a body of water 120 X 45, sport is greatly enhanced in permitting more out playing. Inasmuch as a clear and intelligent description of this game has never been published, and because of the prospect of its becoming a fixture among the pursuits of sportsmen, I shall describe the game pretty fully for the benefit of those that wish to understand and play it.

The game is played by teams of six men, whose formation is somewhat similar to that of a football eleven. It consists of a centre rush, two side rushers (right and left ends), one half back, and two full backs, or goal-keepers. The teams, called reds or blacks, and wearing a distinguishing cap, line up, standing directly over or back of their goal. The referee in the centre holds the ball, awaiting the signal from the captains that all are ready. At the word "Go!" the ball is thrown into the centre, the men dive into the water, getting their positions, while the centre rush of each side, who should be the

fastest swimmer of the team, makes for the ball with all speed — the positions when
in the water being:

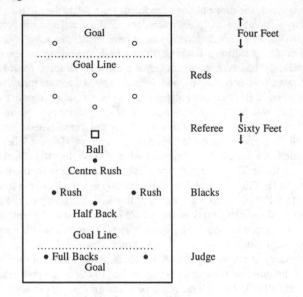

Whichever centre rush reaches the ball first snaps it back to the half back, while he
and the two side rushers continue on to the opponents' goal. The rushers of the side
failing to reach the ball pass on immediately to block the half back of the enemy, and
the position now is:

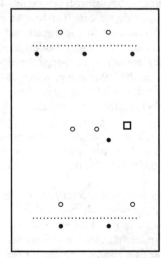

The black half back endeavors to pass the ball down to whichever one of his three
rushers is in the best position; and if he is successful the reds must hurry down to the

aid of their goal-keepers, if it is found necessary. If unsuccessful, the black rushers are likely to be brought back to aid their own full backs. A goal is made then by touching the goal board with the ball, which must be forced through the enemy's line by the three forwards, supported by the half back, while the full backs remain in their own territory to protect their goal in case the ball should be lost to the other side. The most interesting point in the game, and where the greatest amount of skill is required, is when the ball is in play at the goal line or inside. It cannot be thrown to a player who is inside of his opponent's goal line; this would be off-side play. He must either swim across the line with it, or if it happens to have been thrown in, he can follow, at which time his own men join him, and the scrimmage to prevent a goal being made demands the greatest efforts and skill of the home full backs. The goal-keepers are really the most important men on the team, and must be active, cool, and strong. Certainly one of the best, if not the best, I have seen play is E.J. Kintner, of the N.Y.A.C. team. Undoubtedly the strongest centre rush playing is champion distance swimmer Meffert, of the M.A.C.

When the game was first played in this country there was not goal line distinction, and consequently immediately the ball was put in play the men all rushed to one opponent's goal, and the rough-and-tumble scrimmage that resulted upon the ball being thrown in was neither skillful nor interesting, there being absolutely no chance for expert play. Now the struggle on the goal line requires as much manœuvering and neat playing as does the tussle of the football half back to find an opening in the opposing forward. Indeed the goal line rule of water polo formulated by Mr. Wells was patterned entirely after the foot-ball play.

The size of the tanks does not permit of many brilliant individual plays, and experience is proving daily that team work is the one great essential. It is impossible to rely upon the fast swimming or strength of any one or two players, and captains will materially strengthen their teams by schooling them in cool play and strategic passing. There is ample opportunity for the cultivation and display of skill in this direction, but men must be able to act quickly, for a moment's hesitation brings the opposing forwards on him, and down he goes to the bottom of the tank. There is an abundant opportunity for "foxy" playing, such as sinking to the bottom with the ball, and swimming under the surface toward the opponent's goal, or of secreting the ball between the legs or in one hand, and swimming off with it nonchalantly to outwit the enemy's full backs. A player must be extremely quick and cool, however, for with the development of the game the difficulty of losing the ball is becoming greater. Thus far, there has been no great advancement in skillful team plays, there is no reason why water polo should not grow tremendously in popularity and interest.

To the team player in training the best preparation is that which strengthens lung power and endurance. Continued immersion in the water draws heavily on a man's strength, vitality, and weight, and a corresponding increase of tissue-making food is required to counteract it; therefore eat plentifully of good plain food. A player that has once attained good form will suffer no ill effects from a hard fought battle of twenty minutes. The first series of match games ever played in this country was between the Boston A.A. and Providence Swimming Club teams in the season of '89-90, the latter winning two of the three games and the championship. This season Mr. Wells introduced the game at the New York Athletic Club, and has worked indefatigably to make the team expert. It is due to his labors entirely that they have reached their present excellent condition. The Manhattan A.C. organized a team shortly afterward, and though not having the benefit of so experienced and skilled a coach as Mr. Wells, they have made good progress, and especially so in the past couple weeks. The game is about to be started, I hear, at the Columbia A.C. in Washington, and at the Denver Athletic Club. Wherever introduced it has been enthusiastically received, and there is no reason why it should not grow in favor until we shall have some large tanks, as abroad, constructed for it especially, and hold annual championship contests. Indeed, just now the matter is being agitated to form a league next year, such as exists in England, and play a series of games for the championship of the United States. At an early date a meeting of delegates from clubs interested will be held to revise and possibly improve the present rules, which were framed without the basis of experience, and are therefore incomplete in some respects...

The following rules are the latest revised:

RULES

1. The ball to be an Association football (No.3), not less than 8 and not more than 9 inches in diameter.
2. The goals to be boards about 4 feet long and 12 inches wide, marked GOAL in large letters, one to be placed at either end of tank, about 18 inches above water-line.
3. To score a goal the board must be touched by the ball in the hand of an opposing player,and the greatest number of goals to count game.
4. The contesting teams shall consist of six a side, with one reserve man, who can take the place of one of his side in case of disablement, and receive prize if on the winning side.
5. Time of play, 20 minutes; 10 minutes each way and 5 minutes break at half time.
6. The captains shall be playing members of the teams they represent, and shall toss for choice of ends of tank. The ends to be changed at half-time.
7. Game to be started by referee at the sound of whistle, the ball to be thrown into centre of tank.
8. Ball going out of the tank to be thrown in centre opposite where it crossed bounds.
9. No player is allowed to interfere with an opponent unless such as opponent is in actual contact with the ball or within three feet of it. Any player transgressing this rule shall be guilty of a foul. It shall also be a foul to hold any player by any part of his costume.
10. A mark shall be placed on either side of tank, 4 feet from each goal, and no player may come within his opponent's goal line (an imaginary line between these two marks) until the ball is put in play over this line. The goal-keeper alone may stand within it. It shall be foul to cross this line ahead of the ball.
11. Upon a goal being gained the opposite teams go to their own end of the tank, and the ball is thrown by referee into the centre on play being resumed.
12. Teams shall have an umpire at each goal line, who upon goal being made shall notify referee, who will blow a whistle and announce the game.
13. The referee shall decide all fouls; and if in his opinion a player commits a willful foul, he shall be cautioned for the first offence, and for the second the referee shall award a foul to the opposing side. After a foul the ball is to be thrown into

the centre of the tank, when play will be immediately resumed. Waiting the casting of the ball the players may place themselves as they please anywhere in the tank, excepting of course, within the 4-foot goal boundary.

14. Time occupied by disputes shall not be reckoned as in the time of play.

CANADA

Aquatic sports in Canada followed a pattern similar to that of the United States. The Royal Canadian Yacht Club organized about 1840, and the Montreal Yacht Club began in 1877. The Toronto Yacht Club split from the Royal Canadian parent organization in 1880 over competitive differences, resulting in the formation of the Lake Yacht Racing Association in 1884.

Rowing produced Canada's first great national sports hero. Ned Hanlan dominated his competition as a world champion in single sculls from 1877 to 1884. A charismatic and flamboyant figure, idolized by his fans, Hanlan symbolized Canadians' growing nationalistic pride. The Chicago Tribune, 13 November 1887, p. 21, printed bits of Hanlan's wisdom while he was still competitive.

NED HANLAN ON ROWING
THE GREAT OARSMAN'S VIEWS ON
THE ART HE PRACTICES

New York, March 11, (Special Correspondence) Edward Hanlan, the sculler, who lost the world's championship to Beach, the Australian, but hopes to regain it when he meets Beach again in June, laughed a little when asked for an interview on boating, and said he thought he could talk better about politics, because he had noticed that the less a man knew of a subject the more confidently he spoke about it. "Honestly," he said, "I don't know as much about rowing as I thought I did ten years ago, and yet I have picked up a good many little points since then. If I should live to be 100 years old I wouldn't know it all. But I'll try to tell you something. The most striking thing that occurs to me is the steady improvement in sculling made during twenty years and the radical changes in method and style. Before the sliding seat was introduced the only way a sculler could get sufficient length of stroke was by leaning and reaching well forward. Brown used to double up like a jack-knife to take the water, and he had to lean away back to finish the stoke. Now a man cannot exert his strength to much advantage in either of these positions. At the beginning of the stoke he cannot bring his shoulders into play; his strength is being used in getting his body upright again. That style is perpetual see-sawing of the body, using up wind, strength and time in violent movements that do not help the boat along a bit, and it soon tires a man out. In the old style races it was the sculler's stomach or heart that gave out or his wind failed him. If Brown had made three miles in 22:30 in the old style it would have been a great performance. Brown had a good head, and he devised the sliding seat, and then better time was made, although some of the old faults remained for some time. The records I will give all refer to three-mile races. In 1865 Hamill made 22:27, and that held good until 1874, when boats were built lighter and smoother, and then O'Neil lowered the record to 21:19 1/2. In the same year I got it down to 21:14 1/2 in one of his wonderful midnight feats in the dark of the moon. In 1883 Teemer did make it 20:14, and then Hosmer came to the front with a little more skill and lowered the time to 20:02 1/2. Two years later Teemer had learned some more points and made 20:01 1/2 at New Orleans. In June, 1886, at White Bear Lake, Minn., Gaudaur gave a surprise party by getting the record down to 19:54. That was good until I rowed over the measured course on Lake Quinsigamond twice in 19:23. These records are only the milestones, you might say, and they mark the different stages of progress. Thames records are not accepted for time because of the variable tides...

Now, I don't think the men of today are as strong as the men of earlier days were, and it seems to me that the progress in sculling is due to two things in general that is, improved boats and appliances and better knowledge of how to apply their strength. You may call that last skill art or science. Look at this position - arms bent, elbows turned out, knees spread wide apart, body bent forward between the legs - old styles of rowing. Do you think a man can pull his best that way? No two sets of muscles are drawing in the same direction and some strength is spent in getting them into line. What is the use of working the body on that way? Not the least, of course. Now I put my knees close together and straighten my arms. Again, you see, my legs and arms are not pulling in parallel lines and there is loss of power. But when I get my legs and arms in a position to pull all together in the line of the boat's course every ounce of power helps the boat along. I have tried rowing in every possible way, right and wrong, and can tell from my own experience and study what is most effective. This thing I have learned that the less work you make of rowing the better and faster you can pull. You don't want to do it a bit more than is necessary to pull the boat. Avoid extreme effort and try to make every motion in the easiest possible way.... The great difference between the old and new style of rowing is that while formerly only the body down to the waist could be used, now the thighs and legs come into play, greatly increasing the power available. I have been rowing ever since I was 6 years old, and I am now 31, and never have done anything else. I believe I did carry a chain for surveyors on the island where I live just one week and got paid $9, but that is the only money I ever earned by work. During all this time I have been looking and studying for points to make rowing easier. Perhaps natural laziness set me to thinking of it, but that is the fact. No matter how small the point or trivial the advantage I note it and experiment with it, and see just what difference it makes, and I get such points by watching oarsmen, even ordinary boatmen and chaps in yawls. A lot of those little points put together, make the difference of seconds that lower records. I think I have got down pretty low the art of pulling a pair of sculls with the least labor, and that means endurance and ability to keep up a steady pace in the long race. It is the art of making all the muscles act together, so that one set may not to called upon for more than its share of work at any point, and making no effort that does not help the speed of the boat. Consequently I never give out at any particular point and my stomach never goes back on me. When I'm tired, I'm all tired and can't locate the exhaustion. I never felt my heart beat but once in my life and that was when a steamer ran me down. It pounded for a week after that. I never had a pain of any kind, but once. Somehow I got, while in Australia, the rheumatism in the muscles of the left forearm that control the fingers. In the race with Beach I lost my left scull five times through the rheumatism, and twice I saw the handle of the scull three or four inches away from my hand, but I managed every time to recover it and bring in the finish of the stroke even with the right scull. Probably I lost a little speed each time.

I can tell by watching a man's style just where he will give out. Let any man get into a boat and pull three miles pretty hard and I will tell him when he returns just where he feels tired. You see I have rowed in wrong positions just to find out those things. If a man gives out in any particular place, unless there is some special weakness, it is because he doesn't use his strength evenly and intelligently. Great strength is not the only requisite for fast sculling. Many of the men whom I have rowed down are much stronger than I am. My weight is 156 pounds and height five feet eight and five-eighths inches, and most of my antagonists have been six-footers, weighing 200 pounds and more.... All my muscles are long, and I never get muscle-bound, and the circulation is never checked by severe contraction, I never have used dumbbells to any great extend, and I can't swing the clubs without knocking my head. My exercise is rowing, and I have developed my muscles in the work they are called upon to do. It is all nonsense for an oarsman to train his muscles with clubs, and boxing, and all manner of exercises foreign to his work. The way to learn to row fast is to get into a boat and row. If you want to become a singer, you don't train for it by beating a drum or turning flip-flops. If a man wants to be first in any particular line of athletics he must not grow to be an all-round athlete. The all-round men are not first in any one thing. A champion must be a specialist.

Coming now to mechanical progress in boating, it is necessary to say much about the general improvement as every one knows that the builders are making lighter, smoother, and better boats than were thought of twenty years ago. Speed has been increased in that way, of course. The great changes, besides making boats of paper and reducing them to pencil proportions, have been made in the sculls. Josh Ward pulled with sculls that weighed twenty-four pounds the pair, and as most of the weight was outboard, he put lead weights on the handles to balance them. Now we use sculls that weigh only eight pounds to the pair. Up to 1876 nobody used sculls less than ten feet two inches long, nor more than five inches wide in the blade. I showed up in a regatta with sculls nine feet six inches long and six inches wide, and everybody said "Look at the kid with the big sculls," and laughed at me. After that race everybody reduced the length and increased the width of his oars. You see, I had been studying that thing a little. The long scull has to take too wide a sweep through the water, and to get the stroke completed a man must work too fast and too hard. The first and last parts of the stroke are of no use in propelling the boat, but you must take the water forward of the effective point and leave the water astern of the limit of useful power in order to allow for the way of the boat. Too long a scull wastes more power than is necessary in beginning and ending the stroke. The longer the oar the more strength it takes to pull it through the water. But there is such a thing as getting the scull too short and sacrificing speed to power. Experiment has shown the effective medium to be about nine feet six inches. That gives speed without using up a man's strength in useless labor, and the spoon shape keeps the hold to the end of the stroke… Oarsmakers now shape the shank so that it will not bend at all and the whole scull is stiff as a bar of iron. They have got their business down to a science, and an oarsman can now order sculls of a certain size and be sure that the weight will be right and the whole thing just what he wants. It makes a great deal of difference also what style of boat is used in different sorts of weather.

For a straight away race I have three boats. If I had the wind with me and blowing pretty strong, I use a full built boat that rides well out of water. The wind will help it along and make an advantage of fifteen seconds in three miles. A head wind would keep such a boat back fifteen seconds, making in all thirty seconds difference. Should I find the wind against me, I use a thin boat that will race very low and present very little surface to the wind. If the wind is absent or the race is a turn a medium boat is the best. Those points are worth knowing. The wind-sail first brought out by Clasper on the Tyne was quite an invention. It was a thin board set up on edge on the bow of the boat. With the wind abeam or on the quarter, when you pull and lean backward you force the forward part of the boat down and raise the after-part so much out of the water that the wind catches it, throws the stern a little to leeward, and brings the bow into the wind, and you have to pull harder on the windward oar to keep on your course. The windsail corrects that fault. But when the wind is on either bow it catches the sail and throws the boat off the course. To replace the windsail the fin was invented. This is a small centreboard fastened to the bottom of the boat. At first it was quite large and placed about three feet from the stern. It kept the boat from swinging off, but it interfered with quick turning as it acted like a fixed rudder. The size was reduced to lessen this disadvantage, and at last somebody thought of moving the fin up to a point just aft of the centre of the boat, right under the after end of the cockpit, and making it larger. Now the boat can be turned almost as though on a pivot, making a difference of three strokes on the turn, and three strokes means about three boat lengths. Oarsmen used to think that very quick strokes were best for speed. That would be true if a man were a machine that couldn't get tired or out of wind, but I find that in sculling twenty-eight to thirty-four a minute are fast enough for a long race, and thirty-eight strokes at the start, and finish at thirty-two without a spurt or break. At any rate, I could pull strong and steady, making no false motions and keeping my head clear. My breathing was natural, and I wasn't swaying or see-sawing as a man will when he works too fast and too hard. The boat ran along as smoothly and steadily as a steamer. It pumps the wind out of a man and makes his heart jump to row forty strokes a minute in a single scull."

Yacht clubs often served a greater social than athletic function. By their nature exclusionary, such organizations reinforced class lines. Outing, November 1890, pp. 131-134, reported on the affairs of the Royal Canadian Yacht Club.

THE ROYAL CANADIAN YACHT CLUB
By Repard C. Kuarff

The Royal Canadian Yacht Club is fortunate in many things and in nothing more so than in its island home, where, prominent among other buildings stands its club house, the flagship as it were of the Canadian yachtsman. The club launch is ready at its berth: let us pass over with it out of the hurly-burly, the heat and dust of Ontario to the island. Here is quite another world, cool, breezy and fresh, with trim-cut lawns and in every direction the evidence of pleasant pastimes; for, while yachting is by no means neglected, the members of the R.C.Y.C. do not find it at all inconsistent with that more serious occupation to invite, two days each week,"their sisters and their cousins and their aunts" to friendly contests at lawn tennis, croquet and lawn bowls.

These afternoons at the club have become very fashionable. It is the thing of all others to do during the hot summer months, to cross over in the club launch and have your tennis, and your afternoon tea on the club veranda. The upper story is reserved on these occasions for these members who prefer to "flock alone," and in the card room you will usually find one or two tables where the mysteries of the old whist masters are being solemnly investigated by a coterie of bankers, lawyers, doctors and brokers, who silently puff their fragrant pipes and drink in the fresh breezes from the lake through the open windows.

The R.C.Y.C. has been in existence for forty years and has long been granted the privilege of using the prefix Royal to its title. By an amalgamation with the Toronto Yacht Club, a year or so since, both the membership and the fleet were considerably increased in numbers and the union enured greatly to the advantage of Canadian yachting.

The present membership of the club is strong and the fleet is quite a respectable one, the vessels ranging in size from open and half-decked mackinaws up to the stately schooner, cutter and sloop of eighty and one hundred tons.

Toronto's population, like the national bird of the Dominion, is largely amphibious, as witness the sight on her ample bay on almost any summer's day, when the whole surface is dotted with a fleet of skiffs, boats, punts, canoes, shells (four-oared and singles) and sailing craft of all dimensions, cruising about in every direction, all bound on having a good outing.

A better course for rowing over it would be difficult to find. You can see a race almost from start to turning point. On such occasions the whole population turns out, and besides covering the water alongside of the course with everything in the shape of a boat, the water front of the city is lined with thousands on the wharves and docks, and on the roofs of storehouses, rowing clubs and elevators.

If the wind should chance to blow strong enough to make the water bumpy in the bay, the course can be laid out to the west of the island from Hanlon's hotel to the light-house; then the island shore and grand stand afford vantage ground for all spectators who do not go afloat.

But come along and we will climb up into the observatory at the top of the club house and have a look at the cruising ground of the yachts, Lake Ontario. Water in front of you, water to the right of you and water to the left of you, farther than you can see. What more can a man with a fifty-ton yacht ask for than such a glorious stretch of water? An inland fresh-water sea, two hundred miles long by over fifty wide, amply supplied with safe harbors, well lighted and easy of access in all weathers; no currents to puzzle you, no tides to delay you, no sudden storms of any moment to encounter, no shoals or dangerous rocks to avoid, and just enough passing vessels, steamers, propellers and schooners to make it companionable without being dangerous. Here the yachtsman can cruise to his heart's content, but his domain in not limited even by these bounds, for he may, if he chooses, turn to the northward from Timber Island (some hundred miles east of Toronto harbor) and find his way into the waters of the Bay of Quinte, where he will find a further stretch of forty miles or more of good yachting water.

Every yacht makes a cruise or two during the season, varying in duration from one to three weeks, and visits some of the different ports on the lake — Kingston, Cobourg, Port Hope, Hamilton and Niagara on the Canada side, and Oswego and Charlotte (Rochester) in New York State....

The yachts often run as far east as the Thousand Islands of the St. Lawrence and the pretty town of Brockville, and I remember one that extended her wanderings all the way down to Murray Bay, some hundred miles below Quebec; but the general verdict is that for real bonafide enjoyable yachting one does not require to go beyond the eastern limits of the lake itself. The regattas at Put-in-Bay, on Lake Erie, and at Chicago, on Lake Michigan, usually attract some of the R.C.Y.C. squadron, but for ordinary cruising no one thinks of going into either of these lakes....

Probably the most popular cruise of all is that over to the town of Niagara-on-the-Lake, where during the season the weekly Saturday night hops at the Queen's Royal Hotel always attract a goodly number of yachtsmen, who come in for a first rate dinner and dance and a pleasant sail across the lake and back.

As a general rule one can count upon good yachting weather on the lake during the months of June, July, August and most of September. Steady breezes are the rule and heavy gales quite the exception. Thunder squalls come up occasionally, of course, but are not dangerous and they serve a good purpose in accustoming the crews to shorten sail quickly.

When the autumnal equinox sets in in September the lake gets ugly and angry, and only those who want to experience heavy weather and be knocked about venture to put out.

Regattas are held every season and liberal prizes are offered for all classes of yachts, the principal and most coveted one perhaps being the Prince of Wales Challenge Cup, which was presented by H.R.H. many years ago and is open to all club vessels. The course was originally laid out across the lake to a buoy off Port Dalhousie, the entrance to the Welland Canal and return.

It was found, however, that by sending the competing yachts across the lake no one could see anything more of the race than the start and finish. Therefore, with a view to making it more interesting, the present course was some years ago adopted, and the races now start from a buoy in the bay immediately north of the club house, thence westward out of the harbor to a buoy off Mirinco Point, some ten miles distant; thence southerly to a buoy in the lake five miles south of the club house; thence easterly to a buoy some eight miles farther; thence back around the other two lake buoys and through the western entrance to the staring buoy.

This course can be seen from one end to the other from the upper verandas and the observatory at the club house, and the relative positions of the yachts discerned at all times. Each vessel, too, gets plenty of beating and plenty of free sheet, no matter where the wind may choose to blow from, and so has a fair opportunity of displaying her sailing qualities on every point...

For some time the custom prevailed among the members of the club of having a short cruise out on the lake every Saturday afternoon, each yacht taking her turn to lead. On the way out no vessel was permitted under any consideration to pass the leader of the day, but, rather than that, she must shorten sail or lay to, and when the leader chanced to be a slow-going craft the results were sometimes amusing, and a considerable amount of chaff and banter was indulged in.

The leader was free to steer in any direction she pleased, and every yacht was bound to obey all her signals. When the signal for "home and dinner" came everyone headed for the harbor, and cracking on kites, raced for their moorings. These weekly cruises brought all the vessels together on the lake, and their crews met afterward at the dinner table, and they did much toward promoting a friendly rivalry and good fellowship all around...

When the season closes and the yachts are stripped of their sails and safely stored away in comfortable quarters for the winter, and the bay freezes over, the club house is deserted and yachting gives way, perforce, to other sports, and is for the nonce forgotten. Soon after Christmas, however, the invitations are issued for the R.C.Y.C.'s annual ball and society circles are in a flutter at the approaching event. It has long been a distinctive feature among the winter gaieties of Toronto, and for the past twenty-five years has been the ball of the season. It is often held in the pavilion of the Horticultural Gardens, where there are all the facilities at hand.

Here, on these occasions, you will find a large and well-lighted ballroom, with a capital floor, an excellent band from one of the volunteer regiments, a good, spacious supper room, a splendid conservatory and ample dressing rooms; the scene from the galleries, looking down upon the whirling mass of lovely toilettes, fairy figures and flashing eyes, cruising round and round under convoy of yachtsmen and cavalrymen, artillery gunners, rifles and redcoats, goes far to prove that these R.C. yachtsmen do not have all their fun on the water.

More democratic than the yacht clubs in their social composition, rowing clubs had a long history in Canada, which was detailed by Outing in a series of articles, May 1891, pp. 122-127, and June 1891, pp. 244-250.

THE ROWING CLUBS OF CANADA
By Captain Thomas Blackwell

Canada is rather heavily handicapped in the matter of boat racing for, while she has magnificent lakes and noble rivers, King Frost lays an embargo on them for such a long period each year that it makes the rowing season a very short one; yet with these many disadvantages she has held her own well against all comers. When we take into consideration the small number of active rowing clubs there are in Canada it is a matter for nothing short of surprise their producing the marvelous oarsmen and scullers they have. The names of Hanlan, O'Connor, Donahue and others shed quite a lustre on Dominion doings with the oar...

There are but nine active clubs enrolled in the Canadian Association of Amateur Oarsmen, and one or two of these can be styled "active" only by courtesy; yet what a wonderful showing at the N.A.A.O. regattas against the mass of rowing organizations in this country theirs has been! Three times they have won the senior fours, thrice have rowed second; in 1885 the Torontos finished first, but were disqualified for fouling the Columbias. In 1888 they would certainly have won but for the strange illness of the stroke of the Toronto's crew. Twice the junior fours has been theirs; the only other time they entered their crew (the Leander of Hamilton) was disqualified on a foul when in the lead. Twice they have won the senior singles, and would have won it yet again had not William O'Connor been disqualified prior to the start.

In 1888 the Canadian, Donahue was so close a second that but for the opportune "shot" of an amateur photographic crank, standing at the finish line, whose photo showed Psotta to have been a quarter of a length in the lead, there would have been disputing yet as to who really won the race. Ryan, for three years the Canadian champion, through not the fastest sculler in the Dominion, came in third in this race, being sadly handicapped in his boat. Junior singles have twice been won by the Canucks, and in this race both in 1887 and 1888 every heat in which a Canadian rowed was won by him. They have twice won the double-scull race. Pair oars they do not go in for, and there is not an eight oared racing boat in Canada.

In 1886 both the famous Argonaut and Nautilus crews were defeated in this country by the Fairmount crew, of Philadelphia; but there was a crew in Canada at the time that could have beaten everything "hands down" had they competed at the N.A.A.O. regatta. This was the Lachine crew, of Lachine, near Montreal, probably as fine an amateur four-oared crew as ever sat a boat, and whose record of 7m. 50 2.3s, when not really hard pressed, speaks for itself.

In 1888 J.F. Corbett, the N.A.A.O. champion of 1887, winner of races almost without number, was handily beaten at Toronto by J.J. Ryan, beating M. Shea, winner of the junior sculls in this country, by a short quarter length...

The formation of the Canadian Association of Amateur Oarsmen was the inauguration of the meritorious plane upon which rowing in Canada is at present based. It is a "live" organization, ably managed and well off financially. It offers annually for competition a challenge cup for senior fours, valued at $600, and for the senior singles one valued at $300. Another is offered for double sculls, and it is proposed that yet another shall be hung up for pair-oared contests, with a view to popularizing this style of rowing.

The regattas are held alternately at Toronto, Hamilton, Lachine, eight miles distant from Montreal, and Ottawa, the centres of rowing in Canada. The local club or clubs in these places take the management of the regattas through the means of regatta committees nominated by them and approved by the association, on their shoulders. These regatta committees have to raise the necessary funds to meet the expenses which average about $1,200, and are liable for any debts that may accrue...

The active rowing clubs of the Dominion are: The Toronto, Argonaut, Bayside and Don Amateur rowing clubs, located at Toronto; the Leander and Nautilus rowing clubs, of Hamilton; the Ottawa Rowing Club, of Ottawa; the Lachine Boating Club, of Lachine; the Grand Trunk Rowing Club of Montreal, and the Winnipeg Rowing Club, of Winnipeg.... The Toronto Rowing Club may in point of record claim to be the premier rowing organization of America. Time after time the navy blue has been victorious over many a watery course, and their record in 1888 of winning both the N.A.A.O. and the C.A.A.O. junior fours with, necessarily, separate and distinct crews stands unequaled.

Next in seniority to the Atlanta Boat Club of New york, which dates back to 1838, and is the oldest aquatic club on the continent, comes the Toronto Rowing Club.

In the year 1845, the nucleus of the present club was formed, and they at once began holding regattas on Toronto Bay which soon became a regular institution....

Under the presidency of the late Mr. Angus Morrison, the club in 1865 was regularly organized; but it was not until eighteen years later that it became a body corporate with a membership roll of upward of three hundred.

In 1881, after several moves had been made, the club finally settled in its present commodious quarters on the Esplanade fronting on Toronto Bay and next door to the Argonaut's splendid club house....

J.J. Ryan is the representative senior sculler of the Toronto Rowing Club, and outside of the Donahue brothers, of Hamilton, Ontario (both of whom beat him at the C.A.A.O. regatta there in 1889), he has for several seasons been the fastest man in Canada. Jerry Donahue, however, is by long odds the fastest amateur in America, the championship of which he won in 1889 at Pullman. He is five feet ten inches, well built, and weighs about one hundred and fifty pounds, trained.

The Argonaut Rowing Club of Toronto, was organized in 1872, and has now the finest club house and largest number of members of any of the rowing clubs of Canada. It is also the wealthiest, and comprising as it does the best young blood of Toronto among its members, it is not surprising that it exercises a marked influence upon the social life of the city....

During the winter months the members have an instructor who teaches boxing and fencing. The gymnasium is also used for the monthly smoking concerts given by the club during the compulsory close season.... In the years 1883 and 1884 the Argonauts at the National Association of American Oarsmen, at Lake Seneca, won the proud title of champions of America, making the fastest amateur time on record on still water, viz, one and a half miles in 8m.22 3/4s.

It was this victory which induced the Argonauts to send their crew to measure oars with the Englishmen at Henley regatta. The "Henley crew" from this club consisted of R. McCay, bow; Oliver Murphy, No.2; A.G. Thompson, No.3; James W. Hogg, stroke.

They left Montreal on May 22, 1885, taking with them a new paper shell built by E.Waters & Son, of Troy, N.Y., and arrived at Liverpool on June 2. They went to Henley at once and commenced active training...

They had only four weeks to train before the regatta took place, and they entered into work with such zest that they overtrained, as it proved.

On the day of the race for the Steward's Cup — which was the prize they went across the Atlantic to compete for — they rowed in a cedar boat built by Clasper, of Putney, as the boat they took over with them from this side was found unsuitable to the waters of the Thames.

In the race they led most of the way, and while still holding a good lead came to a dead stop when within less than a quarter of a mile from home, owing to No. 2 (Morphy), having to give up, and an almost certain victory was snatched from them. Al of the crew were more or less affected by the severe training, but Morphy suffered more than the others, and was really quite unfit for the effort required on the morning of the race.... The crew was also entered for the Metropolitan Regatta, held the following seek at Putney, but being disabled by No. 2's indisposition had reluctantly to give up the idea and return to Canada without the coveted laurels.

The membership of the club is over three hundred, and the revenue about $4,500. The colors of the club are Oxford and Cambridge blue. Sir Alexander Campbell, the Lieutenant Governor of the province of Ontario, is patron, Col. G.A. Sweeney president, and Mr. H.F. Wyatt honorary secretary.

The records are as follows:

1875	Pair oar, Lambe brothers	Saratoga
1879	Four oar	Lachine
1880	Senior fours	C.A.A.O.
1880	Junior four	C.A.A.O.
1881	Senior fours	C.A.A.O.
1881	Junior fours	C.A.A.O.
1883	Junior fours	C.A.A.O.
1884	Senior fours	C.A.A.O.
1886	Senior fours, finished second	C.A.A.O.
1890	Junior single, A.P Burritt	C.A.A.O.

THE ROWING CLUBS OF CANADA
By Capt. Thos. Blackwell
Part II

Canada possesses more than one small rowing club with energy equal to the largest, and of these, second in seniority, though not in importance, of the Toronto clubs is the Bayside.

Their boat house stands on the shore of Toronto Bay, about a quarter of a mile below that of the Argonauts. The Baysides organized in 1869, and about ninety members are enrolled.

The "bright particular star" of the Baysides, Mr. J.J. Ryan, has left them, having joined the great Toronto Rowing Club.

In senior single sculls this gentleman won for the Baysides first at Lachine in 1886 and first at Ottawa the year after, where he "rowed over." He also won this race at Toronto in 1888...

The Don Amateur Rowing club, of Toronto, is the junior Toronto club, having been organized in 1881. Its career has been a most successful one.

It was in this club that William O'Connor, the present professional champion of America, learned the rudiments of the sculler's art...

The Don's have a membership of upward of sixty, and recently they erected a comfortable new boat house, located on the River Don, about a quarter of a mile above where that stream empties into Toronto Bay...

The Leander Rowing Club, of Hamilton, Ont, was organized in 1877. Some two years ago the Hamilton Canoe Club amalgamated with them, thereby largely increasing the membership. The club house is a fine structure, standing upon the shore of Hamilton Bay...

The Nautilus Rowing Club, of Hamilton, Ont., has at almost every important regatta during the last seven years been successfully represented. This club has no social features to bear comparison with the Leanders, its members being chiefly of the artisan class, but it can turn out sturdy, muscular crews which take a lot of beating. The club house is situated on Hamilton Bay, but is altogether inadequate to meet the requirements of the members.

The Nautilus Club came into prominence chiefly through the rowing of Furlong and Donahue, who carried off the champion double sculls of Canada about eight years ago. The same year, the Nautilus four won the championship of America at Hamilton, at Chautauqua and at Boston....

In 1889 at Pullman, Ill., on August 9, D. Donahue won the singles championship of America, and the following day won at the Mississippi Valley regatta....

The Ottawa Rowing Club is one of the oldest in Canada, having been organized in 1875, succeeding an older organization of the same description which had died out some years before.

The large majority of the members of this club are employees of the civil service, connected with the governmental departments in Ottawa....

The famous Lachine crew of 1886 was a very strong one, as the stroke, D. Robertson, bow; C. Shaw, No.2, and J.G. Monk, No.3, were all six feet in height and averaged one hundred and sixty-two pounds each, trained. This crew won the three-mile race (with a turn) for the Lachine cup in 1886 in the fastest time on record over that course, and the next day won the mile and a half C.A.A.O. four-oared championship in 7m. 50 2-5s, being the best time recorded in Canada, and within three seconds of the best time recorded in America.

Two regattas are held annually — the spring "trial fours" and in the autumn four-oared and sculling races. The prizes for the former are pewter mugs, and for the single-shell race a very handsome silver challenge cup. For the double-scull race there is an even finer challenge cup, presented by the citizens of Ottawa, now held by Messrs, F.H.F. Mercer and P.D. Ross. The Marquis of Lansdowne, ex-Governor General of Canada, presented the club with another challenge cup for single sculls, which is now held by Mr. P.D. Ross.

The Grand Trunk Rowing club, of Montreal, Que., is located at Point St., Charles, a suburb of Montreal, on the St. Lawrence River, has captured its full share of aquatic laurels.

It is made up largely of employees of the Grand Trunk Railway of Canada, whose headquarters are in Montreal.

Mr. Joseph Laing, for so many years champion of Canada and of this country, was a member of this club until he went over to the ranks of the professionals.

The Grand Trunk Rowing Club was organized in 1875 and upward of one hundred members are enrolled. The club boats and those of its members are housed in a series of boat houses, the property of the club, not in one building. Regattas are held each autumn. Mr. Victor Henrichon was their champion single-shell sculler for 1888.

In 1880, 1881, 1882, 1883 and 1884 the justly celebrated Joseph Laing won the senior singles at the C.A.A.O. regatta for the Grand Trunk Rowing Club, and in 1883 and 1884 he also won the championship of this country.

In 1882 he and his brother, R. Laing, won the double-in rigged race, and in 1886 the Messrs. Green won the same race at Lachine....

The Lachine Boating Club is a veteran organization, having sprung into existence in 1864 under the presidency of the late Mr. Thomas Workman. It is almost altogether made up of Montrealers who reside in and around Lachine during the summer months, it being only eight miles distant from the city and situated on the northern shore of Lake St. Louis, a widening of the St. Lawrence River at its junction with the Ottawa....

The active membership at present is about one hundred and seventy-five.... The Lake St. Louis Canoe Club is ultimately associated with the Lachine B.C. A recent innovation in this connection is a big war canoe which so far has made an excellent record. The great four-oared race for the professional championship of the world was rowed over the Lachine course. It was in this race that the celebrated contest took place between the "Paris" crew of St. John, N.B., and the famous "Tyne" crew, of Newcastle, England, stroked by the unfortunate Renforth....

The Longueuil Boating Club, of the village of that name, opposite Montreal, came into existence in the year 1867. In 1871 it absorbed the "St. Lawrence Boat Club," an amalgamation taking place....

The Winnipeg Rowing Club, of Winnipeg, Manitoba, was organized in 1883, when the Hon. John Norquay was patron, Mr. Thos. Renwick president, and G.F. Galt captain. The first club house was a floating one, at the junction of the Red and Assiniboine rivers, and was, unfortunately, carried away by a flood in the spring of 1884, causing a serious loss....

Early in 1886 the Winnipeg and Minnesota Rowing Association was formed and a regatta under its auspices was held at Lake Minnetonka on July 12 and 13 of that year....

The club can look back on their record for 1889 with great pride.... Their success over the remarkably fast crews they met at this regatta suggested the idea of their sending their senior four and hitherto unconquered double to take part in the National Association of American Oarsmen meeting, held the following week at Pullman, Ill., for the championship of America....

By an unavoidable arrangement the senior four and senior double had to be rowed off within half an hour of each other, so that Turnbull and Fox only had thirty minutes rest after one of the hardest races ever witnessed, and before taking their places in the four, not only to compete for but actually to win the championship of America, defeated the Delawares of Chicago., the Atalantas and Athletics of New York and the Torontos of Toronto.

G.F. Galt is one of the best-known amateur oarsmen in Canada and the father of the Winnipeg Rowing Club. Before going to Winnipeg he was stroke of the famous Argonaut four of Toronto, and as such had thrice won the Canadian championship....

J.H. Turnbull was stroke of the junior four when they won the Canadian championship at Ottawa in 1887.... In the coming season the W. and M. Association regatta is to be held at Winnipeg. The principal events at this meeting, the $1,000 trophy presented by Sir Donald Smith and the championship cup, are both at present held by the Winnipeg four...

Chapter 3

AUTOMOBILE RACING

Automobile racing first appeared in France when a newspaper offered cash prizes for motor carriages that completed a trip from Paris to Rouen in 1894. The Chicago Times-Herald promoted an auto race the following year, offering $5,000 in prize money.

The following article appeared in the Sewanee Review, January 1897, pp. 48-62, and provided a brief history of locomotion, but largely neglecting the development of motorcycles, which were first raced in 1895.

THE EVOLUTION OF THE WHEEL-VELOCIPEDE TO MOTOCYCLE.

There is much talk in these days of the "horseless carriage," a term which is certainly not distinctive. What is meant by a "horseless carriage," however, is a carriage propelled by some mechanical power within itself and running on ordinary roads without the aid of rails. The French call such a carriage an "automobile," while in our country the term "motor-carriage" or "motocycle" is used. Within the last twelve months these carriages have attracted general attention, as is attested by the large number of articles on the subject that have appeared in our newspapers and magazines. Another sign that the interest in this new mode of locomotion is real and not feigned, is that quite a number of magazines devoted exclusively to the motocycle have sprung up, and that societies for the promotion of motor carriages have been formed in the United States, in England, in France, in Belgium, and perhaps in other countries. As the caption of this article implies, the writer considers the motocycle as, in a sense, evolved from the bicycle, for this was the pioneer in the field and paved the way for the self-propelled carriage which boasts of more than two wheels and requires no muscular exertion to make it go...

In 1759 Dr. Robinson called the attention of Watt to the possibility of constructing a carriage to be driven by a steam engine, and ten years later Cuynot, a French army officer, rigged up a gun-carriage and a big copper boiler so that it was driven by its own power. There was too much danger of the passengers being scalded to death to make the machine popular and it was soon cast aside. This engine is still preserved in Paris. In 1784 the Cornish engineer, James Murdoch, invented a road engine.

In 1786, Wm. Symington designed a road machine consisting of a carriage with a steam locomotive behind. In the same year the first patent for road engines in America was secured by Oliver Evans, who it seems obtained, from the Maryland Legislature, a monopoly for his sytem of applying steam to the propelling of wagons on land. In 1804 he completed a flat bottomed boat for dredging the Philadelphia docks, and, mounting it on wheels, drove it by its own steam engine to the river bank. Launching the craft, which he named the "Ornkton Amphibolus," he propelled it down the river, using the engine to drive the paddlewheels.

In 1827 Mr. Gurney invented, in England, a steam carriage. In this carriage, which created considerable stir, the engine was made up of several cylinders, transmitting power to the hind axle. There were, besides, "propellers," described as moving like the hind legs of a horse, catching the ground and thus forcing the machine forward, grasshopper fashion. This invention, like earlier attempts, was short-lived, and it did not materialize into anything of real service. Perhaps the chief reason for this was that about 1802 Trevethick and Vivian demonstrated that it was possible to run steam locomotives upon a line of smooth rails, even upon slight gradients, and the attention of inventors was turned in a new direction.

In 1828, however, the subject of self-propelled road carriages came forward, and a great deal of ingenuity was displayed in meeting the supposed demand. It was thought that the days of the horse were numbered, and that the future of these road carriages was assured; steam "buggies" were to supplant horses and steam stage coaches were really built and run for some time for hire.

In 1831, Sir G. Gurney built a steam wagon, which he ran between Cheltenham and Gloucester, a distance of nine miles, and with a coach attached to this motor he carried thirty-three passengers in fifty minutes. He ran this coach for four month and carried over three thousand passengers, and attempted to extend its use throughout England and Scotland. But the success of the experiment of running carriages on rails, and the speedy extension of railways coupled with the difficulties of adapting his road wagon to the varying conditions and gradients of common roads put a stop to further efforts in that direction. So the subject of mechanically propelled carriages for common roads was dropped and was not seriously taken up for many years to come.

It is only within the last decade, or we might say within the last five years that the question of motor carriages has again come to the front. France was the first country to make a public test of the efficiency of the motor carriage, or auto-mobile. Her splendid system of government roads was conducive to the success of the undertaking. The first auto-mobile race, from Paris to Rouen, was held in June, 1894, and this followed in June, 1895, by the great races from Paris to Bordeaux. These contests brought the importance of the subject before the public, and encouraged manufacturers and inventors to renewed efforts looking to the improvement of the horseless carriage.

The Paris-Rouen races were under the auspices of the *Petit Journal,* which enterprising paper offered five prizes, the highest being $1,000.

Security, easy management, and cheapness were essential features of the conditions. Out of one hundred and two carriages which originally entered for the competition, twenty-six finally took part in the race. The greater number were petroleum motors, steam coming next, while there was only one electric motor in the contest. A petroleum motor of the Daimler type got the first prize....

In Germany the motor carriage has been developed to quite a high state of perfection by a number of manufacturers, notably by the firm of Benz & Co., of Mannheim. Many styles of vehicles are made here as in other countries, with seating capacity for one, two, or more persons. When it seats only one, it is usually a motor bicycle or tricycle.

Soon after the Paris-Bordeaux races, the Chicago *Times-Herald,* with most commendable zeal, offered premiums aggregating $5,000 for a motor carriage race to be held in Chicago on Nov. 2, 1895. This contest was not a success, as for various reasons, only one vehicle completed the race. The *Times-Herald,* nothing daunted, announced that its original prizes and conditions would hold good for a contest to be held on Nov. 28, 1895. Any American paper on the history and development of the motocycle would be incomplete without some account of this contest. For nothing has so encouraged the advocates of the motocycle in our country and directed the attention of the public to the subject as this *Times-Herald* contest...

The more important and suggestive conditions of this contest were as follows:

The contest is limited to motor-carriages or, as they are more commonly known, horseless carriages." There will be eligible to competition any and all vehicles having three or more running wheels, and which derive all their motive power from within themselves. No vehicle shall be admitted to competition which depends in any way upon muscular exertion, except for purposes of guidance.

No vehicle shall be admitted to competition unless it shall comfortably carry not less than two persons for the entire distance, one of whom may have charge of the vehicle and the manipulation of the same.

No vehicle shall be admitted to competition except that it be free from danger, not only to its occupants but to spectators and the public users of the highway. The judges at their discretion, may debar any vehicle which, from its construction, gives evidence of defects which would render the adoption of its type an evident impossibility.

For the purpose of limiting the contest to vehicles of practical utility a preliminary test of all vehicles entered for competition shall be held by the judges under such rules and for such a distance as the judges may determine on.

In making awards the judges will carefully consider the various points of excellence as displayed by the respective vehicles, and so far as possible select as prize winners those constructions which combine in the highest degree the following features and requisites, voting them of value in the order named: (1) General utility, ease of control and adaptability to the various forms of work which may be demanded of a vehicle motor. In other words, the construction which is in every way the most practical. (2) Speed. (3) Cost. (4) Economy of operation. (5) General appearance and excellence of design.

The conditions and tests imposed by the board of judges were very comprehensive in character. Each motor carriage should, first, be subjected to a laboratory test and, second, should cover a prescribed course of fifty-four miles inside of seven hours. The time limit was afterwards extended, owing to the bad condition of the roads caused by a heavy fall of snow. The award of premiums was to be made on the record shown both in the laboratory and service tests. The course was over paved city streets and macadamized roads. Six carriages contested and premiums were awarded as follows:

(1) An award of $2,000 to the Duryea Motor Wagon Co., of Springfield, Mass., for best performance in the road race, for range of speed and pull, with compactness of design. (2) An award of $1,500 to the H. Mueller & Co. motocycle, of Decatur, Ill., for performance in the road race and economy in operation. (3) An award of $500 to the R.H. Macy & Co. motorcycle, of New York, for showing made in the road race.

(4) An award of $500 to the Sturges Electric motocycle, of Chicago, for showing made in the road race. (5) An award of the *Times-Herald* gold medal to the Morris & Salom electrobat, of Philadelphia, for best showing made in the official tests for safety, ease of control, absence of noise, vibration, heat or odor, cleanliness and general excellence of design and workmanship....

(1) Duryea Gasoline Motor Carriage: This machine weighs 1,028 lbs., and is mounted on four wheels with pneumatic tires and ball bearings. The power is generated by a two-cyliner 4x4 1/2 inch gasoline engine. The vehicle has a carrying capacity of 8 gallons of gasoline and it also carries a tank of water to prevent the motor from overheating. A vertical movement of a lever changes the speed, starts or stops, or reverses the vehicle if desired. The brake is so arranged that the carriage, under a speed of 12 miles an hour, can be stopped in a few feet. Among the advantages claimed for this wagon are, little noise and odor, four speeds, 5, 10 and 20 miles an hour forward, and 3 miles an hour backward, its fuel costs less than one-half cent per mile, it runs from 100 to 200 miles without refilling, and is not dangerous either from fire or explosion. The retail price of this carriage is from $1,000 to $2,000, according to details.

(2) The Mueller-Benz Gasoline Motor Carriage, which received the second premium, weighs 1,636 lbs., and is mounted on four wheels with solid rubber tires and roller bearings. The power is generated by a one-cylinder Benz Gasoline Engine.

(3) The Moris & Salom Electrobat: This machine is mounted on four wheels with pneumatic tires and ball bearings, the rear wheels being the steering wheels. The power is obtained from two 1 1/2 H P. Sundell electric motors. The weight of the total carriage is 1,650 lbs. The batteries consist of four sets of twelve cells each, having a normal capacity of 50 ampere-hours per cell. There are four speeds ahead and one backward, which are obtained by various groupings of the batteries and motors in series and parallels. The cost of the vehicle is $1,000....

The contest of the year was the Paris-Marseilles-Paris race, held under the auspices of the Auto-Mobile Club of France. The course was from Paris to Marseilles and back to Paris, about 1,000 miles in all....

...It is quite evident that the motocycle is an established fact in the world. We cannot deny that it is here, and we must believe that it is destined to stay. But it is well for us to ask what its sphere of usefulness is and what its possibilities are; for what work is it best suited, and where will it replace the horse, and in what field will it not take the place of the horse?... But even if our roads were all good, the farmers, who do the principal hauling in the country, would have no use for motocycles, for they must have horses for plowing and harvesting, and these horses while not thus employed can be utilized in hauling produce to market, and in taking the family to church on Sunday. In the cities, however, the conditions are very different. For one thing it is very much more expensive to keep a horse in the city than in the country, and then, too, the horse is usually employed solely for hauling freight or passengers, and could be dispensed with if the motocycle can do equally well the same work. Another fact to be considered is that the roads or pavements of the city and vicinity are, generally speaking, much superior to those in the country. For city traffic the motor carriage that would take the place of the horse vehicle must be ready to move at a moment's notice, to take long trips if necessary, to start, to stop, to turn round quickly and with ease. Safety must be the first consideration, and in a large measure the safety of the vehicle depends upon the certainty and promptness with which it can be stopped, and upon the certainty and ease with which it can be steered. Increased speed means increased danger, and it is quite evident that the speed in the streets cannot be much increased. One thing in favor of the horse is his versatility. The horse can vary his speed and his pull by almost imperceptible amounts, and he can exert in an emergency, for a short time, a pull equivalent to three or four horse power. It is a well known fact that accidents, both in crowded streets and country highways, are daily averted by the instinct of the horse itself. But the motor having no instinct, everything depends upon the driver or conductor. The danger from collision would be greatly augmented, and, owing to the greater weight of the vehicles, would be attended with more serious results. On the whole, however, we think that the motocycle, even in its present state of development, is a suitable vehicle under limitations, for city traffic. And it may be that on country stage lines, over good roads, the motocycle could profitably be substituted for the stage-coach or omnibus. There are many such stage lines, even in the more settled parts of the United States, ranging from eight to fifty miles in length. Of course it is mere nonsense to talk of the motocycle taking the place of trolley lines in suburban districts. As to pleasure driving, here the motocycle would play a small part, requiring too much labor and attention, if one elects to drive himself, and, in the other event, great faith in one's coachman. At the same time it is possible that much of the prejudice against such vehicles grows out of the mistaken notion that there is bound to be much noise and vibration, puffing and sissing, and that the brake and steering levers are as formidable as those that the gripman manipulates on cable cars. This is a misleading impression, for even now it is claimed that motors are made practically free from noise and vibration, and with no offensive odor. Indeed, the new machines, with their rawhide gearing and solid rubber or pneumatic tires are said to be almost noiseless.

In closing, we cannot refrain from mentioning one other striking advantage that the motocycles possess, namely, their cleanliness. With motocycles in use, the problem of street cleaning will be greatly simplified, and the health of our cities promoted.

The writer loves a horse too much ever to wish to see a *horseless age,* but he will not be alone in welcoming the day when the motocycle, improved and beautified, shall occupy its proper place in the world's economy.   Samuel M. Barton.

The Chicago Times-Herald announced its contest on the first page of its 28 November 1895 issue. Only six vehicles started the race, won by the gas powered Duryea entry, which used only 3 1/2 gallons of gas but 19 gallons of water in averaging 7 1/2 miles per hour. The Chicago Tribune, a competitor of the Times-Herald, reluctantly and somewhat disdainfully reported the results on 29 November 1895, p. 8.

TIMES-HERALD MOTORCYCLE CONTEST TAKES PLACE TO-DAY
PRIZE OF $5,000 IS AT STAKE

Without fail, notwithstanding the state of the roads and the weather, THE TIMES-HERALD motorcycle contest will take place to-day. This was decided upon by the judges yesterday, and the prizes, amounting to $5,000, offered by THE TIMES-HERALD will be awarded to those horseless carriages which cover the course specified in the rules of the contest and according to the conditions laid down by the judges. Eleven competitors have signified their intention to start in the race this morning, and a good run is expected.

Owing to the condition of the roads the judges decided yesterday to do away with the time limit, reserving the right to add more time for those vehicles which struggle through the snow drifts and finish at Jackson Park. This was deemed necessary, as the test of the motor cycles to-day will be a severe one. The judges considered that the race under such conditions would prove conclusively that the horse will be relegated to the background, and that motorcycles will prove the coming vehicles.

THE TIMES-HERALD contest has aroused so much interest among inventors and wagon manufacturers that to-day's event is looked forward to with more than ordinary enthusiasm. The offering of prizes for the best motorcycles has given an impetus to American invention and manufacturers have been working night and day to perfect their machines. For the benefit of these the judges postponed the contest from Nov. 2 to Thanksgiving Day. Some of them, however, have been unable to get their machines ready in time and will not enter the race. Those who have their wagons in working order are very enthusiastic about the race, though they viewed the snow-storm of Monday night with something of dismay. But they have determined to run the race and are satisfied with the shortened course to Evanston and back and the removal of the time limit by the judges. Everything has been arranged to suit the competitors in the race, as it was felt by the judges that some concession was due owing to the bad state of the roads.

Names of the Competitors

The following have announced their intention of starting in the race this morning, each wagon bearing the number opposite the name of the competitor:

1.- A.C. Ames, 8630 Essex avenue, South Chicago.
   Umpire-T.G. Pilkington.
2.- A. Bauschke and Brother, Benton Harbor, Mich.
   Umpire-William Reardon.
5.- Duryea Motor Wagon Company, Springfield, Mass.
   Umpire-George White.
7.- DeLaVergne Refrigerating Machine Company, New York.
   Umpire-James F. Bate.
10.- Max Hertel, 454 Lincoln avenue, Chicago.
   Umpire-L. Kuhn.
11.- and 12.- Haynes & Apperson, Kokomo, Ind.
   Umpires-J.W. Lambert and W.H. McIntyre.

15.- George W. Lewis, 32 Willis court, Chicago.
　　Umpire-George Hargrave.
18.- Morris & Salom, Philadelphia.
　　Umpire-H.P. Maxin
19.- H. Mueller & Co., Decatur, Ill.
　　Umpire-C.B. King.
22.- R.H. Macy & Co., New York.
　　Umpire-Lieutenant Samuel Rodman
25.- Sturges Electric Motorcycle, 521 Rookery, Chicago.
　　Umpire-F.T. Bennett.
　　Substitute umpires-W.S. Cappeller and William Corbett.

The umpires were appointed by the judges, C.F. Kimball, Professor Barrett, and L.L. Summers, yesterday afternoon, and they are expected to report the progress of the vehicles they ride at THE TIMES-HERALD office as soon after the race as possible. If any accident or breakdown occurs, the umpires are requested to make careful note of everything, and report the matter at THE TIMES-HERALD office this afternoon or evening

DURYEA MOTOCYCLE WINS THE RACE.
TEN HOURS AND SEVENTEEN MINUTES COVERING
FIFTY-FIVE MILES.

Between 9 and 10 o'clock yesterday morning, while crowds of enthusiasts were hastening to the football games, seven motocycles plowed out of Jackson Park for a fifty-five mile race through the snow and slush that lay between the starting point and Evanston. At 9 o'clock last night but two of the horseless vehicles had crossed the finish line. The other five were lost-wandering aimlessly about the streets of Chicago or lying wrecked in some gutter along the way.

The Duryea machine, which in the last race was ditched several miles from anywhere, finished first. The Benz-Mueller craft came in an hour and a half later. Its pilot, however, claims the trophy on the ground the Duryea machine was pushed up the hill to the finish. This is denied by the occupants of the Duyrea motocyle, and there will be a contest.

The time of the winner was 10:17 for the fifty-five miles. No records, but various parts of the mechanism, were broken.

The Duryea machine was first away at 9:01 a.m. No. 22, owned by R.H. Macy & Co. started three minutes later, and the others straggled off at intervals of a few minutes until 10:00, when the Benz-Mueller machine started. After being pushed up the hill at the start the horseless vehicles warmed to their work and reached Rush street without mishap.

Nothing but a carette can successfully combat that roadway, however, and the Duryea machine came to grief at Ontario street. The Macy machine succumbed temporarily at Erie street. After a half hour's delay the damage was repaired and they took up the stern chase.

The Duryea machine showed its fondness for ditches at Sheridan road and Grace street, but was hauled out and started anew. Three of the motocycles reached Evanston after 2 o'clock a.m. and were headed homeward.

Meanwhile the judges had become disgusted and quit and no one witnessed the finish but two reporters.

The Scientific American proclaimed the auto race at the Rhode Island State Fair, the first to be conducted on a track, in its 23 May 1896 issue on page 327. It provided the rules for the contest on 1 August 1896, p. 122.

A NEW HORSELESS CARRIAGE RACE.

The Rhode Island State Fair Association announced that $5,000 will be given in prizes in a series of horseless carriage races to be held during its annual exposition week at Narragansett Park, Providence, R.I., in September. Racing of this kind has been attempted before, but never on so large a scale. The series of races will be held on a regulation trotting track, and the results promise to be interesting. One of the exhibition buildings will be set apart for a horseless carriage exposition. Certainly no "infant industry" was ever so coddled and fostered by the offer of large rewards; up to the present time the results in this country have not been worth the cost.

RULES OF THE PROVIDENCE HORSELESS CARRIAGE RACE.

The following are the rules and conditions of the horseless carriage race and exhibition which will be held on September 7, 8, 9, 10, 11, 1896, at Narragansett Park, under the auspices of the Rhode Island State Fair Association. The race will be twenty-five miles for a $5,000 dividend. The rules are very sensible, and the race will tend to awaken public interest in the horseless carriage. It will be noted that an entrance fee of $100 is charged. This is a step in the right direction and will certainly prevent the pitiable defections from the ranks of competing vehicles which have marked both of the former races.

OFFICIAL RULES AND CONDITIONS.

Entrance fee, $100 per carriage, payable August 10. No coditional entries accepted.

The race to be five heats, of five miles each day of the fair, September 7, 8, 9, 10, 11, 1896.

Ten carriages to enter and five to start, or no race.

Vehicles must be able to show a rate of speed equal to 15 miles an hour to compete in the race.

Vehicles must carry one person in addition to the driver. (Weight carried must be 165 pounds.)

Only vehicles propelled by other than animal power allowed to compete.

Vehicles not limited in number, but no one owner can enter more than one carriage and start in the race. If the starters number ten or more, for reasons of safety the carriages may be divided into classes and started in two or more divisions.

Division of the race purse will be in the following proportion of the winners of the race: 50, 25, 15, and 10 per cent of $3,000. First, $1,500; second, $750; third, $450; fourth, $300.

To the vehicle winning the greatest number out of five heats, first money, etc., but all vehicles must stay in throughout the five heats.

Distance waived, but those vehicles which do not cover the course with an average speed of fifteen miles an hour will be disqualified.

Each vehicle will be required to carry its number in large figures: other printed matter not permitted.

Contestants will be required to conform to such rules and regulations as may be made by the association, particularly in regard to their position on the track. All legal responsibility is thrown upon the contestants, the association declining to assume any whatsoever.

In case that less than five carriages shall respond to the call of the starting judge, the race shall be declared off, and to those answering the call and who are ready with their vehicles, their entrance fees paid in shall be refunded. With ten or more entries received, the association will open, in addition to the speed contest, prizes to be competed for as an exhibition, judging to be made on points of manageability, etc, for $2,000, divided as follows:

First prize, $1,000 and the association's gold medal and diploma.

Second prize, $500 and the association's silver medal and diploma.

Third prize, $300 and the association's bronze medal and diploma.

Fourth prize, $200 and the association's diploma.

In the exhibitive competition the following percentage scale of points shall be made the basis of awards:

Speed	40 per cent.	Cost	10 per cent.
Control	30 "	Maintenance	5 "
Simplicity	10 "	Appearance	10 "

Vehicles may compete, if desired, in both racing and exhibition.

Entries will close August 10, 1896. Entry blanks will be furnished on application to Rhode Island State Fair Association, Providence, R.I.

On 16 December 1899, p. 387, the Scientific American announced the advent of international auto racing competition with the donation of a trophy by James Gordon Bennett, Jr., a controversial American publisher, entrepreneur, sportsman, and expatriate living in Paris. Bennett had already established trophies for yachting, and track and field competition, and he would do so for airplane racing after the turn of the century.

THE AUTOMOBILE CUP.

The cup which has been recently presented to the Automobile Club, of France, by Mr. James Gordon Bennett is to inaugurate a series of yearly international contests between the different clubs of Europe and America, the winning club to hold the cup until beaten, as in the yacht races. This will form a yearly event which promises some interesting sport, as there is no doubt that the cup will be warmly contested by the different clubs. It is now in possession of the Automobile Club, of France, who will hold it until the first contest decides the winner. A series of rules have been established for the conduct of the races; the following is a resume of them:

The cup may be competed for by all the clubs now on the official lists, which includes those of Belgium, Austria, Italy, Great Britain, Germany and the United States. Any club not on this list may be accepted by a majority of the clubs above named. To enter the competition, a letter should be addressed to the president of the club holding the cup, in which will be stated the number of vehicles to be entered, and other necessary details. The time fixed for the races is from the 15th of May to the 15th of August. Each club may send from one to three automobiles, these to belong to the class known as "voitures," as specified in the rules of the Automobile Club, of France, for 1899. According to this they should weigh, empty, more than 400 kilogrammes, and carry at least two persons, these placed side by side. A weight of 70 kilogrammes is allowed per person, this being regulated by the addition of ballast, as usual, to make up the 140 kilogrammes total. The 400 kilogrammes, representing the weight of the vehicle empty, is exclusive of combustibles, accumulators, water, baggage, etc. One of the rules is that all the automobiles entering the contest should be constructed in the countries represented by the different clubs. They are to be conducted by members of these clubs, the two places being occupied during the whole time of the race.

A committee of supervision is to be formed, and for this each club will be represented by a delegate; the donor of the cup is an honorary member of this committee. The necessary officers will be appointed, and also the starters, judges, timekeepers, etc.: these latter are not necessarily chosen from among the members. The races will be run over a route of 550 to 650 kilometers, with stages of not less than 150; they are to take place in the country whose club holds the cup for the year in question: if desired by this club, the races may be held in France, starting presumably from Paris. This will no doubt be carried out in a number of cases, on account of the fine roads in that country and from the fact that Paris, besides being a local center, has all the facilities for the care of automobiles.

Among other rules the most important is naturally that which concerns the winning of the cup; this is decided by the automobile which first crosses the line, and the club it represents will be declared victor. All communications in regard to these contests may be addressed to the secretary of the Automobile Club, of France, Place de la Concorde, Paris.

Chapter 4

BASEBALL

The 1880-1900 period proved critical to the development of baseball. Several events, such as decisive rules changes, volatile labor issues, a players' revolt, and the formation of alternative leagues culminated in the organizational structure, strategies, and post-season championship familiar to modern fans by the turn of the century.

The evolution of baseball rules brought significant changes to the nature of the game as pitchers were allowed to throw overhand by 1884. In 1887 the batter lost his option of calling for a high or low pitched ball, and two years later a base on balls was awarded after the pitcher threw four non-strikes. Previously, as many as nine balls were required for a walk. By the 1890's catchers had begun to wear masks and mitts and managers were allowed to make free substitutions. In 1893 the pitching distance was extended to 60 feet 6 inches, and by 1901 foul balls were counted as strikes. The infield fly rule was adopted in 1895. Professor Hinton developed the first pitching machine at Princeton in 1896.

In addition to such technological advancements, owners constructed specialized sites for baseball. The Polo Grounds was built in New York, and Chicago's Lakefront Park was renovated to seat 10,000 in 1883. Two years later the Chicago team constructed the West Side Park to accommodate 15,000 fans. Albert Reach, owner of the Philadelphia franchise opened his Baker Bowl in 1887.

As baseball became increasingly commercialized, promoters sought the means to garner even greater profits. The first doubleheaders featured Providence at Worcester on 25 September 1882. On 2 June 1883 the Fort Wayne team played the first game under electric lights in Indiana, and the New York Giants initiated a "ladies day" two weeks later. The media accommodated the widespread interest in baseball by providing greater coverage in newspapers. In 1886 Alfred H. Spink, the builder of Sportsman's Park in St. Louis, founded the Sporting News, which became known as the "Bible of Baseball." In 1888 the Chicago White Stockings embarked on a world tour to promote baseball and produce profits for Albert Spalding, team president and sporting goods manufacturer.

The National League led the pattern of commercialization as owners acted as a cartel, consolidating their holdings, and attempting to maximize profits. They did so by monopolizing the best talent and the sites that promised the greatest client base. As early as 1879 owners agreed on a reserve plan, vowing not to employ another team's players and claiming exclusive rights to their own; thus limiting players' options and salaries. The reserve clause soon became a standard feature of players' contracts. Likewise, smaller cities lost their franchise rights in the major league if they could not generate enough paying customers.

National League owners, mired in self-interest, failed to adhere to their own guidelines. Cincinnati was expelled from the league for playing Sunday games and selling beer. In retaliation it led other disgruntled owners, several of whom were brewery owners, to form their own league, the American Association, which started play in 1882. The success of the new organization resulted in a national agreement between the National League, American Association, and the Northwestern League to honor each other's contracts and led to a post-season series between the parent organization and its offshoot starting in 1884.

Owners battled not only each other, but their players as well. Unhappy with the impositions placed on them by owners, particularly the reserve rule, players banned together in opposition. Led by John Montgomery Ward, a star player who was also a lawyer, they organized the Brotherhood of Professional Baseball Players in 1885. When owners initiated a player classification system to limit players' salaries after the 1888 season, players revolted. Meeting secretly throughout 1889 they decided to found their own league based on cooperative management and profit sharing with their wealthy sponsors. The Players' League included most of the star players and outdrew the established leagues during the 1890 season. The American Association soon collapsed, but the National League withstood its losses. Led by Albert Spalding, it scheduled games concomitantly with those in the Players' League, bribed and coopted players and owners in the rebel league to bring about its demise within a year. By 1892 the National League had absorbed the best franchises and players of its competitors and, once again, enjoyed a monopoly. It operated as a twelve team league for much of the decade, and W.C. Temple of Pittsburgh offered a trophy for a post-season championship series between the first and second place teams.

Despite consolidation and such promotional ventures baseball suffered during the 1890s. Bickering and factionalism among owners, unsportsmanlike play, rowdy behavior by fans and athletes cast a pallor over the game. Ban Johnson, president of the minor Western League, led a movement to form another major league that he promoted as a moral alternative. Starting in 1900, the new organization adopted the title of the American League, and its success led to its recognition by the National League and a post-season "World Series" championship in 1903.

RULE REVISIONS

Henry Chadwick, an English immigrant and sportswriter, earned the appellation of "father of baseball" for his tireless promotion of the game. He explained the new rule changes in an article for Outing, April 1887, pp. 77-78.

THE NEW PLAYING RULES OF BASE-BALL
By Henry Chadwick.

THE NEW PITCHING RULES.

The changes made in the rules governing the delivery of the ball to the bat are decidedly of a radical nature in many respects. In the first place, the pitcher is now allowed to send in but five unfair balls to the bat before he is subjected to the penalty of giving the batsman a base on called balls. Last year he could deliver six such unfair balls. Moreover, the penalty for such unfair balls has been increased by adding the charge of a base hit against the the pitcher for every base given on balls. Secondly, the penalty of giving a batsman a base is inflicted every time the pitcher hits the batsman with a pitched ball, provided that the batsman has made all due effort to avoid being hit by the ball. Thirdly, whenever the pitcher makes a balk-as defined in the new code-the batsman, as well as base runners occupying bases, is also given a base as a penalty for the unfair delivery... This largely increased responsibility attached to the position, however, is offset by an important advantage which the new code grants to the pitcher, and this advantage lies in the throwing out of the code the clause in the rules which required the pitcher to send in balls to the bat "high" or "low," as the batsman might choose to designate, thereby relieving the pitcher from the difficulty of delivering the class of balls known as "waist" balls, viz.: balls just above or below the waist. Not only was it quite a task for the pitcher to measure high or low balls in his delivery, but it was one of the most difficult parts of the umpire's duties to judge such balls accurately, and the apparent mistakes of judgment made in this respect were fruitful of disputes by players as to the soundness of the decisions rendered. Under the new code, therefore, the pitcher is now only required to send in balls between the designated height of the batsman's knee and shoulder, all such balls being regarded as fair balls, provided that, at the same time, they pass over the home base...

The letter of the new rule governing the delivery of the ball to the bat is as follows:

"The pitcher shall take his position facing the batter with both feet squarely upon the ground, the *right foot on the rear line of box,* his left foot in advance of the right, and to the left of an imaginary line from his right foot to the centre of the home-plate. He shall not raise his right foot until in the act of delivering the ball, nor make more than one step in the delivery. He shall hold the ball before delivering it fairly in front of his body and in sight of the umpire. In the case of lef-handed pitchers the above words, 'left' and 'right,' are to be reversed. When the pitcher feigns to throw the ball to a base he must resume the above position and pause momentarily before delivering the ball to the bat."

It will be seen that the new rule not only prohibits the pitcher from placing the ball behind his back preliminary to delivering it, but he cannot throw to a base and then throw to the bat with one simultaneous motion, he now being required to resume his standing position after a feint to throw to a base and make a pause before sending the ball in to the bat.

The result of this radical change in the rule will be to reduce the speed of the pitcher's delivery, and to force him to attain a better command of the ball than before, thus forcing him to depend more upon a skillful strategic delivery of the ball for success, rather than, as before, upon great speed in his pitching.

The new rule governing a "balk" in pitching is a more stringent one than ever before enacted and it does away entirely with the undue latitude given the pitcher, under last year's rule, to catch base-runners napping off bases. Under the new code the pitcher commits a balk if he makes any one of the series of movements he is habitually accustomed to make while in the act of delivering the ball to the bat, and then fails to follow up such movement with the immediate delivery of the ball to the batsman, no matter whether such movement is made by his arms or his legs, or by a special motion of his body. He also commits a balk every time he steps outside the lines of his position, or takes more than one forward step in delivery. He also commits a balk if he makes any unnecessary delay in delivery, except the ball be accidentally dropped. He also commits a balk if he makes a feint to throw to a base occupied by a base-runner, and then fails to take his stand in position the same as he stood before attempting to throw to a base.

The Chicago Tribune, 4 February 1894, p. 7, reported on the rules committee meeting of that year. The suggested changes provide some insight into the nature of unsportsmanlike play. The rules committee defined a sacrifice bunt, foul bunts became strikes, and the infield fly rule was adopted.

RULES ARE CHANGED

NEW YORK, Feb. 20.-[Special.]-Baseball and blizzards as a rule do not mix, but the two came into collision at the Fifth Avenue Hotel today. It was the occasion of the nineteenth spring or schedule meeting of the National League of Baseball clubs...
It was nearly noon when President Young of Washington called the meeting to order. The constitution was merely touched upon to the extent of one change, which provides that hereafter no club, without the consent of the opposing club, shall change the time of beginning a scheduled game more than half an hour from the usual time for starting games in that city. This new rule is intended to prevent a repetition of the New York-Washington controversy of last year, when the New Yorks changed the Washington game to 1 o'clock to let the Yale and Princeton teams play on the polo grounds at 4 o'clock.

Rules 2 to 11 inclusive were stricken out and new ones adopted in their stead. The rules refer to the construction of the diamond, and the changes are purely technical. By the new rules a civil engineer is required to lay out or survey every league diamond, and thereby obtain a perfect accordance among them all. As the old rules stood there was a chance left open for various small inaccuracies in the laying out of the various diamonds.

Sec. 2 of Rule 12 was so changed that in the future a new ball or the ball in reserve will be put into play as soon as the ball in use is batted into foul grounds beyond the sight of the umpire and not beyond the sight of the players.

In Sec. 4 of the same rule the word "yarn" was superseded by the word interior. The old rule provided that a new ball should be substituted whenever the ball in use ripped so as to expose the yarn. The new rule changes this so as to read: "So as to expose the interior."

To Prevent Disputes.

The phraseology of Rule 20 was so changed that a dispute which arose last season between the Bostons and Chicagos cannot again occur. It was an extra inning game. The Chicagos scored in their half of the extra inning and the Bostons in the same inning tied the score, with two out. They then had to leave the field to catch a train. They claimed a tie, but Anson disputed their right to count the run. The game went on record as a tie, and the rule as a amended will decide any such case which may arise in the future in the same way. Rule 36 was amended so as to read as follows:

A fair hit is a ball batted by the batsman standing in his position that first touches any part of the person of a player or any umpire or falls within foul lines that whether it first touches foul or fair ground, bounds or rolls within the foul lines between home and first or home and third base without interference by a player.

Then follows a broad new rule, numbered 38, which puts a handicap on the bunt, as follows:

Rule 38. A sacrifice bunt is a ball batted by the batsman standing in his position that falls within fair grounds before reaching the line between first and second bases and second and third bases, as defined in Rule 36, that is made for the obvious purpose of advancing a runner occupying a base which results in putting out the batsman, or would so result if handled without errors.

According to this rule the bunt is described and made definite and certain, as a lawyer would have it, so that a spectator duller of comprehension than the members of the Rule committee can recognize the thing the moment it is made.

Penalizing the Bunt.

To Rule 41 was added a new section (4), which says:

A strike is a foul hit other than a foul tip made by the batsman while attempting a bunt sacrifice hit, as defined in Rule 38, that falls or rolls upon foul ground between home base and first base, or home base and third base.

This is the penalizing of the bunt which has so often been referred to by way of anticipation during the last winter. Hereafter the man who bunts will not do it for the purpose of fouling off fairly pitched balls till he gets his base. That new rule, at least, meets with general approval.

The next change makes another striking innovation in play. Last year when a player was fooled by a pitched ball so much that he struck at it and was hit by it on any part of the person, except the forearm or hand, he was given a base. This year he will get no base, but the ball will be called dead, and a strike instead will be recorded. The new provision, Sec. 8 of Rule 42, reads: "The batsman is out if while attempting a third strike the ball touches any part of the batsman's person, in which event base-runners occupying bases shall retire, as provided in Sec. 5 (old), Rule 47." In order to make this provision apply to any strike Sec. 4 of old Rule 43 is amended so as to provide that the batsman becomes a base-runner when hit by a pitched ball without his making an attempt to strike. In that case it is called a strike, and he does not go to base as heretofore.

To old Rule 48 was added Sec. 9. which says that the batsman is out if he hits a flyball that can be handled by an infielder while first base is occupied with only one out. This new rule effectually wipes out the play of trapping the ball for a double play, which was so successfully worked by McPhee and Pfeffer in particular. It created a good deal of indignation among the ball-players present. Anson especially denounced the new rule as a step in retrogression.

To old Rule 46 was added Sec. 5, which reads: "The base-runner shall return to his base if while attempting a strike the ball touches any part of the batter's person."...

GROWTH AND DEVELOPMENT

Initially played by clubs composed mostly of middle class clerks and artisans during the antebellum period, baseball spread rapidly thereafter. Hundreds of clubs, including working class players abounded in the East, particularly in and around New York city, although the game appeared in many urban areas. By the 1860s intercity play and the Civil War brought the game, and widespread acceptance of the New York rules to the west and south. Newspapers reported on games, and sportswriters, like Henry Chadwick, extolled its virtues.

Cincinnati fielded the first fully professional team in 1869, and Chicago followed a year later. The National Association of Professional Baseball Players organized in 1871 and the National League instituted play in 1876. Professional teams afforded opportunities for commercial entrepreneurs, civic boosters, and working class players. Players earned salaries far in excess of their blue collar occupations, and ethnic immigrant groups soon adopted the game. Many Irish and German-Americans joined the professional ranks during the 1880-1900 period. Only African-American players were systematically excluded from play. In 1887 several star white players, most notably Adrian "Cap" Anson of the Chicago White Stockings, refused to play against teams fielding any black players. That segregationist pattern was reinforced by the Jim Crow laws that permeated American society in the 1890s. African-Americans formed their own teams, and while they still competed against whites, they were banned from the highest levels of play until 1947 when Jackie Robinson made his debut for the Brooklyn Dodgers.

Baseball achieved great popularity on college campuses after intercollegiate play began between Amherst and Williams in 1859. By the 1870s college teams engaged in competitive tours like the professional clubs. The following excerpt from the Richard Dott Papers, at the University of Michigan, dated 20 May 1882, describes the initial season of the Western College Baseball Association. Michigan's black catcher, Moses Fleetwood Walker, later played professionally for the Toledo and Newark teams until 1887, when Anson refused to let his team take the field if Walker was allowed to participate.

WESTERN COLLEGE BASEBALL ASSOCIATION

Realizing that Michigan was too far removed from the older schools of the East and believing that athletics could prosper only by fostering contests with other colleges, the Athletic Association of the University undertook the organization of a foot ball and base ball league with the western colleges... A meeting was called for December 23, 1881, at Chicago, at which Evanston, Racine and Michigan were represented. Illinois, Beloit and Madison had been invited to participate in the meeting. Madison was unable to come but advised us of their hearty sympathy and cooperation. Illinois and Beloit declined. Michigan urged a foot ball association as well as a base ball league but rugby was unknown to the others so we had to content ourselves with the formation of the western college Base Ball Association. At this meeting F.W. Davenport, Michigan, '82, was elected President, C.C. Tybbe, Racine, Secretary-Treasurer. Rules of government were adopted and a committee selected to prepare a schedule of games were so arranged that the clubs had one game at home with each of the others thus making a series of six games for them.

Unfortunately for us only one game was played at Ann Arbor and that was with Madison. Rainy weather prevented the Racine game and Northwestern failed to appear for want of financial support. Scarcity of traveling expenses was not unknown to us and it was with difficulty Manager Olcott gathered together enough for car fare. As it was each player was called on for a double assessment.

We had so arranged the schedule that our games away from home could be played on one trip and on May 26, 1882, nine men and the manager took the train for Evanston to play the first scheduled game. We arrived in Chicago in a rain storm and remained there all night. The next morning the rain still continued but despite the weather and hoping for a change before afternoon we appeared unannounced at Evanston. The rain persisted however, and after consulting with their management it was deemed best to postpone the game until our return from Madison. Accordingly we took the afternoon train for Racine. At the station we were met by Racine's manager, players and students and conveyed to the college grounds, where excellent and ample provision had been made for our comfort and entertainment. We were given rooms in their dormitory and were fed at the college tables. In the evening, an informal reception was held and teachers and pupils gave us good cheer. The next day being Sunday, was spent according to Racine routine in attending college chapel, writing home, visiting and sleeping. On Monday morning the game postponed from Ann Arbor was played and while the score was largely in our favor - 12 to 2, we realized we had found a foe worthy our best efforts. They played an excellent fielding game and only their inability to hit Antle, our pitcher, caused their defeat. Playing second base for them was "Jack" Crooks, who afterwards acquired fame in the National League and even then he was regarded as an exceptional player. Their pitcher, Cowling, was a fine athlete and though pitching both games he showed up stronger in the second than in the first. I afterwards met him at Harvard where he kicked intricute (sic) puzzles as successfully as he threw them on this day. The afternoon game was entirely too close for our comfort, being barely won by a score of 11 to 10. Things had been running along nicely for us up to the eighth inning, for Packard had allowed only two scores, when a wild throw by him to first and a sharp word from the captain put him out of form so that eight runs were added to Racine's score in the eighth and ninth innings. It was only by a fortunate double play that the game was held as it was. With a man on first and one at third and only one out in the ninth, a hot grounder was hit which struck an obstruction in the diamond and instead of being received in the fielders hands, the ball hit him on the shoulder, went into the air but was recovered in time to touch the runner going to second and by quick work was sent to first in time to get that runner and before the man at third could reach home. Considering Racine was a small school with only a limited number of students to draw from, they certainly gave us a bad scare. They had been enthusiastic in the organization of the Association and did much toward its success and the royal way in which they entertained us caused a very friendly feeling for them and it was with regret we bade them good-bye.

With two victories to our credit we all vowed it should be made unanimous and Packard promised he would not make any more wild throws so when we arrived at Madison for their game on the next day, it was with a determination to show the Badgers how base ball should be played. We did show them so far as runs counted, but it was not an errorless game on our part. With the condition of the grounds which were located in a cow pasture with not even the base lines marked out and a drizzling rain most of the game, it was decidedly difficult to keep in harmony with the ball. There was a well back of second base which made it extremely hazardous for both the in and out fielders. The boys that day did not accuse me of encroaching on their territory especially in that direction.

Here occurred the only unpleasant event of the entire trip. At Racine and also at Evanston we were royally entertained and defeat did not detract from their good cheer. That fraternity of feeling which makes student life so enjoyable and which is an inspiration to all college men was entirely wanting at Madison. After their defeat at Ann Arbor they had returned home determined to have revenge on us when we came to play the return game and when they failed so egregiously, they became sulky and accused us of being players hired for the occasion and of not belonging to students at the University. As the names of all players had to be submitted to the officers of the Association and to be certified to by the school authorities, this accusation reflected upon the veracity of President Angell and naturally was vigorously resented by us all. Their papers were filled with comments on the game and our players and in one of their issues they asserted that our catcher, who was a negro, was the whitest man on our team. He certainly was a star player, a fine fellow and popular with us all but Madison's acrimony was entirely uncalled for, insulting to us and proved them the boor. We felt it the more because of the pains we had taken to make their visit to Ann Arbor pleasant and agreeable. We had gone there, it is true, with a determination to win and we would have been unworthy the faithful and hearty support given us by faculty and students had we not done our best. At this distance of time we can be charitable and excuse them on account of zeal for their school and disappointment of defeat, but we felt it keenly then and were nothing loath to take the first train out of town for Evanston.

We had been told we would have an easy game with the Methodists and so it proved for at the end of the seventh inning they cried enough with the score 20 to 3 against them. They had some good players but were especially weak behind the bat. Their catcher had no less than ten passed balls. Plumer and one or two others were good men and hard hitters, but the team lacked practice. We got fifteen hits off their pitcher with a total of sixteen while they solved Antle's delivery for seven with a total of ten. That, together with the passed balls, explains the final result. It was in this game that the Methodists were treated to a new idea in base ball. They had a man at second who was leading off the base a few feet. As the pitcher delivered the ball, Walker gave me the signal to cover second and sent it down so true and speedily that the runner was out before he realized what had happened.

This game ended our series away from home and as it afterwards proved, was the last of our schedule. Evanston should have played us at home, but failed to put in an appearance and forfeited the game to us. Thus was completed the most successful season the base ball club up to that time ever experienced...

Several male entrepreneurs organized women's teams as commercial enterprises with varying results. The following, gleaned from the Chicago Tribune, 8 July 1884, p. 6, reports on one such effort.

FEMALE BALL-PLAYERS STRANDED.

BALTIMORE, Md., July 7.-[Special.]-The 4th of July a man brought to this city from Philadelphia nine blondes and nine brunets, and put them to playing ball at Oriole Park-the grounds of the American Association team, which is now in the West. The audience was very small, not large enough to pay expenses, and the playing was very bad. Saturday the same females played at Monumental Park before an audience of thirty-two people. The manager left Saturday night, and has not been seen since. The result is the female base-ball players are stranded here without a cent in their pockets, and with no means of returning to their homes in Philadelphia. Today they applied to the Mayor for passes to Philadelphia, but he could not grant them. They are half starved and in a sad plight.

In 1886 Alfred H. Spink catered to the interests of the multitude of baseball fans by founding the Sporting News. He detailed the sporting contacts that would make it a national enterprise in the inaugural issue, 17 March 1886, p. 4.

THE SPORTING NEWS.

It is the custom when a new journal of any class is thrust upon an all confiding and unsuspecting public to launch out into a lengthy editorial as to what the new comer will do and as to its aims and objects. Now for various reasons the SPORTING NEWS intends to ignore this custom and to let its readers guess at what its aims and objects are. One thing we must do, however, and that is thank the hundreds of kind friends who have wished us God speed in this new enterprise. From away off on the California slope comes word from a professional we knew in the olden time wishing us a long and successful journey. From New York, Donohue of the *World,* and all the base-ball writers of the Metropolis send their best wishes. From Philadelphia, Richter, the editor of the liveliest sporting journal in the land, sends friendly greeting and hopes the NEWS may live forever a friendly rival of the *Life.* From Chicago, Palmer, Keough and all the sporting writers of the breezy city send words of welcome, while Spaulding, the leader of the National game in the Lake City says the NEWS shall always be welcomed warmly in his "Wig Wam." From away up North among the ice fields of Lake Superior, Lucas, the father of the new Northwestern League, sends word that the whole northwest welcomes the NEWS and will make a warm corner for it for all time. From Dubuque, Loftus and all the old professionals quartered there during the winter write that from its first appearance they will be staunch friends to the newcomer. From the ball fields of the Sunny South, Levis, Sneed and all the leaders in the game, write words of encouragement and good cheer. From the coast of Florida and from far-off Maine comes the same story. And the same kindly help and assistance has been offered by the leaders in all classes of sports in St. Louis. Mr. Lucas, who is rightly considered the Napoleon of base ball, (illegible) has extended his hand in good fellowship and his able lieutenant, Gus Schmaltz, has helped the new enterprise in more ways than one. Genial Chris Von der Ahe and Secretary Weldon of "Der Boss Club" have also put their shoulders to the wheel and they say that they too will do their utmost to push the new venture to a successful issue. And the amateur ball players of St. Louis have also wished us a good and fair voyage. Jake Albrecht, the Nestor of the amateur game, Mose Jasper, Al. McHose, H.E. Hobbs, and all the local managers have all of them lent us a willing hand. Hundreds of turf men, too, from the blue grass region of Kentucky and from the balmy pastures of California have also sent their best wishes. And here at home the gray-haired secretary of the Driving Club has lent us uncalled for but very welcome aid. And we might tell the same story about the lads who put on the mittens here in St. Louis-Tom Kelly and Tom Allen-and the lesser and bigger pugilistic lights, the oarsmen, the wheelmen, the billiardists, the hunters, the athletes, the fishermen and all other class of sportsmen. And the sporting reporters of the old town too, have also given us a good lift. And now, in view of all these kind wishes, how could we in return promise anything but to publish a paper saying good things of all men and ill of none?

Outing chronicled the spread of baseball in September, 1888, p. 538-539.

BASEBALL IN THE SOUTH.
By Henry Chadwick.

Those who are familiar with the position now occupied by the national game in the South, have no idea of the condition of things in regard to outdoor sports which prevailed in the old plantation days "befo' the wah." I had some experience of this while a resident of Richmond, Va., in the fifties, when I undertook to introduce the English game of cricket among the young F.F.V.'s of the City of the Hills. Driven out of Richmond by the breaking out of the civil war in 1861, I revisited that city on its occupation by the Federal forces in 1865 to find a great change in the young Southerners in regard to sports. In fact, the example which the Union forces throughout the war set their Southern adversaries in the way they enjoyed games of ball during the intervals between active service on the field, proved to be contagious, and from that time forth the national game worked its way to the popularity it has since won in every Southern State. In the year 1871 I had occasion to write a chapter on "Baseball in the South," for DeWitt's Baseball Guide. Events which have occurred since that time in regard to field sports among the Southerners fully prove the correctness of the opinions I then expressed, and as a matter of detail, I reprint the article.

BASEBALL AMONG THE SOUTHERNERS.

... The time has arrived, however, when we are to see the last, we trust, of that listlessness and love of indolent pleasures which have too long been a blot on the escutcheon of Southern youths. The late war proved conclusively their powers of physical endurance, as it did the courage, pluck and nerve which they can bring to bear in their efforts to accomplish any task in which their hearts are engaged; and now that peace once more reigns in the land, and that the factionists of both sections of the country are daily giving ground before the advancing steps of a social as well as political reformation, and manly games and trials of athletic skill have taken the place of the bloody contests on the field of battle, we hope to see the many qualifications we have alluded to developed to an extent hitherto unknown in the annals of the South...

Skating, with its joyous exhilaration, their climate excludes them from enjoying, but croquet and baseball afford them, on the one hand, a recreation in which they can actively participate, and, on the other, a most exciting and attractive sport which they can patronize and enjoy without the slightest fear of encountering an objectionable word or action calculated to offend the most fastidious. Henceforth the fair dames and damsels of the South will smile on the champions of the ball-field, as their ancestry were wont to do upon those who, "on faire steeds and in gallant forme," so proudly charged with lance in rest upon their adversaries of the olden time tournament.

During the war, the many games of baseball played by the Northern soldiers on the camp-fields and on some of the prison grounds, led to the introduction of the game among the Southern soldiers, and "when the cruel war was over," the game was generally adopted throughout the South, the students of the University of Virginia being among the advance guard of the Southern army of the fraternity; and as, whatever Old

Virginia takes the lead in, her sisters of the South generally follow, the game has now assumed a popularity from Richmond to New Orleans, making it all the rage...

What brings the subject to my mind now is the receipt of the first number of the new sporting paper published in New Orleans, called the Sporting *South,* which intended to be largely devoted to fostering the national game in the Southern States. Our country is too extensive for one sporting paper to cover the entire ground, and hence we find such journals as the *Sporting Life* and *Sporting Times* devoted to the national game in the East, the *Sporting News* in the Southwest, the *Sporting South* in the extreme South, and the California *Spirit of the Times* on the Pacific coast, all helping the popular OUTING to advance the interest and welfare of the American national game of ball.

Major league franchise sites fluctuated throughout the early years of professional baseball. The Chicago Tribune reported on the selection process on 10 February 1886, p. 3.

KANSAS CITY SELECTED TO FILL THE VACANCY IN THE BASE-BALL LEAGUE

It is quite safe to say that there were few happier men in Chicago yesterday than were those composing the delegation from Kansas City in attendance upon the league committee meeting held at the Tremont House yesterday, and at which the metropolis of Western Missouri was chosen as the eighth member of the league circuit for 1886. The committee, composed of Messrs. Spalding of the Chicago Club, Lucas of the St. Louis Club, and Marsh of Detroit, met in Parlor A yesterday morning, the session being a private one, with President Spalding in the chair. The Milwaukee delegation, composed of Messrs. Forth, Harry Quinn, and G.M. Kipp, were first admitted and their claims for representation listened to and discussed for an hour or more. The advantageous location of the Cream City, the rivalry that had existed between its club and the Chicagos in days gone by, the alleged willingness of the people to support a National League team there, and their readiness to give to the league such reasonable guarantee as it might ask for the faithful fulfillment of their contract were all gone over, after which the Milwaukeeans were permitted to withdraw. Kansas City was then called, and while the members were awaiting the appearance of those representatives President Spalding read to the committee a letter from the Indianapolis Club voicing its claims to recognition. The committee's attention was then given to the Kansas City delegation.

Not until nearly 7 o'clock was this discussion closed, at which time Kansas City was announced to be the unanimous choice of the committee. Downstairs in the hotel office the Milwaukee delegation were waiting to hear the verdict, while near them were seen many base-ball notables. The announcement of the verdict did not create much disappointment, for it seemed to be the general belief that Missouri would beat Wisconsin in the race.

Fully an hour was spent by the committee members and the Kansas City visitors in a convenient quarter of the hotel in talking over the events of the afternoon and discussing the successful candidate's future prospects. Each member of the committee expressed himself as well pleased with the result of the day's work.

The new league city has a population of about 135,000, and that of the suburbs within a radius of ten miles will swell it to fully 180,000. Within two-hours' ride of the city are the populous cities of Lawrence, Atchison, Topeka, St.Joseph, and Leavenworth, with an aggregate population of 140,000. All of these points, it is promised by the Western delegates, will send down generous delegations to the league games. With the advent of league games at Kansas City it is predicted that the game will receive a boom there which it has not before know (sic) west of Chicago.

Outstanding feats created athletic heroes and helped to popularize the game. Outing provided a history of perfect games in its November 1886 issue, p. 181.

PERFECT GAMES.

An EASTERN EXCHANGE says that "the recent feat of Conley, pitcher of the Haverhills, of allowing but twenty-seven men of the opposing team to go to the bat and of the team making no errors has never been equalled." This is a mistake. It has not only been equalled, but surpassed. On June 12, 1880, Richmond, the left-hand pitcher of the Worchesters, retired the Clevelands in order. They did not see first base on a hit or an error. Ward, then pitcher of the Providences, accomplished this feat as well, June 17, 1880, only five days after the above, when the Buffalos went out in one, two and three order. Calvin accomplished it in 1875, and Edward Kent in 1871. Valentine, the present American Association umpire, accomplished the feat attributed to Conley in 1882, while pitching for the Metropolitans.

Youth emulated such heros and modeled their clubs after the professionals, creating issues of eligibility and fair play. The High School Journal addressed such developments in Chicago in February 1890, p. 87, and March 1891, pp. 105-106.

HIGH SCHOOL BASEBALL

The meeting as announced in the January JOURNAL, for the purpose of forming a base ball league among the various high schools, met at the South Division February 7, with the following schools represented: Evanston, Englewood, Hyde Park, South Division, West Division, Harvard school and Manual Training school. Nealy of H.S. was elected president and Benner of H.P., secretary and treasurer. According to the constitution as proposed no person who has played on a college team will be allowed to play in the league games. W.D., it seems has a catcher who is willing to take up a study in the school and play on the nine. The other schools objected and W.D. withdrew, although it is expected they will join as soon as they get over their disappointment. At the Casino gymnasium February 14 a meeting will be held, when it is expected that the constitution, by-laws, schedule, etc., will be arranged and adopted.

BASEBALL.

"Outsiders" have always been the bugbear and bane of High School leagues. No matter with what care the constitution was drawn, provisions prohibiting their participation in the contests providing forfeiture of all games to the opposing side should any such practice be discovered, and placing each school on its honor for the observance of the rule-yet the trouble always exists. It is right to exclude outsiders. Possibly the player, whether it be base ball, foot ball or athletic contest of whatever sort, may be of suitable age, may be only an ordinary man-neither by practice nor talent out-classing his High School mates-yet the principle is sound and should be rigidly adhered to in all High School contests-only High School pupils allowed. That does not mean college graduates who join the foot ball eleven, by virtue of being "specials," who take music or drawing. In the first High School Foot Ball league, the writer captained the South Division and was president of the league. The South Division team had four such specials. We lost the pennant though. The Manual was the only square team of the lot. But the question is how shall this principle be enforced? We offer the following: Arrangements can be made with THE JOURNAL to give space in the April issue for the publication of the league constitution, and a provision can be inserted therein necessitating the sending of a list by each school of, say fifteen, players from whom a nine shall be chosen, to THE JOURNAL, for publication. These lists must first be submitted to the principal and by him endorsed, certifying that each pupil named thereon is a pupil of his school in good and regular standing. In this way the whole school will know who its representatives are, and there will be sufficient honor to prevent "alias" from participating in the games. Even if such a course does not prevent the attempt, it will make discovery inevitable...

ETHNIC BASEBALL TEAMS

For middle class ethnics who had gained a measure of the American dream baseball symbolized assimilation and a degree of inclusion in the mainstream society. The following accounts are derived from the Chicago Tribune, 7 July 1889, p. 12; Svornost, 2 June 1890; and the Dziennik Chicagoski, 10 August 1896, respectively.

THE LITERARY LEAGUE

Six of the Jewish literary societies of Chicago have organized what is known as the Library Base-Ball League. The rivalry existing between the societies has run into the channel of base-ball and the boys are having it out every Sunday morning on the diamond. The societies and B'nai Abraham, Cremieax Haking, Emerson, Voltaire, Laskav, and Fidelity. The clubs are pretty evenly matched and some good games are witnessed. The standing of the league is as follows:

	Won	Lost	Percent
B'nai Abrahams	2	0	100
Cremieax Hakings	2	0	100
Emersons	1	1	50
Voltaires	1	1	50
Laskava	0	2	50
Fidelitys	0	2	50

The following games will be played today B'nai Abrahams vs. Cremleax Hakings at Athletic Park. Voltaires vs. Emersons at South Side Ball League grounds, and Fidelity vs. Laskavs at South West City League grounds. Games called at 9:00 p.m.

BOHEMIAN BASEBALL GAME

Yesterday morning the "Pilsen Sokols" team played the "Klatovsky Sokols," a game of baseball in the field at 20th and Fisk St. The score ended 28 to 8 in favor of the "Pilsen" team. The "Pilsen" battery was pitcher Kostal, Catcher Turek; for "Klatovsky," pitcher Benes, catcher Kalus.

POLISH SOCIETIES PLAY A BASEBALL GAME

Two Polish Societies from the St. Stanislaus Kostka parish, the St. Casimir's Young Men's Society and the St. Cecilia Society played a baseball game yesterday in Avondale.

The St. Cecilia Society team was captained by its president, Mr. John Czekala, and the St. Casimir Society by its president, Mr. John Nering. On Mr. Czekala's team were the following: M. Schultz, P. Marks, J. Marks, J. Kondziorski, J. Petlak, J. Marks, S.

Politowski, Mroz, and F. Arendt. On Mr. Nering's team were F. Budzban, S. Czajka, P. Myks, J. Budzban, M. Budzban, J. Kanabas, Kimlitz, and J. Bogucki.

The game began at three o'clock in the afternoon on a field near the St. Hyacinth church in Avondale, and was very lively, because both teams were in excellent condition. The heat finally forced the players to quit, after three hours of playing. The St. Cecilia team won by a score of thirteen to seven.

By the turn of the century a second major league, under the leadership of Ban Johnson, president of the Western League, emerged to challenge the National League. The Chicago Tribune, 4 February 1900, p. 17, followed the development of the newly organized American League and the resurgent American Association.

BASEBALL VARIETY SHOW PLANNED

Continuous baseball will be the feature of the coming season. It is probable the National league, to forestall the new American association and the American league, will run continuous games in the big cities, starting early in the morning and playing until dark.

With the National league planning to put two clubs in each of four cities and forming two eight club leagues with the new American association planning to put eight clubs in the field, and the American league planning its strengthened eight club circuit. It is probable the baseball public will be sated with baseball before the year ends. The question is where can enough ball players be found to fill thirty-two first-class ball clubs?

The National league, using about 180 players, could never find more than fifty good players, leaving 130 mediocre men. The sixteen National league clubs, the eight association clubs, and the eight American league clubs would need at least 500 men. It would seem the magnates are going to supply quantity in lieu of quality and even under the conditions last year the quality of baseball was enough to make a prairie leaguer groan in commiseration. How any of these teams furnishing the public with a miserable quality of ball can expect to make money is a problem but how thirty-two can hope for success is harder to imagine.

The strategic move of the National league in planning a secondary circuit with a view of crowding out the new American association as a war measure. The baseball trust does not intend to brook rivalry. The magnates do not expect to make money if a war comes. They have simply placed themselves in a position to crush competition. They realize that if the new American association, organized in Chicago and completed in Philadelphia, gets a footing it will mean another baseball war. They know the new American association is not financially strong and is limited in resources, and they know that the National league has great financial backing. They expect to outlast the new association and crush it, as they did the brotherhood, by force of money.

The new American association might appeal to the courts in States having antitrust laws and charge conspiracy, but the outcome of such a move would be doubtful and the trial costly.

The American league, although not friendly to the National, probably will side with the organization for self-defense and keep out of the fight except in Milwaukee and those cities in which the new association may choose to put rival teams.

The situation is not as uncertain as it was a week ago, but it is more complicated. The new American association promoters have met in Philadelphia and showed their hands. They have mustered a fairly respectable amount of capital and if let alone might make a nice snug organization. The promoters do not understand exactly where they stand and the fact they are not spending money shows their indecision. McGraw, once persuaded to join fortunes with the new organization has become its leading spirit, and without him the project probably would have fallen through at Philadelphia. The first failure of the Philadelphia organizers to secure financial backing was a severe blow to the promoters, but they claim to be undaunted.

Providence, St. Louis, Baltimore, and Chicago made a substantial showing at the meeting and Quin was there from Milwaukee. The condition of the league is misty and if quoted among current stocks its stock would not bring par value.

Anson claims to have a lease on the Thirty-fifth street and Wentworth avenue park which is now a stretch of barren prairie without sheds or fences. If he has secured that location he has forestalled Charlie Comiskey, who was considering the project of locating his American league park in that vicinity. Comiskey was considering the Columbia Giants park and speculating on another park on the Illinois Central over near the lake.

There is one class of Chicagoans who are studying the baseball situation carefully, and that is the managers of prairie league teams. These men have been making nice little bunches of money every season without much trouble, garnering most of the coin at Sunday games. The Auburn Parks, the Unions, the Columbia Giants, the Spaldings, and other teams have always paid their players fair wages and made money. If one or two clubs are located on the South or Southwest Sides of town these amateur and semi-professional clubs will be deprived of much of their revenue. In fact, if a club located on the South Side it would not be felt by the National league club on the West Side for most of the South Side baseball lovers attend games where some local pride is involved and would rather see the Auburn Park team play the Spaldings than to make a long trip over to the West Side to see a National league game.

In 1887 members of Chicago's Farragut Boat Club devised an indoor version of baseball while awaiting the results of a football game. The winter game, made possible by electric lighting, became a favorite among militia trainees in city armories. The Play-ground Association adopted it as ideal for its restricted spaces after the turn of the century, where it evolved into the modern game of softball. The Chicago Tribune pro-vided a brief history and rules on 12 October 1890, p. 39.

INDOOR BASEBALL

Indoor base-ball promises to be quite a fashionable fad in this vicinity the coming winter and great preparations are going forward for an active season.

It is remarkable how this game has developed. From a lark with a boxing-glove and broom at the Farragut club-house it has grown under the guidance of George W. Hancock into a popular and scientific game. Mr. Hancock, who, with Augustus J. White, was the originator and promoter of the pastime, from the start had the greatest confidence in its future. When the idea was conceived he boldly announced that the time was not far distant when it would be considered the standard winter sport. It was invented shortly after the roller-skating craze had made its run and sunk into oblivion, and many were firmly of the idea that indoor base-ball would flourish for a time and then go the way of roller-skating. Mr. Hancock did not share the opinion of his skep-tical friends and set to work to perfect the game. He succeeded admirably and that it has become popular cannot be denied. Its popularity is spreading through the surround-ing country, and the small towns in the vicinity are organizing clubs. Plano, ILL. will turn its rink into a ball park, and two of the local teams will open it in a few weeks. Milwaukee also has caught the fever, and teams from here will go up to play there. For the benefit of those who have never seen a game some of the most important rules and regulations will be given.

The ball used is of large size and made of a yielding substance. The bat is 2 3/4 feet long and 1 1/4 inches in diameter at the large end. The four bases are each 1 1/2 feet square, each filled with sand. They are not secured to the floor, and a man may slide in and carry the base with him. The pitcher's box is six by three feet, and is marked on the floor in chalk. The nearest line is 22 feet from the home plate. The bases are 27 feet from each other, forming a diamond. The distance from home to second base by a straight line is 37 1/2 feet. Eight or nine men may be played on a side and only rubber-soled shoes are used.

Only straight-armed pitching, in which the arm and hand swing parallel with the body, will be allowed, and the ball is not to be curved. A batted ball which strikes inside or on the foul line is fair, the first point of contact with the floor, object, or player deciding, regardless of where it afterwards rolls.

A batted ball first striking outside the foul lines shall be foul. The third strike caught before touching the ground is out. A foul tip or foul fly caught before touching the ground is out. Four unfair pitched balls give the batsman first base.

A pitched ball striking the batter is dead ball, but does not entitle him to a base. If it should be the third strike the batter is out and no base can be run on that ball. A base-runner must not leave his base when the pitcher holds the ball standing in his box. A base-runner must not leave his base on a pitched ball not struck until after it has reached or passed the catcher on penalty of being called back. A batted ball caught after striking any wall or fixture shall be considered first bound and is not out.

The above rules will give the reader a fair idea of the game, and shows the difference between it and the regular game of base-ball. The catcher always plays up close to the bat and uses neither masks nor gloves. The only difference in the rules this season from last is that the raise ball has been ruled out as being a curve.

Two Leagues in the City.

There are two regularly organized indoor baseball clubs in the city present. The most powerful of the two is the Midwinter Base-Ball League, which commences its regular games Nov. 10, per the schedule printed two weeks ago in THE TRIBUNE. The members of this league are the La Salles, Kenwoods, Oaks of Austin, Idlewilds of Evanston, Carletons, Marquettes, Farraguts, and Ashlands.

The LaSalles, Kenwoods, Oaks, Idlewilds, and Carletons, will play in their own club-houses. The other clubs will secure suitable halls for the purpose. An effort is being made to secure the Second Regiment Armory for some of the games.

It is intended to make the games as exclusive as possible. For that purpose 2,500 tickets have been issued. Each member of the clubs represented will be entitled to a ticket, which will admit to all games played. Admission can only be secured through those tickets.

There will be a series of fifty-six championship games, and the winners will receive a handsome pennant emblematic of the championship. The first series of these games only have been arranged. Besides the pennant there will be a number of other prizes donated by jewelers, sporting goods houses, etc. They will be given for batting, base-running, and fielding.

A new column has been added to the score, known as "totals." It will represent the number of bases secured by a batter during the game. Batting percentages will be figured on the number of bases secured to outs scored by the batter. It would be all but impossible to score base hits accurately. The present officers of the league are George W. Hancock, President; Edwin H. Hatch, Secretary and Treasurer...

Chicago Indoor League.

Another indoor league, known as the Chicago Indoor Base-Ball League, was organized a few nights ago at the Grand Pacific Hotel. It is composed of the Harvards, Lincoln Cycling Club, Chicago Cycling Club, and South Side Illinois Club. It will begin its season Oct. 23, and its schedule is now in process of formation. Sam A. Crawford is its President and G.E. Battler its Secretary and Treasurer. The teams have not yet been announced.

N. Fred Pfeffer, the well-known second-baseman of the Chicago White Stockings, has determined to organize a team of ball players to contest with the league clubs on off dates. He is of the opinion that he can get together an invincible team. From present prospects Chicago will not suffer from lack of indoor base-ball this winter...

COMMERCIALIZATION

A brief article in Harper's Weekly, 12 May 1883, p. 200, provided insight into the financing and construction of a new ball park in Chicago. Within two years the team moved to a new West Side location, utilizing the facility for other sports to maximize profits.

THE CHICAGO BASE-BALL GROUNDS

The grounds of the Chicago Ball Club, indisputably the finest in the world in respect of seating accommodations and conveniences, are located on what is known as the Lake Front property, the title to which is in the city of Chicago. The inclosure begins at Randolph Street on the north, and extends along the east line of Michigan Avenue southward to a point about midway between Washington and Madison streets. On the east are the tracks and switch yards of the Illinois Central Railroad Company, which has the several years past made a standing offer of $800,000 (not one-half its value) for the property; but as the city has been enjoined either from selling the tract or from permitting its use for permanent buildings, the ball club has continued to enjoy the rare privilege of grounds situated within a two minutes' walk of State Street, the chief retail thoroughfare of Chicago. Partly on account of the convenient location of the grounds, but more by reason of the exceptional management of the Chicago ball team, and its success in winning the National League championship for three successive seasons, beginning with 1881, the game of base-ball is extremely popular in Chicago, and the average attendance at League championship games is considerably greater there than in any other city in the United States. During the season of 1882 the attendance at the forty-five League games played in Chicago was upward of 130,000, or an average of 3000 persons to a game. With this fine patronage, made up in good part of the better classes of the community, the Chicago Club is amply able to maintain its costly team of players, and to equip its grounds and fixtures in a manner that by appurtenances might be termed palatial. At an outlay of $10,000 since the close of the playing season of 1882 the Chicago Club, under the direction of President Spalding, has completely remodelled its seating arrangements. Every exposed surface is painted, so as to admit of thorough cleansing from dust the item of paint alone amounting to $1800. The grand stand seats 2000 people, and the uncovered seats will accommodate 6000 more, so that with the standing room the total capacity is fully 10,000, and this without invading the playing field. A fence six feet high encircles the field in front of all the seats, which are elevated so as to command the best view of the play. Overlooking the main entrance is a handsomely ornamented pagoda, built for a band stand, and to be occupied by the First Cavalry Band throughout the season. Surmounting the grand stand is a row of eighteen private boxes, cozily draped with curtains to keep out wind and sun, and furnished with comfortable arm-chairs. By the use of the telephone and gong President Spalding can conduct all the preliminary details of the game without leaving his private box. Besides club officers and players, the sevices of forty-one persons are required at each game to attend to the grounds and seating arrangements viz, seven ushers, six policemen, four ticket-sellers, four gate-keepers, three field-men, three cushion-renters, six refreshment boys, and eight musicians. Aside from players' salaries, ground rent, and including advertising, the cost per game on the Chicago grounds is $200; add to this the salaries of players, rent of grounds, travelling and hotel expenses, and $10,000 expended this year on improvements, and the total outlay for the season is $60,000, so that the Chicago Club must average $525 for each of the ninety-six League championship games to be played during 1883. But the patronage attracted by the famous champion team both at home and in other cities may be depended upon to make good this large sum, and possibly leave something besides for stockholders. The fact that so large an outlay can be safely made tells its own story of the popularity of base-ball.

A Chicago Tribune article of 31 May 1885, p. 17, describes the new park and alludes to the importance of both a political and transport network necessary for success.

COMPLETION OF THE CHICAGO CLUB'S NEW GROUNDS.

Quite a number of people visited the new grounds of the Chicago Ball Club at Congress and Loomis streets yesterday, and all were loud in their praises of the beautiful park, which the energy, enterprise, and liberality of the Chicago Club management have provided for lovers of the game in this city. The conception of such an enterprise was a daring one: and when President Spalding suggested his ideas to the stockholders of the club they were almost united in their opposition thereto, and for a time it looked as though the club's President would have to abandon the project or else carry it out upon his own responsibility. The opposition thus encountered, however, served only to nerve the old player and present manager to increased effort, and by concessions, promises, and argument a majority of the stockholders were finally induced to increase their shares of stock, and thus furnish part of the funds necessary for the construction of the new grounds and buildings. A lease of the untenanted block of land bounded by Throop, Loomis, Congress, and Harrison streets was secured, and the work at transforming the desolate field into what is now probably the best equipped athletic grounds in the Union was begun. As it stood formerly, the field was below the level of the street and each shower of rain left it little better than a huge mud-hole. Earth was hauled from a distance, and, after a perfect system of drainage had been laid, this was so distributed as to form a lawn gently sloping from the centre of the field in each direction to the base of the 12-foot brick wall which entirely surrounds the grounds. During the building of the wall some residents in the vicinity endeavored through process of law to stop the work upon the grounds, offering many objections to the use of the lot for base-ball purposes, and for a time a serious delay seemed inevitable. The objections entered, however, were not sustained by the City Fathers, and under the personal supervision of President Spalding the work continued without interruption and with all possible speed... The question of providing the park with a bicycle track for racing purposes was suggested to the management by local wheelmen and so earnestly was the idea supported that three weeks ago the Chicago Bicycle Track Association was formed and the sum of $2,500 raised to meet the expense of laying a track which it was intended shall be equal if not superior to any in the country...

The entire outlay of money in the grounds and improvements will aggregate nearly $30,000, the sum or $10,000 alone having been expended upon the brick wall surrounding the square, which is 600 feet in length and 400 feet wide. The grand stand, which is located at the west end of the grounds, facing east, has a seating capacity of 2,500, while the open seats on either side will accommodate 3,000 more. The ticket-office and main entrance to the grounds is at the corner of Loomis and Congress streets, while the carriage entrances are on both Harrison and Loomis streets near the east wall. The diamond has been carefully sodded at an expense of over $500, and the space beyond thickly sown with grass seed, which the spring showers and sun light will soon cause to come up bright and green. The runs forming the diamond are made of crushed stone and cinders, with a top dressing of dust, making the surface smooth, firm, and white. The bicycle track, eighteen feet wide on the sides, twenty feet at the turns, and a quarter of a mile in length, extends around the outer edge of the grounds, its broad white surface forming a pretty frame for the picture of the ball field which it encircles. From two tall flag-poles in the southeast and northwest corners of the grounds stream the flags of the club, one of which, if Anson and his boys mean what they say, will be displaced by the league championship pennant next fall. Taken in their entirety the new grounds are a credit even to the beautiful residence section in which they are located, and that the public will substantially manifest its appreciation of all that has been done for their enjoyment and accommodation can be pretty safely predicted...

Not only will the grounds be used for exhibitions of the National game, and for bicycling, but they are equally well adapted to cricket, lacrosse, lawn-tennis, running races, and athletic sports of every description. They may be reached by a ride of between fifteen and twenty minutes from the business centre over the Van Buren, the Ogden avenue, and the Madison streetlines, the last two lines affording a pleasant walk of five short blocks on Loomis street from Madison street to the grounds, being perhaps the quickest and pleasantest. As compared with those of other cities, the new grounds are most advantageously located, they being but fifteen minutes' ride from the Board of Trade Building: while the St. Louis league grounds are 28 minutes' ride from the business centre: the St. Louis association grounds 45 minutes; the Louisville grounds 35 minutes; Cincinnati, 30; Pittsburg, 40; New York 45 minutes by the elevated road; Philadelphia, 35; Boston, 30; Providence, 30; Detroit, 25; Buffalo, 30; and Baltimore, 30.

In 1888 Albert G. Spalding embarked on the first of his world tours with his White
Stockings and an all-star team to promote America's national game overseas. Outing
provided the itinerary and participants in October, 1888, pp.76-77.

THE TRIP OF THE CHICAGO BALL-PLAYERS

The Australian tour of the Chicago Baseball Team, which is now in everyone's
mouth, is a novel scheme, the credit of which is due to Mr. Leigh S. Lynch, the well-
known theatrical manager. During his travels in Australia Mr. Lynch perceived how
great was the love of outdoor sports displayed by the Anglo-Saxons of that rising
young continent. He also noted the complete ignorance of baseball which prevailed.
The outcome of his observations was the undertaking of the Australian tour by Mr.
A. G. Spalding. Mr. Lynch was dispatched to make arrangements, and on his return
in the spring the work of organizing two teams was undertaken. Not content with instructing the people of Australia in the art of baseball, Mr. Spalding has determined
to take with him men capable of playing cricket and football also. The work of selection has resulted in the choice of the following teams: A.C. Anson, (captain), E.
Williamson, F. Pfeffer, T. Burns, J. Ryan, F. Flint, M. Sullivan, R. Pettit, M. Baldwin
and T. Daly, and this team is to be known as "The Chicagoes." The second bears the
name of "The Picked Club," and comprises: John M. Ward (Captain), M. Kelly,
Boston; F. Carroll, Pittsburgh; M. Tiernan, New York; Wood, Philadelphia; E. Hanlon,
Detroit; Fogarty, Philadelphia; Comiskey, St. Louis; while it is hoped that the services
of Caruthers, of Brooklyn, and McPhee, of Cincinnati, will also be secured. John A.
Rogers, of the Peninsular Cricket Club of Detroit, has been made captain of the
cricket team. All players are bound by strict contracts as if they were playing in a
league or association club.

After a series of farewell games in America, beginning in October at Chicago and
continuing in Milwaukee, Des Moines, St. Paul, Minneapolis, Omaha, Denver, Salt
Lake City, Stockton, Los Angeles and San Francisco, they will embark on November
17 at the last-named place. *S. S. Alameda* has been chartered, the owners agreeing to
do the trip in twenty-five days. The foreign campaign will begin at Honolulu, where
two games will be played, one with a local club, the other between the two teams. It
is hoped that King Kalakaua will honor the field with his august presence. The first
antipodean city visited is Auckland, then Sidney, and hence the route lies to Melbourne,
Adelaide, Brisbane and other cities. Altogether it appears likely that the tour will prove
a phenomenal success.

The sale of alcohol presented a problem for some administrators. Albert Spalding, who
dominated the National League, decried its desultory influence on players and spectators. American Association owners, some of whom owned breweries, found baseball

a means to promote their main product and increase profits, as reported by the New York Times, 14 March 1893, p.3.

BASEBALL AND BEER.

President Drexler and Director Ruckstuhl of the Louisville Club have hit upon a novel plan to outwit the Prohibitionists. They have ascertained that the eastern boundary of the new park is but 130 feet from the eastern boundary of Parkland. Jefferson County, just without Parkland's limits, is but fifty paces. They propose to build a bridge from the top of the grand stand seats over to Jefferson County, where there will be a bar. Decisions in the United States courts have shown that a delivery of liquor doesn't constitute a sale. A thirsty spectator can give a man a nickel and ask him to step over into Jefferson County and buy him a glass of beer. The man, acting merely as a messenger, can walk over the bridge to Jefferson County, buy the commodity desired, and then give it to the person who sent him. The sale being made in Jefferson County and merely being delivered in the park, no law is violated.

As baseball teams vied for fans' support, the initiation of post-season play exacerbated rivalries and generated rabid interest. The Chicago Tribune provided an account of the celebration in Providence, after its team defeated New York. The story appeared on 19 October 1884, p. 14. With the demise of the American Association, post-season play was resurrected when W.C. Temple provided a playoff trophy for the top two National League teams in 1894.

LEAGUE CHAMPIONSHIP
A ROUSING RECEPTION TENDERED AT PROVIDENCE
TO THE VICTORS IN THE NATIONAL BASEBALL CONTEST.

Providence R.I., Oct. 17- Special:-The Providence Base Ball Club had a popular reception tonight on their return from the West as champions of the league. The depot was packed solidly with people. The streets and sidewalks in front of the depot were crowded. A fair estimate of the crowd would be 6,000 people. As the train ran into the depot a detachment of artillery fired a salute, and the military band played "Hail to the Chief," The crowd was so dense in the depot that for a while the special police had hard work to make an avenue through it. As Bancroft and Radbourn left the cars and began to walk through the long line followed by the remainder of the club, the people set up a great shout. Cheer followed cheer. The women frantically waved their hankerchiefs and the small boys yelled like tigers.

After quite a delay the champions got to their carriages which were decorated with new straw brooms and headed by the band, were escorted over the principal streets to the Narragansett Hotel, followed by the crowd. Red fire was burned every few feet and a profuse display of fireworks greeted the procession. The hotel lobby was crowded by Brown University boys, who repeated college cheers for Bussett, late of the Brown nine, and three times three for Bancroft and Radbourn, and three cheers all around for the individual members of the team. The club management gave the boys a neat little supper in the hotel, and later they were entertained at the Hotel Dorrance by some of the wealthy admirers of the game. Tomorrow and Monday they play the Cincinnatis. Tuesday a reception will be given the team at Vue de Lau, in which Managers Mutrie of New York and Cuyler of Cincinnati will participate, as well as several members of the Order of Elks, Bancroft, Radbourn, and Start are Elks. Thursday, Friday, and Saturday, the Greys play the Metroplitans in New York. The reason why these last games were not arranged for until now is that Mutrie wanted: First, to play under the American rules; second, to pay Providence one half the gate receipts, keeping for himself all the grand-stand returns. Bancroft objected to this, but after negotiating succeeded in securing one-half the gross receipts and in having the games played under the American rules with the exception of the pitching. The losing club is to pay for a silk flag, costing $100, which shall be considered as the champion pennant of America.

LABOR ISSUES

The years between 1880 and 1900 proved tumultuous ones for professional baseball. Like their counterparts in industry team owners attempted to maximize their profits by minimizing labor costs. The owners' reserve rule bound players to a single team, denying them the opportunity to obtain their free market value. Under such conditions players likened themselves to slaves, or common laborers at best. Owners' collusion monopolized talent and required conformity, something unattainable among strong-willed individuals.

The inability of owners to adhere to their own policies and the success of the rebel American Association in signing National League players led to the signing of a "National Agreement," explained by John Montgomery Ward in an article entitled, "Our National Game," for Cosmopolitan, October 1888, pp. 443-455.

OUR NATIONAL GAME

In 1881 a new body of professional clubs, called the "American Association," came into existence. The "League" at first made every effort to crush out this rival, but it proved its right to live by withstanding every attack. A compromise was thereupon effected, and the lion and the lamb lay down together on the "National Agreement."

This document is often heard of, but little understood, by the general public. It is, primarily, an agreement between the National League and the American Association, but by "Articles of Qualified Admission," the minor leagues, on conforming to certain stipulations and paying some two hundred dollars, are admitted to certain rights and accorded some privileges. The money thus paid in by the smaller leagues goes to pay the expenses of the two larger associations, but the lesser leagues find it advisable to pay it in order to be able to retain their players and live.

First. It guarantees to each club a monopoly of territory, by agreeing that neither association shall attempt to place a club in any city in which there is already a club of the other association. And, indirectly, both associations agree to make war upon any club of any foreign association which shall make the same attempt.

Second. It provides that all the clubs of each association shall respect the contracts, reservations, suspensions, black-listments and expulsions of every club of the other association.

Third. It provides for a "Board of Arbitration," composed of representatives of the different association-members, which acts as a supreme tribunal for the settlement, in first and last instance, of "all matters specially referred" to it; of "all disputes and complaints arising under, and all interpretations of the agreement;" and "of all differences and disputes" between associations, or between a club member of one and a club member of another association.

By the first feature, guaranteeing to each club a monopoly of its territory, a base-ball "trust" is created, as compact and effectual as the Standard Oil, the Sugar, or any of the other trusts of which we hear so much.

It is true there is nothing to prevent the organization of a new club in, for instance, New York, by parties who are strangers to the National Agreement, but the projectors would have to look to the amateur ranks for players. No player now belonging to any club, in any association, a party to the national agreement, would dare sign with the new club, because he would be at once blacklisted and disbarred. And after the new club had secured its players it would not be able to arrange any games. No club in any association, a party to the agreement, would play with it, and in order to get on games it would have to organize similar clubs in other cities. Then, of course, the prestige of the older clubs with their well-known players would draw all the patronage, and the new clubs would soon starve to death.

The second feature, by which each club agrees to respect the contracts, reservations, black-listments, suspensions and expulsions of every other, may also require some explanation.

By reservation is meant the privilege each club has of claiming for each succeeding year the services of its players, and this "right" is founded, primarily, on an agreement between the clubs themselves of each association. Its effect is that a contract for one season is made perpetual, at the option of the club, and a player, once signed by a club, belongs to that club forever. There is no escape for him, except by the consent of the club which owns him; and if, for any reason, he does not want to engage with the same club, for another year, he is forced out of base-ball entirely. Though guilty of no crime, he becomes a professional outlaw, and no matter how valuable a player, no other club dares open to him its doors. Sometimes the owner is willing to sell, and then we read of this or that "beauty" being transferred at a figure which some years ago would have purchased a half-dozen able-bodied slaves. As I write, the morning's paper announces to the public that the president of a certain Western club is willing to sell his players for twenty thousand dollars, the "goods" to be delivered in October.

These sales of players are sometimes coupled with a condition, and then disputes arise as to who is the real owner. William Sunday was sold last winter by the Chicago Club to Pittsburgh, but there was attached to the sale some condition subsequent. The result is that William is now placed in an awkward predicament, as appears from an article in a local paper under the caption, "Who Owns Billy?" It is bad enough to have a master under any circumstances, but picture the plight of poor "Billy" who knows that he has one, yet knows not which it is.

In justice to the principle of reservation, it should be added that, originally, it contemplated no such mercenary application, but that this feature has been tacked on or rather developed by the cupidity of the club managers. The justification offered, that the sale can not be effectuated without the consent of the player himself, is no justification at all. A man who is dissatisfied with a club, or who, for any reason, wishes to make a change, may be willing to consent to almost anything if that consent is the only way in which he can accomplish the change. So also, the assertion that the player is always benefited by an increase of salary, though not necessarily true, would only prove the injuswtice of his former reservation, by showing that the selling club had paid him a less salary than he was really worth. The reserve rule was made that a club might *retain* its players, not that it might *sell* them. It never comtemplated the creation of such a right, and its prostitution to such a vile purpose, more than anything else, has served to bring the rule itself into disrepute. It is wrong in principle, a reflection on the framers of the rule, an insult to decent players and a dishonor to our national sport.

A black-listment is the disqualification of a player by his own club, which immediately communicates the fact to all other clubs and associations, and the result is that he is completely disbarred; no club under the National Agreement will employ him nor will any such club play against a club by which he is employed. The "black-list" was first made to reach those players who, by dissipation or other disreputable conduct, were injuring base-ball as a business. Had it been confined to this limit, and its exercise properly regulated, it might have always proved an excellent institution. But the offenses for which the penalty may be incurred have been allowed to include too many minor affairs, and insufficient safeguards have been thrown around its application. By allowing any one club to black-list any of its players, more than one of the latter were sacrificed to the spite of some manager or other club official. And, though the player generally had a right of appeal to the representative committee of the association of which his club was a member, his defense was not heard until the following winter, and pending the appeal he was thrown out of employment and, in most cases, through lack of funds or proper instruction, his appeal went by default. And even if he pressed it properly and won, he was only "reinstated," and still lost his salary for the time he had been disqualified.

The public discussion of the abuses of the rule has forced some action, recently, looking to their remedy, but there still remains room for improvement. In every case of black-listment the player should be allowed an appeal to some impartial tribunal, outside of the association of which the black-listing club is a member, and thus entirely free of the latter's influence. His appeal should be heard immediately, and in case it is decided that the club has made a wrongful use of its power, he should be awarded his salary for the time lost. It is true he could recover this at law, but the average player has such a superstitious fear of club influence that he seldom dares to go to that length.

When the Union Association above referred to had succeeded in signing some of the players, whom the League claimed by right of reservation, the latter body passed what was known as "the Day resolution." This declared that if these players did not, within a specified time, sign contracts with the clubs by which they were "reserved," they should be placed on the black-list and forever after made ineligible to play in, or against, any league club.

And it actually did black-list these players, and only reinstated them after the death of the Union Association and upon payment of a fine of five hundred dollars in each case!

In its famous, or, more appropriately, infamous "Cleveland resolution," the American Association went still a step further. They enacted that any reserved player who failed to sign with the reserving club before a given date, should be placed on the black-list. That is, the player was no longer to be given the option of refusing the club's terms, neither could he retire from professional play to go into any other business, but he must play ball and at the club's terms (over a fixed minimum limit), or see himself entirely diqualified and his name placed side by side with those made ineligible on account of vicious habits or downright dishonesty! And these men were deterred from an enforcement of this resolution only by the criticism of the press and the force of public opinion consequently aroused.

It seems, however, that the extreme had not yet been reached. It remained for an organization calling itself "The Tri-State League" to show to what lengths a combination of ignorance and power may lead. At a recent special meeting, this body resolved "that no ball-player hereafter discharged or released from any ball-club in the Tri-State League, can be signed or hired by any other club in said Tri-State League." Here the player is to be virtually black-listed by that league because some club has seen fit, even though through no fault of the player, to discharge or *release* him. And to think that the destinies of our glorious game are in the hands of such numskulls!

The third feature of the National Agreement which provides for a Board of Arbitration, makes possible the enforcement of these absurd pieces of base-ball legislation. If base-ball clubs were forced to settle their disputes in the courts of law, many of the practices now in vogue would be impossible. The general public may not know that there is a law in this land higher than the common law. "Base-ball law" is a law unto itself, and so reckless have these legislators become, in the undisputed exercise of their powers, that they make but little pretense to conformation with the rules laid down by courts of law and equity. I do not wish to be understood as denouncing the National Agreement, or even its most radical feature, the reservation of players. Base-ball owes much to its restraining influence upon the piratical tendencies of club managers. I speak only of its abuses and the methods by which it is sought to visit the sins of these managers upon the heads of the players.

In addition to internal disputes baseball owners ran afoul of some local magistrates, who steadfastly applied sabbatarian laws that prohibited Sunday games. In many locales such legislation persisted well into the twentieth century. The Chicago Tribune, 29 June 1884, p. 13, reported on the dilemma of the Columbus, Ohio team.

NO SUNDAY BALL-PLAYING IN OHIO.

COLUMBUS, O., June 28.-Judge Wylie, of the Common Pleas Court, this morning rendered a decision in the case of the State against Fred H. Carroll, catcher of the Columbus Base-Ball Club, on an application for a writ of habeas corpus. A number of the players of the Columbus and Brooklyn clubs were arrested last Sunday for violating the State law by playing Sunday. The Judge held that the phrase, "breach of the peace," in the statutes, includes all indictable offenses, and that arrests Sunday are legal. He therefore refused the writ, and remanded the prisoner to the custody of the Constable. The President of the base-ball club says this is the death blow to the game in Columbus, as it cannot be supported without Sunday games.

The Directors of the Columbus Base-Ball Club and the Citizens League came to an agreement this evening by which the game with the Metropolitans tomorrow shall not be molested if order is preserved, and the club agrees this shall be the last Sunday game on the local grounds. This compromise is the result of the decision of the court this morning.

Players bristled under the reserve rule and owners' impositions on their lifestyle. Owners felt that excessive drinking affected players' production; while athletes resented incursions into their leisure time. The Chicago team stunned the sports world when it sold one of the game's biggest stars, the flamboyant, but incorrigible Mike "King" Kelly to Boston for an astronomical sum. The Chicago Tribune detailed the particulars on 10 February 1887, p. 3.

KELLY WILL NOT PLAY WITH THE CHICAGO NINE.

Mike Kelly says he will not play base ball with the Chicago Club during the year 1887. W.A. McConnell, the theatrical manager, saw Kelly and McCormick in New York the latter part of last week, and took occasion to sound them on this, to ball players, all important question... all during last season Clarkson and McCormick were put in against the weakest clubs in the league as Washington, Kansas City, and St. Louis, while Flynn and Ryan were selected to face such clubs as the Detroit, New York, and Philadelphia. This naturally angered McCormick and was not at all pleasing to his friends. Then the boys were to receive a certain sum of money in addition to their salaries if they won the championship and abstained from drink. Well, they won the championship, but they never got the money that was promised for abstaining from liquor and this is the particular reason why neither of them will play here this year... I can tell you that the Metropolitan Athletic Club has offered him (Kelly) more money to stay in New York and coach its members than he can possibly earn in the league area, and you can depend upon it that if he plays ball at all this year it won't be in Chicago. And they talk about McCormick drinking: Suppose he does drink? Didn't he win the first eighteen games he pitched in the last season, and in the season of 1885 didn't he win twenty one out of twenty four games? I tell you Kelly hasn't any love for Anson, either. He said to me last week, to say, 'You know Anson can't play any ball, and he couldn't hold a balloon after he got both hands on it.' He says: 'I'll tell you what it is. If somebody were to knock a string of sausages towards Anson he couldn't hold one of them unless he was hungry, and then he'd have to pick it up from the ground.' He says: 'Anson ain't no good except at the bat, and he put in the weak men so's to work 'em up and reduce salaries of good men, cause he's one of the stockholders in the club, and cause every dollar saved that way goes into his own pocket.' That's what he says, and he says lots of things about Anson and they ain't nice things, either. Kel don't like Anson, and you can bet he won't play here this year."

On March 6, 1887, p. 16, the Chicago Tribune reported the sale of Kelly to Boston.

THE SALE OF KELLY

Kelly's release, $10,000; salary for season, $15,000: Boston's investment, $15,000.

The players forced the issues of ownership and control by starting their own league. The short-lived organization was chronicled in an article by the Chicago Tribune, 16 November 1889, p. 3.

MAGNATES DECLARE WAR.
THEY WILL FIGHT THE BROTHERHOOD TO THE BITTER END.
LEAGUE DIRECTORS AUTHORIZE THE EXPENDITURE OF UNLIMITED BLOOD AND TREASURE IN DEFEATING THE "CONSPIRATORS"

NEW YORK, NOV. 15.-[Special.]-The National League finished up its business today and adjourned...

The league men met about 11 o'clock and devoted three hours to the consideration of the desertion of their players and the Players' League. Director John I. Rogers stated that it was a notorious fact that a number of players reserved by league clubs have declared their intention to violate said reserve, notwithstanding notices of their respective clubs of said reserve and of the latter's option to renew the usual form of contract with such players for the season of 1890. Also that the opinions of eminent counsel had been received affirming the legal and equitable rights of said clubs under said contracts to the services of their reserved players for the season of 1890, and that therefore he moved the following resolution:

"Re*solved*, That this league hereby declares that it will aid each of the club members in the enforcement of the contract rights of said clubs to the services of its reserved players for the season of 1890 and that a committee of three be appointed by the league with full power to act and so formulate and carry out the best methods of enforcements of said contract rights of said clubs, and that said committee be authorized to draw from the guarantee fund of the league such amount as may be necessary to carry out the intent and purpose of this resolution."

The resolution was adopted and Messrs. John I. Rogers, Charles H. Byrne and John B. Day were appointed as the law committee.

SPALDING DECLARES WAR.

Mr. Spalding then introduced the following resolutions:

"*Resolved*, That no league club shall from this day enter into negotiations or contract with players not under league reservation or enter into negotiations with any club for the transfer of any of its players until Feb. 1, 1890.

"*Resolved*, That a committee of three be appointed, to be designated as the Negotiations Committee, of which the President of the league shall be Chairman, to which shall be referred all applications from players desiring positions on league teams as well as applications from club members of the national agreement wishing releases of their players.

"*Resolved*, The Chairman of the committee shall be the exclusive channel through which applications and negotiations can be conducted by the National League or any of its clubs, and said committee shall ascertain the terms upon which any such releases can be procured or any contracts executed.

"*Resolved*, That all league clubs, in order to secure the services of such players, will indicate to the Chairman the position to be filled and the names of the players wanted, and upon the unanimous vote of said committee a contract may be executed between a club and any player so approved and promulgated in the usual manner.

"*Resolved*, That the committee by its unanimous vote be authorized to draw from the guarantee fund of the league such funds as may be necessary to carry out the purposes of this resolution, to be repaid to said fund by the clubs benefited thereby."

These resolutions were adopted and Messrs. Young, Byrne, and Reach were appointed as members of the Negotiations Committee. The league then adjourned to meet at the Fifth Avenue Hotel Jan. 28, 1890...

CALLS IT A CONSPIRACY.

In answer to a question as to what the policy of the league would be towards their revolting players, Mr. Spalding said that "no one could speak definitely for the league, but his personal idea was that if the players persist in their "conspiracy" and show in some more substantial way than empty threats that they really intend to carry their scheme into operation he had no doubt that the league clubs would make every possible effort to enjoin the players from playing in any other organization. Mr. Spalding said that it was the opinion of some of the most prominent lawyers in the country that such an injunction will hold. He has as yet seen no opinion from any lawyer on the other side indicating the reverse.

"In case the injunctions are not obtainable, what will the policy of the league be then?" Mr. Spalding was asked.

"In that event there will be nothing left for the league to do but to expel all the players who enter into the conspiracy, which will practically mean their retirement from professional baseball should their rebellious scheme prove a failure. I have too high a regard for the general intelligence of the rank and file of the league players to believe that they will be led into such a dangerous experiment by a few hot-headed Anarchists urged on and abetted by a few enthusiastic long chance capitalists whose only possible interest in the matter, according to their own statements, is the amount of money they hope to realize out of it."...

On 22 November 1890 the Chicago Tribune listed the economic casualties of the baseball wars.

HERE ARE THE FIGURES
THE LOSSES OF THE BASE-BALL YEAR
MADE PUBLIC AT LAST.
Chicago Lost $76,000 With Its Two Clubs -Other Cities Even Larger Losers-

CLEVELAND,O., Nov. 21.-[Special.]-Players' National League figures are full of deep interest to the poublic at this time. The losses of the league during the season through the playing side of the game footed about $125,000, divided as follows: Boston, none; New York, $15,000; Philadelphia, $20,000; Cleveland, $15,000; Pittsburg, $20,000; Buffalo, $20,000; Brooklyn, $19,000; Chicago, $16,000. Total, $125,000

In the conferences the following admissions as to losses have been made by National League men about National League clubs: Boston, $60,000; New York, $45,000; Chicago, $35,000; Brooklyn, $25,000; Cleveland, $23,000; Philadelphia, $16,000; Cincinnati, $15,000; Pittsburg, $12,000. Total, $231,000. Against the latter item stands a claim by J. Palmer O'Neil that the Pittsburgs lost but $3,700 last season. He also has a claim for $2,000 for extra mileage traveled, but doesn't hope to get it all.

Added to the losses in case the Players' League does not go on, may be added the following sums spent in building and equipping grounds: Boston, $40,000; New York, $60,000; Philadelphia, $38,000; Brooklyn, $41,000; Chicago $25,000; Cleveland, $20,000; Pittsburg, $18,000; Buffalo, $13,000, Total, $215,000. Grand total invested: $340,000. The Brooklyn club did not pay for its ground or stands. They were furnished virtually rent free by the railroad and land companies. Of Buffalo's $13,000 $10,200 was paid Rowe and White in stock, cash, and debts assumed. They were paid for the old International franchise. A good deal of money was wasted in New York and Philadelphia through bad management, and a good deal in every city through hurry incident to a late start and an early opening. It cost $45,000 to run the Players' League, of which nearly $18,000 went for umpires and $10,000 to lawyers. For 1891 a reduction averaging $9,000 per club can be made, and with a non-conflicting schedule, a matter entirely within the control of any single organization, a serious loss is almost impossible.

At this time there may as well be told an important piece of secret history which throws light upon the refusal of the National League to meet the second conference committee of the Players' League with three ball players among its members. The first committee had bungled and the non-consolidation men, in the majority, put the players on the committee to make it equal in

voting strength and experience with that representing the National League and American Association. It presented itself and was not received, but the question of receiving it was discussed by the old committees. Just before a vote on the question was taken A.G. Spalding drew E. B. Talcott, one of the Players' League men, aside and asked:

"How shall I vote on the question?"

"Vote against it," was Talcott's prompt answer.

Spalding did so and the players were not received. Spalding's query shows that the National League wanted a fix, and if Talcott's "tip" to him was not an act of treachery Players' League people cannot believe it. Had not a sudden change come up during the last minutes of the Pittsburg meeting a resolution expelling the New York club for violating its agreement with the other clubs would have been offered.

All now hangs on Chicago. An agreement between Spalding and Addison has been reached, but the sale may be prevented. It it is, there will be a six or eight club Players' League next season. If a six club league, Boston, Brooklyn, and Philadelphia will be the Eastern cities, and Chicago, Cleveland, and Cincinnati the Western. Should it be an eight club league, Washington stands ready to take New York's place, and another Western town can be secured. The present Brooklyn team would play on new grounds, it being well to keep one club in the Metropolitan district.

The Chicago Tribune divulged the plans for resolution on 17 January 1891, p. 6.

BIG DEALS IN BASE-BALL.
END OF THE LONG WAR BETWEEN RIVAL ORGANIZATIONS.

NEW YORK, Jan. 16.-[Special.]-The clouds have rolled away at last and the base-ball sky is almost clear. It is true a few masses of apparently gloomy significance hang over Cleveland, Brooklyn, and Cincinnati, but they will not prove so formidable as they look, and will soon melt away under the logic of events and necessity. The National League magnates have finally persuaded the Boston triummvirs to consent to an association club in Boston and the late Players' League organization of the city has been granted a franchise by the American Association. The conditions of the deal were pretty tough, but the association and Mr. Prince were obliged to assent to them because they were the best attainable. They signed a contract which provides that the Boston association club shall not have the word "Boston" in any way connected with the name of the club; that the club shall charge 50 cents for admission to its games, and should it find that a 50-cent tariff cannot be maintained then the club agrees to give up its franchise in Boston; it agrees to return to their respective clubs all the league players now under contract to or held by them; it agrees not to play games in Boston Decoration-Day in any year; the leaguers get June 17 and the association Labor-Day.

In return for these concessions Messrs. Prince and company get a franchise and the privilege of non-conflict July 4 and Sept. 2. This deal leaves the new association club Morgan, Murphy, Swett, Irwin, and Tom Brown as a nucleus for a new team. Stovey and Kilroy of course revert to the association, and the chances are that it will allow the Boston Club to retain them.

Money for the Retiring Clubs.

The association met and received and accepted the resignations of Toledo, Rochester, and Syracuse. The exact amounts received by them for vanishing from the baseball map are Syracuse $7,000, half cash, half notes; Rochester, $8,500, in notes; and Toledo, $,500, in cash. The Athletic franchise was formally given to the Wagner brothers of Philadelphia. Washington was admitted to membership and Boston was admitted also. All the clubs are assessed $3,000, each to pay bonuses given the retiring clubs.

The league finished its consideration of the new National agreement early in the afternoon. It took a recess at 7 o'clock and the association immediately convened, Col. John J. Rogers, as a committee of one, went before the association and explained the league's ultimatum in regard to Boston. The contract was accepted and signed.

It is understood that the association can have a Chicago franchise whenever it desires, and Chris Von der Ahe and Henry Vonderhorst are to be granted a franchise and run the club under conditions somewhat similar to those imposed upon the Boston people. Neither of the Spaldings would say a word about the matter this evening.

The Philadelphia (P.L.) Club gives up all its League and Western Association players and has been told the Athletic players may not be able to get them. The Milwaukee people, after having been held here by diplomatic assurances, got the "dinky dink" and return home much disgruntled. They made heroic efforts but could not convince the association that Milwaukee was a better ball town for it than Chicago.

Last of the Players' League.

The Players' League held several meetings today. At the first one the clubs were represented as follows: Boston, C. F. Prince and A.A. Irwin; Chicago, James A. Hart; Brooklyn, Messrs. Linton, Ward, and Wirth; Cleveland and Cincinnati, Al Johnson; New York, Frank Robinson; Philadelphia, J. Earle Wagner. F. H. Brunell was Secretary. The appearance of Messrs. Wirth, Hart, and Robinson, all National Leaguers, caused a sensation and the remnant froze them out of the meeting by appointing

Messrs. Prince, Wagner, Johnson, and Linton a committee to consider the prospects of the organization and report later. This done, an adjournment was taken.

Later on, after the settlement of the deals, the Players' League met at 8 o'clock. A motion to adjourn sine die was made and carried. Frank Robinson "touched the button," and amid the sparkling of the juice of the grape and the tinkling of glasses the "wine went round" for the last time and the light of the Players' League went out forever.

At 9 o'clock the three associations convened in joint session and formally signed the new Natinoal agreement. The meeting was public and the seventy-five persons present formed the greatest assemblage of base-ball men ever gathered together in this country. Johnson, Brunell, and Ward were about the only prominent absentees. It was a regular love-feast. The lions and lambs sat down together, and eloquent speeches were made by Messrs. Thurman, Prince, Krantaff, Byrne, Rogers, and Spalding.

The league and association will meet again tomorrow and take up the question of the disposal of the players of their respective organizations and other details.

The New National Agreement.

The following is a digest of the National agreement that was signed by N.E. Young, President of the National League; A.W. Thurman, President of the American Association; and L.C. Krauthoff, President of the Western Associaton:

The purposes of the agreement are well expressed in the preamble, and to accomplish these has been steadily kept in view in preparing the instrument. The experience of the past has all been brought to bear with a view of avoiding as far as possible all cause for irritation and complaint, and for alleviating and adjusting such instances as are inevitably incident to any large business concerns in which so many interests are involved.

The Western Association has shown itself to be stable and qualified to full recognition, and has been admitted as a major league. All rights under existing legislation are preserved. A board of three is established with authority to elect a Chairman and such other officers as may be necessary. This board will establish an office open all the year round. Incidental questions are decided by the Chairman on the spot. Important matters receive the consideration of the full board.

Hereafter all contracts with managers and players will be approved and promulgated by the board. All umpires and scorers for any association requesting it will be appointed and assigned by it. All playing records will be compiled by it. The board will also act as a joint playing rules committee and secretary.

This will effect a great saving of time and expense and also produce uniformity. The secretaries of individual associations will be relieved of most of their duties. The board has jurisdiction over all controversies and grievances which can grow up and is given large powers to be exercised in its discretion to preserve discipline and harmony and to protect against injustice or oppression. Very wisely these powers stand unhampered, but are left to be exercised by what may be deemed the general welfare of the game and the spirit of this legislation. All parties in interest may be heard as a matter of right. A classification is provided by which other bodies may be entitled to the benefits of the agreement. This takes the place of the qualified articles under which minor leagues have heretofore acted, and particularly gives the classified bodies the same privileges and benefits under one and the same instruments; thereby the minor leagues are elevated, and not assigned under a separate qualified recognition as heretofore.

For the Advancement of Players.

A new feature is also presented for the advancement of players, by which a club, instead of incurring the expense of carrying substitutes to be available in case of accident to a regular player, may supply the vacancy by selecting a player from one of the other bodies of a lower classification which has consented to such selection being made.

During the playing season this can only be done when it will not operate to the detriment of the club called on. The players must receive an increased salary and must consent to the change. Indeed, it is provided in the broadest terms that no player can even be transferred or undertaken to be, directly or indirectly, without his fullest consent. This destroys all criticism upon the "reserve rule," and forever ends the existence of what has been called the "sales system." The corner-stone grievance claimed by the brotherhood is thus carefully and judiciously met.

It is conceded by all that the "reserve rule" is absolutely essential to preserve the game and that it contains of itself no element of injustice to the player. The brotherhood contract with the league recognizes this fully. That rule has been preserved intact in connection with the provisions to prevent and remedy any attempted abuses under its cover. Players can be contracted with for a series of years instead of only from season to season as heretofore.

The Black List Abolished.

There will no longer be such a thing as a black list. It has been abolished-in fact, many years ago; but the very name is now removed. When a player is released he is open to negotiations from any club of the same association which may desire to enter into them for a period of ten days. When the release results from the disbanding of a club the association thus losing a member has ten days in which to supply the vacancy and to negotiate with the player to join the new club.

The territory rights of clubs are preserved for the same city or county and within five miles thereof. The board is given power to enforce all agreements fairly made, and to release any player whose salary is in arrears, or to whom a contract is not tendered before March 15, or who will be prejudiced by a transfer of the membership of the club with which he is under contract to some other association.

The plan adopted by this agreement contains no chance which can work a hardship to any one; a central body is provided as the arbiter and protector of every grievance and all rights, and this power is to be exercised equitably and with due regard to the inherent justice in the premises.

Great care will be used in selecting the membership of this body so that all will have confidence in the fairness and ability of the organization. Its membership will be elected for five years, so as to insure permanency and to avoid the shifting of views. This board will also be placed on so high a plane of independence that complaints and criticisms which have at times been made upon particular rulings and decisions will be unavailing.

CANADA

Historians have reported a baseball game in Canada as early as 1838. The game reached particular popularity in Ontario in the latter nineteenth century. Toronto joined the International League in 1886, and won the league title the following year. The Canadian Amateur Baseball Association was organized in 1893.

The Montreal Base-ball Club, an affiliate of the Montreal Athletic Association, organized in 1886, and issued its first annual report a year later, which was supplied by the National Archives of Canada.

FIRST ANNUAL REPORT
OF THE
MONTREAL BASE-BALL CLUB,
SEASON 1886

GENTLEMEN:-

I have the honor of presenting you with the first annual report of the above club.

We were formerly organized and officers elected July 29, 1886.

Our season began so late and the difficulty of obtaining special days for practice has been so great that the first year of the club has not been marked by any special feature.

We made our debut Saturday, August 21st, when we met the Gordon B.B. Club, of Point St. Charles, in a practice match of 7 innings and were defeated by a score of 24 to 17.

Nothing daunted we accepted a challenge from the Clippers, and met them on the grounds of the M.L.C. September 4th, winning the match and our first ball by a score of 15 to 14, with an innings to spare. Time of game 1 h, 50 min.

The following players donned their new uniforms to meet the Clippers:-

Jos. Bruce, Jno. Heenan, T.S. Brophy, A.G.Walker, E.A. Cowley, W.G. Slack, J.A. Walker, E.S. Putman, J.G.Cornell, Captain.

September 11th, we met the Gordons and through want of practice sustained a defeat, the score standing 24 to 17 at the end of the 7th innings when game was called to allow the M.J.L.C. the use of the grounds. This match was advertised and netted us a small balance.

When it is taken into consideration that practice was limited to August and the first half of September, our practices were fairly well attended.

Our membership now numbers over 70 and should be tripled by the middle of the coming season.

For the coming season we will have the pick of a very large number of men and should become the possessors of the championship pennant of the City League just formed.

We have purchased 9 uniforms, 9 caps, a mask, catcher's gloves, &c..and with the exception of, perhaps, a new mask, and bats and bases, we should begin the season of 1887 fully equipped...

FINANCIAL STATEMENT MONTREAL BASEBALL CLUB.

Receipts.

Subscriptions	$ 58 00	
Proceeds of match	15 10	
		$ 73 10

Expenditures.

By Sundries	61 10	
Cash on hand	$ 12 00	

CAPITAL ACCOUNT.

9 Uniforms	$ 26 10	
8 Bats	2 00	
1 Mask	1 50	
1 Pair Catcher's Gloves	5 75	
1 Home PLate	1 00	
1 Set Bases	2 40	
Total	$ 38 75	
Add cash on hand	12 00	
Net worth of club		$ 50 75

E.A. Cowley,
Treasurer Pro tem.

Chapter 5

BASKETBALL

In the winter of 1891 Luther Gulick, gymnasium director at the YMCA training school in Springfield, Massachusetts, found himself with a group of restless athletes. Bored with formal gymnastics, the young men had little to hold their attention between football and baseball seasons. Gulick assigned the problem to James Naismith, a student and part-time instructor from Canada, for solution. Naismith experimented with several existing games before deriving at basketball by utilizing a soccer ball and peach baskets as goals. The first game was played at the YMCA on 21 December 1891 with two nine-man teams. The rules were published in the YMCA Physical Education magazine, 15 January 1892. The game spread rapidly thereafter. It became particularly popular in the YMCAs, women's colleges, and high schools.

The game underwent several rule changes before a number of sports governing bodies agreed to some standardization in 1915. An iron rim and cord net came into use as early as 1893. In March of 1897, Yale defeated Penn utilizing five players per side; harbinger of the modern game. In a conference held in June 1899, rulesmakers for the women's game agreed on a three court system of play, using two or three players in each zone. Such rules were designed to limit physical exertion for women and to disallow any one player from becoming a star by monopolizing the ball. Senda Berenson, who had introduced the game to women at Smith College shortly after its inception, published the women's rules in the 1899 Spalding Guide.

YMCA instructors, publications, and traveling teams promoted basketball throughout North America. On 25 January 1893, the Toronto YMCA engaged Toronto University in a game, and the University of Chicago played a full schedule of seven games in the winter of 1894. In 1895 the YMCA founded the Athletic League of North America to promote state and regional competition, while attempting to suppress games with contingents that violated amateur standards. Professional teams appeared in Trenton and Buffalo by the mid-1890s. Intercollegiate play for men started on 9 February 1895 when Hamline vied with the Minnesota State School of Agriculture. Stanford's women opposed a female squad from the University of California on 4 April 1895. The Berkeley women had lost an earlier game to a girl's prep school on 18 November 1892. On 24 April 1896, an American championship was conducted in Brooklyn. Largely an eastern affair, the East Division YMCA defeated Brooklyn Central, 4-0. An eastern circuit, known as the National Basketball League organized in 1898; and Columbia, Cornell, Harvard, Princeton, and Yale formed a collegiate league in 1900.

Amos Alonzo Stagg, an All-American athlete at Yale in the late 1880s, served as captain of one of the teams in the first game, while enrolled at the Springfield school. He described the game and its enthusiastic reception in a letter to his sister, Pauline Stagg, on 10 March 1892. The letter excerpt is part of the Stagg Papers in the Special Collections at the University of Chicago Library.

A.A. STAGG TO SISTER, PAULINE STAGG, MARCH 10, 1892

"There is a great furor among the boys in the school over a new game which Naismith our center rusher invented, called basket foot ball. It is played indoors in the gymnasium or some good sized room. Any number of persons on a side. A basket with large enough opening to take the ball easily is hung at each end about eight feet from the floor. The object is for the ball to be thrown or pitched into these baskets. The ball cannot be run with, although no limitations are placed on any one when not having the ball. This of course places a premium on passing the ball to others and so work it down the field. Fouls are declared for running with the ball and for kicking it. Any one has a right to the ball at all times if he can get it. I think the game could be easily adapted to girls - the main point being to get a basket as big as a house. The faculty of the school play the best team composed of the Secretarial men tomorrow. We expect a great time."

In 1893, James Naismith published a revision of the original thirteen rules in a booklet entitled Basket Ball for 1893 (Springfield, Mass., 1893). The following excerpt from pages 3-9, provides insight into the nature of early play as well as the ways in which players modified Naismith's original intentions.

BASKETBALL FOR 1893

"Basket Ball," the rules of which were first published in PHYSICAL EDUCATION as an experiment one year ago, has proved its right to a place among our games and has been more popular than was anticipated. It has spread from Nova Scotia to California, especially in the gymnasiums of the Young Men's Christian Associations, and there is no reason why it should not become just as popular among our colleges and athletic clubs. It has been found preculiarly adapted to business and professional men, as it is interesting and may be played by men of any size and in any condition of training. It has also been found valuable for girls and women, as there are few games which they can play that are not a strain on the nervous system rather than on the bodily functions. It is peculiarly adapted for giving health without involving a severe mental strain.

It has survived the various tests that have been applied to it, which instead of killing has developed it, until to-day there is need for a new edition of the rules with a good many amendments...

Basket Ball is not a game intended merely for amusement, but is the attempted solution of a problem which has been pressing on physical educators. Most of the games which are played out of doors are unsuitable for indoors, and consequently whenever the season closes, the game together with all the benefits to be derived therefrom, is dropped...

There were certain definite conditions to be met by the game which was required, and these had to be complied with before it could be pronounced satisfactory.

1st. It should be such as could be played on any kind of ground, - in a gymnasium, a large room, a small lot, a large field, whether these had uneven or smooth surface, so that no special preparation would be necessary. It has been played in a gymnasium 12 x 20 and can be played on an ordinary foot ball field.

2nd. It should be such as could be played by a large number of men at once... If a great number of men wish to play at once, two balls may be used at the same time, and thus the fun is augmented, though some of the science may be lost. The men, however, are required to keep their positions a little more carefully. As many as fifty on a side have been accommodated.

3rd. It should exercise a man all-around. Every part of his body should get a share of attention. His legs are used to sustain his body and his arms are exercised in handling an object, which is a normal function. In the bendings and twistings of the trunk and limbs the vital organs receive such exercise as will make them healthy and strong. Thus in a manner, it serves the same purpose as the sum total of the appartus in a gymnasium, while the main development is in strict accord with the idea of unity in man. It should cultivate the different energies of which he is capable. Agility is one of the prime requisites... This also gives us grace as the perfection of action. Physical judgment is required and cultivated in handling the ball, receiving it from one of your own side, and eluding an opponent. This reqires that a man should keep complete control of himself or his play is more than likely to count for nothing...

4th. It should be so attractive that men would desire to play it for its own sake....The thorough abandonment of every thought but that of true sport makes it entirely recreative, while the laughable side of the game may be appreciated by both players and spectators....

5th. It should have little or none of the reputed roughness of Rugby or Association foot ball. For this reason, kicking at the ball and striking at it with the fist were prohibited. All running with the ball was done away with because when a man runs with the ball we necessarily have tackling to stop him... A man's whole attention is thus centered on the ball and not on the person of an opponent, and thus opportunity for personal spite is taken away...

6th. It should be easy to learn... any one can learn to play Basket Ball at a single lesson...

These were felt to be the conditions that would determine the usefulness of a game that might be played summer and winter, in any climate, and under varying conditions.

To play the game, divide the men into two teams, hang a basket at each end of the room, let each side defend one of these goals while endeavoring to put the ball into that of their opponents'... Passing the ball from one to another and trying to throw it into the goal.

The object of a player should be whenever his own side has possession of the ball to gain an uncovered position so that his own side may pass it to him. On the other hand, his opponent should see that he does not gain this favorable position....Indiviudal play does not count for much, for very often a man has to sacrifice his own *chance* of making a goal that he may be *sure* of it from the hands of another...

... when a match game is to be played it is necessary to have a definite number of men on the floor; for a small gymnasium, five men make the best sized team, while for a large gymnasium nine men may be put on the floor.

Basket

---

home

L. Forward   R. Forward

....

Center

L. Center   R. Center

....

L. Back   R. Back

Goalkeeper

Basket

Diagram of Basket Ball - position of players

...This is not a hard and fast division, but merely to let the men know for what part of the field they are responsible...

Basket Ball Rules

1. The ball is put in play as follows: The teams line up in their respective positions and the referee throws the ball up in the middle of the field. This is done at the beginning of the game, at the beginning of the second half, after each goal, when a foul has been made and whenever time has been called.

2. The ball may be thrown in any direction with one or both hands.

3. The ball may be batted in any direction with the open hand or hands.

4. The ball cannot be struck with the fists or kicked.

5. A player cannot run with the ball either in or out of bounds except as specified in rule 11. He must throw it from the spot on which he catches it, allowance to be made for a man who catches the ball while he is running, if he tries to stop. (This does not exclude turning around on the spot.)

6. The ball must be held by the hands; the arms, legs or body must not be used for holding it.

7. When the ball is passed from the field of play out of bounds in order to claim exemption from interference, or when it is passed between players, outside of bounds, the ball shall be given to the opponents.

8. When the ball is held by more than two men for any length of time, the referee shall blow the whistle and throw the ball straight up from the spot where it was held.

9. No shouldering, holding, pushing, tripping or striking shall be allowed. The first infringement of this rule shall count as a foul, the second shall disqualify him but a substitute may take his place.

10. The ball is not out of bounds until it crosses the line.

11. When the ball goes out of bounds, it shall be returned by the side first holding it. The thrower in shall walk as directly towards the line as the apparatus, etc., will admit, he may then (1) bound it in and catch it, (2) throw it to some one in the field, or (3) roll it along the ground. He is allowed five seconds (to hold it) and if he holds it

longer than that, it goes to the opponents. In case of doubt in the mind of the referee as to which side first held the ball he shall throw it up in the field of play.

12. A foul is a violation of rules 4, 5, 6, 9, 16 and 19.

13. A goal shall be made when the ball is thrown or batted from the ground *into* the basket (directly or by a rebound from the sides) provided it stays in. If the ball rests on the edge of the basket and an opponent moves the basket, it shall count as a goal.

14. The score shall be counted by points. A goal shall count 3 points, a foul 1 point for the opponents. A majority of points shall decide the game.

15. The goals must be protected against interference from the specators, this protection to extend at least six feet on each side of the goal, and in case of a screen or other contrivance, to be at least six feet high. In case of doubt *in the mind of the referee or umpire* arising from the presence of the spectators, the visiting team shall have the benefit of the doubt.

16. Any persistent intentional delay of the game shall be counted as a foul against the team so delaying.

17. The time shall be two halves of twenty minutes each or such time as the captains may mutually agree upon. This is time of actual play.

18. The referee shall be judge of the ball and decide when the ball is in play, to which side it belongs; shall keep the time, decide when a goal has been made; keep account of the goals and fouls made; and any other duties not covered by the umpire.

19. The umpire shall be judge of the men, shall note the fouls made, report to the referee, keep an account of them, and notify the offenders. He shall have power to disqualify a player according to rule 9. In case any player is needlessly rough in his efforts to get the ball, the umpire shall warn him, even though he does not make a foul, and if he persists, the umpire shall call a foul upon him or even disqualify him if he thinks it necessary.

20. Any player has a right to get the ball at any time while it is in the field of play, provided only that he handles the *ball* and not the opponent.

21. The team shall consist of five men when the actual playing space is less than 1200 square feet, and nine men when it is more than this and less than 3600 square feet.

The position of the umpire is a very responsible one and on his ruling depends, to a great degree, the value of the game. If he deliberately overlooks violation of the rules he is responsible for a great deal of unnecessary roughness and consequent ill feeling, but if he is firm and impartial in his decisions he will soon win the respect of all, even those who suffered at the time.

A player may stand in front of the thrower and obstruct the ball, but he must not violate Rule 9. (sic) One aim of the rules has been to eliminate rough play, and for this reason the umpire must interpret them with this aim in view.

It is difficult for an umpire to see what every man is doing in every play, but if he watches where the ball is going to alight he may note the few men who are actually engaged in the play and may detect fouls. He does not need to watch the ball but the men. This will simplify the work of the umpire which is difficult at best.

On 21 March 1897, p. 3, the New York Times reported the Yale-Penn game of the pre-vious day which featured five-man teams. Quintets, pioneered by the Universities of Chicago and Iowa in 1893, ushered in the modern version of the game.

YALE WINS AT BASKETBALL

NEW HAVEN, Conn., March 20.-Yale defeated the University of Pennsylvania here this evening at basket ball by the score of 32 to 10. Yale's players took the lead at the start, and maintained their advantage until the close of the contest. The team play of the visi-tors was inferior, although several fine individual plays were made. The summary:

Yale	Position.	Pennsylvania.
Clark	Right forward	Milligan, Capt.
Beard	Left forward	De Loffre
Sharp	Center	Hedges, Schrack
Peck, Capt	Left guard	Stewart
Rockwell	Right guard	Margraff

Goals-Milligan, (2) De Loffre, Schrack and Stewart, Beard, (3) Clark, Sharp, (6) Peck, (3) Rockwell, (2) Goals thrown from foul-Beard and Sharp. Referee-Louis A. Leyerzapf, New Haven, Umpires-Messrs. Mannager and Abbott of Pennsylvania, and George A. May of the Yale Gymnasium.

WOMEN'S BASKETBALL

While women took to the new game quickly and enthusiastically, particularly in the colleges, female physical educators voiced concerns over the nature of play and feared that women would adopt the overly competitive and commercialized male model. As a result the women were often sequestered from male spectators; while women's rules limited exertion by restricting players to one of three zones on the court.

In a letter to her mother, dated 6 March 1892, Josephine Wilkin related the first game played at Smith College. The letter is obtained from the school's archives.

LETTER FROM JOSEPHINE WILKIN, CLASS OF 1895, TO HER MOTHER, MARCH 6, 1892

Friday afternoon at the Gym, we played a game, instead of going through the or-dinary performances. Two waste-paper baskets were hung, one on either side of the Gym about three feet above our heads. Two of the girls choose sides, + those on our side were distinguished from the other by handkerchiefs tied on their arms. Three girls from each side were sent over to the other and the game began. We had a football which was to be touched only with the hands, + the object was to get it into your opponent's basket + keep it out of your own. When it was sent over to our side, the girls on that side who had been sent from the other, tried to get it and throw it into the basket while the rest tried to catch it + throw it back to their helpers on the other side. See? It was great fun, + very exciting, especially when we got knocked down, as frequently happened. The side I was on had the misfortune to be beaten, but we had the ball in their basket several times, including the first time.

The New York Herald Tribune, 27 March 1893, p. 4, reported an intramural contest at Smith College.

SMITH COLLEGE

Northampton, March 26 (Special). - On Wednesday evening an exciting game of "basket Ball" was played by the sophomore and freshmen teams. The running track of the gymnasium was crowded with spectators, and gay with the colors of the two classes. One side was occupied by sophomores and seniors, the other by juniors and freshmen, and a lively rivalry between the two parties was maintained throughout the contest. The game consists in the two sides trying to get the ball into their respective baskets, which are suspended at opposite sides of the gymnasium, and each tries to prevent the other from accomplishing that. Every time the ball is put in it counts one point. All the playing must be done by throwing, as no running while the ball is in the hands is permissible. In spite of the fact that the sophomore captain was disabled at the beginning of the game, the score was 5 to 4, in favor of the sophomores after a close conterst of fifteen minute halves. The winning side gained a gold and white banner, which will be handed over to the next victorious team....

The Boston Sunday Globe, 18 March 1894, provided greater detail of the growing importance of the game and the class spirit that it generated the following year.

NO MAN IN IT.
SMITH COLLEGE GYM HELD 1000 EXCITED GIRLS.

NORTHAMPTON, March 17- The annual match game of basket ball between picked teams from the sophomore and freshmen classes at Smith College was played today amid great enthusiasm.

For weeks the two teams and their substitutes have been practising under the direction of Miss Senda Berenson, the instructor in gymnastics. Both teams were in splendid condition, and it was a toss-up which was the stronger. There has existed great rivalry between the teams and classes.

The game took place in the new gymnasium. A running track was built for the occasion.

The floor of the gymnasium was divided by the chalk lines between which the center players stood. The other players were arranged around the baskets hanging at either end of the gymnasium, at opposite sides on the running track.

The baskets were about 100 feet apart. The gymnasium is 60 feet wide. No running with the ball was allowed, nor holding it over a certain time. It must be thrown almost immediately after being received into the hands, and thrown from one to another.

It is slowly advanced towards the goal, until finally, unless secured by their opponents or in some way stopped, it safely landed in the basket. Each time this is done one point is scored.

The only way which the game played at the college differs from the prescribed game is that the ball when once in any player's hands cannot be knocked out or snatched away from any other player.

This, of course makes the games a great deal less rough. The ball used was the regular Rugby football.

Around each basket stood players of both sides, those guarding the basket to prevent their opponents getting the ball in and if possible to send it toward the other, and those who were to try to get it in.

The tallest girls were chosen for this position, to catch the ball as it fell.

The baskets were of iron and netting. To the basket was attached a string, which the girls pulled to jerk out the ball when a goal was made.

Such was the arrangements preceding the battle.

The spectators, about 1000 girls, were seated in galleries running across and along the sides of the gymnasium. One gallery was tastefully hung with violet, the sophomore team's color, and the other with yellow, the color of the freshmen.

Hundreds of violet and yellow flags fluttered violently at the exciting periods of the game.

Yelling was prohibited by Miss Berenson, so the girls sang rival snatches of song.

The scene in the gymnasium at 3:30 was most inspiring. Not a man was to be seen. The thousand girls kept up a continual hum.

One thousand pretty faces turned repeatedly in the direction of the two little rooms each side of the stage.

The rival teams occupied these rooms. The substitute teams occupied the stage in readiness to recruit either side in case of accident.

The handsome silk banner won by the class of 95 hung with the class pennant of green on the same pole during the game.

At the close of the game Miss Kristine Mann of Orange, N.J. as captain of the team last year, took off the banner and presented it to the captain of the winning team amid the excited, deafening cheering of the students.

At a few minutes after 4 o'clock the two teams issued from their respective rooms and took their places.

The uniforms of both teams were the regulation gymnasium suits of navy blue, consisting of loose blouse and bloomers.

Around the sleeves of the sophomore players were bands of violet ribbon and the figures 96 in the same color were on the fronts of their suits. They wore neckties of the same color. The freshmen wore similarly decorated, the color of their ribbon being yellow.

The teams lined up as follows: Sophomores-Centers, Katherine Von Hovenberg, Eau Claire, Wis: Marian Baker, Providence, RI; Litz Dustin, captain, Rushton, N.Y.; Laura Ulrich, Decatur, Ill; guards Katherine Van Wagner, Northampton; Laura Crane, Scarsdale, N.Y.; Lucy Daniels, Jacksonville, Ill; home. Eleuthera Smith, Franklin, Penn: Clara Bates, Brooklyn, NY; Josephine Percy, Worcester; Martha Hale, Chicago, Ill.

Freshmen-Centers, Mary L. Nare, Chicago, Ill: Lillian Blaikie, Englewood, NJ; Mary H. Johnson, Hartford, Conn; Frances Hale, Minneapolis, Minn; guards Julia Boles, Chicago, Ill; Alice S. Tallent, Capt. Boston; Edith Blake, Newark, NJ; home, Mary Rossetter, Boston, Ethel Dixon, Boston; Henrietta S. Seelye, Northampton.

The game was a close one and during the first half was equal. The sophomore team entered the hall first followed closely by the freshman. Both teams indulged in a few minutes' practice.

Amid an almost palpable silence among the 1000 spectators, Miss Berenson called the game.

The first two goals were made in rapid succession after the ball was put in motion, the first by the sophomores, the second by the freshmen.

These goals, though scored so rapidly, showed clearly that as clever and sure throwers Miss Rosseter and Miss Smith 96 could be relied upon. Miss Blaikie, 97, and Miss Bates, 96, improved good opportunities for interference.

The scoring after this was rapid. The ball zigzagged from one goal to the other. The freshmen missed some goals on account of the nervousness of their putter-in. Time for the first half was called at 4:30.

A great sigh rose to the oaken rafters from the anxious freshmen as the score was posted 10 to 3 in favor of the sophomores. This sigh was all the more intense because three successive goals were scored by the sophomores off of fouls by the freshmen.

To give vent to their suppressed emotions the girls sang snatches of original songs. The favorite lines of the freshmen was a parody on George Goldsmith's song, "The Baby on the Shore," ... The sophomores sang:

Here's to 96, that's a class of perfect bricks,

And here's to 97, they are wanted up in heaven.

In this first half the sophomores plainly showed their training of last year. They played with more head, and had several team plays that were not appreciated by the freshmen until the second half.

Miss Huntington and Miss Ware 97 made some combination plays, but the strong chain which they had to oppose, consisting of Misses Baker, Crane, Bates and Van Wagner, succeeded in getting the ball to the sophomore goals in spite of noble interference.

These four players passed the ball with great skill, often from one end of the gymnasium to the other. This play was made much more effective by Miss Van Wagner's rolling the ball along the floor when apparently hemmed in by freshmen.

At 4:40 the second half began.

The freshmen walked into the hall with sober determination, which was most effectually shown in the plays with which they began the second half.

They had in the interval apparently mastered the puzzling sophs ways. Their interference showed marked improvement and they exhibited more science and gave the sophomores hard work to hold their ground.

The last goals were made by the freshmen. The whole score for the second half was 4 to 3 in favor of the freshmen, making the total score 13 to 7.

The best plays for the sophomores were made by Misses Ulrich, Perry, Bates, Van Wagner and Dustin and for the freshmen by Misses Ware, Rossitter and Huntington.

At the close of the game amid a wave of handkerchiefs, flags and ribbons, Miss Dustin, the captain of the winning team was hoisted on the shoulders of her victorious team.

Thus proudly borne the girl captain was presented with the victors' banner by Misses Marrs and Martin of last Year's winning team.

The gymnasium was the scene of wild enthusiasm, and everybody collectively and individually on the winning side and off congratulated and received congratulations.

Venerable Register Marsh of Amherst college wore in his buttonhole this afternoon a huge yellow chrysanthemum and Rev. Henry T. Rose, well on in years, was enthusiastic as any of the girls and was similarly decorated.

Prof. Seelye wore a yellow ribbon on his coat, surmounted by a cluster of violets and thus honored both teams.

After the game the girls flocked into the city, and until supper time the streets presented a lively spectacle.

Some of the girls wore huge yellow violet bows, some had their hats decorated with ribbon of the color of their class and some carried flags.

All were brilliant with their favorite color, and all were much excited.

The Chicago Tribune, 25 February 1900, p. 18, reported on the growth, popularity, and lack of standardization in the women's game. Chicago high school girls had formed a league as early as 1895.

GROWTH OF BASKET BALL
MOST POPULAR OF INDOOR SPORTS FOR YOUNG WOMEN.

Attention to the Game Is Steadily Increasing Among Colleges, Institutes and High Schools Both In the East and The West -Advantages of the Exercise and Mental Training - Three Sets of Rules in Vogue at Present.
By Frances A. Kellar

Interest in the game of basket ball in Chicago is grouped about the Y.M.C.A. teams, and the acme of interest will be reached in the Fond du Lac - Ravenswood Y.M.C.A. game, which is the first of a series to determine the championship of the West.

Basket ball within the last five years has grown to such an extent in women's organizations that it is often viewed as a woman's game. In Chicago its interest is at its height, the various colleges and institutions and high schools having teams. Hull House and the University Settlement, Armour and Lewis Institutes, Lake Forest, University of Chicago, Chicago Normal School, and many other colleges and high schools have enthusiastic teams and rooters. The high schools have shown the most systematic work, and this year have organized a league for league games.

If one were to name the indoor sport for which women are most devoted it would undoubtedly be basket ball. Almost without exception the Eastern colleges have teams. This includes such institutions as Smith, Wellesley, Oberlin, Bryn Mawr, Cornell and many normal schools. In Chicago all the teams play outside teams except the University of Chicago. In the East only Cornell and Syracuse exchange games, and the other universities and colleges being content with class games. The normal and training schools permit outside games to the East.

In any game in which women indulge there is a keener question of merits and defects, and basket ball by no means escapes the rule. Women have three ways to play basket ball; men only one, and many of the institutions are at strife, contending for their especial way. The one most in vogue is the game as played by men under the Spalding rules. This requires five players on a side and permits the snatching or snapping the ball from another player's hands. This is in use in the high school league, consisting of the Austin, Hyde Park, Englewood, and West Division High Schools, and by the settlements. Then there is the non-interference game. The only change from the Spalding rules is that the ball cannot be interfered with until it has left the player's hands. All must wait until the player throws the ball. This method has been adopted by the University of Chicago and Wellesley.

Owing to the roughness and overfatigue a movement was started in the East for special basket ball for women, or line ball. This prohibits snatching and modifies minor points to rules. It permits the playing of eighteen people at one time, nine on a side. The Chicago Normal School, Smith, and Oberlin represent this method. The result of these changes is a different style of playing in each case.

Where Mass Plays Are Frequent

The first, where interference is permitted, insures swift, snappy playing and quickness in securing and disposing of the ball. It is a passing, ground floor game, often involving mass plays and deadlocks. In this style of play more than any other there is danger of roughness and overfatigue because of the close personal interference and violent attempts at snatching. Mass plays have a tendency to produce injury. Massing prevents good, clean, team work and exercise of judgment. In the interference game the inevitability to irritation is also great, and this is no small consideration, especially of teams consisting of the younger girls.

Chapter 6

BICYCLING

Introduced in North America in the mid-nineteenth century, the bicycle underwent several technological changes, enjoying episodes of popularity. By the 1870s the high-wheeled ordinary allowed daring young men and a few adventurous women to achieve high rates of speed. Such "scorchers" endangered other riders and pedestrians, engendering a ban on cycles in many areas. The League of American Wheelmen, organized in 1880, campaigned for better roads and cyclists' rights. It enjoyed some political leverage as its membership soared and its publications reached more than 100,000 voters by 1898.

The modern safety bicycle, with a tubular frame and tires of equal size, appeared by the 1880s. Mass production made such vehicles accessible to the middle class, fostering a cycling craze throughout the 1890s. Cycling clubs proliferated in urban areas and women riders increasingly challenged conventional standards by adopting pants or bloomers in order to ride. Bicycle excursions also allowed women to avoid watchful chaperones.

Bicycle racing enjoyed a surge of popularity during the 1890s as manufacturers sponsored events and professional riders to advertise their wares. Among the best cyclists, Marshall W. "Major" Taylor won the American sprint championships from 1898-1900 and set several records; but as an African-American he was subjected to discrimination and partisan tactics on the track, causing him to pursue the remainder of his career in Europe. The League of American Wheelmen had already excluded blacks in 1894 in deference to its southern membership. By 1900 cycling interest waned as the bicycle began to be eclipsed by the automobile.

ORGANIZATION

The Bicycling World, 12 June 1880, pp. 254-256, provided an account of the founding of the League of American Wheelman.

THE GRAND MEET AT NEWPORT.
THE PRELIMINARIES.

Small as compared with the Hampton meets of England, but large under the circumstances of its unofficial call, the wide distances between the places represented, and the yet limited numbers of the increasing army of bicyclers, was our first national assembly at Newport, R.I., for a convention and a parade, on Monday, the 31 May. Representatives from New York, Boston, Philadelphia, and Chicago, were on the ground as early as Friday the 28th, and on Saturday evening the 29th there were about 100 riders in the city, and more than 20 clubs represented. These numbers were augmented on Sunday morning and evening, until the Monday proceedings opened with 150 riders in the city, representing 32 clubs and the unattached....

The 29th and 30th were passed without formal proceedings ... "PROGRAMME.- Route of parade and rules governing the first grand meet of American Wheelmen, Newport, R.I., 31 May, 1880.

All captains and acting captains of clubs will report to Capt. E.C. Hodges, at Aquidneck Hotel, at 9 o'clock, a.m. A convention, to which all wheelmen are invited, will be held in Skating-Rink, near Ocean House, at 10 a.m. But two votes will be allowed each club represented.

The parade of all clubs and all unattached wheelmen who have previously reported to the Secretary of the New York Bi. Club, will be in the afternoon....

Procession will then re-form, return as it went, and will disband at Touro Park.

A bicycle dinner will be given at the Aquidneck House, at 5:30 p.m., to which all wheelmen are invited. Tickets for dinner may be procured at Hotel office, for $1.00 each.

ROAD RULES.- Assembly and retreat will be sounded by the bugle; all other orders will be given by means of whistle calls, which will be as follows: One long whistle, mount.-One short whistle, single file.-Two short whistles, double file.-Three short whistles, dismount and half.-Four short whistles, form fours. During the progress of the procession no bugle or whislte calls will be sounded except by order of the commander....

THE CONVENTION.

Here the meeting was called to order by Mr. C.K. Munroe, who, after securing the quiet attention of the large audience, briefly stated the object of the meeting to be the formation of a national organization of the bicyclers of America.

On motion of Mr. Pratt, of Boston, Mr. S.T. Clark, of Baltimore, was chosen temporary chairman, and assumed the chair with a few appropriate remarks. Mr. K.N. Putnam, of New York, was then chosen temporary secretary; and the organization of the meeting was completed by calling the roll of the clubs, and recording the names of responding delegates, each club being allowed two representatives, with each a vote, or two votes by one representative where but one was present ...

On motion, the chair appointed as a Committee on Constitution, C.E. Pratt (Boston Bi.C.). C.K. Munroe (N.Y. Bi. C.), and H.A. Blakiston (Phila. Bi.C.)...

On motion, the chairman appointed a Committee on Organization, consisting of J.M. Fairfield (Chicago Bi.C.), E.C. Hodges (Boston Bi.C.), and A. S. Parsons (Mass. Bi.C.)

The committees, having retired, found their work expedited and lightened by the deliberations of quite a body of representatives of the leading clubs the evening before, who had come together in a preliminary conference and agreed upon a name, constitution, and list of officers, to be presented for adoption or amendment in the convention....

CONSTITUTION.

1. This organization shall be known as the LEAGUE OF AMERICAN WHEELMEN.
2. Its objects are: to promote the general interests of bicycling: to ascertain, defend, and protect the rights of wheelmen; and to encourage and facilitate touring.

3. Any amateur wheelman of good standing may become a member of this League, upon payment of an initiation fee of one dollar, and approval by the board of officers, or a committee thereof, after the publication of his name in a list of candidates in the official organ of the League at least two weeks previously; provided that the entire active membership of any recognized amateur bicycle club may be received at one-half the above-named initiation fee per member.

4. Its officers shall be a President, a Vice-President, a Commander, a Corresponding Secretary, a Recording Secretary, a Treasurer, and two Directors for each State in which there is a regularly organized bicycle club; and these officers shall form a Board of Officers, of which eight shall constitute a quorum, who shall direct and decide in all matters not provided for in this Constitution, and shall have power to fill all vacancies....

The chairman of the committee on organization reported the following names to the convention for

OFFICERS FOR 1880-1.

President, CHARLES E. PRATT, of Boston.
Vice-President, THOMAS K. LONGSTRETH, of Philadelphia.
Commander, C.K. MUNROE, of New York,
Corresponding Secretary, ALBERT S. PARSONS, of Cambridge.
Recording Secretary, J. FRANK BURRILL, of New York.
Treasurer, HUGH L. WILLOUGHBY, of Saratoga....

On motion of Mr. Longstreth, of Philadelphia, it was unanimously voted that THE BICYCLING WORLD be made the official organ of this League....

COMPETITION

Sporting Life, 28 November 1882, p. 6, reported on a world cycling tour that featured Louise Armaindo, one of the few women who braved Victorian strictures to become a professional athlete.

THE WHEEL.
MATTERS OF INTEREST TO DEVOTEES OF THE SILENT STEED.
A NEW COMBINATION.
PROFESSIONAL BICYCLING STARS GO ON A TRIP AROUND THE WORLD.

A combination of bicycle riders, to be known as "The League of Champions," was formed in Chicago week before last. Chicago's favorite, Mlle. Armaindo, the champion long-distance rider of America, heads the list. John S. Prince, short-distance champion; Henry W. Higham, long-distance champion of England; Fred S. Rollinson, ex-champion, and Thomas W. Eck, professional, comprise the party. All are under the management of Fred J. Engelhardt, the well-known manager of sporting celebrities. It is the

intention of the "League" to give exhibitions and races in the leading cities throughout the West, thence to Australia and England. Armaindo, with a record of 843 miles
in 72 hours, Price, with 486 miles to his credit at the end of 30 hours; Higham, with
1,040 miles in 72 hours; and Rollinson with 50 in 3 hours, is a sufficient guarantee of
the strength of this organization. The "League" has entered into an agreement, a portion of which is decidely novel. A pool is made of the earnings from which the expenses are paid. From what remains of any and all earnings of any member or the
League collectively, 10 per cent shall be paid into a racing fund, which shall be used
only for stake-money with outside challengers and for the expenses incident to a preparation for a race if no challenges are received from persons outside the League within
a reasonable time, then the amount on hand will be put up to be contested by
Armaindo, Higham and Prince in a six days race. Even then any outsider can by de-
positing a third of the amount on hand, enter and start in the race, the winner to take
the entire stake. On the evening of Nov. 16th this combination left Chicago for Kansas City. At San Francisco Prince is to meet Charles Smith, champion of the Pacific
slope, still a six days match will take place there for 10 percent of the gross receipts
of the tour, which will be contested for by Prince, Higham, and Armaindo. They expect to sail for Australia on February 1, where Higham will try conclusions with Rolf,
and Australian champion. Each one of the party takes two machines on the trip. The
return home will be by way of England.

F.P. Prial provided a brief history of cycling in an article for Harper's Weekly, 30
August 1890. The following is excerpted from pages 671-672.

CYCLE RACING

The possible speed of the cycle has always been a fascinating inquiry. Habitual
tourists and confirmed constitutional riders pretend to care nothing for "record" or for
speed trials, but the majority of riders take some interest in this branch of the sport;
sometimes it is a mild, indirect interest, and at others almost a mania, and men who
suffer from it devour every word about training and racing, and spend a lot of time and
energy in attempting to develop speed, either on the path or road.

Racing was in the early years of cycling essentially the sport of the English, the
pioneers of the game being Jack Keen; Stanton, and others. The record may be said to
have started at three minutes for one mile....

RACING IN AMERICA.

The racing history of this country commences with a race held at Lynn on July 4,
1876, the time being 3 minutes 13 seconds. Between 1876 and 1880 the records was

gradually cut to 3 minutes 8 1/4 seconds, and ... George M. Hendee ... cut it to 2 minutes 50 seconds.

In 1884 the newly built half-mile track at Springfield, and the great interest it attracted to racing, caused a general lowering of the records. In the one-mile event, John S. Prince, an Englishman, cut the professional record to 2 minutes 39 seconds. In the same month, on the new Hartford track, Hendee reduced the amateur record to 2 minutes 39 seconds.

In 1885 a new American rider appeared who threatened Hendee's reign, which had lasted from 1881. This was William A. Rowe, who won many races that year, and reduced the record to 2 minutes 35 2/3 seconds where it stands to-day. The next year, 1886, Rowe became a professional, and going into strict training, he reduced the one-mile record at Springfield, on October 23, 1886, to 2 minutes 29 4/5 seconds, which remained the fastest time ever made on a cycle until July of this year. Rowe also rode 22 miles 150 yards within one hours.-Passing from the mile it is to be noted that at least a score of men have ridden over twenty miles within one hour, the record standing as follows: one hour, 22 miles 150 yards, W.A. Rowe; two hours, 39 3/4 miles. F.F. Ives; three hours, 54 3/4 miles, F.F. Ives.

SAFETY RACING

Within the past year a new phase of the sport has developed in safety racing, which has been kept entirely distinct from racing on "tall" of "ordinary" bicycles. Until July of this year the safety record stood at 2 minutes 36 1/3 seconds, or over six seconds behind the ordinary record. During the past six weeks a complete revolution has been witnessed and the safety is now regarded as faster than the ordinary....

FLIGHTS OF SPEED ON THE ROAD

Road racing is another branch of competition. It is at its best in England, where some remarkable bursts of speed have been made. The English "scorcher" is usually a man of powerful physique with great staying power. Such a man, trained and mounted on a light safety bicycle is capable of great work....

The greatest ride ever recorded was the notable feat of riding 324 miles in 24 hours. The credit of this wonderful record is shared alike by S.G. Whitaker, an American rider, and M.A. Holbein who is at present the fastest man in England....

In America we are just commencing to develop ability at the game of road racing....

The most popular races in this country-races which have a national reputation-are the Pullman and the Irvington-Milburn road races. Both are held each year on May 30th, and the pick of the Western riders enter at Pullman, while the supremacy of the East is practically decided in the Irvington-Milburn race. The Pullman course is a 14 7/10 mile stretch between Chicago and Pullman. In the race held on May 30, 1890, there were 71 starters at Pullman, and the fasest time, 56 minutes 38 seconds, was made by Arthur Lumsden, of Chicago.

The Irvington-Milburn course is a five-mile stretch between the two villages of the name at Orange, New Jersey. The road is smooth but hilly, and it is a most punishing course. In the race held last May, 69 men started, and 51 finished. The fastest time was 1 hour 28 minutes 29 seconds; five men finished inside of 1 hour 30 minutes for the 25 miles, the ocurse having to be traversed five times; three men rode the first 15 miles inside of 53 minutes; and 44 men rode the first 15 miles within one hour.

Outside of these two classic events a number of minor road races are held, the
majority being five and ten mile handicaps....

Speed, endurance, and technology fascinated Americans. The first national championship at one mile occurred at the League of America Wheelmen convention at Boston
in 1882. The next year Karl Kron rode more than 1400 miles from Detroit to Staunton,
Virginia, and H.L. Cortis set an endurance record of more than 200 miles in 24 hours.
In 1884 Thomas Stevens' ride around the world was duly chronicled by journalists.
When the League of American Wheelmen banned professionals, they retaliated by
forming the American Cyclists Union in 1886. Pneumatic tires replaced the hard rubber types by 1890, and the construction of velodromes made cycle racing a commer-
cially viable sport in the 1890s. The International Cyclists Association organized in
1893 and held its first world championship that year, as reported below by the Chicago
Tribune, 13 August 1893, p. 7.

Intercollegiate racing in the United States started at the Manhattan Beach Track in
New York in 1896, and Madison Square Garden featured a six day endurance race for
women the same year. The National Cycling Association formed in 1898 to govern
professional racing.

BICYCLE RECORDS GO.

The last day of the bicycle tournament was fittingly distinguished by some spendid
racing and the breaking of all former, competitive records for distances between
twenty-five and sixty-two miles.

All the cracks, A.A. Zimmerman, Herbert Githens, J.P. Bliss, L.S. Meintjes, G.F.
Taylor, J.S. Johnson, F.H. Tuttle, "Billy" Rhodes, and others, were out in full force, and
as a result several close finishes and some speedy runs were scored.

The day's great event was the sixty-two mile international championship. L.S.
Meintjes of South Africa won it easily and established a score of new long distance
records.

The starters in this took their places at 4:15. Besides the stocky forms of the two
foreigners, L.S. Meintjes and William Hyslop, there was a field of eight American
contestants, among others Frank Waller, L.D. Munger, and E. Ulbrecht of Chicago,
Conn Baker of Columbus, J.W. Linneman and M. Dirnberger, the Buffalo long distance
riders, and J.P. Clark of Boston.

The pacemakers were all the fast riders who have competed during the tournament-
Zimmerman, Tyler, Taylor, F.J. Osmond, the English crack, John S. Johnson, G.F.
Taylor, J.P. Bliss, C.T. Knisely, F.H. Tuttle, A.T. Crooks, Hoyland, Smith, Rhodes,
Gary, White, and a dozen others.

Osmond Sets a Merry Pace.

F.J. Osmond started as pacemaker. It was his first appearance on the track, and he was lustily cheered. He immediately set a cracking pace the others following in single file. At the second mile A.A. Zimmerman took up the pace in scorching style. At the fifth mile the eleven starters dwindled to five with Linneman leading. The plan was to have a new pacemaker every mile. Only once or twice the riders lacked a leader. The first record to go was that for six miles. Linneman's time was 15:15.

The announcement that the records were going spurred Menitjes to the lead and he scored the now eight-mile record, 20:27, three seconds faster than the old one. Linneman was leading again at the twelve-mile post and looking fresh as at the start. It was on him and Ulbrecht that America's honors were conceded to depend.

As Linneman rounded the lower turn on the thirteenth mile his wheel slipped, throwing him heavily and making him turn a complete somerset right in front of the grand stand. The others evaded him. In a jiffy Linneman was up and after his men. His plucky action was loudly cheered. He had nearly made up his loss of half a lap when he found his machine disabled. A new one was run out and he made a flying change. There were loud shouts for a pacemaker for Linneman at this time and at last one was sent. But the Buffalo man couldn't make up his loss and both he and Hyslop the Canadian champion, dropped out at the sixteenth mile.

Only Meintjes, Ulbrecht, and Baker were left. They pedaled on and on with seemingly tireless effort, though each mile brought a new burst of speed to keep up with the fresh pacemaker. The distance for the first hour was 23 miles 473 yards. Never once did Meintjes flag, but several times pushed past the pacemakers, demanding more speed. At the thirteenth mile F.J. Osmond again set the pace and was followed by Bryne, Blauvelt, Githens, and Grosch, all fast men. Each traveled a mile or two and then covered with moisture from their efforts yielded to a fresh man, and still the three racers pounded on with the tireless energy of machines rather than men.

Conn Baker Wabbles and Quits.

Conn Baker showed weakness at thirty-five miles. He wabbled noticeably at the turns and gave up at the thirty-seventh mile. Only two were now left; it was South Africa against America. Meintjes led and Ulbrecht followed close after him and both looked fresh. Things went on thus until the forty-second mile post was passed and meanwhile the spectators' minds were diverted by the trick riding of Sydney Black of Cleveland in the oval. At this juncture Ulbrecht, the Chicago man, began to lag. Meintjes spurted away and virtually raced alone to the end. Meintjes' distance for the two hours was 45 miles 1,530 yards. The time for fifty miles was 2:11:00, breaking both the American competition record of 2:10:41 and that of the French champion, Jules Dubois, 2:11:10, made in 1892. Ulbrecht's time for the fifty was 2:14:10.

At the sixty miles E.L. Blauvelt was pacemaker and Meintjes' time 2:30:47, over seven minutes better that the previous record for that distance. On the last lap Meintjes showed his wonderful reserve power by sprinting around the turn, passing and finishing five feet ahead of his pacemaker and more than seven laps ahead of Ulbrecht.

The latter declared his intnetion of finishing his time was 2:55:31 2-5.

L.S. Meintjes the winner at the finish, was escorted off to his quarters by the crowd and the track was with difficulty kept clear for Ulbrecht's finish. It was 7:15 o'clock when the race ended. Over 8,000 people witnessed yesterday's races and fully 5,000 staid to see the finish of the sixty-two mile contest.

There were some lively contests in the other races. J.P. Bliss of Chicago carried off the first race, the one mile handicap, from such cracks as H.A. Githens and M. Dirnberger. It was one of the closest finishes of the week. Bliss led Githens by less than two feet at the post. Bliss had fifty yards and Githens 80 yards handicap. Bliss showed his generosity as well as his speed in the sixth event, a one mile invitation race. He and H.C. Tyler came down the straight side by side. Ten yards from the line Tyler led by a few feet. He slipped his pedals, however and instead of winning narrowly escaped a fall, while Bliss passed him by three feet. Few in the grand stand saw Tyler's accident. The spectators were accordingly astonished to hear that Bliss had yielded the race to his opponent. When the motive was made known the doughty Chicagoan received greater applause than had been given any winner.

Zimmerman Shows His Quality.

Zimmerman's winning of the fourth event, the one mile international championship, was too much like his other performances to need description or comment. There was a time limit of 2:40 but Zimmerman's time, 2:27 1.5, left plenty to spare. It was another of the New-Yorker's cyclone finishes. J.P. Bliss and J.S. Johnson rode almost a dead heat for second place. Zimmerman's winning by twenty feet was remarkable, since he was over one hundred feet behind C.L. Knisely at the last turn, less than 150 yards from the finish.

C.F. Nelson of Springfield won the mile consolation race over a field of eight unfortunates who haven't had a place during the week. The time, 3:07 2-5, was no consolation.

The second event, the quarter of a mile open race, was also Zimmerman's. He took it honestly by fifteen feet or more in 31 2.5 seconds.

G.L. Gary of Boston and Paul Grosch of Passaic, N.J., rode a dead heat for second place, the first one of this meet. In the toss up Gary won.

Last night all visiting wheelmen were invited to the smokers held at the various clubs after the evening ride down town.

The American records broken yesterday between twenty-five miles and sixty-two miles were those made by F.E. Spooner. The previous sixty mile record was 2:47.20 2.5; made last July by Frank Shorland of England....

While sport might assimilate it also allowed opportunities to promote ethnic consciousness and the retention of traditional customs and values. Although ethnic immigrants adopted some American sport forms they often practiced them within the context of exclusive nationalistic organizations, as reported by the Polish newspaper, Dziennik Chicagoski, 12 July 1897.

CHICAGO POLES VICTORS IN ANNUAL BICYCLE MEET IN SOUTH BEND

During the annual convention of the Polish Falcons in South Bend, Indiana, bicycle races were also held.

Stanislaus Paczynski of South Chicago took first place in the ten-mile event by breaking the tape in 30 minutes and 20 seconds.

Of the various entrants the following received awards (ten-mile event):

The first to reach the tape was S. Adamkiewicz of Chicago, 30 minutes and 40 seconds (handicap, 2 minutes and 30 seconds); awarded gold medal.

Second place, J. Malewicki of Chicago, 31 minutes and 15 seconds (handicap, 2 minutes and 30 seconds); silver medal.

Third, J. Wojtecki of Chicago, 33 minutes and 13 seconds (handicap, 4 minutes);

Charles Murphy garnered worldwide acclaim when he covered a mile in less than a minute by drafting behind a train on 30 June 1899. The Scientific American reported the logistics of the feat on 15 July 1899, pp. 41-42.

A MILE IN LESS THAN A MINUTE ON A BICYCLE

As our readers are aware, it is not the custom of the SCIENTIFIC AMERICAN to lend its columns to the announcement or discussion of feats of speed or endurance, and it is only when such performances have a distinctly scientific bearing that an exception is made. The remarkable ride recently accomplished by the bicyclist C.W. Murphy, however, who covered a mile in 57 4/5 seconds, has such an important bearing upon the question of air resistance, while the distance and time were surveyed and recorded by such unimpeachable authorities, that the facts are well worthy of being carefully recorded, both for their scientific value, and as data for future reference.

The Long Island Railroad, at the request of Mr. H.B. Fullerton, who is the special agent of the road and holds the position of vice-consul of the League of American Wheelmen, arranged to give Murphy an opportunity to ride a mile, paced by a locomotive, on a five-mile stretch of local track which is used only on special occasions for the transfer of trains between the two main branches of their system. Murphy, who is a well-known cyclist, has for many years been anxious to prove that if fast enough pace could be secured, a mile could be ridden within 60 seconds. His remarkable and, as the event proved, successful attempt was arranged by the railroad company as one of the attractive features of the State meet of the League of American Wheelmen, which took place a few miles further up the road, at Patchogue, Long Island, the railroad company running special trains to the scene of the trial course....

The measured mile was laid off on a straight and approximately level stretch of road about 2 1/4 miles in length. Three quarters of a mile was allowed on which to get up speed and half a mile on which to slow up. The bicycle track was supported on 2 by 4-inch ties, which were cut to exact length and laid on the inner flanges of the rails. Upon these were laid five 1 by 10 inch planks, which were dressed on both edges and the upper side, and laid close together, the abutting ends being arranged to break joint on the ties. The railroad, track and roadbed were of the light construction used 20 to 25 years ago, consisting of 56-pound rail laid on 6 by 8-inch ties, upon a sand and gravel ballast.... The bicycle track, of course, extended the whole 2 1/4 miles of the course. The mile was measured with an engineer's steel tape under the personal supervision of Mr. P.D. Ford, the chief engineer of the Long Island system, and was personally remeasured just before the race by Mr. James E. Sullivan, secretary of the Amateur Athletic Union, who acted as the referee of the trial.

The pacing outfit consisted of an engine and one passenger car, at the rear of which had been constructed a wind shield ... in the preliminary preparations, it began to be a question as to whether the locomotive ifself could, on so short a track, develop and hold a speed of a mile a minute.... Altogether six trials were made with three different engines.... It was then decided to use a more powerful engine with larger boiler capacity, and No. 74, with 18 by 24-inch cylinders, was given a trial. This is an 8-wheel engine of the American type, with 68-inch drivers and large firebox and heating surface. The weight on each pair of drivers is 35,000 pounds, and the total weight of engine and tender 91 tons. On the first trial No.74 covered the mile in 56 seconds, the steam falling from 180 to 170 pounds, and Sam Booth, the engineer, was satisfied that he could take the bicyclist over the course at the speed requested which was 58 to 59 seconds, or just within the minute.

The shield was built of 1 by 3 inch tongued and grooved sheathing, laid over a light frame work of 2 by 4 scantiling. It was built flush with the sides and roof of the car and extended for a distance of 5 feet beyond the rear of the platform. Below the level of the floor of the car platform its sides sloped inwardly until its bottom edges were between the rails and the board track. Projecting forward below the car platform and extending down to within an inch of the track was a plow-shaped projection which served to deflect the wind, dust, etc, to each side of the shield. The latter was thus perfectly closed at the front, top, and sides, the only entrance for air being by way of the one inch of clearance between the shield and the track. To enable the rider to keep the middle of the track a vertical strip of wood 3 inches in width and painted white was nailed to the rear of the car platform. To prevent his wheel from touching the rear of the shield a fender of 1-inch round iron projected rearwardly 2 1/2 feet at a height which would allow the front wheel of the bicycle to pass beneath it, but would cause the head of the machine to bring up against the bar, which was covered with rubber to lessen the shock.

The beginning and the end of the mile were each marked by large flags, one green and one red, and the quarters were marked by white flags, placed on the right hand side of the track. The timers, five in number, were all men who are well-known judges and timers in the various athletic gatherings in the East. They were stationed at the last five open windows of the car... They carried split-seconds stop-watches, and each quarter was taken by two timers to avoid error. In the only case where they differed the referee accepted the slower time.

The rider, who is twenty-eight years old and weighs 154 pounds, was mounted on a Tribune racing wheel, which weighed; 20 1/2 pounds, had 6 1/2-inch cranks, and was geared to 120. For the trial ride, made in 65 seconds, he had used a 112 gear. On the car were Messrs. W.F. Potter, the general superintendent of the railroad; P.D. Ford, the chief engineer; J.H. Cummin, superintendent of bridges and buildings; H.B. Fullerton, who had charge of the trial, together with representatives of the press and several engineers, who were interested in the scientific side of the experiment. In pulling the engine up to a mile-a-minute speed the engineer with one hand on the throttle and the other on the sand-lever, gave the cylinders all the steam they could use without slipping the drivers, the throttle being pulled gradually open to one-half with a 3/4 cut-off. The acceleration was wonderfully rapid, and the first quarter of the mile was made in exactly 15 seconds, the last three-quarters being covered in 14 2/5, 14 2/5, and 14 seconds, or 57 4/5 seconds for the mile. The average speed for the mile was 62:28 miles per hour, and for the last quarter the speed was 64:29 miles per hour.

Murphy kept inside the shield and within a few inches of the iron fender bar until he entered the first quarter when it was noticed that he kept falling a foot or two back and then running up and striking the head of his wheel against the bar. He finally fell back about fifteen feet, and rode for the rest of the mile entirely outside the shell and just ahead of a perfect maelstrom of dust which whirled and eddied behind the shield. Then as the mile flag was passed, he sprinted forward and closed up until he struck the fender when he commenced to climb aboard the car, assisted by those on the platform, the wheel, which was held by the toe-clips, being dragged up with him. This was certainly the first time that anyone over-took and boarded a train going at a speed of over sixty-four miles an hour.

In the trial ride of a week before, it was arranged for the rider to back-pedal when the mile flag was passed, the engineer at the same time making a final spurt to run clear, thereby allowing the resistance of the air to assist the rider in slowing up. This was done; but as should have been foreseen, the violent eddies in the air nearly threw Murphy from his wheel, and it was, no doubt, the determination, to stay within the shield on the second attempt that prevented a fatal accident.

We are informed by the rider that at no time during the ride was he working up to his full power. All went well until he entered the first quarter, when a violent vertical vibration set up in the track, "as though the boards were rapping the bottom of my wheel" At the same time, although he was riding "in perfectly still or dead air," the effort necessary to drive the wheel varied, the effect being as though he were riding over an undulating instead of a level track thinking that the track might be less "lively" further back from the train, he dropped back 15 feet, and here, though a slight wind resistance was felt at his sides, making harder pedaling necessary, the vibration was not nearly so marked. There is no doubt that the vibration and undulating sensation were due to the natural elasticity of a light track under the rapid passage of a 91-ton engine. The rebound of the rail joints after the passage of the train would produce a rapping effect on the plank track, and the "wave-action" of the whole track at such a high speed would easily have a retarding or accelerating effect on anything so light as a bicycle, according as the wave moved to the front or the rear of the rider.

In view of the fact that Murphy assures us he was not riding up to his full power, the question arises as to how fast a bicycle could travel if the proper pace were supplied. Probably on a rock-ballasted track, laid with 100 pound steel, where the vibrations would be greatly reduced, one of the younger racing men who are accustomed to paced riding, or Murphy himself, could cover the mile in 50 or even 45 seconds. Of the three kinds of resistance to bicycle propulsion, the internal friction and the rolling friction ... are very slight in a carefully constructed racing wheel, with the tires inflated to the full limit; and in the recent trial the most serious resistance, that of the atmosphere was entirely wanting. However it is possible that Murphy is right when he says that on a perfectly quiet track a bicyclist can follow any pace the locomotive can set for him. It is more a question of rapidity of pedaling, and a cool head, than of strength and endurance. Although he was using a 120 gear, equivalent, as we showed in the special bicycle number of the SCIENTIFIC AMERICAN of May 13, to a 10-foot driving wheel covering over 31 feet at each revolution of the pedals, the rider was spinning his feet at the rate of 2.91 revolutions a second or 175 revolutions a minute.

Without disparaging in any degree the persistence and pluck of the bicyclist, the most interesting feature of the ride is the impressive object lesson it affords as to the serious nature of atmospheric resistance on moving bodies, a question which is discussed at some length in our editorial columns.

The most prolific American cyclist at the turn of the century was an African-American, Major Taylor, the world record holder at several distances. The Chicago Tribune published accounts of his achievements on 4 August 1899, p. 4, and 17 November 1899, p. 4, before racism proved unbearable. After 1900 he chose to race on European tracks.

TAYLOR MAKES A RECORD
CYCLIST, PACED BY MOTOR, GOES A MILE IN 1:22 2-5.

After repeated trials for the one-mile record, Major Taylor, the colored wonder, whirled around the Garfield track cement path in 1:22 2/5 the fastest time ever made by a rider on a regulation track. Three times Taylor tried to turn the trick at Ravenswood, but Munger's infernal machine was out of order at each attempt. Twice he tried at Garfield Park and failed because of his pace. Yesterday, however, everything was ready. The day was almost at a close, there was not a breath of air stirring, and for the first time the machine was in perfect shape.

At 6 o'clock "Birdie" Munger announced all was ready. A triplet manned by "Jimmy" Bowler, Charles MacCarthy, and Charles Lavin was placed at the south end of the track to catch the streak of ebony if the steam failed. With Taylor tacked on for a little warm-up the motor spun around. The record for the first time seemed in danger, for Munger announced the machine would not fail. He had been working on this arrangement of tubes and boilers ever since he came to Chicago, three weeks ago and has, in spite of continual jeers, been convinced it would go all right, for in the two trials of half a mile each he clipped off the distance in 43 and 41 seconds, the last quarter of the latter trial in 19 1/5 seconds.

Off Like a Flash

After all the officials had been selected, and in their places, Munger nodded for the word go, and motor and rider were off like a flash, fairly flying around the first turn, and to the one-quarter mile pole in 20 1-5 seconds. Taylor's legs worked like the piston rods that drove the motor and tacked behind the flying machine, he hung within a foot of the whirling spokes. The watches registered 39 2-5 seconds for the half mile, the second quarter being done in 19 seconds, which is faster than any rider ever traveled for even a quarter mile record. This terrific clip was kept up to the three-quarter pole which was turned in 59 3-5 seconds, and Taylor looked to be a part of the pacing machine, so close did he cling to the rear of the motor.

As Taylor entered the one-half mile stretch the triplet team was started from the south end of the track and they got under headway fast. They rushed over the bridge on the back stretch, the motor closing on them in a moment's time. They would have made a beautiful pickup, but as the motor was going all right they took the Major only at the home stretch, carrying him to the finish in 1:22 2-5, which is 6 3/5 lower than the world's record.

Taylor finished strong, and it looked as though he could have gone a trifle faster. The colored boy made the turns in wonderful shape. His jackknife position made wind shields unnecessary, and he lay behind W.F. Blanchard throughout the terrible mile seeming hardly to move so fast did he go. Watches on the outside announced the time as 1:21 and 1:22.

Cheers for Taylor.

A cheer went up from the 400 people who witnessed the ride and they fairly swarmed on the track and over to the place where the official timers were when the official time was announced. The crowd made for the colored wonder and escorted him to his dressing-room, congratulating him on all sides. The official time was as follows: Quarter, 20 1/5; half, 39 2/5; three-quarters, 59 3/5: one mile, 1:22 2/3, The following acted as officials: L.A.W. representative, O.C. Dennis; judges, George Leander, Eugene Holway, T.A. Padgett; timers, J.P. Bliss, James Temple, O.N. Stenstrum, T.W. Eck.

When Representative Dennis examined the watches they registered as follows: Bliss, 1:22 2-5; Temple, 1:22 1-5; Stenstrum, 1:22 2-5; Eck, one watch 1:22 2-5 and his other watch 1:22 3-5 Dennis then decided 1:22 2-5 as the one accepted....

TAYLOR'S DAILY RECORD GRIST.
LOWERS THE THIRD MILE AND HALF MILE MARKS AT GARFIELD PARK.

"Major" Taylor added two more world's records to his already creditable list at Garfield Park yesterday afternoon. He now possesses the one-third, one-half, and mile marks.

Taylor captured the third and half mile marks yesterday, when he clipped a fifth of a second from each. They formerly were held by Eddie McDuffie.

Both records were made at the same time, Taylor first going the third mile and continuing to the half.

The third mile was accomplished in :27 1-5, which is one-fifth of a second faster than McDuffie's record of :27 2-5. Taylor made the half mile in :40 1-5, which also beats McDuffie's record of :40 2-5, made at Garfield Park track last Monday.

Three timers were stationed at the third mile post, and the same number at the half....

Taylor intended to go for the two mile record of 3:57, now held by McDuffie, but the wind, which had increased prevented.

To close his day's work Taylor tried for the quarter mile record, but the wind was too strong for even this distance, and the "Major" after going a quarter in :20 2-5 concluded to let the record stand until the conditions were better....

Women, too, gained a measure of recognition for their athletic feats. The "Gibson Girl" and the "new woman" of the 1890s portrayed athletes as healthier, more vivacious, and spirited women, a departure from the fragile Victorian damsel of the past. Female cyclists helped to fashion the new image and the New York Times took notice on 18 September 1899, p. 4.

WOMEN IN CENTURY RUNS.

On the smooth macadam roads of Long Island a little woman on a bicycle flitted hither and thither all day yesterday bent on accomplishing a task which the average woman, or the average man, for that matter, would no more undertake than she or he would attempt to fly. The little woman on the wheel was Miss Jane C. Yatman of Brooklyn, whose century riding feats this season have won her fame in the cycling world. The task which she has set for herself this time is that of riding 700 miles in eighty-four hours or less. Paced by several male riders of speed and endurance, Miss Yatman started at 7 o"clock on Saturday night from the Bedford Rest, Bedford Avenue and Eastern Parkway. Brooklyn, on her long ride. She hopes to finish the ride at the same place either late to-morrow night or early on Wednesday morning.

When the plucky young woman started she had plenty of company besides her pacemakers, the Century Road Club starting out at the same time on a moonlight century run. Miss Yatman is doing most of her riding on the fine triangular course from Valley Stream, along the Merrick Turnpike to Freeport, to Hempstead, and back to Valley Stream through Lynbrook. This course has been measured, and West's Hotel, at Valley Stream, has been made the checking headquarters.

Miss Yatman's present ride is the out-come of an interesting rivalry for century riding honors between herself and Mrs. Jane Lindsay and Mrs. Irene Brush, also of Brooklyn. Mrs. Brush set a mark for her rivals by riding 400 miles in forty-eight hours. A few weeks later Miss Yatman eclipsed this performance by riding 500 miles in fifty-eight hours. But this record didn't stand, for soon afterward Mrs. Lindsay broke it by riding 600 miles in seventy-two hours. And now Miss Yatman is bent upon regaining her lost laurels by pedaling 700 miles in eighty-four hours. If Miss Yatman succeeds, even this record may be broken by Mrs. Brush, who is preparing herself for a still longer ride. Mrs. Brush, about two weeks from now, will attempt to ride 1,000 miles in five days, doing the first 600 miles in sixty hours, then after a rest of twelve hours, riding the remaining 400 miles in forty hours.

GOOD ROADS MOVEMENT

The League of American Wheelmen crusaded not only for the right to use roads; but for better roads on which to pursue their interests. Charles E. Pratt, league president and a lawyer, carried the matter to court. In an 1880 test case versus the Haddenfield, New Jersey turnpike, the LAW won the right to use the roadway. In 1883 it succeeded in opening New York's Central Park and Riverside Drive to cyclists. By 1887 its widespread "liberty bill" movement provided access to state roads and parkways. Pratt provided a history of LAW successes and its rationale in an Outing article, May 1887, pp. 157-161.

LEGISLATION AS TO BICYCLES IN HIGHWAYS.

... For more than twenty years bicycles have been used as vehicles on our American roads. It is ten years since the renaissance of bicycling began to send the more modern and better perfected wheel as a swift and easy carrier of young and middle-aged men about all our cities and through all our States. And yet the inexpert might look in vain through most of our State statute books for any "law of the land" upon this particular carriage. In two or three States, indeed, he would find special local statutes; but these are interesting chiefly as curiosities or absurdities of legislation; they are neither of them in a legal sense, law of the land in those States....

Public roads are the oldest monuments of civilization; memorials of one of the oldest rights. Before all bills of rights and constitutions and legislatures in this country, were highways and the common right of travel therein. There are three provisions in our State constitutions, and one or more in the Federal, which guarantee the right of the wheelman to ride his bicycle in every public road of the United States. And as these muniments of title to the roads are not always kept in view, it may be worth while to refer briefly to them here. In the State constitutions are reserved to the people the right peaceably to assemble, the right to possession and enjoyment of property, and immunity from being deprived of any common fundamental right, unless by the law of the land. Now, carriages are private property, and the enjoyment of them is in their use of travel. There can be no assembling without travel, and the public highway is the only place for lawful travel....

It requires some reflection to realize how much the existence and the genius of our institutions of government and social order presupposes the existence of highways and the common inalienable right of travel therein. And this right of travel includes the right of movement on foot, on horse, with carriage, or in any reasonable manner; and is coextensive with the limits of the United States; to move without unreasonable restriction with person, conveyance, and property from one extremity of this broad land to another, in any direction, into and over the lines of towns, counties and States.

How well, indeed, this right is recognized in all lands, is illustrated in the course of Thomas Stevens' remarkable tour of the world on a bicycle. Whatever other vicissitudes he met with, no one in any tongue disputed his right to travel. And yet, an American explorer, with an American vehicle, backed by American enterprise, representing an American magazine, and winning for America the results of his indomitable energy in his whole circuit of the earth could find his only prohibition of travel on the meridian of our own Atlantic coast. From Wilmington, North Carolina, to the sea, he could not ride on his own proper and universally possible carriage!...

The key to the law of bicycling, not only constitutional, but legislative, which we now come to consider, lies in the fact that the bicycle is a carriage.... No correct definition of carriage or vehicle can be found or framed, or could have been found or framed, fifty years or a century ago, that will not include the most modern bicycle.... Only make the wheelman and the non-wheelman appreciate this fact at its value, that the bicycle is a carriage, and the bicycler a wagoner, and most of the misunderstandings and friction will disappear. The present status of wheelmen as to rights and remedies is then easily understood.

The law of highways is simple and clear. Every person has an equal right with every other to use any public highway at any time for travel, either on foot, on beast, or with any vehicle or conveyance by which he simply passes over the road and leaves it reasonably undisturbed for the next passer; and upon every traveler rests the duty of so using the road as not to injure or unreasonably impede any other who may be exercising the same right and observing the same duty thereon. This is the sum of all statutes and decisions throughout this country. All other laws are but regulations as to direction, speed, warning or other requirement for the common safety....

The present and almost universal legislative regulations of travel applicable to bicycling are that the carriage shall be in roadworthy condition; that the rider shall turn to the right of the middle of the roadway on meeting another and allow passage on the left when overtaken by another who wishes to pass; exercise reasonable care to prevent collision; yield reasonably to a more heavily loaded team, and use reasonable care in respect to foot-passenger crossings....

The first special statute relating to the bicycle in this country was obtained in the Kentucky Legislature a few years ago, practically prohibiting bicycling in certain counties of that State. Of course it was not constitutional, and is not "law of the land" for two reasons,-discriminating unequally against certain travelers, and not applying to the whole State.... But a more serious instance of special legislation occurred two years ago in North Carolina. The Wilmington and Coast Turnpike Company quietly obtained the passage of an act amending their charter to the effect that "no person shall use upon the roads of said Company a bicycle, or tricycle, or other non-horse vehicle, without the express permission of the Superintendent of said road." This extraordinary delegation of authority used as it is as an absolute prohibition, was promptly challenged by the local wheelmen of Wilmington, who, with the backing of the League of American Wheelmen, have brought the matter before the Supreme Court of that State, where it is still waiting decision on questions of constitutionality.... When a bill restricting bicycling was presented to the Ohio Legislature, it was rejected on preliminary consideration, as not only unconstitutional, but as against equitable right and good public policy....

One other mischievous piece of present legislation exists in Oregon, where a rash regulation is made oppressive to the wheelmen, without being of any advantage to the remainder of the public. Unreasonable everywhere, in the cities it is substantially prohibitive. That law requires every bicycle rider to dismount one hundred yards in front of any approaching team, and to remain so until it has passed. That the non-wheelmen may appreciate the bearing of this regulation, let him imagine that every horseback rider is required to dismount one hundred yards before he reaches any crossing and walk by it, in order that foot-passers may not be what?-trampled upon? no; may not be frightened! ...

In the large cities of Chicago, St. Louis, Philadelphia, Baltimore, Boston and San Francisco, these questions of the rights of wheelmen and of reasonable regulation have long since been considered and acted upon, in more or less practical consistency with the principles of law and justice. Nowhere else, as in the State of New York, are public parkways controlled so much as if they belonged to the owners of private and livery stables instead of to the whole people. In Prospect Park, Brooklyn, wheelmen have for years been allowed to ride, but, singularly enough, they were relegated to the sidewalks and foot-paths, instead of the carriage-ways. Recently the Commissioners have restricted them from all riding in this park, excepting the west side route to Coney Island. The Commissioners of the Central Park in New York some years ago passed an order that no bicycle or tricycle be allowed in that park. Several gentlemen were arrested for violation of the ordinance, and a rather unique and celebrated case arose in the courts, popularly known as the "Central Park Case." That case began in a mistake and ended in a virtual withdrawal; but while both the unconstitutional and u*ltra vires* ordinance and the strange suit were pending, there occurred an annual meet of the League of American Wheelmen in New York City. The Park Commissioners courteously gave them the freedom of the parkways. A thousand bicycles took their noise-less way through the drives that day, to the equal pleasure of thousands of pedestrians, equestrians and occupants of more costly carriages, without an accident or an annoy-ance. And after that the Riverside drive was open to wheelmen, and in the main park more privileges [nay, rights!] were accorded them than they had ever asked for, lim-ited and restricted though they were.

But justice is not done. Such use as is permitted to bicyclers and tricyclers within certain hours and on certain ways, is accorded as a privilege and not as a right, and would anywhere else be considered substantially prohibitive. The parkways are con-trolled principally in the interest of the wealthy and the stablekeepers. The owners and drivers of other vehicles than velocipedes are unjustly excluded; the honest tradesman who uses his horse and wagon to earn a living through the week, and who would give his team a few extra brushes, and put in another seat of a Sunday and take his family to drive amidst the beauties his earnings have helped to pay for, is turned away. Room for varnish and livery. Style and influence in the park. Horses, a million dollars, or a deal in votes, are these only to move a Park Board's action to justice? Perhaps the hundred ladies with tricycles living near Central Park, and denied its privileges except at unreasonable hours, might gain a recognition of their rights, but the two thousand gentlemen have so far failed....

A Harper's Weekly piece, 11 April 1896, p. 362, detailed the influences of cycling on road building.

THE BICYCLE'S RELATION TO GOOD ROADS

The first concerted movement for improved roads within the United States must be credited to the wheelmen....

Now and then, to be sure, a stray article appeared in some American newspaper in which a wheelman writer gave words to his belief in the general need of better high-ways; but it was not until 1889 that the League of American Wheelmen appointed its first committee on Improvement of the Highways, and adopted a by-law in which the duties of this committee were defined.... The new committee went vigorously about its work by first publishing a convenient little hand-book on the general subject of road-making, of which the first edition of 20,000 copies was soon exhausted by free distri-bution. Following this came "The Gospel of God Roads," an illustrated pamphlet con-taining a collection of half-tone pictures from photographs showing the marvelous contrast between the roads of Europe and those of our own country with about sixty pages of text and statistical tables.... Sixty thousand copies of the "Gospel" had been distributed, and several newspapers had reproduced it in their pages for special use among their farmer readers. The executive officers of the League came together in

November, 1891, and after carefully reviewing the work done, and gauging the probable field of work for the future, established Goo*d Roads Magazine*, an illustrated publication of which about a million copies were distributed during the three following years....

What have been the practical results? ...

Within the last three years sixteen of our States have passed laws looking to the betterment of their public roads. California has now a State commission, or "Bureau of Highways," appointed to visit the several counties gather and compile statistics, hold public meetings, and publish information by means of periodical bulletins. Connecticut has a State Board of Highway Commissioners appointed to approve specifications, supervise road construction, and make reports. One-third the cost of construction of new roads is borne by the State, and a like proportion by the town and by the county. Iowa has passed a law providing that all unused building and refuse stone shall be broken by convicts in the State penitentiary, and that the broken stone shall be distributed among the counties in lots of ten car-loads each on application by the county supervisors to the warden:

The new road law in Kentucky provides that all persons in county jails and workhouses under sentence of hard labor may be required to work on the public roads. In Massachusetts the Legislature of 1893 passed an act providing for a permanent State Highway Commission, and for the construction of State roads under its direction. The members of this commission are all members of the League of American Wheelmen, and have been prominent in urging the advance of the movement from its beginning....

New Jersey supplies another example of the splendid impetus and good results given to the work for good roads by the beneficent provision for State aid supplied under the general law. Under the New Jersey law of 1891 the owners of two-thirds of the property fronting on any public highway (being at least one mile in length) may petition the board of chosen freeholders for the construction of an improved road, and in case the petition is granted only one-tenth of the cost is paid by the owners, one-third by the State, and the balance by the county....

The relation of the bicycle to good roads is therefore a most direct and important one, and the influence of the bicycle had doubtless been more potent than any other factor in bringing about the results thus far obtained. Upon every essential point affecting good roads legislation and road construction all well informed cyclists are substantially agreed, and more than ninety per cent of the expert road builders and success agitators for better roads in America are found among the ranks of the wheelmen....

Almost equal in value to the good road surface, and of great importance to the touring wheelman, is a knowledge of routes and distances. To supply this knowledge, as well as to indicate the quality and direction of each of the several different roads within the State, the wheelmen have prepared road books and maps for the use of the members of their several State organizations.

Touring is the cyclist's popular diversion. So popular, indeed, is it becoming that many a country hostlery, almost abandoned a decade ago for want of patrons has taken new life to itself and assumed the vigor of a new prosperity. From every populous centre each Sunday and public holiday takes thousands of cyclists of both sexes into the pleasant highways and byways of the surrounding country, and the keen strife to

which country innkeepers lend themselves in their effort to hold the wheeling patronage is shown in no better way than by the numerous special sign-boards and "official
hotel" advertisements by which the host so often seeks to lure the touring cyclist.

The rejuvenation of the old tavern is one of the happy incidents of cycling growth.
It insures to the country a greater joy and a stronger life, takes away much of its lone-
someness, brings many of the people of city and country into closer touch with one
another, insures an interchange of benefits, and helps the development of that undevel-
oped section of every county which becomes only the more pronounced in its unde-
veloped appearance as one proceeds outward from the populous town....

And so it shall come to pass that when all our farmers ride bicycles the country road
will reach the full splendor of its excellence, and when all our merchants and manufacturers are wheelmen the street pavements of the town will be made fitly to co-operate with the wagon wheel in the movement of merchandise. And then will the great
mission of the bicycle have due acknowledgment, and the efforts of the wheelman for
better roads be placed in the schedule of things that are not altogether selfish.

ISSUES

Cycling generated issues other than that of roads. Physicians, mostly male, aired their
concerns relative to the advantages or disadvantages of cycling on women's health.
Others were more bothered by the participation of women in a speed or power sport
and the dress reforms, such as the wearing of pants or bloomers, that symbolically
threatened their masculine status.

Physicians warned of various maladies caused by cycling, such as deformities,
bowed legs, over-enlargement of leg muscles, and overexertion of the heart. The following reprint from Scientific American, 1 July 1893, p. 10, provides a typical example.

KYPHOSIS BICYCLISTARUM.

One evil traceable to bicycling is the confirmed stoop which has already declared
itself in many wheelmen, a result so common in the less strongly built bicyclists of the
Continent as to have found its way into classification as the "kyphosis bicyclistarum."

The dorsal curvature posteriorly, which used to be rare in boys under 14 years of
age, is now that the bicycle is so largely used, very frequently met with, particularly
among those young bicyclists whose spinal column is developing more rapidly than the
ligaments and muscles, and in whose case, therefore, the equilibrium between those
parts is more or less disturbed.

Were it merely an unsightly deformity, the stoop in question ought to be combated
in every way; but confirmed dorsal curvature posteriorly has consequences of its own

quite mischievous enough to call for immediate counteraction. The displacement, embarrassed functional activity, and arrested or diseased development of these organs, which kyphosis inevitably induces are all too serious to warrant the slightest neglect in remedying them.

Exercise of a kind to accustom the spinal column to an action directly antagonistic to the inclination forward of the bicyclist's attitude is what is needed. The use of the Indian clubs or such similar means of incurvating the spine anteriorly, throwing out the chest and maintaining the head erect, should be practiced with that object. All the undoubted advantages of bicycling may thus be retained, without that cultivation of the stoop which tends to take a cubit from the stature of its inveterate exponents and to impose a hunchbacked development on what it would then be a figure of speech to call the rising generation.-*Lancet.*

Women's cycling attire also engendered controversy. Some municipalities even outlawed the wearing of pants or bloomers; but women were able to circumvent such prohibitions when Hilda S. Peterson invented a cycling clip that gathered skirts in the same fashion. The following selections, reprinted from the Atlanta Constitution, 14 July 1895, p. 14; and the Chicago Tribune, 31 July 1895, p. 6, respectively, present more than the practical difficulties.

NO BLOOMERS THERE
MAYOR OCHS, OF CHATTANOOGA, WANTS THEM KEPT OFF THE STREETS.
HE DOES NOT THINK THEY ARE MODEST
AN ORDINANCE IS TO BE INTRODUCED IN COUNCIL PROVIDING
A FINE FOR WOMEN WEARING THEM OUTDOORS.

Chattanooga, Tenn. July 12-(Special)- Municipal matters in the city of Chattanooga are engineered on a 16 to 1 ratio- that is, sixteen aldermen and one mayor. The mayor has laid wake nights during his term of office and concocted many sensations to let the people know, perhaps that he was not a figurehead in the celectial chair, but he never dreamed of such a sensation as Alderman Crabtree will spring at the next meeting of the council. Mr. Crabtree is a young man, and a handsome young man at that. He sells farms and makes lots of money. The girls admire him for his good looks and want him for his money. He was born in Georgia and in the country, and though rather up-to-date himself is violently opposed to the creeds of the new woman. When he saw a leading society woman go down the street on a bicycle in bloomers the other day he was, therefore, deeply pained. He pondered the evil tendency of the times, and finally drew up the following ordinance against bloomers, which he will present for passage at the next meeting of the council:

"Be it ordained by the board of mayor and aldermen of the city of Chattanooga, that from and after this date that the wearing of bloomers by females shall be prohibited upon the public streets of the city of Chattanooga.

"Be it further ordained that this board does declare that the wearing of the said bloomers or bifurcated garment in plain view is a menace to the peace and good morals of the male residents of the city.

"Be it further ordained that any one violating the ordinance or any part of it shall be subject to a fine of not less than $5 or more than $50; said fine to be assessed by the city recorder upon the conviction of a defendant.

"Be it further ordained, that all ordinances or parts of ordinances in conflict with this ordinance are hereby repealed, and that it takes effect from and after its passage, the public welfare requiring it."

BLOOMERS IN THE SANCTUARY.

The theory of the Rev. Mr. Hawthorne of Atlanta, Ga., that women ride bicycles and wear bloomers because a personal devil has possessed them who spurs them on from one dreadful act to another seems to be borne out by what happened last Sunday in a small Ohio town, the home of a peaceable and religious community.

A young and accomplished woman was the organist of the Methodist church of the place. For two years she had filled that difficult position to the satisfaction of the congregation. Satan saw with displeasure the peacefulness of the town and the serenity of the congregation and he set to work to destroy both by means of his favorite weapon, the bicycle, and he seems to have succeeded.

First he put it into the head of the organist to buy a bicycle. It is only the first step that costs. Not long after that she appeared in public in aggressively red bloomers. There are some eccentricities which cannot be tolerated, even in an organist. This was one of them. Last week a delegation called on the minister and requested him to preach a sermon denouncing bloomers. He failed to do so. Then he was given his choice-either to bear testimony against the red trousers of the organist or to leave the church.

The probabilities are that the organist, who is comely, had found favor in the eyes of the minister, and that he was called on to choose between giving up his sweetheart and his church. For while he may not have approved of the bloomers, he must have felt that denunciation of them in open meeting would lead to an estrangement. No woman can be expected to stand such treatment as that.

The prayer-meeting evening came. The minister was in his pulpit and his grieved parishioners were in their places. Down the aisle, through the horrified audience, strode the organist in her scarlet bloomers, took her seat at the organ, and began to play. Most of the members rose up and fled from the polluted sanctuary. The minister, the organist, and a few others remained, and went through the services. Ordinarily the inhabitants of this little town are abed and asleep by 10, but not so that eventful day. "At midnight," says the dispatch, "the streets were still alive with people discussing the event."

The bicycle had done its deadly work. The church is rent in twain. The minister has wandered off after strange gods. The peace of the community had departed. Satan alone is happy. This fall the general convention of the Methodist Church is to be held. It ought to speak out in no uncertain tone on this bicycle question. It should banish bloomers from the churches and should forbid the wearing of them by organists, choir, singers, and all church members under any circumstances. A new danger threatens. Daily the news may come of the invasion and disruption of other congregations by the bicycle. The convention must act.

The following article, written from a woman's perspective, expresses some of the lure in cycling. It appeared in Athletic Sports, 1897.

WOMAN AND THE BICYCLE

The collocation of woman and the bicycle has not wholly outgrown controversy; but if the woman's taste be for the royal pleasure of glowing exercise in sunlit air, she will do well quietly but firmly to override argument with the best model of a wheel to which she may lay hand....

Once purchased, it needs only to be stabled in a passageway, and fed on oil and air.... The woman of affairs has learned that an hour, or even half an hour, may be stolen from the working day, with profit to both woman and affairs.... An hour of the wheel means sixty minutes of fresh air and wholesome exercise, and at least eight miles of change of scene; it may well be put down to the credit side of the day's reckoning with flesh and spirit.

Like all costumes, the regimentals of the wheel are affected by locality and racial prejudice....

In cosmopolitan New York the eye of the spectator has long become wonted to costumes of all kinds. Bloomer and tailor-made alike ride on unchallenged; tunicked and gaitered Rosalinds excite no more comment than everyday people in everyday clothers. Knickerbockers and the skirt composed of twin filibegs have their advocates; Pinero's youngest Amazon has set a pretty fashion for the girl cyclist, and many riders make their records in the conventional walking-dress with cone-shaped skirt worn over the silk trousers of an odalisk, or the satin breeks of an operatic page.... So far the large majority of American women have declared in favor of the skirt in one form or another. Short rides on level roads can be accomplished with but slight modification of ordinary attire; and the sailor-hat, shirt-waist, serge-skirt uniform, is as much at home on the bicycle as it is anywhere else the world over. The armies of women clerks in Chicago and Washington who go by wheel to business, show that the exercise within bounds need not impair the spick-and spandy neatness that marks the bread-winning American girl. On the excursion a special adaptation of dress is absolutely necessary; for skirts, while they have not hindered women from climbing to the topmost branches of the higher education, may prove fatal in down-hill coasting; and skirts, unless frankly shortened or discarded, must be fashioned so as to minimize the danger of entanglement with the flying wheel.

The pastime does not lend itself to personal display; and in criticism the costume must be referred, not to the standards of the domestic hearthrug, but to the exigencies of the wheel, the rider's positions to the mechanical demands of the motion....

Regarding bicycling purely as exercise, there is an advantage in the symmetry of development it brings about, and a danger in riding too fast and far. The occasional denunciation of the pastime as unwormanly is fortunately lost in the general approval that a new and wholesome recreation has been found, whose pursuit adds joy and vigor to the dowry of the race....

TECHNOLOGY

The machines produced by relentless technological advancement fascinated Americans. Science held the potential to overcome natural limits, and the bicycle, a relatively simple machine accessible to many, brought individuals to such a realization through the ability to provide rapid self-propulsion.

The Scientific American enthusiastically recorded such improvements in a number of articles: 13 May 1899, p. 292; and 14 July 1900, p. 27.

THE CHARM OF THE BICYCLE.

The philosophers tell us that one of the most powerful motives that govern human life is the love of power...

It is when we consider the modern pastime of bicycling, however, that we meet with the most striking exhibition of the strength of this desire to do much and do it with comparatively little effort. It is because the bicycle enables us to travel so far afield with such an astonishing small expenditure of effort that it has achieved its sudden and world-wide popularity. Of course, there are other contributory causes, such as the desire for exercise; the opportunity given to those who cannot afford to keep a carriage to get out into the scenes and sweet air of the country; and to many people the saving of time and expense in transacting their daily business; but these considerations alone do not account probably for one-tenth of the millions of people who day by day and week by week are to be found reeling off the miles with a persistence which might make one suppose that wheeling was as necessary a part of their existence as breathing or the circulation of the blood-and to not a few of them, indeed, it is as necessary.

Fresh air, green fields, the song of birds, the ever changing panorama of the countryside, the quickened sensibilities of mind and body all are accessory pleasures of the wheel; but the deep, underlying charm of it all is the sense of achieving this swift motion at as little expenditure of effort as would be necessary in walking for half a dozen blocks in a city thoroughfare. Who will ever forget his first bona fide country ride on a good level road, undertaken as soon as the problems of equilibrium had been mastered, and the thrill of exultation with which he found that the same muscular effort which moved him at three miles an hour on his legs, is now sufficient to carry him at twelve miles an hour on his wheel. The result seems so absurdly disproportioned to the effort, as to create a half belief that one's own physical strength must have redoubled. Certain it is that one's sense of power is most pleasurably affected, and the persistent protest of the mind against the inertia of things material is silenced for the while.

And, after all, speaking of the inertia of things, the bicycle is only one expression of the great world-struggle of mind to overcome the inertia of matter.

The history of the arts and sciences, and especially of those which concern travel and intercommunication, is the history of man's successful effort to set in motion the latent energies, the inert masses of nature, and hence there is a strict relation between the development of transportation and the growth of our material wealth and comfort. The craze for "breaking the record," whether it be on the train, the steamship, or the wheel, is prompted by something more than the mere love of the spectacular; for the world recognizes that every new performance is a further breaking away from that universal stagnation in which all matter lay before its present evolution began-a stagnation which it is the constant effort of out modern arts and sciences to overcome.

A CALIFORNIA CYCLEWAY.
By Charles Frederick Holder.

Among the many new constructions that are to be seen in Southern California none are of more practical interest than the Pasadena cycleway, now nearing completion and already opened to the public for bicycles and motorcycles. Southern California has especial attractions to the wheelman, as the season is the whole year.... This fact and the assurance of good roads all over the State brings out numbers of wheelmen, and a conservative estimate places the wheels in Los Angeles and Pasadena, resident and visiting, at thirty thousand, and the inventors of wheels at five thousand.

The Pasadena and Los Angeles cycleway is a movement to provide the wheelman with a perfect road, with a minimum grade between two cities nine miles apart and at different altitudes. The inventor and promotor of the novel scheme is a wealthy resident and trustee of the city of Pasadena, Mr. Horace Dobbins, he being the president of the company, the vice-president is ex-Governor H.H. Markham. The cycleway, which it is believed is the only one of its kind in the world, is an elevated perfectly adjusted road running from the heart of Pasadena to the plaza of Los Angeles. In appearance it somewhat resembles the elevated road in New York, being apparently as high in places; but it is built of wood instead of iron, yet strong enough to bear the equipment and car service of an electric road.... but a few days ago an automobile owned by a resident of Pasadena, was run out upon the cycleway and went speeding toward Los Angeles under the most perfect conditions; and it was evident that if the road permitted an automobile to run upon it, it would soon become very popular-a literal sky route to Los Angeles for these vehicles.

A critical examination of the cycleway is interesting, showing it to be a somewhat remarkable piece of engineering. The proposition has been to give wheelmen a grade from Los Angeles to Pasadena up hill and a decided rise at that which will not be appreciable, and this has been accomplished. The roadway ranges from 3 to 50 feet in height, giving a maximum grade of but three per cent; and this but for two thousand feet; at all other points it will not be greater than 1 1/4 per cent.... It is at present wide enough to hold four wheels abreast, and has the right of way for a duplication in width. The timber used in the construction is Oregon pine; 1,250,000 feet were required to complete it, and twenty miles of heavy wire netting.

At intervals of 200 feet over the center, incandescent lights are being placed, which at night will convert the cycleway into a gleaming serpent. The terminal stations are Moorish in design; one being placed near the Hotel Green in the business center of Pasadena, and the other at the plaza in Los Angeles. At these buildings, which will be equipped with the facilities of a railway depot, will be a department for renting bicycles and motorcycles; also a repair shop. So one may rent a wheel at Pasadena, and run down to Los Angeles and leave it there if desired, or vice versa; or a motorcycle can be taken at either city, leaving the cycleway and carrying the passenger to any part of the city.

The route of the road was selected by the inventor with great care, and as a result of several years work in securing rights of way and legislative action.... Merlemount, as the casino is called, stands in the center of a part of one hundred acres, reached from the cycleway by walks, wheel or motorcycle. This is being laid out into walks and various conveniences for wheelmen. The casino itself will be delightful in its beauty of situation and equipment. The building will be 200 feet in length, surrounded by a broad piazza and protected by a wealth of tropical and semi-tropical plants. At one end will be a circular rack for ladies' wheels and a ladies' waiting room fitted up in the Turkish fashion. Besides these there will be reception rooms, cafe and restaurant, while part of the basement is to be a Swiss dairy complete in all its furnishings....

The cost of this cycleway is insignificant when everything is considered, being but $187,500. The toll is ten cents by book tickets between Pasadena and Los Angeles (eighteen miles), the park and other features being free. This toll permits a bicycle or motorcycle to enter the cycleway, and ride up and down all day, if desired. It has been estimated that if half of the wheelmen in the two cities patronize the road once a month it will give the cycleway an income of $20,000 per year, which would seem a very conservative estimate as the roads on Sunday between Los Angeles and Pasadena are often filled with wheelmen, who ride through the dust, taking the heavy grade between the cities without question; and that the majority of them would choose the perfectly smooth road is without doubt. It is to be hoped that the cycleway will be the financial success, as it promises to be a boon to thousands of devotees of the wheel in Southern California and, doubtless, will be the initiative for such roadways all over the country-certainly in the vicinity of the large cities.

CANADA

Like the United States, cycling took hold in Canada as well. The Montreal Bicycle Club was formed in 1878 and it soon assumed great importance in Canadian sporting life. In 1881 the Montreal Bicycle Club joined with the Lacrosse and Snowshoe Clubs of that city to form the Montreal Athletic Association. By 1884 it had assumed national status as the Canadian Amateur Athletic Association and the major promoter of sport in Canada.

The Canadian Wheelmen's Association organized in 1882, shortly after that of the United States. Canadian cycling assumed international proportions when Montreal hosted the World Bicycle Meet in 1899.

Chapter 7

BOWLING

Bowling has a long history dating back to antiquity. Bowling implements have been discovered in an Egyptian tomb from 5200 BC. By the middle ages the game enjoyed widespread popularity in Europe. It was practiced in many regional variations from lawn bowling to skittles. Colonists brought the many varieties to America; but the game, often centered in taverns, came into disrepute for the gambling associated with it. Colonial bans, and later, those imposed by states proved unenforceable. The game of tenpins reportedly originated when an innovative bowler circumvented the prohibition on ninepins by adding a pin in a triangle rather than a diamond configuration.

In 1875 nine bowling clubs in New York city and Brooklyn presumptively formed the National Bowling Association and offered a set of rules. The game was played largely in private clubs, and particularly, among German-Americans in their beer halls and Turnvereins over the next twenty years. The National Bowling Association evolved into the American Bowling League with a new set of rules by 1890. The newly organized American Amateur Bowling Union adopted the new rules; but failed to eliminate the prize money associated with bowling matches and professionalism. Factionalism over the professional issue resulted in a revolt by 1895, when a group of New Yorkers held a series of summer meetings that culminated in the founding of the American Bowling Congress on 9 September 1895. The ABC convention standardized rules and equipment that remain largely intact, with the exception of hard rubber balls which have replaced wooden ones.

In January 1896 the Quebec Bowling League joined other affiliates in the United States in the ABC membership, and other Canadian leagues followed. The ABC issued a new constitution and by-laws in 1897. Their publication and distribution, as well as the ABC rules, were financed by equipment manufacturers who stood to profit from their adoption. With standardization of the rules inter-city matches increased. By 1899 manufacturers sent an all-star team on a twenty-four city tour throughout the East and Midwest. By the summer of 1900 the United States and Canada engaged in international competition at Union Hill, New Jersey. During the week of 15 July 1900 an international tournament held in New York City included duckpin, candlepin, headpin, and ten pin bowling. On 14 September 1900 the ABC initiated its annual tournament in Chicago with individual, doubles and team championships.

The ABC Constitution and By-Laws are a reprint of the 1903 edition. The rules are largely unchanged from the 1897 and 1899 versions; but the new document unified the myriad local associations under a strong, national, executive body.

AMERICAN BOWLING CONGRESS, CONSTITUTION AND BY-LAWS

ARTICLE 1
Name

This organization shall be known as the American Bowling Congress.

ARTICLE 2
Objects

The American Bowling Congress is formed for the following objects and purposes:

1. To provide, adopt and enforce for and among its members, uniform rules and regulations governing the manner and method of playing the game of American Ten Pins.

2. To provide, adopt and enforce uniform qualifications and conditions governing regulation tournaments and match games of the game of American Ten Pins, and fixing and determining by rules and regulations, the qualifications to be required of all bowlers, clubs, leagues and associations participating therein, and to hold, conduct and manage annually, either directly or under its direction and auspices, a National Tournament of the game of American Ten Pins.

3. The Congress shall have power to sanction special tournaments or match games of the game of American Ten Pins, provided that such tournaments or games are conducted and managed in full compliance with the rules and regulations of the Congress, and comply in all respects with the requirements of the Executive Committee of the Congress.

It shall also have power to issue in all proper cases and in the manner provided by the rules adopted for such purpose by the Executive Committee, certificates to the owners or lessees of alleys certifying therein that the alleys so certified are in all respects constructed in compliance with the rules and regulations of the Congress, and to receive and collect therefor a proper fee to be fixed and determined by the Executive Committee and in compliance with this Constitution.

4. To encourage and foster among its members and all bowlers in general, the spirit of good fellowship; to maintain and increase the interest in the bowling game, and to have and exercise a general care, supervision and direction over all bowling interests in the United States.

ARTICLE 3
Membership and Organization

Section 1. The American Bowling Congress shall be the National body in Bowling affairs, and it shall be a representative, legislative and executive body. Its membership shall be composed of Bowling Associations, represented in the parent body by delegates and alternates, elected to such office by and from regularly organized Bowling Associations, composed and organized in manner provided by this Constitution.

Section 2. The Congress, through its Executive Committee, shall organize or adopt in and for each City or Town in the United States, one central Association as subsidiary and auxiliary to this organization, except that in the City of Greater New York such organizations may be organized or adopted by Boroughs of one or more Boroughs each, as may be determined by the Executive Committee of the Congress.

Section 3. Such association shall be composed of such Bowling Clubs in their respective jurisdictions as are regularly organized in manner provided by the laws of this Congress, and such associations must have a Constitution and laws providing for their regular organization, the election of their officers, which shall in no manner conflict with the provisions of this Constitution, laws or regulations of this Congress. Such associations shall be named after the City, Town, or Borough in which they are organized, and such City, Town or Borough shall be the limit of their jurisdiction.

Section 4. Each association shall, on or before October 1, 1903, and each year thereafter, elect from its members as its representatives to the Congress one delegate and one alternate, and for each ten clubs or major part thereof in its membership over the first ten clubs, such association shall be entitled to an additional delegate and alternate. The terms of office of such delegates and alternates to begin with the date of the annual meeting of the Congress following such election, and to continue for one year from such date. Such delegates and alternates shall be elected annually for the term of one year, as provided above, at least thirty (30) days prior to the annual meeting of this organization, and the names and addresses of such delegates and alternates shall, within ten (10) days after their election, be certified to the Secretary of this Congress, by the President and Secretary thereof.

ARTICLE 4
Admission to Membership

Section 1. All regularly-organized Bowling Associations in the United States, the members of which hold annual club, league, city or state tournaments of the game of American Ten Pins, or engage in regular weekly or bi-weekly practice of such game, and whose tournaments and games are conducted and played in full compliance with the rules and regulations of this Congress, shall, subject to the provisions of this Constitution, be eligible to membership in this organization.

Section 2. Such organizations shall be admitted to membership by a majority vote of the Executive committee, upon written application made by and through its Board of Directors or managing body, but no application shall be approved unless the required dues and all other fees provided by the rules of the Congress shall accompany the application.

Section 3. uch associations shall remain members of this organization so long as they comply with the rules, regulations and constitution of the Congress, and maintain their individual organization.

Section 4. The several associations shall, through their secretaries, mail to the Secretary of the Congress a complete and correct list of the names and addresses of the President, Secretary, and Treasurer of such association, and of the clubs comprised in its membership, and notice in writing shall be given the Secretary of any and all changes occurring thereafter.

ARTICLE 5
Management

Section 1. The management shall be vested in the Congress composed of the delegates and alternates elected by and from the several associations, and such body shall be known as the American Bowling Congress.

Section 2. The Congress shall have full control and management of all the affairs of this organization, and shall carry out and enforce all the objects and purposes for which it is organized, and shall have full power to adopt, amend or rescind rules and regulations governing the manner and method of playing the game of American Ten Pins, and shall provide and define the qualifications of all participants therein.

Section 3. The Congress shall have full power to hear and determine all protests arising from or under a construction of the rules of the Congress and its decision thereon shall be final. The Congress shall have original and appellate jurisdiction over all violations of the rules and regulations of this organization, and shall have power to suspend, expel or otherwise discipline any bowler, league, association or club identified with this organization, or of any tournament association, owner or lessee of any alley sanctioned or certified by this Congress, for all violations of the terms of any sanction or certificate so issued.

The Congress shall have appellate jurisdiction of all matters taken to it by appeal from any decision of a Bowling Association wherein are involved questions pertaining to the proper construction of any of the rules, regulations or provisions of the Constitution of the Congress, and its decision thereon shall be final. For the purpose of determining all such matters the Congress may through its Secretary issue to the several parties and witnesses its citation to appear at the hearing of the questions in controversy, and may also inspect the records and papers involved in the case.

Section 4. The Congress shall name from among its members such committees as may from time to time be deemed necessary.

Section 5. At all meetings of the Congress, the regularly elected and certified delegates to the Congress shall act as such, and during the absence of any delegate his duly elected and certified alternate shall act in his stead, provided that should both the delegate and alternate be absent, then the other delegates present representing such association may select from the other alternates of such association who are present one who shall act in the place of the absent delegate and alternate.

Voting by proxy shall in no case be permitted at any of the meetings of the Congress or of the Executive Committee.

ARTICLE 6
Officers and their Duties

Section 1. The officers of the Congress shall consist of a President, a first, second and third Vice Presidents, a Secretary and a Treasurer, and such officers together with nine other members shall constitute the Executive Committee. The Secretary may by consent of the Executive Committee name such assistants as are deemed necessary, who shall be entitled assistant secretaries, but they shall not, ex-officio, be members of the Executive Committee.

Section 2. The officers of the Congress and the members of the Executive Committee shall be elected by ballot, at the annual meeting of the Congress, and they shall hold their respective offices for the term of one year, and until their successors are elected and qualified. Vacancies occurring in such offices, either by death, resignation or otherwise, shall be filled by election of the Executive Committee, and the person or persons so elected shall fill the unexpired term of the office to which he has been elected.

Section 3. The President shall preside at all meetings of the Congress and of the Executive Committee. He shall sign all warrants drawn on the Treasurer ordered paid by the Executive Committee. He shall appoint the members of all committees created unless otherwise provided in the motion ordering such committee to be named. He shall be the Chief Executive of the Congress, and as such shall enforce all the provisions, objects and purposes thereof. He shall also perform such other duties as pertain to his office, and shall make a report in writing with his recommendations at each annual meeting of the Congress.

Section 4. The Vice-Presidents, in the order of their election, and in the absence of the President, shall perform the duties of that office, and shall discharge such other and further duties as may from time to time be required of them.

Section 5. The Secretary shall keep a true record of all the proceedings had at the meetings of the Congress or of the Executive Committee, in books provided for such purpose. He shall also in books, provided for such purpose, keep a true account between the Congress and its members, and a membership record, and such other records and books as may be determined by the Executive Committee. From the reports made to him by the members of this organization and from all tournaments sanctioned and alleys certified, he shall compile, prepare, and in books provided for such purpose, keep a true and correct Bowling record, and only the records made by a bowler or a team a member of this Congress, and the records of any tournament sanctioned or upon alleys certified by the Congress, shall be entitled to be received and recorded upon such record.

He shall have charge of and conduct the correspondence of this organization, and shall notify in writing the members of any and all meetings of the Congress and Executive Committee as the case may be, and he shall also perform such other duties as may from time to time be required of him by the President, or by the Executive Committee. At the close of his term of office, he shall make a written report with his recommendations to the Congress.

The Secretary shall receive and receipt for all dues or other fees paid to the Congress, and shall, within five (5) days from the receipt thereof remit the same with a detailed account of the several items to the Treasurer, taking his receipt therefor.

The Secretary shall furnish a good and sufficient bond for the faithful performance of the duties of his office, the amount of the penalty of the bond to be fixed from time to time by the Executive Committee. The Secretary shall draw all warrants for bills allowed by the Executive Committee.

Section 6. The Treasurer shall receive from the Secretary any and all moneys or other property paid or donated to the Congress and shall disburse or deliver this same on the vote of the Executive Committee upon warrants signed by the President and countersigned by the Secretary. He shall keep a true and correct account of all receipts and disbursements, and at the annual meeting of the Congress he shall submit a written report and statement of all the financial transactions of the Congress, its officers or Executive Committee, during their term of office. He shall also make such reports and statements to the President and the Executive Committee as may from time to time be required by them. He shall furnish such bonds for the faithful performance of his duties as the Executive Committee may from time to time require.

Section 7. All proposed amendments to the Constitution, By-Laws, Rules and Regulations of the Congress shall be first submitted in writing to the Executive Committee, which shall consider the same and shall report with its recommendations thereon to the Congress for final action. The Executive Committee shall audit all bills and accounts of the Congress and, if the same are found correct, shall order the same paid. The committee shall provide ways and means for defraying the expenses of the Congress, and make its recommendation to the Congress for action thereon.

When the Congress is not in session, the Executive Committee shall have and exercise all the powers granted by this Constitution in the matter of issuing citations for persons or papers required in any hearing had by the Committee for violations of the rules and regulations of the Congress, or in matters involving a construction of the Constitution, rules and regulations of the Congress, and to enforce the penalties provided for such offenses. An appeal from the decision of the Committee in any such case may be taken by any interested party to the Congress, provided the same be taken in writing and the notice thereof be given the Secretary within ten days after the decision is rendered.

The Executive Committee shall act upon all applications for membership in the Congress, and shall have supervision and charge of the organizing work of the Congress, and it shall have power to strike from the rolls of membership any and all associations which are in a state of suspension under the laws of the Congress for a period of thirty days, and it shall have power to annul or cancel any sanction for holding any tournament issued, or certificate issues upon proof satisfactory to it, for a violation of any of the terms or conditions of such sanction or certificate, or the terms or conditions upon which the same are issued.

The Executive Committee shall by proper rules and regulations provide for the issuing of sanctions for tournaments and match games other then those conducted by the members of this Congress, and also to provide proper rules for the issuing of certificates to alley owners or lessees certifying that the alleys are constructed in compliance with the rules of the Congress, and shall provide and adopt a reasonable and uniform charge for such service.

During the time when the Congress is not in session, the Executive Committee shall have and exercise all the powers thereof, except that it shall have no power to alter, adopt, rescind or nullify any part or provision of such Constitution, By-Laws, Rules or Regulations.

The Executive Committee shall supervise, manage, conduct and control all national tournaments held by the Congress, or by its direction, and shall have power to change the location of such tournaments and to annul and cancel any grant or privilege for conducting any such tournament, if at any time the city, person, or corporation to whom such sanction, grant or privilege was given, shall default in any of the terms, conditions or provisions of such sanction, grant or privilege.

The Committee shall have power to name from among its members such sub-committees as it may from time to time deem necessary to carry out its duties and also to prescribe the duties thereof. The officers of the Congress shall, ex-officio, be the officers respectively of the Committee.

The committee, through its Secretary, shall make a full report of its acts and doings at each annual meeting of the Congress.

ARTICLE 7
Dues

Section 1. Each Bowling Association shall pay to the Secretary of the Congress as annual dues for such association the sum of One Dollar ($1.00) for each club represented in its membership.

Section 2. The annual dues shall be due and payable to the Secretary on or before twenty (20) days prior to the date of the annual meeting of the Congress, and if not paid as above provided, the Secretary shall mail a notice to the delinquent association, and failure to pay the same within ten (10) days prior to the annual meeting shall cause such association to be delinquent and shall be cause for the suspension or expulsion of such delinquent association, and during the time such association shall be delinquent its delegates or alternates shall not be entitled to either voice or vote at the meetings of the Congress, and on the expulsion of such delinquent, its delegates and alternates shall cease to be representatives to the Congress, and any and all offices held by such delegates shall, ipso facto, be vacant.

The basis of representation in the Congress from any association shall in all cases be determined and controlled by the amount of the payment of the dues made hereunder. The first payment of dues made hereunder shall be made on or before ten (10) days prior to the annual meeting of February, 1904. No payment shall be received except for a Club duly certified to the Executive Committee.

ARTICLE 8
Meetings

Section 1. The annual meetings of the Congress shall be held on the second Monday of the month of February in each year at such place in the United States as shall have been selected by the Congress upon recommendation of the Executive Committee. The meeting shall be called to order by the President at the hour of 1:30 o'clock of such day. If the Congress fail to make such selection then the Executive Committee shall on or before October 1st, select the place for holding the next annual meeting and tournament. If for any satisfactory reason appearing to the Executive Committee after the selection of the place of holding such annual meeting is made, it shall be deemed inadvisable or inexpedient to hold such meeting at such place so selected, then the Executive Committee is hereby empowered to change such place of meeting to such city in the United States as it may by vote and made not later than the 15th day of November, immediately prior to the date of the annual meeting.

Section 2. The Congress shall also hold such other meetings from time to time as may be deemed necessary by the President and the President shall call the meetings of the Congress upon written request of not less than twenty-five (25%) per cent of the total membership. The Secretary shall give each delegate and alternate fifteen (15) days notice in writing of the time and place of any and all meetings of the Congress.

Section 3. The annual meeting of the Executive Committee shall be held immediately after the adjournment of each annual meeting of the Congress. The Executive Committee shall also hold a regular meeting at 9 o'clock A.M. on the day of the annual meeting of the Congress and also immediately preceding each other meeting of the Congress, and the Committee shall also hold such other meetings as may be deemed necessary by the President, and the President shall call a meeting of the Committee when requested in writing to do so by not less than seven (7) members of the Committee. Ten days written notice shall be given each member of the Committee by the Secretary of the time and place of such meetings.

The President may in his discretion submit by mail to the members of the Committee any questions requiring a vote of the members, and on such submission each member shall in writing and on the proposition so submitted, record his vote thereon, and a vote so taken shall have the same effect in deciding the action of the Committee as if taken at a meeting where the members were present in person. The Secretary shall record such vote on the minutes of the Executive Committee and note thereon how such vote was taken.

Section 4. A majority in number of the delegates to the Congress of the members of the Executive Committee shall be a quorum for the transaction of the business of the Congress or of the Executive Committee respectively.

ARTICLE 9
Amendments

This Constitution may be amended or repealed at any annual meeting of the Congress by a two-thirds affirmative vote of the delegates present, provided that such proposed amendment or repeal shall have been submitted in writing to the Executive Committee for its consideration and report thereon as provided by this Constitution and By-Laws of the Congress.

BY-LAWS
OF THE
AMERICAN BOWLING CONGRESS

Section 1. Robert's rules of order shall govern the proceedings at all meetings of the Congress and of the Executive Committee, when not inconsistent with the Constitution and By-Laws of the Congress.

Section 2. The regular order of business at all meetings of the Congress shall be as follows:

1. Call to order.
2. Roll call of officers and delegates.
3. Report of the Executive Committee on new members. Report of the Secretary on delinquent Associations.
4. Reading of the minutes of last meeting and action thereon.
5. Report of officers in their order.
6. Report of the Executive Committee.
7. Reports of other standing committees.
8. Reports of special committees.
9. Unfinished business.
10. New business.
11. Election and installation of officers.
12. Report of Executive Committee on selection of place of next annual meeting, and action thereon by the Congress.
13. Adjournment.

Section 3. The order of business at all; meetings of the Executive Committee shall be as follows:

1. Roll call.
2. Reading minutes of last meeting and action thereon.
3. Reports of officers.
4. Reports of committees. Standing committees. Special committees.
5. Unfinished business.
6. New business.
7. Adjournment.

Section 4. Any and all proposed amendments to the Constitution, By-Laws, Rules and Regulations of the Congress shall be submitted in writing by the proposer thereof to the Executive Committee not less than thirty (30) days prior to the date of each annual meeting of the Congress and unless so submitted the same shall not be acted upon or discussed at any such meeting unless ordered by a two-thirds affirmative vote of all the delegates present. The Executive Committee shall consider all such proposed amendments so submitted, and report its conclusion and recommendations thereon to the meeting of the Congress immediately following their submission.

Section 5. All applications for membership in the Congress shall be made upon blanks prepared for such a purpose by the Executive Committee, and shall contain such information as may therein be required by such committee, and such application shall be signed in the name of the Bowling Association by its President and Secretary, and mailed to the Secretary of the Congress with the required dues and fees.

Section 6. At the close of each tournament or special match game, held by or under the direction of the members of this Congress, or sanctioned by this Congress, it shall be the duty of the Secretary or persons in charge of such tournament, to immediately forward to the Secretary of the Congress, a full, true and correct report of the results of such tournament, showing the bowling records or averages made thereon, and specifying the individuals and teams winning the championship in such tournament and such report shall also contain such other and further information, as may be required by the Executive Committee.

Unless such report is so made within thirty (30) days after the close of such tournament, the record so made shall not be entered in the official records of the Congress.

Section 7. The Executive Committee shall be a Nominating Committee for the purpose of placing in nomination at each annual meeting of the Congress, such persons for the respective offices to be filed as they may by vote decide, and the report of the Committee on nominations shall be made under the order of "Election of officers." After such report is read, any delegate or set of delegates may make other nominations for any or all of the said offices.

Section 8. These By-Laws may be amended or repealed at any meeting of the Congress by a two-thirds affirmative vote of all the delegates present, provided such proposed amendment or repeal shall have been submitted in writing to the Executive Committee for consideration as provided by the Constitution and By-Laws of the Congress.

Resolved, That the Constitution and By-Laws as read be and the same are hereby adopted as an amendment of and in lieu of the present Constitution and By-Laws of this Congress, and that the said Constitution and By-Laws so adopted go into *immediate effect.* Be it further

Resolved, That the present delegates and alternates of the Congress qualified under the present Constitution, be and they are hereby declared to be the qualified delegates and alternates to the Congress under the Constitution as amended, to hold such offices until the next annual meeting of the Congress, except that in all cities or towns where there shall, prior to the next meeting of the Congress, be organized or adopted an association as provided by the Constitution, such association shall elect its quota of delegates, and alternates to this Congress, then such delegates and alternates so elected shall act and serve as such in lieu of the present delegates and alternates from all leagues identified with such association. This resolution shall not, however, be held to in any manner vacate any elective office held by and officer of the Congress elected at this meeting, but such officers shall serve until their successors are duly elected and qualified...

Harper's Weekly commented on the resurgence of bowling in it's issue of 14 June 1890, pp. 470-471. The ABC, in standardizing the rules, later reduced the number of balls per frame from three to two, and adopted the 300 point scoring system.

THE GAME OF BOWLS

During the last two or three years there has been a great revival of interest in the game of bowls or in the more particular form of that sport in this country — American tenpins. Especially during the last winter the pastime has become more wide spread and has obtained more followers than perhaps any other indoor sport. Indeed, bowling has much the same prominence in winter that base-ball has in summer, but with the distinction that while the great majority of those interested in base-ball are spectators, most of the adherents of bowling are actual participants of the game. In New York, Brooklyn, and adjacent cities the popular favor of the game has been marked. Clubs without number have sprung up and tournaments have been held, bringing together the best teams and individual bowlers.

Bowling had an interesting history and had been the subject of many legal enactments before it was finally evolved into the highly respectable and scientific game that it is today. The sport, as is proved by historical references and court records, dates back to the twelfth century...

The American game of bowling is a survival of Dutch rubbers, which, in turn, was an evolved form of one of the ancient varieties of bowls. The original sport was doubtless introduced directly into this country by the Dutch. The staid Dutch settlers marked out a space at the lower end of the island of Manhattan, and here as they rolled were heard sounds similar to those that greeted the ears of the legendary Rip Van Winkle. Thus the spot where the game was played has been made historic by the name of Bowling Green. Just as in England, alleys soon followed the outdoor bowling lawns; but there was not here, as there, a return to the out-door sport, so the American game became a purely indoor pastime. The game was first played with nine pins, but as a law was passed against it, on account of the evils of gambling and drinking that had grown up about the sport, a tenth pin was added in order to evade the law; and thus tenpins has become recognized as the national sport of the kind, though many other forms of bowling are played more or less.

On November 13, 1875, eleven clubs met and formed the National Bowling Association and from that time bowling has been recognized as a standard sport.

Bowling as now played is a highly perfected game, with rules and regulations quite as exact as govern any other sport. The regulation alley is sixty-four feet long and three and a half feet wide... sixty feet from the regulation line, ten pins are arranged in a triangle, the pins being equidistant from each other, with the apex toward the player. The regulation pin is fifteen inches high, fifteen inches in circumference, and measures two and a quarter inches across the bottom. The player tries to knock down as many pins as possible with large balls of polished wood. This seems an easy task, but the persistency with which some pins cling to their bottoms even when the ball crashes into the triangle is disheartening to the beginner.

A game consists of ten "frames" and each player rolls thirty balls in all, three in each "frame." If ten pins are knocked down by the first ball a "strike' is secured; if all the pins are knocked down by two balls, a "spare" is made; and if three balls are rolled, the result is a "break" and the bowler counts as many pins as are knocked down. The method of counting is somewhat complicated, but easily mastered by a careful study of the game in progress. It is thus seen that the individual limit of play is 300 points, and the team limit will be a multiple of this number, teams usually consisting of either five or ten men.

Among the changes that have rendered the game more scientific and therefore more popular has been the introduction of balls with finger holes. In the old style of play, balls necessarily smaller, but in any case unwieldy, were grasped in the palm of the hand, and thrown rather than rolled. Counterbalancing the greater difficulty of bringing down the pins, their bases were smaller than now, and they were placed nearer together. Now the balls have finger holes which give the bowler more perfect control at the moment of delivery...

Alleys are provided with balls from about two pounds to slightly less than sixteen pounds in weight. The beginner should take a small ball that is easily controlled, gradually increasing the size to the largest that can be used effectively. Put the thumb and third finger in the holes, and stand just back of the regulation line. Hold the arm perfectly straight and let it swing like a pendulum. Swing the ball backward until the arm is on a level with the shoulder, then bring the ball downward so that it comes within an inch of the floor, and, if possible just brushes the alley. At this very instant release the ball, when it will go without jar or bound. One of the most common mistakes of bowlers is that the moment of delivery of the ball is postponed until it is on the upward swing, when it is thrown rather than bowled, and goes bounding down the alley. The bowler should not lose control of the ball at the moment of delivery. In order to make a "strike," the ball should not hit the head pin directly in the centre, but a trifle to one side, between the first and second pins; otherwise a path is quite likely to be cut through the triangle, leaving some pins standing on both sides, and consequently a difficult "spare".

Finally, in order that the pins may be scattered as much as possible, a twist should be put on the ball at the instant of delivery. A great question among bowling experts is as to the relative excellence of the centre ball, which is rolled straight down the alley, and the cross ball rolled from the side. Opinion is about equally divided on the subject, and a somewhat critical analysis of the last season's playing fails to show any marked superiority in the work of either style of bowlers. The cross ball obviously is the more difficult. Perhaps the work of straight ball rollers is more steady, while that of the cross-bowlers is at times more brilliant, occasionally high scores being made, and often poor ones. There are a few who roll a curved ball, but as this style of play depends on the power of the ball to catch the wood, it is evident that until all alleys are of uniform smoothness, like a billiard table, this style of play cannot be rendered scientific. It requires, of course, considerable skill to roll a ball sixty feet and hit the head pin, but it requires more to pick off the difficult "spares"; and it is here that pretty and scientific play comes in.

That the game has the elements of enduring popularity is shown by the fact that ... The elements of scientific play and skill are applied to a sport of a not too violent nature, and there is an entire absence of danger. In driving balls with precision at a distant point there is required keenness of vision and coolness of control, and there comes greater muscular development and an increased grace and freedom of carriage. Some sports require more skill, others more exertion, but few, if any, unite these qualities so admirably. The game is adapted alike to women, men of sedentary habits, and to those most proficient in athletic sports. There is, further, a clearly defined limit to team records — a limit that may be more and more nearly approximated, but doubtless never reached. It may be said in this connection that the Phoenix Club of this city has a record of 1885 out of a possible 3000 points. While it would be hazardous to say that this has not been excelled in some remote alley or unheard of game, yet it is regarded as about the record score of a ten-men team made on a regulation alley. In the recent Herald, Amateur Bowling Tournament, which doubtless brought together the best individual bowlers and teams that ever met in a bowling contest, the highest record for a five-man team was 969 out of a possible 1500, and the highest individual record was 258 out of a possible 300. The Jersey City Athletic Club won the championship with an individual average of 175 4-45... It is almost needless to say that every athletic club has its picked team of representative bowlers. The Produce Exchange has an excellent team; so has the Consolidated Stock Exchange; and there are teams selected from the big houses of Wall Street, from the national banks, from the silversmiths, and a host of other organizations, many of the representatives being expert bowlers...

Nor is bowling confined to men. Women have recently taken it up, and have shown an ability to surmount those difficulties which are supposed to obtain against their acquiring proficiency in sports requiring free play of the arm, as in throwing the ball. Some excellent bowling has been done during the season by women. The new Ladies' Berkeley Athletic Club has some finely constructed alleys devoted exclusively to women's use. Some very creditable scores have been made also at the Knickerbockers Bowling club's tournament by the women as well as the men. The number of clubs composed of both women and men is very large, bowling parties having become a social feature, alleys being rented one evening each week.

So popular, indeed, has the sport become that even now, before the season has fairly closed, most of the alleys have been engaged for next season, new ones are being projected, new clubs are forming, and everything indicates increased prosperity and interest in the game.

Although a national women's tournament was not conducted until 1907, and the Woman's International Bowling Congress was not founded until 1916, women had a long history of participation in the sport. An article appearing in Outing, April 1890, pp. 33-36, provided some historical speculation along with instruction and conditions for women.

BOWLING FOR WOMEN

... bowling, not only on a green but in covered alleys, as far back as the thirteenth century was a favorite pastime at court and in the country, and ... women have not always officiated in their usual capacity of enthusiastic spectators, but often actively warred, ball in hand and full of deadly purpose, against the unoffending pins...

Up to the time of King Edward the Fourth lovers of bowling had evidently been satisfied with playing a simple game on a level lawn, deriving much amusement therefrom. These lawns were great level green squares as carefully marked out as a tennis court, the grass closely clipped and with a trench running about the four sides much after the pattern of a huge billiard table. But the game then as now played in England on the green, is even more intricate and requires more skill and calculation than our tenpins... Balls were rolled at cones of wood varying in size and number as the game went through the process of evolution, so to speak, and thus, behold! In the thirteenth century we discover the very venerable progenitors of our modern game and alley. King Edward, seeing great opportunities for amusement in the covered alleys, signified his royal approval of the same by commanding one to be built in the palace grounds, and here the ladies-in-waiting joined their husbands, fathers and friends in the practice of rolling a ball, and did this with such deft skill and force that the pins would be easily and often displaced. During the reign of King Henry the Eighth... we find bowling in alleys under his patronage vigorously practiced, with not a few improvements in building and with far better balls and pins.

The game found favor in the eyes of King Harry, who with kingly prodigality ordered, among "divers fair tennice courts and cockpits," that a "bowling alley" should be built for his use at Whitehall...

Again we read that Charles the First was a fair bowler on the green and in the alley, as was his son, who ordered an alley built in the palace at Turnbridge. So the history of the game is easily traced to the date when certain sturdy Dutch settlers of New Amsterdam introduced it into America... At first, the game was played in America with but nine pins and the three balls, but by the legislative action of the athletic union another pin was added, and on November 13, 1875, the National Bowling Association, consisting of eleven flourishing clubs, met, and bowling was recognized as a standard sport.

Perhaps from that time dates the active and widespread feminine interest in the exercise that grows with advancing years. Today in New York and Brooklyn, not to speak of the suburban cities, each one of which boasts a well-equipped athletic club, there are innumerable and most prosperous bowling clubs for women. The names of these are legion collectively, but most fanciful individually, and there is not one but is well attended every evening or afternoon that a meeting is called. Better and more encouraging than any recommendation put forward in favor of these clubs is the fact that not only young women blessed with health and a comfortable portion of this world's goods are numbered among the members, but many ladies bowl with their daughters and workingwomen find the exercise of incalculable benefit.

In not one but many ways does this sport present itself to feminine favor. Its methods and regulations are easily mastered without the aid of a teacher, by practice — careful, well-directed practice — and a somewhat large share of patience. Bowling is easy, oh, very easy! There is a perfectly rounded ball to roll down a wonderfully level alley at a triangle of slender pins that seem a large and easy prey at the distance of sixty-four feet...

There are for every well-appointed alley something like thirty balls, the largest weighing not quite sixteen pounds and the smallest about a pound and a half. Between these two weights it should be easy to choose a ball that may be swung up to the level of the waist without visible effort, yet not so light that it will bound and swerve from its path down the alley. The choice of a ball, especially for a woman, depends upon her length of arm and the amount of muscle she possesses, and these latter should not be unduly strained by initiatory practice.

Select a ball that, on putting a thumb and third finger into the two holes, can be lifted, by a swinging back movement, level with the waist or shoulder. This is done standing almost on the line that marks the regulation sixty-four feet of alley. Let the left arm swing easily; then, by bending the left knee and bringing the whole body forward, the right hand, holding the ball, falls within an inch of the floor and is propelled forward with double force. This gives to the body a most natural position and does not, as by the false method of running when the arm swings down, force one across the line and often into misdirection of the ball.

Beginning with a light ball and assuming the proper position in delivery may not bring success the first, second, nor even the third time; yet, if practice is encouraged, it will not be long before the slim, white arm is able to lift and swing a ball of nearly twice the weight of the one first used... provided the pretty aspirant to honors in the alley practices ardently and carefully three or four times a week.

She will, in the course of time, be able to alternate the well-known feminine method of always bowling a centre ball by trying side balls, and perhaps attempting that much discussed and often condemned twisted ball that experts alone can use with effect in tournaments... It is urged by writers on bowling that women especially can scarcely hope to ever become really very expert with a ball, owing to physical weakness, the shoulder and arm being differently shaped from those of men, and, more than all, on account of the full skirts preventing the ball being swung close to the side.

This would seem true enough till women practically demonstrated their ability to overcome these obstacles by various means devised by the ingenious. A woman should wear low, comfortable shoes when bowling. Tennis shoes are the best, but the ordinary walking shoe, if the sole is well chalked to prevent slipping, quite answers the purpose. The uncomfortable corset must be worn loose, with a waist that will afford absolute freedom to movements of body and arms. These, with a full skirt escaping the floor, will perfectly equip any woman for her bowling practice. She may learn to bowl with left or right arm almost equally well, and the benefits will be doubled. Care should always to given with regard to proper ventilation of the alley when the bowlers are at work, for there are no good results from exercise in a close atmosphere.

In New York, during the past few winters, bowling has been a popular amusement among young people, who entertain their friends by giving bowling parties where pleasure and a good bit of healthy exercise are enjoyed. These parties formed the nucleus of the clubs, for it was found that many good alleys might be rented by the evening for a modest sum. Each member of the club subscribed, so that the expense fell heavily on no one, and it was this fact that recommended bowling in parties and clubs so strongly to women who would not indulge in more costly and elaborate exercises.

At the Knickerbocker Bowling Club the women take as vital an interest in the bowling of a good score as the men, and some very nice work has been done with the balls in their erstwhile "lily white hands." The ladies of the United Bowling Club in Brooklyn rolled some very remarkable scores during the winter and once something very near the full three hundred was bowled by one of them.

At the Ladies' Berkeley Athletic Club, that temple of feminine sport and gymnastics, is found a most complete and well-furnished alley for women's use exclusively. Passing down the stairs to the well-lit, well-ventilated basement, one is shown into the long hall where the double alleys are laid. These measure the regulation sixty-four feet, and admirable lavatory arrangements are situated at the end of the room for further convenience of the players...

But it is not in New York alone that bowling has taken such a hold upon the public fancy. In nearly all of the large cities of America bowling clubs, counting many female members, have quietly organized for exercise and pleasure, and some have even attained great importance in sporting circles...

And, ladies, when some jealous and false prophet arises to decry your noble efforts by drawing a forbidding picture of your great-great grandchildren as huge, muscular amazons divested of sweet womanly charms by too steady encroachment on the field where men alone are fitted to excel, believe him not! By some happy provision of kind nature, no matter if the woman's biceps grow as hard as iron and her wrists as firm as steel, the member remains as softly rounded, as tenderly curved, as though no greater strain than the weight of jeweled ornaments had been laid upon them. This is a comforting assurance, and one that may perhaps induce many hitherto prudent ladies to lay aside old-fashioned prejudice and join the growing host of womankind in the bowling alley.

On 22 March 1894, p. 8, the Montreal Gazette printed an article that exemplified the difficulty of arranging matches before clubs agreed to standardize the rules and equipment.

INTERNATIONAL BOWLING
A POSSIBILITY OF CANADIAN AND AMERICAN TEAMS MEETING

For a couple of weeks there has been an agitation in bowling circles looking to the meeting of the champion Canadian club, the Victoria Rifles, and the champions from the other side of the border. Bowling in the United States is a bigger sport than most people in Canada have any idea of, and in the American Amateur Bowling union there are over fifty clubs. It was with the idea of playing the champions of this union that Mr. E.E. Belcourt, of the Victoria Rifles wrote to New york endeavoring to arrange a match. This was about two weeks ago, but no answer was received until yesterday morning, when the president of the A.A.B.U., said that a match could be played on Saturday evening. This was hardly what the Montreal bowlers expected, as in the first place they expressed the desire to play on Good Friday, and, secondly, they naturally expected an answer in time to make some arrangements as to the style of play, because the methods on both sides are widely different. For instance, the custom here is to play a team of six men, three strings each, while in New York they play teams of five, one string each. Then, again, the Victorias want to play the champion team of the A.A.B.U. Had a chance been given for fuller correspondence the arrangements to be suggested by the Montreal bowlers would have been eminently fair and would in substance have been about as follows: Play one match according to the American style, a team of five, one string each, and alleys changed after each square; the second match to be played after the Canadian fashion, three strings each, changing alleys at the end of each string. Considering that the Canadians were playing both matches on American alleys and with American balls and pins, which are smaller than the Canadian regulation, the proposition that would have been offered could hardly be looked on other than as acceptable. As it is, the letter received yesterday gives no information on any of these points, simply stating that the suggestion of the Victorias has been accepted, and setting down Saturday evening as the date of play. Then, again, after playing the two matches, the Montreal men wanted the aggregate to count instead of match for match, which in the case of each team winning once would necessitate a third match, a difficulty which would be obviated by counting the aggregate. Under the circumstances the Victorias held a meeting last night, at which the conclusion was come to that it would be impossible to play in New York on Saturday; but this by no means does, away with the possibility of both teams meeting. In fact, the Victorias suggest that the match be played about April 7. This would give ample time to make all necessary arrangements, and, no doubt, will be agreeable to both sides.

Increased newspaper coverage of bowling results helped to promote interest. On 21 July 1900, the Chicago Tribune reported on the victory of its hometown representatives in an intercity match on page 6. Such competitions instilled civic pride and fostered urban rivalries.

CHICAGO'S SCORE IS THE HIGHEST
BOWLING TEAM WINS FIRST PLACE — BRILL TAKES INDIVIDUAL PRIZE.

New York, July 20. The sixth day of the International bowling tournament was highly successful. The main event was the series between New York and Chicago in the intercity championship contest. Each team rolled three games, the highest aggregate score winning. Chicago was in fine form and showed the New Yorkers how to win an up-hill game. The Westerners had a small band of rooters with them, and they gathered in a good sum of money when the result was announced. Brill won the first game for his side with a score of 246, while Harb pulled Chicago out of the second game by striking out, and in the final he again came to the rescue in the last three frames. Chicago's total score was 2,615, an average of 871 2-3 per game. The score was the highest of the tournament, and the Western men captured first prize. New York was second, both passing the Columbus (O), and Wheeling (W.Va.) men...

The Chicago Tribune detailed preparations for the first national championships in an article on 16 September 1900, p. 19. The Illinois Bowling Association represented a hotbed of bowling activity by 1900 and soon usurped the New Yorkers power within the ABC.

NATIONAL CHAMPIONSHIPS TO BE HELD IN JANUARY

It took but a few minutes on Friday night for the delegates to the Illinois Bowling association to decide in favor of holding a national championship in January. Having so decided, they instructed the Executive committee to also act as a Committee on Ways and Means.

As a starter each league in the association was assessed $5. Twelve hundred dollars in cash prizes will be guaranteed. This amount will be raised within the next few weeks and deposited in one of the local banks. A facsimile of the certificate of deposit will be printed on all of the stationery used in promoting the tournament, and out-of-town bowlers can rest assured the prizes will be forthcoming. The local bowlers do not intend to stop at this amount, but will secure as much more as possible and add it to the prize list.

The various events will be decided upon later, but the chief will be the team championship of the country and the individual championship. It is more than likely a women's event will be added, as the game in this locality is rapidly becoming popular among the fair sex. On a large number of the local alleys women bowlers can be seen every day, and no less an authority than Sam Karpf, Secretary of the American bowling congress, says the Western women have made greater progress at the game than have their Eastern sisters.

Championships in January

The annual meeting of the American Bowling congress will be held in this city from Jan. 6 to 14, and the championships will be held then. Expert bowlers from all parts of the country will be in attendance at the congress and the local bowlers assert the championship will be the greatest bowling tournament ever held, not excepting the big one last summer in New Jersey…

A knotty point was brought up when the question of whether the team winning the championship of its league or the high average men of that league should compete for the State championship. In the tournament of last season the high average men were chosen to do duty for their leagues, and this method seems to be favored by many of the delegates. The team plan, however, is not without its supporters, and a motion was submitted by them…

At present Illinois is the only state with a regularly constituted state organization, although New York has an association which to some extent controls the sport in Greater New York. The Illinois Bowling association has proved a great success, and those at the head of it say that similar associations in other states where bowling is popular would do much to benefit the game.

New Constitution Drafted

It is with this idea in view that President Langhenry has drafted his new constitution which will give the American Bowling league a much greater scope than it now possesses. With a number of the States having regularly organized leagues the matter of holding the national championship would be simplified. The winning team in each state as well as the individual champion of that state would be eligible to compete for national honors. With the financial backing of their state league it would be comparatively easy for the winning team to attend the national championship. Under the existing conditions it is a difficult matter to get the best players to go any distance to compete in a championship. The players not being in a position to stand the expenses incidental to a long trip…

Chapter 8

BOXING

During the period between 1880-1900 boxing shed some of its rough and tumble image to become a commercialized business. Unregulated by any centralized governing body, individual fighters and agents promoted the sport by issuing challenges and sponsoring awards or money prizes. Richard Kyle Fox, publisher of the National Police Gazette, was particularly instrumental in the process. Fox offered opulent championship belts for various weight classes, which brought some sense of order and equanimity to contests that previously disregarded differences in size. Fox's paper catered to the sporting interests of the bachelor subculture and he increased his circulation and profits as a showman and chief antagonist of John L. Sullivan, heavyweight champion and idol of the working class Irish-American community.

Sullivan, a hard-drinking slugger, known as the "Boston Strong Boy," won the championship in 1882 by knocking out Paddy Ryan in a bare-knuckle bout. Sullivan held the title for the next ten years, building his reputation by touring the country and offering $1,000 to anyone who could last four rounds with him. But Sullivan refused to engage black fighters, as did suceeding champions until 1908. Such a policy denied Peter Jackson, the Austrialian champion, his rightful chance at the boxing crown. Jackson fought a sixty-one round bout with James J. Corbett that ended in a draw in 1891. Corbett, a scientific boxer, conquered Sullivan the next year.

The lighter weight classes imposed no color ban and George Dixon became both bantamweight and featherweight champion in the 1890s. His particularly brutal knockout of Jack Skelly in New Orleans led to a ban on interracial fights in the South, as black victories challenged Social Darwinist perceptions of white superiority.

Boxing had a particular allure for various ethnic groups, who found champions within their ranks. For working class immigrants who appreciated toughness and physical prowess, boxers symbolized a measure of socioeconomic status consistent with their own values.

The interest of upper and middle class males in the "manly art of self-defense" allowed boxing to overcome some of the social stigma associated with its brutality and concurrent gambling. As champion from 1892 to 1897 "Gentleman Jim" Corbett lent an air of respectability. Elite athletic clubs hired boxing instructors, brought the manly art indoors, and charged admission to gloved exhibitions, circumventing the laws that banned boxing in many states during the 1890s. The Olymic Club of New Orleans utilized such a strategy to become the first modern boxing arena, hosting the Carnival of Champions, a three day series of title bouts in 1892.

The adoption of the Marquis of Queensberry rules also helped to alleviate some of the concerns about boxing. Originally fashioned in 1867, the new rules provided for padded gloves, three minute rounds, a ten second count for knockdowns, and the barring of rough and tumble tactics, such as wrestling holds. Paddy Ryan won his championship in an eighty-seven round knockout of Englishman Joe Goss in 1880 but Sullivan's 1889 defeat of Jake Kilrain in seventy-five rounds proved the last of the major bare-knuckle affairs. The adoption of gloves did not eliminate violence or gambling. Several fighters died in the ring and Bob Fitzsimmons faced a manslaughter trial for killing his sparring partner in 1895. Fitzsimmons defeated Corbett for the heavyweight title in 1897, in a fight filmed by a motion picture camera. Such technology afforded boxing even greater opportunities to reach popular audiences. Despite such growth promoters struggled to gain acceptance and continued to face regulations or bans in most states.

THE BUSINESS OF BOXING

By the 1890s contenders preferred business arrangements conducted by agents or managers rather than public challenges. The New York Times printed such a case on 14 March 1893, p. 3.

FITZSIMMONS GETS HIS MONEY.
SATISFACTORY SETTLEMENT MADE BY THE CRESCENT ATHLETIC CLUB.

New Orleans, La., March 13.-At 3 o'clock this afternoon Robert Fitzsimmons, champion middle weight; Martin Julian, his manager, and Judge Henry L. Lazarus, attorney for the party, had a meeting with President Charles Noel and Directors Frank Williams, R.M. Frank, Louis C. Grovenig, and others of the Crescent Athletic Club. The conference lasted two hours, and at the close the parties drank to each other's health and announced that a satisfactory settlement had been made. Both sides were reticent as to the terms of the settlement, Mr. Noel thinking that it came under the head of private business, but it is understood that Fitzsimmons was given a check for a large part of the forty-thousand dollar purse, and the rest was represented by notes secured by ample property.

President Noel was asked as to the attitude of the club on the Corbett-Mitchell battle in face of the seventy-five-thousand-dollar bid from Buffalo, and replied that if the bid was bona fide and was considered so by the fighers the Buffalo concern would certainly have no opposition. Such a bid was entirely out of the question and only meant heavy loss to the concern undertaking the contract. There would hardly be a bid, from New Orleans in opposition to the figures named, and if the match was made at that price the officials of the New Orleans organizations would save money and charter a special car and go to Buffalo as spectators....

The following articles from the Chicago Tribune trace the commerical evolution of the boxing business. The first article, printed 18 February 1886, p. 6, depicts an exhibition at a socially acceptable athletic club.

IT COULD ONLY OCCUR IN BOSTON

Boston, Mass., Feb. 17-[Special.]-The Athenian Club, a new sparring association composed of a number of the wealthiest citizens of this city, had its opening tonight. The event of the evening was a six-round glove fight for a purse of $150 between Jack McGee and Jerry McManus of Lowell. The fight was one of the most brutal witnessed in this city for many months. The men pounded each other until both were covered with blood, and the disgraceful affair ended in the fourth round, when McManus was knocked insensible. It was almost half a minute before his seconds could stand him on his feet. The winner receives $100 and the loser $50.

The following article, from the Chicago Tribune, 20 March 1892, p. 6, presents the increasingly legalistic atmosphere.

OLYMPIC CLUB'S NEW ARTICLES.
COPIES HAVE BEEN SENT TO SULLIVAN AND CORBETT FOR SIGNATURE.

New Orleans, La., March 19.-[Special.]-The Olympic club today forwarded the articles of agreement for the Sullivan-Corbett battle to the principals. The Olympics insist upon having their own articles govern, and they also insist upon a forfeit from the men. The historic document is as follows:

We the undersigned, John L. Sullivan of Boston and James J. Corbett of San Francisco, Cal. do hereby agree to engage in a glove contest to a finish before the Olympic club of New Orleans Wednesday, Sept. 7, at 9 o'clock p.m. sharp, for a purse of $26,000 the winner to receive all of said purse, the contest to be with five ounce gloves and according to Marquis of Queensberry rules.

The club is to select the referee and official time keeper, each of us reserving the right to appoint a time-keeper to represent us, said time keeper to be subject to the approval of the club.

The referee shall have power to stop and decide the contest if in his opinion the same becomes too brutal or when humanity may demand it.

Should either of us commit a deliberate foul, thereby injuring the other's chances of winning, the one so doing shall lose all interest in the aforesaid purse.

To guarantee the faithful performances of the above obligations we each hereby agree to deposit the sum of $2,500 in the hands of the Olympic club should either of us fail to appear at the proper time and place the one so doing shall forfeit his deposit....

On 29 January 1894, p. 11, the Chicago Tribune summarized the profit oriented commercial enterprise that boxing had become within the decade.

NEW SUBTERFUGE MUST BE INVENTED TO REVIVE PUGILISM

SAN FRANCISCO, Cal., Jan. 24.-[Special Correspondence.]-American pugilism has had its last prosperous year for some time. It always has been a spurty sport, and would have died a natural death long ago but for a few operators who with rich prizes in view took the glove and club routes and dodged legislation thereby. A new subterfuge must be invented if pugilism is to be sustained. The past prosperous era has taught the pugilist a trick worth two of fighting for his own money. During 1893 some $170,000 was given by various real and sham clubs to American pugilists in purses of from $45,000 down to $100. The Fitzsimmons-Hall $40,000 purse was not half as large in reality. More than half has not been paid. The era of big purses closed with 1893. The Smith-Goddard $10,000 prize was a joke considering the attraction and the Fitzsimmons-Hall $45,000 a failure. Before that had come the Sullivan-Corbett $25,000 and $20,000 stake Corbett-Mitchell, $20,000; Myer-McAuliffe $10,000; Carroll-McAuliffe, $13,000, and Fitzsimmons-Dempsey, $12,000. The old prize ring, grown unfashionable long ago, yielded no such profits to its men. There are only three total stakes of over $10,000 on record, Jack Cooper and Woolf Bendoff fought at Johannesburg, South Africa, July 20, 1889, for $22,500; the Sullivan-Kilrain stake at Richburg, Miss., July 8, 1889, was $22,500, and the Kilrain-Smith prize, fought for in France, Dec. 10, 1887, was $12,000. There are no less than twenty-two $10,000 prizes on the books, dating from the Hyer-Sullivan match of 1849.

Coney Island Club Profits.

But who can wonder at these prizes when the records also show that the Olympic club of New Orleans, La., win to $150,000 by its fights, the Columbia club $10,000 in the face of enormous expenses, and the Coney Island club $237,600, as follows:

Events	Profile
Kelly-Plimmer	2,500
Lannon-Godfrey	2,300
McCarty-Burns	1,800
Dixon-Johnson	25,000
Siddons-Pierce	22,000
Griffin-Lynch	18,000

Choynski-Godfrey	22,000
Costello-Greggains	15,000
Goddard-Maher	25,000
Plimmer-McGrath	20,000
Griffin-Murphy	22,000
Smith-Williams	18,000
Dixon-Smith	22,000
Dixon-Siddons	15,000
Total	$337,000

During 1893 there were six fatal fights, Feb. 24, here, Dal Hawkins killed Billy Miller in the ring, and actual pugilism on the Pacific coast died with Miller, April 4, at Maple Bay, near Syracuse, N.Y., Joe Dunfee killed Dan Donovan of Cleveland in the ring after seven rounds of fighting. March 15, at Grand Rapids, Mich., in the Ottawa Athletic club arena, Albert Taylor, a colored fighter, killed Edgar Broom, white. There were three other fatal accidents during the year.

Winning Fighters of 1893.

The leading winners of 1893 with their earnings are shown in the table below:

Winners	Amount	Winners	Amount
R. Fitzsimmons	42,500	Pat Cahill	1,450
Geo. Dixon	12,000	Dick O'Brien	1,600
Ed Smith	9,000	P. Smith	2,000
Dan Croedon	8,000	J. Van Hoest	1,500
Solly Smith	5,250	G. Lavigne	1,500
John Griffin	6,000	James Slusher	1,500
Billy Smith	5,100	Jack Burke	1,250
Austin Gibbons	4,750	Jim Burge	1,250
Billy Maber	4,150	Peter Maher	1,250
John Daly	3,000	Jim Barron	1,250
Martin Flaherty	2,750	J. Cattanach	1,250
Jo Butler	2,750	Tom Tracy	1,250
Tom Ryan	1,500	F. Childs	1,000
Jim Hall	2,500	Bobby Burns	750
Andy Bowen	2,750	M.J. Daly	750
Billy Plimmer	2,500	Rich Dobbs	750
Dick Moore	2,800	J.C. McGee	700
Charles Vokes	2,250	Henry Baker	750
Hugh Napier	2,000	W. Ernst	650
Billy McCarthy	2,000	Buff. Costello	500
S. O'Donnell	2,000	Joe Fielden	500
Jack Dempsey	1,750	W. McMillan	500
Billy Murphy	1,100	Fred Norris	500
Jim Ryan	1,000	Geo. Siddons	500
Joe Goddard	1,000	T. Williams	500
George Green	1,000	Ike Weir	500

A. Greggains	1,000	Ed Myer	500
G. LaBiancho	900	Miscellaneous	5,000
Dolly Lyons	800		
Jas. Sullivan	800	Total	$ 166,800

In the transition from bare-knuckle to Queensberry rules, proponents of each debated their merits. The rules suggested by Charles E. Clay appeared in Outing, April 1887, p. 31, and provide a glimpse into the nature of anything goes rough and tumble bouts.

A BOUT WITH THE GLOVES.
THE RULES

At present there are two recognized codes under which all boxing contests are held, viz: the London Prize Ring Rules, which regulate all championship fights with bare knuckles, and are only used by professionals. They admit of every license, and are not fit to be considered by amateurs. The rules that govern all amateur-meetings both in this country and in England, are known as the "Marquis of Queensberry's Rules," but even these, although they are free from most of the worst features of their prototype, still leave much to be desired....

FAIR-PLAY RULES TO GOVERN BOXING-GLOVE CONTESTS.

1st.-The contest should take place in a twenty-two foot roped enclosure, or as near that as the space will allow, with eight (8) posts padded on the inside, and three (3) ropes of one inch diameter, each one foot apart; the top one to be four (4) feet, and the lower one two (2) feet from the floor. There should be a circle drawn in the middle of the enclosure to be known as the "Center," to be three (3) feet in diameter, where all contests shall commence.

2d.-Each principal shall be allowed one attendant, who shall remain in his corner, and not advise or speak to either of the principals while the contest is in progress. A violation of this rule may be punished by the referee excluding the offender from the enclosure. While resting, each principal may be allowed the use of a light chair in his corner, which must be placed outside of the enclosure by the attendants while the contest is in progress.

3d.-No wrestling, clinching, bugging, butting, nor the use of the *inside* of the hands in any way shall be allowed, or anything done to injure an opponent except by fair and manly boxing. A contestant shall not go to the floor to avoid punishment or obtain rest, nor shall he strike his opponent when down, or on one or both knees, nor be allowed to strike below the belt or waist.

4th.-The gloves shall not be less than five (5) ounces each in weight, and of soft, thin glove-leather, properly filled with curled hair, so distributed as to be thickest over the knuckles. Only slight shoes or slippers may be worn.

5th.-Rounds to be of three (3) minutes duration, the number of them to be mutually agreed upon, and not to exceed eight (8), with one minute between rounds for rest.

6th.-If a glove shall burst or come off, it must be replaced immediately to the satisfaction of the referee. Any tampering with the gloves, by forcing the hair from the knuckles or otherwise, shall be considered foul.

7th.-If either man is knocked down or accidentally falls to the floor, he may be helped to his feet by his attendant, and shall be allowed twelve seconds from the time of his fall to walk unassisted to the centre. In the meantime his opponent shall retire to his corner and there remain until the twelve seconds have expired, when time shall be called and the round continued. If, however, the man fails to come to the centre within twelve seconds, the referee shall decide he has lost the contest.

8th.-If a man is forced on to the ropes in such a manner as to be in a position where he is unable to defend himself, it shall be the duty of the referee to order both men to the center.

9th.-Spectators should not be allowed within five feet of the enclosure.

10th.-A responsible timekeeper should be appointed, who shall take his position near the ropes, and he provided with a proper time-watch.

11th.-No ill feeling should exist, and the custom of shaking hands before and after a contest should never be omitted.

12th.-An honest and competent referee, who is familiar with the rules, shall be chosen, whose orders must be promptly obeyed, and his decisions in all cases shall be final.

13th.-In order that exhibitions may be conducted in a quiet and pleasant manner, it is suggested that the referee should always request all persons present to refrain (while a contest is in progress) from any loud expression or demonstration.

R.C. MacDonald posted rules for the Boston Athletic Association in Outing, October 1892, pp. 23-24, which adhered to Amateur Athletic Union guidelines. The AAU instituted its amateur boxing championships in 1888.

SCIENTIFIC BOXING UNDER THE BOSTON A.A. RULES.

When it was announced that the B.A.A. intended to give an exhibition of boxing under the new rules, the organs of the professional punchers devoted columns to matter and pages to cartoons ridiculing what they called "gentleman" sparring. All this, though personally unpleasant, was not unexpected. What was unexpected, however, was the very widespread interest which was manifested. From all parts of the country, from the South and from the West, from Canada and from New York, comments and inquiries poured in upon the management. Owing to the errors and haste of the newspaper reports of the proceedings, much misunderstanding arose concerning the object and scope of the new movement, many papers even believing, or affecting to believe, that the new rules were intended as a substitute for the old system. To this misconception can be attributed much of the opposition encountered....

For the last three years I have acted as judge at nearly all the amateur boxing tournaments held in and about Boston, and I had been forced to the conclusion, reached, I doubt not, by all judges of amateur boxing, that science was becoming more and more conspicuous by its absence, and that slugging, pure and simple, was becoming more and more the order of the day. Boys with the merest rudiments of boxing skill enter competitions, depending solely upon their strength and endurance; little effort is made for defense; the competitors hammer each other like savages, and the one who is the luckiest, the strongest, or the most enduring, gets the decision. This is not boxing; it is fighting. This is not the art defensive, but the art offensive.

It will be admitted readily, I think, that there is need of reform and improvement in boxing; the only difference of opinion which can exist is as to the method. Whatever the method, it must be radical; merely instructing the judges to consider form and points will have no effect. The A.A.U. rules contain such a clause now, but is rarely considered, nor can it justly be, for it is undoubted that when two men come together to fight, the one who whips the other should receive the decision, even if he made less points or did his work less gracefully. I doubt if any judge or referee would have the courage to give a decision to a whipped man because he showed more cleverness; and yet such cases occur in every tournament. It is manifest to me that rules to compel science in ordinary competitions will be useless.

There is, however, another method; namely, to separate the two forms of boxing, leaving the ordinary form as it is now, and instituting a separate system of distinctively scientific boxing. This was the object of the new rules, which are here given:

RULES FOR SCIENTIFIC BOXING.

These rules are not intended as a substitute for the ordinary boxing rules, nor are they expected to interfere with the holding of regular boxing competitions, from which the question of strength and endurance can never justly be eliminated; they are framed solely to encourage exhibitions and competitions, if desired, of purely scientific boxing.

RULE I.-The A.A.U. rules shall govern all contests, except as they conflict with these rules.

RULE II.-Contests shall be decided entirely on scientific points. The question of endurance, condition or strength shall not be considered.

RULE III.-If, in the opinion of the referee, a competitor shows a determination to "slug" or maliciously injure his opponent, he shall caution him. If, after two cautions, the offense be repeated, the referee shall disqualify the offender.

RULE IV.-If, during a contest, a disabling accident occurs, the decision shall be given on the points made previous to the accident, unless in the opinion of two judges, or one judge and the referee, the accident was caused deliberately, in which case the offender shall be disqualified.

The question to be considered is this: Are the rules practicable? It is an undoubted fact that men do spar in a friendly way in private; that in the boxing room men can and do give clever and interesting exhibitions without any intention or desire to injure each other. If they can spar thus for points in private, there is no reason why they cannot do so in public.

I am not so infatuated with the new rules as to imagine that an anxious public, debauched by the modern methods, is clamoring for them; on the contrary, I believe that it would be impossible, at the present time, to give a paying exhibition under them, for the public has been educated, unfortunately, to look for something more stimulating. These rules, however, are not framed for the purpose of money exhibitions. They are intended to stimulate an interest in sparring in clubs and in private. They are intended to bring back, at least in part, the pre-Sullivanite method under which two gentlemen, even if strangers, could spar for scientific mastery without being compelled to undergo a long and arduous prize-fight training. In former times rules such as we are now considering were not necessary, because the idea of "killing" each other rarely entered into the minds of competitors. The rules here presented amount, indeed, to little in themselves. Their sole object is to place the contestants at ease, to inspire them with confidence. As in former times, and as now in private, men sparred as gentlemen, seeking only to show superior science, so, in the confidence inspired by these rules, men will compete with each other and will each endeavor to show greater cleverness. Of course, there will be hard hitting; there always was hard hitting when two friends sparred a friendly bout; but there is a very material difference between hard hitting and "slugging," between a blow which is quick and sharp by its very method of delivery and a deliberate, nerve-concentrated blow dealt with the desire to injure. There is a difference between the leads and counters, the parries and shifts of a clever, gentlemanly set-to and the vicious swings, the bull-rushes, the foul elbow and shoulder jabs now too often present in the style of so-called amateur boxing. Who can doubt that, when under the new rules men come together, each will do his cleverest work? Who can doubt that such a spirit will result in true science? The science of boxing will be improved; there will be more good boxers, and as there is nothing to prevent a man from entering into both kinds of competitions, the result would be a more scientific lot of boxers in the ordinary competitions.

The scientific competitions would be, as they should be, schools from which would graduate every now and again some who have not only science, but strength and endurance and the fighting desire. Such men, fitted against men equally as good physically but with little science, would so easily show their superiority that the mere sluggers would be more chary of entering competitions until, in mere self-defense, they had required some cleverness. The result could not fail to be more scientific if less extended.

While men can spar friendly bouts in private, while professionals can spar for points, we cannot reasonably deny the practicability of these *rules*. The whole matter depends upon the contestants. If men desire to spar under these rules, they can do so, and that very desire will keep them from "slugging." As in an ordinary contest each man goes in with the consciousness that he must "slug" and be slugged," so, under the new rules, each man would compete with the confidence that not only that he will be slugged, but that slugging will injure rather than help.

The object of boxing is, of course, to make fighters; not, however, fighters who can only attack, for that is a natural instinct, but true fighters, who cannot only act on the offensive, but on the defensive. In a few words, the science of boxing seeks to enable one to incapacitate an opponent with as little injury to one's self as possible. The science of boxing is an artificial method, and can only be acquired by study and practice; the science of fighting is a natural instinct, greater in some than in others. The figher is "born, not made," but the opposite is true of the boxer. That our present system of so-called boxing is merely natural fighting is beyond need of proof; and as fighting and scientific boxing are by no means necessarily conjunct, an experiment which separates them should be welcomed by all true amateurs. R.C. MACDONALD, M.D.

ISSUES

The Brooklyn Eagle reported on the revival of boxing in New York in its 1 July 1892 issue, p. 4. In 1896 New York City legalized boxing when it passed the Horton law, later repealed due to inadequate regulation. Nevada became the first state to authorize boxing in 1897.

THE REVIVAL OF BOXING IN NEW YORK

Last winter, when the Coney Island athletic club was first projected by John W. Murphy. Frederick Baden, Robert Sutherland and several other ambitious youngsters of John Y. McKane's island, the idea caused a smile among those professional boomers of boxing matches who have killed the business in town. The Coney Islanders soared at once into the realm of finish fights and gave it out that they would challenge the fame of the Olympic club of New Orleans. This caused a still broader smile on the faces of the scrapping managers. Even with ex-Register McLaughlin at the ring side in Brooklyn the police did not allow the continuance of anything that looked like finish fighting, and during the season stopped more than a dozen such battles. The announcement of a "ten round sparring bout for points only" was enough to put the Brooklyn police on edge, and one or the other of the inspectors always stood by the ring to close up the show in case of any obvious disobedience of the law. A number of these local "tournaments," as they were called, had Police Justice James G. Tighe as a backer and manager. Some were in the name of the Varuna boat club and some were not, being run by the men who did the fighting.

Under these circumstances, and with the manifest pull that such exhibition had it was natural that the towering ambitions of the Coney Islanders should cause a laugh. But soon, a wonder came to light. The Coney Island athletic club was incorporated with Justice Kenneth F. Sutherland and Justice R.V.B. Newton among its list of trustees. These young justices of Coney Island are acknowledged to be very near to Chief McKane and do very little which has not his sanction. Another move which showed the power which was behind the project of the Coney Island youngsters was the hiring of the West end casino which belongs to the estate of the late Paul Bauer. Chief

McKane is the trustee of the estate, and the hiring of the casino which has been a financial elephant on the estate for several years, was made from him. The statements that finish fights would be brought off in Coney then looked less like an idle boast and more like something which had been guaranteed or at least tacitly agreed to by the chief authority of the island.

Move second came when the carpenters went into the rink and transformed it into a permanent fighting arena on the plan of the great club of the south. Fully $15,000 was expended on the alterations and improvements which were made. Here first appeared the engagement of considerable capital in the enterprise and that capital was furnished in part by individuals who have no connection with the island. The opening fight of the club was on Monday, May 9, when Plimmer and Kelly were advertised to fight "twenty rounds or more." At this contest the personal interest of Judge Tighe in the club was manifest. He appeared as a director and adviser of the show and the underlings openly referred matters in connection with the arrangements to him. The same solicitude was exhibited by the justice at the Burns-McCarthy fight, and also in the last of the fights, the Dixon-Johnson battle.

Not withstanding that the contests so far held at the Coney Island athletic club have been on the whole second rate affairs it has been clearly shown that the authorities of the island stand ready to allow finish fights of all kinds. These battles were "finish fights" in the sporting sense inasmuch as, both the audience and the participants were given to understand that no decision of the referee would be made unless one or the other of the principals was knocked out. Kelly was knocked out by Plimmer. Lannon was similarly treated by Godfrey. Cal McCarthy would have been knocked out by Burns if he had not laid down and quit, and in the last fight Johnson was knocked senseless by George Dixon. The prices which were demanded by the club, $5 for admission, $10 for reserved seats and $50 for four seat boxes were also such as could not have been maintained unless the club was in a position to let the fights go on to a finish.

When it is remembered, as stated above that the Brooklyn police would hunt down such shows in platoons with night sticks if they were attempted in Brooklyn, it can be inferred whether or not the Coney Island athletic club is violating the law. Chief McKane's police are in the Coney Island rink on every night of a fight in large numbers and the announcement is made from the platform at each show that people in the audience who cause a disturbance will be put out by the police. This is a strange reversal of the judicial aspect of the case, where a cordon of police surrounds the law breakers and threatens anyone who interferes with them.

At the conclusion of the last fight of the Coney island club a crowd of 5,000 sports were turned loose upon the island and thronged the trains returning to town until morning. Those who had gone to the resort from Brooklyn for the day and had women and children with them had to mix with a crowd of intoxicated individuals unusual even from Coney Island. It is unnecessary to say that those who had experience with the first big crowd which a prize fight has drawn to Coney Island will avoid the Island on prize fight nights hereafter.

At the present time the building rented by Chief McKane to the association of people who want to make money out of prize fights is the only building outside of New Orleans and San Francisco in all the broad United States where such fights can be carried on without police interference. Even in the wild West and Southwest the battles have to take place in woods and barns at the heel of sheriffs' posses. At Coney they take place under the glare of the electric lights, where the cries of the excited spectators can be heard at police headquarters.

The New York Times carried several stories of attempts to abolish boxing in different areas of the country. The first appeared on 24 May 1899, p. 4; the second on 13 November 1900, p. 9.

MAY FORBID ALL PRIZE FIGHTS.
BILL TO REPEAL THE HORTON LAW REPORTED TO THE ASSEMBLY.

ALBANY, March 23.-After several attempts Assemblyman M.E. Lewis of Monroe this morning succeeded in getting out of the Codes Committee his bill to repeal the Horton Law, which allows sparring exhibitions with gloves not less than five ounces each in weight, conducted by an athletic association owning or leasing the entire building in which the exhibition takes place.

The repeal of the law will prohibit sparring exhibitions or prize fights entirely and make it a misdemeanor to hold such exhibitions. The vote by which the bill was reported favorably stood 7 to 3. The Democrats who voted against it were Messrs. Collins, Sharkey, and Dillon of New York, the absentees being Messrs. Reddington, Brown, and Delaney.

BOXING BARRED IN ORANGE.
PROTESTS OF CLERGYMEN STOPPED THE PROPOSED PUGILISTIC SHOW.
SPECIAL TO THE NEW YORK TIMES.

ORANGE, N.J., Nov. 12.-Objection by ministers and officials of various organizations resulted to-day in Mayor Henry Stetson of Orange announcing that an exhibition of boxing,-set for to-night under the auspices of the Orange Amusement Company, would not be permitted. The Orange Amusement Company, recently organized, had arranged to give bouts every Monday night this Winter, and had leased the old Orange Armory for that purpose. The first exhibition last Monday night attracted a big crowd, including men from Brooklyn and New York. No decisions were given.

Big placards announcing the bouts set for to-night were posted all over the Oranges, the vaudeville feature of the show being announced in small type. Clergymen and others who had not observed the modest advertising of last week could not fail to notice the conspicuous advertising of the bouts arranged for to-night, and many of these appeared before Mayor Stetson this morning to protest against the show....These protested to the Mayor to save young men from the influence of the boxing bouts. Mayor Stetson told his visitors that the exhibition proposed was clearly illegal. He assured the clergymen that no license for the show would be issued, and that if any attempt was made to give it, the police would interfere.

The difficulty of stamping out boxing is evident in a New York Times article, 14 November 1900, p. 10; for just as the reform elements of New Jersey met with some success, the wealthy enthusiasts of Pittsburgh were able to circumvent such attempts.

PITTSBURGERS TO FOSTER BOXING.

PITTSBURG, Penn., Nov. 13.-Twelve of Pittsburg's wealthy citizens, lovers of boxing, have formed themselves into a club under the name of the Rankin Athletic Club, and have erected a clubhouse at Rankin, just outside the city limits, for the purpose of pulling off all the big pugilistic events possible, and also to give a good fistic show every two weeks.

The clubhouse is up to date in every respect, and has a seating capacity of 10,000. Sergt. "Tom" Sterck, who resigned from the city police force to accept the position, will be matchmaker. He has arranged for the opening of the club on Thanksgiving night, with a match between "Spike" Sullivan and "Eddie" Kennedy of this city. A bid will be made for the coming Jeffries-Ruhlin fight, and every effort put forward to secure it for the new house.

MEMORABLE BOUTS

The Chicago Tribune ran a story of a vicious bout between two New York fighters, on 26 October 1881, p. 3. The account, which follows, gives an indication of working class physicality, the concept of honor, and the collusion of law enforcement officials.

SEVENTY-NINE ROUNDS.
THE YOUNG PUGILISTS ENGAGE IN A PRIZE FIGHT NEAR WEEHAWKEN-BOTH SHOCKINGLY DISFIGURED.

Frank McGowan and Dennis Lyons, both of this city faced each other through seventy-nine hot rounds in a sanguinary prize fight in a field between Bull's Ferry and Weehawken yesterday morning. McGowan is the son of the Fourth Ward pugilist of that name. The fight had its origin in a meeting in a Fourth Ward saloon recently, in which McGowan's father was beaten by Lyons. The son thereupon challenged the victor to a contest, either in a room or according to the rules of the prizering for $100 a side. Lyons accepted the challenge.

At day break the ring was pitched about two miles from Weehawken, Jack Gallagher, the pugilist, and Jac Boliver a Fourth Ward bruiser, seconded McGowan, and John Morris better known as "Yorke" the English pugilist, attended Lyons. At seventeen minutes past 7 o'clock the referee shouted, "Are you ready" and then called them. The pugilists promptly stepped up to the scratch. First blood was drawn by McGowan with a lefthander on Lyon's nose and he got the first knock down by planting a left hander on Lyons' jaw and sending him to grass.

Round after round was now fought, both pugilists being either fought down or knocked down. After twenty-seven rounds had been fought the faces of both were shockingly disfigured. Neither betrayed any willingness to give up and neither had gained any advantage. Lyon's was the most scientific, behaving like one who had been fighting all his life. The twenty-eighth round ended in McGowan's knocking Lyons down.

Now a New Jersey constable arrived on the scene, and bade the crowd stop the fight. But they threatened him, and he demanded of the referee, "What is this now?" "Only two fellows had a row over a girl and they are fighting to see who shall have her," was the reply.

The fight went on, both McGowan and Lyons punishing each other horribly. On time being called for the sixtieth round both men were weak and barely able to stand. The New Jersey constable was still at the ring and enjoying the show. Seventy rounds were fought Lyons' eyes were both fast closing, and McGowan was frightfully punished. Still neither would yield.

Time was called for the seventy-ninth round, and it was an open question whether either man could reach the mark. McGowan staggered to the scratch and it was all that Lyons could do to stand, so frightfully had he been punished. McGowan met him and by the advise of the seconds forced the fighting. He planted a telling blow on Lyons' damaged eye, and Lyons staggered and tried to retaliate. He failed in his effort and fell senseless to the ground. His seconds quickly carried him to his corner. He was unable to stand, and his face had been beaten out of semblance to that of a man. His seconds tried to revive him, but the New Jersey Constable shouted, "He's whipped, sure, don't let him fight anymore!" The sponge was thrown up, and McGowan was declared the winner. The fight lasted one hour and twenty-seven minutes. More than 300 persons were on the ground.

On 9 February 1882, p. 7, the Chicago Tribune gave a round-by-round account of the John L. Sullivan-Paddy Ryan fight for the American heavyweight championship.

HOW SULLIVAN DID IT.

The St. Louis *Globe-Democrat* has the following account of the fight and its results:

As the rivals advanced to the scratch, Ryan's massive proportions loomed up in all their splendor, and it looked as though Sullivan had assumed an impossible task. Ryan's underpinning was perfection, but his upper-works were not as symmetrical as those of Sullivan. The latter, though lacking in inches, was undeniably more muscular, and apparently as heavy as his opponent. All superfluous flesh had been removed, and the skin, clear and tight-drawn, looked as durable as parchment. The hands and face of each, tanned by hard training, were nut-brown in color, and their eyes, clear as crystal, denoted that nothing had been left undone to bring them to the top mark. They were perfect specimens of physical manhood. The disparity in the size of the men was not as great to the eye as had been anticipated -Sullivan's shapely contour almost offsetting Ryan's gut. The latter was considered by old stagers as rather soft, but the Boston boy, on shedding his blanket and raising his arms above his head to be rubbed by his attendants, looked the gladiator all over.

Round 1. The passes made by the men as they toed the mark were more scientific than at any subsequent stage of the battle, Sullivan appeared to be brimful of confidence, and it was soon at a glance that he had been counseled to force the fighting from the word "time," Feinting with his left, he sent out his right with the force of a catapult. Ryan evaded the blow by ducking, and without endeavoring to counter closed with his antagonist. Half-arm fighting of the most desperate nature then ensued. The men, locked together, fought all over the ring, into Sullivan's corner. Johnny's blows were backed up by much more steam than those of his opponent, and Ryan thus early in the fight was made aware of the fact that he had undoubtedly met his master. In endeavoring to evade Johnny's fierce onslaught Paddy laid himself open to a swinging left-handed blow, and first knock-down was claimed for and allowed Sullivan. As the men were carried to their corners the air rang with shouts for Sullivan. The enthusiasm of his partisans knew no bounds, and offers of $100 to $50 on him went begging. Ryan's friends had circulated that if he could avoid Johnny's rushes he could win by infighting, but the very first round had demonstrated that Jack was even better than his master.

Round 2. Both men responded with alacrity to the call. Ryan acted on the defensive, his hopes of winning evidently being based on a prolongation of the fight. Sullivan, however, was not to be denied. He went to work at once, fighting with both hands like a veteran. A feint, followed by blow with his left, no receipt being rendered, increased Sullivan's confidence, and he again made a ferouious drive with his right. Ryan dodged successfully, and, securing an advantageous upper hold, did his utmost to throw his opponent. It was a desperate struggle for supremacy, and was to decide which was the better wrestler of the two. The rivals strained every nerve to secure the fall, and as Ryan's huge frame gradually tottered and went down, such a shout went up as was never heard before in the precincts of Mississippi City. Ryan, who had begun to bleed from Sullivan's handiwork in the first round, not only lost his fall but was covered with gore, and Sullivan placed the second coveted event-first blood-to his credit early in the combat.

Round 3. Sullivan this time could not get across the scratch and into Ryan's territory quick enough, but the Trojan was slow to respond, and loath to commmence operations when he did so. The Boston Boy was averse to having any breathing spell on
the program, and skirmishing beautifully with his left, again sent a vicious right-hander
at Ryan's coconut. Paddy got his headgear out of the way by his favorite method of
dodging, and seizing his antagonist, went in for bail-arm work. As in the first round,
he had all the worst of it. Sullivan pegged away merrily with both hands, while the big
fellow was doing nothing effective, and wound up with a wicked smash in the ribs that
Ryan failed to avoid, although he went down for that purpose. It was patent to every
one by this time that Sullivan could not lose, and Ryan's adherents, who had stuck to
him with unflinching loyalty since the match was made, began to look down in the
mouth.

Round 4. Sullivan, at the word, capered nimbly to the front, but Ryan again took
his time. The round was one of the most terrific ever witnessed. Ryan went in to do
or die, and took his punishment wonderfully well. For the first time, he endeavored to
counter when Sully led, but his attempts were so feeble and futile that he again resorted
to in-fighting and had all the worst of it, being thrown heavily at the close. When
picked up he was covered with blood and visibly giving way under the terrible punishment dealt out so unsparingly.

Round 5. This round was as desperate as its predecessor, Ryan manifesting more
strength and vim than could possibly have been anticipated by his appearance. He was
quick to close, and, after hot work at short range, the Bostonian administering the lion's
share of the punishment, Ryan secured the only fall credited to him during the fight.
When Sullivan was picked up by Chambers and Goss he was covered with Ryan's
blood.

Round 6. Sullivan lost no time in getting at his man, and went at him with the fe-
rocity of a tiger. Ryan, though game to a fault, was utterly unable to do anything in his
own defense at long range, owing to Sullivan's superior science, and the original tactics of closing were persisted in. Sullivan brought the round to an end with a left-
handed shot, from which Ryan reeled and fell.

Round 7. It was now dollars to doughnuts that Sullivan could not lose. There was
not a mark visible on his face or body, while Ryan was a mass of blood. Paddy faced
the music with Spartan courage, but was met with such a rush as is rarely seen.
Outfought at every point, the Troy man, as a dernier resort, again closed with the
smaller man. Sullivan quickly cross-butted his man, and as Ryan was thrown heavily
all thought that the life had been knocked out of him, but his seconds succeeded in the
next round in sending him again to the scratch in a presentable condition.

Round 8. Ryan was not in readiness until the last second permitted him, while
Sullivan was all impatience. He evidently wanted to finish the job that was now apparently so easy. On getting within reach Sullivan smashed his man right and left, and
this time assumed the initiative in closing. Ryan, however, succeeded in effecting a
separation, partially falling as he did so. Sullivan, thinking his opponent was going
down, failed to follow up his advantage, at which both Goss and Chambers manifested
their displeasure by gestures and urging Johnny on. The round was resumed. It ended
in the Boston man's corner, Paddy being terribly punished in the exchange of blows

at short range, a telling uppercut followed by a couple of blinders full in the face sending Ryan to grass as limp as a rag.

Round 9, and last. Hardly anyone expected that the big man would again respond
to the call of time, but skillful handling placed him in a condition to do so, Sullivan
barely missed fierce lunging hits right left, receiving in return a feeble tap over the left
eye. This netted the Bostonian, who quickly put the finishing touches on his antagonists, and, after seeing that he was beyond aid, ended the round by pushing Ryan down
with his open hand. When time was again called Ryan's hat was slung in midair as a
token of defeat, and Sullivan was hailed.

CHAMPION OF AMERICA.

Sullivan's fast fighting told its tale, and he was a very tired man at the finish. Had
his handiwork not been so effective, there was a bare possibility of his losing, as he
was undoubtedly well-nigh exhausted. Ryan, however, was a mere chopping hook,
without a particle of science, and how he ever obtained backing against such a man as
Sullivan can only be accounted for as the wound of partisanship. No novices ever made
a more brilliant debut in the roped arena...

The longest fight on record occurred in 1892 when two fighters battled more than 100
rounds and nearly seven and a half hours. One of the participants, Andy Bowen, was
killed in a match two years later. The Chicago Tribune provided coverage of both
bouts, on 8 April 1892, p. 6; and 24 December 1894, p. 11, respectively.

PUGILISTIC RECORD IS BROKEN.
THE BURKE-BOWEN FIGHT LASTS 109 ROUNDS
AND IS DECLARED "NO CONTEST."

NEW ORLEANS, La., April 7.-[Special.]-The only remarkable thing about this
morning's Bowen-Burke fight was its length and the peculiar decision at the end of the
109th and not the 110th round as the official announcement had it. The gong sounded
for the first round at 9:24. When Referee Duffy announced "no contest" it was 4:49
a.m. The men had been fighting seven hours and twenty-five minutes, just the time for
109 rounds. This broke the world's record, made by Danny Needham and Patsy
Kerrigan at San Francisco Feb. 17, 1890. This pair fought a 100 round draw. This
morning's fight broke ring recrods of any time for length. The decision was peculiar
in that it meant nothing. John Duffy called it "no contest." The San Francisco clubs
invented the "no contest" decision to prevent being worsted by crooked fighters. Duffy
explained today that he made his decision because he did not want to handicap the club
by a draw. The fight was fifty-four rounds too long for humanity's sake. Burke broke
his right hand in the forty-ninth round and his wrist was sprained. The tough Texan
finished with one hand. Bowen and the referee knew of the trouble. In the 100 rounds
there were only fourteen of fair fighting. From the forty-seventh to the fifty-first either

man would have gone out to a good punch, but neither had one in him. Whenever the fighting was mixed Bowen came off best. The other rounds were merely bits of pedestrianism. There was one show of blood on Bowen's face in the second round. The men mauled and fell over each other in the last rounds. There were 8,200 paying people in the ring and the receipts were about $16,000. The men will not be matched again.

NEW STORY TOLD OF BOWEN'S DEATH.

Several local sporting men who went to the recent fatal fight at New Orleans have broken silence concerning the tragedy and have revealed a story that was smothered in the Louisiana town. The death of Andy Bowen, they declare, was the result of a tricky play of Bowen.

They say Bowen, a fast fighter and shifty on his feet, went to the club officials some time before the contest and asked that the padding be removed, as he did not feel at home on the padded floor, and could not move with quickness. Bowen was the pet of New Orleans, the Crescent City's gamest fighter, and a favorite in local betting. The club directors seeing the force of his argument ordered the padding taken away.

And so the padding was removed. Lavigne was given some plausible excuse, and the fight was brought off with a floor protected only by a canvas. But things did not turn out as had been anticipated. Bowen's agile feet could not keep him from Lavigne's staggering blows, and the New Orleans man was shipped almost from the beginning. At last came the knockout. Lavigne had been expected to receive the blow, but the knocked out man was Bowen; weak and dazed, he fell heavily, his head struck the canvas, and Andy Bowen lay dying in the ring.

∞

The Olympic Club of New Orleans sponsored a boxing spectacle, billed as the Carnival of Champions, 5-7 September 1892. Among the title fights were the George Dixon-Jack Skelly fight for the featherweight crown, and the John L. Sullivan - Jim Corbett heavyweight championship. The New Orleans Times-Democrat gave front page headlines and in-depth coverage to the event. Dixon's mauling of his opponent engendered a racist backlash to ban interracial fights. Sullivan's defeat stunned the country for he had been invincible for a decade and brashly predicted an eighth round knockout. Dixon's story appeared on 7 September 1892, p. 1, with the editorial following the next day on page 4.

CORBETT WINS
JOHN L. IS THE CHAMPION FIGHTER NO LONGER.

OLYMPIC CLUB, NEW ORLEANS, La., Sept. 7,-[Special.]-James J. Corbett is the champion fighter of the world.

He knocked out John L. Sullivan tonight in the twenty-first round.

From start to finish the Californian had far the best of it and left the ring without a scratch. On the contrary, John L. was unable to deliver an effective blow. For the first time he was confronted by a man who would stand up close to him; so close that their toes were together frequently. But Corbett, though standing close, dodged nearly every blow. He showed great generalship and delivered wonderfully effective blows. He laughed at the ferocious "Sullivan look" and did what he pleased with his opponent.

Won the Lucky Corner.

When the men tossed for the choice of corners and Corbett won his friends almost danced the Highland fling. Fighters and their friends are superstitious almost to the verge of idiocy, and when they found their man had won they felt that things were coming their way to be sure. When asked what corner he would take Corbett replied promptly: "Why, the lucky corner of course." The lucky corner in the Olympic club has become a famous one. It is the one across the ring from the entrance gate and nearest the gong. Only two losers have ever come out of it... Sullivan's friends smiled at the antics of Corbett's admirers and declared that before the fight had gone ten rounds Corbett would not know whether he was in a corner or on horseback.

Boasted Too Early.

When it began to rain just before the men entered the ring one of the Sullivan party, who was present when corners were tossed for, turned to a Corbett man and remarked:

"Happy the bride the sun shines on; happy the corpse the rain falls on." Corbett, he opined, would fill the bill for the last line nicely when Sullivan was through with him.

Special chairs had been provided for the contestants higher and more roomy than the ones that had been used in the two previous mills. Corbett had had the back sawed off his chair, preferring to give his seconds plenty of room. Sullivan's remained intact.

President Guillotte had not finished speaking before the contestants came down the steps and entered the ring. Sullivan was stripped down to a pair of green trunks, and his enormous frame showed up to its best advantage. The awful air of determination which invariably rests on the big fellow's features was there in its entirety, and as he calmly surveyed his surroundings the crowd broke into a cheer that almost raised the roof.

"Sully" the Favorite.

It was a Sullivan crowd from pit to gallery. Corbett came so close behind the big fellow that he was almost lost sight of. He seemed trained to the bone, but looked like a middle-weight before the massive frame of the champion. Corbett, during the preliminaries, tapped his foot nervously while the gloves were being weighed and thrown into the ring. The mysterious plush box was opened and found to contain a tankard which the club presented to Referee Duffy for services rendered. Capt. Barrett went around to each corner of the ring and warned the crowd that if anybody attempted to get into the ring or in any way interfere with the proceedings it would go hard with him. The crowd cheered this statement. It was evidently a most orderly gathering and intent on seeing the best man win without regard to sentiment.

The contestants and seconds were called to the center of the ring and the club rules explained to them. Jack McAuliffe, Phil Casey, Charley Johnson, and Joe Lannon were in Sullivan's corner, while Jim Daly, Mike Donovan, and McVey, the wrestler, were in

Corbett's corner. Bat Masterson kept time for Corbett and Frank Moran for Sullivan. The gloves were made of brown leather and were fitted snugly to the hands of the contestants. The crowd cheered lustily as the gloves were donned, and when the gong sounded for the first round the applause fairly shook the building. It was 9:03 when time was called and the men faced each other.

Sullivan Meets His Match.

When the gong sounded for the first round and Corbett walked up and pushed his glove in the big fellow's face and then began to run around, the crowd saw at once that Sullivan had more than his match in science and the fight simply resolved into a question whether Corbett had strength enough to whip the champion of champions. When Corbett started his walking tactics the crowd commenced to hiss, but the demonstration affected the Californian not a bit. Sullivan had not been in the ring five minutes before his miserable condition began to show itself. He was fat as a pig and when he moved around the great layers of fat on his back and stomach shook like so much jelly. He seemed in even poorer shape than when he fought Kilrain. Corbett devoted the first four rounds to feeling his man, but went at him in the fifth. Sullivan was not expecting this and when Corbett's left came like a flash into his nose it seemed to stagger him for the moment. Corbett was at him like a demon and there is no mistaking the fact that had there been more power behind the Californian's blows the famous fight would have ended then and there. Sullivan's nose was cut right across the bridge and when the blood spurted from it in a stream it almost blinded the champion.

With this mark and Sullivan's enormous build to shoot at Corbett kept the big fellow busy. His work was done almost exclusively with the left hand and was not a straight punch, but a sort of round-arm swing that Sullivan seemed unable to gauge at all. Corbett would walk up to him and shoot the left into his stomach, and when the big fellow's hands would go down, Corbett's left was on the damaged nose in a trice. That was the story of the fight right through.

Watched for an Opening.

Corbett would walk around the big Vulcan like a cat watching a mouse. When an opening was presented he was at it, and landed every time he led. Whenever Sullivan would lead the blow was short and the Californian's left was right back in his damaged visage. When the sixteenth round was reached Sullivan went back to his corner a sick and tired man. Before the gong sounded for the seventeenth round the big fellow vomited, and the lynx-eyed seconds at once noted the champion's weakness, and Corbett's orders were to work for his stomach at once.

When time was called Corbett went right at the big fellow's immense stomach and made him fairly sicken under his bombardment. If Sullivan ever had a chance to win it ended there; from that time on he grew perceptibly weaker and was made a punching bag of by the skillful Californian.

After this round there was never any doubt as to the result. The champion grew weaker and weaker with each succeeding round, and it was in the twentieth round that Sullivan really met his Waterloo. It happened in a mixing up near the ropes and in the exchanges Sullivan had all the worst of it. He staggered against the ropes, fell back against Corbett only to receive the volley of blows he seemed unable to ward off. Corbett was unable to knock him down, but he staggered him time and and again until the big fellow's body fairly shivered. When the round closed he was a pitiable sight.

His wretched condition showed itself in his face, which puffed and discolored under every blow.

He was receiving only what he had administered to scores of men before him, and there was scant pity in the faces of the frenzied mob that had commenced to realize that a new champion had arisen. When a man is well conditioned the blood is drawn from his face and he does not bleed readily, while his face scarcely puffs at all. Corbett was such a trained man. Sullivan's rest between the twentieth and twenty-first round did not help him, and, despite McAuliffe's herculean efforts, Sullivan was wabbling when he advanced to the center. The first sign of a weak and groggy man is a trembling of the right leg, and Sullivan seemed unable to straighten that member. Corbett was quick to note, and he was at the champion like a bull. He had no longer become even cautious, and went right to mixing it up near Sullivan's corner. He landed with the left, throwing Sullivan off his guard, and was on to him like a demon.

Down at Last.

He fairly rained blows on the helpless champion, who threw up his hands in a pleading manner, but there was no mercy for him. The fiend incarnate could not have been more infuriated than was Corbett at that moment.

Corbett finally steadied himself and swung his right with fearful force. It landed on the mouth of the weakened Vulcan, and he fell a helpless and inanimate mass in the river sand of the ring. The blood was gushing from his mouth in a perfect stream and he must have bled a quart during the next minute. The brute courage which has been part of the man during his career asserted itself, and with the effort of desperation he staggered to his feet, but before Corbett could reach him to hit him he fell back again helpless. He was up again only to fall in a tangled mass of bruised flesh and fat-covered brawn. Before he could attempt to rise again the gong sounded and the fight had gone down to history.

Was Put to Sleep.

Sullivan was carried to his corner insensible and slumbered in his chair for a full minute while his seconds worked with all kinds of restoratives to bring him to. They succeeded finally, and with wonderful vitality he walked to the center of the ring and made his speech.

He said that he had entered the ring once too often and was sorry, but was glad that the championship remained in America.

Never was a heavy-weight championship won more easily. Sullivan did not land hard enough on Corbett to hurt him during the entire fight. Corbett was fresh and strong when the fight was over and did not show a mark. Sullivan had met his master; science and skill had triumphed over brute force. The new champion is American born, talented, and clean cut, and he cannot fail to become popular. He will become the public idol and fill more gracefully the place Sullivan has so long occupied.

THE NEGRO WINS.

GEORGE DIXON, THE featherweight champion, again proved his claim to the title by knocking out Jack Skelly in the Olympic Club arena last night in eight rounds. From the beginning the fight was the negro's, the white man giving his supporters scarcely any hope of success at any stage of the contest. The white boy could not stand the severe blows of the negro. He grew weaker with each round and finally "went out" with a stiff blow on the neck.

The first feather-weight battle of any account that has taken place in the arena of the New Orleans Olympic Club was that of last night, in which George Dixon, the wonderful little negro, and John Skelly, a clever Brooklyn amateur were the contestants. The Olympic Club, in preparing for the great September contests, had not counted on a battle of this kind in its programme, but after every effort to secure a fight for Fitzsimmons had been exhausted, the directors fell back upon Dixon as the best drawing card remaining available. Skelly was anxious to risk his amateur standing and the reputation he had won with it in a trial against Dixon for a purse of $7500, and a stake of $5000 a side and Dixon, being always ready to meet all comers-American, English or Australian, white or black interposed no obstacle. The preliminaries were easily settled and though the majority of sporting men looked upon the coming battle as a probable walk over for Dixon, there were not wanting enthusiastic admirers of the young amateur who were ready and willing to back him at the long odds offered against him. The management of the Olympic Club expected this to be the least attractive of the three September battles and they were not disappointed, though the financial results of last night's entertainment were, at the same time, highly satisfactory. Many had predicted that it would be imprudent for the Olympic Club to permit a negro to fight in its arena, and there were not a few who feared that should the colored boy make anything like a victorious showing over his white antagonist, it would be difficult, if not impossible, to prevent outside interference. The Olympic Club, however, entertained no such fears; they felt confident that a large majority of those present would be so actuated by a spirit of fair play that they would scorn to interfere or in any way improperly influence the result of the fight, no matter how pronouncedly it might be going against their sympathies. In addition to this, ample police protection had been provided, and every one felt confident that Dixon would be as safe on the club premises as his antagonist.

Appearance of the Men.
DIXON.

It was just 9 o'clock when Dixon entered the ring and took his seat in what is commonly called the lucky corner. At first it was difficult to judge of his form, and only his coffee-colored limbs and his small round head were visible, he being enveloped in a thick, knitted shirt of white wool, which covered him from his neck to his thighs. His hair was cropped so closely that his head assumed the same coffee-colored hue as his skin elsewhere. His head is small and round, and a retreating forehead does not improve his otherwise bright and very good natured expression of countenance. His knee, are shapely and muscular, while his thighs are long, straight and finely developed. Like all great fighters, Dixon has a grand chest, shoulders and loins, and though the sympathies of a majority of those present were undoubtedly against him, a cheer burst from all parts of the pavilion when he stood in his corner and, pulling off his loose white wool shirt exposed his magnificent development from his ears to his thighs. His neck has the tower-like pyramidal shape common to so many of the most successful prize fighters. His shoulders are simply wonderful for a man of his weight both in breadth and thickness, while his arms, chest and loins are made to match his shoulders. Though beautifully shaped down to his knees, and showing a great, clean muscular development Dixon appeared to be a shade too high in flesh for a long, hard battle, though this impression may have been partly due to the fact that his whole physical conformation is smooth and shapely.

SKELLY.

Skelly has not the face of a pugilist though elsewhere he has all that would seem necessary to success in the ring. His face is narrow and sharp looking, and his jaw and nose are not of the kind to withstand punishment. His nose is rather long and narrow at the base of the nostril, and will always be a trouble to him in fighting until he shall have become clever enough to guard it under any and all circumstances. His chin is pointed and somewhat receding, while the jaw behind it is narrow, light and thinly muscled. These peculiarities aside, Skelly has the conformation of a featherweight pugilist. He is very tall for one of his weight, has a fine reach, good broad shoulders (though much narrower than Dixon's), and a full, well-muscled chest. Though his arms and shoulders do not appear heavy, he has fine, clean-cut and sharply defined muscles about the shoulder blades, indicating more than ordinary hitting power. He has a good loin and limbs, his calves being larger and his thighs smaller than Dixon's. He appeared to have been trained down much finer than the negro, as his muscles stood out very sharply defined all over his arms, chest, shoulders and limbs. He had certainly been trained down finely enough, and possibly a shade too fine.

Both men looked happy and contented as they sat in their corners, but, if possible, Skelly looked the more confident of the two.

THE ARENA.
A Large Crowd Present-A Space Set Apart for Negroes.

The appearance of the arena was in every respect similar to the picture it presented Monday night when Myer and McAuliffe faced each other for their great struggle, except that a portion of the north gallery had been set apart for negroes, a goodly number of whom availed themselves of seeing the diminutive champion of their race display his powers in the ring....

Just Before the Battle.

From 8:30 to 9 o'clock the crowds surged in, filling the reserved seats in twenty minutes' time and swelling the number in the general admission seats. The spectators knew when they saw Skelly's backer, Reynolds, come into the amphitheater that it would only be a few moments until the fight, and there was no manifestation of impatience, as on Monday night.

About 8:45 Referee Duffy came into the amphitheater and received the customary ovation, and in a few minutes later the scales for weighing the gloves were brought in. Telegraph instruments were clicking, the buzz of conversation sounded through the building, and everybody was on the alert.

At just 9 o'clock, without introduction or announcement, Dixon walked into the ring, accompanied by his seconds and trainers. He was dressed in his trunks and had on a white woolen shirt. He took the winning corner which McAuliffe occupied last night.

Ex-Mayor Guillotte came into the ring to make the opening talk, but his cries were drowned in the wild applause that followed the entrance of Skelly, which took place at this time, Skelly was clad in the same manner as his opponent, and was accompanied by his seconds and trainers. Dixon had received but few cheers in comparison with the ovation that Skelly got, and he must have felt that he had few friends in the crowd.

Skelly walked over and spoke to Dixon, shaking hands with him, and the crowd applauded.

Skelly's seconds were Jack McAuliffe, Prof. Robertson, Jimmy Carroll and Joe Choynski; timekeeper, Johnnie Griffin.

Dixon's seconds were Jack Houlin, Morris Kelly, James Dobert and Tom O'Rourke. R.M. Frank was timekeeper for the club.

The customary explanation by the referee in the centre of the ring was made, and in ten minutes the gloves were adjusted and Duffy said "Shake hands."

FIRST ROUND.

They faced each other at 9:11, and as soon as he was within range Dixon sprang forward and landed his left on Skelly's nose heavily, but the blow was too high to have much effect. Then Skelly appeared warm and followed the negro all around the ring, but he failed to land, Dixon closing with him whenever they came to close quarters. They clinched three times, and each time Dixon had the better of it. Twice, they came within range. Dixon led sharply for the head, but each time Skelly ducked cleverly and caught the blows on his forehead, where they did no harm. Just before the sound of the gong Dixon got home with his left between Skelly's eyes, but again it was too high up to have much effect. Skelly showed a disposition to force the fighting in this round, but Dixon stopped him each time.

SECOND ROUND.

The round opened with both men wary. Skelly began forcing the fighting, but when he had his opponent on the ropes his rushes were cleverly evaded. Dixon's left hand leads and right hand swings were cleverly warded off by Skelly. Dixon began to rush matters after a bit, and swinging heavily for the right ribs, dealing Skelly terrific upper cuts in the stomach. Dixon was a perfect demon on the ribs, but Skelly showed decided cleverness in guarding. In the clinches both men guarded cleverly, and only on one occasion was there the slightest shadow of a foul. While in a clinch Dixon dealt his white opponent a heavy blow on the ribs. Cries of "Foul" rang out from all sides of the ring, but Referee Duffy properly declined to allow the claim. Dixon's tactics became painfully evident to Skelly's friends. He would rush in and swing viciously for the right ribs, landing on nearly every occasion. The white boy jabbed the negro every time in the face, but the blows were not backed by sufficient muscle to hurt Dixon. At the close of the round Skelly's right ribs were a deep pink color, and he showed marks on his neck of Dixon's blows.

THIRD ROUND.

Dixon led several times but failed to reach. He landed soon, however, on the chin and secured the first knock-down. It was a clean blow. When Skelly got up he got a swinging blow in the stomach from the colored bantam. It ended in a clinch. The fighting was then fast and furious. Skelly saving himself by clever clinching. He stopped several dangerous blows in this way. Dixon landed his terrible left in the stomach, neck and stomach again. Skelly did some remarkably clever dodging with his head. He landed three times following on Dixon's face. The latter got in a stiff body blow just as the gong sounded.

FOURTH ROUND.

Dixon led with his usual hard blow for the right side and landed. Skelly made a jump at the negro, hit him and ran on against him, forcing Dixon against the ropes. Dixon got out from under him and turning, started toward Skelly with a rush. Skelly made a good dodge, and coming up in front of Dixon with his guards up ready to hit surprised him. Dixon led and landed, and on the next lead Skelly made a very nice stop. Dixon found the right side with his left again, and then with his left grazed Skelly's head. He led for the side again and landed. The place was swollen and red. Dixon led again, and Skelly countered on the stomach, the men coming forcibly tgogether. When Dixon led for Skelly's head again, the latter made a beautiful duck, bringing forth wild applause. Dixon landed in the face. Dixon led again and landed on the right side twice in rapid succession.

FIFTH ROUND.

Skelly led for the neck, but was prettily stopped, as usual. Then they closed, Dixon landing his left on Skelly's ribs as they came together. Then Dixon danced away, and Skelly refusing to follow him Dixon ran in and landed twice on the ribs with his left in rapid succession. Skelly was not inclined to force matters this time, but finding he could not draw him out Dixon rushed in and did some terrible execution. He landed his left heavily on the mouth and nose in rapid succession, each blow bringing copious streams of blood, which ran down his chest to his waistband. Again, as they came together Dixon landed his left on the ribs and countered over the eye with his right, bringing another big crimson stream which flowed down the white boy's check and over his neck and shoulder, following the outside of his left arm. Skelly, still game, kept on with his utterly hopeless up-hill struggle, and as Dixon ducked and, running in, landed his left once more heavily on the ribs, upper-cut the negro smartly on the nose with his right, bringing the blood freely. After breaking away Dixon made another rush, and driving Skelly into his own corner, punished him horribly at short range with both right and left, making the blood spatter from his swollen mouth and nose till that portion of the white boy's face looked like a ragged piece of blood-soaked sponge. Freely as Skelly was bleeding from both mouth and nose it was clear that a portion of the blood was flowing into his throat and choking him. It was a sickening sight, but the negro, with a cold vicious look in his eye, smiled as he went on with his horrible work as though the thought of pity or forbearance could find no place in his small round head until after he had heard the sound of the gong.

SIXTH ROUND

Skelly came up game and followed Dixon to his corner only to receive a swing on the ribs from the left. The fighters got into close quarters, and Dixon led with his right for the head. Skelly ducked to avoid punishment, but received a vicious uppercut from the left in the face. The blow dazed Skelly considerably, and Dixon, at once perceiving his advantage, went in to bring matters to an early issue. He led heavily for the ribs, and whenever he landed it would smash his right into Skelly's face. Skelly would invariably clinch to avoid punishment, but exhibited gameness and cleverness in close quarters. Clinches and hot rallies were frequent. Dixon was aggressive from the start, while Skelly, though willing and as game as a pebble, seemed to be a mere tyro in his hands. Again and again the colored featherweight swung for the ribs, landing nearly every time without return. It was plainly evident that Skelly was doomed to defeat and that nothing short of a chance blow could save him from being whipped in short order. Dixon's blows on the head had dazed the plucky little fellow, and his body blows had wounded him considerably.

SEVENTH ROUND.

In this round Dixon adopted McAuliffe's tactics and did the leading. For four successive times he led with the left, but fell short. He landed on the face, and, a clinch followed. He lead again, but it was short. He landed on the face and was countered on the neck. Three clinches followed. Then the colored featherweight walked in to Skelly and nearly knocked him out. He landed repeatedly. Three times sharp, quick blows smashed Skelly's face. The latter fell, and as he rose he clutched his opponent round the neck, and a clinch followed. The men were parted with difficulty. Dixon led sharply with his left and Skelly attempted a counter. A clinch followed; and just before the breakaway Dixon punched Skelly a light one in the stomach. An awful yell of "foul" arose, but Referee Duffy held up both hands and Capt. Barrell followed suit. Quiet again reigned, but nothing was done up to the time the gong sounded.

EIGHTH ROUND.

During the intermission between this and the seventh round the seconds of Skelly did valiant work trying to get their man into condition to wind out another round. As fast as the blood was wiped from his face it flowed anew, and Skelly sat there looking the picture of disconsolation. He looked over toward Dixon's corner in an appealing kind of a way, and when the call for time was sounded he arose from his corner with a pitiable attempt at liveliness, and went out to meet his fate. Before he had been up a second the blood began to flow anew from his face, and ran in a stream down to his chin. Skelly, evidently realizing that he was getting weaker and weaker, and that his only chance to avoid Dixon's rushes was to hit him a good blow and stop him, rushed at Dixon and led as savagely as he was able, but Dixon nimbly avoided the blow, smiling as he did so, and immediately after landing on the left side of Skelly's face with his right hand. Skelly made another futile attempt to hit the negro and Dixon, landed on his face and right side, forcing him against the ropes. In this position Dixon landed several hard blows on the face and stomach of his opponent, and when they separated Skelly went wide of his mark in an attempt to retaliate by a blow on the face. Skelly was now hopelessly weak, and every man in the amphitheatre knew that he had no chance to win. He was panting, and his face, bruised, bloody and swollen, presented a sickening sight. He was at the mercy of Dixon, and, finding that he could not hit him, edged away from the centre of the ring to a place just to the left of his own corner. Here he was again attacked by Dixon, who hit him at will in the face, knocking him against the ropes. Skelly staggered up to as erect a position as he could assume, and Dixon, poising himself, swung his right, and catching Skelly on the right jaw, sent him to the ground. Skelly made a noble effort to arise, but was unsuccessful and even as the referee was counting the time aloud one of Skelly's seconds reached through the ropes and wiped the blood from the face of the prostrate amateur. Duffy counted ten with the regularity of clockwork and on the last count as Skelly was still on the ground, he said "out" and Dixon was still the champion, after a battle lasting just exactly one-half hour....

GEORGE DIXON.

George Dixon, the saddle-colored champion bantamweight of the world, who fought Jack Skelly in the arena of the Olympic Club last night had previous to his appearance in New Orleans achieved a success in the pugilistic world of which any pugilist that ever lived might be proud. He had fought the champions of America, England and Australia, and had conquered every opponent whom he had faced, in the most impressive style. His list of victories speaks for itself and there is little that can be added to his record, which is as follows:

Defeated	*Rounds*	*Year*
Elias Hamilton at Boston	3	1886
Young Mack at Boston	3	1887
Jack Lyman at Boston	8	1887
Charley Parton at Boston	5	1887
Barney Finnegan at Boston	6	1888
Ned Morris at Boston	7	1888
James Bracket at Boston	4	1888
Paddy Kelly at Boston	10	1888
Billy James at Haverhill	2	1889
Eugene Hornbacker at New York	2	1889
Jack Carey at Jersey City	4	1890
Joe Farrell at New York	4	1890
Paddy Kearney at Paterson	4	1890
Ned Wallace in England	18	1890
Johnny Murphy at Providence	40	1890
Cal McCarthy at Troy, N.Y	24	1890
J. Allen at Baltimore	2	1890
Virginia Rosebud at Baltimore	2	1890
Leeds Andrew at Washington	4	1890
W. Dyson at Washington	3	1890
Nick Collins	4	1890
Abe Willis at San Francisco	5	1890
Fred Johnson at New York	14	1892

The above record does not include the names of the numerous men who have attempted to stand-before the Bostonian during his theatrical tours. Were these added to the list, it would be swelled to over 100. Many of them were ambitious novices, wholly unknown to fame, but whether novices or veterans all shared the same fate. Every one was impressively "bested." Dixon stands five feet five inches high and is twenty-two years of age. His battles, though termed victories in the long run, often resulted in his receiving terrible punishment at the hands of men to whom he was giving a great deal of weight, and it was this wonderful faculty which he seemed to possess for taking punishment almost as much as his extraordinary hitting powers that caused O'Rourke, his present backer and manager, to single him out for a pugilistic phenomenon.

THE OLYMPIC CONTESTS

The Olympic Club has certainly managed its "pugilistic carnival" admirably. Whatever one may think of these ring contests, whether he believes they help athletics or encourage fighting, no one can deny that the "affairs" before the Olympic were most admirably conducted and disciplined. There was not a fault to find in this respect. The contests were carried to the end and the audience was given the full value of its money. There were none of these fake contests which have become quite common in some other athletic clubs, but everything was conducted honestly and fairly.

As for the order preserved, we cannot be too complimentary. There was applause when a favorite struck a good blow, but no jeers, calls or abuse were allowed, and the arena was as orderly and well behaved as any theatre could be.

The Olympic Club deserves the credit of having fully carried out its promises and made the prize ring as little objectionable as it can be made.

On one point, however, we disagree with the policy of the Olympic Club, and that is in respect to the match between Dixon and Skelly; and we sincerely trust that this mistake-for it was a mistake and a serious one to match a negro with a white man-will not be repeated.

Out of respect for the Olympic Club the people of this city and the audience present Tuesday night did not resent this match as they would otherwise have done. It was already made, and it was too late to prevent it without causing some scandal that might have reflected on the club. The latter had promised that there should be no discrimination because of color; that the fight should be perfectly fair and equal in all respects. It carried out its pledge faithfully, and the audience helped it to do so. But it was a disagreeable duty to all Southern men present, and we hope the club will not subject them to any more unpleasantness of this kind.

It was a mistake to match a negro and a white man, a mistake to bring the races together on any terms of equality, even in the prize ring, and especially a mistake to arrange a fight where representatives of the two races were placed in antagonism; for, among the ignorant negroes the idea has naturally been created that it was a test of the strength and fighting powers of Caucasian and African. No one can doubt who saw the reception of Dixon when he arrived and the interest and enthusiasm felt over the fight by the colored population of this city, that they regarded "the little darky" as the champion of their race; and that because of his victory they are far more confident than they ever were before of the equality of the races, and disposed to claim more for themselves than we intend to concede. We have heard some instances of this already; we shall probably hear more as some impudent negro becomes filled with the idea that he is another Dixon, the equal if not superior of the white man he meets; and we need not say that such a belief is liable to lead to still greate unpleasantness than that exhibited in the ring between the two featherweights. We of the South who know the fallacy and danger of this doctrine of race equality, who are opposed to placing the negro on any terms of equality, who have insisted on a separation of the races in church, hotel, car, saloon and theatre; who believe that the law ought to step in and forever forbid the idea of equality by making marriages between them illegal, are heartily opposed to any arrangement encouraging this equality, which give negroes false ideas and dangerous beliefs. They have their legal rights; they should have no more; and the white race of the South will destroy itself if it tolerates equality of any kind. Some may argue that there is no race question in the prize ring. We think differently. It was not pleasant to see white men applaud a negro for knocking another white man out. It was not pleasant to see them crowding around "Mr." Dixon to congratulate him on his victory, to seek an introduction with "the distinguished colored gentleman" while he puffed his cigar and lay back like a prince receiving his subjects. There were a number of other unpleasant features about the matter which should have been avoided.

Mr. John L. Sullivan has set a good example in this matter. Although a Northerner, a native of Massachusetts, and, therefore, free from the racial sentiment of the Southern whites which tells them that white civilization and blood can alone be preserved by refusing any equality with the negroes, he (Sullivan) has persistently refused to meet a negro in the ring. No one can believe that he has done this for any other reasons than his confidence that such contests place the races more or less on terms of equality. The champion is a Northern man, and what he feels on this subject should be felt in even greater degree by the member of the Olympic Club, who are Southern men.

We understand that some of the members did not approve of the fight, and did not want negroes admitted to the clubhouse; and that the match was made simply to prove that the club was able to give a fight of this kind, fairly and above all suspicion, and that no race discrimination would be shown. If it was desired to prove the perfect fairness of the Olympic Club, which no one doubted, this has been fully done; and now let us have no more negro fights here, or, if they are to occur, let them occur before a negro club. As we have said before, there have been many growls on this subject, and a very strong feeling about it. Respect for the Olympics has kept that feeling down for some time. It would do well not to try the experiment a second time.

We can inform the Olympic Club, as its members doubtless well know, that fights between negroes and whites are not popular here; that the people believe they are likely to stir up strife and create unpleasantness, and that any more of them will be regarded with decided disfavor.

"Gentleman Jim" Corbett lost his heavyweight title to Bob Fitzsimmons on 17 March 1897 in Carson City, Nevada. Fitzsimmons held the title until 9 June 1899 when he was beaten by Jim Jeffries. The Chicago Tribune printed a round by round account of the first encounter on page 2 the following day.

STORY OF THE FIGHT BY ROUNDS.

[SPECIAL BY W.W. NAUGHTON] Carson, Nev., March 17,-[Copyright, 1897] It was given out that the men would be called into the ring at ten minutes to 12, and precisely at that time Fitz was seen approaching from his dressing-room, which was situated in the east end of the arena. Martin Julian led the procession, and Fitz, attired in a red and blue bath robe, followed. Next to him was Roeber and then Hickey and Stelzner. They walked clear around to the opposite side of the ring, and Fitz came clear around to his corner. Before entering the ring he kissed his wife, who sat in a box near by. The Cornishman had his face puckered up on account of the strong sunlight, but he did not seem to be at all nervous.

Corbett, attired in a brown dressing gown, was in the ring a few seconds after Fitz. Jim was attended by Billy Delaney, Jack McVey, Charley White, Billy Woods, and John Donaldson. Jim walked around the ring nodding to his friends, while Fitz stood with his hands on the ropes.

Charley White took the Irish and American flags, which together were Corbett's colors, and tied them around the corner post. Fitz paced slowly up and down the ring with his hands in his robe pockets, while Martin Julian walked over to Corbett and began discussing matters pertaining to ring etiquette.

While Corbett and Fitz stepped slowly around the ring waving their hands to friends who offered greeting, Billy Madden, the master of ceremonies, announced the conditions of the contest and the names of the officials. The officials named were: George Siler, referee: William Muldoon, official timekeeper; James Colville, timekeeper for Corbett; Lou Houseman, timekeeper for Fitz. Corbett's seconds were Charley White, Billy Delaney, Billy Woods, Jack McVey, John Donaldson, and Jim Jefferies. Fitz had for henchmen, Martin Julian, Jack Stelzer, Ernest Roeber, and Dan Hickey. Several bottleholders were engaged outside the ropes in uncorking bottles of mineral water, and in dampening sponges for the fighters.

After Siler had been introduced, Madden stepped down and left the referee, principals, and seconds in possession of the ring. Delaney examined Fitzsimmons' gloves while the Cornishman was putting them on, and Julian stepped over to Corbett's corner and performed a like service.

The men quickly shed their robes. Fitz had on black shoes and stockings, and dark navy blue trunks, and an American flag belt. Corbett wore black shoes and grey stockings, low down, the red trunk and the Stars and Stripes and green sash entwined in a belt. The loins and body of both men were bare.

Siler went over to Fitz, and convinced himself that the Cornishman surely understood the rules under which they were to fight. Then he walked over to Corbett's corner and had a similar understanding. It was remarked by some of Corbett's friends that Fitz was shaking like an aspen but if such was the condition of the Cornishman's nerves, he concealed it very well.

Corbett walked over to Fitz to give him a preliminary hand shake, and Julian stepped in between. "No hand shake," said he. Fitz also shook his head. There was a big laugh, as this was evidently for Corbett's treatment during the meeting on the country road. Corbett said, "Very well," laughed, and strode back to his corner. The men stood a little distance from their corners.

ROUND 1.

At 12:05 o'clock the gong clanged and the championship battle was on.

Both men went to the center of the ring and feinted rapidly. Fitz made a slight movement with his left and Corbett stepped back. Again Fitz made a motion and Jim side-stepped. He was smiling and walking around so as to keep the sun in the

Cornishman's eyes. Corbett backed away towards the ropes and Fitz made a violent left lunge at him. Corbett ducked and got out of the way and Fitz came back again with the left hand.

Again Fitz went in. Corbett swung with his left, missed the Cornishman's chin by a few inches. Fitz was forcing Corbett. He worked him back towards the ropes again and Jim grinned. There was a light exchange of left-handers but no harm was done, the men breaking away immediately. Fitz started with his left: Jim ducked and caught him with a body blow. They clinched for a moment, breaking away almost immediately at a word from the referee. Fitz followed Corbett and led off with the left, but Jim backed out of the way. Fitz worked Corbett towards the corner, and Corbett ducked out of danger.

Fitz as he faced around, had the sun in his eyes and Corbett made a lead at him. They clinched. Corbett balked with the left and swung his right on the ribs lightly. Fitz forced Corbett into his own corner and tried twice with the left. One blow missed and the other caught Corbett on the shoulder. Corbett stepped in and gave Fitz a right above the heart. Fitz feinted at Corbett. Corbett poked out his left hand. Fitz ducked under it and clinched. They broke away instantly. Corbett was fighting very cautiously. Fitz advanced and Corbett swung and hit the Cornishman high on the left hand side of the head. Fitz worked Corbett towards the ropes and led full with his left. Corbett ducked and got out of danger.

Corbett led with his left and there was a clinch. Fitz hit him on the temple with his right during the clinch and Corbett made a motion with his mouth, as saying "O," and looked towards the referee. Fitz tried for an opening and Corbett caught him in the body with his left. They hung together for a few seconds just before the gong rung.

What honors there were in the first round Corbett was entitled to. The Cornishman forced the fighting, but failed to land effectively. The blow on Corbett's temple with the right in the clinch was the only one he scored. Fitz was breathing heavily and was pale, while Corbett's breathing was not distressed.

ROUND 2.

Corbett went briskly to the center of the ring at the call of time. He feinted repeatedly with his left. Fitz led at him, and there was a clinch. Corbett catching Fitz a slight right-hander on the ear as they clinched. They hung together for some time, Fitzsimmons vainly endeavoring to push Corbett away. When they finally broke away Fitz was backed up in Corbett's corner. Corbett kept him there by feinting, but Fitz made two or three leads and worked out. None of the blows took effect.

They clinched in Corbett's corner, and when they turned around Corbett's back was to his own corner and the sun in the Cornishman's face. Corbett drove with his right, and then they clinched. They broke away immediately. Fitz pressed Corbett again and Corbett backed around the ring, backing out of danger. They stood still for a moment and Corbett swung his left on Fitz's temple. They hung together a moment and Fitz pushed Corbett away. Corbett got in a straight left-hander on Fitz's forehead and they clinched. Corbett this time rushed the Cornishman away.

Corbett feinted with his left and Bob ducked. Fitz forced Corbett into a corner and let fly with left and right. The blow with the right caught Corbett on the shoulder and they clinched. They swung around and worked into the center of the ring and Corbett hit Fitz in the ribs with his right. There was another clinch, and as they broke away Corbett put in a little right hook on the jaw. Fitz made a swing with the left and the right, but missed. Corbett came back at him with a right swing which went too far around and it resulted in a clinch. Corbett swung his left, grazing Fitz's chin. He tried again with similar success, but neither of the blows was a hard one. Fitz led with his left and Corbett ducked. They went into a clinch, and Fitz threw his forearm up across Corbett's neck. Jim landed a hard left half-round jab on Fitz's stomach. Another from Jim's left goes to the same place. Jim jabs Fitz hard right and left on body when bell rings.

ROUND 3.

Corbett starts right in with that left hook on the body. Fitz gets savage and tries his left and right on Corbett's head but does very little damage. Corbett lands another left jab on the body and follows with right short on the ribs. Jim clinches, Corbett lands right hand over heart. Fitz mixes it up and puts the heel of his glove in Corbett's face. In the clinch Jim keeps his right working like a piston rod on Fitz's body. They clinch and Fitz roughs it in the breakaway. As the gong sounds Fitz seems anxious to continue, but Corbett laughingly sticks his right glove in Fitz's face and they go to their corners.

ROUND 4.

Corbett rushing, lands the left again on Fitz's body. Fitz is short with his left, Fitz follows it with a stiff left in Jim's stomach and they clinch. They rough it again. They are fighting at a terrific rate and it is a beautiful contest. Fitz rushes and Jim meets him with a stiff right hand short in the stomach. Fitz is doing the rushing and hitting in the breakaways. Corbett is by long odds making the cleverer fight. He is playing systematically with right and left on body.

They clinched again. Corbett came in with a left on the face and a right under the heart, and clinched. Fitz acted as if he was tired. Fitz led with his right and Corbett with his left, just as time was called. Fitz's blows took effect on Corbett's stomach and Jim's did not reach. They clinched and parted at the sound of the gong.

ROUND 5.

Corbett opened the fifth round with a left hand punch fair on the jaw. They clinched and broke away. Fitz rushed and Corbett side stepped in a lively fashion. Fitz crowded him near the ropes but did not get in a blow. They clinched for a moment and then broke away. As Fitz was coming in Corbett reached him with a left hander on the chin and they clinched again. Jim made two short attempts with left and right, and they clinched. Corbett having his hand around Fitz's neck and swinging around. Fitz went towards the ropes and Corbett landed a very heavy heart punch.

They hugged and worked their way over to the center of the ring, where they dropped their arms and stood away. Fitz and Corbett both landed a heart punch at the same time. It would be hard to say which one was the most severe. Fitz landed another heart punch and received a left on the jaw. Jim also landed a left on the jaw and they clinched. Jim swung with his left and Fitz with his right, but the blows were smothered ones and it simply resulted in a clinch. Corbett let fly with his right for heart and hit a bit too high, and they clinched again. Corbett tried with his left and was short. Fitz blinked and grinned, and they clinched. Corbett tried another left, and they clinched.

Corbett tried another left, which was short. Fitz still grinning, Corbett tries with his left, but Fitz was there first, landing on Jim's chin. They clinched. Fitz let fly a left hander and Jim placed his forearm against the Cornishman's throat, driving him away. Corbett landed a swift left on the face and another with the right. Delaney and White called "First blood for Corbett," as they were clinched. The blood showed on Fitz's upper lip. When they drifted apart Corbett landed another swift left on the nose. They clinched again momentarily and then Corbett scored again with his left, and his seconds sung out, "Take your time, Jim, you've got him."

The sun was now in Fitz's eyes. Corbett landed three blows in succession, two lefts and a right on Fitz's face. The right took effect on the chin and jarred Fitz. They clinched, and Fitz passed a heart punch. His eyes were rolling and he appeared to be in distress. Corbett led with his right for the heart, but Fitz got the blow with his glove. Corbett swung with his left on Fitz's jaw. Corbett reached Fitz's face with his left again, and they clinched. Fitz hit at the heart before breaking away, and Corbett uppercut him with the right on the chin. This round was decidedly in Corbett's favor. He scored twice to the Cornishman's once, and Fitz looked very tired. The referee walked to the ropes and announced first blood for Corbett. Mrs. Fitz arose in her seat. She was pale, and apparently very much disturbed. She shouted to the seconds and worked her hands up and down as if instructing them to ask Fitz to alter his style of fighting in some way.

ROUND 6.

As soon as they came to the center of the ring Fitz feinted and there was a clinch. He got his forearm across Corbett's throat and forced his head back, jamming him so that it looked as if he would crack Corbett's nose. Corbett himself looked around at the referee. They parted at the ropes and met again in the center of the ring, where a slight lead from Fitz ended in a clinch. This time Corbett got Fitz's head under his arm and squeezed it.

A lead from Fitz resulted in a clinch, and Corbett caught him with a right in the chin on the breakaway. Fitz this time clinched again. Corbett uppercut him on the breakaway and sent the Cornishman's head back. Another right hand punch from Corbett brought the blood in showeres from the Cornishman's nose. He was very much distressed. He clung to Corbett, and the blood went all over Corbett's chest. Corbett's seconds were excited and were shouting "Take your time, Jim." After they parted Corbett smashed Fitz right and left on the face. Fitz was powerless.

A succession of lefts and rights from Corbett made him dizzy and he clinched on every available occasion. Corbett worked him towards the ropes, holding him with his left and smashing him in the face with his right. Fitz was a dilapidated man. Once he swung at Jim, but his feet went from under him and he fell to the floor. He rested on his knees and Corbett walked away from him. The referee stood between them. Julian came to the rope and Fitz got up just as time was called. Corbett went at him again and scored a left and right in the face. Fitz stood back and feinted and then he clinched and hung on to Corbett.

Corbett got in a right uppercut which sent Fitz's head back. Fitz clinched at every opportunity. He was helpless, for Corbett kept pumping the right-hand uppercut into him. Once Corbett varied it by giving a right-hand punch fair in the stomach. They clinched and broke away momentarily and Fitz clung around his neck again Corbett punched him in the body and occasionally in the face. Fitz swung his arms, but with no force to his blows. Corbett drew back so as to be out of range, and then would lead first with his left and then with his right, reaching Fitz's face every time. Fitz caught Corbett in the face. Jim came to the corner with a little blood in his nostrils and on his lip. As Fitz sat in his corner he was very weak.

When his head went down the fresh blood fell from his lips. The seconds sponged his mouth, but couldn't keep the blood from flowing. There was great excitement. Corbett was evidently anxious, but in good shape. His wind was good and he was perfectly strong. While the other man was badly rattled, and his strength was waning. The end looked very near when the gong sounded at the end of the sixth round.

ROUND 7.

As they came to the center of the ring Fitz led with his left. The blow missed and there was a clinch. In the breakaway Corbett got in a right-hander on the nose and started the blood afresh. After the breakaway Fitz came in swinging wildly. Corbett steadied him up with a flush left-hander on the nose, which increased the flow of blood. Corbett then stood away and watched Fitz keenly, as if to size up his condition. A lead from Fitz resulted in a clinch. Bob attempted to get in a right-hand blow in the breakaway but Corbett was too quick for him. Fitz led with his left, but was short. They clinched. As Fitz came in Corbett let out his right, reaching the Cornishman's jaw. The blow was only a kind of a balk to prepare the way for a right-hand body blow, which Corbett drove in with considerable force.

Fitz bounded away from it, and then they clinched. Corbett feinted with his left and Fitz ducked. Again Corbett feinted with his left. This time Fitz made no motion and Corbett hit him a swift left-hander in the nose. Fitz tried with his left and right, being short with the blows and getting a left counter which spurted the blood all over his face. He clung to Corbett and flecked Corbett's body with the gory fluid. Fitz tried a right-hander at the ribs, which Corbett drew back from. They clinched. Everything seemed going Corbett's way. He was taking his time and punching Fitz alternately in the face and body with his left, and Corbett got his forearm against Fitz's neck. Fitz made two or three swings with his right and left hand but they were so feeble that Corbett evidently made up his mind that the danger point was passed. He went in and hit Fitz a swinging right-hander in the cheek. As the gong sounded Corbett drew his right hand around, scoring again on Fitz's ear.

ROUND 8.

Fitz fiddled for an opening and Corbett sidestepped in a bewildering manner. When the Cornishman finally launched out Jim ducked and they clinched. Fitz hit him and tried again. Corbett ducked under the blow. Fitz tried again and Corbett ducked and threw a hard left into the pit of the stomach. Fitz let fly with his left and nearly threw himself off his balance. Corbett drew away laughing. Fitz had his right poised now, evidently waiting to get in a right-hander, but Corbett was wary. At every motion he would draw back, not far, but just far enough to be out of the way of the blow. Fitz led with his left and was short, his glove dropping on Corbett's chest. Corbett stood watching Fitz intently. Fitz led with his left and Jim ducked the blow and brought his own left into the pit of Fitz's stomach. Then Corbett came in with a heart punch, which landed. Fitz followed Corbett and was met by a right swing on the nose, which started the blood again. He drew back for a moment and Corbett in turn made the pace, driving a right in the heart and two lefts on Fitz's damaged countenance. There was a big daub of blood on Corbett's right shoulder where Fitz's face rested in the clinches. Corbett led short with the left once or twice. The blows looked as if he didn't intend them to reach, but was evidently waiting for something. Finally Fitz came toward him and Corbett swung hard, reaching Fitz's chin. Fitz swung with his right, but missed Corbett by about a foot.

Jim clinched and gave him a blow with the right in the mouth. They broke away and went around the ring. Corbett swung with a left and right landing. They clinched. Corbett held Fitz's head under his arm. Corbett put in two or three left-handers now, which covered Fitz's face with blood from the roots of his hair to his breastbone. Corbett wound up the round with a straight left-hander which took effect on Fitz's nose and sent the Cornishman's head back with a jolt.

Corbett was fighting with wonderful carefulness. He wasn't taking any chances and at the same time he was doing all the scoring. Brady sung out to him frequently during the round to look out for that right, but the caution seemed unheeded.

ROUND 9.

They both feinted for a while at the opening of the ninth round. Finally Corbett led with his left and Fitz drew back. Corbett tried to put another left hand swing in the stomach and Fitz caught the blow on his glove. Fitz led with his left for the stomach, and the referee complained that the blow was rather low. Bob said he would be careful in the future. Corbett put in a left-hander fair in Fitz's belt and he doubled up like a jack-knife. As he came in again they clinched. Fitz forced Corbett back, swinging with his left. As he came again Corbett gave him a left rap in the face and started the blood again. They clinched. Fitz forced Corbett back, swinging right and left, but failing to score. As they came to the center of the ring Corbett got in a jarring left fair on the chin. Fitz shook his head as they clinched. Corbett put in another left-hander and they clinched.

Fitz seemed very feeble. Another left-hander and a clinch, and Corbett gave Fitz a nasty one under the heart with his right before breaking. Fitz worked Corbett into a corner and scored with two lefts in the face, neither of which left a mark. They clinched again. Fitz tried a left swing, but Corbett threw the blow off with his shoulder. He countered Fitz with a left in the jaw, rattling him badly. As they came in now Corbett placed his gloves slowly on Fitz's mouth and clinched. Fitz laughed and said something. Fitz tried a right-hander and was short. He was given a left in the nose on return and they clinched again.

Fitz led lightly with his left and Corbett ducked. Jim put in a left-hander in the nose and clinched. Fitz tried to hit him with a right in the breakaway but Jim threw the blow off with his shoulder. As Jim looked towards his own corner he looked to Delaney as much as to say: "it is all right: I have got him."

Fitz was bleeding freely. His back was humped and his legs seemed to drag as he moved around. One of Corbett's seconds sung out: "Look out for him, Jim; he's faking there; he isn't as bad off as he looks."

At this point the gong clanged and the ninth round was over. As Fitz sat in his corner Julian and Roeber were rubbing and slashing his legs vigorously. The Cornishman's under lip protruded. It was swollen and his nose was in such a state it was hard to stop the flow of blood.

ROUND 10.

Fitzsimmons forced Corbett and let fly a wild left swing. He missed and stumbled and went to the ropes. As he turned around Corbett crowded him a right-hander on the ear. There was a clinch. They swung over to mid-ring and parted. Fitz led with his left and Corbett countered on the nose. They clinched again. Fitz tried a left for the ribs and the blow fell against Corbett's left elbow. Corbett put one in on the face and there was a clinch. After they got away Fitz swung his left on the face and put in a blow over the heart. They clinched again. After the breakaway Corbett led with his left and reached Fitz's neck.

Fitz clinched and placed his forearm across Corbett's throat, forcing Jim's head back. Corbett swung for the body with his left and missed. Fitz a left hander on the cheek. Corbett worked Fitz over to Corbett's corner and put in a heart blow. After that Jim landed two to the pit of the stomach. He let fly a left on the mouth and got a left counter in return. They clinched. Corbett put in a blow under the heart and they clinched again. Fitz swung with his right and missed. He followed it up with a left hander which took Corbett on the neck. They clinched in Corbett's corner. As they broke away Fitz swung heavily with the left, landing on Corbett's mouth, and there were cries of: "Good boy, Fitz."

They clinched and as they broke away Fitz swung with his right on Corbett's neck. Corbett clinched again. There were more cries of "Good boy, Fitz."

Corbett at this point was very tired or pretended to be. He led with his left for Fitz's chin and Fitz countered with a much heavier left on his chin. Then they clinched, Jim's seconds shouted out to him to take his time. Fitz reached Corbett with another left-hander and they clinched again. Fitz led with his left and Corbett ducked the blow and clinched. Fitz tried to hit him and in the breakaway Corbett threw his head down and Fitz held him wrestler fashion around the neck and dragged him towards the ropes. There were cries of "Ah, don't do that."

Fitz let go and Corbett went to the center of the ring. A left-hander from Fitz took effect on Corbett's chin and they clinched again. The gong separated them.

ROUND 11.

Fitz tried with his left. Corbett smothered the blow and clinched. When they broke away Corbett landed a left swing on the chin. Fitz tried repeatedly with his left, but was short. Corbett put in a heart blow with his right. They separated. Fitz put in two left handers on the chin. Corbett then forced the pace, striking with left and right. He reached the face and caused it to bleed afresh. They clinched and parted, and Corbett put in a right-hander under the heart. He tried a left swing, which reached Fitz's shoulder, and they clinched again. Both men appeared to be tired. They hit short and clinched at every opportunity, hanging together without punching. Delaney said: "Look out for that right, Jim."

Fitz swung twice with the right and was short, Corbett clinched. Fitz ducked a right-hander and clinched. Fitz led off with the right and the blow caught Corbett on the upper arm. Corbett let fly with his right, and Fitz promptly ducked the blow. The men clinched again, and before breaking away Fitz put in a right uppercut, which grazed Jim's face. Fitz left-hooked Jim, and they clinched again. They clung together without hitting. Corbett tried a left-hander, and Fitz threw the blow off with his right arm. They clinched. Fitz put in a short right in the breakaway. Fitz led, catching Corbett twice on chin. They clinched, and Corbett appeared to be as tired as Fitz. Corbett put in two or three straight lefts, but there wasn't a great deal of steam in them. Corbett put a left-hander straight in the face, and Fitz responded with a heavier one. Fitz tried a wild left swing and was short. He got Corbett into his corner and let fly with right and left. One of the right-handers caught Corbett on the ear, and he clinched. Fitz made a terrific right hand swing just as the gong sounded. Corbett ducked under the blow, and they hung together. The issue seemed in doubt as the men went to their corners.

ROUND 12.

Fitz came up quickly, starting after Corbett with a vicious left for the head. Corbett ducked and Fitz's arm passed fully a foot above his back. The energy of his blow swung Fitz clear around and he staggered, almost falling down in Corbett's corner. He rallied quickly, however, and put his right on body before Corbett could catch him. Corbett missed a left jab pointed at the jaw, and Fitz went through a similar performance, but swung back with his right, catching Corbett on the head, and then followed it up with a straight poke in the nose. Fitz repeated this performance, and with a left hook. Corbett put his left on the body very lightly and then put his left hand on the jaw, receiving a severe counter in the same place. Jim then landed hard to the head and rushed Fitz to the ropes, where a clinch followed. Men were apart just long enough to allow Corbett to put a light left on the jaw and a hard left on the nose, and they clinched again. During the clinch Fitz cleared his throat of blood, which he spat over Corbett's shoulder in the coolest manner possible. Then he wiped the blood from his nose with the thumb of his glove.

His toilet being completed, Fitz broke away, catching a hard left on the nose as he did. He missed another of the same sort and clinched, uppercutting Jim with his right on the breakaway. Both men ducked left swings and clinched again. Corbett then landed a rain of blows on Fitz, catching him repeatedly on the jaw and body. He landed on the body just about as he pleased, although the latter was fighting strong.

ROUND 13.

Fitz landed a left on the body and a hard right on the jaw. Jim missed a left-hand swing, but landed a left on the jaw and the men clinched. Fitz missed a hard right for the head, following Corbett around the ring, Corbett with his guard down in a careless fashion, Fitz following him up and pushing him to the ropes. No harm was done, both men taking it easy. Corbett landed a light left on the face and another on the body but missed a right uppercut. He then landed a hard straight left on Fitz's nose, following him to the ropes and missing a left-hand swing, receiving only a light tap on the ear in return and the men clinched. Fitz's bleeding nose seemed to be troubling him, but he assumed the aggressive and made Corbett dance around the ring to avoid him, receiving a hard left on the body before he desisted. Fitz landed a hard left on the body, staggering Corbett and then landed on the body. Both men laughed. Jim put in a straight left on the nose and a right uppercut on the jaw in the clinch that followed. Corbett landed his left on the face twice and missed a lead for the head. While following Jim. Fitz got a light left on the face. Both men were in the center of the ring as the round closed. Fitz's face being again covered with blood from his nose.

ROUND 14.

Up to this Corbett had the better of the fighting. He hit Fitz whenever he pleased and pretty much where he pleased. His generalship was far superior to that of Fitz and he got away and came in again with marvelous speed. He was tiring rapidly, however, and was far from having the stamina that Fitz showed. The latter had been punished fearfully throughout the proceding rounds, but he was still strong and game to the core. The round opened with a left swing for the jaw by Corbett. It missed the mark, burt he tried again with better success, reaching the jaw good and hard. Fitz was all there, however, and he sent his left to the body with terrific force. The blow sent Corbett staggering backward several feet and evidently hurt him badly. Fitz lost no time and followed closely and sent his right to Corbett's face, causing him to totter again. He then put his left hand on the body and was hot after his man, but Corbett gave ground to get away.

Corbett came up strong, however, and put his left hard on Fitz's body. The latter put in a hard right on the head. Jim was looking tired, his strength was going, and he clinched. After the breakaway Fitz put a hard right and left on the jaw and the men clinched again, Corbett fighting Fitz into the southwest corner of the ring. Jim put his left on the jaw and Fitz sent his right to the chin with fearful force. The blow made Corbett lean backward and turned him partly around. He raised his guard a trifle, and, quick as lightning, Fitz shot his left glove on Corbett's body just below the heart.

The blow was one that would have shivered a plank, and Corbett's face paled instantly, his arms fell to his sides, his eyes closed, and he fell forward to the ropes, catching at them with his right hand. His face bore a look of intense agony and he was evidently suffering the most excruciating pain. He tried to rise, but Fitz, with his right on him, caught him with a right jab on the chin. Corbett was not knocked out in the common acceptance of the word. He was not unconscious, but the pain resulting from the blow under the heart was so great to make him careless of anything else.

He tried several times to rise, but was unable to do so and was counted out by the referee.

The New York Times provided commentary on the Fitzsimmons-Jeffries bout on 10 June 1899, p. 2.

JEFFRIES WINS FROM FITZSIMMONS

THE WINNER IS NOW CHAMPION OF THE WORLD - GREAT CROWDS GATHER TO OBTAIN NEWS OF THE EVENT.

The long-heralded prizefight, known by a pleasant fiction of New York law as a boxing contest, between Robert Fitzsimmons, who held the championship of the world, and James J. Jeffries, the aspiring boilermaker from California, was fought last night in the building of the New Coney Island Sporting Club.

It resulted in an indisputable victory for Jeffries in the eleventh round. Consequently the world has a new champion pugilist this morning, and Fitzsimmons, who knocked out Corbett, who knocked out Sullivan, has taken his place in the long procession of fistic heroes known in ring circles as "back numbers" or "has beens."

The work of changing champions occupied a little less than forty-four minutes. How much the two men gained in money nobody knows. On a rough estimate it is said that Fitzsimmons, whose dignity demanded large pecuniary inducements to tempt him to display his prowess upon a comparatively unknown man, will receive about $25,000 of the gate receipts as his share, besides contingent profits from the vitascope, which took photographs of the fight and will reproduce them indefinitely.

Jeffries will do as well and is probably richer by a comfortable amount in side bets, to say nothing of gratuities from winners, who are naturally all his enthusiastic friends....

A WELL-DRESSED CROWD.

It was a well-dressed gathering. There was not a shabby man in sight anywhere, nor were there many whose dress indicated the sporting man. Immediately about the ring there were rows of middle-aged and elderly men, some of them with white hair and beards. These had a distinctively well-fed and well-groomed appearance, and diamonds flashed from their fingers and shirt fronts in the electric light. But for the diamonds and the formidable cigars at which many of them pulled, they might have been taken for vestrymen waiting for the opening of a religious service, so tranquil was their demeanor so calm were their countenances and the peace of their attitudes.

There were old and young men who had traveled more than a thousand miles and spent hundreds of dollars to reach the ringside, and they were content to be there. Some of them had thousands and ten of thousands of dollars at stake, but it is against sporting ethics to display emotion and the prevalent face was impassive, even though it might sometimes pale or flush....

JEFFRIES LOOKED ANGRY.

There was a great cheer and a rattle of applause when Jeffries walked in a little after 9 o'clock, pushing his way through the men packed along the arena. He looked huge and rather angry than pleased, and, with his red sweater under a sack coat, and a flimsy cap on the back of his head resting on his thick black hair, was the most carelessly dressed and the roughest-looking man in the room. There was a fainter cheer as Fitzsimmons was announced, and after his disappearance there were symptoms of impatience and cries and hoots began to sound from around the house.

The rumor that there was a dispute over the rules had gone abroad, and it caused impatience and dissatisfaction. The uncertainty of Chief of Police Devery's intentions added to the uneasy feeling. The men there had not come to see whether Fitzsimmons or Jeffries was the better boxer. They wanted to see which was the "best man," which could hit hardest, endure the most pain and fatigue, keep his head, and use his skill the better when breath was coming hard and short and the body was sore and the muscles tired and resenting the fearful strain upon them.

At 10 o'clock there were yet vacant patches in the expanses of reserved seats opposite the ring on each side....

FLOWERS FOR FITZSIMMONS.

But the annoyance of waiting seemed to be forgotten when a cheer began at the eastern end of the great building, and the men there were seen to rise in their seats. The mass of humanity surged up like a great wave as a mound of roses appeared moving through the throng down o the floor. This was a gigantic horseshoe of pink, white, and crimson roses, with American flags above it, and bearing the inscription, "Good Luck to the Champion."

Behind this aesthetic proclamation, which was carried by two men, Fitzsimmons stalked solemnly, like the chief figure in a classic spectacle. His bearing was solemn, like that of a man who felt that he was about to perform a rite with the eyes of an admiring world concentrated upon him. He wore a bath robe of pale blue, gathered at the waist, and his head was bare. His three attendants, in white flannel undershirts and long trousers, followed him, two of them bearing galvanized iron buckets and broad palm-leaf fans, one of them with a long bottle driven into his hip pocket.

Jeffries was more on the rough-and-ready order. He moved briskly and swung his shoulders and wore a red sweater, with ordinary, commonplace humanity; but his three seconds carried the galvanized iron buckets and the bottles and fans and were also in their undershirts.

AN AESTHETIC FEATURE.

A stray wounded moth had been fluttering about the padded surface of the ring, and as the big floral piece was carried in many of the roses tumbled to places. Therefore, it was another aesthetic feature of the affair that the first actual preliminary was to clear the ring of moth and rose leaves, which was done with one of the big fans.

Fitzsimmons, sitting on his wooden stool in his corner, watched this operation with interest. Jeffries, from his stool in his corner, twisted his neck and peered between the men who surrounded him, trying to catch a view of his antagonist.

Then came the referee, George Siler, in blue and white striped undershirt, collarless and bareheaded. He leaned negligently against the ropes in an unoccupied corner while the seconds inspected the gloves and other seconds fitted them on.

Fitzsimmons rubbed his hands together before he submitted to be gloved, his air being that of a man who rather expected to enjoy himslef. Jeffries leaned over and rubbed his palms on the floor to get resin upon them. Billy Brady leaned against the ropes opposite the press stalls, and bit the top one idly. Nobody in or around the ring was excited or hurried. One of the seconds held a fan over Fitzsimmons's head as Eastern attendants hold umbrellas of state above potentates.

By this time the spectators had all arrived and it was seen that men of several classes were elbow to elbow and cheek by jowl. There were sporting men and business men, financiers and actors, society men and jockeys, and distributed among them all were the denizens of South Brooklyn, who always can afford to buy a front seat at a prize fight in or around New York.

MRS. FITZSIMMONS PRESENT.

Mrs. Fitzsimmons got into the clubhouse, and was in her husband's dressing room while he was preparing for the battle, but she decided not to attempt to witness the fight. She saw William A. Brady, the manager of Jeffries, shook hands with him, and remarked:

"We will beat your man again to-night, as we did the other at Carson City."

Brady smiled and replied that he hoped not, and Mrs. Fitzsimmons, after seeing that her husband was properly equipped for for the fray, kissed him, and wishing him good luck, sent him out into the arena.

George E. Smith, ("Pittsburg Phil,") a man who never in his career on the turf even when a decision of $100,000 depended on an inch of ground, was known to betray excitement, caused some surprise by becoming one of the most enthusiastic of the shouters. He was a Jeffries man, and his excitement was in marked contrast to the cool demeanor of some of the others.

About 10:17 Jeffries's seconds, with serious demeanor, began to withdraw his trousers, and a hundred pencils in the press stalls were instantly busy with the chronicle of this portentous fact.

Two journalists with split second watches had quite an energetic dispute as to whether the ceremony began at 10:17 or 10:17 1/4. There was also a solemn drawing of corks from the bottles and an unfolding and laying aside of large towels. About the same time Fitzsimmons untied and put away his pale-blue robe and revealed himslef naked but for trunks and shoes with black stockings turned down nearly to his ankles. The trunks were ornamented with rosettes of red, white, and blue. Jeffries also wore trunks, shoes, and stockings. His trunks were plain white.

PERFUNCTORY HANDSHAKE.

Then they gargled their throats from the bottles and met each other at the centre of the ring, where they shook hands coldly and perfunctorily.

There was silence throughout the house by this time. The contrast between the two was startling. Fitzsimmons looked little and white confronting his antagonist. Jeffries is a dark man. His eyes and hair are black and his skin almost a tan. Fitzsimmons is light-eyed and what hair he has is pale red. No woman has a skin whiter or smoother than his.

The word was given and the men rose from the stools to which they had returned. Neither looked cheerful. Jeffries swallowed hard: Fitzsimmons moistened his lips with his tongue, and as he faced his man and they slowly and cautiously circled about, feinting, advancing, and retreating, never within arm's length, their eyes intently fastened on each other, he began to work his lips nervously.

THEY FACE EACH OTHER.

If the crowd had been a crowd of dead men, the stillness could not have been deeper than it was. The two pugilists trod softly as cats. Nothing could be heard but the gentle thud, thud of their ever restless, shifting feet as they circled.

Then there was a sudden rush and the sharp slap of a glove landing, a gleaming of arms and twisting and violent motion of white bodies in the ring, a storm of cries, with applause and some roaring laughter from arena and encompassing seats.

Jeffries had led. He was not afraid to fight. That was one point settled.

Fitzsimmons' light blue eyes opened wide and blazed angrily. Jeffries crouched low, keeping his tremendous left arm well thrust out, his head down, looking from under his eyebrows.

In the second round the cheering and shouting began again. The crowd then felt that it would see what it had gathered to see-a fight with hard knocks. The two men in the ring smiled at each other as both missed and they came together in a clinch, but the big muscles in their thighs were already quivering and they did not relax their watchfulness the fraction of a second.

CROWD WITH JEFFRIES.

The crowd was evidently with Jeffries, and after Fitzsimmons had tumbled on his back, looking a much-surprised man, joy was unrestrained. It was evident then that the ideas of Chief of Police Devery on slugging were liberal, and that there would be no interference. The older sporting men around the ring, their last fear removed, settled down more placidly and calmly than ever and looked entirely and supremely happy.

After the sixth round a new change came into Fitzsimmons's face. He had looked furious at times and amused at times, as he felt that he had scored a point or that his antagonist had missed one.

FITZSIMMONS WORRIED.

Now he looked old and worn and anxious. Wrinkles seemed to come into his cheeks. He was aggressive, crafty, watchful, always moving, his rather cruel lips working and working as if he would like to bite; but he seemed like a man who is hunted. Once or twice thereafter his lips broke into a smile. When he and Jeffries broke out of a clinch and separated at the end of the eighth round, their mutual grins were almost affable. But as he sat on his stool and breathed fast and his seconds fanned him furiously with towels and fans and gave him from the bottle to gargle, he looked harassed.

When the end came it seemed very quick and easy. The blow that really did the work was given with Jeffrie's left glove. After it was delivered Fitzsimmons stood an instant, his hands hanging by his side, his knees bowed. The knock-out with the right came swiftly. It was given from the hip, much like a quick slap. It was not like one of the long, hard swings Jeffries had aimed at him several times, and which had gone over his head.

When it landed Fitzsimmons fell and turned on his right side. There was no need to count. His body was limp and doubled up. He passed the back of his hand wearily over his bald forehead and straightened out on his back, his lower lip hanging foolishly his long upper lip scarlet.

Jeffries looked at him an instant and walked to his corner, breathing hard. A thousand men were storming and swirling about the ringside then.

Hats were waving and the big hall was ringing with yells and cheers and exultant laughter.

Fitzsimmons was dragged to his stool, his heels trailing helplessly on the floor. It was all over.

DEVERY AND SILER TALK.

After the knockout blow had been dealt Chief of Police Devery jumped to the outer edge of the ring and waited for the referee to count the fatal tenth second. He stepped into the ring then and his men surrounded it. He was asked in the ring by a reporter for the THE NEW YORK TIMES whether, in accordance with his declaration of a few days ago, he would arrest the principals.

"Wait a few moments and we will see," he replied. And then as he saw that Fitzsimmons had recovered sufficiently to sit up and answer the greeting and handshake Jeffries offered him, he added: He is as well as when he entered the ring, according to the report of Dr. Creamer, who examined him; so an arrest is not necessary."

"I wish it to be said, and said distinctly, that neither Mr. McLaughlin nor any other man made me change my opinion regarding the stand I took two days before the fight. I would have stopped the fight in a minute if I had seen anything that was a violation of the law."

George Siler, the referee, and Chief Devery had a short talk, and then the referee declared to a reporter for THE NEW YORK TIMES that the fight was one of the best he had ever witnessed.

"It was Jeffries' fight from start to finish," he said, "and if the fight had been stopped at any time previous to the knockout, the decision would have to have been in Jeffries' favor. Several times during the fight it looked as if one or the other was tired, and some little hugging was attempted, but I stepped in and stopped this. There were positively no fouls in this fight."

Padded gloves could not eliminate the violent nature of the sport, and incidents, such as the following one recorded in the New York Times, 21 March 1897, p. 4, continued to cast a pallor over boxing.

TWO BOXERS ARE KILLED.
ALLEGED FRIENDLY CONTESTS IN PHILADELPHIA,
RESULTING IN THE DEATH OF THE PRINCIPALS.

PHILADELPHIA, March 20.-A blow near the heart, similar to the one with which Fitzsimmons defeated Corbett, caused the death at 12:30 o'clock this morning of Edward Gibbons, who late last night met Samuel S. Perry in a boxing bout at the Tenth Ward Democratic Club.

The contest was one of a number on the programme of an entertainment of the club, and the men were good friends.

For two rounds the contest continued without much damage being done, although it was clear to the spectators that Gibbons was no match for Perry. In the third round the men sparred for a minute, and Perry, who had decidedly the better of the argument, suddenly stepped in close and shot a hard blow at Gibbons' body. His glove landed just under the heart, and the recipient staggered back, but did not fall.

At this point referee Gillespie ordered the bourt stopped, declaring that Gibbons was clearly unmatched, and the men took off their gloves. Perry went home, while Gibbons, after dressing, staid about the clubhouse some time.

Suddenly he complained of feeling sick and began vomiting blood. This alarmed the crowd, and Dr. Curry was called in. The physician found the man badly injured, and, as he continued to sink, ordered his removal to a hospital. Gibbons was taken to the Hahnemann Hospital in a comatose condition, and with blood coming from his mouth. No marks were visible to show where the blow landed, but the patient continued to sink until midnight, when he expired.

Perry was arrested at his home. He declared that the bout was friendly, and that he did not hit Gibbons very hard. Martin Comber, a well-known Custom House employe and the President of the club, was arrested this morning, as were also James O'Neill, who seconded Gibbons, and William Farrell, a spectator. They were held in $800 bail each, excepting Perry, who was committed without bail to await the Coroner's investigation.

Another death as the result of a boxing bout occurred this morning at St. Mary's Hospital. Christian Keilnecker, aged forty-six years, was the victim. On Thursday night Keilnecker and Frank Connelly, aged thirty-five years, engaged in a glove contest in a room over a blacksmith shop at Fourth and Oxford Streets, and Keilnecker was badly worsted. The latter went to his home, and yesterday he was found unconscious in bed, and was removed to the hospital. Keilnecker's face presented a sorry spectacle. His right eye was closed and his nose and forehead were badly contused. Shortly after his admission to the hospital the injured man developed delirium tremens, which the doctors say was superinduced by the punishment he received. Connelly was taken into custody yesterday. It is not known whether gloves were used, although it is claimed by mutual friends of Connelly and Keilnecker that it was a friendly bout. Connelly is much larger than Keilnecker. The latter had been drinking heavily. This morning he died.

Connelly was given a preliminary hearing by Magistrate Gillespie this morning, and was held without bail to await the result of the Coroner's investigation.

Chapter 9

EQUESTRIANISM

After the disruption caused by the Civil War, horseracing enjoyed a resurgence in the postbellum period. Wealthy owners and promoters formed governing agencies promoting greater standardization, commercialization, and more scientific breeding practices. New tracks were constructed, often at a distance from the cities and the disparaging influence of gamblers, although racing never completely shed that stigma. Between 1875 and 1900 the governing councils shortened the distance of races, but increased their number and prize money.

The National Trotting Association, founded in 1870, was followed by the National Association of Trotting Horse Breeders in 1876. More scientific breeding and training procedures were initiated, along with better technology, such as the introduction of pneumatic tires, the use of hobbles to keep pacers on gait, and new sulkies. The low-wheeled sulkies proved more maneuverable and less wind resistant, and new sulkies dramatically lowered times for trotters and pacers. By 1892 more than 1000 tracks featured harness racing, most in the Midwest. More than 400 operated in Canada.

The first Kentucky Derby was run in May 1875 at Churchill Downs in Louisville. In 1881 the Ontario Jockey Club organized in Canada and offered its first races at the Woodbine track in Toronto. In 1883 Woodbine became the site of the Queen's Plate races, the oldest continuously run stakes race in North America. On 28 June 1884 Washington Park in Chicago hosted its first American Derby, which became the premier event of its day and the social event of the racing season for high society. New York legalized betting at its tracks in 1887, and Belmont Park opened in 1890. A year later the American Jockey Club instituted a board of control, which eventually registered horses, codified racing rules, appointed officials, and licensed trainers and jockeys. New York installed a state racing commission in 1895, a year after construction of the Aquaduct Race Track.

While New York racing prospered, the Midwest center in Chicago faced difficulties. While eight tracks operated in the Chicago area, some were run by disreputable gambling syndicates. Beginning in 1892 moral reformers led a successful campaign to close Garfield Park, and the prestigious Washington Park was shut down in 1894. Violence and riots at other tracks cast darker shadows on racing and fostered bans in other areas as well.

Despite such troubles racing enjoyed several highlights during the latter nineteenth century. Maud S. earned acclaim as the world champion trotter of the 1880s. In 1892 the trotter, Nancy Hanks, set a world record of 2:04 in the mile, while Star Pointer broke the two minute barrier for pacers in 1897. Jockeys, such as Tod Sloan, revolutionized riding techniques and tactics. Isaac Murphy, a black jockey, won three Kentucky Derby races and a host of other honors before the stress of racism contributed to his early death.

HARNESS RACING

In dispatches from New York, the Chicago Tribune reported on the National Trotting Association Meeting and its attempt to address cheating at the tracks. The articles are reprinted from the 12 and 13 February 1880 issues, p. 3, and 5, respectively.

MEETING OF THE NATIONAL TROTTING ASSOCIATION IN NEW YORK.
UNUSUALLY LARGE ATTENDANCE FROM ALL PARTS OF THE COUNTRY.

NEW YORK. Feb. 11.-The biennial Congress of the National Trotting Association began work Sunday in the Fifth Avenue Hotel. There was a large attendance of turfmen from all parts of the country. First Vice-President Edwin Thorne, of Millbrook, N.Y. called the delegates to order at 2:00 o'clock, and the Secretary, Mr. Thomas J. Vail, of Hartford, Conn., read the call for the Congress. Mr. Thorne read a short speech, asking that all discussions be governed by calmness and moderation, and then the Secretary began the arduous task of calling the roll of Associations entitled to send representatives, and receiving credentials of delegates....

The Treasurer's report showed a surplus $6,244.12 in the Treasury.

After a Committee had been appointed to nominate officers Secretary Vail began reading the report of the Special Committee to review the report of the Special Committee on revision of the by-laws and rules the special feature of the Congress. After a few unimportant amendments by the Revising Committee had been disposed of, Sec. 11 of Art. 7 of the by-laws was reached. This it was proposed to amend so as to provide that the next meeting of the Board of Review should be held in this city on the first Tuesday of December next. Over this there arose a very lively discussion. The Western men were determined to have some meeting held some time in Chicago, and demanded at least an equal standing in the rules with New York. Nearly every Western delegate had an amendment of his own designed to bring this about and although the Eastern delegates were quite willing to recognize Chicago yet they too desired to have it done in a dozen different ways. Amendments and amendments to amendments followed each other so fast that everybody became thoroughly confused. Finally after an hour's talk it was decided to substitute the word Chicago for that of New York in the by-Laws. A motion to adjourn for supper followed immediately, and recess was taken until 7 o'clock.

As soon as the meeting was called to order after supper Mr. C.M. Smith moved a reconsideration of the last vote, which was agreed to, and the delegates voted to leave the whole matter of future meetings just as the Committee at first recommended.

A new by-law was adopted, allowing the President of the National Association to employ trusty men to attend trots and see that the rules of the Association are enforced, the reports of these Supervisors to be received by the Board of Review as competent evidence in all cases. When the Committee's changes in the rules came to be voted upon, Rule 2 was changed so that entries by registered letter or telegraph may be eligible, if received at the office from which they are sent on or before the hour of closing entries.

It was also decided that judges and their assistants shall be allowed in the judges' stand.

Another change was in Rule 20, which was amended so that no warning shall be necessary on the part of the judges of a race before enforcing a penalty.

A long debate arose over a new section proposed to Rule 30, providing that it shall be the duty of one of the judges at each race to call out every break made by any horse which breaks and it shall be at once recorded in writing. The amendment was carried.

Rule No. 43 was stricken out, and for it was substituted a rule declaring that hereafter a record can only be made on a track belonging to a member of the National Association.

Rule No. 51, regarding suspensions and expulsions, caused the most interesting debate of the session. The Revision Committee proposed to so change Sec. 4 that hereafter no penalty of expulsion for fraud shall be removed or modified after confirmation by the Board of Review, and on appeal to the Board the burden of proof shall be upon the applicant. Expulsion for offenses not fraudulent, however, may be modified.

Nearly every delegate spoke two or three times on the amendment, the opponents claiming that it was too harsh to condemn a man to eternal punishment without any hope of pardon. Mr. Smith contended for the Committee that, when we have made it known that banishment for fraud once is banishment forever, we will have turned to a brighter page in the history of the National Association. A majority of the delegates agreed with Mr. Smith, and the Committee's recommendation was adopted.

Mr. Goldsmith tried to get some changes made to take the power of expulsion away from the judges but was summarily shut off by a successful motion to adjourn. The Congress will meet again tomorrow at 11 o'clock, and will elect officers for the ensuing two years.

NEW YORK, Feb. 12.-The National Trotting Association met again to-day at 11:30 o'clock. The Committee appointed to examine the accounts of the Secretary and treasurer reported that so far as they knew, the accounts were all right, and then the Committee to nominate officers for the ensuing two years made its report, which was unanimously adopted, as follows:

President-Judge James Grant, of Davenport, Ia.

First Vice-President-Edward Thorne, of Millbrook, N.Y.

Second Vice-President-S.K. Dow, of Chicago, Eastern District Board-Measrs. W.S. Tilton, Tagus, Me: Burdett Loomis, Hartford, Conn., and Lewis J. Powers, Springfield, Mass.

Atlantic District Board-Messrs. George Sturges, Philadelphia; M.P. Bush, Buffalo, and G.M. Rieder, Easton, Pa.

Central District Board-Messrs. Jabez W. Fitch, Cleveland; Richard West, Georgetown, Ky., and Charles L. Hunt, St. Louis.

Western District Board-Messrs. M.M. Morse, Earlville, Ill: J.T. Kinney, Nebraska City, Neb; and E.H. Broadhead, Milwaukee, Wis.

Pacific District Board-T.W. Hinchman, San Francisco; N.T. Smith, San Francisco; and Christopher Green, Sacramento.

The first-named gentleman on each of the District Boards, together with the President and Vice-Presidents of the Association, constitute the Board of Review, The President and Vice-Presidents are always ex-officio members, but it is a rule that at each meeting of a District Board the Chairman shall be changed. Hence, the make-up of the body of the Board of Review is constantly changing. The Secretary and Treasurer hold their officers by appointment from the Board of Review.

Judge Grant accepted his new honor in a short speech, in which he expressed his opinion that the present revision of the rules would prove a step in advance in the work of purging the turf from disgraceful frauds.

A resolution expressing the many obligations of the turf and its supporters to Secretary Vail was adopted, and then Mr. D.J. Robinson read a long address in eulogy of Mr. Alden Goldsmith, embodying a resolution to relieve the latter's son, Mr. James Goldsmith, from the penalty of expulsion under which he now rests. This provoked a great deal of discussion, and the matter was finally settled by laying the whole subject upon the table.

Mr. Hamilton Busby offered a resolution of thanks to retiring President Woolley, which was adopted as were similar resolutions regarding Col. William Edwards retiring from the Board of Review and the Committee on Revision of the Rules. Mr. Morris Holcombe made an earnest effort to secure the passage of all amendment to Rule 31, providing that any offer remaining in a race after having been ruled out should have such share of the premium money as he was entitled to when ruled out. After sharp discussion, the amendment was voted down.

On motion of Mr. Vail, a resolution was passed declaring it to be the sense of the Congress that Art. No. 5 of the by-laws should be interpreted as giving ex-offcio members of the Board of Review and District Boards the right to vote at meetings.

Mr. W.H. Wilson then offered the following important resolution, designed to detect ringers:

"It shall be the duty of the members upon whose track a suspicious horse appears to order the animal photographed, and take his full description as to size and other peculiarities and forward the same, say one-half-dozen, to the Secretary of the National Association, one copy to be kept on exhibition in the office; the other five to be subject to the call of the members; which copies shall as soon as practicable be returned to the Secretary. The copies of photographs of all suspicious horses on exhibition in the office of the Secretary shall be known a the 'Rogues' Gallery! In case the party controlling the horse should refuse to allow his animal to be photographed, he or they shall be expelled.

This was adopted almost unanimously, and then the President was authorized to appoint a new Committee on Revision of the Rules to report at the Congress of 1882.

It was decided that the next Congress should be held in this city, and then Mr. Frank E. Shaw made an ineffectual effort to have a new class of members formed, for whom the fee should be $30.

Mr. William A. Owen proposed a resolution calling upon the new Committee on Rules to carefully consider the questions now being agitated relative to time bars. This was carried, and then the Congress adjourned to meet in this city in 1883.

The delegates expressed themselves as much pleased with the work of the Congress in general. It is believed that its beneficial effects will be especially felt in the operation of the new rules relative to fraud on the turf. While the now rule that no sentence of expulsion can ever be repealed after being confirmed by the Board of Review, and the resolution adopted to-day regarding the "rogues gallery" of suspicious horses are thought to be very stringent, they are looked upon as being no more than just in their severity, and much good is expected to result from their enforcement.

Seven years later, on 3 March 1887, p. 8, the Chicago Tribune recorded the reorganization of the association and its continued attempts to regulate the sport.

THE MEETING IN DETROIT.
ORGANIZATION OF THE NEW TROTTING ASSOCIATION.

DETROIT, Mich., March 2-[Special.]-The advocates of the new trotting association did not anticipate so large an attendance of delegates at the first meeting as arrived in the city today. Sixty-six associations were represented at the meeting which began its session at the Russell House this afternoon. The States represented were: Ohio, Michigan, Illinois, Connecticut, Wisconsin, New York, Kansas, Kentucky, Nebraska, Iowa, Missouri, Minnesota, Pennsylvania, and Indiana.

D.J. Campau of Detroit called the meeting to order, and stated its object. Rufus W. Gillett, President of the Detroit Driving Club, acted as Chairman, and a Committee on Credentials was appointed consisting of F.C. Pillsbury of Minneapolis, G.G. Watson of Terre Haute, Frank Brannan of Montpelier, O: W.L. Smith of Canandaigua, N.Y.,: and George Forbes of Cleveland, O. Short addresses were made by Fred A. Baker of Detroit and Judge Beaman of Ottumwa, Ia., in which they referred to the necessity of the formation of a new trotting association.

Mr. Boardman of Jackson thought the desire to form a new association should be stated explicitly, and he made a motion that was the sense of the meeting that such steps be taken. This was carried unanimously.

D.J. Campau read a telegram from Charles Green, President of the St. Louis Fair Association, which explained his absence from the meeting on the ground that he was detained by legislation which affected his association. A telegram from W.R. Armstrong, Orrin Hickok, and Ames Crawford from San Francisco said that all the tracks on the Pacific coast would join the new association. A telegram from Gov. Luce, at Lansing, said that the Legislature had passed a bill for the incorporation of the new association, and it had been signed by the Governor. A recess was then taken till 7:30 p.m.

At the evening session the articles of incorporation were signed. They provide for the organization of the American Trotting Association, with a capital stock of $10,000. The principal officers are to be located in Detroit. The time of incorporation is thirty-five years. Subscriptions for stock were then asked for and were taken by most of the associations represented. Election of officers being in order, J.J. Baird of Lansing nominated for the Presidency D.J. Campau of Detroit, who declined the honor in a neat speech. Mr. Campau suggested the name of William R. Marion of St. Paul, who was thereupon elected President by acclamation. D.C. Beaman of Ottumwa, Ia., was elected Vice President. The directors are W.T. Hams of Terre Haute, Ind., C.M. Cottrell of Milwaukee, R.W. Gillett of Detroit, H.G. Toler of Wichita, Kas., E.C. Long of St. Paul.

In the By-laws which were adopted there is a slight departure from the by-laws of the old association, but the trotting rules remain the same. The officers of the new organization are elected by the members thereof. The old district boards are dispensed with. A board of Directors, of which the President and Secretary are members, has control of affairs and becomes a Board of Appeal for the consideration of complaints. All protests must be supported by competent proofs, and if no proofs are furnished the money shall be refunded and the protest withdrawn, unless the Board of Appeal has good reason to believe the protest is well grounded. All appeals must be settled within two months after the decisions are rendered. Annual dues are apportioned on the basis of premiums offered, ranging from $10 to $100.

The by-laws provide for the establishment of a Board of Review in each State, which shall have complete jurisdiction over all matter appertaining to the turf in the States; and also form Board of Appeals, to which all appeals from the Board of Review must be presented.

An excerpt from an Atlantic Monthly article by H.C. Merwin, in July 1889, pp. 111-122, provides a contemporary description of harness racing at that time. The development of the kite-shaped track, with its longer straightaways, less and wider turns, improved times but created debate over the legality of such non-traditional courses.

TROTTING RACES.

Since 1824, when trotting may be said to have begun as a sport, the record has been reduced from 2 minutes 40 seconds to 2 minutes 8 3/4 seconds. Whence comes this great advance? It is due to improvements in trotting-courses, in sulkies, in horseshoes, in boots and toe-weights, in harness (particularly in the device of the overdraw check),

in training and driving, and finally in the speed and endurance of the trotters themselves. The gain in actual speed for a short distance has been much slighter than is
commonly supposed. So long ago as 1866, Hiram Woodruff drove Mr. Bonner's gray
mare Peerless (who was bred like Dexter, being in part Messenger and in part Star) a
quarter of a mile at the rate of a mile in two minutes,- and this not to a sulky, but to
a skeleton wagon, a four-wheeled vehicle, which is much heavier. It is doubtful if this
rate of going will ever greatly be surpassed, though it is, I think, commonly believed
by horsemen that some time or other a mile will be trotted in two minutes. The gain
will probably be not so much in speed for a short distance as in the ability to maintain speed for a full circuit of the track. Even Maud S. flagged a little on the last quarter
of her fastest mile.

For the past fifty years, and especially for the latter half of that time, much ingenuity and inventive skill have been employed to afford the trotter all the mechanical
assistance that is possible. Tracks are made of a elliptical instead of a round shape,
because the two long stretches or straight pieces thus obtained give the horse, particularly a big-striding one, the opportunity that he requires to get up his speed. Courses
laid out in this way are found to be much faster than the old tracks, which were more
nearly round. Then, two, the footing has been improved. The best tracks now have an
underlayer of turf, which makes them springy, and the surface is soft without being
deep or heavy....

Equal mechanical skill has been exerted in another direction. Many horses cannot
be driven at anything like their highest speed without danger of cutting themselves, by
striking one foot or leg against another, expecially when they "break;" and to protect
them from injury in this manner a great variety of "boots" has been invented. Counting different sizes of these articles separately, the number of them now on sale is over
two hundred. Very few trotters are able to dispense with boots entirely, and many of
them could not be used as race horses at all except for these appliances. The shoeing
of trotting horses, again, is an art in itself, and so is the use of toe-weights, which are
small pieces of brass screwed or otherwise attached to the hoofs of the fore-feet. Heavy
shoes and toe-weights are employed to make horses trot who otherwise would pace,
to keep them level in their gait, and sometimes to cause a lengthening of their stride.
The difficulty and importance of these matters may be gathered from the fact that a
change of no more than two ounces in a trotter's fore-shoes or toe-weights would, in
many cases, make a difference of several seconds in his speed for a mile, and consequently of thousands of dollars in his value as a race horse. The necessity for toe-
weights or heavy shoes lies in some defect of conformation or of gait, and when a trotter is obliged to carry a heavy load in this manner his feet and legs suffer. The famous
Smuggler, a noble brown stallion with a white blaze in his face, a heavy and powerful animal, was originally a pacer, and in his races he wore shoes on his fore-feet
weighing two pounds each; in fact, he is said to have carried at one time three pounds
on each fore-foot. His great strength and courage enabled him to bear this burden, but
eventually it disabled him. Smuggler was once sold for $40,000, the highest price, until
a few months ago, ever paid in this country for a horse; and though he was capable of
very high speed, he must be regarded as on the whole a failure. If he made a single
break in a race, he lost so much ground that he was pretty sure to be distanced. This

peculiarity is explained by Mr. H.T. Helm, an intelligent writer, who says that Smuggler's stride with his fore-legs is not long enough to correspond with the tremendous stroke of his hind-legs, and consequently that he is apt to lose his balance....

The last factor in the development of the trotting horse is the driver; and here we touch upon the great difference between running and trotting races. A running race may be described, with some exaggeration, as a brief but spirited flight of colts ridden by boys, whereas a trotting race is a long-drawn contest between seasoned horses and mature men, who are commonly the trainers as well as the drivers of their steeds. Not all running horses, to be sure, are colts, nor all their riders boys, but the limit of age in the horse and of weight in the man is quickly reached. In trotting races, the jockeys are always men; the standard weight is 150 pounds, and if the driver falls below that he must carry lead enough on his sulky to make up the deficiency. In running races, steeplechases excepted, the weight (including that of the rider) varies, roughly speaking, from 75 to 130 pounds, and a Fred Archer who tips the scales at anything over 120 must retire to private life. Then, again, running races, nowadays at least, almost invariably consist of a single dash, whereas trotting races are in heats, the best three in five: and this affords an opportunity for stratagem and patience on the part of the driver; for courage, endurance, and even for recuperation on the part of the horse. There is, therefore, in the trotting race, an element of subtlety which gives it a peculiar fascination. The typical driver who has been evolved from these conditions is a spare but sinewy man, with a quiet manner and a firm mouth,-as distinctly American a person as any that can be found. His chief qualities, so far as the horse is concerned, are sympathy and resolution. "Confidence between the trotting horse and his driver," said the great master of the art, "is of the utmost importance: it is all in all. Some men inspire it readily, so that a horse will take hold and do all he knows the first time the man drives him. For another man the same horse will not trot a yard. The truth is that the horse is a very knowing, sagacious creature, much more so than he gets credit for. If a driver has no settled system of his own, or if he is rash or severe without cause, it is not likely that confidence will be inspired in the horse even in a long time."

It is a fact often remarked that some drivers succeed much better with certain equine families than with others, the reason doubtless being that they are better adapted to them in disposition. A trainer, for example, who did very well with a well-known high-spirited and willful breed failed conspicuously with another strain, of a milder and more gentle nature.... Hiram Woodruff was the first to take this mental grip of the powers of the trotting horse; and the result in his case was that, by dint of his own mind, he carried him triumphantly over the gap which lies between 2.40 and 2.18."...

To drive a trotter with art is, first, to get from him the highest speed of which he is capable; secondly, to keep him from making a break; and, thirdly, to bring him back to the trot with as little loss as possible after a break has actually occurred. To do this well requires a light and "sensational" hand, a sympathetic intelligence, and a vast deal of practice. The break is prevented, sometimes by restraining the animal with voice and rein, when it is simply a case of too much eagerness, but more often by moving the bit in his mouth. If the break happens, the horse "leaving his feet," as the phrase is, and going to a gallop or a run, he must be "caught" by pulling his head to one side, so that he will have to come back to a trot in order to keep his balance; and in extreme cases it will be necessary to pull him first this way, and then that. The break does not come without premonitory signals; there is a sort of general unsteadiness of the horse's gait, when the change is in contemplation, and at the last moment he moves his ears backward. "The sign of a coming break," says Hiram Woodruff, that excellent writer from whom I have quoted so much already, "will be discovered by watching the head and ears of the horse. The attention of the driver ought always to be fixed upon the head of his horse. Many a heat is lost by neglect of this matter. A driver is seen coming up the home stretch a length or a length and a half ahead. Both the horses are tired, but the leading one could win. The driver, however, when he gets where the carriages are, turns his head to look at the ladies, or to see whether they are looking at him. Just then the horse gives a twitch with his ears; the driver doesn't see it; up flies the trotter, and the ugly man behind holds his horse square, and wins by a neck.".... Mr. Vanderbilt drove Maud S. and Aldine, harnessed to his road wagon, a mile in 2.15 1/2; at Cleveland, some years ago, a four-in-hand accomplished the same distance in 2.40; and a moderately fast horse, a moderately light wagon, and a smooth road supply all the necessary conditions for artistic driving.

There is another function of the bit scarcely less important, and that is to encourage and restore a tired horse. When, at the end of a stoutly contested heat, two trotters are struggling for supremacy, they can be urged by the voice, reinforced either by the whip or by the bit. A coarsely bred, sluggish animal may, at this critical moment, require the lash, but its application to a beast of any spirit is pretty sure to disgust and dishearten him. In some subtle way, however, when the driver moves the bit to and fro in his mouth, the effect is to enliven and stimulate the horse, as if something of the jockey's spirit were thus conveyed to his mind. If this motion be performed with an exaggerated movement of the arm, it is called "reefing," and it sometimes appears, when it is "neck or nothing," at the end of a heat, as if the driver were actually "sawing" the horse's mouth, whereas in reality he is only giving the bit a loose but vigorous motion therein....

The race is over a mile track, almost elliptical in shape, and the judges are perched in a two-story balcony close to the track, and pretty near one extremity of the ellipse, so that at the end of a heat the horses have a long, straight stretch before reaching the goal. Across the track from the judges' stand, and high enough to clear the trotters' heads, is stretched a wire, by the aid of which, in a very close finish, the judges can determine which horse has won. The race is usually "best three in five;" that is, in order to win, a horse must come in first three times, not necessarily in succession. Thus it will be seen, if there are many contestants in the race, it may be prolonged to seven, eight, and even ten heats, before any one trotter has secured three. But if a horse has taken part in five heats without winning a single one, he is rules out, or "sent to the barn," as the expression is, and cannot start again. So, also, he may be ruled out if at the close of a heat he is very far behind the winning horse. At a point in the home stretch one hundred feet from the judges' stand (one hundred and fifty, if eight or more horses are engaged in the race), a man is stationed with a flag in his hand, which he drops when the winner reaches the wire; and if any lagging horse has not passed him when his flag falls, that horse is "distanced," and cannot start again. It is possible for a driver to "lay up" a heat, as it is called; that is, if his horse be tired, or for any other cause, he may content himself for that heat with just "saving his distance," making no effort to win. The start is a flying one. When the judges ring their bell, the drivers turn about at or near the distance point, and come down past the judges' stand almost or quite at full speed. If, when they pass under the wire, they are upon pretty even terms, the starter (one of the judges) cries out, "Go!" and on they rush. If, however, the start would not be a fair one, the bell is rung as a signal that the drivers must come back and try again. Sometimes the scoring, as these attempts are called, is prolonged for a long while; but the judges are authorized to fine any driver who comes down ahead of or behind the "pole" horse; that is, the horse who has the inside position, or that nearest the poles which mark the quarter, the half, and the three-quarter mile points. All the positions are assigned by lot. The attempt is occasionally made by a combination of drivers to tire out or excite some particular horse by unnecessary scoring, and in former years this nefarious plan was often practiced successfully, but of late the rules are enforced with more strictness. Even with the best intentions on the part of all the drivers concerned, it is sometimes difficult to get a fair start, especially if the horses are young or badly behaved, and the scoring is frequently spoken of as a great drawback to the pleasures of a trotting race. These false starts, however, afford a most interesting exhibition of horses and men; the spectator has such an opportunity as he could not otherwise enjoy to study the gaits of the various trotters, to note how well or ill they "catch," and to observe the skill, temper, and courage of the jockeys. There is a great difference in the behavior of the different horses. Some pull and tug on the bit, despite the signal to return, carrying their drivers down to the first turn in the track before they can be stopped; whereas others, old campaigners as a rule, will slacken speed at once when they hear the bell, stop, and turn around of their own accord....

Close to the fence, but inside of it on the track, opposite the judges' stand or thereabout, there is always a motley group of "rubbers," grooms, and helpers, with pails of water and sponges in their hands, and blankets, thick or thin according to the weather, thrown over their shoulders or deposited conveniently on the fence. Here, very often, the driver pulls up for a moment, on his way back to the starting-point, after the bell has rung for a recall, while the groom hastily sponges out the horse's mouth and nostrils, adjusts the check-rein, takes up a hole in the breeching, or makes some other slight change in the harness.

These are tense moments in an important race, especially if the contestants are known to be pretty evenly matched, and each driver is anxious that the others shall take no advantage of him. At such times, a reputation for courage is of some service; it is always a temptation for one jockey to "cut out" another, or unfairly drive in to the "pole" ahead of him, just as one boat in a rowing race may take another boat's water. Under these circumstances, it is the right of the driver whose territory is invaded to keep on, even though a collision may result; and a resolute man will do so, undeterred by the fact that spokes are flying from the wheel of his own or of his adversary's sulky, as the two gossamer vehicles come together. "The quarter stretch looked more like a tooth-pick factory than a race-course," was facetiously remarked of one occasion, when the driving had been reckless.

Aided by the new, faster bicycle style sulky, the trotter, Nancy Hanks lowered the mile record three times during the 1892 racing season, eventually achieving a 2:04 mark. The Chicago Tribune reported one of her great runs on 1 September 1892, p. 6. The Tribune also detailed Star Pointer's world record on 29 August 1897, p. 1.

NANCY HANKS. 2:05. 1-4
MR. FORBES' GREAT MARE TROTS A WONDERFUL MILE.
HER CHICAGO RECORD CUT TWO SECONDS OVER THE INDEPENDENCE KITE
YESTERDAY-THE JOURNEY
WONDERFULLYWELL DONE AND SUSTAINED WITH A FIRST QUARTER IN
30SECONDS AND A LAST IN 31 1/4-FLYING JIB,
THE PACER, ALSO BEATS THE RACE RECORD

INDEPENDENCE, Ia. Aug.31.-Nancy Hanks, the queen of trotters added to her corwn and glory today when she trotted the Independence kite track in 2:05 1/4, clipping two seconds off her Chicago mark, made two weeks ago. She was brought out at 2:30, and as soon as she was recognized in the loop the cheering began. She looked well and was heartily cheered during her two warming up miles. At just 5:15 Doble and Nancy Hanks appeared again for their trip against the record. She was now jogged up the loop and turned to face the kite before her. The mare was not going well and came back and scored down again. Frank Starr had the runner, Abraham Lincoln, who prompted her in her great mile at Chicago, near her, while Williams, with Ned Gordon, was waiting at the post.

When she reached the wire she was going square and true and Doble nodded for the word. From the word "go" Nancy trotted, as only Nancy can trot, steady as clockwork and swifter than a bird. With her long and frictionless gait she reached the quarterpoll in thirty seconds. "Too fast" is the verdict of the crowd. The half was reached in 1:01, and men found it hard to believe their watches. The third quarter flag was down at 1:34, and fearing that she was lagging Williams closed up with his runner, Ned Gordon. He was not needed. Doble had loosed Nancy's head and was urging her on gently with whip and voice. As she darted under the wire watches were consulted. They ranged all the way from 2:05 1/4 to 2:06. Cheers flooded the track. The great mare was driven back to the stand and a hush fell over all as the bell was tapped. Starter McCarthy announced the official time of 2:05 1/4 and his voice was drowned with yells.

A strong breeze was blowing from the Northwest and situated as the kite track is from the half to the home wire the force of the wind increased with every step. The breeze begun to strike her after the half was passed, and the third flag was reached a second or two slower than was intended, but here Nancy was given her head and she finished the last quarter strong and in the face of a Northwest wind in :31 1/4.

"A noticeable feature," says Doble, "was the condition of the mare after her mile. Within fifteen minutes after she reached her stall she was as fresh and lively as a young colt, and no one would dream she had made the greatest trial of her life. Yes, the kite tracks are faster than the regulation shape. How many seconds I would not say, but there is not the shadow of doubt about it."

Nancy Hanks' three fastest miles were made by quarters in this way:

Richmond	33 1/4	31 3/4	33 1/3	32 1/3-2:09
Chicago.................	31 1/3	32 1/4	32 3/4	30 1/4-2:07 1/4
Independence	30	31	33	31 1/4-2:05 1/4

There were 8,000 people out and the weather was perfect for the time.

STAR POINTER, B.H., 1889, BY BROWN HAL-SWEEPSTAKES, BY KNIGHT'S SNOW HEELS; READVILLE, MASS., AUG. 28, 1897-1:39 1/4

Boston, Mass., Aug. 28-[Special.]-The two-minute horse has come at last. He is no other than Star Pointer, the gallant, homely bay, whose owner, James A. Murphy, lives in Chicago. Today on the Readville track Star Pointer paced a mile against time in 1:50 1/4, surpassing the goal that has been the dream of harness horse drivers, owners, trainers, and breeders for a decade.

While the day was ideal for a supreme effort, no one dreamed that the big bay stallion had it in him to do more than come comfortably near the record of 2:00 1/2, which gave John R. Gentry the championship last year. When the crowd that filled the grand stand and the hundreds of horsemen who stood on the concrete walk that slopes down to the track realized that not only had a higher mark been reached, but that Star Pointer had paced a mile in 1:50 1/2, there was at first a general paralysis of surprise. This was followed by a veritable tornado of enthusiasm as the new king of the sulky and his driver returned to the wire they had just passed at such an unheard of rate. To improve world's record by a second and a quarter is nothing new in harness racing, but to see the two minute goal-once a visionary improbability-so safely passed set the most lymphatic horseman half wild with excitement.

Laurels for Driver McClary.

The mile was one of the most evenly rated ever driven and reflects the highest credit on young McClary who has not had anything like the same experience at this sort of work as Geers and other reinsmen who steared champions to victory against the sun dial.

It was about 4 o'clock when Star Pointer was brought out to try to get a new mark for pacers. He had previously been sharpened up with a mile in 2:11 1/2 the last quarter of which was at a 2:01 clip.

Half an hour later the regular card was suspended and everybody with a chronograph got as near to the wire as possible... Nobody hazarded the prediction that he would beat Gentry's time. In the betting ring it was even he would not go faster than 2:01 1/2. When the runner carried the Pointer horse down for the preliminary score the pacer made a break, though he was not anything like up to speed. His owner, James A. Murphy of Chicago, who sat with a party of turfmen noting every movement of the horse he paid $15,000 for last winter, called out nervously: "What can be the matter, something is wrong," as he saw the stallion lose his stride. It developed afterward that Pointer's mouth is a trifle sore and the bit pinched the tender place a little, causing him to protest with a short gallop.

McClary let his big pupil jog more than a furlong before he turned to come back. By that time the horse forgot his troubles and was ready for a do or die battle. He fell into his easy, powerful stride as soon as his head was pointed for the wire, and the little man who held the rains nodded vigorously that he was ready. The first eighth was not officially timed, but dozens of the practiced spectators caught it in fifteen seconds. That was the clip to start with if it could be carried, and, sure enough, Star Pointer was at the quarter pole in exactly thirty seconds. As he turned into the backstretch the eye could see little variation, but the next quarter was a fraction more rapid, making the half 50 3/4. Now it was evident that a new marvel in speed was transpiring, for the third quarter was passed in twenty-nine and a quarter seconds, making the time for the six furlongs 1:29. That was better than a two-minute gait for three-fourths of the journey, and the only question was whether Star Pointer could stand the strain.

"If he lasts we've got the record," shouted the delighted owner of the peerless pacer as the latter came round the last turn. The great horse was apparently as full of go as ever, though it seemed impossible he could carry such an unheard of clip home.

Art of the Driver.

Here the driver's art came into play and McClary's heart and soul were in the reins as he talked to the flying giant in front of him. The runner remained at his wheel, and as gamely as when he set out the noble descendant of the Tennessee saddlers came straight and true for the goal. As a matter of fact, he took 30 1/4 seconds for the last quarter, but there was no apparent slackening and a stronger finish for a record breaking effort never was seen. It did not require the official announcement to tell what happened. Hundreds of men were dancing about and yelling like demons as they exhibited their watches with the hand stopped on the winning side of the two minute mark....

Before he could dismount the driver was lifted from his seat and carried on the shoulders of his brother professionals to the weighing-room. Here he was invited to the judges' stand and introduced as the "first driver to ride in two minutes."

After that came the official verification of the fact that Star Pointer had paced a mile in 1:50 1/4. Then Mr. Murphy was asked to come up the steps and be presented as the owner of the new king of the sulky.

Later on the Chicago turfman said to your correspondent: "I must admit that I was surprised to see the horse so good. He has raced against anything that came up and we have not given him any special preparation for time trials. Since the season began Pointer has traveled 4,555 miles on the cars, and, as you know, came from Chicago this week. I expected to beat two minutes with him in the year, but he has fooled all of us by doing it the first time of asking."

From his debut on the turf in 1895 Star Pointer has given promise of reaching a higher mark than any other horse that goes in harness. He carried everything before him that season, when he was 5 years old, and was sold at auction the next winter. Up to that time Ed F. Geers had driven him and since that time Bird McClary, a Boston trainer, has had charge of the stallion....

TECHNOLOGY

Clark's Horse Review paid tribute to the new bicycle sulky on 2 August 1892, but misjudged how rapidly owners embraced the new technology, as evidenced by its own announcement issued two weeks later, 16 August 1892 and the following excerpt from The Horseman, 18 August 1892, p. 1473.

The advent of the pneumatic tire and ball-bearing sulky is acknowledged and given a place beside the many new and legitimate aids to speed-making in harness races. Some indication of its adaptability to actual race contests was given in the free-for-all trot at Detroit last Thursday, when the gray son of Pilot Medium carried Doble the fastest three heats ever trotted in a free-for-all race. The usefulness of this make of a track vehicle is not alone in its easy draft, as its cushioned tires lessens in a great measure the jar and concussion which the driver in the old sulky was wont to endure, and which has undoubtedly sent many a trainer and driver to private life long before his usefulness had disappeared. In the event of a few more races such as the above the demand for this form of wheel may become great enough to induce manufacturers to put the bicycle sulky upon the market. It would seem that our standard sulky makers could add the ball-bearing and pneumatic tire features to the regulation sulky without disastrous changes being necessary. It will probably be a long time before the improved sulky will find its way into general use, but among the leading trainers and drivers it will no doubt find immediate and lasting favor and, incidentally, it may be mentioned that this improvement is a step in the direction of the two-minute goal that is in the mind's eye of so many hopeful horsemen today. It is, indeed, an open question at this time whether upon a straight away rubber top track, with automatic electric start and stop arrangement, there could not be found a horse who could be tempered fine enough to do the mile in even time.

The sulky wheel equipped with the ball-bearing axle and pneumatic tire, seems to have been pretty generally accepted by trotting horse men as a legitimate aid and improvement in the line of turf advancement. Many of the important eastern meetings have already sanctioned their use, and so far as we have been able to learn thus far neither of the great national associations have made any move in the direction of questioning the legality of records made with the improved sulky. The propriety, therefore, of the act of the judges of the Cincinnati meeting in compelling Madge Hatton, who was harnessed to a pneumatic sulky, to perfrom in one of the old style may be open to question. The new vehicle has attained great popularity and it is extremely doubtful if an edict from the judges' stand alone can check its onward march.

Sterling Elliott quickly patented the successful innovation, as reported by The Horseman, 25 August 1892, p. 1552.

The inventor of the "bicycle sulky," Sterling Elliott, of Newton, Mass., a gentleman whose business has been the manufacture of hickory bicycle wheels, said to us the other day that he had just come from Washington, where he had filed patents covering about all the recent improvements in sulky building. Mr. Elliott's invention was first tested on the farm of Charles Clark, and Mr. Clark has contributed greatly to its success, but did not invent it, as generally reported. Mr. Elliott tells us that instead of enlarging the wheels he looks for better results from even smaller wheels than those now used. The limberness of the old-fashioned sulky wheel is its greatest defect. It yielded and "wabbled" under lateral pressure. The smaller the wheel the greater the rigidity, the less the vibration, and the truer the running.

THOROUGHBRED RACING

Urban rivalry and civic pride contributed greatly to the growth of sport. When wealthy patrons constructed luxurious tracks in other areas, Chicago's social leaders endeavored to surpass them. The Chicago Tribune described the opening of Washington Park on 28 June 1884, p.12, and its inaugural event, the American Derby, the following day on page 13.

WASHINGTON PARK.

Today the grounds of the Washington Park Driving Club will be thrown open to the public for the first time, the races being begun, and the event has been looked forward to with great interest, so that the turnout this afternoon of the votaries of the turf and their friends will probably be such a one as has never before been witnessed in Chicago. On this occasion a glance backward at the origin and growth of the club and something about its grounds may not prove uninteresting.

About two years ago the Washington Park Club was projected by men who felt that Chicago needed a place where their speeders would have a chance to show them power and the lovers of the turf in the Northwest have a track whereon the best racers of the country could show their mettle. From this feeling came the present Washington Park - a park second to none in America, ranking with Saratoga, Coney Island, Jerome Park, Monmouth, Pimlico, and Washington. It was begun by men who put not only their names but their money into the work....

These men elected the following officers President, Gen. P.H. Sheridan, Vice-Presidents, N.K. Fairbank, S.W. Allerton, J.W. Doane, and A.S. Gage; Treasurer, John H. Walsh; Secretary, J.E. Brewster, Executive Committee in addition to the officers, H.J. MacFarland, C.D. Hamill, James Van Inwagen, M.A. Ryerson, and M.R. Hull.

The certificate of Incorporation was filed Feb. 9 of last year, the capital stock was $100,000, 1,000 shares of $100 each.

THE MEMBERSHIP.

When the club was organized it was decided that the membership should be limited to 300 the first 200 to pay an initiation fee of $150 and the fee of the rest to be seated up to $300. The annual dues are $10, which insured an income of $20,000 per annum in sum sufficient to run the club if nothing is made on the outside. At the time the officers were elected a statement was made of the objects of the association. It was intended to furnish the members and their friends with a club house and pleasure grounds for their entertainment and the promotion and good fellowship and to encourage by providing proper facilities raising, improving breeding, training, and exhibiting horses at the annual meetings. It was proposed as stated above, to do for the citizens of Chicago what the Jerome and Coney Island Clubs have done for New York and the Pimlico for Baltimore.

The management of those clubs are in the hands of some of the most influential businessesmen and are conducted in such a manner as to furnish a fine retreat for members and their friends at all times and give the public the very best entertainment and sport during the meetings. Before the opening of Jerome Park in New York, which is how perhaps the most fashionable and popular resort about the metropolis, there was but little pleasure driving by the richer classes in consequence of poor roads after leaving the city limits and a still poorer class of houses to entertain guests. The construction of a club house at Jerome Park, however, necessitated the building of a new road, and at once a boulevard was laid out and called Jerome avenue. The construction of Jerome Park has thus far resulted in giving New York what she never possessed before-fine drivers and also the title of having the largest number of fine horses and equipages of any city in the world.

HOW THE WORK WAS DONE.

Those who have undertaken the enterprise in Chicago were confident that this city presented advantages far above New York for such a pleasure-ground. Believing this, nothing was done by halves, and a careful generosity was shown in all details, from the laying out of the grounds to the preparation of plans for the club-house and other structures. While strict attention was paid to the arrangement of the park so that it should be in fact a gentlemen's pleasure-ground, nothing that would contribute to the comfort or enjoyment of those whose patronage would be solicited was neglected. It was believed that a special feature should be an American Derby-Day, though large amounts of money would be required to do this. That point has now been reached, and the American Derby is an accomplished fact. The faith of the managers was strong that Chicago and the West possessed elements interested in witnessing honest trials of speed of horses sufficient to support every effort they might make in that direction, basing their hopes upon the patronage of people who want to see pure sport.

THE CLUB-HOUSE.

The club-house has a fashionable and exclusive side as well as a public one. With this view the house will be open only to holders of membership tickets and the same care is exercised in the admission of members of the leading clubs of the city. The house is open at all times and managed on the same plan as any other private club-house. The idea carried out is that it shall be a place where a member may drive at the close of the day with his family or friends, a place where all the pleasures of a country retreat may be enjoyed. The club-house has a length of 136 feet by a width of ninety-seven, and is two stories, basement and attic in height. The kitchen, storerooms, heating apparatus, and so forth, are in the basement, the attic containing the servants' rooms. There is a spacious entrance hall on the main floor, club office, cafe-thirty-three by seventy-five feet with serving and wine rooms, billiard-room twenty-four by thirty-two feet, ladies' waiting-room, a parlor thirty-two by twenty feet for the Directors, lavatory, and five private dining-rooms, each twelve by twenty feet. Extending around the entire building on the main floor is a veranda sixteen feet wide, provided with chairs, settees, and other conveniences for witnessing races. The ground floor is in reality an immense hall off from which are the other apartments. The floor above is reached by a broad oak stairway, guarded by a balustrade richly carved in open designs. Half-way up is a broad landing, and the stairs take an opposite direction from this point. The second floor has a dining room of the same dimensions as the cafe. There are ladies' parlors, toilet and retiring rooms, sewing-rooms, and seven private dining rooms. Above are the living rooms of the Superintendent, sleeping-rooms, and servant rooms. Upon the roof are two open observatories from which every part of the park and surrounding country can be seen. A covered balcony sixteen feet wide runs around the second story. The exterior of the building, all of which above the foundation is of wood, is broken with towers and gables so disposed as to secure a very pleasing and picturesque appearance from all points of view, and especially harmonizing with the general landscape effect. The general style of the exterior is rural English.

THE GRAND STAND.

Off to the left of the club-house is the grand stand, 504 feet in length, fifty-five feet wide, and three stories high. From the club-house to the stand there is a broad walk. The stand is back from the track, and is a model of such structures, being upon an elevation of five and one half feet. Greensward slopes to the tracks, and from no position on the stand or from the lawn in front will not the horses feet be visible from any point on the track. Ten thousand people can really be accommodated. There are no benches or fixed chairs, but there is an ordinary chair for each visitor so that there will be no crowding or jamming. Along the front railing and separated from the other seats by a high railing is a row of seventy-two boxes, each of which will accommodate four persons. These boxes will be rented per day or season. The judges' stand is on the same side of the track as the grandstand, so that the judges and the public will have the same idea as to which is the winning horse. In the basement of the grand stand is a room 300 feet by 55 feet, where all the bookmaking and betting will be done, as it will not be permitted in the other portion of the ground. Access to the second story is gained by five flights of stairs, and on top of the building is a promenade extending its entire length. From this can be obtained a magnificent view of the surrounding country. On the ground floor is a cafe, where the public can secure refreshments. There are also private dining rooms for those who have not the privileges of the clubhouse.

THE GROUNDS

The club's property consists of eighty acres, bounded on the north by Sixty-first street, to the east by Cottage Grove avenue, on the south by Sixty-third street, and on the west by South Park avenue. Lying as it does midway between Woodlawn and Englewood it is accessible by the Illinois Central Railroad, Pittsburg and Fort Wayne Railroad, Michigan Southern Railroad, and Chicago and Rock Island Railroad, besides, from its contingency to West South Park, by both Grand and Drexel boulevards and the Hyde Park Street Railway. The land has a gentle natural slope from the east and north twelve feet above the city datum in elevation to the west and south, allowing a feature acceptable to all turfmen-viz: a track of gentle up-and-down grade which is considered faster than a dead-level run. The natural flatness of the track has been broken by artificial depressions and raises. The management has considered rapid and complete surface drainage first, and all else has to subserve that most important end. The track has many of the features of the popular Saratoga course, although wider and having on the same grounds a practice track, resembling in that respect the track at Louisville. The home and back stretches have a length of 1,414 feet the turns 1,226 feet, thus affording longer straight runs than the stereotyped method of having stretches and turns of equal length. This alteration has been highly commended by turfmen. The widths are: Homestretch, eighty-five feet; back stretch, sixty-five feet; turns, sixty feet. These widths have been carefully determined after an examination of all the tracks of the country. Immediately inside of the course proper, and separated from it by a ten-foot drainage sod space, is the practice track, forty feet in width, constructed with the same care as the track itself.

In three-quarter mile dashes it has formerly been an objection that the horses were started on the mile course at such a distance from the spectators that they could not get a good view. To obviate this a diagonal "short" has been constructed similar to that at Saratoga, which allows a start near the wire and directly in front of the grand stand. The steeple is so arranged that the water jumps occur over natural lake-necks, a feature unknown on any other course in the country. The awkward artificial water-jumps now in vogue are not unnatural in appearance, but do not acquaint the horse with the presence of water until its brink.

THE CLUB RACES
A BRILLANT AND SUCCESSFUL OPENING
OF THE SEASON AT WASHINGTON PARK.

_____

BY TRAIN.
REACHING THE GROUNDS VIA THE ILLINOIS CENTRAL.

That Chicago was en fete and bent on having a good time must have been obvious to the dullest observer on the streets yesterday. As 1 o'clock drew near crowds of people in every variety of holiday attire could be seen pushing their way along the main streets towards the Illinois Central Depot. The weather was everything that could be desired-pleasant sunshine, with a cool, delicious breeze that seemed to make every one feel bright and buoyant. When one looked around the depot it was quite plain that the crowd of plea-sure-seekers did not belong particularly to any age or class. The portly-looking elderly man of business in white hat and vest, throwing to the winds his financial cares, was out for his holiday, and looked to be enjoying it to the full. The wealthy speculator and gam-bler, the low-salaried clerk, the store-keeper, and the son of toil alike bent on pleasure, jostled one another in the scramble to get on board. Even a few detectives could be seen here and there among the throng to remind one that amid the crowd there were some at least, who had very indistinct notions of the rights of property. But even they had on their summer suits and looked as bright as any around.

At 1:15 a train of nine cars, packed to its utmost capacity, moved off, only to make room for another to accommodate an ever-increasing crowd. As the time drew on for the 1:30 train troops of all kinds of citizens, chiefly arrayed in white plug and straw hats and suits of every summer hue, kept pouring into the depot. The ticket clerks could scarcely meet the demands of the crowd, and numbers were generally left behind as each train moved off. Venders of "official programs" of the races at 10 cents apiece seemed to gather a rich harvest of dimes. When any one grumbled at the price he was instantly told that each copy cost the seller nine cents, and such information generally seemed to satisfy the purchaser and engage his sympathy for the small dealers who could only realize profits by making heavy sales. At 1:45 a train still larger and more densely crowded than the preceeding, filled with a similar miscellaneous holiday crowd, steamed off to the races. The only class of the community that was not largely represented was the ladies, the gentler sex having evidently preferred the more secret method of reaching the course-by means of carriages and horses. Quality atoned for quanity, however, and the bright looks and brighter costumes of the ladies who did travel by the race-trains helped materially to enliven and freshen the scene.

White plug hats and light clothes for the men, wide straw and flowing plumes for the women, gave character to the 2 o'clock train. The women were in the minority, and there was an absence of young people in the coaches, the benches of which were mostly taken up with business-men, young and old, who had apparently been detained in their offices and counting houses until the last moment. They came single and in pairs, usually hurrying into the cars and landing themselves down in the nearest seat. In the absence of women smoking was allowed on nearly all the coaches. From the general drift of conversation it appeared that most of the females of the families of the passengers had gone ahead behind fast trotters by way of the boulevards, and many deplored the fact that their engagements had delayed them so long as to deny them the privilege of reaching the destination in the same inviting way.

The next train, which left at 2:15, was almost empty. Its passengers gathered about the corners of the cars to explain to one another how it was that they had been left by previous trains. As the 2:15 train was to reach the course after the first heat, it may well be termed the "kicker's" train, for there was hardly a man on it who did not complain. From the general drift of remarks the idea might be caught that the company ought to try to make some arrangement by which a train starting after the races began should get to the track in time for the beginning. Still the people were good-natured, and, after a few words expressive of their disappointment and ill-luck, they fell to smoking and reading the programs for the races. This last train was as long as any of the first, although a single coach of the seven might have taken all the passengers. Its special mission was to help bring the people home at the close.

THE CROWD.

IT WAS THIRSTY, NOISY, AND GOOD-NATURED.

The inaugural meeting was most satisfactory in every respect. The races were exciting and well contested, the attendance was good, and the weather was all that could be desired. The club-house and the grand stand, though not crowded, were fairly well filled with the representatives of Chicago's wealth and beauty, and striking and picturesque costumes were to be seen in every direction. On the ground floor, at the east end of the grand stand, where all the betting was conducted, the scene was one of the wildest imaginable. Auctioneers shouted themselves hoarse in their attempts to sell pools, Paris-mutuals men yelled themselves black in the face, and about fifty bookmakers joined in a shrieking chorus to let the public know what odds they laid against the favorites. The space beneath the grand stand where the betting went on was filled with a wild-eyed, surging crowd, each one yelling for his favorite. It was very much like the floor of the Board of Trade, only more so. Thousands-perhaps tens of thousands-of dollars were put up on each event, and in every case the "suckers" and the bookmakers came out ahead. That is, the few of the "suckers" who happened to bet on the right "dark horse." The liquor-stand was surrounded by a howling mob all day long. Whisky and beer were served out as fast as a hundred hands could take payment, but there was no satisfying the thirsty crowd. Every man who won, and every man who lost, and every man who "didn't bet anything" alike clamored at the liquor-bar. But it was a very thirsty day. The touts with "tips" were there by the dozen, as usual. Each one had a "dead-sure thing" for any one who was willing to listen. Altogether, the Washington Park Derby Day was a fair imitation of the famous myriad-gathering English Derby.

Despite elaborate facilities and the patronage of the rich and powerful, racing faced a constant battle with gamblers that tainted the sport. Moral crusades during the Progressive era succeeded in closing many of the tracks and brought reform legislation that fostered greater regulation by government rather than private agencies. Both the Chicago Tribune and the New York Times followed the political repercussions throughout the period. The first two stories appeared in the Tribune, 31 May 1885, p. 17, and 10 March 1887, p. 4.

POOL-SELLERS COME TO GRIEF.

NEW YORK, May 30.-[Special.]-Manager George Engeman kept up his work at the Brighton Beach race-course today. He said Wednesday last that the pool-sellers would be ready Decoration-Day, and they were. But their readiness did not last throughout the day, for their sale of "short horses" was checked by the police. The Paris Mutual machines were put in order, and long before the first race was called this afternoon the sale of pools was begun. The first race was run, and the holders of tickets on Weasel were not dilatory in cashing them. The sellers had just begun to put out tickets on the second race, when a sharp-eyed watcher caught sight of Chief McKane in the throng. Distributed through the crowd of betters he had a dozen ununiformed special policemen. Under the command of Capt. Hilman. The sharp-eyed watcher communicated his discovery to the pool-sellers, and at once there was a hurried attempt made by them to get out of the way with the boxes containing the cash and unsold tickets. Only three of the pool-sellers were arrested. The prisoners were arraigned, gave bail, and went back to the track. While on their way thither they passed George Engeman and Charles Hoff, the chief of the pool-sellers, who were on their way to court, having been arrested on warrants procured by Chief McKane. Engeman and Hoff refused to plead and were held in $500 each for examination. The effect of the stoppage of pool-selling will probably be the abandonment of the Brighton Beach course. After the pool-selling was stopped but little interest was manifested in the races.

THE POOL BILL.

A bill is now pending before the General Assembly entitled "An act to prohibit bookmaking and pool-selling." Strenuous effort is being made to amend it by restricting its operation to pool-rooms and betting-places entirely disconnected with any race-course. As it stands the bill is narrow and unsatisfactory in its scope, but thus amended it would be worse than no law at all. Better let the matter entirely alone than say in effect: It is all right for those who witness a horse-race to bet on the result, but those who are too busy or too poor to indulge in that luxury must not. The original bill contains only one section and reads as follows:

Be it enacted, etc. That any person who keeps any room, shed, tenement, tent, booth, or building, or any part thereof, or who occupies any place upon any public or private grounds within this State with any book, instrument, or device for the purpose of recording or registering bets or wages, or of selling pools, or any person who records or registers bets or wagers, or sells pools upon the result of any trial or contest of skill, speed, or power of endurance of man or beast, or upon the results of any political nomination appointment, or elections or being the owner, leasee, or occupant of any room, shed, tenement, tent, booth, or building, or part thereof, knowingly permits the same to be used or occupied for any of these purposes, or therein keeps, exhibits, or employs any device or apparatus for the purpose of recording or registering such bets or wagers, or selling of such pools, or becomes the custodian or depository for hire or privilege of any money, property, or thing of value staked, wagered, or pledged upon any such result, shall be punishable by imprisonment for one year, or by fine not exceeding $2000 or both.

All this is now condemned and punishable under the criminal code of the State. If the Mayor of Chicago would only obey the law and respect his oath of office pool-rooms would not exist. But the responsibility for allowing the law to be a dead letter is not all on his shoulders. Every organization which allows betting to be done on its premises must share in that responsibility, whether it exist for the promotion and management of a country fair or a city trotting park. So long as the glamour of respectability is thrown around gambling or jockeys and horses poolrooms will thrive, especially if those who claim eminent respectability set the example of giving zest to the excitement by wagering on which nag will come under the wire first.

A plea is made for exempting race-courses from the provisions of this bill on the ground that they are useful and could not exist if gambling were shut off. The utility is more imaginary than real. Improvement in horse-flesh is encouraged by the demand for rapid roadsters rather than by the profits of racing. But conceding that point it by no means follows that gambling is a necessary feature of the track. A case in point is furnished by the diamond field. A few years ago a Chicago gentleman now dead was confessedly at the head of base-ball management in this country. That gentleman was by no means a Puritan. He had no hesitation in using high-spiced English in his speech, but he drew the line at allowing public gambling at ball matches. Against great opposition he persisted, and he had his way, too. Instead of ruining the business it proved a brilliant stroke of financial policy. That example is commended to the especial attention of all who are trying to emasculate the Anti-pool bill by exempting gambling on race-courses.

The following article, from the New York Times, charged collusion between gamblers and telegraph operators on 20 May 1891, p. 1.

AN ALLY OF GAMBLERS

THE WESTERN UNION COMPANY IN ITS TRUE COLORS.
GOULD'S REPRESENTATIVES TELL THE RACING BOARD OF CONTROL
THAT THEY WILL HELP THE POOLROOMS IN THEIR FIGHT FOR EXISTENCE.

The Western Union Telegraph Company has now come out flatly as an ally of the city poolrooms, and will probably prove as strong a one as the police authorities, as Jay Gould has a large "pull" in this town. Yesterday a committee of the Racing Board of Control called at the executive offices of the company to ascertain if the racing associations were to have the assistance of the company in the fight with the city poolrooms, or were to expect the opposition of the company.

The outcome of the interview was a complete surprise to the representatives of the race tracks. They were informed in the plainest possible language that the Western Union Telegraph Company was against the race tracks and hand-in-hand with the keepers of the gambling dives in this city. The telegraph people they said, had no favors of any kind to ask of the racing associations, and no favors to extend.

Their present policy was to be their future policy they said, plainly. The company proposed to steal the news which was wanted in the city dives in any way that they could, and, having stolen it, proposed to furnish it to poolroom keepers in this and other cities at a tariff which would amply repay them for all the trouble they were put to and for all the danger they run as accessories of the New-York City pool-room keepers in the violation of the laws of the State.

The race department of the Western Union Telegraph Company is the most profitable department in its entire service, and it is very natural that the company should make a fight to get for nothing the news for which it has heretofore paid the racing associations for the exclusive possession of. It has now no rival in the field, as it had when the Baltimore and Ohio Company was in existence and when the Western Union employed a force of men to cut and ground the wires of its rival in its attempt to obtain news exclusively.

Without a rival, therefore, it expects to be able, by use of signal flags, carrier pigeons, messengers, and other devices, to defeat the attempt of the jockey clubs to keep the news from them, and supply all the "Pete" DeLacys, "Shang" Drapers, "The" Allens, and "Barney" Michaels it can get as customers with the information they want.

These men will, in turn, furnish the Western Union Company with all the means of protection which they employ and enjoy through their "pull" with the chiefs of the police officials of the city to hold them safe from prosecution. As the police dare not arrest "Pete" DeLacy, they will hardly dare move against his rich and powerful ally, the Western Union Telegraph Company.

There was great rejoicing among the poolroom men last evening when the position of the Western Union managers was learned, and, backed by this corporation, they will now resume their business more openly and carry it on more defiantly than ever, believing that with such a man as Jay Gould behind them at the head of a powerful corporation; a man who buys his law by the year, and Legislatures and other bodies of law makers and law expounders in job lots, they are safe from any prosecution or annoyance, no matter what they may do.

The proprietors of the poolrooms conducted gambling operations with greater audacity and with apparently fewer annoyances yesterday than any day since Fisher's conviction. If all the laws had been wiped off the books and all the police and other officials whose business it is to stop the commission of crime had been suddenly made private citizens without authority the nefarious business could not have opened up any more briskly than it did yesterday.

The Western Union wires were apparently in good working order, for the races were described just as they used to be when the betting was done on horses at the Guttenberg track, and the winners and place horses were posted within a few minutes after the events became matters of record at the tracks.

Mr. DeLancey Nicoll, District Attorney, who has a number of indictments which he is promising to prosecute, said to a TIMES reporter that he was giving some attention to this particular class of lawbreakers. He said that he would not discuss the case he proposed to make, or give any hint of what evidence he had against the indicted men, because the poolsellers were watching closely, and if they got a shadow of an idea of the way he intended to charge upon them they would at once hunt up a way to get around him.

"The Wynan case will be argued before the Court of Appeals some day next week," he said. "The briefs are being prepared in this office now. If the holding of the court below, in that case, is reversed, then the 'contract' business may be declared a farce and prosecutions may be carried on until the rooms are closed up tight."

"Why are they not closed up now! Why are not lawbreakers of this class treated like any others and the proprietors made to quit committing crime or pay the penalty?" Mr. Nicoll was asked.

He fell back upon that tottering old excuse, the "commission business, which THE TIMES has repeatedly shown is a fiction pure and simple.

"The poolroom keepers allege that they are doing a commission business," he said, "and they have contracts to that effect on the alleged orders which those persons who do business with them execute. Suppose these orders and contracts are nothing but a farce, it will not do to bring a case hurriedly on such imperfect evidence as a policeman may secure and take the risk of losing the case. If the prosecution were once thrown out of court on a weak case, then all that has been done toward closing the rooms would amount to nothing, and business at all the places would go on unchecked."

Mr. Nicoll said that he did not know the precise day when the Court of Appeals would listen to arguments in the Wynn case. There were opinions, he said, from lawyers of good standing that some of the points in that decision would be reversed.

Violence contributed to the vile atmosphere of some tracks which were controlled completely by bookmakers. When a police raid on Garfield Park in Chicago resulted in two deaths in 1892, the track was closed. Gamblers in Chicago enjoyed strong political connections but eventually succumbed to a coalition of reformers known as the Civic Federation. Other municipal reform groups adopted the Chicago model. Harper's Weekly provided a forum for the reformers in its issue of 25 March 1893, p. 291.

THE DEGENERATION OF HORSE RACING.
By John A. Hennessy.

What is known as the legitimate racing season of 1893 will begin at Washington in April and end at Linden or Elizabeth, New Jersey, in November. There is every promise now of brilliant success, but as in 1892 this promise may be blighted by general mismanagement and a failure on the part of the jockey clubs to properly protect the public from the fradulent plans of men who care nothing for the good advancement of the turf. Public condemnation was soundly set on jockey club management in 1892, and the reports filed with the State Comptroller at Albany-show that every racing association within the jurisdiction of the Board of Control suffered a great falling off in gate receipts. The paying attendance did not average four thousand persons a day which does not speak well for the gentlemen who control the management of the Eastern turf.

The lack of confidence by the public grew day by day in 1892 and was especially noticeable at the meetings of the Coney Island Jockey Club at Sheepshead Bay. The grand stand was rarely half filled during the spring and autumn meetings. The Coney Island Jockey Club has been going back steadily in public favor since the death of Mr. Leonard Jerome, who was its efficient president, and the fact is now generally recognized that a complete reorganization of the club's management must come to pass if the old-time prestige is to be regained. What is true of this once prosperous jockey club is in a lesser degree true of the New York and Brooklyn jockey clubs and the Monmouth Park Racing Association. Men beyond the prime of life, chained to old traditions of the turf, not alive to the new conditions which exist and not strong enough to be independent in their convictions, form one element in the turf management of today. The present and the future seem a blank to them; they live in the past. The other element in control comprises men prominent in the political life of the cities of New York and Brooklyn and the State of New Jersey. This element has a very dense idea of turf morality, if it has any idea of morality at all, and insists on managing racing matters after the style most in favor with political machines. The members in this latter class own stock in the race-tracks, have race horses, employ jockeys, and in some instances are interested in the profits made by certain book makers. All of these men gamble, and are under obligations to other men who own race horses and speculate in the betting ring.

The result is the growth of a privileged class of horsemen who have "influential connections," or what in public life would be termed a "political pull." They can take daring chances in the running of their horses. Their jockeys may ride in slovenly fashion and escape official censure, and, generally speaking, they can do pretty much as they please so long as they have the political elements of the turf behind them. Sometimes one man more hardened than the others may overstep the broad line of protection afforded him, in which event his jockey may be made a scapegoat until public clamor has subsided. The amiable old gentlemen who act as figure-heads and draw salaries are too discrete to challenge the opinions of those officials or stockholders whose political affiliations have much to do with determining the decisions of the stewards of racing. The horseman, trainer, or jockey who has no influence at court must walk a pretty straight line, unless he wishes to suffer condign punishment at the first lapse from morality. He is in the position of the unprotected liquor dealer who is pounced upon by the virtuous policeman. He must come in out of the wet and divide the spoils occasionally, or take chances of having no friends to plead his cause if the necessity should arise. This evil has grown measurably with the increase of the political element on the turf. The gentlemen who raced for sport have been crowded out of turf management, although still factors in actual racing. They no longer have any power in the making of turf laws, or in the settlement of allegedly fraudulent races. Such men as Perry Belmont, August Belmont, O.P.H. Belmont, J R. Keene, Foxhall Keene, Pierre Lorillard, Frederick Gebberd, S. S. Brown, Nathan Straus, Chester C. Chapin, and others of the same class are not represented in the Board of Control or in the steward's stand. All this explains why the attendance, which fell off notably in 1891 and 1892 may not be appreciably increased in 1893, unless the acceptable stockholders assert themselves and determine that the rules of racing shall be lived up to by all, and shall be applied in the interest of the public.

Another evil which has grown to hurt the turf in the last few years is the employment by the jockey clubs of gentlemen who are employed as turf writers on metropolitan papers. These gentlemen are employed in various stations at a rate of pay ranging from $10 to $50 a day. Nearly as many more have applied from time to time for employment. These gentlemen can hardly be expected to do justice to their newspapers in the matter of fearless cirticism while receiving the money of the clubs they are called upon to write of. This has led to an increased lack of confidence on the part of the public, and to a belief that fraud underlies almost everything in racing. As a matter of fact, abuse is not one-tenth of the fraud in racing which turf goers believe exists, but the failure of turf officials to take notice of flagrant cases has naturally increased the suspicion of fraud which always finds lodgement in the finds of many. Turf goers look to the proprietor of the Coney Island Jockey Club to set the pace in turf reforms. The other clubs will have to follow. He is independent, if he chooses to be, of political dictation. He should compel his employees to be so and he can do so. He ought not to permit persons who are not stockholders to manage his property. A renewal of excellent management that obtained three, four, five, and six years ago would regain for the club and the turf of the prestige that has been lost. Judges who are competent and independent would work a great reform in racing. Otherwise than is suggested above the outlook for racing is bright. Good management can make a brilliant season....

The Scientific American reprinted an article on 4 January 1896, p. 9, that had appeared previously in the Quarterly Journal of Inebriety that exposed one of the nefarious means used to doctor races.

USE OF COCAINE ON THE RACETRACK

Within a recent period cocaine has come into use on the race track, as a stimulant. Horses that are worn and exhausted, or are uncertain as to speed and endurance, are given ten to fifteen grains of cocaine by the needle under the skin at the time of starting, or a few moments before.

The effects are very prominent, and a veritable muscular delirioum follows, in which the horse dsplays unusual speed, and often unexpectedly wins the race. This agitation continues and the driver has difficulty in "slowing down" the horse after the race is over; not unfrequently the horse will go half round again before he can be stopped. The exhaustion which follows is not marked, except in the great thirst and loss of appetite. Sometimes diarrhea and trembling follow. But good grooms give unusual attention to rubbing and bathing the legs in hot water and stimulants. The general effect on the horse is depression from which he soon recovers but it is found essential to give cocaine again to make sure of his speed. The action of cocaine grows more transient as the use increases, and when a long period of scoring follows before the race begins, drivers give a second dose secretly while in the saddle. Sometimes the horse becomes delirious and unmanageable, and leaves the track in a wild frenzy, often killing the driver, or he drops dead on the track from the cocaine, although the cause is unknown to any but the owner and driver. Some horses have been given as high as twenty grains at a time, but this is dangerous and only given to worn-out animals, who may by this means win a race. It appears that cocaine is only used in running races, and as a temporary stimulant for the time. It is claimed that the flashing eyes and trembling excitement of the horse is strong evidence of the use of cocaine. - Quarterly Journal of Inebriety.

The backlash to such deeds produced a rash of closings, as reported by the New York Times, 11 March 1893, p. 2, and 22 March 1894, p. 11.

TO ABOLISH RACING.

A BILL RECOMMENDED TO THE CONNECTICUT LEGISLATURE.

HARTFORD, Conn. March 10.-The movement in this State, organized and led by the Rev. Dr. Newman Smyth of New-Haven, against pool selling and horse racing culminated in the Legislature this afternoon in a recommendation from the Judiciary Committee favoring stringent legislation.

Should the bill receive the Governor's signature, it would drive horse racing from the State and reduce Charter Oak Park to an outlying farm.

The bill provides that every person, whether as principal, agent, or servant, who shall own, possess, keep, manage, maintain, or who shall assist in keeping, managing, maintaining, or occupying any building, office, or place with apparatus, books, boards, or any device for the purpose of making, recording, or registering bets or wagers, or of buying or selling pools upon the result of any trial or contest of skill, speed, or endurance of man, beast, bird, or machine, or upon the result of any game, competition, political nomination, appointment or election, whether in Connecticut or not, shall be fined $500 or imprisoned not more than one year.

In exceptional cases both penalties can be imposed. The person registering these bets or holding the stakes shall be treated in the same way. While the bill was under consideration by the committee, strenuous efforts were made to exempt horse racing from its provisions and penalties.

It is a question whether the bill, being so radical in character, can be carried through the House. In sporting circles the measure is regarded with consternation, and one of the most desperate contests of the session will be made over it.

KILLS RACING ON JERSEY TRACKS.
SUPREME COURT DECISION SEALS THE GATES AT ALL COURSES.

NEW YORK, March 21.-[Special.]-The news of Chief Justice Beasley's decision in the Supreme Court at Trenton, N.J., to the effect that the Democrats should vacate their seats in the Legislature, came as a thunderclap to turfmen in this city today. The big owners and members of the New Jockey club regretted the news for the reason that Monmouth Park will again lie idle, whereas the smaller "fry" were disconsolate because Guttenberg, Clifton, Gloucester, Elizabeth, and Linden would have to keep their gates closed. A large proportion of the latter element has remained in the city hoping against hope that one or the other of smaller tracks would commence operations, and when it was announced that George Engeman in an unguarded moment had placed himself on record by stating that Clifton would surely race, many who had resolved upon going afield abandoned the idea. Relating to the decision a prominent turfman said today; "I am deeply sorry for Monmouth Park's sake, as this means there will be no racing in New Jersey this year at least. On the other hand when you come to consider the injurious effect arising from Gloucester, Clifton, and Guttenberg I am not sure but that it is the best thing that can happen for racing in the long run."

ANNAPOLIS, Md., March 21.-[Special.]- In connection with the bill to prohibit pool selling at Arlington, near this city, it is reported here that the gamblers who expect to be driven out of New Jersey by the acts of the present Legislature of that State, with regard to pool selling, are making arrangements to move their busines to Arlington in case the bill before the General Assembly here fails to pass. A strong lobby is at work trying to defeat the bill.

Some state governments eventually opted for a more pragmatic approach, attempting to regulate and tax the perpetrators by setting up racing commissions that brought revenue to the state. The organized crime rings continued to try to evade the authorities, as well as their own corporate co-conspirators, such as the telegraph companies. The developments can be traced in the reports of the New York Times, 15 February 1893, p. 3, and Chicago Tribune, 19 March 1897, p. 8.

NEW STATUTES PROPOSED

Albany, Feb. 14.-One of the most important of all the amendments offered to the Ives pool law was introduced in the Senate to-day by Gen. Parker, (Dem, Albany.) The bill was drawn by Controller Campbell, and imposes a tax of 5 per cent on the gross receipts of racing associations except those received for entries for horses.

Deputy Controller Huson explained the bill in these terms: "The present law merely taxes the gross amount of the admission receipts to the tracks. Our amendment taxes all the receipts of the racing associations except those for the entries of horses. Formerly the State received $60,000 from the Ives pool law; now it receives only $30,000 yearly. We feel that we ought to have the legal right to look at the books of the racing associations and determine whether or not their statements to us about their gross receipts are true. That is a new provision, also, in our bill. Controller Campbell intends to push the bill, and I think we shall be able to pass it."

The proposed law will tax the bookmakers, who now pay $100 a day to the racing associations for the privilege of making books....

The second bill is an amendment to the Penal Code. It provides punishment by imprisonment for one year or a fine of $2,000, or both, for any person who receives money bet or wagered of to be transmitted by him or by any other person to be placed as a bet or wager or for the purchase of pools upon the result of any trial or contest of skill, speed, or power of endurance of man or beast. Both bills will be introduced in the Assembly to-morrow.

TO PERMIT POOL SELLING
BILL FOR SIXTY-DAY MEETINGS INTRODUCED AT SPRINGFIELD.

It Is Put In by Representative Kilcourse-Wasted by Hawthorne and Garfield Park Crowds-Puts a Tax of $50 a Day on the Privilege-Bets Must Be on Horses at Meeting Where Pools Are Sold-Penalties for Violation.

Springfield, Ill., March 18-[Special]-The Kilcourse bill which was introduced here today in the House on the subject of racetracks provides for sixty-day meetings. The bill to be introduced in the Senate on behalf of the Northwestern Horsebreeders' Association declares for thirty-day meetings.

The Kilcourse bill is wanted by the Hawthorne and old Garfield Park crowd: Representatives of these organizations have been banging around here from time to time ever since the session began. The General Assembly will not stand the sixty-day bill, and it is a question if a thirty-day measure would be sanctioned. The old race-track crowd does itself no good by keeping people here, and if a pooling bill is wanted some other class should be sent to push it.

The Kilcourse bill is to permit poolselling and bookmaking on race tracks, and provides that racing may not continue more than sixty days on one track in a year. It also says that a tax of $50 a day must be paid to the County Treasurer of the county in which the track is located. The County Treasurer must remit the tax to the State Treasurer every six days, deducting the 2 per cent allowed him by law.

The section permitting the making of books and pool selling reads:

At the time of every race meeting it shall be lawful to make books and buy and sell pools upon the result of any race between horses to be actually had within such racing enclosure during the meeting being then and there held, but no books shall be made or pools bought or sold at any other time upon any race that takes place outside of the said inclosure.

The next secion provides for the regulation of the size of the track. It says that every racing inclosure under this act where books are made and pools bought and sold on races shall be not less than one mile in length and the owner of the inclosure may offer prizes and charge fees for entries.

The next section provides that all race meetings shall be held within the period of time between the first day of May and the first day of November, thereafter following of each year and at no other time. It also says that the aggregate racing in each year shall not exceed sixty days and the meeting shall be conducted between the hours of 12 o'clock noon and 7 o'clock in the afternoon of every day.

The penalties provided that whoever shall permit books to be made and pools to be bought or sold upon such racing inclosures excepting as provided for in the act shall pay the country in which such meeting is held not less than $200 nor more than $1,000 for each and every offense. Any person who shall make books or buy and sell pools contrary to the provisions of the act is liable to a fine of not less than $200 and imprisonment in county jail not less than thirty days nor more than six months, and any person or corporation who shall fail to pay the tax imposed upon it by the act shall pay to the State of Illinois the sum of $1,000 for each day it so fails to pay.

The following is from the New York Times, 10 March 1900, p. 2.

BIG POOLROOM TRUST.
FORMED TO REDUCE TELEGRAPH EXPENSES, WHICH AMOUNTED TO MILLIONS

The poolroom keepers have organized a trust, and the figures indicate that it has effected a great saving. The combination was formed against the Western Union Telegraph Company and the "touts." The poolroom business in the State of New York was worth nearly $10,000,000 per annum to the Western Union Telegraph Company.

When poolrooms first started they made an arrangement with the racing bureau of the telegraph company. The latter was to be paid $5 for information furnished on each race. This included a list of the entries and weights, the riders, the scratches, the first and second betting, the description, and result of the races. The poolroom keeper had to pay his operator, and also had a man on each racetrack to whom he paid $5 or more per day to wire the needed information.

Week in and week out throughout the year the poolrooms receive information from an average of fifteen races daily, six days in the week, and fifty-two weeks in the eyar. There are 400 poolrooms in the city, and the estimate is probably below rather than over the correct figure. Before the formation of the combination the proprietor of each of these 400 rooms paid the telegraph company $65 per day. That means $26,000 per day for the 400, $156,000 per week, and the enormous sum of $8,112,000 per year.

While the poolroom business is very profitable, the keepers realized that the telegraph company and the "touts" who sent the information from the tracks, were getting about all of the profits after the fees for protection had been paid. They did not object to the $20 or $25 paid the telegraph operator, weekly, because some one to do this work was necessary under any circumstances.

So the big poolroom men got together and in this city they established four telephone stations. One of these is in "honest" John Kelly's place on West Forty-first Street. Another is located in the central portion of the city, further west; a third in Harlem, and a fourth near Fulton Street.

It is to these four places that the telegraphic dispatches from the racetracks go, and from these bureaus it is distributed by telephone to the poolrooms. So that where the poolroom owners were paying $26,000 a day to the Western Union, the combination pays less than $1,000.

It is the report in the poolrooms that the owners have to pay the combination $1 on each race for telephone service, a daily average expense of $15, exclusive of telephone rentals. The telegraph operator is superseded by the telephone man, who sits at a desk with a receiver constantly attached to his ear.

On 14 May 1891 the Louisville Courier-Journal paid tribute to Isaac Murphy on page 6. Murphy, who had just won his third Kentucky Derby aboard Kingman, enjoyed the rare praise of a black man in American society. The accolades proved short-lived as Murphy was falsely accused of practicing a dissolute lifestyle and driven from his profession.

KINGMAN'S GREAT RIDER

Isaac Murphy, who rode Kingman to victory, showed the same dexterity which has made him famous, and gained for him the reputation of being the greatest jockey on the American turf. Probably without an exception Murphy has piloted more horses to victory than any other jockey in this country, and has ridden some of the finest races. His success is especially attributed to his ability to judge pace. He never punishes his animal, and yet his ability to control an unruly horse is regarded as something wonderful.

Above all things he recognizes the right time to set the pace, and never takes unnecessary speed. It was this careful avoiding of anything like fast riding at unnecessary moments yesterday which gained for Kingman his victory. Yesterday's Derby is the third at Churchill Downs in which he has ridden to victory, the other two horses being Buchanan, whom he rode in 1884, and Riley in 1890.

Murphy is the wealthiest jockey on the turf. His income has ranged from $10,000 to $15,000 for over five years, a great part of which sum he has placed in safe investments. He lives in Frankfort when not with the races, and when at home devotes his idle time to study and reading. Though he is reserved and said not to be a good mixer, yet he has a great many warm friends. His reputation for honesty and integrity is a matter of great pride among turfmen, and they never lose an opportunity to boast of his qualities, both as a horseman and a man. The great rider is only twenty-seven years of age, but he has been a conspicuous figure on the turf since he was a mere boy.

QUARTERHORSES

The following appeared in Harper's Weekly, 9 June 1894, p. 534.

PONY RACING AND THE BRONCO

... The bronco is in truth not only the native American type, but the only racing pony known even to the effete East for many years, and his blood flows through the veins of many winners on the race-tracks to this day.

But the East is a very small part of pony-racing in America. It is in the great West that we must look for typical American ponyracing, for out there it has been a recognized sport ever since the advance column of pioneers found the tough little cayuse ready at hand, and almost for the asking. And yet earlier than that it flourished with the Indians, and in Mexico long before Westward Ho! became the watchword.

It seems altogether incomprehensible that with such favoring traditions, and the article ready-made at our very door, the sport of racing ponies should have had no organized recognition on the Atlantic coast until four years ago. The home of the bronco is only three days travel from New York, and although as he first comes to us he is not an ideal as compared with the bred-up type of recent years, yet a very few generations serve to make him so. Moreover, not infrequently it is possible to pick up a bronco which is a very fast sprinter, and in such a case it is safe to conclude that he comes from across the Rio Grande (where there is more of the sport than elsewhere), and is no stranger to racing....

Probably Mexico and the southern portion of New Mexico, Arizona, and California furnish the more picturesque side of the sporting bronco, but they do not limit the field of his racing. The cow-pony of the West is a well-known sprinter, that can start almost with the revolver's report, and at top speed turn on a blanket. There used to be a great deal of racing in the mining-camps when the West was "wild and wooly," and every other man was a prospective millionaire; and there was, and of course is to-day, quite a bit of it on the cattle ranges, though not so much as the average "tenderfoot" might suppose. Cow-punchers, in season, are too busy by day and too weary at night to give much thought to the sport....Yet there are races, generally impromptu and at catch weights, during the dull season, which usually result from the purchase of new ponies by individual herders, or from a discussion over the respective ponies of rival ranches.

With the exception of the Apaches, the Indians, generally speaking, have always been devoted to pony-racing. Like the Mexicans, many of their games are on horse-back, some of the sort that requires instant stopping and quick turning - all attributes of the cow-pony. Unlike the Mexican, however, the Indian racing pony goes to the post with the simplest of trappings; he carries no elaborately decorated and expensively made saddle; the gag-bit he has, very probably, but it is not likely to be of the hand-made pattern, nor silver inlaid, and the Indian jockey is very likely to drum the ribs of his mount with his heels minus spurs. Many times I have seen them race without saddle, and with the end of a rawhide lariat twisted about the pony's jaw for a bridle. But this type is more often on the artist's easel than in the Indian camp.

The Mexican and Indian bronco is not fitted (without breeding up) to the distances prevalent on the Eastern tracks. Of course it is well known that blood and bone give a horse staying power at top speed, and it is not to be supposed that a raw bronco could hold his own against a thoroughbred or a half-breed at half-mile, or at any distance the latter could cover at his uttermost gait. The same nervous, catlike alacrity that has made the mustang the greatest cow-pony in the world makes him also undoubtedly the fastest starter of his kind; add to this a natural turn of speed for a short distance, and you have a sprinter that as a rule is unequalled. He is quite as unbeatable at long distances, for there is no quadruped that can travel so far and so long with so little care as this same unkempt, unattractive little best, called according to locality, cayuse, mustang, bronco....

Although pony-racing had no organized recognition until 1890, yet there was plenty of scattered sport before that among the polo and hunting men. Polo, started by James Gordon Bennett in 1876, led, the following year, to the organization of hunt clubs, and racing among these sportsmen followed as a natural sequence. An attempt was made later to hold race meetings in conjunction with steeple-chasing, but it all ended with little sport and less credit to the projectors.

The American Pony-Racing Association was organized in '90 through the efforts of a few sportsmen, including H.L. Herbert, Jenkins Van Schaick, Elliott Roosevelt, A. Belmont Purdy, August Belmont, J.R. Wood, J. Clinch Smith, F.T. Underhill, Louis V. Bell, and others, and about two years later broadened its scope to include the hunt club races, changing its name accordingly to the American Hunt and Pony-Racing Association. It has been growing steadily, wisely profiting each season by its experience of the one before, and has been taken up by the Country Clubs, whose meetings have furnished the brightest and cetainly the most successful scenes of the pony-racing year.

The season of 1893 brought out larger fields, with a more general distribution of winnings, and sustained an interest to the end.

How it has thrived may be judged from these figures:

	Meetings	Races Run	Members	Registry of Ponies and Horses
1890	9	47	215	221
1893	35	171	500	500

At Washington, Philadelphia, Baltimore, New York, Long Branch, Boston, where the meetings are held at the Brookline Country Club, one of the best club courses in the country, also Saratoga, Danbury, and Chicago, pony-racing has made its way into public favor; all of this goes to show that the Steeple-chase, Hunt, and Pony-Racing Association has not only increased its membership, but has outgrown the mere local character it had at the beginning.

POLO

James Gordon Bennett introduced polo to America after witnessing the game in England. He and his friends formed the Westchester Polo Club shortly thereafter. Wealthy socialites played polo during their summer retreats to Newport, Rhode Island and by the 1890s Boston Brahmins and Philadelphia's elite had taken up the sport. The Polo Association was formed in 1890 to promote expansion and standardization of play. The following is excerpted from Lawrence Timpson's article in Outing, August 1891, p. 412-414.

AMERICAN POLO

... Below are given the rules of play as adopted by the Westchester Polo Club. They have been essentially the same all along in America, the only changes of any moment made being the reduction of the number of players allowed on a side, a larger number than four having been found to impede the play and to largely increase the chance of accidents. Hooking mallets, too, was first allowed, but was afterward prohibited, as it was not at all a question of skill, and the limit for the height of ponies was raised in 1879 from thirteen hands to fourteen one.

RULES

1. The grounds to be about 750 feet long by 500 feet wide, with a ten-inch guard from end to end on the sides only.

2. The height of the ponies must not exceed fourteen hands one inch.

3. The balls to be of wood, with no other covering than paint, and about three inches in diameter. The mallets to be such as are approved by the steward.

4. The goal-posts to be twenty-four feet apart and light enough to break if collided with.

5. Match games between pairs shall be for periods of thirty minutes, time between goals included, unless otherwise specified.

6. Match games between teams of four shall be for periods of twenty minutes each, actual play, time between goals and delays not counted, with ten minutes between the periods for rest, unless otherwise specified.

7. Each team to choose an umpire, and if necessary the two umpires to appoint a referee, whose decision shall be final.

8. Each team shall have a substitute in readiness to play when a match is on.

9. There shall be a captain for each team, who shall have the direction of the positions and the playing of his men.

10. No captain shall allow a member of his team to appear in a game otherwise than in the club uniform.

11. No person - players, umpires, and referee excepted -shall, under any circumstances, be allowed on the ground during the progress of the game.

12. It is forbidden to touch an adversary, his pony or his mallet, with the hand or mallet, during play, or to strike the ball when dismounted.

13. The game to begin with a charge, the contestants taking their positions behind the chalk line, which is to be thirty feet from the goal posts. When the signal to charge has been given by the referee the first and second players must keep to the left of the ball until it has been touched.

14. In the case of an accident to a player or pony, or for any other reasonable cause, the referee may stop the game, and the time so lost shall not be counted. When the game is resumed the ball shall be thrown between the players, who shall be lined up at the point at which the ball stopped. But if the game is stopped on account of a foul the ball is to be thrown in at the place where the foul occurred.

15. When the limit of time has expired the game must continue until the ball goes out of bounds, and such overtime shall not be counted.

16. In case of an equal number of goals having been made at the end of the third period, the game is to be continued until one side makes the winning goal.

17. When the ball goes out of bounds at the sides it must be thrown in from the place at which it went out, by the referee or an impartial person, between the two sides, which shall be drawn up in line facing each other. When the ball goes out at the ends the side defending the goal is entitled to a knock-out from the point at which it crossed the line. When the player having the knock-out causes unnecessary delay the umpire may throw a ball on the field and call play. No opponent shall come within fifty feet of the player having the knock-out until the ball has been hit.

18. A player requiring a mallet during a game must ride to the end or side line. It must not be brought on the field to him.

19. Foul riding is careless and dangerous horsemanship and lack of consideration for the safety of others. A player in possession of the ball has the right of way, and no one shall cross him unless at such a distance as to avoid all possibility of a collission.

20. The referee may suspend a player for the match for foul riding, or he may award the opposing side a half goal.

As the game developed on the East Coast, Anglo immigrants introduced it to the West, replete with connotations of social elitism, as reported by Harper's Weekly, 10 February 1894, pp. 142-143.

POLO IN SOUTHERN CALIFORNIA

Scattered through the orange counties of southern California is a considerable number of Englishmen engaged in fruit culture and kindred industries. Everywhere, even in the little frequented mountain valleys, the traveller happens upon the athletic tweed-clad figure and brier pipe that betoken Brittania's sons the world over, and where a dozen are living in the same locality a tennis court or race track is apt to be found serving as the assembly ground for the colony. Tennis is widely played and on occasion there are cricket matches; but chief in interest, both to the sporstman and general public, of the games brought from across the Atlantic is polo.

In southern California the game has been going since '87. At Santa Monica, a charming little town on the sea some sixteen miles from Los Angeles, the Englishmen have long been used to gather during the hot weather for a holiday after the orange harvest.... In the spring of 1887 an Australian named Edmonds turned up and began to discuss the feasibility of starting polo. The seed fell upon good ground. There was a young Englishman who had played the game in Iowa; there was another who, down in his luck, had started a riding academy in Los Angeles, and several others who were good horsemen that fell in with the idea heartily. They got a field, made some mallets, and with the ponies at hand started in. A couple more turned up later, and that summer polo went on more or less regularly under conditions which, though hardly favorable to scientific play, permitted good sport. At the end of the season Edmonds drifted away, but he left in Santa Monica, among other things, a well-established polo club, alas, the founder of such is still venerated.

The next summer the play was continued under more favorable conditions. The holes in the field were in a measure filled up; there were better ponies and some new players.

The second season was finished up successfully with pony races and gymkana sports. Each succeeding summer, although in the spring the outlook for players has sometimes been ominous, the game has gone on with a constantly increasing standard of excellence. Good ponies have become the rule, and the beginners have grown seasoned and skilfil....

In California polo is played on dirt, for turf is the triumph of watchful gardening and a prodigal use of precious water.... Brown Mexican ragamuffins lead the spare mounts to and fro, for grooms are unknown in Santa Monica. One of the more prosperous members of the club, I believe, keeps a man, but livery and the word "groom" are out of place with the democracy of southern California. Shortly the sides, respectively in orange and black, ride out, and the game begins, and pretty sharply, too.

In the early summer of '92 there were only two or three men who lived up to a very definite idea of team play, but as the season advanced the sides fell into a system of mutual support that was the more effective, perhaps, because it was undefined. Out there the game is played under the English rules, with the off-side principle and the privilege of hooking mallets. With fours sometimes a "flying man" is played, as in the English game, to watch the opposing back - a purposeless combination, of course, under our rules of always on side. Generally, however, all but the backs play up. The hour is divided into fifteen-minute periods, with ten-minute intervalsls. Between the quarters the ladies serve tea, and the afternoon assumes a social character. The players, with their "greaser" esquires, rub down and blanket the hot ponies, and then gather round the shandygraff for their own refreshment.

When the day has been won and lost, the ponies put up, and the rider bathed and clad in fresh duck, the pipes are lit, the soda and decanters are brought forth, and in little groups on the rose-trellised verandas the afternoon is talked over. After dinner the little club is the gathering place, and the talk goes on again till bedtime, the eternal topic, of course, being "pony," the diversity of types found in Santa Monica giving rise to endless discussion.

Under the American system of rating, the Los Angeles players, Captain Bolton, Messrs. Proctor, Waring, Woodhouse, and Young, would probably be handicapped from four to six goals. Mr. Woodhouse, who is an exceptionally clever hitter, would perhaps give seven. A team picked from these men and shaken together would make a good showing at Newport, but would hardly be in the same class with a team like the Independents.

While Santa Monica is the home of polo in California, many of those who play there in the summer have orange groves at or near Riverside, and a couple of years ago winter play was started with great success. The Americans have begun to take hand, and the continuance of the experiment is well-nigh assured. On the whole the future of the game is very bright, for it is probable that in the near future polo clubs will be started at Pasadena and Santa Barbara. At San Francisco I believe some such move has already been made.... With the advantage of winter practice, California should put a team in the field which would make a good match with the best fours of the East....

RODEO

A new work-related sport surfaced during the period in the western states. Although the contests lacked formal rules or a governing body until 1929, rodeos began testing cowboys' work-related skills as early as 1883, when the town of Pecos, Texas sponsored a calf-roping contest on the Fourth of July. Prescott, Arizona and Canadian, Texas organized rodeos in 1888. The latter included roping competition for a collected sum of money and wagers, horse racing, bronco riding, and dancing. Female competitors appeared in the 1880s, and gained acclaim as bronco riders within a decade.

In 1896 Canadians organized their first formal rodeo competition at the Regina, Saskatchewan Territorial Exposition. The event evolved into the famous Calgary Stampede, initiated in 1912.

In 1896 Seymour, Texas began offering prize money for its rodeo, and the Cheyenne Frontier Days were established the following year. The following accounts, reprinted from the Cheyenne Daily Sun-Leader, 15 September 1897, p. 1; and 27 September 1897, p. 4, indicate the objectives of promoters, such as the newspaper and the Union Pacific Railroad, in the invention of tradition and the realization of civic and pecuniary profit. Within a few years the celebration drew competitors from throughout the West and thousands of spectators. The greatly expanded scope of activities included baseball games, a bicycle race, and a horserace for women.

THE DAY WE CELEBRATE

Since the idea of Frontier Day was proposed and the committee appointed by Mayor Schnitger began the important work, the scheme of the day's amusements has broadly developed from day to day. Owing to the limited period allowed for preparation, the cowboy and pony events were promptly arranged in order to give those desiring to enter from a distance the necessary time to prepare and bring in horses. The amount of purses and prizes to be awarded and the conditions attched to each event, appear below, that portion of the program being complete.

The additional events which will be most picturesque and entertaining features of the day have not all been arranged, but will be announced from day to day as they are prepared for, and added to the program.

Among the frontier exhibits already secured may be mentioned, the emigrant schooner and ox train, the pony express, the overland stage, the stage hold-up and the pilgrims of the old Mormon and California trail. These will indicate the general nature of the program. The committee has other pleasant and exciting events under consideration, and will secure the best of everything in the line of entertainment that their limited time allows that is in keeping with the spirit and character of the occasion.

COW PONY RACE, HALF MILE HEATS

2. Cowpony race, half mile heats, purse $50; entrance fee, 5 per cent - First horse, 75 per cent; second horse, 15 per cent; third horse, 10 per cent.

WILD HORSE RACE, HALF MILE

3. Wild horse race, distance half mile, purse $75, 5 per cent to enter - Conditions: Horses eligible for this race are those that are only halter broken. Riders will not be permitted to ride their own horses but will be assigned to horses by the judges. The

rider finishing the half mile first will get 75 per cent of the purse and entrance money; the rider finishing second 15 per cent, and the rider finishing third, 10 per cent. Each rider can have an assistant on foot to help him.

COWPONY RACE, 250 YARDS

4. Cowpony race, distance 250 yards, purse $25; 5 per cent to enter - First horse, 75 per cent; second horse 15 per cent; third, 10 per cent. In this race the ponies run 125 yards, turn stake and return to starting point.

FREE FOR ALL RACE, ONE MILE

5. Free for all race, distance one mile, catch weights, purse $50, 5 per cent entrance - First horse, 75 per cent; second, 15 per cent; third, 10 per cent.

PITCHING AND BUCKING HORSES

6. Pitching and bucking horses, purse for the best pitching and bucking horse, $100. $25 prize for the best bronco rider. No entrance fee for this contest.

FREE FOR ALL

7. Free for all, distance one-half mile, catch weights, purse $50; 5 per cent to enter - First horse, 75 per cent; second 15 per cent; third, 10 per cent.

ROPING CONTEST

8. Roping contest, purse $50. To be given to the man who ropes and "hog ties" a steer in the shortest time; 5 per cent to enter - First man, 75 per cent; second, 15 per cent; third, 10 per cent.

In all contests where an entrance fee is charged, the entrance money will be added to the purse.

Cowponies to carry regular standard saddles.

In all contests five to enter, three to start.

Entries now open to close Wednesday evening, Sept. 22.

EXCURSION RATES

The Union Pacific round trip rates for the Frontier Day celebration will be as follows from Colorado points:

Denver	$2.00
Greeley	1.00
Carr	.60
Eaton	.95
Evans	1.15
LaSalle	1.25
Platteville	1.55
Lupton	1.75
Brighton	1.90

Tickets good only on special train in each direction.

Cheyenne and Northern round trip:

Chugwater	$2.40
Wheatland	3.20
Badger	4.10
Orin Junction	5.15

COMPLIMENTARY THANKS
TO RAILROAD OFFICIALS AND OTHERS WHO AIDED THE
FRONTIER DAY COMMITTEE

Courteous and Appreciative Letters From the Committee to E.L. Lomax, L. Malloy, J.W. Angier and E.A. Slack, Recognizing Their Valuable Services for Wyoming's Big Day.

In closing up the business connected with the Frontier Day celebration, the committee were pleased to find everything in good shape and that the management were especially succesful financially. Sufficient funds were contributed by our citizens, in addition to the receipts from the grand stand, to meet every obligation promptly. The committee will go out with a clean sheet and will in a few days make a report of their doings to our citizens, showing the amount of receipts and disbursements.

Through general co-operation of our citizens and their contributions and the enterprising and liberal action of the railroads in giving very low excursion rates, advertising and otherwise aiding them, the committee feel that a great success has been achieved, especially considering the brief time allowed them to prepare and place a program. While they feel under obligation to all who have aided by their efforts or contributions, they have received special and generous assistance from the parties whose services they have recognized by letters of thanks ...

The Cheyenne Leader provided the program of events on 11 September 1900, p. 4.

FRONTIER DAY FESTIVITIES

Another Frontier day is here in all its gaiety amd excitement, lacking none of the captivating features of former years to make it a grand success, a pleasure alike to or own citizens as well as to the hundreds of visitors that throng our pretty city, and the visitation to the celebration is very large. This is particularly true of state people.

The Colorado bands brought in a number of visitors as did the Rock Springs band. Last evening the Loveland band serenaded various members of the committee, and early this morning both bands were out playing around at various business houses.

THE INDIANS

The Indians are here in full force and they have all kinds of paint and seem to be imbued with the warlike tendencies of olden times....

These were the times when the variety theaters were running full blast and the cow puncher was "it" on the streets, and brought his revolver into play frequently, though as a rule, he was a good natured, harmless fellow...

Frontier day recalled all these little incidents and brought together old friends and enabled our neighbors to come in and see what we are.

Last evening at the fair grounds the Indians gave their first war dance. It was intensely interesting and was witnessed by quite a crowd.

AN INTERESTING CHIEF

One of the Indians here is Chief Brave Boy, whose father was in the Custer massacre. Brave Boy has been in several battles, also, and he does not conceal the fact that in old times when it was considered the proper thing among Indians, he had a number of scalps attached to his belt.

THE DAY'S SPORTS

In the morning occurred the ball game. Denver didn't do a thing but run in a number of professional league players to play our boys. The fact was that Denver was frightened. Every nine that the town has sent to Cheyenne has gone down before the mighty Indians. The result was that Colorado was searched from one corner to the other for ball players. They were paid big money and are considered as expert ball tossers as there are in the west.

But even so, the Indians didn't collapse, and in yesterday's game showed that they were there. The score was 17 to 10 in favor of the visitors.

BALLOON ASCENSION

Cheyenne never had a successful balloon ascension and parachute jump before today. This event was extremely interesting. The areanaut was no amateur and he said it was extremely difficult to manage the balloon here, but he did it and succesfully too. As he jumped from the sky he looked a mere speck. Certainly it requirees an unusual courage to follow this sort of life. The areanaut was Prof. Haddon.

COW PONY RACE

The first event was the cow pony race. These races are always interesting and are more typical frontier than any others.... The race today was half mile, purse $60, 5 per cent to enter; first horse, 75 per cent; second horse, 15 per cent, and third, 10 per cent. Standard saddles, horse to carry 180 pounds. Open to Wyoming horses only....

The winners in this race were Cricket first, Frankie second, Cuba third. Time, 55. The horses finished close together and the people were on their feet in excitement.

RUNNING RACE

The running race was a half mile, free for all, purse $60, 5 per cent to enter; first horse, 75 per cent; second, 15 per cent, and third, 10 per cent....

The winner in this race was Chicken, with Annie Won second and Cashier third. Time, 52.

INDIAN PONY RACE

The Indian pony race was one of the most entertaining races of the day. The Indians have always taken great interest in racing from time immemorial. It was a half mile, at catch weights, no entry, purse $20; first horse, 75 per cent; second horse, 15 per cent, and third horse, 10 per cent; open to Indians only.

There were twenty starters in this race, which was won by Chief Judge Martin First, Jeff Davis second, Luther Shakespeare third, Johnnie Washakie fourth, Jeff Davis fifth. Time, 58 2-5.

THE WAR DANCE

The war dance was one of the best ever seen here. The Indians were most fiercely made up and went through the barbaroues antics as if they were in earnest, giving those present a realistic idea of the festivities that preceded the massacre of the early days.

A TROTTING EVENT

A Greeley racing man gave a very interesting exhibition trot after the Indian war dance was over.

BUCKING AND PITCHING

The bucking and pitching contest has always been the best event on the program and was today and the number was more exciting this year than ever before. Some of the meanest, liveliest, and trickiest broncs in the western country were entered, and ... the riders comprised the best "busters" in Wyoming. This event beggars description and must be seen to be appreciated.... The prizes for this event were, $130 for worst horse and best rider, no hobbling or stirrups, no entry fee, best rider gets $50, second best rider gets $30, third best rider gets pair of shapps donated by F.A. Meanea, Cheyenne; worst horse gets $30, second $20....

LADIES RACE

The ladies' race exhibited to some of the admiring visitors some of Wyoming's accomplished ranch girls, with a health and vigor that the life of the city aristocracy is unaquainted with. The Wyoming ranch girl manages a bronc as cleverly as a man. Thus also does she handle fire arms and is master of all the requisites that make the successful ranch owner. This event was loudly cheered and was one of the most pleasing of the day. It was half mile, open to Wyoming horses only, purse $50, no entry fee; first horse, $25; second horse, $15; third horse, $10....

This race was won by Mrs. Clara McGee; Hila Granstian second, Kitty McPhee third. Time. 57 1-2. In this race little Jennie Pawson, a little girl, was first almost to the finish, when her saddle turned and she was thrown to the ground. She sprained a leg, but was not otherwise hurt. She would certainly have won the race and cared not for her injuries nearly so much as she did for not winning the race....

GOT A PURSE

The committee collected a snug purse for the gallant little lady who was thrown.

RUNNING RACE NO. 2

The race was a quarter mile free for all, 5 per cent to enter, purse $50; first horse, 75 per cent; second, 15 per cent; third, 10 per cent....

STAGE HOLD UP

The stage hold up was better this year than last year and it was one of the best things on last year's program. This is really exciting and as the Indians suddenly made their appearance, seeming to come out of the earth, and with their heart trending yells attacked the little body of passenges in the coach, modern westerners appreciated the dangers of stage travel in the early days.

STEER ROPING CONTEST

The eastern tenderfoot that imagines all that is required to be a cowboy is a big hat and a gun was very much surprised today when he witnessed the steer roping contest. The skill of the roper and his dexterity is simply wonderful and the proficiency shown by all the ropers brought forth the enthusiastic applause. The purse was $100, no entry fee, animals to have 100 feet start of rider, to be "hog tied," and man to jump back and signal judges by waving hands; best time, $65; second best, $25....

EVENTS THIS EVENING

The illuminated parade and grand mask carnival wiil take place at 6:30 this evening.

Parade will form as follows

First division; bands, fire department and floats.

Second Division; Troop A, Wyoming National Guards. National Guards, cow boys and lady riders.

Third division; private conveyances, Indians and masquers....

At 7:30 the Indians will give a war dance. The cake walk at 8 p.m. will be one of the most interesting events of the celebration. This cake walk is for the championship of the west.

Tommy Smith and many other champion walkers have entered for the contest. Prize, $50; first couple, $5; second, $15; third, $10.

Immediately after the cake walk the grand march led by two bands of Shoshone and Arapahoe Indian warriors in full war paint and dress, will start to the music if two brass bands. Don't miss this, the leading feature of the great Frontier day celebration. Band concerts by the best musical organization in the west on the street corners each evening.

Cheyenne Wins

The ball game today was won by Cheyenne, the score being 12 to 10 in favor of the Indians. It was a great game and was witnessed by a large and enthusiastic crowd. Our boys played exceptionally well and made but few errors. Mr Ed. F. Stahle umpired the game.

The same teams will play tomorrow morning.

Tonight's Opera

One of the most interesting features of the Frontier celebration will be the Arnold Opera company's presentation of the popular opera "Boccaccio" and "The Bohemian Girl" tonight and tomorrow night....

Grand Frontier Ball

Lovers of dancing and music should attend the grand ball at Turner hall on Wednesday evening September 12, given under the auspices of Capitol Camp, Modern Woodmen of America. The famous Naporstek's orchestra will furnish music for the occasion. Visiting Woodmen, their friends, and everybody cordially invited to attend. Admission, $1. Ladies free.

Attention, Sir Knights

Cheyenne Lodge No. 2, Knights of Pythias, desire to welcome visiting knights present in the city during the Frontier day festivities and invite all such to visit their lodge rooms, 312 Seventeenth street at all hours of the day....

Merry Go Round

The merry go round, the same one that was here three years ago, is doing good business on the vacant lot on the corner of Ferguson and Nineteenth streets.

Chapter 10

FOOTBALL

The meteoric rise of football on college campuses occurred largely between 1880 and 1900. During that period the game underwent a transition from a mostly localized, student-intiated, intramural exercise to a national, commercialized enterprise supported by the schools and their alumni. Winning teams generated school spirit; but also hired professional coaches and used ineligible players to achieve success. Such practices led to involvement by school faculty and administrators, who organized athletic associations to govern intercollegiate play.

The nature of the game changed dramatically during the latter decades of the nineteenth century from one akin to soccer, with its emphasis on kicking, to a running game that featured mass plays and violent collisions. The brutality of football caused grave concerns and led to a reform movement that culminated in the establishment of the Intercollegiate Athletic Association of the United States (NCAA) in 1905.

Much of the credit for significant rule changes is bestowed upon Walter Camp, who is known as the "father of American football." Camp attended, played for, and coached Yale University, the dominant football team of the era. He served on the rules committee for nearly half a century (1878-1925) that engineered the evolution of the modern form of the sport. In 1889 Camp collaborated with Caspar Whitney, a prominent sportswriter, to choose the first of his All-America teams. Selections recognized star players and fostered the cult of the athletic hero, often idealized in children's literature.

Other teams copied Yale's remarkable success by employing professional team managers and specialized training systems. In 1892 the newly-founded University of Chicago hired Amos Alonzo Stagg, a Yale All-American, and awarded him faculty status. The university president, William Rainey Harper, clearly intended to utilize athletics as a marketing tool.

Football games drew tens of thousands by the 1890s, bringing prestige and profit to sponsoring institutions. The annual Thanksgiving games, featuring the "Big Three" of Harvard, Yale, and Princeton were major events on the social calendar. The Army-Navy game, instituted in 1890, soon became an annual tradition as well. Football spread rapidly throughout the land, and even small colleges fielded teams. In the South, two black colleges faced each other for the first time when Biddle (now Johnson C. Smith) met Livingstone in 1892. That same year Stanford defeated the University of California in the first big game on the West Coast. By 1894 the University of Chicago traveled to San Francisco for a game with Stanford.

Several factors may have contributed to the outburst of interest in football. Among a generation of college men who had lacked the opportunity for valor and glory accorded their fathers in the Civil War, football may have served as a symbolic substitute. As the rising tide of feminism encroached upon male domains, football provided a bastion. Moreover, as European immigrants swelled American cities, nativists felt a threat to their culture and status. The males most endangered by such movements, the sons of the New England elite, led the football crusade. Proponents rationalized football as training for life, arguing that it taught both teamwork and aggressiveness, and leadership skills necessary for the corporate life. Opponents questioned such values and the undeniable violence and professionalism associated with the overemphasis on winning. Such issues were hotly debated throughout the nation.

RULES

In 1887 Outing published an article by Walter Camp listing the intercollegiate football rules in its October issue, pp. 79-85. The rules had been amended several times, but by 1880 a line of scrimmage had replaced the rugby scrum and each team fielded eleven players, who held possession of the ball for a half. When teams simply monopolized the ball, the rules were changed, requiring a gain of five yards in three downs to retain possession. Camp included the changes for 1887, most significantly, the new scoring system. The emphasis at that time still remained on the kicking game.

INTERCOLLEGIATE FOOTBALL RULES

As amended by the American Intercollegiate Association, November 23d, 1876; October 9th, 1877; October 14th, 1879; October 13th, 1880; October 8th, 1881; April, 1882.

1. Grounds must be 330 feet in length and 160 feet in width.

2. Each goal shall be composed of two upright posts exceeding twenty feet in height and placed eighteen feet six inches apart, with cross-bar ten feet from the ground.

3. The game shall be played by teams of eleven men each.

4. Time of game is an hour and a half, each side playing an inning of forty-five minutes from each goal. There shall be ten minutes intermission between the two *three-quarters*. Should the two *three- quarters* result in a tie, ten minutes after the end of the second inning, two fifteen minute innings shall be played, subject to the same rules and conditions as the three-quarters, with the exception that there shall be only five minutes intermission. The game shall be decided by the score of even innings.

5. A match shall be decided by a majority of touchdowns. A goal shall be equal to four touchdowns; but in case of a tie, a goal kicked from a touchdown shall take precedence over touchdowns, or a goal otherwise kicked. Any player guarding his own goal who shall receive the ball from any player of his own side, either by a pass, kick, or snap-back, and shall then touch it down behind his own goal line, or who shall himself carry the ball across his own goal line and touch it down, makes a *safety touchdown*, which shall serve against his side, as hereafter designated. A side which makes four or more safety touch-downs less than their opponents shall win the game, in case nothing else is obtained. No player shall put the ball, having received it from one of his own side, in his own touch in goal, under penalty of a safety touch-down.

6. There shall be two judges and a referee in every match.

7. No one wearing projecting nails, iron plates, or gutta-percha on any part of his boots or shoes shall be allowed to play in a match. Ordinary rubber soles allowed,

but not rubber tips. No sticky or greasy substance shall be used on the persons of the players.

8. No hacking or throttling, bucking or tripping up, or tackling below the hips shall be allowed under any circumstances.

9. A drop-kick or drop is made by letting the ball fall from the hands and kicking it the *very instant* it rises.

10. A place kick or place is made by kicking the ball after it has been placed on the ground.

11. A punt is made by letting the ball fall from the hands and kicking it before it touches the ground.

12. The captains of the respective sides shall toss up before the commencement of the match; the winner of the toss shall have the option of the choice of goal or of kick-off. The same side shall not kick off in two successive innings.

13. A kick-off is a *place kick* from the center of the field of play and cannot count as a goal. The opposite side must stand at least *ten yards* in front of the ball until it has been kicked. The side which has the kick off must be on side when the ball is kicked. This applies to all free kicks. Disregard of this rule shall constitute a foul.

14. The ball shall be *kicked off* at the beginning of each inning, and after a goal has been obtained.

15. A goal may be obtained by any type of a kick except a punt. (See Rule 13.)

16. A goal can be obtained by kicking the ball from the field of play direct (i.e., without touching the ground or the dress or person of any player of either side) over the cross-bar of the opponents' goal. A ball that strikes the post or cross-bar and goes inside the posts and over, the bar shall be scored as a goal.

17. Whenever a goal shall have been obtained, the side which has lost the goal shall then kick off.

18. A player may throw or pass the ball in any direction except towards his opponents' goal.

19. Knocking the ball (i.e., deliberately hitting the ball with the hand), and throwing forward (i.e., throwing the ball in the direction of the opponents' goal line), are not lawful. If the ball be *knocked or thrown forward*, the captain of the opposite side may (unless a fair catch has been made, as provided by the next rule), require to have it brought back to the spot where it was *knocked or thrown forward*, and there put down.

20. A fair catch is a catch made direct from a kick or a *throw forward,* or a *knock* by one of the opposite side only, or from a *punt out* (see Rule 52), provided the catcher makes a mark with his heel at the spot where he has made the catch, and no other of his own side touch the ball. (See Rules 21 and 22).

21. A player who has made and claimed a *fair catch* shall thereupon either take a *drop kick* or a *punt,* or *place* the ball for a place kick.

22. After a *fair catch* has been made, the opposite side may come up to the catcher's mark and (except in cases under Rule 54), the catcher's side shall retire so that they shall be even with or behind the ball kicked; the ball shall be kicked from such mark, or from a spot any distance behind it on a line parallel to the touch line.

23. A catch made when the ball is thrown out of touch is not a *fair catch.*

24. In cases of a *fair catch* the opposite side may come up to and charge from anywhere on a line drawn through the mark made by the player who has made the catch

and parallel to their own goal line; but in the case of a *fair catch* from a *punt out* or a *punt on*. (See Rule 53.)

25. The ball is dead (I.) when a player holding it has cried "Down," and it is then put in play by Rule 33; (II.) when a goal has been obtained and is then put in play by Rule 14; (III.) when it has gone into *touch in goal* and is then put in play by Rule 43; (IV.) when a *touch down* has been obtained and is then put in play by Rules 51, 53, or 59; (V.) also when a *safety touch down* has been made and it is then put in play by Rules 57 and 58.

26. The ball is *dead* whenever a goal has been obtained; but if a *try at goal* be not successful, the kick shall be considered as only an ordinary kick in the course of the game.

27. It is not lawful to take up the ball when dead (except in order to bring it out after it has been touched down in touch or in goal) for any purpose whatever; whenever the ball shall have been so unlawfully taken up it shall at once be brought back to where it was taken up and there put down.

28. A player may *take up* the ball whenever it is rolling or bounding, except in a scrimmage.

29. It is lawful for any player who has the ball to run with it.

30. It is lawful to *run in* anywhere across the goal line.

31. A tackle is when the holder of the ball is held by one or more players of the opposite side.

32. If any player holding or running with the ball be tackled, and the ball fairly held, the man so tackling shall cry "Held'" and the one tackled must cry "Down," and there put it down.

33. (a) A scrimmage takes place when the holder of the ball, being in the field of play, puts it down on the ground in front of him, and puts it in play when on side by kicking or snapping it back. (b) The *quarter-back* is the man who first receives the ball when snapped back from a *down* or thrown back from a *fair*, and he shall in neither case be allowed to carry the ball forward. If a player be off side in the act of snapping back, the ball shall be snapped back over again. If he is off side three times on the same *down* the ball shall go to the opposite side. If in three consecutive *fairs* and *downs* a team shall not have advanced the ball *five yards* or lost *ten,* they must give up the ball to the opposite side at the spot where the *fourth down* is made. Consecutive means without leaving the hands of the side holding it.

34. In a scrimmage it is not lawful for a man who has the ball, nor the man opposite and opposed to him, to pick out the ball with the hand, under any circumstances whatever; but if the ball touch a third man, either may.

35. Every player is *on side*, but is put *off side* if he enters a scrimmage from his opponents' side, or being in a scrimmage, gets in front of the ball, or when the ball has been kicked, touched, or is being run with by any of his own side behind him (i.e. between himself and his goal line), no player can be off side in his own goal.

36. Every player when *off side* is out of the game and shall not touch the ball in any case whatever either in or out of touch or goal, or in any way interrupt or obstruct any player until he be again *on side*.

37. A player being *off side,* is put *on side* when the ball has been kicked by or

touched the dress or person of any player of the opposite side, or when one of his own side has run in front of him either with the ball or having kicked it when behind him.

38. Touch (bounds). If a ball goes into *touch*, whether it bound back or not, any player on the side which touches it down must bring it to the spot where it crossed the touch line; or, if a player, when running with the ball, cross or put any part of either foot across the touch line, he must return with the ball to the spot where the line was so crossed and then return it to the field of play in one of the modes provided by the following rule. If the player only has his hand over the line it is not out of bounds.

39. He must then, by himself or by one of his own side, either (I.) *bound* the ball in the field of play at right angles to the touch line, and then run with it, kick it, or throw it back to his own side; or (II.) throw it out at right angles to the touch line; or (III.) walk out with it at right angles to the touch line, any distance not less than *five* nor mor than *fifteen* yards, and then put it down, first declaring how far he intends to walk out. The man who throws the ball in must face the field or his opponents' goal. No player but the man throwing the ball in shall have either foot entirely outside the touch line. In putting the ball in play from *touch,* any man who places his person, hands or feet between the ball and his opponents' goal is off side. This, however, does not apply to the hands of the man holding the ball.

40. If two or more players holding the ball are pushed into *touch* the ball shall belong *in touch* to the player who first had hold of it in the field of play and has not released his hold of it.

41. If the ball when thrown out of *touch*, be not thrown out at right angles to the touch line, the captain of either side may at once claim to have it thrown out over again.

42. The goal line is in goal and the touch line in touch.

43. Touch in Goal. - Immediately the ball, whether in the hands of a player (except for the purpose of a *punt out* - see Rule 51), or not, goes into touch in goal, it is at once *dead* and out of the game, and must be brought out, as provided by Rules 57 and 58.

44. A maul in goal is when the holder of the ball is tackled inside goal line, or being tackled immediately outside, is carried or pushed across it, and he, or the opposite side, or both, endeavor to touch the ball down. In all cases, when so touched down, the ball shall belong to the players of the side who first had possession of it before the maul commenced unless the opposite side have gained complete possession of it.

45. In case of a *maul in goal,* those players only who are touching the ball with their hands when it crosses the goal line may continue the maul in goal; and when a player has once released his hold of the ball after it is inside the goal line, he may not again join in the maul, and if he attempts to do so may be dragged out by the opposite side.

46. But if a player, when *running in,* is tackled inside the goal line, then only the player who first tackled him, or if two or more tackle simultaneously, they only may join in the maul.

47. A touch-down is when a player, putting his hand upon the ball on the ground in goal, stops it so that it remains dead.

48. When the ball has been touched down in his opponents' goal, none of the side in whose goal it has been so touched down shall so touch it, or in any way displace it or interfere with the player of the other side who may be taking it up or out.

49. A side having touched the ball down in their opponents' goal, shall *try at goal* either by a *place kick or a punt out.*

50. If a *try at goal* be made by a *place kick,* a player of the side which has touched the ball down shall bring it up to the goal line in a straight line from and opposite to the spot where the ball was touched down, and there must make a mark on the goal line and then walk straight out with it at right angles to the goal line, to such distance as he thinks proper and there place it for another of his side to kick. The kicker's side must be behind the ball when it is kicked, and the opposite side must remain behind their goal line until the ball has been placed on the ground.

51. A punt out is a *punt* made after a touch down by a player from behind his opponents' goal line, and from touch in goal, if necessary, toward another of his own side, who must stand *outside* the goal line not less than fifteen feet, and endeavor to make a fair catch, or get the ball and *run in or drop* a goal (see Rules 53 and 54), but he cannot pass it. The *punter* shall not touch the ball after punting it until it has been touched by some other player.

52. A punt on is a *punt* made in a manner similar to a *punt out,* and from touch, if necessary, by a player who has made a fair catch from a *punt out* or another *punt on.*

53. If the *try at goal* be by a *punt out* (see Rule 51,) a player of the side which has touched the ball down shall bring it straight up to the goal line opposite to the spot where it was touched down and there make a mark on the goal line and then *punt out* from touch in goal, if necessary, or from any part behind the goal line not nearer to the goal post than such mark. The opposite side may line up anywhere on the goal line except in the space of five feet, extending from the mark made by the punter out towards the touch line. The punter out must not be interfered with. (See Rules 59 and 60.) If punter does not make his mark he must punt over again. A *punt out or punt on* must be a kick from the foot.

54. If a *fair catch* be made from a *punt out or a punt on,* the catcher may either proceed, as provided by Rules 22 and 53, or himself take a *punt on,* in which case the mark made on making the fair catch shall be regarded (for the purpose of determining as well the position of the player who makes the *punt on* as of the other players of both sides), as the mark made on the goal line in the case of a *punt out.*

55. A catch made in touch from a *punt out or a punt on* is not a *fair catch;* the ball must then be taken or thrown out of touch, as provided by Rule 38; but if the catch be made in touch in goal the ball is at once dead, and must be *kicked out,* as provided by Rules 57 and 58.

56. A player may touch the ball down in his own goal at any time.

57. Kick out is a drop kick by one of the players of the side which has had to touch the ball down in their own goal, or into whose touch in goal the ball has gone (Rule 9), is the mode of bringing the ball again into play, and cannot count as a goal. If a ball from a *kick out* pitch in touch three times in succession, it shall be given as in touch to the opposite side on the twenty-five yard line on the side where the ball pitches in touch, without however, the privilege of Rule 39 (III.)

58. Kick out must be a *drop kick,* and from not more than *twenty-five yards* outside the kicker's goal; if the ball, when kicked out, pitch in touch, it must be taken back and kicked out again. But if the ball touch a player of the opposite side before *pitching* in

touch, the game continues. *(Pitch* means either on the fly, bound or roll.) The kicker's side must be behind the ball when kicked out, and the opposite side must be on the twenty-five yard line, or nearer their own goal.

59. If a player having the ball, when about to *punt it out,* goes outside the goal line, or when about to *punt on,* advances nearer to his own goal line than his mark, made on marking the *fair catch,* or when a *fair catch* has been made, if more than one player on the side which made the fair catch touch the ball before it is again kicked, the opposite side may *charge* at once.

60. Charging (i.e., rushing forward to kick the ball or tackle a player), is lawful for the opposite side in all cases of a *place* kick after a fair catch, or upon a *try at goal,* immediately the ball touches, or is placed on the ground, and in cases of a *drop kick or punt* after a *fair catch,* as soon as the player having the ball commences to run or offers to kick, or the ball has touched the ground; but he may always draw back, and unless he has dropped the ball or has actually touched it with his foot, they must again retire to his mark. The opposite side, in the case of a *punt out or a punt on,* and the kicker's side, in *all* cases, may not *charge* until the ball has been kicked.

61. If a player, when *off side,* interferes with an opponent or the ball when he (the opponent) is trying for a *fair catch,* the opponent's side may either have the ball *down,* where the *foul* was made, or take a *free kick.* Waving hat or hands before an opponent's face shall be considered an interference.

62. No player shall intentionally lay hands upon or interfere with an opponent, unless he has the ball.

63. The penalty for fouls, where judged as intentional by the referee, except as before provided, will be a *down* for the other side.

64. The referee shall disqualify a player whom he has warned three times for intentional *off side* play.

FOOT BALL RULES FOR THE SEASON OF 1887

Rule 1. - A *drop-kick* is made by letting the ball fall from the hands and kicking it at the very instant it rises; a *place-kick,* by kicking it after it has been placed on the ground; a *punt* by letting it fall from the hands and kicking it before it touches the ground.

Rule 2. - *Kick-off* is a place-kick from the center of the field of play, and cannot score a goal.

Rule 3. - *Kick-out* is a drop-kick or a place-kick by a player of the side which has touched the ball down in their own goal, or into whose touch-in-goal the ball has gone, and cannot score a goal.

Rule 4. - When the ball is carried across the goal line it shall be a *touch down* at the place where it is held or down, and when it is carried into touch-in-goal it shall be a *touch-down,* and the try shall be from a punt-out at the intersection of the two lines. In opponents' goal this entitles to a try-at-goal; in player's own goal to kick out; and if any player guarding his own goal receives the ball from a player of his own side either by a passs, kick, or snap-back, and then touches it down behind his own goal, or if he himself carries it across his own goal line and touches it down, or if he puts the ball into his own touch-in-goal, he makes a *safety,* which shall score against his side.

Rule 5. - A side having touched the ball down in their opponents' goal, must try at goal either by a *place-kick or a punt-out.*

Rule 6. - If the try be by a place-kick, a player of the side which has touched the ball down shall bring it up to the goal line, and, making a mark opposite the spot where it was touched down, bring it out at right angles to the goal line such distance as he thinks proper, and then place it for another of his side to kick. The opponents must remain behind their goal line until the ball has been placed on the ground.

Rule 7. - If the try be by a *punt-out,* the punter shall bring the ball up to the goal line, and, making a mark opposite the spot where it was touched down, punt out from any spot behind line of goal and not nearer the goal post than such mark, to another of his side, who must all stand outside the goal line not less than fifteen feet. The opponents may line up anywhere on the goal line except space of ten feet extending from the punter's mark toward touch on each side, but cannot interfere with the punter, nor can he touch the ball after kicking it until it touch some other player. If a fair catch be made from a punt-out or on, the mark shall serve to determine positions as the mark on the goal line.

Rule 8. - A *punt-on* is made like a punt-out by a player who has made a fair catch from a punt-out or on.

Rule 9. - A *goal* may be obtained by kicking the ball, in any way except a punt, from the field of play (without touching the ground, or dress, or person of any player, after the kick), over the cross-bar of opponents' goal.

Rule 10. - A *fair catch* is a catch made direct from a kick, throw forward, or a bat by one of the opponents; or from a punt-out or on by one of the same side; provided the catcher make a mark with his heel at the spot where he has made the catch, and no other of his side touch the ball.

Rule 11. - The ball is *dead:*

I. When the holder has cried down (see 12 and 29), or when the referee has cried down.

II. When a goal has been obtained (see 23).

III. When it has gone into touch (see 13 and 30), or touch in goal, except for punt-out (see 3).

IV. When a touch-down has been made (see 4 and 5).

V. When a fair catch has been heeled (see 33).

No play can be made when the ball is dead, except to put in play by rule.

Rule 12. - A *scrimmage* takes place when the holder of the ball puts it down on the ground, and puts it in play by kicking or snapping it back.

Rule 13. - A ball goes into *touch* when it crosses the touch line, or when the holder puts part of either foot across the touch line. Putting it in play is called a "fair." The touch line is in touch and the goal line is in goal.

Rule 14. - A player is put *off side* if, during a scrimmage, he gets in front of the ball, or if the ball has last been touched by his own side behind him. It is impossible for a player to be off side in his own goal. No player when off side shall touch the ball, or interrupt, or obstruct opponent until again on side.

Rule 15. - A player being off side is put *on side* when the ball has touched an opponent, or when one of his own side has run in front of him, either with the ball, or having touched it when behind him.

Rule 16. - "Will be decided at the October convention; and will probably result in two referees - one for the players and one for the ball."

Rule 17. - For intentional delay of game, or off side play, or intentional violation of Rule 26, a player shall be disqualified and his side shall lose five yards for each offense. No delay arising from any cause whatsoever shall continue more than five minutes.

Rule 18. - The grounds must be 330 feet in length and 160 feet in width, with a goal placed in the middle of each goal line, composed of two upright posts, exceeding 20 feet in height, and placed 18 feet, 6 inches apart, with cross-bar 10 feet from the ground.

Rule 19. - The game shall be played by teams of eleven men each, and in case of a disqualified or injured player, a substitute shall take his place.

Rule 20. - The time of a game is one hour and a half, each side playing forty-five minutes from each goal. There shall be ten minutes intermission between the two halves. The game shall be decided by the score of even halves. Either side refusing to play, after ordered to by the referee, shall forfeit the game.

Rule 21. - No one wearing projecting nails, iron plates, or gutta-percha on his shoes, shall be allowed to play in a match. Ordinary rubber soles allowed, but not rubber tips. No sticky or greasy substance shall be used on the person of players.

Rule 22. - The captains shall toss up before the commencement of the match and the winner of the toss shall have his choice of goal or kick-off. The same side shall not kick-off in two successive halves.

Rule 23. - The ball shall be kicked off at the beginning of each half, and whenever a gaol has been obtained, the side which has lost it shall kick off.

Rule 24. - The penalty for fouls and violation of rules, where judged as intentional, except otherwise provided, shall be a down for the other side.

Rule 25. - The following shall be the value of each point in the scoring: Goal obtained by a touch-down, 6; goal from field kick, 5; touch-down failing goal, 4; safety by opponents, 2.

Rule 26. - No unnecessary roughness, hacking, butting, tripping up, tackling below the hips, or striking with closed fists shall be allowed.

Rule 27. - The side which has a free kick must be behind the ball when it is kicked. At kick-off the opposite side must stand at least ten yards in front of the ball until it is kicked.

Rule 28. - A player may throw or pass the ball in any direction except toward opponents' goal. If the ball be batted or thrown forward, unless a fair catch is made, it shall go down on the spot to opponents.

Rule 29. - If a player having the ball be tackled and the ball fairly held, the man so tackling shall cry, "Held;" the one so tackled must cry, "Down," and some player of his side put it down for a scrimmage. The snapper-back and the man opposite him cannot pick out the ball with the hand until it touch a *third* man. If the snapper-back be off side in the act of snapping back, the ball must be snapped again, and if this occur three times on the same down, the ball goes to opponents. The man who first receives the ball when snapped back from a *down* or thrown back from a *fair*, shall not carry the ball forward under any circumstances whatever. If, in three consecutive *fairs and downs,* unless the ball cross the goal line, a team shall not have advanced the ball five or taken it back twenty yards, it shall go to opponents on spot of fourth. Consecutive means without leaving the hands of the side holding it.

Rule 30. - If the ball goes into touch, whether it bound back or not, a player on the side which touches it down must bring it to the spot where the line was crossed and there either (I.) bound the ball into the field of play at right angles to the touch line and then run with it, kick it or throw it back, or (II.) throw it out at right angles to the touch-line, or (III.) walk out with it, at right angles to touch-line, any distance not less than five nor more than fifteen yards, and there put it down, first declaring how far he intends walking. The man who puts the ball in must face field or opponents' goal, and he alone can have his foot outside touch-line. any one, except him, who puts his hands or feet between the ball and opponents' goal is off side. If it not be thrown out at right angles either side may claim it thrown over again, and if it fail to be put in play fairly in three trials it shall go to opponents.

Rule 31. - Kick-out must be a drop-kick or a place-kick from not more than twenty-five yards outside the kicker's goal. If the ball go into touch before striking a player it must be kicked out again; and if this occur three times in succession, it shall be given to opponents, as in touch on twenty-five yard line, on the side where it went out at kick-out opponents must be on twenty-five yard line, or nearer their own goal.

Rule 32. - Charging is lawful for opponents if punter advances beyond his lines, or in case of a place-kick, immediately the ball is put in play by touching the ground. In case of a punt-out, not till the ball is kicked.

Rule 33. - A player who has made and claimed a fair catch shall take a drop-kick, or a punt, or place the ball for a place-kick. The opponents may come up to the catcher's mark, and the ball must be kicked from some spot behind that mark on a parallel to touch line.

Rule 34. - If a player, when off side, interferes with an opponent trying for a fair catch, by touching him, or the ball, or waving his hat or hands, the opponent may have a free kick, or a down, where the interference occurred.

Rule 35. - No player shall lay his hands upon, or interfere with, an opponent, unless he has the ball.

Excerpts from Spalding's Guide, 1894, pp. 74-83, denote several rule revisions aimed at reducing the brutal aspects of the game. Officials duties were specified, interference clarified, piling on penalized, and mass plays, such as the flying wedge, banned.

REVISED CODE OF FOOT BALL RULES

... Rule 8. - A fair catch is made direct from a kick by one of the opponents (or a punt-on by one of the same side), provided the man intending to make the catch indicates that intention by holding up his hand when running for the ball, and also makes a mark with his heel upon catching it, and no other of his side touches the ball. If he be interfered with by an opponent who is off side, or if he be thrown after catching the ball, he shall be given fifteen yards, unless this carries the ball across the goal line. In that case he shall be given but half the intervening distance. After having raised his hand he cannot run with the ball, but must take his fair catch if he succeed in making one....

Rule 14. - There shall be an umpire, a referee, and a linesman.

Rule 15. - (a) The umpire is the judge of the conduct of the players, and his decision is final regarding fouls and unfair tactics. The umpire may appeal to both the linesman and referee for testimony regarding cases of unnecessary roughness, off side play, or holding, but they shall not volunteer their opinion, nor can they be appealed to upon these points by the captains or players.

(b) The referee is judge of the position and progress of the ball, and his decision is final in all points not covered by the umpire.

(c) Both umpire and referee shall use whistles to indicate cessation of play on fouls and downs. The linesman shall use a stopwatch in timing the game.

(d) The umpire shall permit no coaching, either by substitutes, coaches or any one inside the ropes. If such coaching occur he shall warn the offender, and upon the second offense must have him sent behind the ropes for the remainder of the game.

(e) The linesman shall, under the advice of the referee, mark the distance gained or lost in the progress of the play, and upon the request of the umpire shall give testimony upon any unnecessary roughness, off side play, or holding; but he may not be appealed to by any player or captain. He shall also, under the direction of the referee, keep the time.

(f) Only one official representative for each side shall come upon the field of play in case of an accident to a player.

Rule 16. - (a) The time of the game is seventy minutes, each side playing thirty-five minutes from each goal. There shall be ten minutes intermission between the two halves. The game shall be decided by the final score at the end of even halves. Either side refusing to play after being ordered to by the referee, shall forfeit the game. This shall also apply to refusing to commence the game when ordered to by the referee. The linesman shall notify the captains of the time remaining not more than ten nor less than five minutes from the end of each half.

(b) Time shall not be called for the end of a half until the ball is dead; and in the case of a try-at-goal from a touchdown the try shall be allowed. Time shall be taken out while the ball is being brought out either for a try, kick-out or kick-off, and when play is for any reason suspended....

Rule 25. - No player shall lay his hands upon, or, by the use of his hands or arms, interfere with an opponent, unless he himself or that opponent has the ball. That is, the players of the side which has possession of the ball can obstruct the opponents with the body only. But the players of the side which has not the ball can use the hands and arms, as heretofore; that is to push their opponents out of the way in breaking through when the ball is snapped....

Rule 27. - (a) A player shall be disqualified for unnecessary roughness, hacking or striking with closed fist.

(b) For the offences of throttling, tripping up or intentional tackling below the knees, the opponents shall receive twenty-five yards, or a free-kick, at their option. In case, however, the twenty-five yards would carry the ball across the goal line they can have half the distance from the spot of the offence to the goal line, and shall not be allowed a free-kick....

Rule 30 (a) ...As soon as a runner attempting to go through is tackled and goes down, the referee shall blow his whistle and the ball shall be considered down at that spot. Any piling up on the man after that, shall be punished by giving him fifteen yards, unless this carry the ball across the goal line, when he shall have only half the intervening distance....

(c) No momentum-mass plays shall be allowed. A momentum-mass play is one where more than three men start before the ball is put in play. Nor shall three men group for that purpose more than five yards back of the point where the ball is put in play....

Rule 33.- ...(b)The placer in a try-at-goal may be offside or in touch without vitiating the kick.

ORGANIZATION

The following selection from the Richard Dott Papers at the University of Michigan provides insight into the informal nature of football between 1880-1883. As a member of the Michigan football team, still referred to as rugby, Dott recorded the team's initial eastern tour.

RUGBY AT MICHIGAN, 1881

Rugby at Michigan was scarcely two years old when the desire to try issues with the Eastern Colleges began to show itself. In this short time our teams had secured victories from all the nearby elevens including the Chicago Athletics and Toronto University. The game at Toronto in the fall of 1880 gave such a decided victory for us that immediately upon our return the Athletic Association opened up negotiations and arranged a schedule for the next Fall with Harvard, Yale and Princeton.

On the afternoon of October 29, 1881, the foot ball "squad" consisting all told of thirteen men boarded the day coach for Boston. Each man had his round trip ticket which as I remember cost $7.00 to New York by way of Boston. Sleepers in those days were too great a luxury for all our energies were directed to placing money into the "gym" fund and no such extravagance could be tolerated by the Board. The man who possessed a whole seat to himself was fortunate and the short fellows were extremely so, for by piling the baggage between the seats they were able to span the chasm with a reasonable degree of comfort to themselves, while the elongated fellows like "Gay" Depew, Frank Wormwood, "Pa" Ayres and "Billy" Olcott had a hard time of it especially at night. The fellows who could not sleep saw no reason why the others should and as their was no trainer to send them to bed, the result was none of us had much rest. Two days and one night were spent in this way so it may be imagined that when Boston was reached it took considerable limbering of joints before "getting into the game".

Imagine our consternation when we appeared on Jarvis Field for the game, to have thrown to us, instead of the round association ball with which we were familiar, one of those lively, small and egg shaped balls which had just been adopted as the Rugby ball. None of us had ever seen one much less handled it and when we 'tackled' the monstrosity we found it as elusive as a maiden. We tried to kick it, to throw it and to catch it with such poor and varied success that Captain Horton protested against its use but as it was the adopted ball his protests were unavailing. It was that ball which enabled Harvard to score her one and only touch down which came early in the play.

If it had not been for "Billy" Olcott's large feet and their persistence in getting 'offside', the score would have been reversed with one goal to our credit. "Billy", however, was not to blame for the size of his feet. It was the fault of the Referee in declaring "Billy's" right foot to be "off side" while he was in the very act and did actually kick a goal with his left foot.

"Pa" Ayres contended that if we had possessed the right sort of a mascot, the referee would have over-looked "Billy's" feet, and to guard against its repetition in the other games that very evening he started out in quest of a mascot to his liking and some time before midnight returned with a "bull pup". He was highly elated with his success and was recounting his adventures and narrow escape from the owner's wrath and while in the midst of this very interesting experience, the owner appeared with a blue coat and brass buttons at his heels. It was only the persuasive eloquence of Horton, the lawyer of the team, that saved "Pa" for the rest of the games. (It was in this game that one of our number made the longest run ever made at that time on Jarvis Field. He carried the ball unassisted through Harvard's whole team from our two yard line to within five yards of their goal line. Had the interference of modern Rugby been used a touchdown would surely have resulted from that play)

On that trip three hard games were played within a week besides we traveled over a thousand miles in an ordinary coach and in looking back, I often wonder how it was accomplished....Of course, we were bruised and lame but strange as it may seem, not one of the regular team was so disabled that he was compelled to give way to the substitutes and they, poor fellows, had no opportunity of distinguishing themselves....

Two years later, another schedule was completed with Weslyan, Yale, Harvard and Stevens, the Yale and Harvard games being on successive days. This eleven had four of the old team and three substitutes were thought necessary. Of the fourteen men, '84 boasted eight. The trains should have put us into Hartford on Sunday afternoon, but on arriving at Niagara Falls we found that the railroads were to inaugurate the Standard Time on that day so instead of making immediate connections for New York, we were compelled to lay over eight hours. This time passed in sight seeing and some of the more enterprising secured a foot race with a local sprinter for Conine, one of the substitutes, and who had a record of nine and three-fourths seconds. Our fellows carried away all of the money in sight and secured a substantial increase of spending money.

When New York was reached on Monday, there was barely enough time to get the train for Hartford and as none had breakfasted, it was deemed best for all but two to remain and secure a substantial meal while these two should go on without breakfast and make the necessary arrangements for the afternoon game. The result was the balance arrived just in time for the game and without dinners, while the two had dinners but no breakfasts. This was a bad beginning boded ill for our success. If Prettyman and Killelea could have had good dinners, there would have been no doubt about the result. It was Prettyman's great regret that he had not brought along his boarding house....

Four games were played in eight days. We lost some, won some and tied one. This time it was necessary to use some of the substitutes, as one or two of the boys having been given permission to visit friends missed their trains and did not arrive until the game was over. They were tried, convicted, and compelled to pay a fine, and were glad to escape solitary confinement.

These trips were object lessons not only in teaching the eastern style of play, but in showing that western grit and brawn, though raw and untaught, was able to successfully compete with the trained veterans of the eastern colleges. With rugby a fixture interest in all athletics was awakened and the successful erection and equipment of Michigan's magnificent gymnasium in a very large measure was influenced by the spirit and enthusiasm engendered by these pioneers.

High schools followed the model set by their collegiate brethren. Chicagoans organized a football league as early as 1885. The High School Journal, October 1886, p. 5, at the Chicago Historical Society, called for another organizational meeting the following year.

HIGH SCHOOL FOOTBALL, 1886

The following letter was sent out Sept. 29th, by the Lake View school, to the players represented in the Journal:

Wright's Grove, Ill., Sept. 29, '86.

To the foot-ball interests of the _____ H.S.:

Sirs - In consideration of the fact that the officers of the Chicago Foot-Ball league, as far as we are able to ascertain, have graduated from their respective schools, we do hereby suggest that delegates, two from each school, be appointed to meet and arrange for the games of the season of '86; and we do hereby invite said delegates to hold their first meeting at our school, at 3 p.m., Wednesday, Oct. 6.

An immediate answer, stating your opinion as to the advisability of such a meeting, will be of value to all....

By order of the Executive Board of the L.V.H.S. Athletic Association.

In response delegates from the North, South, and West Divisions, and the Manual Training School, met at the stated time. A letter was also received from the Oak Park school, saying that, although they could not send delegates, they might be able to join a league, if formed. At this meeting no definite business was done, but another was held Tuesday, Oct 12, for the completion of all the arrangements. On this occasion the intercollegiate rules were adopted. Another meeting to make out the schedule will be held on the 19th inst., at the Harvard Preparatory School, South Side. The schools which have thus far sent representatives are the North, South, and West Divisions, Manual Training, Englewood, Harvard Preparatory, and Lake View.

The Spalding Guide, 1894, printed the Constitution of the American Intercollegiate Foot Ball Association, pp. 84-88. The agreement actually constituted a reorganization plan, for Harvard excluded itself after an ongoing series of charges and countercharges alleging the use of ineligible players. The University of Michigan team used seven players who were not students in 1893, resulting in intervention by school authorities. In 1896 the Intercollegiate Conference of Faculty Representatives (later the Big 10) was formed by seven midwestern schools to address such problems.

AMERICAN INTERCOLLEGIATE FOOTBALL ASSOCIATION CONSTITUTION

ARTICLE I.

The name of this association shall be the AMERICAN INTER-COLLEGIATE FOOTBALL ASSOCIATION.

ARTICLE II.

Section 1. This association shall consist of Yale, Princeton and such other colleges as may be admitted from time to time.

Sec. 2. No college shall be admitted to membership except by an unanimous vote.

Sec. 3. The annual assessment shall be $25 from each college, and this shall be expended for the championship pennant.

Sec. 4. Any college failing to pay the annual assessment on or before December 1st of each year shall forfeit its membership in the Association.

ARTICLE III.

Section 1. The officers shall consist of a President, Secretary and Treasurer. The Presidency shall be held by the college last holding the championship. The Secretary and Treasurer shall be elected by ballot. The Secretary shall call meetings subject to the order of the President and shall preserve the minutes of the meeting in a book.

Sec. 2. There shall be a Graduate Advisory Committee; one member being elected by the alumni or appointed by the Faculty of each of the colleges in the Association.

Sec. 3. This Advisory Committeee shall meet and propose the rules, or changes in the same, on the first Saturday in March of each year, and shall submit the said proposed rules or changes to the Secretary of the Intercollegiate Association on or before the first Saturday in April, to be forthwith transmitted by him to the respective college Associations before the Spring meeting of the Intercollegiate Association, to occur on the first Saturday in May. At that meeting the said proposed rules or changes shall be acted upon, and be returned by the Intercollegiate Association, with its approval or disapproval, to the Advisory Committee at its Summer meeting, to occur on the day of the Intercollegiate Track Athletic meeting in May. Those rules or changes approved shall forthwith take effect; those disapproved shall go over for consideration until the following Spring, unless they shall receive a two-thirds vote in the Advisory Committee, in which case they shall take immediate effect.

Sec. 4. Each of the members of the Advisory Committee shall have a full vote. Any one may vote and act by representative with a written proxy. Three-fourths the members of the committee shall constitute a quorum.

Sec. 5. At the written request of one-half the members of the Advisory Committee or delegates of the Intercollegiate Association, the Secretary of the Committee shall convene a meeting both of the Advisory Committee and the Intercollegiate Association, but the same shall be only on a five days' written notice to the various members and delegates, which notice must contain a statement of the object of the said meetings. The meetings of the present year shall be governed by this section.

Sec. 6. There shall be an umpire and a referee. The referee shall judge for the ball, and the umpire for the player. No man shall act as an umpire who is an alumnus of either of the competing colleges. The umpires shall be nominated and elected by the Advisory Committee. The referee shall be chosen by the two captains of the opposing teams in each game, except in case of disagreement, when the choice shall be referred to the Advisory Committee, whose decision shall be final. All referees and umpires shall be permanently elected and assigned on or before the third Saturday in October of each year.

Sec. 7. The Advisory Committeee shall act as a Committee of Appeals, and shall hold its regular annual session on the third Saturday in October of each year, at which time it shall hear and finally determine any appeal, which must be in writing, from a decision or determination which substantially affects the interpretation or construction of any provision of the Constitution, or the rules of the Association, during the year preceding; but this section shall not be construed as affecting any question of fact, the determination of which rests in the discretion of the referee.

ARTICLE IV.

Section 1. The series shall consist of one game with each college, and shall be played upon grounds mutually agreed upon.

Sec. 2. The two leading colleges of the preceding year shall play in or near New York.

Sec. 3. The Championship shall be decided by the greatest number of games won. In case of a tie in games won, the team losing the fewest games shall have the championship.

Sec. 4. In case there is a tie for second place in the championship series, the record of the previous year shall determine which of the two colleges so tieing shall play with the champion in New york, according to the provisions of Section 2 of this article.

ARTICLE V.

In all the championship games the net receipts shall be equally divided between the contesting colleges.

ARTICLE VI.

Any team failing to meet its engagements shall, unless the failure be caused by an unavoidable accident in traveling, or by postponement with the consent of the other team, forfeit its membership. Any college failing to put a team in the field each year shall forfeit its membership. A certificate signed by three members of the Faculty shall be considered sufficient excuse for failure to play.

ARTICLE VII.

There shall be two meetings of this Association, one to be held on the first Saturday in May, the other on the first Saturday in October.

ARTICLE VIII.

The printing of the Rules and Constitution shall be done by the Secretary of the Advisory Committee, and fifty copies shall be forwarded by the Secretary to each college of the Association free of charge.

ARTICLE IX.

No man shall play more than four years in this Association.

ARTICLE X.

No professional athlete shall take part in any contest of this Association, nor shall any player of any university or college be paid or receive, directly or indirectly, any money or financial concession compensation for, or as prior consideration or inducement to playing, whether the same be received from, or paid by, or at the instance of the Foot Ball Association, Athletic Committee or Faculty of such university, or college, or any individual whatsoever. And any player who is specifically challenged under this section by any member of the Association in writing, shall, within five days after the filing of such such challenge with the Secretary, file with the Secretary of the Committee an affidavit, duly verified under oath, showing that he in no way violates the provisions of this section, and upon his failure to make and file such affidavit he shall be barred from participating in any contest of the members of this Association. And in case the sufficiency of such affidavit be questioned by the challenging party, and the Committee of Appeals be notified thereof, the player challenged shall submit to oral examination on two days' notice by said challenging party before said Committee, who shall then and thereafter decide regarding the eligibility of said challenged player to take part in contests of members of the Association. The date of such examination shall not be set on the day of nor within forty-eight hours of a championship game. No challenge or protest shall in any way affect a game which has been played previous to the filing of such challenge or protest. Furthermore, no one shall be eligible to take part as a player in any championship games of the Association who is not a bona fide student of the college on whose team he plays, matriculated for the then current college year, and regularly pursuing a course which requires his attendance upon at least five lectures or recitations a week; and in case a player's qualifications are questioned he shall furnish to the Advisory Committee an affidavit stating that he is a bona fide student of the college on whose team he plays, matriculated for the then current college year, and regularly pursuing a course which requires his attendance upon at least five recitations and lectures a week, and that it his intention to continue in said course until the expiration of the then current college year.

Amendment adopted at a special meeting of the Intercollegiate Association, 1893: "No member of a graduate department, nor a special student shall be allowed to play, nor any undergraduate who has registered or attended lectures or recitiations at any other university or college; nor any undergraduate who is not pursuing a course requiring for a degree an attendance of at least three years."

ARTICLE XI.

A majority vote shall be necessary to pass any vote, and a two-thirds vote to amend this Constitution.

The following brief announcements from the Chicago Tribune, 17 November 1899, p. 4, pointed to some of the problems of the period.

ANOTHER ROW IN HIGH SCHOOL GAME

Lake View High School and North Division High School met yesterday afternoon at Lincoln Park. At half time neither side had scored. With only a few minutes to play in the second half Lake View made on off-side play. Referee Lejeune of the English High School gave North Division the option of taking the ball or the distance. North Division elected, of course, to take the ball, but Umpire Roy insisted it was only entitled to the distance. North Division refused to abide by this decision and left the field, the score at this time being 0 to 0. Lake View, with no one to oppose them, made three touchdowns, kicked three goals, and claim the game by a score of 18 to 0.

The Tribune's prognostication about the Carlisle School proved prophetic. A small government institution designed to assimilate American Indians, it played a national schedule against the football powerhouses of the day. The Carlisle team later featured Jim Thorpe, star of the 1912 Olympics.

INDIAN SCHOOL REPRESENTATIVE HERE

Dr. A.C. Eastman of the Carlisle Indian School was in Chicago yesterday looking over plans for an Indian game in Chicago next season. He said the success of the Indians at football caused the game to be the a big topic at the school. Even the smaller boys were becoming so proficient that in the every day practice the playing was fierce. The Indians entering the school are almost perfect specimens of development, and the material is such that the teams of the next few years will be able to cope with any of the larger teams in the country. Dr. Eastman is considering several offers of games from the Western schools and has not yet decided on any.

COMPETITION

An article in Harper's Weekly, 10 December 1887, p. 903, recounted the football season and provided a measure of approbation for the game.

THE FOOT-BALL CHAMPIONSHIP

The foot-ball season of the Intercollegiate League came to an end on Thanksgiving Day, after a series of remarkable contests among the teams of Harvard, Princeton, and Yale. Rarely has the issue of the championship been so clouded with doubts, conjectures, and uncertainties, which had placed each successive college in the lead, until the final struggle between the magnificent elevens of Yale and Harvard culminated in a victory for "the blue."

For two years the strong and clever men of Princeton had preserved the champion football which their phenomenal half-back, LAMAR, had wrested from Yale in the memorable struggle at New Haven in the fall of 1885, and in the third year the contest for the leathern trophy promised to be as bitterly close as the contention which involved the fairest divinities of the Roman mythology. The opening games were akin to the preliminary "moves" in a chess match, each college defeating the teams of the University of Pennsylvania and Wesleyan with apparent ease, and without disclosing the methods of play or the vulnerable points of attack. November 12th will long be regarded as a crimson-letter day in the calendar of the Cambridge collegians, for it marked the second victory which Harvard had ever gained over Princeton since the founding of the League in 1876. The further defeat of Princeton by Yale on November 19th, at the Polo Grounds, utterly checked the aspirations of "the orange and black" of Nassau, and the Princetonians were forced to seek proleptic consolation in the season of 1888.

The fact that Harvard and Yale had each defeated the old enemy by the same score - 12 to 0 - gave an additional significance and interest, if any were needed, to the decisive struggle on Thanksgiving Day between these teams. The Polo Grounds have rarely, if ever, been the scene of such a glorious and well-fought contest. It was a veritable field-day for the college men and their friends - perfect in its atmospheric conditions, tempered by a clear, bracing air, which gave an added brilliancy to the masses of blue and crimson ribbons, the costumes bright and vivid, as a WATTEAU coloring, and the gay panorama on coach, field, and grand stand. The enthusiasm and merriment of the 17,000 people within the enclosure could scarcely find expression in the good-natured shouts and encouraging calls of "the outsiders," and the peculiar cries of the college men - the barking "rahs" of Harvard and Yale, the "rocket" cheer of Princeton, the orthographic exercise of Columbia's undergraduates, and the thanksgiving shouts of the men of Wesleyan, triumphant, but far from fresh, from their morning victory over the University of Pennsylvania. Not a single untoward event marred the climax of victory, and the scenes during the game, which have been so admirably reproduced by the artist, vividly recall the Oxford-Cambridge contests and the picturesque incidents of an Eton-Harrow cricket match.

Under these inspiring influences, it is not to be wondered that the rival teams gave an exhibition which in point of brilliancy, skill, and the display of the technical points of the "science" of foot-ball was only excelled by its freedom from harmful tendencies to brutal play, and its indications of a rivalry which was burningly intense without descending to vulgarity or barbaric display. The matchless team play and wonderful discipline of the Yale eleven, resulting in a resistless mechanism of movement, and emphasized by the brilliant individual plays of Captain BEECHER - a sort of KEELEY-motor with ubiquitous attachment - and of "rushers" WALLACE and CORBIN, proved too powerful for the no less heroic play of Harvard, which redeemed its lack of an effective method of aggressive play by an exhibition of vigor, impetuosity, and onslaught which has made the Harvard team of this year the finest eleven which the college has ever sent out. The final score, 17 points to 8, gives but a faint idea of the closeness of the struggle.

The salvation of the game of foot-ball, which, after it had fallen into disrepute in 1884 through the declaration of the Harvard faculty that it was "brutal and dangerous to life and limb," passed a quiet provincial existence under the fostering care of Princeton and Yale until the times should be ripe for its return at the old arena at the Polo Grounds, has been conscientiously wrought out by the leading teams in the struggle of the season just ended, and the newspaper press, the public, and the college faculties have again stamped the game with probationary approval. The crowning stroke in the diplomatic changes which led to this restoration waas achieved in the appointment of the *umpire,* who in the exercise of his preventive and retributive functions has reduced the pernicious activity of "slugging" to a minimum, and has visited foul and unmanly play with the disgrace of dismissal from the field.

The future of foot-ball as a recognized game will never be in doubt if its best tendencies as a manly game for the development of manly qualities are carefully preserved and cherished by the only ones upon whom his responsibility rests -the college men.

Outing followed the spread of football throughout the country, providing histories of its regional development in its issues of September, 1893, pp. 448-458; and December 1894, pp. 257-264.

FOOTBALL ON THE PACIFIC SLOPE
by John Craig

... Football on the Pacific slope has not seen many years of life; it is yet in its infancy, and perhaps not more than ten years have seen the game in progress there. About the first clubs to organize were the Phoenix and Wanderers. These were composed, in the main, of grown men - the Wanderers pricipally from the English residents - and all their matches were under the rugby rules. Some exciting games were played at the old Recreation Grounds, in San Francisco, in the Fall and Winter of 1880-81, the "punting" of Nicholson, captain if the Wanderers, and the "tackling" of Coubrough and Woolrich of the same club, with the clock-work "passing" and the running of Dean and Sime, of the Phoenix team, being the features of these contests....Sime was a wonderful runner, doing 100 yards very close to 10 seconds, and was selected by the Olympic Club of San Francisco, with Belcher and R.B. Haley, for whom a record of 9 4/5 seconds for 100 yards is claimed, to represent that club at the championship games in the East several years ago.

Not long after this a number of other clubs entered the field. The Merion Cricket Club organized a team, and then the Union Club was formed from members of the San Francisco Boys' High School. The Unions soon showed the great advantage of constant practice which, as school boys, they were enabled to get, and in a game with the Merions at the Presidio of San Francisco, early in 1882, easily defeated their older opponents.

The Unions had a heavy team, and many brilliant players. Edgar Foster, the captain and "half-back," proved himself a wonder in the foot-ball line, and seldom failed to carry the ball from fifteen to twenty yards with each run....The Unions were especially strong in "tackling and "blocking," a trait that they handed down to the Wasps, ...a team that many of the Unions joined in after years.

After defeating the Merions, the Unions decided to try conclusions with the older clubs, which were composed in the main of grown men, and which had in consequence a decided advantage over their younger rivals in the matter of weight, an important factor in the Rugby game, with its "push scrimmage." In two very close games played early in 1882 with, first the Phoenix team, and then the Wanderers, the younger men were defeated ...

The next game played on this coast was at San Mateo, in the fall of 1882, between the Union team and one from Brewer's Academy. The town turned out *en masse* to witness the contest, which proved very close and exciting, finally ending in a victory for the San Francisco club....This was the last match the Union team played, as on leaving school many of its men engaged in business pursuits, which precluded giving the proper time for training and practice.

The University of California now began to manifest considerable interest in football, and the Merion team soon tried conclusions with the "U.C.s" on the campus at

Berkeley, in a game wherein the University team made a wonderful showing. Soon after, they were able to defeat all comers, among them the crack Phoenix team.

Though the "Phoenix never dies," the football club did, and with it its rival, the Wanderers, and for some time after 1883 the only contests were between the University and Merion teams, and these were few and far between....

Early in 1885 a number of ex-Union men organized The Wasps, a powerful organization, which afterwards became the pride of San Francisco football enthusiasts. This club soon had a large and active membership, and did much to revive the declining interest in the game. At the outset it was captained by Kenneth Mount McKay, with Felton Taylor as vice-captain, but later Frank Hittell took the club in hand, and Taylor organized the Reliance team of Oakland.

In February of 1885, The Wasps met the University team on the college campus, and here took place probably as brilliant a game of football as was ever witnessed. The game was played under the Rugby Union Rules, but not a "goal" was kicked nor a "touchdown" made by either side, although the game was characterized throughout by brilliant plays on the part of both teams.... A return match was played a few weeks later and again no goal was kicked nor "touch-down" made, though at the last moment, on call of time, the University men claimed a 'touch-down' in "touch-in-goal," which was not allowed, and the score once more was *nil*.

The Reliance Club had by this time formed a football team, and a good one too, nearly all of its men being fine athletes in other lines. All were heavy men, the "rush line" averaging over 180 pounds to each man, while Felton Taylor, one of their half-backs, weighed 190 pounds when in condition. This team soon threw down the gauntlet to The Wasps, and a contest was played on the Oakland grounds, resulting in a victory for The Wasps by a score of 10 to 0.

The public now began to take great interest in football, for it had found these games full of excitement, and the season of 1886 found five clubs in the field - the University, The Wasps, Orions, Reliance and Law College teams. These organized the California Football League, and for the first time on the Pacific coast the game was played by eleven men instead of fifteen, though at first the intercollegiate rules were not adopted as a whole.

A series of twenty games was played by the league teams in 1886, and they proved to be the greatest treat yet offered to the public in the way of out-door sports. From 4,000 to 5,000 spectators would fill the grand stand each Saturday at Fourteenth and Centre streets, Oakland, to witness the contests; among the fair sex there was never before on the Pacific coast so much interest manifested in athletic games.

At the outset of the series the Orions, though all younger and lighter men than on the other teams, took everything by storm, but The Wasps and the University men soon forged ahead and came out with an equal number of games to their credit. The University men won the series through The Wasps being obliged to let the concluding game go by default, for the reason that all their "backs" were damaged in the game with the Reliance team on the previous Saturday, which The Wasps had won by a score of 14 to 0....

In 1887 another league was organized among younger players than those who formed the teams of the previous season, and was in consequence dubbed the Little

League." These clubs were, however, not far behind their predecessors in any particular, and many large audiences witnessed the contests. The teams represented were the Unions, Alerts, Orients and Wideawakes, and they developed some good men ...

The third league series, in 1888, in which the Posens, with Nourse as captain, carried off the honors, brought out new teams and new men ...

When Joseph Tobin came home from Georgetown College in 1890, he brought with him the latest tactics in vogue with the crack 'varsity teams of the East. He soon introduced the close play of the Eastern elevens into the work of the San Fransisco team of which he was captain. Before this time the coast teams had played the half-backs and full-back many yards behind the rush-line, relying on a long pass from the quarter to give them opportunities for gaining headway in going around the "end." The close play and center-rushing tactics introduced by Tobin soon showed the inferiority of the old-time method, and a game between the San Francisco and University teams resulted in a victory for the former by a score of 44-0. The "long pass" game has never been used on the coast since.

In November of 1891 the San Francisco team reorganized under the auspices of the Olympic Athletic Club, taking the name of that organization. It proved the victor in all of the five games played by it during the season of 1891-2. The first game of the season was played at San Francisco between the Olympics and the Los Angeles team, in which the visitors were defeated by a score of 22-0. The Napa College team was the next to succumb to the Olympics, who were then playing first-class football under Tobin' tuition, and the college boys went home to the Valley of Vines with a score of 44-0 against them to think about on the way. The only team that succeeded in scoring against the victorious Olympics was the eleven of the Leland Stanford, Junior, University - the new university at Palo Alto that has since done so much to develop football and bring it into favor in California.... The University of California next went against the sturdy Olympic athletes, but failed to score against them, while the local team had six points to their credit when time was called. The final game was played with the team from the United States Cruiser *Charleston,* at whose hands the Olympics, when known as the San Franciscos, had suffered defeat the previous year. This time they turned the tables on the blue-jackets, who were captained by Catlin, formerly of the Annapolis Naval Academy team - winning the game by 16-0.

The great game of the season was yet to be played. When the new university of Palo Alto sprang into life, there was naturally an intense rivalry between it and the University of California in all matters pertaining to athletics. On March 19, 1892, the teams from the rival colleges met at the Haight Street Grounds in San Francisco. This was the first inter-collegiate game played on the coast, and the throngs who witnessed it attested the esteem in which football is now held in the West. The Berkeley men were much heavier and relied entirely on a "wedge" game, while the wiry boys in red from Palo Alto played an "end" game that won the day.... When the Stanford men won by a score of 14-10, the rivalry between the two universities increased to such a degree that their efforts this year brought football into a more prominent place in the public mind here than it has ever held before. To the enterprise displayed by the managers of these two elevens is due entirely the interest shown by sport-loving people during the football season just closed.

The football season of 1892-3 opened with a game between the Olympic Football Team and the eleven of the University of California. The former team outweighed their opponents and won the game handily by a score of 20-10....

The next game of the season was played on November fifth, when the University men turned the tables on their opponents, winning by a score of 16-0. They also took the next game from the Olympics, who lost these last matches by reason of entire lack of training and poor team work....

Soon after the Olympics tried conclusions with the eleven from the Stanford University. The defeat of the Olympics by the men of Berkeley had the effect of waking them up, for they put in a much better game than in the two previous matches. The game resulted in a tie score, 14-14.

It was not until December seventeenth last, when the two rival universities of the State met, that the great game of the year was played. The managers of these teams were enterprising enough to secure the services of Walter Camp and Thomas Lee McClung, of Yale, to act as coaches for their teams; the first named to teach the boys of Palo Alto how to play football according to the most approved methods, and McClung to act as coach for the State University. Immediately after the Yale-Harvard Thanksgiving Day game, these two celebrated lights of the football world left for the coast. Their coaching soon demonstrated that both teams had much to learn, for while they contained many good individual players, their team work was poor, and their play slow and lacking in snap. Fully 15,000 people assembled to witness the great game, by far the largest gathering of its kind in the West, and the charities that received the proceeds are many of thousands of dollars richer. The Berkeley men once more had a decided advantage in weight, which was their only salvation, as it gained them ground on their wedge plays, while the boys in red outplayed them in every other particular.

The play throughout was snappy and quick. The Berkeley men relied solely upon the "wedge," and Hunt did some very clever "line bucking." Oscar Taylor did good work for the "U.C." team, and his was the only punting in the entire game.... In interference and tackling the Stanford men were the better, and twice they used the Dellant Flying Wedge with good results. At the end of the first half the score stood 6-0 in favor of Stanford, and it began to look as though the blue and gold would once again be draped in black, but when time was called at the end of the second half their whirling wedges and center-rushes had told; the score stood 10-10, and a trophy to be presented to the victor by the University Club of San Francisco was to remain in the club rooms for another year.

After the game between the universities, the Stanford team made a tour of the State, defeating the teams at Los Angeles, Pasadena, Colton and San Jose. The eleven at the last named place was the only one that really showed any form against the boys in red, and promises to develop into a formidable rival of some of the leading clubs of the State....

After the close of the football season proper with the great game between the two universities last December, its devotees arranged other matches which were not without public interest. Principal among these were the charity game at the High Street Grounds in San Franciso, between the two teams styled respectively the University Veterans and the Army team. While neither were composed strictly of old varsity men or players from the Army posts about, they were made up of splendid material, and a vast throng witnessed the game....

The next game played here under intercollegiate rules, was that between the football men who were members of the various tennis clubs about San Francisco and Oakland. Very poor football was played, but the game succeeded in bringing out the leading lights of the social world to witness it, and aided in creating sentiment in favor of the game here....

The three leading football teams of California are now in active preparation for the coming games, which begin early in the autumn. The Olympic team has secured the services of Laurie Bliss as coach, and for weeks past he has been carefully training the men at the Olympic Club's grounds....The Palo Alto team has secured the services of Laurie Bliss's brother...

Heffelfinger, the famous guard of McClung's Yale team, will coach the U.C. boys for the coming season....

The securing of crack Eastern players as coaches for our coast teams has done more to bring the game here on a level of that played by the Eastern 'varsity teams than all the former years of playing, and it is not too much to expect that before another year the leading teams of the East and West may meet on the football field.

There are besides the teams mentioned, football clubs in Los Angeles, Pasadena, Stockton, Napa and San Jose. The Amateur Academic Athletic Association, formed by members of the preparatory schools about San Francisco, maintain a Football League, of which the Hopkins Academy carried away the pennant in '91, and the Oakland High School in '92.

The game has now taken such a solid hold upon the affections of the Western people that the future will see teams on the coast that will rival those of the Eastern universities.

Until within the past year this coast has seen nothing of Gaelic football, but the several teams formed early in the year among the Scotch and Irish residents soon developed an interest in the game among that class. The Pacific Coast Gaelic Football Association was formed, and the following teams contested for the championship pennant: Pacific Wanderers, Parnells, Scotch Thistles, Emmetts, Sarsfields, Wm. O'Briens and Sheridans. The Emmetts succeeded in carrying off the prize, after a series of some thirty games, together with a trophy offered by the *Examiner,* the San Francisco daily that did the most to foster interest in the sport....

Besides the University, Stanford and Olympic teams, there were in the field in the last year several others which contained many good individual players, but which were defective in team-work, and too light in the rush-line to withstand the heavier men of the teams referred to. Among these were the elevens of Cogswell Polytechnic School, Hopkins Academy and, Boys' High School of San Francisco, and Berkeley Gymnasium.

The tendency of the game in the West has been to produce hardy, manly men....

Farther up the coast, at Victoria, British Columbia, our English brothers cling to the Rugby game, and the Beacon Hill and Victoria teams are regular in their practice and games.

Several teams have organized among the English and Scotch residents about San Francisco to play the association game, but the public has never manifested any great interest in that game.

FOOTBALL IN THE SOUTH
by Lovick Pierce Miles

SOUTHERN college men have long heard the development of the ancient Greeks commended in the classroom, but until recently their instructors have been strongly opposed to modern college athletics. Indeed, within the past five years one of the best universities prohibited all Intercollegiate contests, while another forbade any student to appear upon its grounds in an athletic uniform. Happily, it seems, a great change has taken place, and to-day the athletic student in Southern colleges receives liberal encouragement; old things have passed away, and the spirit of manly sport, which has always been characteristic of life in the South, is being recognized in the schools. This is certainly largely due to the excellent results, consequent upon the encouragement of athletics in the universities of the North. Yet the instinct of self-preservation has been a strong factor, for the the athletic colleges of the North were every year attracting great numbers from the South. Something had to be done to stay the pilgrimage, and the encouragement of athletics wisely followed.

Football was first played, according to the Intercollegiate rules, in 1884, by Johns Hopkins, which university is justly a pioneer in this field of sport. It stood practically alone for three years. In 1887 the University of Virginia presented its first regularly organized team. The same year, John F. Crowell introduced it at Trinity, of North Carolina, and they began making football history. Two years later, in 1889, the University of North Carolina and some minor Virginia colleges began to organize. The year following, Vanderbilt University appeared on the field, and in 1891 the University of the South, at Sewanee, Tennessee, made its first "down" in a game against Vanderbilt, which Vanderbilt won, 22-0. The same fall, the University of Georgia and the Alabama Agricultural and Mechanical College presented their first regular elevens. They met in Atlanta before a great crowd and played the first important game ever seen in the city. Alabama won. In the fall of 1892 the adoption of the sport became general - Central Kentucky, of Kentucky; Tulane, of New Orleans; Universirty of Mississippi; Southwestern University, of Georgetown, Texas, and the University of Texas, being among the last to adopt it.

There are many obstacles in the way of the best football development in the colleges of the South, and until these are overcome no team can be produced equal to the best Northern elevens. Not only is the number of student, as a rule, comparatively small, but many of those physically well qualified show absolutely no interest in the game. Alumni coaches, too, are hard to find, there being few capable graduate players; while the number of Southern men who have played on the elevens at Yale, Harvard, Princeton and other Eastern colleges is so small that little, if indeed, any, benefit is derived from them. Consequently, coaches have to be imported, and aside from the difficulty of securing the right man, it necessitates a considerable expense. But this handicap will be removed as colleges advance in football and turn out skilled players.

This point, however, leads to the question of finance. The treasurers' reports show that many of the elevens have failed to pay expenses, Virginia being several times among the number. This college would probably have met her expenses, had it not been for her desire to play Northern tams which demanded and received large guarantees.

The chief causes of the deficits have proven to be the extensive traveling necessary, and the difficulty of securing a profitable attendance at the games. The most important contests have rarely attracted fifteen hundred people in Richmond; in Nashville the game is little better patronized, while in Atlanta, where the greatest interest has been manifested, a crowd has not yet exceeded five thousand. There is not that intense college spirit in the Southern alumnus which works the Northern ex-college man into a fever of excitement on the eve of a great intercollegiate struggle.

In addition to embarrassments in coaching and finance, the Southern captains are handicapped in the matter of time at their disposal. The greatest time that any team was permitted to devote to training last fall did not exceed four hours each day, while some were forced to do their best in two and a half; not being allowed to encroach on any degree upon class-room work.

Another difficulty that is met is the dearth of Intercollegiate practice. Of course, the "scrub" eleven is essential to any team in training, but the development is by no means perfect without an abundance of the varied experience which is derived from meeting the teams of other colleges. The games of a Southern eleven number rarely as many as eight; the average is only six....

The system of training in the South is not elaborate. Prior to 1893 the training table was little used. In that year the Universities of North Carolina, Virginia and Vanderbilt kept regular tables, and the University of the South employed one for a few days prior to each game. As a rule, the candidates have not been governed in their diet except by the pledges which are required of them. The daily practice most often adopted consists of thirty minutes' passing, punting, and falling on the ball. This is followed by some special attention to the timing of interference, and then comes an hour and a half or two hours of play with the scrub, which is followed by a team run. The matter of bathing is left entirely up to the player. All work is done in the afternoon, for the morning is required in the class-rooms.

At Johns Hopkins the conditions have never been favorable to football ... The chief difficulty lies in the training. The campus ...is three miles from college, so that it has been impossible to practice more than twice a week. Then, too, the dormitory system is not employed at Hopkins, thus scattering the students throughout the city; while the well-known rigid requirements of the university also militate against superior football.

The game as generally played by American colleges was, as we have already noted, introduced at Hopkins in 1884, though the year previous the English Rugby had found followers ... In 1885 Richard Harding Davis captained the team and played center. His enthusiasm and untiring zeal "boomed" the game, though the results were most apparent in the years following....

The year 1886 marked the turning point in football at Johns Hopkins. In former years the teams had been composed largely of men who had learned their football at other colleges, and were at Hopkins pursuing post-graduate courses. Now, however, the undergraduates, who have greatly increased in number, were aroused, and the candidates became so numerous that undergraduates soon composed the back-bone of the elevens....

For two years, 1890 and 1891, there followed a football requiescence at Johns Hopkins. The material in college appeared so poor, and so little was the general interest, that no university team was put out, and the game, poorly played, was confined to class elevens....

At Virginia the progress of the game has been more consistent. In 1886, Wilcox, of Yale, was at the university and aroused much interest in the sport. The result was that in the following year Virginia put her first regularly organized team in the field. It was some years before the eleven found opponents in the South, so that its early games were confined to teams farther North. This was very fortunate, for the men thus secured much valuable knowledge....

The team of 1891 was not successful ... and resulted in Virginia's candidates in the fall of 1892 being under the university's first coach, in the person of William C. Spicer, a former Princeton half-back. It was due to his coaching that Virginia won the 1892 championship ...

The opening of college in 1893 found John Poe, half-back of Princeton the previous year, at the university in the capacity of coach....

Football was introduced at the University of North Carolina in 1889, when Hector Cowan, famous among Princeton players, spent two weeks at Chapel Hill teaching the rudiments of the game. Two years later, "Billy" Graves came down from Yale for three weeks, and his coaching developed the best men of the strong eleven of 1892. Notwithstanding these fine advantages in training, the progress of the sport was not satisfactory. The authorities of the university objected to Intercollegiate games, and in 1890 stopped the growing prominence of athletics at Chapel Hill by summarily prohibiting all Intercollegiate contests. The lack of wisdom in this order became apparent almost with its enactment and it was soon rescinded....

The fall of 1892 found the athletic spirit of the college fully recovered from the blow received in 1890. The growing interest manifested in football throughout the country, together with the prominence given it at the University of Virginia and at Trinity, North Carolina's chief rivals, caused the game to fairly "boom."...

In 1893... North Carolina... played on Manhattan Field, New York City, against Lehigh on November 25th, resulting in a victory for the latter, 34-0. This was the first appearance of a Southern eleven in New York, and though defeat was anticipated, the event gave evidence of the progress of college sports in the South and spoke volumes for the progressive spirit of the athletic management at Chapel Hill....

Until 1893 Vanderbilt had made little progress in football. The Nashville men first lined up against a college in 1890, when they defeated the eleven of the University of Nashville, 40-0, in a poorly played game on Thanksgiving....

The fall of 1893 opened with strong evidence of a new and vigorous athletic spirit present at Vanderbilt. The prospect for an excellent season soon became apparent. William J. Keller, who played on A.A. Stagg's Springfield eleven ... entered the medical department and was at once made captain. Under his coaching the applicants developed into good individual players, and their team work closely rivaled that of the strongest Southern elevens....

At the University of the South football was introduced in 1891, and had constantly received the hearty encouragement of the authorities. The first game was played against Vanderbilt in November, resulting in a victory for the latter, 22-0. At this time only two men in college had seen a contest. In 1892, under the coaching of Frederic G. Swett, an old Bowdoin player, the team was defeated by Virginia alone, 0-30....

Among the smaller colleges, Trinity, of North Carolina, has done especially well. Though some attempt at play was made as early as 1887, it formally adopted the game in 1889, and the following year demanded a championship contest with Virginia. The game was played in Richmond, and the greater experience of the latter proved too much for the North Carolinians, who lost, 10-4. In the summer of 1891 Captain Daniels went North to study the game. When he returned in the fall, he developed an eleven much superior to their previous conquerors an ddefeated them, 22-0, for the Southern leadership. Since that season Trinity has experienced the varied success that is characteristic of all small colleges, where the attendance is never large and only occasionally is there sufficient good material to compose a strong eleven....

The Virginia Military Institute has made a very creditable record, considering the amount of conflicting work in the matter of drills and other militrary requirements... The teams are not permitted to leave Lexington, which militates against them.

The game as played in Georgia and Alabama is the most primitive in the South. The development of athletics at the University of Georgia was seriously retarded by authorities, until the spring of 1893, when all grave obstacles were removed. The Alabama Agricultural and Mechanical College has maintained a team for three years and has evinced admirable spirit.

Central University of Kentucky presented a strong eleven in 1893, which succeeded in taking the championship of the State. The University of Tennessee has turned its attention to football within the past two years, and has manifested great enthusiasm. Texas University and the Southwestern University, at Georgetown, Texas, are the latest acquisitions to Southern football colleges. In the far South, Tulane and the University of Mississippi are playing the game, and the rivalry between them has developed considerable skill.

The preparatory schools and the academies are fast being wedded to the sport. Many of them have clever young players. From these the larger colleges will draw their best men. Especially in the connection should be mentioned the Episcopal High School at Alexandria, Virginia, that has constantly manifested a progressive athletic spirit ... St. Albans School at Radford, Virginia, was only established in 1892, yet it has already completely outstripped its smaller rivals and easily stands the equal of the High School and many of the minor colleges. Shaw, of Yale, was with the school in 1892, and the season of 1893 was passed through without a defeat under the leadership of Symmes, Princeton's old center, and Biggs, the strong end of North Carolina in 1892.

The athletic clubs in Baltimore, Louisville, Nashville, Atlanta, Birmingham and New Orleans have appeared in the field, and many old college players have donned their well-worn jackets. The sport is no longer confined to college men and towns, but nearly every city now has its eleven.

As reported in Harper's Weekly, 9 December 1893, p. 1170, the annual Thanksgiving Day game had become a social and economic spectacle in New York.

THE THANKSGIVING-DAY GAME
by Richard Harding Davis

THERE is nothing more curious or more interesting in the history of New York city within the last decade than the development of the Thanksgiving-day game. Ten years ago the game was a sporting event and nothing more of interest to but a few thousand faithful ones, and to others a public and private nuisance, because for them it disturbed the peace of Broadway at night, and left a vacant chair at the dinner table of every family in which there was a boy worthy of the name. To-day the sporting character of the game has been overwhelmed by the social interest it has aroused in itself, and which has enveloped it and made it more of a spectacle than an athletic contest. But it is still the greatest sporting event and spectacle combined that this country has to show. It is one of the things every foreigner should be taken to see, and which no foreigner could possibly appreciate. No one who does not live in New York can understand how completely it colors and lays its hold upon that city, how it upsets and overturns its thoroughfares, and disturbs its rapid routines of existence, and very few of those even who do live in New York can explain just why this is so; they can only accept the fact.

And they accept it gladly. The enthusiasm of the few faithful ones ten years back is mocked at and set at naught to-day by the thousands who do not know a touch-down from a three base hit, or whether Yale is a city, State, or club, or its eleven a traveling combination of ex-pugilists. They are only certain that two teams of young men are going to fight it out in Harlem, and that "the Yales" are blue, and "the Princetons" are generally referred to as "tigers," which fact makes them the choice among the voters of the east side.

Ten years ago, Thanksgiving day in New York was an event of moment and of meaning; there still clung to it the semi-religious significance that gave it its place in the calendar, and it was as heinous an offence to be absent from the dinner table on that day as to substitute duck for turkey at that meal. But the game up at the polo grounds caused many desertions and annual mutinies; and the family idea which was first lessened by the absence from the table of one was further spoiled when the head of the family followed his son, and then the uncles and poor relations, and at last the daughters and mothers, learned to prefer the nipping winds and tingling feet of the polo grounds to the heavy dinner in the middle of the day at home. It was not so much that they cared for football pure and simple, but that the day was a holiday, and that there ws nothing better offered, and that they could see the other people, and could be seen by them, and it, in short, became "the thing to do"; and the significance of that day which once centred in New England around a grateful family offering thanks for blessings received and a fruitful harvest now centres in Harlem about twenty-two very dirty and very earnest young men who are trying to force a leather ball over a whitewashed line.

Ten years ago a solitary "haberdasher," as he delights to call himself, used to deco-
rate his windows before Thanksgiving day with orange and black and blue handkerchiefs, and those of us who were in college then considered this as a rare piece of
condescension on his part, and as a sign that the public, as represented by this solitary
shopkeeper, was interested in the struggle of the college boys up on the polo grounds.
To-day - But this is not the place to tell how it is today: this but tells how it used to
be. It used to be that there were two games - one in the morning, between Pennsylvania
and Wesleyan, and the great game in the afternoon - and all "true sports" went out early
to see both, and remained on the damp muddy grounds until late in the afternoon. The
first game was not scientific, but it was desperate, and served to whet one's appetite
for the game to come. At this, 8000 people formed what was considered in those days
a magnificent audience - an audience in which the young men outnumbered the young
women fifty to one, and the numbers of which strayed over the field, and lost themselves on the big grand stand, and spent the greater part of their energy in shouting
"Get off the field!" at the two or three hundred politicians, newspaper men, actors, and
attaches of the polo grounds, who walked complacently around the lines. It was only
necessary in those days to take a few sheets of writing paper with you, and to say that
you were a reporter, to get a place inside the ropes. There was no system worthy the
name, and no order.

The real reporters, with very few exceptions, never saw a football match from one
year's end to another except this particular one, and so gave only descriptive accounts
of the game, in which they spoke humorously of the splints and bandages and ambu-
lances and gallantly of the girls with "eyes of Yale blue" and those who "wore Harvard
crimson in their cheeks." And the fact that a Tammany politician had attended the game
in a white greatcoat was of much more important news interest to them than that either side had scored. In those days a man who drove out to the game in a cab, instead
of taking the elevated, was considered a profligate, and there was seldom more than
twenty of these to be seen on the field, seated on the driver's box, and waving a large
flask and a small flag. I do not know why it should have been so, but even the clerk
of the weather disregarded the college men entirely in those days, and never took the
trouble to see that they had any accompaniment for their game other than a drizzling
rain, with gust and flurries of snow, and a bleak wind. He knows better than that now.

After the game in those earlier days all the students massed themselves in Koster
& Bial's, which was then at Twenty-third Street, and packed it so full that after nine
o'clock a man who wished to leave it had to be passed out over the heads of a crowd;
and this the crowd would do for him with a cheerful alacrity that landed him hatless
and breathless in the lobby, with the impression that he had been caught up by the sails
of a windmill and hurled into space.

It was a most envious sight. The hall was very small, very dirty, badly lit, and with
a low ceiling, against which the smoke rolled and clung like waves on a shore. Below
this, and in the single balcony that ran like a horseshoe around the building, were more
men than the floor could hold, and who overflowed upon each other's shoulders, and
stepped from table to table, or dropped from the boxes to the heads of the men below.
These were all very young men, in what were known in those days as Newmarket coats
and high curly-brimmed hats, and with silk kerchiefs bound around their necks inside

the collar of these green greatcoats. The silk kerchief was one of the fashions of that day, and it gave the unknowing ones the impression that every well-dressed young man of New York was suffering from a severe cold. These young men, whose garb made them look like an army of coachmen, hung three deep over the railings of the boxes, blocked the aisles, balanced themselves and embraced each other on the tops of the tables, and stepped forth from these unsteadily on to the heads of the crowd without exciting any ill humor on the part of the gentlemen so trampled upon. They yelled the entire time, and gave the particular college cheer of every known institution of learning, and at moments of greatest enthusiasm clambered upon the stage, and were pitched-off into the arms of their companions and on to the heads of the frightened orchestra by the irate German managers.

There was an attempt at a performance going on meanwhile, but no one noticed it, and on one night I remember an audience of over a thousand students sang the chorus of one song throughout the entire evening in a monotonous roar that turned the performance on the stage into a pantomime. The actors came on and went off, embraced or fought or sang or danced as their part on the programme suggested, but it was as silent a performance as that of the *L'Enfant Prodigue*. One could see the leader wave his baton, and the actresses open their lips, and the comedians fall down and get up again, but all one could hear was the audience shouting cheerfully,

"They're af-ter me,
They're af-ter me,
For I'm the Individual they require."

They were singing it when I left, and with such evident self-satisfaction that if it were not that Koster's has moved, I would not be sure that they were not sitting there yet and singing still.

Now all this is changed, and the city surrenders herself to the students and their game as she never welcomes any other event, except a Presidential election, which only happens once every four years, or a Columbian celebration, which has occurred but once in four hundred. She begins to prepare for them early in November, and shops in which there is nothing the student could possibly wish to buy fill their bow-windows, in spite of that fact, with the colors of the two rivals, and from Ninety-fourth Street in Harlem to lower Broadway, where the battle of business is thickest, and from the east side to the North River, the same colors in every form and texture hang on the outer walls, and the cry is that "they come." But long before they come, every other young woman you meet, and every little boy, and elderly men even, begin to parade Broadway with bows of blue stuck on their persons, or long strips of orange and black ribbon, like those of the floor committee of an east-side ball, which proclaim their allegiance and their hopes. It is not at all probable that the brothers of all these young women have ever enjoyed the benefits of a collegiate education - if they have they should certainly take better care of their sisters - or that the little boys can expect to "follow the ball," but they like to feel that thay are in whatever is going on, and though they have the vaguest ideas of what it is about, they are nevertheless proud of their colors and that they are championing something. There are two or more facts which tend to show how the development of the Thanksgiving-day game has affected those in high places. One of these is that service in many of the churches of the city were held one hour earlier than usual last Thanksgiving day, because the rectors found they could not get a full congregation unless the service was over in time to allow the worshippers to make an early start for Manhattan Field. And another is that the manager of the Yale team wrote the secretary of the President of the United States to inquire if he could not get prompt information as to just what day the President intended to proclaim as the day of general thanksgiving. Whether he received this information promptly I do not know, but they tell in Boston how that other fine Democrat, ther Governor of Massachusetts, wrote to the Harvard team to ask when it would best please that august body to have Thanksgiving day in that commonwealth. These facts are interesting as showing that Church and State both recognize the national importance of the Thanksgiving-day game.

Three days before the eventful day fakirs from Nassau and Ann streets swarm up town like an invading army, or like two invading armies, with banners and flags and artificial flowers in the true colors, and with tiny leather footballs and buttons and rosettes and ribbons and tin horns and countless varieties of badges. They give the streets as much color as the flowers give life to the Paris boulevards, and the city is *en fete* and divided into rival camps. Photographs of the players show in every shop window; and their pictures appear and reappear with each edition of the daily papers. The legitimate gambling on the floor of the Stock Exchange is neglected for the greater interest of betting on the game, and the odds given and taken are quoted in the papers as regularly as the rise and fall of railroad stock. Seats for the game sell at fifteen dollars apiece, and boxes at a hundred and fifty, and the men who took the few solitary cabs to the polo grounds ten years ago have now to engage a coach *one year in advance,* and pay twenty dollars to reserve a place for it.

The collegians begin to arrive in town on Wednesday, and one sees nothing but young men enveloped in huge greatcoats and ulsters, with yellow shoes, and canes wrapped in ribbons. They make Broadway between the Fifth Avenue Hotel, where the Yale team lodges, and the Hoffman House, where odds are given and taken on the game, almost impassable. In the corridors of these two hotels men who graduated in the seventies are sure to meet men who graduated with them, and they gather here from all over the United States, from Texas and Oregon, with that disregard for distances that the Western man soon learns, to talk football, and to wager large sums of money with utter strangers, who agree with them readily enough to leave large sums of two and three thousand dollars in the hands of a man who is also a stranger to both of them. This man is "Billy" Edwards, an ex-prizefighter, who keeps guard over the glass-ware of the Hoffman House bar, and who has become a most important figure in this great sporting event. He is the depository of almost all bets, and gives nothing in return for the bundles of bills left in his charge but a piece of paper, and yet so great is the confidence in him and in his integrity that he goes to sleep on the eve of Thanksgiving day with as much as $50,000 in his possession, belonging to men he had seen but a few hours before, and the faces of whom he has quite forgotten.

Everything on four wheels and that will hold twenty men on its top in the city of New York goes up Fifth Avenue on Thursday morning. It is like a circus procession many miles long. It begins at ten in the morning, four hours before the game, when the coaches meet in front of trhe Fifth Avenue and the Brunswick hotels, where a crowd has gathered to cheer them as they start. The streets are empty, for it is a holiday, and the sounds of the bugle calls and the coach horns and the riflelike cheer of Yale and the hissing sky-rocket yell of Princeton break in on the Sabbath-like quiet of the streets like the advance of an army going forth triumphantly to war. There is everything from the newest English brake to omnibuses; draped from their tops to the level of the street with cloths of yellow and blue hung in festoons or dropped in four straight curtains from each corner and dragging in the mud, and with wheels covered up entirely or decorated with ribbons around their spokes, and suggesting monster revolving pin-wheels. Some of the brakes have six horses, none less than four, all blanketed in the true colors, and every coach carries twenty shouting men and excited young women smothered in furs; and the flags, as they jerk them about, fill the air with color; and the coaches themselves toss like ships in a heavy sea, rocking from side to side, and sinking as the men on top jump up and down in time to the rhythm of the rival cheers.

Every coach-load yells for all the pretty girls on the next coach if they were the proper colors, and race scornfully past those who do not; and from the Washington Arch to the layers of flats in Harlem there are holiday-makers out along the route to see the procession pass, standing in some places three and four deep along the side-walk. And from the houses all along the course there are bits of bunting and big flags; sometimes it is only a strip of paper muslin fluttering from the eighth story window of a cheap apartment house, and again it is a big silken banner swinging from the housefront of some important friend of one or the other of the two colleges, who has built a dormitory or given a son to the football team. And as the decorated horses and the bedecked hansoms and brakes and coaches and omnibuses go galloping up the Avenue there are special cheers for the orange flag and the big black P in front of the Sloanes and the Alexanders and the Scribners, and for the blue banners and white Y before the homes of the Whitneys and the Vanderbilts.

Manhattan Field, where the game has been held of late years, and where it took place last week, looks to the spectators as if it were laid out on the top of a table-land, with the grand stands built up around its edges. In almost all other athletic grounds in this country you can see, above the sky-line of the stands, the roofs of houses and the tops of trees beyond; but in Manhattan Field it is as though you were in a big bucket, with green turf at the bottom and grand stands for sides. At one end back of the stands there is a steep hill with a face of bare rocks and this and the Washington Viaduct, which stretches high in air beyond the south side of the field, are the only objects one can see from the ground that are not part and parcel of the immense stands towering on every side. It is exactly as though you were in a pit or in the mouth of a monster crater lined to its edges with human beings. Last week these human beings numbered thirty thousand. They were ranged around the whitewashed gridiron and separated from it by a stout board fence, four feet high. Inside of this fence were the reporters and the telegraph operators, and the coaches and substitutes lying on the ground or crouched out of sight against the board fence.

Back of the fence, boxes stretched around one-fourth of its circumference, and behind the rest of its extent people stood in a solid mass until they reached the grand stands, where they rose skywards as closely packed together as fir trees on a mountain side. But just as human beings are much more interesting than fir trees, so this portrait gallery of faces was more impressive than a forest of pines. It was as if all the faces of the portrait gallery had been cut out of their canvases, and pasted together on a wall a quarter of a mile in circumference and fifty yards high, and at places much higher; for those on Dead-head Hill and on the Washington Viaduct were so far above the heads of those on the ground that it was impossible to distinguish them except with an opera-glass. When every other one of these forty thousand human beings stood up and yelled and waved a blue or an orange and black flag, the effect was worth crossing an ocean to see. There are certain traditions of these games which are interesting, and which were observed last week with much enthusiasm. One of these is the singing of words expressive of the sentiments of the rival colleges to the tunes of hymns and popular songs, in which the names of the "star" players are handed down to immortality, as were the heroes of the ancient Goths in their war-songs.

It is also interesting to the stranger to note how systematically the cheering is given, how it is timed to destroy the effect of the rival cheering, and that certain men are selected to lead and give the time for these yells, who hold a position similar to that of a leader of an orchestra. This year there was a new and unintentionally pretty effect in the introduction of blankets by the substitutes, in the place of "sweaters." They found that it took too long to pull a jersy on and off a player while he was waiting for a comrade to revive, or for the two captains to discuss a disputed point with the referee, and that throwing a blanket around him kept him warmer. So this year the substitutes lay around the lines, stretched at full length on blankets of double length, and whenever time was called, as it was at almost every fifth minute of each half, they would swarm over the field, waving their blankets like matadors in a bull-fight, and smother the eleven men of their college, transforming them in an instant into a dancing group of blanketed Indians.

There is no change so noticeable in the Thanksgiving-day game as the difference in the manner in which it is reported for the daily papers. It is no longer considered enough to cover it with two men - one to write the introduction, and the other to describe the play. Now each paper sends its star men, its artists, and photographers, and engages many ex-players of reputation to describe the game from the points of view of adherents of each college, and to make diagrams which show where the ball was at every minute of the two halves and to denote who advanced it and who stopped it. At the last Thanksgiving-day game that I helped to report for the *Evening Sun* there were seventeen men assisting one another in covering it for that paper, and every one helped, from the proud reporter who came out on a coach and sent us word by a policeman that Chauncey M. Depew had just arrived, to the new reporter who raced five blocks after an ambulance to get the story of the wounded player whom he supposed to be inside, and which he finally found, on overtaking it, to be empty.

This last game was perhaps the very best, as a sporting event and as a spectacle, that New York has ever seen.

The weather was perfect weather, and the football was perfect football. It was particularly interesting to old players, as Walter Camp has already pointed out in the New York *Herald*, on account of the revival, and the most successful revival, of the double pass and the long pass, which plays had been given up of late for the wedge. No one, no matter how hardened he may be to the roughness of football, can look at a wedge forming without a shudder od apprehension and disgust, and no one who saw "Bobby" Baker's old trick of the long pass so beautifully executed last week but felt that the open game is the cleaner and safer and better one.

In enthusiasm I do believe I have never seen a more remarkable game than this last; and as an exhibition of delight there was never anything so complete and satisfying as an illustration of that feeling than was the sight of the Princeton substitutes, with their chins in their hands, and their elbows in the mud, and the rest of their bodies balanced in and kicking and trembling with ecstasy. Nor was there ever a more excellent example of Yale grit than that showed by the eleven within three minutes of the last half, when they prevented Princeton from scoring a second time, though the ball was within a few feet of the goal line.

People who live far away from New York, and who cannot understand from the faint echoes they receive how great is the enthusiasm that this contest arouses, may possibly get some idea of what it means to the contestants themselves through the story of a remarkable incident which occurred after the game in the Princeton dressing room. The team were being rubbed down for the last time after their three months of self-denial, and anxiety, and the hardest and roughest sort of rough work that young men are called upon to do, and outside in the semi-darkness thousands of Princeton followers were jumping up and down, and hugging each other, and shrieking themselves hoarse.

One of the Princeton coaches came into the room out of this mob, and holding up his arm for silence, said, "Boys, I want you to sing the doxology." And standing as they were, naked and covered with mud and blood and perspiration, the eleven men who had won the championship sang the doxology from the beginning to the end as solemnly and as seriously, and , I am sure, as sincerely, as they ever did in their lives, while outside the no less thankful fellow-students yelled and cheered, and beat at the doors and windows, and howled for them to come out and show themselves. This may strike some people as a very sacrilegious performance, and as a most improper one, but the spirit in which it was done has a great deal to do with the question, and any one who has seen a defeated team lying on the benches of their dressing- room sobbing, like hysterical schoolgirls, can understand how great and how serious is the joy of victory to the men who conquer.

On 24 December 1894, p. 11, The Chicago Tribune followed the post-season western tour of the University of Chicago team. Such athletic excursions generated much publicity for the institution.

READY FOR THE GAME

San Francisco, Cal., Dec. 23.-[Special}-Stagg's eighteen husky young football play-ers from Chicago have arrived and the town is on the qui vive to see them play. They were due at 10:40 this morning, but their train was caught in the terrific snowstorm in the Sierras and was several hours late. Manager Hiscks, President Hinsdale of the Associated Students, H.C. Hoover, and Tom Cobb of Stanford; Manager Lang and Capt. Benson of the University of California; Managers Ewing and Morrow of the Reliance club, met the train at Port Costa.

Stagg's party are all in the best of health and spirits. Ewing was in a bad way when he left Chicago, but the trip improved him wonderfully and he will undoubtedly be able to play his position. The journey across the continent was made without incident fur-ther than having their meals in their own car. Stagg was enabled to take men out at each meal station and give them twenty-five minutes' run, which has landed them here with their pipes wide open and ready to meet a team of wildcats.

The long continued rain is apparently at an end and a great crowd is assured at Tuesday's game if the weather holds good. The visitors were delighted to learn thast the Haight street grounds, where the game will be played, is ankle deep in mud. That's the kind of ground they prefer. Stanford would prefer to see harder soil. New Year's day the Chicagoans will play Reliance team at Haight street and then will go to Los Angeles for a trial game with Stanford. The game scheduled with the University of California has been abandoned as five of the Berkley men are ill and no substitutes are available. After Los Angeles the Easterners will go to Austin and play the University of Texas team one game, and will reach Chicago Jan. 7.

When wedge plays produced a multitude of injuries, manufacturers sought to meet the needs of safety. Coaches and players also desired equipment or strategies that provided a winning advantage, as shown by the Chicago Tribune, 28 January 1894, p. 6.

LEATHER FOR FOOTBALL SUITS
PENNSYLVANIA FOLLOWS HARVARD IN ADOPTING THE NEW STYLE

New York, Jan. 27.-[Special]-Will the leather football suits be adopted by all the university teams next year? There is no question but what Harvard will use them, and the Pennsylvanians have already notified the tailor who made them for Harvard last fall that they shall want to be supplied. They propose, however, to have the suits made in a new way, with the upper section of mole skin, according to the old style, and the breeches of leather. In this way it is hoped to secure the advantages of the new style and none of the disadvantages. Butterworth, the Yale full back, said, after the Spring-field game, that he found the slippery leather aided him in diving through the Harvard players. It is argued that if the upper section is made in the old way this objection will be largely corrected, and, on the other hand, the slippery leather breeches will prevent a player from being easily tackled, as most of the tackling is done below the waist.

ISSUES AND IDEOLOGY

Football provoked much debate and extreme positions for and against its practice. The Nation decried the lack of sportsmanship inherent in the game on 20 November 1890, p. 895.

THE FUTURE OF FOOTBALL

FOOTBALL is obviously gaining in popularity, and bids fair soon to become a national sport. A few years ago it was played only in two or three of the leading col-leges, now it is established in all of the colleges and in the preparatory schools. More-over, it is getting a hold outside the college circle; athletic clubs in the cities have their elevens; and every year the game attracts a larger and larger audience from the mis-cellaneous public. The combination of discipline, individual skill, and brute strength which it calls for; the splendid fierceness of the game; the element of personal com-bat; which delights the savage instincts lingering in the breasts even of the most civi-lized lingering amongst us - these qualities account for its growing popularity, and promise a vogue even wider than it now enjoys. There would be little rashness in pre-dicting that within ten years we shall have in the great cities professional elevens, like the professional baseball nines, and that thousands will gather to shout themselves hoarse at the exploits of hired rushers and backs.

This prospect suggests some questions as to what will be the quality of the game when it is no longer exclusively in the hands of the gentleman amateur. It differs from sports like baseball and cricket in some important respects. In the first place, violations of the rules of the game are easy, and give distinct advantages to the side that practises them. Thus, if you violate the rules by running ahead of a comrade of yours who is carrying the ball, and harass the member of the opposing team who tries to tackle him, you help most effectively toward scoring. If a rusher "holds" his *vis-a-vis* in the rush line -i.e., not merely blocks him by getting in his way, but grabs him and holds on - he enables his own half-back to get through so much more easily without being seized. This is "foul play," in the technical sense; and, unfortunately, there is also abundant room for foul play in the literal sense. If your opponent in the rush line is an effective player, it is a fine thing to disable him, by "winding" him, or gouging in the stomach, or strangling viciously when you tackle, or giving him a smart blow on the nose if you happen to know his nose is very sensitive (this illustration is from a notorious case). There is a constant suspicion by each party that the other side is trying to "lay off" its good players; sometimes the opposing rushers fall into regular fisticuffs, and in any game a brutal fellow has abundant opportunity to abuse its possibilities.

Further - and this is another distinguishing feature of the game - the foul plays, technical and literal, are very difficult to detect and prevent. When the ball is put in play, there is a confused mass of running, rushing, blocking players, with heads, arms, legs, heels intermingled; and it is impossible for any umpire to see more than a small part of what is going on. The unfair or brutal player has more than an even chance of escaping detection; and at worst, he will only be disqualified, and a fresh, unfatigued hand takes his place.

Given these peculiarities, and given also the extraordinary feeling which the college public, graduate and undergraduate, has about the success of the college team, and it is easy to see why the game, even in the hands of the gentleman amateur, tends to degenerate into a competition of underhand play and of "slugging." Not infrequently it is tacitly understood that the referee is to close his eyes to fisticuffs, and to let the opposing rushers fight it out to their heart's content. To such a pass had the sport come a few years ago that the Harvard Faculty prohibited its undergraduates from engaging in intercollegiate matches, and removed the prohibition only when certain changes were made in the rules with the design of removing the objectionable features. The most important of these changes was the addition of a second umpire or referee, whose special duty it is to watch the players; an acknowledgement of the absence of honor among gentlemen which gives the strongest evidence of the temptaions to unfair play in the game. The immediate result was some improvement; but the improvement was not great, and promises not to be permanent. The spirit of the American youth, as of the man, is to win, to "get there," by fair means or foul; and the lack of moral scruple which pervades the struggle of the business world meets with temptations equally irresistible in the miniature contests of the football field.

Transfer these conditions to contests between professional athletes, before the sort of public that now goes to baseball games, and the development is not likely to be in the way of moderation. There is as much of the savage left in the average citizen that nothing draws like a prizefight; and if we permitted gladiatorial shows, they would be enormously profitable. If football reaches the stage in which baseball now is, it will be the slugging matches that draw, and the managers will respond to the demand. Possibly in the end its brutalizing effects will become such that, like the prizefight, it will have to be prohibited by law. Meanwhile, the game grows apace; and the world is treated in the curious spectacle that the one absorbing question for the graduates and undergraduates of two great institutions of learning is whether eleven Yale boys can beat eleven Princeton boys at football on Thanksgiving day.

Even proponents of football could not deny its violent nature and newspapers called public attention to the problem. The Chicago Tribune monitored the ongoing problem in the following reports; 21 November 1893, p. 11; 24 December 1894, p. 11; and 17 November 1899, p. 4.

FOOTBALL GUARD FATALLY INJURED

NEW HAVEN, Conn., Nov. 20, At the football game in Farmington Saturday between the Yale senior team and the Farmington Athletic club eleven, John White, guard on the Farmingtons, was probably fatally injured. In a rough scrimmage he fell beneath both Warner, Yale's center rush, and Griswold, half back on the Farmingtons, who weigh together about 400 pounds. His head was twisted; and he was picked up apparently lifeless. Physicians have been working over him since and found that he is paralyzed below the seventh vertebra. He is still unconscious and will be take to the Hartford Hospital tonight.

ANOTHER FOOTBALL PLAYER IS DYING
THOMAS CAHILL OF THE SCRANTON TEAM NOT EXPECTED TO LIVE

PHILADELPHIA, Pa., Dec. 23. - [Special] - Thomas Cahill, manager of the Scranton (Pa.) Baseball Association, who also played with the Louisville American Association team, is a victim of football. He overexerted himself, brought on hemmorhages, and is dying.

FOOTBALL INDIRECTLY CAUSES DEATH

Sioux City, Ia., Nov. 16, - George Shoup, the 14-year-old son of Professor J.S. Shoup, formerly Superintendent of Schools in Woodbury County, died at Merill as the result of an accident on the football field. While playing last Friday Shoup sprained his knee quite badly, the injury soon developing a serious inflammation. As a result of the extreme pain he became a victim of nervous prostration, which is assigned as the cause of his death.

While numerous critics assailed the sport, apologists countered with their own rationales, a sampling of which follows. In 1889 Caspar Whitney, assisted by Walter Camp, selected the first All-America team; all of the players chosen represented Harvard, Princeton, and Yale. Whitney reprinted previous selections and a rationale for the 1891 team in Harper's Weekly, 12 December 1891, p. 1003. The All-America selections set an arbitrary criteria of excellence that idealized the athletic hero, connoted patriotism, and raised the status of sport on college campuses.

THE ALL AMERICA TEAM

CLASSIFYING FOOTBALL PLAYERS is not so simple as it looks. It should be borne in mind that the opinions advanced in this column are the results of a season's work. The men are not chosen for the national team from their showing in any one game, but from what they have done throughout the football year. Bearing this in mind, therefore, I should pick the All America eleven of '91 as follows:

Homans, full back.

McClung and Lake, half backs.

King, quarter.

Adams, centre.

Heffelfinger and Riggs, guards.

Newell and Winter, tackles.

Hinkey and Hartwell, ends.

SUBSTITUTES

Poe, Bliss, Barbour, and Trafford behind the line.

Holly, Balliet, Warren, Hallowell, and Newton in the line.

It may be interesting, and serve for matter of record as well, to reproduce here the All America teams of '90 and '89.

That of '90 was;

Homans, full back.

McClung and Corbett, half backs.

Dean, quarter.

Cranston, centre.

Heffelfinger and Riggs, guards.

Rhodes and Newell , tackles.

Hallowell and Warren, ends.

SUBSTITUTES

Hartwell, Upton, and Morison in the line.

Poe for quarter.

King, Lee, Lake, and Bliss for halves.

Trafford, full back.

That of '89 was:

Ames, full back.

Lee and Channing, half backs.

Poe, quarter

George, centre.

Heffelfinger and Cranston, guards.

Cowan and Gill, tackles.

Cumnock and Stagg, ends.

SUBSTITUTES

Dean, Trafford, Black and McBride behind the line.

Janeway, Stickney, Donnelly, and Rhodes in the line.

THERE WERE SOME OPINIONS at variance with mine when a year ago I wrote down Homans as full back on what would be the picked American team, but his work this season has, I think, thoroughly vindicated my judgment based upon his kicking ability a twelvemonth ago. He has easily out-punted any man on the field, and shown himself equal to making good gains with the ball. He tackles well, is safe nine times out of ten under a kick, and is not rattled by opposing ends rushing down on him.

Of the half backs, McClung has won the first place not only by his straight gaining abilities, but by his certainties to make distance in a game. Unlike half backs generally, even of the first class, he has been brilliant not only in small games, but also in the final ones. He follows interference with better judgment than any half on the field to-day, his dodging is a revelation, and a hole in the line must be closed up very quickly to keep him from getting through.

LAKE SHOULD BE the side partner of McClung, and it would indeed be a perfect line that did not yield to either the dashing plunges of the former or the remarkable dodging of the latter. Lake has by no means had an opportunity this season to show off his prowess. He is undoubtedly the most difficult to bring down of all the half backs; he runs very low, and with considerable speed, and his 175 pounds makes a difficult armful for even the surest tackler. His forwards this year have given him little support; they were unable to make holes for him in the Yale line, and several times I saw Lake actually dive into the line for a gain of a few yards, carrying the men along by the very force of his battering. Had he been behind the Yale line, this young man would have had several brilliant runs to his credit. The man to feed the ball to these three players is King; not because he is a better passer or so strong in his judgment of what plays to try as Barbour, but because he is so marvellously active in interference and tackling. In the latter respect he is one of the best on the field, while the coolness with which he directs a runner for whom he is interfering gains many a yard in the course of a season.

IN THE CENTRE, Adams of the University of Pennsylvania, flanked by Heffelfinger and Riggs, would make a formidable trio for any team to face. Both Yale and Harvard have had new men to develop at centre this year, and though Sanford and Bangs are promising, they are much behind the University of Pennsylvania man. Symmes's play this season has greatly improved over that of last, and of Yale, Harvard, and Princeton, he would be the choice. Should he continue next season as he has this, he would be the man for the picked team. There is another centre whose play has greatly impressed me this year, and that is Balliet of Lehigh. He runs Adams very close for choice; so close, in fact, I have heard men whose opinions carry weight declare him to be the best centre on the field to-day. Choosing guards is a very easy matter, for Heffelfinger and Riggs clearly out-class all other candidates. Newton, of Wesleyan, has shown form of the first class, and, more acceptably than any of the others, would fill a vacancy at that point of the line. Both Heffelfinger and Riggs have been commented on in this department until there remains nothing new to be said. Riggs played a much stronger game this year than last, and, so far as line work goes, there is little if any difference between the two. Heffelfinger, however, has an advantage in speed, and the style of Yale's play has brought this prominently to the front in his interference. In guarding a runner, he makes the life of an opposing tackler a veritable burden, and to his skilful work in this respect is to be credited a good share of Yale's gains. Despite his two hundred pounds, he is able to move his body as quickly as a man weighing one hundred and fifty, and it is this combination of weight and activity that makes him so valuable as a rusher.

NEWELL AND WINTER, the former as a terror to opponents' attacks and the latter as a ground-gainer, would make a pair of tackles to any captain's liking. Newell's work has not shown this season as it did last, simply because he was a picked man, and like Heffelfinger in the Yale-Harvard game, received an extra amount of attention. It gives rise to great expectations for a player to be chosen for the All America team the first year he makes' the 'varsity, and Winter may consider himself indebted to Billy Rhodes for the compliment, as it certainly was the coaching of Yale's ex-captain that brought him into such shape. But Winter owes his ground-gaining to his own stout legs and heart. His playing in the Princeton game was far stronger than at Springfield. Out on the ends the shadowy Hinkey and Hartwell would complete an almost invincible individual team. Freshman Hinkey has been one of the year's surprises. No one outside of his preparatory school had ever heard of him before the season, when he appeared on the Yale grounds as a candidate. He played on the scrub side awhile, but soon gave ample evidence to the Yale coaches that he knew too much football for some of the 'varsity candidates. He was too much for Hallowell at Springfield, and that is equal to writing him down as one of the best playing. Hartwell has earned a place on the All America team in spite of strong competition. The ends he faced (Emmons and Vincent), although not so experienced as those Hinkey had to handle (Hallowell and Warren), were wide awake and active, but Hartwell succeeded in getting his own runners by or through repeatedly, while his end was never passed by an opposing runner. Beginning with the U. of P. game in New York, and followed by Springfield and Thanksgiving day, Hartwell put up the strongest play of his football career, and his record will live in the memory of Yale as one of her best ends.

THE WORRY OF DEVELOPING a team out of green material has worked strongly against Warren's chances for a regular end on the picked team. His individual play has been sacrificed to a considerable extent to the captaincy in a year when to gain a place he must have played his very best game. He has played a careful, steady game, not what he is equal to, or what we shall probably see next season, when there is not so much bother. I should want him as substitute end in case the others were laid up. Emmons is going to make a first class man, and if he plays on Harvard's end next year, his opponents will realize the truth of this remark.

AMONG THE SUBSTITUTES I should take Barbour first, and in the event of a half back being laid up, would drop King back as a half, and play Barbour at quarter. Trafford would go next as a substitute for Homans, though it is not very likely he would be used, as the Princeton back appears never to get injured to any serious extent. In case Adams were laid up, I should not consider my team weakened by putting in Balliet, and if both of them went off the field, I should continue to feel my eleven superior to the best by placing Riggs in centre and putting Newton guard. As change tackle I know of no better man than Holly, who, although not so experienced as Wallis, was too much for him in many respects on Thanksgiving day. Holly has the right idea of the position, is strong and aggressive, and it would not take him many days to rank with the best in the country. With Hallowell at change end, and Warren in reserve in case of calamity, the line of the All America team would be well taken care of.

BEHIND THE LINE there is such a wealth of fine material that one hesitates before picking substitutes; but it seems, after looking it over from all sides, that if King were disabled after he had been taken back from quarter, I should call on Poe, and later,

Bliss. I am not forgetting Corbett, but I should be afraid to trust him after his exhibition at Springfield of very miserable high tackling and dropping the ball. It is possible, of course, this came from lack of practice, but it stands against him until he shows to the contrary another season. Neither am I forgetting Osgood, of Cornell, nor Thayer, Camp, and Branson, of the University of Pennsylvania, nor, among the New England colleges, Street, of Williams; they are all good - very good. Bliss is a clever experienced half, and uses his interference to the best possible advantage. Poe is a natural-born player, but has his brother's deadly tackle, is very fast, and dives into the line with the same dash that characterizes Lake's plunging. His weight, of course, prevents him carrying the line on his head and shoulders for a few yards' gain, as Lake did at Springfield, but he managed to squirm a few yards through Yale's stiff line even when unaided - in fact, he was the only one that could.

Give an eleven chosen from these picked men steady coaching - for without it they would be easy prey to one with strong teamwork - and the All America team of '91 would be invincible....

Proponents of football argued that sport, and football in particular, built character. Among them, Joseph Sears, published an article in the North American Review, 53 (1891), pp. 750-753.

FOOT-BALL: SPORT AND TRAINING

A young student who has left home and a parent's watchful care, especially if the home be at some distance from a large city, arrives under the shades of the college he has chosen in a peculiar state of mind. In most cases a healthy, vigorous youth, he is full of life and spirits, and rather overfilled with his own importance and freedom. He comes among three or four hundred like himself, young bucks who do not wish it to appear that they have come into any different atmosphere from that of the home circle. The first few months are times of hazing, - happily now almost extinct,- of the making of new acquaintances, and of introduction to new pleasures. Two or three hours a day must necessarily be given to recitations, but the rest of the time belongs to each student to use as he pleases for study or pleasure. Even the most exacting of parents would confess that some of this time should be given to relaxation.

Such a number of young bloods huddled together within a small area and full of animal spirits are apt to set each other on to actions that at another time would never enter into their precious heads. It is all quite harmless and natural, and may never amount to anything more. Most of it has no unfortunate results in after life; some of it, indeed, is far better than mere acres of books that have no life or stimulus in them. But occasionally it hits some hopeful heir very hard, and it is such as he who give the university its bad name, if it has one.

The call for members and candidates for a foot-ball team, or for a dozen foot-ball teams, for a crew or a nine, is a very opportune thing at such a time, and the first-named sport issues its summons on registration day. It is difficult to realize, perhaps, how much wholesome restraint such an athletic sport exerts over new men at college, coming at a time when they are at their weakest; to realize how much influence the system of training the members of the team has over others who merely stand by and watch. Each one who offers himself must be on the field at a certain time every day, must stop smoking, - perhaps he only began yesterday, - must stop drinking, and, in fact, put an end to all those villainies that have not yet been born, but for whose arrival preparations are being made by their mother, the devil.

Order and regularity is the first principle of the team. The trainer insists upon this, and the candidate does not object, because it is a point of honor with him to do his best in the defence of the larger honor of his college. He can do his studying if he wishes, at any time during the day, except for the pair of hours in the afternoon. He may put off the team at an early date, but he has the opportunity of joining others, and in any case he has had a little suggestion of something respected by his mates much more than the perpetration of some outlandish prank. The two are not very different from one another, except that one is permitted by the community and the other may be - and probably is - contrary to civil and moral law. They serve, however, precisely the same purpose as far as the perpetrator is concerned. They are both the overflow of this new sense of freedom, of naturally bouyant spirits that can be turned into athletic sports as easily as into cards or something worse.

Much of the danger at a university can be traced to its source in the need of wholesome recreation and exercise. It is not the exercise tht detracts from study, but the inaction which detracts from both. College morality in a large sense is a thing maligned. The few who do not see fit to put themselves under its protection furnish the material for gossip and journalism which both of these estimable mediums for spreading news credit to the entire university. The morality there is not a perfect thing, but, without detracting from the respect that is justly given our honored parents, it is infinitely better than it was thirty years ago, and "progress is better than perfection."

Close upon the restraint enforced by the training comes that which is the first essential of education, and which has justly been said to be next to godliness. After two hours of strong, vigorous exercise comes a hot and cold bath, a "rub-down" with all sorts of healthy liniments, and a phenomenal dinner of soup, roast beef, potatoes, and custard pudding: what could be a better preparation for morality and health and success? It may be too much for a year, too strong exercise for the heat of spring and summer, but three months of it can easily add twenty pounds to a young man's weight and 10 per cent to his examination marks, and finally, - let us be conservative - at least 50 per cent to his manly self-respect and his ability to reason with clear common-sense on whatever comes before him. One needs but to step into the dining room of the team or into the huge shower-baths of the gymnasium to see that human manners and human morals are being straightened day by day as well as human bodies. Those whose allowance from the parental exchequer is large must forego fancy dinners and indigestible concoctions, liquid or otherwise; those who know of no parental exchequer are under a like necessity of eating a stunning meal three times a day. Far be it from me to taboo a mellow pipe after dinner or a glass of mellower Burgundy. Many a hard-worked brain playing at foot-ball with the world finds infinite solace in these relaxations. They have their admirable uses; but where they serve no other purpose than that of firebrand to start the flame, it is fortunate that in some cases they can be withheld for a time.

Then too, the game, in conjunction with others, has a small education in it that would, if they were compared, equal several much more dignified occupations and revered studies. It is a peculiar game, familiar no doubt, or should be, to all; for though at every instant during the hour and a half required to play it out there is the same repitition of a scrimmage, yet the instant the ball is again in motion, and the twenty-two men are started after it, the field is in a situation it has never been in before. Signals there are, schemes piled upon schemes, tricks, feints, and rules that are with difficulty followed or totally disregarded; but the history of each play is unique; it has never been known before. Active thinking, self-reliance, power to carry out what is attempted, and ability to decide at once and in the right way - these are not qualities to be disregarded, nor is any training that tends to perfect them....

The great trouble, however, at home and abroad, with the game of foot-ball is in its *brutality* (the word has been so abused that it deserves to be put in italics). Here is another point on which journalism has called up all that could be found in the dictionary and elsewhere to help it condemn and at the same time highly color the sport. The newspaper 'story' must be a bright, readable account, free from dull detail, and it takes advantage of the extraordinary amount of scratches, which cannot be avoided in a personal contest, to give that spice to its narrative that is demanded by the delicate palate of the American reading public....

Injuries, however, slight, are less frequent than ever, and in the more important games of last season there is scarcely an instance of rough, brutal, or unfair play. As for accidents, there is an important distinction to be made in estimating them -the distinction between very slight and serious injuries. In an admirable report prepared by a committee appointed for that purpose in 1888 at Harvard University, it appeared from replies sent in by 1,016 students that 912 had received no injuries at all, that 88 had been hurt once, 13 twice, and 3 three times. Of these 104 accidents, 42 resulted from foot-ball, in which 165 students practised regularly every day during two months and about 200 more played games occasionally. Out of the 42 accidents 35 were slight and amounted to nothing. Consequently seven men supplied the material which filled the newspapers with the brutal details of injuries for nearly two months; nothing being said of the injuries received in other sports.

That is, the accidents in foot-ball are almost entirely such as a result from any sport where human beings come in contact with each other, and the serious injuries there are not more common than in daily life. Nor are those that do occur more lasting than or so much to be regretted as some of the moral and mental injuries that the game helps to prevent. On the other hand, the moral brutality supposed to be called up by this contest is still more of a myth.

Men do lose their tempers, - not so much as they did, however, - but such carelessness is in direct violation of rule and is disobedience, and it is punished with discharge.

There can be no better school for the cultivation of self-control than one in which the test is so severe as it is here... if a boy cannot learn to control himself here and stand up for his own, it will go hard with him when he tries to stand up against the world outside....

The continuation of abuses and excesses led faculty and school administrators to regulate interscholastic athletics, but the task proved arduous and had limited success. The New York Times reported some headway on 14 November 1900, p. 10.

FOOTBALL PLAYERS BARRED

Four members of the Manhattan College eleven have been excluded from playing during the remainder of the season, and the game scheduled between the Manhattan and Columbia University teams, which was to have been played Nov. 24, has been canceled, as the result of a Faculty order promulgated yesterday, whereby students taking special courses are prohibited from representing the college on any athletic team.

The men dropped from the football team as a result of the new rule are Full Back Gonder, Right Tackle Owens, Left Tackle Payne, and Centre Rush Murphy. All are special students, and do not reside at the college. Payne, Murphy, and Owens are the heaviest men in the rush line - in fact, the only heavy line men in the squad. Their loss is felt so severely that Manager Lynch and Capt. Garrett Cotter deemed it impossible to meet the Columbia eleven with the lightweight men who will have to succeed the excluded players, and word was at once sent Manager Shoemaker of the Columbia team requesting a cancellation of the game.

The other games remaining upon the Manhattan schedule, however, will be played. Capt. Cotter said last night that the training would continue without interruption and that members of the scrub team would be developed to replace the four men dropped from the 'Varsity. The most important game yet to be played is one on Thanksgiving Day against the strong eleven of the Harlem Catholic Club.

The action of the Manhattan College Faculty in excluding special students from further participation in athletics occasioned no great surprise among the student body of the institution, as complaint against the conduct of certain special student members of the football squad during recent trips of the eleven has been frequent. The Faculty action is commended by the majority of the resident students of the college.

PROFESSIONAL FOOTBALL

Talented football players soon learned to capitalize on their skills. Pudge Heffelfinger, a former All-American from Yale, accepted $500 from the Allegheny Athletic Association to play against its rival, the Pittsburgh Athletic Club on November 12, 1892. With larger wagers dependent upon the outcome, Heffelfinger proved the difference as he scored on a recovered fumble that he had caused in a 6-0 win. Other players soon pedaled their abilities to the highest bidder. Pennsylvania and Ohio remained the center of pro football in the ensuing years, but early attempts to organize leagues proved short-lived. The Pro Football Hall of Fame supplied the following ledger accounting for the first known case of professionalism.

EXPENSE ACCOUNTING ALLEGHENY ATHLETIC ASSOC.
- FOOTBALL CLUB -

Game of Oct. 29, 1892 - AAA vs. Washington, D.C.

balance carried over (account)	$ 432.20
guarantees gross profit (check)	$ 258.00
team traveling expenses (cash)	$ 221.85
net profit	$ 36.15
total balance	$ 468.35

Game of Nov. 12, 1892 - AAA vs. Pittsburg A.C.

balance carried over (account)	$ 468.35
game receipts gross profit (cash)	$ 1,683.50
visitors guarantee expense (check)	$ 428.00
park rental expense (check)	$ 50.00
Donnelly, Malley, Heffelfinger expenses (cash) ·	$ 75.00
Schlosser hotel bill for above (check)	$ 9.00
W. Heffelfinger for playing (cash)	$ 500.00
total expenses	$ 1,062.00
net profit	$ 621.00
total balance	$ 1,089.85

The following newspaper accounts are excerpted from Richard M. Cohen, et. al., *The Scrapbook History of Pro Football* (Indianapolis, 1977). The first is from 1894.

THE PROFESSIONALS NEED TO MEND THEIR MANNER AND SPEECH

The managers of the professional football teams of this city, says the New York Sun, will find it necessary to call their players to pretty shary account, as far as their talk is concerned, if they expect ladies and people of refinement to visit the Polo Grounds. In the game between the New York and Brooklyn clubs the other day there was an amount of profanity, obscenity and general abuse utterly unprecedented in the history of first-class sport in this city. There were very few ladies present, it is true, but those who were there and attempted to follow the game had their ears assailed with such talk that it is not likely that any of them will visit the grounds again. The effort of the football managers is attracting a great deal of attention, for it is still an open question whether professional foot ball can succeed professional baseball in public favor. The game under the Association rules was apparently new to most of the spectators, and they found some difficulty in following it at first. Undoubtedly most of them looked for a game such as the college clubs put up. The new game is exciting, despite the fact that the men are not allowed to use their hands, but the first duty of the managers is to make it possible for the ladies and schoolboys to follow the sport without being shocked by hearing the sort of epithets which have thus far characterized the players.

The following selection is also from 1894, as printed in *The Scrapbook History of Pro Football*.

THE AMERICAN LEAGUE OF PROFESSIONALS FORCED TO GIVE IT UP.

A meeting of the American League of Professional Football Clubs was held in New York last Thursday. All clubs were represented, After a full discussion it was deemed for the best interest of all club members that the season be brought to a close on October 20. The late period at which the Association got under way, on account of the prolongation of the base ball season, and the difficulty of avoiding conflict with the regular college foot ball games proved a serious obstacle to carrying out a schedule of games, but the Association feels that with the experience it has gained it will be in good condition to reorganize in the opening of 1895. The Association will, during the winter, arrange to formulate a new association on somewhat different lines, ready for spring work.

Following is the valedictory of the secretary, Mr. George Stackhouse, who backed the New York Club and became tired so very soon:

"After the full discussion of the situation and receiving reports from the various clubs it was deemed for the best interest of all club members that the season be brought to a close October 20. It was determined that all clubs should pay salaries in full up to November 1, 1894."

A prominent member of the Association says the failure to make a success of the enterprise was largely due to the fact that the members had failed to take the advice of persons who could have aided them, and since the opening of the season over $2000 had been lost. The clubs interested were: New York, Boston, Baltimore, Washington,

Philadelphia and Brooklyn. It is pretty safe betting that this league will not be revived for some years, at least not by those who have just had their fingers burned.

The following selection from *The Scrapbook History of Pro Football*, 1895, represents a typical situation in early pro games. Latrobe had won a previous meeting of small town rivals and when large bets were involved one or both teams sought an advantage by hiring college stars for the occasion, and eventually, for the whole season.

RED-HOT FOOTBALL WHILE IT LASTED

Yesterday's game between Latrobe and Greensburg football teams was the most unsatisfactory of the big contests of the season. It was advertised to begin at 3 o'clock, but it was 20 minutes after 4 before the ball was set in motion. Three thousand people gathered in the grounds and sat in the dampness alternately yelling to keep up their enthusiasm and stamping to keep the blood warm in their veins, while the two teams stood in the middle of the field doing nothing but jawing at each other. The whole trouble was caused by the fact that Greensburg had Core, the W.& J. guard, in their line. According to an agreement between the two sides neither side was entitled to play any man yesterday who was not either in the game last Saturday or among the subs. Latrobe claimed that Core, although on the side lines on Saturday, was not in uniform, and therefore could not be classed among the subs. Greensburg claimed that it had a right to use him, as he was designated a sub by wearing a Greensburg sweater on that day. Latrobe insisted that a sweater was not a uniform, and strenuously opposed the enrollment of the W. & J. guard. Latrobe did not object to Crookston or Flowers, both of whom were in the line-up, as they were in uniform on the side lines in Saturday's game. But the line was strictly drawn on Core. Latrobe agreed to leave the matter for decision in the hands of two Pittsburg gentlemen, but Greensburg declined to submit. Bluffs good and hard were hurled to and fro, and finally the Greensburg bucks boarded their bus and drove out of the grounds. The Latrobe players a moment later crawled into their conveyance and also drove out of the grounds. On the outside the teams met again and another wordy warfare ensued. Both sides, however, were not so strong in the bluffing business, and the upshot was that the wagons returned to the grounds, where they were received with a mixture of hoots and cheers. Core was sent to the side lines, and as the sun began to sink in the western skies the game commenced.

That there is a bitter feeling between the hamlets of Greensburg and Latrobe was evident to anybody who was in Latrobe yesterday. The feeling was without a good-natured coating, and was shared by people of all conditions and sexes. The female population of Latrobe was particularly loyal. Not a female in the burg could be seen who did not wear the colors of the football team. It is said that not an inch of blue or red ribbon could be secured in Latrobe for love or money after noon yesterday. Large

and noisy delegations of Greensburgers invaded the powerful village, but at every twist
or turn loyal female Latrobists glanced disdainfully at the shouting marchers, and some
even grew livid with rage. This was the case among old and young. An old lady turned
her back after spitting at a Greensburg crowd and then defiantly waved a yard or more
of red and blue ribbon. It would be supposed that the defeat of the pets would have
stunned the loyal female population. Not so. After the game, although not being altogether successful in hiding their disappointment, the ladies began cheering for W. &
J. whenever the colors of Greensburg met their gaze. "It took two teams to beat us"
shouted a lovely beauty as she jumped the fence for a short cut to town, and all Latrobe
took up the cry....

Professionalism entered the game in Ohio about the same time; the following account
is from an unidentified local paper, 3 November 1895, in *The Scrapbook History of
Pro Football*.

THE CANTON ELEVEN DEFEATS THE WEST END TEAM IN A GOOD GAME

The game Saturday afternoon between the Canton and West End teams resulted in
a victory for the former in a hard fought contest. The game was the first participated
in by either eleven this year and both teams being anxious for the victory the playing
was quite rough at times.

The West Ends won the toss and took the ball, Canton taking the north goal. Atkins
kicked off, Bald securing the ball and made a fine run of 30 yards, the Canton backs
then bucked the line for 25 yards more. Cantons lost the ball on a fumble, the West
Ends securing it and making 30 yards on the play. The West end boys forced the ball
to Cantons 25 yard line, Cantons then braced up and West Ends were forced to punt.
Here they sprung a surprise on their opponents. Atkins played close to the line but
instead of bucking the line made a beautiful drop kick, kicking a goal from the field,
scoring 5 points. The Cantons were taken completely by surprise as they were playing low for Atkins to buck the line.

The teams again lined up for the kick off. Johnson kicked the ball well into W.E.'s
territory, Stokey securing it, but was downed in his tracks. The W.E.'s sent Hallam and
Stokey around the ends for good gains until they were in the center of the field. The
Cantons line played good, tackling by Bald, Johnson and Herbst secured the ball for
Canton on downs.

The teams scrimmaged fiercely, Johnson bucked the line for several good gains.
The ball was next passed to Piero who broke through and made a run of 35 yards
within two yards of the W. Ends goal. The ball was then shoved over the W. Ends line
for a touchdown. John failed at goal.

The teams lined up for a kick off. Atkins kicked out of bounds on the second trial.
He again made a failure. The ball was then given the Cantons. Kaufman kicked off the

W. Ends making a poor return of the ball. The teams lined up. The W. Ends could make no gains and the ball went to the Canton team on downs. Time was called with the ball with W. Ends territory.

In the second half Pumphrey replaced Pfouts at left guard and Lynn was put on at right end in place of Bald. Johnson kicked off and the W. Ends could not advance the ball five yards and Canton took it. By good line play and end runs they gained rapidly. Piero secured the ball and went through right end for a 15 yard gain. The ball was within six inches of the W. Ends goal. Canton then massed for a center buck and the ball was pushed over with ease. Johnson failed at goal.

Both teams lined up for the kick off. Johnsod secured the ball and by good interference by Locke, Piero, Herbst and Kagle made 25 yards. By good runs by Piero and Kagle and bucking the line the ball was rapidly advanced into W. End territory. The ball was fumbled and the W. Ends secured it but could make no gains as Canton's line was invincible and Atkins was forced to punt. Carkness was now rapidly coming on and Herbst had a chance to secure the ball but could scarcely see it and Lyttle fell on it. W. Ends soon lost it again and Piero now made the star run of the game. Securing the ball he whirled rapidly and ran around right end making a run of 70 yards for a touchdown. Johnson failed at goal owing to darkness. One of the features of the game was Kagle's superb tackle of Cunningham when the auburn haired captain tried to get around left end tackling his man low he carried him back for a seven yard loss.

The game was an interesting one and from the start both teams were on their mettle. Considerable trouble was experienced in keeping the crowd off the field, and it should not be allowed in games to follow: The line-up was as follows:

CANTONS		WEST ENDS
Mayforth	left end	H. Hallam
Herbst	left tackle	Parrott
Pfouts ⎫	left guard	Gauchet
Pumphrey ⎭		
Eitner	center	Quinlan
Beebout	right guard	Turnbull
Locke	right tackle	Lyttle
Bald ⎫	right end	Cunningham
Lynn ⎭		capt.
Kagle	left half	J. Hallam
Piero	right half	Stokey
Kaufman	quarter back	Jahn
Johnson, Capt.	full back	Atkins

Referee Kirby, Umpire Rowlen, Lineman C. Pumphrey
Punts.

The Canton team has some splendid materially and with more team work will make a strong eleven. The boys will meet some fast teams in the near future. Oscar Pfouts is manager and Lennie Anderson secretary and treasurer.

The Cantons have secured Eitrer, of last year's team for Canton, and are to be congratulated in getting this fine player.

The West End boys have a good team in the field this year, much stronger than last year.

The Cantons have secured quarters for practice, and will try hard to have a winning team this year.

Eitner and Quinlan had quite an argument at center, but the Canton center outplayed his man at all points.

CANADA

Modern Canadian football did not develop until the twentieth century as Canadian schools adhered to rugby rules. The Montreal Football Club reported on its activities during its fourteenth year of operation in 1884, from the National Archives of Canada.

ANNUAL REPORT OF THE MONTREAL FOOTBALL CLUB

Gentlemen:

The 14th Annual General Meeting of the Montreal Football Club was held in the Montreal Gymnasium, Monday, March 30th, Mr. R. Esdaile in the chair.

Never has the Club had such a successful season as that of 1884. The practices have been well attended; the membership has increased; and as nearly all the new members have been playing members it has had the effect of making the Club very strong in every way.

For the last two seasons, 1883 and 1884, not a single match has been lost.

During the season 1884 the Quebec Rugby Union was formed, and ties were arranged for Clubs in the Province of Quebec. In Ontario they also formed an Ontario Rugby Union.

We won all our Quebec matches, thus winning the championship of Lower Canada.

On November 6th, Thanksgiving Day, we went up to Toronto, to dispute with the Toronto Football Club the title Champions of Canada. We won the match by 30 points to nothing, thus holding the right of callling ourselves "Champions of Canada."

In January, 1885, the Committee decided to lay the question of affiliating with the M.A.A. Association before the Club, and at a special meeting held on Thursday, March 28, 1885, it was unanimously resolved to affiliate.

We have played 8 first fifteen matches, 4 second fifteen matches, and 3 Association matches....

Outing reported on the state of football in Canada in December, 1892, pp. 247-251.

THE CHARACTERISTICS OF CANADIAN FOOTBALL

THE English game of Rugby football was introduced into Canada about 1870, and continued to be played, under nearly the same conditions, until six or seven years ago, when important changes began to be made; though not so radical as those made by players in the United States, where the amount of scientific team play introduced has really resulted in a new game.

In Canada, we have adopted a middle course, and, by so doing, appear to have escaped the faults, while we have retained the advantages of each system.

Our game, though less complex than that of our American cousins, is easier to follow, while abounding in combined skill and team play unknown to English experts. Fifteen men a side are played, as in England, but the introduction of "wing play" and the lessening of the number of men in the scrimmage has introduced much more skillful team play than the English game, though, at the same time, giving great opportunities for individual prowess and less roughness than seems inseparable from the American game.

The Canadian football field is one hundred and ten yards in length and is quite unlike the American in its markings. Along the edges, from one end to another, run the "touch lines," and when the ball goes over these it is not in play.

This touch line play is quite an interesting feature of Canadian football, and affords many an opportunity for team play.

There are six lines only crossing the field of play - one at each end, marking its limits, two twenty-five and two fifty yards from these, and one at the centre...

These lines, however, are only marks to indicate where the ball is to be put in play after certain points have been scored. For instance, after a touchdown, it is put in play or kicked off at centre, and after a rouge at the twenty-five yard mark. They are not useful beyond this; which fact, perhaps... will enable a novice to appreciate the difference between the Canadian and American game.

It is of no importance in the former to know how much ground has been gained, since the ball does not change hands because of a failure to make five yards or five inches. When a man is tackled and holds the ball, his side still has the ball in the next scrimmage, so long as the other side does not gain lawful possesion. It will thus be seen that any further lines would, in the Canadian game be unnecessary, since in it the rule of gaining five yards on three downs or relinquishing the ball does not exist.

What chiefly strikes a Canadian in American football is the system of training which obtains at the American colleges. In Canada, players are content with a moderate amount of this-holding... that one may eat or drink what one likes, in moderation. Too much preparation, they argue, makes a man a mere machine... incapable of strenuous efforts at unlooked for critical points, and unable... to rise to the occasion... Short, sharp practice generally lasting about an hour, is the general custom....

Canadian men rarely train at all until two weeks before the season opens, and even then, only by practicing hard for about an hour daily, with perhaps, an occasional run.

They make no change to speak of in their diets, nor do they eschew smoking, though it is indulged in moderation.

The most successful team in Canada, in late years, has been that of Osgoode Hall, an institution where only the most moderate practice is at all possible; where, indeed, by reason of lectures, only occasional practices in the afternoon can be had, so that the players are compelled to do all their team work before breakfast in the mornings, and yet their untiring efforts and invincible rushes secured to them the Championship of Canada for two years in succession....

To describe the game as it is played, and compare it with the American... The first point is the well-known difference in the number of men. In our game a team is composed of fifteen men, and when lined up on the field they are distributed as follows:

Full back

Half-back   Half-back
Centre half-back
Quarter
Wings   Scrimmage   Wings
. . .   .   Rush Line

The full back must be a good catch, kick and tackle well, and also be possessed of more than an average degree of nerve. It is, perhaps the most responsible place on the field and the hardes to fill. In many ways he resembles the American back, though he is not called on to "buck the line," while he stands at greater distance behind his halves than in the game across the line.

Again, we play three halves instead of two... They stand further from the scrimmage than the American halves... and are required to do more kicking than our American cousins...

The quarter-back's duties in both games are very much the same, only with us, instead of having the ball "snapped back" to him by the centre, it is heeled out for him by his scrimmage. When he obtains possession of the ball he is required to use his judgment as to whether it would be more advisable "to go through the line" himself or pass the ball back to his halves.

The wings, which are seven in number, correspond to the American guards, tackles and ends, and the extra man is called a "flying wing." Thus we have inside, centre, outside and flying wings. Their two main duties are to follow up the ball when kicked by their halves and to tackle the opposing backs. Of course, they are paired off so as to mark each other, and thus neutralize the most effective work of each.

The greatest difference in the style of play lies in the scrimmaging. In this we have preserved something of the English game, where ten men play in scrimmage and no "wing work" is done. For years the Canadian game remained, in this respect, the same; but finding it too cumbrous, and endeavoring to facilitate a greater accuracy and a higher degree of science, we reduced the number of men from ten to three and converted the quondam scrimmage men into wings.... Our system of scrimmaging, then, consists in a centre man with a man on either side of him. When one side has possession of the ball, it is given to the centre, who, together with his confrerees, endeavors to keep the opposing scrimmage in check and, at the same time heel the ball back to his quarter; the object of the other scrimmage being to prevent this, either by kicking the ball through and following it up, or by pushing their opponents to their knees. It is this "scrimmaging" which is the weak point of our game and... which... agitates our football world... to devise some other means of setting the ball in play than this awkward and clumsy fashion.

Imagine then, both teams "lined up"... The ball is kicked off... The opposing half catches it and returns it by a kick to one of the advancing rush line, and he, in turn, is tackled and thrown down with the ball. Then a scrimmage follows.

The centre heels the ball to his quarter, and he passes to his half, who runs, and when tackled, passes to his brother half, who is following him up, and thus the game progresses.

There are two points, however, peculiar to the Canadian game which remain to be touched on.

On either side of the field run "touch lines," and when the ball is kicked or carried "into touch,"... both teams line up straight across the field from where the ball went "into touch." The ball is thrown out from touch by the side that carried it in, or by the opposite side to that which kicked it in. This "punting into touch" is a very favorite means of gaining ground, for though the team which kicks the ball "into touch" loses possession of it, so much ground is gained, and possession does not mean to us what it does in the American game.

...Any man... in front of the ball when kicked by his own team is off-side, and is not allowed to touch the ball or interfere with his opponent, on the penalty of a free kick....

A "touch-down" or "try" consists of four points with the privilege of trying a kick at the goal, which, if successful, nets the team which scored two points more. A "touch-down" is simply one side carrying the ball over the goal line of the opposing team, and touching it down; whence the origin of the name. A "rouge" occurs when a man, in order to save his team from a try being tallied against them, himself touches the ball down behind his own goal, and thereby gives one point to the opposing side. A goal dropped from the field counts five points, and a place kick two. A "maul in goal" scores four without the privilege of trying a goal, while a "safety touch" means two points, and a "touch in goal" one less....

...The following are a few ideas prevalent among football men in this country.

First of all, unnecessary roughness, as far as possible, should be avoided. Here, indeed, the Canadian game shows the advantage, for by the "off-side" rule, which is always strictly enforced, all interference and wedge plays are excluded... this is the very nucleus of the American game... which causes all the roughness...

In conclusion, it may be interesting to note the effect which the American game has had on us here. For instance, attempts have been made... to introduce interference, although nothing can be more opposed to our rules. These attempts have failed.

There have been, also, agitations to reduce the numbers of players. The supporters of this movement argue that... it will be possible... to pit our best teams against the best that the United States can produce...

In our football clothes, too, the influence of the American game may be seen. Before 1890, a Canadian footballer's costume consisted merely of a jersey, canvas knickerbockers, which barely reached to the knee, and light shoes and stockings. Neither shin-pads nor canvas jackets were worn.... Heavily padded knickers, canvas jackets and all the other paraphernalia which are used to protect the different parts of the body, are now universally seen. This metamorphosis is entirely due to our American cousins. It is to be hoped that experts in the game, on both sides of the line, may soon see their way to modify the rules, so that international contests may take place. Such modifications as will render this possible must, however, come from the American side....

Chapter 11

GOLF

Golf arrived in the United States relatively late. Having been played in England and Scotland for centuries, and in Canada for more than a decade, it was not adopted south of the border until well into the 1880s. Historians disagree as to the introduction. Joseph Fox allegedly started play at Foxburg, Pennsylvania as early as 1885, but most historians credit John Reid, a Scottish immigrant, with a primary role in 1888. Localities in West Virginia, Kentucky, and Georgia claim golf activity before that date, but Reid definitely instituted the St. Andrew's Golf Club in Yonkers, New York by that time.

In 1891 Shinnecock Hills, in Southampton, on Long Island, became the first professionally designed course and the first incorporated club. In 1892 it was the first to add a clubhouse and featured nine holes. The Chicago Golf Club, organized in 1893, built the first eighteen hole course in the western suburb of Wheaton. The following year both the St. Andrew's and the Newport Club in Rhode Island sponsored national tournaments. In 1895 five clubs organized the United States Golf Association, which governed play thereafter. The first U.S. Open took place at the Newport Club in October, 1895. A national women's tournament occurred the next month at the Meadowbrook Club on Long Island. By 1897 an Intercollegiate Golf Association had been formed, and within two years a sufficient number of courses had been constructed on the west coast to organize the Southern California Golf Association.

During the early years of its development golf served a significant social function. As a sport that required expensive equipment and a large tract of land, it restricted participation to the wealthy. As a socially elite amateur sport it carried distinct class connotations, separating its practitioners from their perceived inferiors geographically, in exclusive country clubs, and socially, by restrictive membership covenants in such associations.

Technological advancements improved play as the rubber cored ball appeared by 1898, and the old gutta percha ball became obsolete. As golf clubs became less expensive the game became more attractive to the middle class. The first public golf course opened in Van Cortlandt Park in New York city on 5 May 1895, but middle class participation did not become widespread until after 1900.

ORGANIZATION

The Chicago Tribune reported the initial meeting of the United States Golf Association, 25 December 1895, p. 8.

NATIONAL GOLF ASSOCIATION

New York, Dec. 24. -[Special}-A National Golf Association was organized Satur-day. All the clubs in the United States and Canada are merged into a new association. At the meeting were H.O Talmadge, Secretary, and John Reid, President of the St. Andrews Golf club, the oldest in the United States; Lawrence B. Curtis and Philip Sears of the Country club of Boston; Theodore A. Havemeyer and Winthrop Rutherford of the Newport club; Gen. I.H. Barber and Samuel L. Parrish of the Shinnecock Golf club; and Charles Blair McDonald and J.L. Ryerson of the Chicago Golf club. They were Mr. Talmadge's guests at dinner prior to the business meeting. The main purpose of the organization will be to further the interests of the sport by the adoption of uni-form rules, the establishment of a circuit of club meetings, and the regulation of the amateurs' professional championships. Permanent organization was formed with the following officers: President, Theodore A. Havemeyer; Vice-Presidents, Lawrence B. Curtis and Charles Blair McDonald; Secretary, H.O. Talmadge; and Treasurer, Samuel L. Parrish. It was decided to hold a tournament annually to settle the single and four-some championships. The conditions of the tournament were finally left to a committee made up of John Reid, St. Andrews club; C.B. McDonald, Chicago club, and Gen. I.H. Barber, Shinnecock club, who will also draft the constitution and the by-laws and the playing and handicap rules and report at a future meeting.

The original constitution and by-laws are reprinted from James P. Lee's *Golf in America* (New York, 1895), pp. 70-87.

CONSTITUTION OF THE UNITED STATES GOLF ASSOCIATION

ARTICLE I.

The name of this organization shall be "THE UNITED STATES GOLF ASSOCIATION."

ARTICLE II.
OBJECT

The objects of this Association shall be to promote interest in the game of Golf; the protection of the mutual interests of its members; to establish and enforce uniformity in the rules of the game by creating a representative authority; its Executive Committee to be a Court of Reference as final authority in matters of controversy, to establish a uniform system of handicapping, to decide on what links the Amateur and Open Cham-pionships shall be played.

ARTICLE III.
MEMBERS

Sec. 1. This Association shall consist of Associate and Allied Clubs.

Sec. 2. The following clubs shall be Associate members:

    1. Chicago Golf Club.

    2. The Country Club of Brookline, Mass.

    3. Newport Golf Club.

    4. The St. Andrews Golf Club of Yonkers.

    5. Shinnecock Hills Golf Club of Southampton, L.I., and such other representative club or clubs as may hereafter be admitted as hereinafter provided.

Sec. 3. Allied members shall be such regularly organized clubs in the United States as shall enter into an alliance with this Association as hereinafter provided.

ARTICLE IV.
CLUBS ELIGIBLE

Sec. 1. Older clubs eligible to be admitted to membership in the Association as Associate Clubs shall be any representative clubs in an accessible part of the United States where the links, accommodations, constitution and by-laws of the club are such as to make it nationally representative, and such clubs may be admitted on a four-fifths vote of the Executive Committee of the Association.

Sec. 3. Any regularly organized golf club in the United States may at any time be admitted as an Allied Club by a two-thirds vote of the Executive Committee upon subscribibg to and fulfilling the conditions of the Association Constitution and By-Laws.

ARTICLE V.
ANNUAL MEETINGS

Sec. 1. The regular annual meeting of this Association shall be held on some day in February in each year, at such time and place as might be designated by the President, thirty days' notice being given and published.

Sec. 2. Each Associate Club of the Association shall have the right to be represented by two delegates duly authorized and their appointment certified to by their Club Secretary.

Sec. 3. Each Allied Club shall have the right to be represented by one delegate, but he shall have no power to vote.

ARTICLE VI.
ELECTIONS

Sec. 1. At the annual meeting the Association shall elect from its Associate Clubs a President, two Vice-Presidents, a Secretary, and a Treasurer.

Sec. 2. The election of officers shall be by ballot at the annual meeting in each year. They shall be voted for separately and receive a majority of all the votes cast to entitle them to an election, and they shall continue in office one year or until their successors be elected.

Sec. 3. At any regular or special meeting of this Association seven delegates shall constitute a quorum representing at least three Associate Clubs.

ARTICLE VII.
EXECUTIVE COMMITTEE

Sec. 1. The management of this Association shall be intrusted to an Executive Committee, consisting of the officers of the Association.

QUARTERLY MEETINGS

Sec. 2. Regular meetings of the Executive Committee shall be held at the time of the annual meeting, and if necessary quarterly thereafter, on such dates as may be designated by the President, fourteen days' notice of which shall be given to members.

SPECIAL MEETINGS

Sec. 3. The President may call a special meeting of the Executive Committee of the Association at such time as he may deem expedient, and he shall call a special meeting of the Association upon the written request of three Associate Clubs within fifteen days of the receipt of such request. At special meetings no other business shall be transacted than that for which they were called, and such business shall be specified in the call, which shall be sent out ten days previous to the time appointed for the meeting.

PROXIES

Sec. 4. Proxies may be voted at all meetings of the Association.

QUORUM OF EXECUTIVE COMMITTEE

Sec. 5. Three members shall constitute a quorum of the Executive Committee.

ARTICLE VIII.

Sec. 1. The President shall preside at all meetings of this Association and of the Executive Committee.

A Vice-President shall in the absence of the President perform the duties of that office.

ARTICLE IX.
SECRETARY

Sec. 1. The Secretary shall keep records of all meetings of this Association and of the Executive Committee, and he shall issue calls for such meetings. He shall keep a roll of membership and take charge of all correspondence and papers belonging to the Association. In his absence, Secretay pro tem. shall fulfill his duties.

TREASURER

Sec. 2. The Treasurer shall collect all moneys belonging to the Association and dispense the same under the direction of the Executive Committee.

He shall report in writing the state of finances when required by the Executive Committee, and at the annual meeting he shall present a written report showing all the receipts and expenditures during the year.

ARTICLE X.
APPLICATION FOR MEMBERSHIP

Applications for Associate and Allied membership shall be in writing to the Secretary of the Association, accompanied by a copy of the Constitution and By-laws of the Club making Application, a list of officers and a full year's dues, and an election shall be held at the next meeting of the Executive Committe, provided such application shall have been filed with the Secretary at least fourteen days previous to said election.

ARTICLE XI.
OBLIGAT'ONS AND DISCIPLINE

Sec. 1. The acceptance of membership in this Association shall bind each club to abide by all the conditions of the Constitution, By-laws and Rules of this Association, and to accept and enforce all decisions of the Executive Committee within its jurisdiction.

Sec. 2. Refusing or neglecting a strict and honorable compliance with the Constitution, By-laws or Rules of this Association, or with the decisions of the Executive Committee, shall render such club or member liable to suspension or expulsion by two-thirds vote of the Executive Committee, from whose decision an appeal may be taken to the delegates at the annual or special meeting.

Sec. 3. No club or member, however, shall be disqualified or deprived of any privilege without due notice and formal charges, with specifications, having been made, and an opportunity having been given to be heard in its or his own defense.

ARTICLE XII.
DUES AND EXPENSES

Sec. 1. Each Associate Club shall pay to the Treasurer before the annual meeting $100 annual dues.

Sec. 2. Each Allied Club shall pay to the Treasurer before the annual meeting $25 annual dues.

Sec. 3. Failure to pay such dues within the prescribed time shall preclude delinquent clubs from representation or voting at any meeting of the Association.

Sec. 4. The receipts from dues shall be devoted to defraying the cost of championship medals or other tokens, and for printing and other necessary expenses incurred by the Executive Committee in the performance of their duties.

ARTICLE XIII.
FISCAL YEAR

Sec. 1. The fiscal year shall end on the 31st of December.

ARTICLE IV.
AMENDMENTS

Sec. 1. Amendments to this Constitution may be made at any annual meeting by a vote of at least two-thirds of all the votes cast, providing twenty days' notice has been given associate and allied members, stating the proposed revision or amendment.

BY-LAWS OF THE UNITED STATES GOLF ASSOCIATION

Sec. 1. The following order of business shall be observed at the annual meeting of this Association:

(1) Roll call.
(2) Reading minutes of previous meeting.
(3) Secretary's report.
(4) Treasurer's report.
(5) Election of officers and committees.
(6) General business.
(7) Adjournment.

Sec. 2. In the event of an appeal from an order of discipline imposed by the Executive Committee it must be heard at the next regular or special meeting of the Association, and any member or person who is proved, to the satisfaction of the Association, to have been guilty of fraudulent or discreditable conduct of any kind may be declared ineligible to compete at any competition, suspended or expelled.

Sec. 3. All complaints or disputes between clubs of this Association shall be decided by those members of the Executive Committee who are in no way connected with the clubs interested.

Sec. 4. The president shall appoint such special committees as shall be found necessary.

Sec. 5. The Executive Committee shall interpret the Rules of Golf.

Sec. 6. The Amateur and Open Championship tournaments shall take place on the links of an Associate Club, in selecting which due consideration shall be given accessibility, accommodations and condition of course.

Sec. 7. It shall be determined at the annual meeting each year over which links the Championship prizes shall be contended for that year.

Sec. 8. The Executive Committee may delegate the power of naming the time and regulating the order of starting and determining the handicap of players to the Green Committee of the club over whose grounds the Association competitions are played, and of appointing such other committees as are necessary to govern such a competition.

Sec. 9. An amateur golfer shall be a golfer who has never made for sale golf clubs, balls, or any other article connected with the game; who has never carried clubs for hire after attaining the age of fifteen years, and who has not carried clubs for hire at any time within six years of the date on which the competition begins; who has never received any consideration for playing in a match or for giving lessons in a game, and who for a period of five years prior to the 1st of September, 1890, has never contended for a money prize in any open competition.

Sec. 10. Only persons members of clubs belonging to the Association, season subscribers thereto, and those who under the rules of any Associated or Allied Club are entitled to the use of the links in whole or in part for a period not less than the current season, can compete for the Amateur Championship, and competitors must enter for the competition through the Secretaries of their respective clubs, who, in sending in the names, shall be held to certify that the players are bona fide Amateur Golfers in terms of the foregoing definition.

Sec. 11. In both the Amateur and the Open Championship Golf competitions the entrance fee shall be $5, and must be received by the Secretary of the Association not later than 6 P.M. one week previous to the opening of the competition.

Sec. 12. The Amateur Golf Championship shall be played by holes. The Open Golf Championship shall be medal play.

Sec. 13. The competition shall be played in accordance with the Rules of Golf as adopted by the Royal and Ancient Golf Club of St. Andrews, Scotland, in 1891, with such special rules as are in force and published on the green over which the competition takes place.

Sec. 14. In the Amateur competition each game shall consist of one round of eighteen holes, with the exception of the last or final game, which shall be played on a separate day and consist of thirty-six holes.

Sec. 15. The draw shall take place three days before competition, and shall be conducted as follows: Depending on the number of entries, such number of byes shall be first drawn as shall after the completion of the first round leave 4, 8, 16, 32 or 64 players, and one draw shall decide the order of play throughout the competition, those who have drawn byes being placed at the head of the list of winners of the first round, and taking their place in the second round in the order in which their names then stand.

Sec. 16. In the event of a tie in any round, competitors shall continue to play on until one or the other shall have gained a hole, when the match shall be considered won.

Sec. 17. The winner of the competition shall be the Champion Amateur Golfer for the year, and the trophy shall be held for that year by the club from which the winner shall have entered. The winners shall receive - the first, a gold medal; the second, a silver medal; the third and fourth, bronze medals.

Sec. 18. All entries are subject to the approval of the Executive Committee of this Association.

Sec. 19. All disputes shall be settled by the Executive Committee of this Association, whose decision shall be final.

Sec. 20. It shall be incumbent upon clubs over whose green the tournament is held to admit all members of the Association as visitors without payment during the tournament; also to bear the necessary incidental expenses.

Sec. 21. Open Championship prizes shall be as follows:

First - $200 to the winner of the championship, of which $50 shall be expended on a gold medal and $150 given in money to a professional or in plate to an amateur golfer; the winner to have custody of the championship cup, but he must, if required, give security for its safe keeping.

Second - $100.

Third - $50.

Fourth - $25.

Fifth - $10.

The last four prizes shall go to professionals only.

Sec. 22. Any person paying his entrance money shall be considered thereby to have submitted himself to the Rules of the Association, both as to restrictions enjoined and penalties imposed. On these conditions alone he is entitled to enjoy all the advantages and privileges of the Association competition.

Sec. 23. These By-Laws may be altered, amended or suspended without notice, at any regular meeting of the Executive Committee, by two-thirds ...

The By-Laws of the Chicago Golf Club, gleaned from the 1909 edition, provide insight into the exclusivity of such groups.

CHICAGO GOLF CLUB BY-LAWS

ARTICLE I.
ORGANIZATION AND OBJECT

Section 1. This club is incorporated under the laws of Illinois as Chicago Golf Club, and its corporate seal is a circular disk, bearing the words, "Chicago Golf Club," and the figure of a golf player, and the motto, "Far and Sure."

Section 2. The Chicago Golf Club is organized for the purpose of promoting the game of golf and other outdoor sports, for pleasure and for acquiring and maintaining the grounds, Club House and appurtenances necessary to these objects.

Section 3. Its principal places of business shall be in Chicago and at its Club House, near Wheaton, Illinois.

ARTICLE II.
MEMBERSHIP

Section 1. Any male person over eighteen years of age may be elected to membership in the Club, provided not more than one adverse ballot be cast by directors, and shall become a member upon the payment of an initiation fee of not less than $100, as the Board of Directors shall prescribe, and the dues for the current half year.

Every candidate must be proposed and seconded by two members, in their own handwriting, at least one week before election, and his name posted at the Club House in a conspicuous place for the same length of time. The candidate must be personally known to both proposer and seconder, as well as to some member of the Board of Directors. His full name, place of residence and the names of proposer and seconder shall be entered in a book to be kept for this purpose by the Secretary.

Section 2. The membership of the Club shall be limited to two hundred and fifty. The annual dues shall be $75, payable $37.50 on January 1 and $37.50 on July 1 of each year.

Section 3. Every member shall furnish his postoffice address to the Secretary for the purposes of notice; and failing to do so, shall be deemed to be properly served with any notice when the same shall have been addressed and mailed to him at the general postoffice in Chicago.

Section 4. Any person elected to membership who shall fail to qualify within ten days after notice of his election shall be considered to have declined to become a member.

Section 5. Officers of the army and navy, clergymen, professors of universities residing in Chiacgo and vicinity, and foreign consuls who are not permanent residents of Chicago, may be admitted to the Club as subscribers, paying a subscription of $15 per month or $75 for the calendar year, which shall entitle them to the privileges of the Club, without ownership or vote.

Section 6. Non-residents (male) may be admitted to the Club as subscribers paying an initiation fee of $50, with annual dues of $25, which shall entitle them to the privileges of the Club without ownership or vote, provided that subscribers who may become permanent residents, will not be permitted thereafter to renew their subscriptions on expiration, but may become regular members upon paymentr of $50, or the difference between the non-resident and regular initiation fee. Persons not residing or having places of business within fifty miles of the Club House shall be deemed non-residents.

Section 7. Ladies over sixteen years of age, who are members of the immediate family of a member of the Club, and youths from sixteen to twenty-two years of age, may be granted the privileges of the Club as subscribers on paying a subscription for each calendar year as follows: For lady and her family (not including males, themselves eligible for election), $40; for a single lady, or youth from sixteen to twenty-two years of age, $25.

Section 8. Subscribers shall be proposed and elected in the manner prescribed for members, and must be re-elected each year.

Section 9. Any person may be proposed by a member of the Club, as a summer guest, for one summer only. Such person to be duly elected by the rules governing the election of regular members, and upon election and payment of $75 shall be granted the privileges of the Club for the summer from May to October 15th and ahve the same privileges as a regular member of the Club, except that such person shall not be entitled to vote or have any interest in the assets of the Club....

By the turn-of-the-century professionalism had entered golf circles to a greater degree and the USGA felt a need to address the problem. The New York Times printed the USGA's very narrow interpretation of an amateur on 28 May 1899, p. 25.

AMATEUR GOLFERS DEFINED

Golfers in general heartily commend the new rules defining the status of an amateur golfer which went into operation last week by act of the Executive Committee of the United States Golf Association. The rules are practically amendments of the amateur regulations which went into effect Jan. 1, 1897. Although made at that time as strict as was thought necessary to preserve the highest amateur standing of the game, two or three weaknesses have appeared from time to time, and other features have arisen which it seemed advisable to embody in the rules.

Among these was the gradually growing practice of assumed names, and the clear understanding that a professional in golf is not only one who has used golf for financial gain in any way, but who is considered a professional in any other sport. The new rules have been compiled with the aid of advice from several able lawyers who are well-known as golfers, and they draw the amateur line as clearly and strictly as it is, probably, possible to be done. They are in full:

Section 9. No person shall be considered an amateur golfer who has played for a money prize in a match or in an open competition, or who has received money for giving lessons or exhibitions of his skill in the game of golf; or laid out or taken charge of golf links for hire; or who has ever carried clubs for hire after attaining the age of fifteen years; or who has ever personally made for sale golf clubs, balls, or any other articles connected with the game of golf, or who, after the adoption of this section as amended, shall be classed as a professional in any athletic sport.

Section 10. No person shall be eligible to compete for the amateur championship of this association who does not conform to the conditions of Section 9, or who, after Jan. 1, 1897, has received compensation for services performed in any athletic organization, or who plays the game or frequents golf courses, for the purpose of exploiting his business; nor shall any be eligible to compete who hereafter shall enter any golfing competition under an assumed name. Any person having become ineligible by a violation of any of the provisions of this section may be duly reinstated upon his giving satisfactory evidence of meriting it. Only members of clubs belonging to this association, and those entitled under the rules of an associate or allied club to the use of the links, in whole or in part, for a period not less than the entire current season, may compete for the amateur and women's championships. Competitiors must enter for the championships through the secretaries of their respective clubs, who, in sending in their names, shall be held to certify that the players are qualified amateur golfers in accordance with the terms of Sections 9 and 10.

Any case not covered by the foregoing sections will be decided by the Executive Committee on its individual merits....

An important change in Section 10 clearly defines just what business shall be considered subject to golf professionalism. That is, any one shall be classed as a professional who "plays the game or frequents golf courses for the purpose of exploiting his business." Under the old rule it was somewhat ambiguous as to whether a manager or member of a firm whose goods were used in golf in any capacity should be classed as a professional....

It has further been pointed out that the rule might be so stretched as to include writers on golf subjects. Could it be claimed that they "frequent the links for the purpose of exploiting their business"? It might be so claimed in that it surely is necessary to see golf contests in order to become properly qualified to write upon the subject. If the rule should be so construed, which, by the way, seems unlikely, it would make Horace Hutchinson, the popular writer on the game in England, a professional in America, as well as Whigham, Findlay Douglas, W.G. Van T. Sutphen, and a score of others who do more or less writing on golf. With the exception of this possible ambiguity, the rules are firmly and clearly defined....

GROWTH AND DEVELOPMENT

The Chicago Tribune noted the St. Andrews' tournament, one of the first of the annual national competitions, on 13 October 1895, p. 7.

HE WINS BOTH CUPS
STODDART THE STAR OF THE ST. ANDREW'S GOLF TOURNEY

Captures the Willard Brown Trophy and the St. Andrew's Club Cup in Magnificent Exhibitions of Scientific Playing- Sands Has Bad Luck - Willie Dunn of Shinnecock Captures the Professional Match

New York, Oct. 12 -[Special}- The four days tournament of the St. Andrews Golf club ended today. Three contests were decided, and, from a golfing standpoint, it was an important day in spite of the rain. C.B. Stoddart, the ex-amateur champion, had W.H. Sands as his opponent in the contest for the Willard Brown cup. The match for this trophy, the hansomest that has ever been offered for a club tournament, was played by strokes, eighteen holes. It was a hot, close match, but Stoddart finally won by a score of 93 to Sands' 100. In the second round Sands showed up in much better form and succeeded in placing the game at a tie at the sixteenth hole. But then a bad drive landed his ball in the sand and when he got it out, after three shots, he drove it back in again. The last hole Stoddart took in one less than Sands, beating him by seven strokes. As none of the other competitors did the course less than ninety-three Stoddart had no difficulty in getting first place. A.L. Livermore came second with ninety-seven, and George E. Armstrong and J.F. Gray tied for third place at ninety-nine each. The committee ordered all ties to be played off, but Gray could not play in the afternoon, so he let the third prize go by default to Armstrong.

W.H. Sands was beaten in the afternoon by L.B. Stoddart in the final for the St. Andrews club cup. Stoddart won by two holes.

The professional tourney for four money prizes, $100 to first, brought out the finest professional golfers in the country and close scores were the result. Willie Danny of Shinnecock won by the fine score of 80. Davis of Newport came second, only two behind. Horace Rawlins of Newport, the new professional champion, got third place, and W. Campbell of Brookline, Mass., and Samuel Tucker of St. Andrews divided fourth money. The summaries:

WILLARD BROWN CUP TOURNAMENT

L.B. Stoddard	93	C.W. Barnes	102
A.L. Livermore	97	W.R. Innis	103
G.E. Armstrong	99	J. Lynch	107
J.F. Gray	99	W.F. Gray	107
W.H. Sands	100	R.S. Peters	111
H.G. Trevor	100	H.W. Taff	111
R.B. Kerr	101	F.A. Walthew	112

John Reid, J.B. Upham, and J.C. Teneyck withdrew from the match before completing their rounds.

The scores in the final of the St. Andrews cup contest are: L.B. Stoddard, 87; W.H. Sands, 90.

The scores in the professional match were: Willie Dunn, 80; W.F. Davis, 82; H. Rawlins, 84; W. Campbell, 86; S. Tucker, 86; W. Norton, 88.

H.J. Whigham offered suggestions on course construction in *How to Play Golf*, p. 215. He criticized Americans for their impetuous character, having failed to adhere to traditional British designs in their haste to adopt the sport.

COURSE CONSTRUCTION

...For the purpose of making an eighteen hole course, look out first for at least two hundred acres of the best pasture land, provided that you cannot get the genuine golf land by the sea. Avoid a clay soil.

Make your course seventy-five yards wide at every hole and remove every tree, ditch and stone from its surface.

Locate your putting greens first with regard to natural situation, and then model your distances upon the St. Andrews links in Scotland. Roll your course every spring, and keep it close cut with mowing machines in summer. Make your putting greens as perfect as the abundant use of water and the mowing machine will permit.

Let all your hazards be sand bunkers, with the addition of a water hazard if nature supplies it.

Make your bunkers large and varied in shape - you cannot make them too large - and guard all your putting greens either on one or upon every side.

Harper's Weekly, 6 November 1897, p. 1113, provided an example of such a transition.

A PHILADELPHIA GOLF COURSE

THE Country Club at Philadelphia, with its fine house and spacious grounds at Bala, has always been one of the leading social organizations of the Quaker City, but in its later development and present prosperity golf has been the active and indeed the magic agent. Three or four years ago, through the influence of Dr. Charles R. Claxton, the club laid out a tentative nine-hole course around the race course, and a few enthusiasts startd in to learn to play the game....

"A player who has done a round at the club will have passed over various points of avenue, steeple-chase course, race-track, polo-field, and pigeon-shooting grounds; but will have come triumphantly through a purgatorial stone-wall jump, a sand bunker and bastion, and, finally, a vast gravel pit or crater ... Stone walls, ploughed fields, quarries, fences, and chasms are among the other excellent sporting requirements of the course."

Now some one of an exact turn of mind may file an objection to this catalogue of horrors ... it gives point to Mr. Whigham's comment upon our American golf, that "this sort of thing is exactly what a golf links ought not to be, since a golfer is neither a jockey nor a quarryman."...

But now we have changed all that. In the spring of 1896 the club employed Willie Dunn to rearrange the course in conformity with recognized golfing conditions, and this was done at a cost of over $3000. The change was a great improvement, but it was found that a nine-hole course was too small to accommodate all who wished to play, and it was considered inadvisable to depend upon the good nature of the Park Commissioners for the use of that portion of the course that lay outside of the club property. And so, early in the present year, the Roberts farm of ninety-four acres was acquired by purchase, and plans were made for the laying out of a regular eighteen holes. The new ground was well fitted for the purpose, since the greater part of it had been used as a pasture for twenty-five years. The new course measures 5600 yards in playing distance, and when it is finally in shape it should rank with any in the country. The putting greens have been laid out upon a generous scale, the hazards are paced with excellent judgment, and, as before noted, the turf on the mid-green is of good golfing quality.

The club has now over six hundred names upon its membership list, divided into three classes of resident, non-resident, and army and navy. Resident members pay $50 in annual dues, and the other classes $25 yearly. The club-house is one of the largest and best-appointed in the country, and contains every possible luxury and convenience. W.G. van T. Sutphen

As golf became increasingly available to the middle class urban park districts began to supply sites for its practice. New York's Van Cortlandt Park course was the first; with others being established after 1900. Such public courses somewhat diminished the exclusive nature of the sport and made it more accessible to urban residents. The social nature of such undertakings was still evident in a New York Times article, 14 November 1900, p. 10.

VAN CORTLANDT GOLF CLUB

The Van Cortlandt Golf Club is going to close its season of activity with a concert to-morrow night in Carnegie Hall.... It is the intention to have on view at that time most of the silver trophies played for during the season, including the O'Connell Championship Cup, and Park Commissioner Moebus will present them to the various winners. H.E. Brown and P.F. Gilmartin will play the final round for the Championship Cup before the day of the concert.

As the year's activity of the Van Cortlandt Club will practically close with the coming concert and Vardon's exhibition on Saturday, it may not be amiss to say a few words regarding the success of the club's first year. If it has not accomplished all that some of its ardent organizers hoped for at the start, it has surely stimulated competitive golf at Van Cortlandt, and had given a more clublike tone to the public links. When the new golf and skatehouse now being erected by the side of the lake is finished the club will very likely secure a permanent room for its headquarters, and it will be enabled to exert a still more beneficent influence upon golf and its management at Van Cortlandt....

Enterprising entrepreneurs accommodated urban golfers by developing indoor practice sites as well. The Chicago Tribune, 10 November 1895, p. 5, described such an operation.

INDOOR GOLF FOR A WINTER GAME

Indoor golf is the latest development of the golf craze. It is a new game, and is a Chicago invention designed to furnish a winter substitute for the real outdoor article. H. Boakes, the Superintendent of the racket courts at the Chicago Athletic club, is the inventor of the game, and expects to have it in operation shortly at the club.

The main feature of the game that distinguishes it from other golf substitutes is the fact that the ordinary golf clubs and balls can be used. A canvas sheet is suspended from the ceiling across the end of the room or court. In the sheet are holes or pockets of various sizes, and heights from the ground. By placing the ball at different distances from the sheet the best of practice can be obtained in driving and lofting, and considerable skill will be necessary to strike the differnt pockets. The game will consist in playing into the different holes in rotation, and counting the number of strokes needed, much as in the genuine sport.

Mr. Boakes expects to install the new game in the court tennis court at the Chicago Athletic club. The court is 100 feet long by 40 feet wide and will give plenty of room for practice. The sheet will be hung across one end on a roller, so that it can be let down or raised out of the way. A mat will be used to drive from. As there are fifty or sixty golf enthusiasts in the Athletic club, it is expected the new game will prove popular as soon as started.

The amateur code, which the USGA wished to enforce, adhered to the principle of play for play's sake, as exemplified by a Harper's Weekly piece on 25 December 1897, p. 1298. The game, however, lent itself to wagering, and under such circumstances the idealized code of honor crumbled.

"CHEATING" AT GOLF

..."There is no cheating at golf." Certainly we had supposed that there was none ... the writer must confess that he regards it as very singular, if there be so much cheating on the links, that during a tolerably long experience, extending over a quarter of a century and over many greens, he cannot recall a single instance ... in all that time....It is so easy to transgress thoughtlessly, either in careless forgetfulness of a rule, or in careless grounding of a club, or stepping where the foot shall not fall. All these things are done, no doubt, and done by people who should know better....But all this is as far removed from cheating, with its horrid sense of moral depravity, as light is from darkness. ...And surely it is those thoughtless acts of inattention that form the slender basis on which all this momentous fabric of accusation is reared. Cheating - real intentional breaking of a rule in order to derive an illegal advantage - is, we may be confident, virtually unknown.... It is said that there are errors in counting -it may be so- but who is to prove that they are perpetrated of malice or forethought? ... Golfers who commit to their caddies the task of scoring for them are perhaps almost criminally careless, and put every temptation to cheating in the way of irresponsible little boys ... And if any transgressions are at all often committed ... they are far more frequently in the nature of those transgressions of the laws of etiquette, such as standing still and silent while the opponent is playing ... Cheating is really such a dreadful word, and conveys such a heinous degree of moral obliquity, that the very clearest proofs ought to be forth-coming before it is ever whispered....But really it is comforting to be able to assure America that this is not the spirit in which we play golf in this country. We break the rules now and then by accident ... But we do not cheat. No one cheats. Cheating is virtually non-existent, and even those golfers who are disposed to take every inch that the letter of the law allows them, while violating the purity of its spirit, are very rarely met with.... Let Americans be assured of this - that we try to play golf for pleasure, and not for profit, nor on the "win, tie, or wrangle" principle, far less do we cheat intentionally, or find such an odious practice as cheating at all common amongst us.... The game has its rules, and it should be played according to those rules, or else, ..."you don't know where you are." And the more strict the adherence to these rules the more pleasant the game becomes - only when the rule is transgressed it becomes the part of the transgressor, not of his opponent, to insist on the exaction of the uttermost penalty. All the opponent ought to be compelled to do - and he ought never to be compelled to do that much - is to inform the transgressor, in all courtesy, of his breach of the rule....

As golf became popular, gambling became prominent, even extraordinary, as shown by a Chicago Tribune story, 21 July 1900, p. 6.

UNIQUE WAGER BY GOLFERS
W.J. PATTON DRIVES FOUR AND A HALF MILES IN 119 STROKES

Pittsburg, Pa., July 20. -On a wager of $300, William J. Patton, the crack golfer of the Allegheny Country club, easily accomplished the unique feat early this morning of driving a golf ball along four and one-half miles of city streets in less than 150 strokes. Mr. Patton did it in exactly 119 strokes, or 31 inside the limit. The ball was driven from the house of the Allegheny Country club at Benton and California avenues, Allegheny, to the fashionable Pittsburg club on Penn avenue, this city. The task was undertaken as a result of an argument over driving a golf ball in city streets.

The start was made at 5 o'clock. The route was almost entirely over asphalt paving. The first part of the course was hardest and fifty strokes were required to cover the first mile. After that Patton did better and at one stage about a quarter of a mile was covered in two strokes. A pedestrian, a window, and a street car were struck by the flying ball at different points along the route. Several balls were lost on the route and Patton broke three clubs. Mr. Patton was followed over the course by a large crowd of clubmen and several thousand dollars were bet on the result of the experiment.

The "new woman" of the 1890s took readily to both cycling and golf. Both provided healthful exercise in the open air and an acceptable means to socialize with the opposite sex. Margaret Abbot, a Chicagoan on sojourn in Paris during the Olympic Games of 1900, won the gold medal in the golf competition, the first by an American woman. Chicago women were particularly visible on the links, as evident by a front page story in the Chicago Tribune, 10 September 1895.

IS WON BY A CHILD

Little "Johnny" Carpenter won the women's match in the golf tournament on the Wheaton links yesterday. She easily defeated the fashionable women who were her opponents, and as the child is far from being a society favorite some of the women said they wouldn't play. But "Johnny" beat them all and carried off the medal.

In spite of her masculine name "Johnny" is a girl. She was christened John Anna Carpenter and is the 14-year-old stepdaughter of Archibald H. Smith of Oak Park. The trouble began when she first came upon the links. Her costume was not exactly the regulation thing; at least it did not resemble those worn by other women present. But it answered the purpose. She wore a short, brown skirt with a white shirt waist, the sleeves of which were rolled up to the shoulders and displayed well-formed but muscular arms, browned by exposure to the sun. Most of the players knew her, as she has frequently acted as a "caddie" on the grounds of the Illinois Golf club, and she was soon surrounded by a group of men. With them she was a favorite; with the women she wasn't.

When she marched upon the link she carried under her arm a bundle of golf sticks and several balls. The sticks were a dilapidated lot and were some that the child had picked up after they had been discarded by grown-up players. The balls were in as disreputable a condition, but they suited "Johnny," being the best she had. Before she could begin play she found it necessary to repair some of her sticks which had renewed their former fractures and splits. She bravely began the task without help, but Stuyvesant Le Roy soon came to her assistance and had sticks and balls in working shape.

Then when the time came for the women's match there was a little trouble. Some of the other contestants objected to "Johnny" taking part and said it would be unfair. Just why it would be so they did not say. Perhaps it was because the child was known to have shown much proficiency in practice play. But the men came to the rescue and said "Johnny" had a right to enter the match, as she had been elected an honorary member of the club a year ago, before the other women joined. In spite of this the women didn't think it fair that "Johnny" should compete. Several of the woman had positively refused to play with the child and it looked as if the match might have to be called off when Mrs. C.W. Cramer came to the rescue and offered to play with "Johnny." Then Mr. LeRoy again appeared as her champion and picking up her sticks agreed to act as her caddie.

That settled the trouble and everything began to move smoothly. The contest between Mrs. Cramer and "Johnny" was watched by a majority of the spectators who followed them over the entire course. Both players started off well, "Johnny's" first drive sailing skyward ahead of any previous effort. Her performance was applauded as was that of her magnanimous opponent. They played a fast game and fine strokes on both sides elicited frequent applause. "Johnny" made the first hole by a score of 6 strokes to her opponent's 7. The next hole was made more easily than the first by a score of 8 to 11. The next hole "Johnny" increased her lead by one point, winning 8 to 12. Mrs. Cramer now began playing a stronger game and the next was a tied hole, 7 to 7. The playing now became a little slower, but Miss Carpenter took the rest of the course.

"Johnny" Wins the Match

At the finish her total score was announced when it developed that the child was the winner of the medal. Mrs. Cramer was the first to congratulate her on her success.

The other matches in the contest were all well contested. The scores:

Mrs. C.W. Cramer .... 101 strokes
Miss J. Annie Carpenter .... 69 strokes
Mrs. Adams .... 75 strokes
Miss Julia Day .... 98 strokes
Mrs. Shearson .... 82 strokes
Mrs. Chatfield-Taylor .... 74 strokes
Miss Annie Day .... 104 strokes
Mrs. McBirney .... 93 strokes

The course in the women's match was but half the regular course, being nine holes in extent.

Little "Johnny" has had a good deal of practice in golf, though she has never been in a match before yesterday. Last year she frequently acted as a "caddie" at the links of the Illinois Golf club at Belmont, and, like most "caddies," indulged in practice play when the grounds were not in use. In this way she acquired the skill which enabled her to win the match yesterday....

Outlook provided an historical glimpse of early women golfers, the development of golf etiquette, and the social dynamics that insured male privilege on the golf course in an article on 3 June 1899, pp. 249-257.

THE GOLFING WOMAN

NOT long ago a young woman entered a shop where golfing goods are sold and asked the salesman to make her up a set of clubs, as she intended to go in for golf in earnest. The shopkeeper handed her a beautifully balanced driver, with the remark that it was a new model and especially designed for ladies' use.

"But I don"t want a lady's club," explained the young woman indignantly. "I am going to play real golf over the men's course, and I want a man's club to do it with."

Well, of course she got what she wanted, but in getting it she probably threw away at the outset whatever chance she might have had of playing "real golf." And now for the moral of this profitable little tale....What sort of "real golf" can a woman expect to play?

It is only within a comparatively few years that women were supposed to play golf at all; and their position abroad is largely a matter of sufferance. It was customary at one time in England and Scotland to set aside a small portion of the regular links to be used as a woman's course ... The holes were necessarily of the shortest, varying from seventy-five yards down to ten; but in the aspirations of the feminine golfer were supposed to be confined to the noble exercise of putting....

In this country the feminine golfer has received due consideration from the very start; but then it must be remembered that golf in the United States owes a great deal to women. One of the largest and best known clubs in the country, the Morris County, of Morristown, New Jersey, was originally started and managed by women alone; and women have had a very considerable part in the organizing and maintenance of the thousand and one other clubs at which golf is now played....

In the vast majority of American clubs men and women hold membership on virtually equal terms, and the latter have, consequently, been entitled from the beginning to the use of the full or regular course. In some cases, as at St. Andrews (Yonkers), the women players are restricted to certain days in the week, and at many of the popular and overcrowded courses the men have exclusive rights on Saturdays and holidays. The one prominent exception to this general rule is the Shinnecock Hills Club on Long Island.

The Shinnecock Hills Club ... added an entirely separate one of nine holes, to be known as the "red" course, and intended for the use of the feminine and junior members. No woman could play regularly over the "white" or full course until she had qualified by making the "red" course three separate times in certain minimum figures. It should be said that the "red" course is not a mere succession of putting-holes, the links varying from two hundred yards down to seventy-five.

...One of the "graduates" of the "red" course is Miss Beatrix Hoyt, for three years holder of the woman's championship; and among the other members of the club we may note the names of Mrs. Charles Brown (winner of the first women's contest at Meadowbrook, 1895) and Mrs. Arthur Turnure (silver medalist at Morris County in 1896). But of even more significance is the fact that the "red" course is soon to be enlarged and rearranged under the direct supervision of the women players themselves....

Miss Beatrix Hoyt can outdrive, on the average, seven out of ten of her masculine rivals. She has acquired the knack of getting the ball away clean, and can count upon an average distance of one hundred and twenty to one hundred and sixty yards.... But let Miss Hoyt be matched against Mr. Findlay Douglas, and what happens? Miss Hoyt hits the ball clean, and gets, let us say, a carry and a roll of one hundred and sixty yards - her best ball. Douglas does the same thing, and drives over two hundred yards. Up to a certain point, skill may equalize matters, but after that it is simply a question of muscle. The amateur champion of Great Britain is credited with a drive that (carefully measured) was a few inches over three hundred and forty-one yards. No feminine golf-player has ever come within one hundred and fifty yards of that record, or ever will, so long as men are men and women women.

But we must look for the average and not the exception. First-class driving, from the masculine standpoint, may be anything over one hundred and sixty yards, and it will be fair to place the average ... at one hundred and forty yards.... how many feminine players may be fairly counted as coming up to this average standard of one hundred forty yards of loft? At the championship meeting in 1897 Miss Madeline Boardman won the long-driving competition by a carry and roll of 137 yards, 6 inches, and Miss Hoyt drove 131 yards, 7 inches. At Ardsley, last October, the victor in the same competition was Mrs. Edward Manice with 134 yards 1 1/4 inches. Well, granting that my point is made, what does it prove?

Simply, then, that it is the average standard of play that must be taken into account in the laying out and subsequent development of the first-class golf course, and this average cannot be the same for both men and women players.... our American courses are being gradually conformed to first-class standards, and this implies rearrangement of the holes, not in length alone, but in the position of the hazards. And for these changes it is inevitable that the masculine average will alone be taken into account.

...Other things being equal, the woman's long game must lose to that of the man; and, indeed, the two quantities are incommensurate. For the highest exercise of her art, the woman golfer of the future must not only have her clubs but the course fitted to her hand.

There is one variety of golf, however, in which the woman does hold her own, and that is the "mixed foursome," in which she is partnered with a masculine player against another pair similarly constituted. Here her comparative driving weakness is halved, and if her short game is brilliant it may be of inestimable service. A mixed foursome at golf is much more satisfactory form of amusement than a mixed double at tennis. In the latter case, the man usually would do all the work, or else had to. In golf there is a fair division of labor ... Moreover, the mixed foursome is an admirable school for the disciplining of one's temper ...

"It is a hard lot to follow a party of ladies, with a powerful driver behind you, if you are troubled with a spark of chivalry or shyness." So speaks one of the Badminton authorities ... The tender mercies of the long-driving male golfer are cruel, and a three-ball match between women players is apt to be a trifle slow. In justice to the feminine golfer it must be said that she is generally quick to recognize the situation, and to beckon the unhappy one to come on...

As a matter of reference, I append a few statistics relating to the National competitions for the women's championship of the United States.

The first meeting was held on November 10, 1895, upon the course of the Meadowbrook (Long Island) Club. The contest was under the rules for stroke play, and was won by Mrs. Charles S. Brown, of the Shinnecock Club, with a score of 132. Miss Sargent, of the Essex County (Mass.) Club was second.

At the beginning of the next season it was announced that Mr. Robert Cox, M.P., of Edinburgh, Scotland, had presented a silver cup to the United States Golf Association as a perpetual trophy in the women's championship meeting. The gift was accepted, and the Association took formal charge of the annual event.

The first regular championship meeting was held upon the course of the Morris County Club, October 6-10, 1896. There were twenty-five entries, and the winner was Miss Beatrix Hoyt, of the Shinnecock Hills Club. Mrs. Arthur Turnure (Shinnecock Hills) received the silver medal, and the bronze went to Miss Anna Sands (Newport) and to Miss Cora Oliver (Albany).

The second championship meeting was held upon the course of the Essex County (Mass.) Club, August 24-27, 1897. Miss Hoyt repeated her victory of the year before. Miss Sargent, of the home club, was the runner-up, and the bronze medals went to Miss Frances C. Griscom (Merion Cricket Club, Philadelphia), and to Miss C.E. Longworth (Cincinnati).

The third championship meeting was held upon the course of the Ardsley Club (Irvington-on-Hudson), October 11-15, 1898. For the third time Miss Hoyt became the champion, Miss Maud Wetmore (Newport) taking the silver medal, and the bronze ones going to Miss Frances Griscom (Merion Cricket Club, Philadelphia), and to Miss Carl Eidlitz (Ardsley)....

CANADA

Given to more direct British influence, Canadians adopted golf more readily than their American cousins. There is some evidence of short, three hole golf courses operating in Quebec during the 1860s; but the founding of the Montreal Golf Club by Canadian Scots in 1873 is considered to be the first in North America. The Montreal Golf Club offered women's competition by 1881. Interprovincial matches occurred by 1893 and the Canadian Golf Association was established by 1895. That same year Canada hosted a tournament billed as the American championship, and the Royal Canadian Golf Association hosted the first national amateur championship.

The Montreal Gazette offered only a terse announcement of the local championship, 1 November 1887, n.p.

ROYAL MONTREAL GOLF CLUB

The champion belt for colts was played for on Saturday last, notwithstanding the unfavorable weather, the winner being the Rev. G.C. Heine, with a score of 91.

James P. Lee's *Golf in America*, pp. 88-93, provides greater detail.

GOLF IN CANADA

... a few words should be added concerning golf in Canada. The Scottish pastime there has an older history than we can boast of on this side of the border....As early as 1873 the game was started by the foundation of the Royal Montreal Golf Club; in the year following, the Quebec Club was organized, and shortly afterwards, in 1876, the game was played for the first time in Toronto. These three clubs are the chief amongst the Canadian homes of golf, although the game is played in many other places. The Niagara Golf Club, on the Canada shore of the Niagara River, was founded in 1882, and a little later an excellent club was organized at Kingston, and another at Ottawa in 1891. The Deer Park Club in Toronto, and the London and Hamilton Clubs, which were both founded last year, must also be mentioned.

Of all these, the Quebec green is by far the most interesting and picturesque. Here the game is played over the Cove Fields, which are not far distant from the citadel ... the course abounds in hazards of various kinds ... The old French bastion forms one of the hazards; and, indeed, it may be said, that there is every possible hazard upon the course, with the exception of sand; of that there is none. But the old French fort and earthworks, and precipices, together with moats, rocks and swamps, provide more than enough to harass even the expert.

...the Royal Montreal Golf Club ... is well known for its open hospitality and welcome to strangers. The game is played here over Fletcher's Field, which lies at the base of a mountain ... The course is much smaller than is the case at Quebec ... The distances between the holes are rather short, for in most cases a good drive and an iron shot is sufficient to bring the player upon the putting-green.... These two clubs are old rivals, and the great golfing events of the year to them are the two semi-annual matches, one of which is played in Quebec and the other in Montreal. These matches have been played for the past twenty years, and never fail to excite the greatest interest in that part of the country.

It is the boast of the Toronto Golf Club that it possesses the only eighteen hole course in the country. The game was started in that city as early as 1876, but it was not until 1882 that it obtained a strong footing at "Fernhill," the present links of the Toronto Golf Club....A characteristic of the Canadian links is their great natural beauty; especially is this true of Quebec, Toronto, and Niagara....

Visitors to Niagara certainly remember the Queen's Royal Hotel upon the Canadian shore of the river. It is upon the grounds of this hotel that the golf course of the Niagara Golf Club is laid out. The course is only a mile and a half in extent at present, and consists of nine holes; it could easily be lengthened, however, so as to afford eighteen holes. The hazards are broken ground, old fortifications, embankments, water-ditches and a sandy shore....

Chapter 12

GYMNASTICS

Formal gymnastics became a part of the school curriculum in the 1880s, largely through the efforts of immigrant groups. In cities with sizeable German populations, such as Chicago, St. Louis, Cincinnati, and Milwaukee, the Turner societies held power and influence on school boards. Other areas favored the Swedish or French systems. By the 1880s Dudley Sargent, director of the Harvard gymnasium, had introduced his American system.

By that time the interest in interscholastic athletics began to displace formal gymnastics, although they remained a part of high school curriculums well into the twentieth century. Gymnastics continued to flourish in the ethnic fraternal societies, where they helped to imbue a nationalistic spirit and cultural traditions. The ethnic groups tried to maintain contact with their mother country and other American groups through gymnastic competitions.In 1881 the German Turners traveled to Frankfurt for a month; and in later years Czech and Polish contingents followed their example or hosted their foreign compatriots.

In 1881 the Germans instituted the North American Gymnastics Union in Milwaukee as a teacher training school. The Sargent School and the Boston Normal School of Gymnastics, the latter of which became part of Wellesley College in 1909, trained instructors on the East coast. In 1889, Mary Hemenway, a Boston philanthropist, sponsored a major conference on the various gymnastic systems, but it failed to establish any one system as dominant.

The first gymnastics championship in the United States was held in 1885. Tumbling was added the following year, and the rope climb became an event in 1888. Gymnastics appeared as part of the original Olympic program in 1896. The Amateur Athletic Union obtained governance of the U.S. championships in 1897, when the long horse, side horse, and all-around competitions were added to the program. New York University hosted the first intercollegiate championship with eighteen schools participating in March, 1899. Eight of the schools organized as the Intercollegiate Gymnastics Union.

ETHNIC GYMNASTICS

Ethnic gymnastic societies included all classes; but the Germans, and some Czech units, known as sokols, favored a socialistic philosophy. Both were very active in the labor movement of the latter nineteenth century. Women sometimes served in auxiliary units, but often formed their own gymnastic groups. Czech women, in particular, held prominent leadership positions within the sokol system. Polish falcon units, however, were more clearly tied to the Catholic church, and usually operated within the context of clerical dictates.

The following excerpts from the Foreign Language Press Survey of ethnic newspapers give an indication of such operations. The first three are reprinted from the Svornost, a Czech paper, on 8 November 1883; 28 August 1884; and 8 September 1890.

LADIES GYMNASTIC SOCIETY

Our continuous calls, that the young Bohemian girls should organize a gymnastic society is now an accomplished fact. Bohemian girls, assembled in our Bohemian "Pilzen" Hall, unanimously decided to found such an organization and judging from the accomplished deed, we are assured that this new society will properly proceed in its work toward prosperity.

Yesterday at 7 p.m. they started the exercises for the first time and the number of "Falcon" girls was considerable. Many new members filled out the membership applications. We hope that, in the future, the "Ladies Falcon Association" will reach the high point of prosperity. The new association will operate and exercise under supervision of the "Pilzen-Falcons" until the ladies shall be able to choose a capable instructress from among themselves.

THIRD GYMNASTIC COMPETITION

After two days of strenuous competitive gymnastics, results and prizes were published yesterday. Today we give the report of the results of the competition, which was conducted in a manner satisfactory to all sokols.

Yesterday afternoon the judges were busy counting the points, and as it usually happens, there were some disagreements about fencing: whether it should be regarded in the same class as the ordinary exercises on the gymnastic apparatus. Opposition was voiced by those Sokols who do not fence, but, finally, the sokols who do fence forced their motion over and fencing points were counted the same as points received on other competitive exercises on the gymnastic apparatus.

While the judges perspired counting the points made by individual competitors, thre Sokols employed their leisure by sightseeing the city and its parks. After the sightseers returned home, they made preparations for a dance in the Bohemian-American Sokol Hall, at which the results would be announced and where the fencing would be held. The dance hall was filled with the participants in the festival. Our pretty young girls dressed in white attracted everybody. After 10 P.M. there started on the stage the fencing contest in which eight Sokols participated.... After the fencing between individual Sokols, the first prize was awarded to Kostlan from Milwaukee; second to Kadlec, New York, and third to Novy, Chicago. The curtain was lowered and the Sokols and their guests continued to dance. Late in the evening Sokol J.B. Belohradski, chairman of the National Sokol Union, announced the results.

Three prizes for exercises in formation were granted: first to the contingent from New York Sokols; second to the Bohemian-American Sokols of Chicago; third to the Pilzen Sokols of Chicago. For individual exercises thirty-three prizes were awarded to various Sokols... The dance entertainment continued until early in the morning and we can state positively that the excellent exercises were rewarded with complete success and attracted unexpected attention from other nationalities.

"SOKOL" DAY

How the Bohemian public values the sincere gymnastic efforts and rewards their earnest unselfish work was shown yesterday. The gigantic premises of the second regiment State militia, the largest place of its kind in the city, was filled to overflowing with our public yesterday and the attendance, the enthusiasm which prevailed in the Armory, the enthusiastic shouting, which welcomed the ranks of the "Sokols," should be an incentive for our "Sokols" to further united efforts.

The gymnasts, marching to the music of Mr. Kounovsky's excellent band, and with the sprightly women gymnasts in their midst, proudly strutted through the streets, loudly greeted by strangers; our women gymnasts especially were pleasing to everyone. It was unnecessary for anyone to ask what the parade represented - Bohemian Sokols are well known to the local public and who ever had time joined the parade and accompanied the Sokols to the Armory in order to witness their exercises.

At three o'clock, when the building was filled (it is estimated that there were fully three thousand people present) the signal was given and the gymnasts with their instructor Karl Stulik appeared in a body; the applause which greeted these hearty men, fairly shook the building. When the gymnasts took positions preparatory to the calisthenic exercises, Mr. J. Cermak delivered a short welcoming address, explaining to the gathering that the Sokol Societies are not merely pleasure societies, but that their gymnasiums are teachers of a better, more sturdy generation; that in gymnastic institutions can be gained that which makes men on earth more fortunate, that is health, that it is possible through proper exercise to develop those characteristics which are the aim of every ideeal man, these are strength, courage, manliness and morality. After the speech the calisthenic exercises were performed; fairly difficult combination acts were performed correctly with such apparent ease as to cause a continuous outburst of applause; the Americans present were entirely enraptured and today's papers repeat the praises of Bohemian Gymnasts and liken the Bohemian people to the Spartans who laid such great importance upon physical development.

Our women gymnasts awakened justified enthusiasm by their appearance. Their exercises with wands, were performed with such elegance and perfection, that a storm of applause greeted their every movement, and there is no doubt that the ranks of our women gymnasts will grow even more from now on....

The next two selections appeared in Polish newspapers, Zgoda, 14 August 1892; and Dziennik Chicagoski, 23 August 1893.

ANNOUNCEMENT OF THE POLISH FALCONS

On the 17th of this month, the delegates of the Polish Falcons gathered in Chicago and decided to take energetic steps to encourage the establishment of Polish Falcon organizations in every Polish community throughout the continent. In order that this important matter be thoroughly considered, the delegates decided to call a mass meeting of Polish Falcons for August 27, to which all well-wishing Poles are invited to attend. As a result of this decision, the following article... was submitted for publication:

"'A sound mind in a sound body'" - this is the principle upon which all gymnastic and Falcon societies have been founded. The mind can be strong and active only if the body is strong and healthy. A deed conceived in the mind can only be executed by a strong, enduring hand. Thus, the body should be trained so that, through its physical strength and health, it may constitute the foundation for action. The aim of the Falcon organizations is to provide this training, but ordinarily they serve still another purpose - that of giving us a chance to work and struggle together. By bringing us together, they foster a greater sense of brotherhood among young men, binding them in friendship and teaching them discipline. 'Unity is life, disunity death,' is the motto adopted by some of the Falcon nests.

"It is needless to expain further the usefulness of Falconry. Its usefulness was well understood in Poland. In Galicia and Poznan, wherever political conditions permitted, hundreds of Falcon nests have been organized - hundreds of Falcon banners unfurled. Solemn days such as those of the Falcon Jubilee in Lwow last year awaken and elevate the spirit; they strengthen the ties of brotherhood and tend to give the Falcons the character of a national organization.

...Do the examples of our brethren in Poland and by our Bohemian cousins mean nothing to us here in America? ... "No! We Poles, occupied with a desparate struggle for existence, perhaps do not lead in certain respects, but in this case, we can keep up with others....

"Let us therefore spread our wings in flight! Polish Falcon activities have already begun in Chicago, and though the number of Falcons is still small, there will be enough for a nest ... in other cities and towns wherever Polish hearts beat... A few dollars for gymnastic equipment; good will on the part of the youth, who instead of spending their time in saloons at immoral pastimes will find decent recreation and spiritual and physical gain in the Falcons' hall; a teacher or organizer ... is all that is necessary for the creation of a new Falcon nest....

NEW GYMNASTIC SOCIETY FOR YOUNG POLISH WOMEN

There was organized in the northwest part of Chicago a Polish gymnastic society for young Polish women. Its practical uses are extensive. The organizers of this new society are concerned above all about the beneficial results derived from it for the health of Polish women, who sometimes work hard and waste their strength. Secondly, it is our intention to furnish our young ladies pleasant exercise, in their own circle, and above that, awaken in their hearts and souls the desire for higher accomplishments through elevating the spirit by mutual work for the good of all.

...We will direct our work toward national aims.... The next meeting will take place, September 18, 1892, at 5 P.M. in Greenwald's Hall ... In this hall we have our gymnastic exercises every Wednesday, beginning at 8 o'clock.

As evidenced by the announcement in Svornost, 8 February 1892, the ethnic societies hoped to influence the mainstream culture to accept their beliefs. At the World's Fair, held in Chicago in 1893, thousands of German Turners displayed their skills in a synchronized routine. While the Germans in particular had some success in introducing gymnastics into the schools and specific events into American competitions, the fraternal groups eventually fell victim to the assimilation process as their offspring adopted American sport forms and World War I taxed their allegiance.

GYMNASTIC EXHIBITION AT WORLD'S FAIR
BOHEMIAN-AMERICAN SOKOLS PREPARE FOR DIGNIFIED APPEARANCE

A meeting was held last Saturday by the Gymnastic Teachers Club of the Public Schools in which was discussed the feasibility of holding a great intrnational gymnastic celebration in Chicago during the period of the World's Fair. German gymnasts have already taken preliminary steps in this direction and have worked up a partial program, according to which, the celebration is to be of such colossal proportions as have never before been seen here. The main purpose of this gymnastic exhibition is to show Americans the results of systematic gymnastics, such as are cultivated by the German Turners, the Bohemian Sokols and gymnastic clubs of other nationalities, and thereby convert Americans to this system.

On 5 May 1895, p. 13, the New York Times featured an historical sketch of one of the prominent turner societies in the city.

A PIONEER TURN VEREIN

The history of the New York Turn Verein "Bloomingdale" is replete with the vicissitudes that all German societies of antebellum origin had to encounter. All of the

German societies of the past generation had to battle hard for existence, but this institution had more than its share of hardships, and its present existence is due to an allegiance of unusual faithfulness. So impecunious was this club during its first few years that its members frequently expressed considerable surprise when they found the headquarters in the same building for two or three consecutive months.

The first organization of this association was formed in 1851, under the name, "Bloomingdale Turn Verein School and Gymnasium." It was the outgrowth of the New York Turn Verein, some of whose members lived on the west side of the town, who, with their friends, came to the conclusion that that section was ripe for a German association whose object should be to promote physical and intellectual culture, according to the plan of these institutions.

...They obtained a short lease on a small piece of ground on West Thirtieth Street, which exhausted all their means.... irrespective of the fact that there was no probability of a treasury ... they started to build a meeting house.

... This little force of builders contained mechanics of almost all trades ... but they were novices of that particular branch of industry.... The down-town turners viewed this quaint shanty with much amusement, and many a pleasant joke was had with its impromptu builders. But it answered their purpose, and the one large room was utilized as a gymnasium, a school for the children, and a hall where the entertainments and meetings also took place.

...The cheerful melodies of the Fatherland were frequently heard in this crude hall, and even German comedies were presented in it...

These few stalwarts ... frequently found it cheaper to move than to pay rent, and the first few years the society changed its quarters often on very short notice.... The enthusiasm of these turners attracted new members, and in 1859 there were one hundred and fifty names on its rolls.

With this membership list a large wooden building at 316 West Thirty-sixth Street was converted into a turner hall, and there they remained during the war. Fully one-quarter of these turners joined the Union Army at the outset of the war, and this, again, crippled the society.

One of its members, Adolph Senger, was one of the captors of John Wilkes Booth, after the assassination of President Lincoln, for which Mr. Senger received $700 as his share of the reward offered by the government....

Two lots were purchased on Forty-seventh Street, upon one of which a hall of brick and stone was erected in 1873. This hall was dedicated January 26, 1874 ... the property was sold to satisfy the debts of the Turn Verein ... in 1882 there were just seventy faithfuls ... eighteen men reorganized under the name of the New York Turn Verein "Bloomingdale," July 26, 1883.

At that meeting Otto Pullich was elected Speaker, and, the members having paid their monthly dues of fifty cents each, there was a fund of $9 in the treasury. An energetic canvass was made among the Germans of the west side, and at the close of the year there were two hundred members enrolled.

The old premises at 341 West Forty-seventh Street were rented, and there, in May, 1884, the ladies organized, and presented a flag to the Turn Verein. With the aid of the women the Verein became more active....

A mass meeting ... was held May 23, 1886, for the purpose of devising ways and means to give the Turn Verein the needed financial aid ... It was finally decided to hold a fair...

It was largely owing to the efforts of the women that this project met with a successful outcome.... The fair netted $10,000, and to this the members succeeded in adding $5,000 in donations.... with this amount the subject of erecting a large hall... was agitated.

...during the latter part of 1887... Manhattan Hall...was purchased and arranged to suit the plans of the turners. The dedication took place on June 4, 1888...

...It became a member of the North American Turner Bund, and has taken part in all of the national turnfests. At the twenty-fifth national festival, held at Cincinnati in June, 1889, the company from the Turn Verein "Bloomingdale" received four honorary prizes. At the fourteenth district festival the groups of the Bloomingdale turners won first prize. At this exhibition the school of this society was represented by seventy turners of the younger classes.

At all subsequent festivals the society was seen to advantage, and frequently was among the prize winners. At the last national turnfest, which was held in Milwaukee last year, its delegation captured one of the honorary prizes of the highest grade....

In addition to this are the classes of the boys and girls, and the schools in German under the supervision of Franz Graf, who is aldso the editor of the society's paper, "The Bloomingdale," published weekly. These classes number about five hundred, and show a high standard of advancement. The hours of these schools are arranged so that they do not conflict with the public schools, in which the turners are stanch believers. There are industrial classes and object teaching, besides lessons in German, drawing, and singing. This is one of the first requisites of a turn verein, and upon these schools do they build the hope of future existence.

CANADA

In a document obtained from the National Archives of Canada the chairman of its gymnastics committee reported to the Montreal Amateur Athletic Association on the very limited accomplishments of the club in 1881.

REPORT OF THE GYMNASTICS COMMITTEE

GENTLEMEN:

I have much pleasure herewith in presenting the Report for the past season of the department of this Association over which I have the honor to preside.

The season has been a successful one as far as attendance is concerned, the average being greater than last year, viz: 32 3/4, as against 26 for last season; the largest for any one night being 53 and the smallest 12. The average was greatest in November, viz: 44, and the least in February and March, viz: 20. For each month, the average attendance was as follows: Oct., 40; Nov. 44; Dec., 39; Jan., 28; Feb., 20; Mar., 21.

The standard of proficiency, however, has fallen short, which may be attributed mainly to the great proportion of new members and comparatively inferior gymnasts attending the classes, among whom, however, the progress made is more noticeable than among older members, who might be expected to do better. This is especially noticeable in the results of the late competition, the winner (Mr. Gwilt) failing to score sufficient marks to enntitle him to the "Championship" medal, which was accordingly withdrawn under the regulations governing the competition. In contrast to this, Mr. Paterson, the winner of the "green" medal, may be complimented on the degree of proficiency attained.

...our late instructor, Mr. Liddell ... deserves praise ... for the attention given to the interests of the classes under his charge.

The Association may be congratulated on the efficient condition of the apparatus, the same being now very complete and in good order with the exception of the mattresses, which will require restuffing and repairs for next season.

I have the honor to be,
SAMUEL L. BAYLIS,
Chairman. Gym. Com.

Chapter 13

LACROSSE

Lacrosse, a game indigenous to many native American Indian tribes, never achieved the status in the United States that it enjoyed in Canada. A National Lacrosse League started in 1879 with the adoption of Canadian rules, and a championship match was held at Newport, Rhode Island that year. Most competition occurred between Boston and New York teams and those from Canada. In 1880 the Americans achieved their first victory over a touring Canadian team in Boston. Harvard won an intercollegiate title in New York the following year, and the Intercollegiate Lacrosse Association was established in 1882. A select All-American team made a trip abroad in 1884, winning nine of its eleven games in England and Ireland.

Lacrosse spread throughout the Midwest, but internecine squabbles led to the termination of the national association in 1888. The AAU took over governance of lacrosse in the United States in 1890 and established regional tournaments. The use of professional players brought controversy and expulsions within a year. The AAU offered its last national championship in 1893. By that time the Crescent Athletic Club of Brooklyn fielded a team which was to dominate American lacrosse for more than forty years. In March, 1897 the Crescent team embarked on a successful tour of the British Isles.

The latter part of the century witnessed a number of technological innovations. Stevens Institute of Pennsylvania initiated the use of goal nets in 1897. The next year a Johns Hopkins University player experimented with a short stick that allowed for greater control and a more proficient passing game. The resultant "Hopkins system" allowed it to win several intercollegiate championships and was widely copied. The interest in lacrosse remained largely an eastern phenomenon and its growth and development occurred mainly in New England and the mid-Atlantic states.

An Outing article of June, 1894, pp. 212-215, described lacrosse as played by two Indian teams.

AN INDIAN BALL GAME

A number of different tribes of Indians, more especially those living in the Indian Territory, such as the Choctaws, Cherokees, Chickasaws, etc., have a national game of ball which they have played for generations. The game has never varied from year to year, though the methods of playing it differ slightly among the several tribes. The sticks used are made of strong pieces of oak or hickory about two feet in length. At the end a thin flat piece of the wood is bent in the form of a loop and laced across with thongs of buckskin. This is just large enough to hold the ball, which is much smaller than a base ball. One stick is carried in each hand; the wrists are crossed when the ball is in play. The player is not permitted to touch the ball with anything but the sticks. In fact the game is lacrosse to all intents and purposes, though it also offers an interesting analogy to football.

...Nowadays the games are only between different counties of the same nation. In such games from twenty to thirty men play on each side. The contest I shall describe was between the Sugar Loaf and Gaines County teams of the Choctaw Nation and took place in a beautiful open prairie surrounded by old oak trees, above which the peaks of the Cavinal Mountains frowned.

The ball players came on the field just as the setting sun cast its long shadows from the monarch oaks almost across the glade. From far away came a series of weird sounds, a low deep monotonous chant given in regular time, but occasionally varied by the most ear-piercing screeches. The chanting became almost appalling as it grew gradually louder and louder, but it never abated. Soon the players rode into view, about thirty fine-looking Indians ... A dozen Choctaw boys ,.. rode with the cavalcade, darting round and round the dignified men... Last of all came the squaws and children in wagons and on ponies.

Then from the opposite direction came similar sounds and the opposing team appeared at the other end of the prairie. Following their respective captains they dashed forward at full speed, uttering their war cries and brandishing their ball sticks. When they reached the center of the field each band halted, saluted, and wheeling their horses rode back to their own goal post. Circling around their goal posts, each party shouted its war cry and chanted an incantation to their god of sport to grace their banners with victory on the morrow.

After this ceremony the players returned to partake of the supper prepared by their squaws, who always attend, and evince the liveliest interest in the games. While the play goes on they carry pails of hot coffee to the players and encourage them with their cheers.

The ball field is laid out on a piece of level prairie and is marked by two goal posts about one thousand feet apart. The game consists in driving the ball against the opponents goal so that it rebounds inside a line drawn through the posts at right angles to the axis of the field. Two planks set up side by side about fourteen feet long are now used as goal posts in place of the old hewn posts which were put up by the Choctaws in 1857 when they first came to this reservation from Mississippi.

Nearly all the games take place during the full moon, and after the evening meal the two parties assembled again in the moonlight on the ball gorund. The older men from both sides formed a circle in the exact center of the field and there agreed upon the rules governing the next day's play and settled any complaints about "imported" or "professional" players. The athletes, meanwhile, where in charge of the medicine man who, dressed in some fantastic garb, got them into their ball costume, which consists of a breech clout. He then led them to their goal posts, around which they circled, beating them with their ball sticks and singing all the while some incantation which was supposed to bring good luck. The conjurer also led them in a march, during which they chanted, as they walked, until he decided that sufficient had been done to gain them the victory on the morrow. Then they dispersed to join the squaws in a wild dance on the turf by the light of the moon....

The next morning the whole camp was up at sunrise, and soon all the country for miles around turned out ... the ball players came running out of the woods on the opposite side of the prairie. The dusky figures, naked except for gay breech clouts and daubs of red paint on their faces, whirling their ball sticks and yelling and screeching like demons ...

The captain of each team called all his men together and seated them in a circle while he instructed them in the rules made the night before. All the available men in each county were thus seated, and the captain, standing in the middle of the circle, studied all the faces carefully. Then, walking around the circle, he touched each player that he wanted to take part in the game. A number of very sour visages were left after this choosing. There was no appeal, however, from the captain's decision; and so, after a bit of guttural grumbling, those who were not chosen left the circle to resume their every-day garments and take the chaffing of their friends as best they could.

When two counties are playing, local feeling runs high, and one of the features of the day is the "bettor" or go-between. He is mounted on a pony, loaded down till he looks like the White Knight in "Alice Through the Looking Glass," and carries anything and everything that is betted. He ties the articles together; thus you will see a pair of boots traded for a shawl, or several small aticles for a coat, and if the owner of the coat wins he takes everything tied to it. Sometimes the betting is carried to such lengths that the Choctaw trades everything he owns, pony and all, but the clothes he stands in....

At last all the final arrangements were completed, all the bets were made, and the two teams, led by their captains on horseback, ranged up facing each other in the center of the field. The ball sticks were laid on the grass in front of each player and carefully counted to prove that the number of players was the same for each county. The captains then distributed their men over the entire field, leaving about six of what might be called rushers in the center to follow the ball as closely as possible. The balance of the players were scattered from one goal post to the other in couples, one from each side in every pair. Each team placed its best players to protect its goal. The lightest and fleetest runners were stationed about halfway between the goals, while the heaviest men, the rushers, followed the ball to tackle an adversary if he had it or to ward off attacks on their own players when running with the ball.

To put the ball in play the umpire threw it in the air so that it fell among the rushers in the middle of the field. A wild scramble ensued ... the ball was finally brought out by one of the light runners; but his race was short, for in less than a second he had three men on top of him. He quickly toossd the ball back toward one of his side. That man was also quick, but his adversary was very much alive; so instead of his securing the ball he was grabbed by one leg and thrown with a thud. He pulled his assailant down with him, and they rolled over and over in the grass until the bystanders rushed in and separated them. This was repeated all through the game. What lacrosse players would term close hard checking was the rule, and whenever the ball was thrown to a certain part of the field all the players in that vicinity grabbed each other and hung on and wrestled until separated by the onlookers, who were kept constantly employed in this business.

A sudden fierce yelling marked a new phase of the game. Running down the edge of the field was a light, finely built Choctaw, protected by a big, heavy man on each side. The runner held himself straight with his pair of sticks well in front of him and the ball between them. One opponent darted for him, but was intercepted by one of his big protectors and both rolled over in the grass. The runner held himself in, knowing the time for speed had not yet come. Another adversary almost reached him, but his second "interferer" pinned the foe. Another man on his side joined him, and helped to ward off the enemies who rushed at him from all sides. His last interferer was tied up in a wrestling match with one of the other side, and he had to trust to his own legs. With a quick dodge he darted at right angles across the field, eluding all attempts to tackle, and went down the other side like the wind. The goalkeepers rushed for him in a body that he knew he could not pass. The goal post was a hundred feet off yet; he must reach it with a single throw or not at all. He swung the sticks over his head and, like a stone from a sling, the ball flew straight for its mark. It looked like a sure goal, and the friends of the runner's side set up a victorious whoop; but they forgot the old veteran of a hundred games who was guarding that goal. With a spring like a panther he leaped up and caught the ball in his sticks not two feet in front of the post, and with a mighty swing sent it a hundred yards into the cente of the field, where the fight began all over again.

Twelve goals constitute a game, and after five hours' play the score stood ten goals each. The game had gradually been growing rougher, and several players had been obliged to leave the field more or less injured. But now the blood was up on both sides; the captain of the Gaines County team called his men from the field and changed their positions, putting the goalkeepers, who were comparatively fresh, in the front and placing the tired rushers at the goals. He admonished his new rushers that when they tackled a player they were to do it so effectively that he would not bother them again. Some of them followed his directions quite literally, for I saw one man I knew pick an adversary up by the legs and dash him head downward onto the ground, not only once but several times. I remonstrated with him after the game, saying he might have broken the man's neck.

"No; wouldn't break," he replied, "I tried."

The spectators, Indian and white, were now all thoroughly aroused, and followed the game up and down the field, some on foot and some on horseback, yelling and cheering their men on. When a mass of players were bunched in a scrimmage the spectators even went so far as to strike the bare backs of their favorites with quirts, or whips, to urge them on. Toward the end of the game the Sugar Loaf rushers were obviously flagged. The strategy of the Gaines County captain was successful, and in less than half an hour the decisive goal was won.

The game lasted five hours and a half, and we all agreed that few if any outdoor sports equaled in excitement, skill and picturesqueness a Choctaw ball game.

In January of 1887, Outing summarized the previous lacrosse season on pages 395-396. The synopsis touched upon the problems affecting the sport throughout the period.

THE LACROSSE SEASON OF 1886

THE season of 1886 has been the most successful one that has fallen to the lot of the game of lacrosse in the United States. The promising signs, in the order of their importance, to be noted are, the growth of junior clubs in number and efficiency; the increased rivalry between the senior clubs; the international visits, Ireland to the United States, and, lastly, the removal of the championship from the distant West to the East, where it will be more constantly an object of sharp competition.

It is always difficult to ascertain the number of juniors who take part in any game....But an inquiry among dealers in lacrosse goods reveals the fact that the number of boys that are playing the game is very large, and is constantly increasing....

The rivalry among senior clubs was never as great as has been this season. The Oelrich Cup Tournament, last spring, emphasized this fact. The long journey that the New York club took to St. Paul, to obtain the championship, is a further illustration of it. The rivalry has once or twice expressed itself in very unpleasant words and deeds. Clubs have not been as tender of each other's feelings, mental and physical, as true sportsmen should be. There was hot blood in the championship game in St. Paul, and we read of exceedingly rough play in the games in Boston between the local clubs. The college games have been entirely free from it. ...Several times the National Association have disqualified players because of rough play; once they disqualified an entire club. Perhaps such action does some good. But the real remedy lies with the referees. They should be carefully chosen, and fearless in enforcing fair play. Rough play is as yet a rare exception in the United States, and we do not believe that it is to become less of an exception. The movement seems to be in the right direction among all the clubs of the better class.

Four championships have been contested by the senior clubs during the year.

THE OELRICHS CUP TOURNAMENT, played May 22 and June 5, was won by New York; the other contestants being Princeton, Stevens Institute, New York University, the Druids of Baltimore, and the South Boston Club.

THE INTER-COLLEGIATE CHAMPIONSHIP was won by Harvard ...

THE UNITED STATES CHAMPIONSHIP has been contested by clubs upon the lacrosse field, and by others upon paper, in the council of the association. The New York Club went to St. Paul, in July, and played the holders of the Westchester Cup, the emblem of the championship, and won the game by a score of 3 to 1. The Calumet Club, of Chicago, put in a claim for the championship, on the ground that the New York challenge to St. Paul was lacking in necessary formalities, and that their own challenge was the only one that St. Paul could legally accept, and their non-acceptance gave the championship to Chicago. After much delay ... the council decided almost unanimously against the claim of the Calumet Club.

The New York Club only held the cup for a few weeks after the decision, when the Independents, of Boston, relieved them of its care by winning a game at Staten Island by a score of 4 to 2.

The Independent Club almost immediately received challenges from the Boston, South Boston and New York clubs. The season was so nearly over that they were only bound to play one game. They accepted the challenge of the Boston Club as being the first received, and still retain the Westchester Cup. The South Boston Club now claims it, and the championship, on the ground that the Boston Club does not in fact exist, and that their own challenge, being the first received unanswered, the Independents have forfeited the championship to them.

All this shows very clearly that some change is needed in the rules relating to challenges.

The columns of OUTING have already contained accounts of the international trips of Irishmen, Americans and Canadians. Each of these in its own way has contributed to the growth of the game by the interest excited both by the games and the victories of the United States clubs.

An Outing report, July, 1889, p. 362, indicated problems that still plagued lacrosse. With the growth of clubs in the Midwest, factionalism developed, resulting in an eastern and western division after the dissolution of the national association. Only the eastern circuit conducted a championship.

THE GAME OF LACROSSE

THE season which closed November 1 has not been so productive of good results as those interested in the success of Canada's national game anticipated. Certain innovations, which were introduced last spring and promised well, have proved to be impracticable. Then, again, the splitting of the old National Association into two minor leagues has not brought about closer relationship between the clubs. Not one of the New England clubs has signified its intention of joining the Eastern Association. A local championship series and a few games with outside clubs have satisfied them.

The Western Association, and its doings during the first season of its existence, remain unknown to the lacrosse men in the East. For some reason efforts to bring about cordial relations between the two sections of the country have failed. The Western men appear to think that enough deference is not paid them on account of their possession of the National Championship, which was gained, not on the field, but on paper.

The Brooklyn Club will have the honor of being the champion club until 1889. It has made astonishing strides forward....The Staten Island Club, on the other hand, may safely be, relied upon making every effort next spring to recover the coveted honor which so long was theirs.

The other clubs in the Eastern Association - Philadelphia, Baltimore, Jersey City, Staten Island Cricket Club - have not done much during the summer ...

That nothing encourages so much as success, is seen in the vigor and enthusiasm with which Princeton, the champion of the College League, has gone to work since the opening of college.... class games have been played, and the University team has also had several games with outside clubs. This has not escaped Harvard, her most dangerous rival. The *Crimson* has repeatedly called upon the college to give better support to the lacrosse team, which has at times been almost the only one to bring back a championship. In the spring the time is too limited to get the men into first-class condition, and fall and winter work should be indulged in when possible.

Lehigh is thoroughly delighted with lacrosse and Cornell is taking it up. Williams is considering whether it will not draw too many men from the other sports, and other colleges and schools are getting ready to introduce the game....

Harper's Weekly published an article by Caspar Whitney, 14 April 1894, pp. 349-350, that made several key points. In addition to providing a brief history, Whitney claimed that Americans did not appreciate the game, perhaps because it was not perceived as an "American" sport like baseball or football. Ironically, the Canadians had learned the game from the native Indians. By the 1890s Indians were excluded from championship play on the basis that they were professionals. Whitney conceded their "natural" ability; but asserted that whites played a more scientific game, consistent with the Social Darwinian principle of Anglo superiority.

AN UNAPPRECIATED GAME

One of the least appreciated and yet most thoroughly enjoyable games, to participant and spectator alike, is lacrosse. Why it has never been more popular in the United States, why not generally taken up, as baseball and football have been, is a question I have asked myself very often. I think those who have seen lacrosse played will agree with me that, especially for the spectator, it has even more charms than our two most popular games, football and baseball. It is a sport in which every player on each side is constantly being called upon, and always with a chance for brilliant work. It differs from football in being absolutely intelligible to the most uninformed layman, and from baseball in giving more opportunities for play to more men on the same side simultaneously.... I really think, from an all-round point of view, that there is no game that excels it ... not even football. It ... takes the timidity out of a boy ... it makes a man of him.... It abounds in open and beautiful plays...

It has been asserted that lacrosse resembles, and may possibly have its origin in, the Irish game of comah, but careful research fails to discover anything more than the generic resemblance which exists between all games played with ball and bat. Lacrosse is an Indian game ...

The most satisfactory record of the early history of lacrosse is the result of Mr. W.G. Beers's research. His little pamphlet put forth in 1860 was the first publication, I believe of the game, and about twenty years later... he brought out the best volume on the subject we have ever had, and from which we gather most. It is to this little volume that we are indebted for what we know of this typical American game in its infancy.

Lacrosse originally bore the name which each tribe of Indians gave the ball. The Iroquois, who were counted the most skilful players in those early days, called the game Tehontahiksakeks; the Algonquins, Teiontsesiksaheks; the Ojibways, Baggataway; while the cross the Iroquois called Teionstikwahektawa, and the Algonquins, Tessanaton. The goal (which at first was a single pole, or, as occasion required, a tree or rock that happened to be near) was called by the Iroquois Iorhenoketo-Ohikta.

With no formal history and such formidable names to burden it, small wonder the early record of the game is wanting.... Of one thing we are certainly assured, the early Indian game could not have been more vigorous. It was practically a combat ... 600, 800, and even 1000 players emerging in the play, while the field was ... 500 yards to one-half mile in length ... Regular tournaments were held from time to time ... of tribes against tribes, or villages against villages ... Such matches consisted sometimes of even as many as one hundred games, and lasted several days.

... Even with teams that sometimes consisted of hundreds of players the team work was, from accounts, astonishing. It goes without saying that the game was not so scientific as that of to-day.... Even to-day in their advanced form the Indians do not play a scientific game as do the whites. Nor is it a fact that all Indians are good players, though the expertness of Indian boys is surprising; but they appear to have a natural aptitude for the game, and certainly when brought together their best teams seem to have more wind than their pale-faced opponents.... the Indians played the game probably generations before the whites ever saw it.

When we first began to play lacrosse it is hard to say, though certainly the scene of our first efforts was in Canada, to whose players, indeed, we are indebted for the game as it comes to us in its present scientific form....

As we see it to-day, lacrosse began to crystallize about '76. The first sign of development was the repudiation of the old bagged cross, and the making of the netting of the stick ...This was followed by reducing the size of the field ... and restricting the number of players ... and the beginning of the remarkably clever checking ...

From that time the game has had as marked growth in Canada as football has had in the United States. Its popularity has spread over all the Dominion....It is beyond doubt the national game of Canada ...

I have written to the principal colleges in the different sections of the country, and, of them all, lacrosse is played at only the Johns Hopkins, Lehigh, and Stevens Institute Universities. At Harvard, Yale, Princeton, and the Univ. of Pa., in the middle West, the South, and in the extreme West, the game so far as I can learn, is not played at all, and in some localities is hardly known....Here and there an athletic club sports a team, the best known being the Druids of Baltimore, the Athletic Club of the Schuylkill Navy, the Staten Island Athletic and the New York Athletic clubs, the last being practically the old Brooklyn team....

The game came into the United States shortly after it began to fluorish in Canada, the first club being the Mohawks, of Troy, which was shortly followed by the Maple Leaf, of Buffalo.... In 1882 the United States Intercollegiate Lacrosse Association was organized, and some excellent contests were had ... but the game was probably at its height in 1886 when Lehigh defeated Stevens. The following season, '87, Lehigh won five out of six matches ... Lehigh in '88 applied for admission to the Intercollegiate Association, and ... gained third place, Princeton winning the championship ...

In '90 Lehigh ... won the championship ... In '91 and '92 Lehigh took third place, being defeated by Johns Hopkins and Stevens respectively. Last year Lehigh ... won the college championship with ease, defeated all the best amateur teams of the country, and lost to the University of Toronto, the champions of Canada, only after a hard struggle.

... Here in New York we have the Staten Island and the New York teams, and in Philadelphia the Schuylkill Navy, but in the last two seasons they seem to have been following in the footsteps of some of their track athletic brethren, for the championship of the year was not awarded because the teams had transgressed the amateur rules....

CANADA

Canadians witnessed the game of lacrosse among American Indians for many years. They apparently began to play it after an Indian exhibition in Montreal in 1834. The Montreal Lacrosse Club formally organized in 1856, and William G. Beers, known as the "father of lacrosse," set down the rules in an 1860 book. Between 1868 and 1884 the Montreal Shamrocks, a team largely composed of working class Irish Catholics, dominated the sport against Protestant middle class players. Such ethnic and religious rivalries played out in athletic competition helped to establish lacrosse as a major sport in Canada.

Practiced mostly in the eastern provinces, the sport assumed international dimensions in the Anglo world. In 1883 a Canadian team toured England and Ireland, playing sixty-two matches in forty-one different cities. The game was introduced to Vancouver in 1886, and the British Columbia Amateur Lacrosse Association initiated play four years later. It soon became the most popular spectator sport in the region.

Despite the growth and popularity of lacrosse, the sport experienced problems during the 1880s as professionalism crept into the game. The early middle class proponents of the game adhered to the amateur ideal, and factions developed as professional players attempted to capitalize on their skills. Teams who hoped to gain a winning edge by employing such talents found amateurism obsolete or infringed upon the ideal in their quest for victory. Despite their desire to win the Canadians intentionally excluded some of the best players from amateur championships by declaring native Indians to be professionals. Indians were forced to compete in separate championships; but some who possessed Anglo physical characteristics became highly valued on white teams during the period.

With or without the Indians, Canadian teams were considered the best in the world, a fact usually proven in international competitions. Lacrosse enjoyed immense popularity in Canada; but did not officially become Canada's national sport despite references to that effect.

The Montreal Gazette, 14 August 1883, p. 8, provided in depth coverage of the Canadian tour of the British Isles with its own correspondent.

HOME AGAIN
THE RETURN OF THE CANADIAN LACROSSE TEAM

Leaving behind us the fashionable precincts of Scarsborough, its Spa and its grand hotel on Wednesday evening, the 25th July, in order to reach Liverpool in time for the steamer Dominion, booked to leave the Mersey at 2 p.m. on Thursday, another (the fifth or sixth since our arrival) night's journey in the peculiarly built cars of the country was indulged in; and I must say, from sad experience, that it is not a berth to be envied....

Arrived at Liverpool, little or no time was lost in transferring our goods and chattels to the steamer Oregon, which looked staunch and trim as she lay at anchor. About 3 o'clock anchor was weighed, and we steamed slowly out past the "bar" and quietly (but sadly to some) we said

"GOOD BYE TO OLD ENGLAND"

where we had received many kindnesses, but at the same time had put in a lot of hard work without an over amount of appreciation.... the desire to reach Belfast supplanted every other feeling.

Thither already had gone Mr. Bowie, who has been some time acting as the "advance agent," we having found that it was absolutely necessary for some one to look after the secretaries and others who were supposed to manage local affairs, Dr. Beers being unable, owing to press of emigration and other serious matters, to devote the whole of his time to this special kind of work.... A very quiet night was passed on the good ship, which reached Belfast Lough about day-break. An early breakfast, which was hardly finished when the tender from the wharf steamed up, having on board Dr. Beers, Mr. Bowie and Dr. Hickey of our own party, and several representatives of the local press. A photograph was taken ... and reached our hotel between 10 and 11 o'clock.

IN BELFAST

At 3 p.m. a coach-and-four drove up to the Queen's Hotel, and the horn being sounded a tour around the city (or rather suburbs, as we were not now on "show" but on a tour of inspection), *en route* to the grounds, was enjoyed at the invitation of the Belfast clubs....The ... North of Ireland Cricket Club Grounds, were reached at 4 p.m. ... At 4:30 the first match of the series or tournament, as it has not inaptly been called here, began between the Belfast team (selected from the various clubs of the city) and the Indians. The latter were *minus* Norton, who had left in the morning for home, and thus played eleven against ... twelve ...

There was not a vacant space to be seen around the vast enclosure of the ropes ... Prompt on time the teams were drawn up, with Mr. H.C. Kelly as captain of the home team, and Big John at his usual post, While Mr. R.B. Walkington (the champion football player of Ireland) acted as referee, and Messers. J.N. Hamilton, of Belfast, and D.E. Bowie, of Montreal, as umpires. On the face, the Indians immediately begun the attack, and Dominique, securing the ball, began a series of his beautiful manipulations, and in 15 seconds secured the first game amid hearty applause.

In the second game the Irishmen seemed much cooler, and tackled their work with a vim, and although time and again it seemed as though the Indians would have an easy victory, the goal-keeping of Dill and the play of the other defence men completely negatived the efforts of Hamrock and Dominique, who time and again got about there but never in. A long shy from Childs sent the ball to the home, where, after some very pretty passing between the "homes," J. Sinclair scored a goal in seven minutes, amidst vociferous cheering.

A third game was at once begun, with again the advantage to the Indians, and shot after shot rained on Dill, some being beautifully stopped and others being narrow shaves. The Indians threw well down from defence whenever it got up amongst that dangerous attack, while the Irishmen were hardly so far, and they again had great difficulty in repelling the attacks of the Indians; however it seemed to be their day, for up it went, and White Eagle having uncovered his man the passing began, and again Sinclair scored in nine minutes.

John did not look very happy at this turn of the wheel, but still wore a look of confidence, which broke into a beam of satisfaction when Dominique again scored in five minutes. No time was lost in changing ends, and the play here seemed to fall off a bit, their hard struggle telling considerably against the home team, and the Indians kept the ball on the flags until Hamrocks scored in four minutes, thus winning, according to our tallying, the match. However from this time out they did not get another game, the home team taking the sixth, seventh and eighth games in 2, 8 and 5 minutes respectively, when time was called. The

SUCCESS OF THE IRISH TEAM

was loudly applauded, and it deserved all the praise received. They played a plucky, sharp and scientific game, were especially dangerous at home, and had the particular style of attack which Indians seem scarcely ever able to repel....

The Indians, after a short rest, then went out in the field to face the Canadians. After the defeat, it seemed any odds on the white men, and although the full strength of the team ... were on ... the result was a great victory for the Caughnawaga, who went to work and beat their opponents 3 to 2 in one full hour's play, the games being turn about with the rubber in favour of the "red."

This turn of affairs set all the prophets at sea, and many were not found wanting to prognosticate a defeat for the Canadians in the international match and quite ready to back their opinions.

In the evening the members of the North of Ireland Cricket Club entertained the Canadians to dinner in the pavilion on the grounds where the '76 team had their banquet, and a most enjoyable evening was spent....

On Saturday morning a drag-and-four called to take the team out for a drive, which lasted a couple or three hours, when home was reached and preparations for the grand match of the day entered into.

THE INTERNATIONAL MATCH

Arriving on the ground a few minutes before three, we found an immense assemblage of the wealth, beauty and fashion of the northern capital of Ireland. The pavilion and reserved seats for members were packed; the galleries and promenade crowded, while the ropes which encircled the vast grounds were lined five and six deep in some places; improvised grand stands of benches and chairs were jammed to the height of twenty tiers. The Irish team, which was the same as the day before, first came on the grounds and were well received. The Canadians, who, recognizing the mettle they had to play against, had a long confab the evening previous as to whom they should play, decided, with Dr. Beer's kind consent, to have Mr. Bowie act as field captain, and make up the team from the balance of the men present....

Cleghorn, goal; Bonnell, point; Dwight, coverpoint; Garvin, McNaught and Cravin, defence fields; Griffin, centre; Fraser, Nicholson and McKenzie, home field; Struthers and Smith, home; Mr. D.E. Bowie, field captain.

Messrs. F.W. Schofield (Liverpool) and J.N. Hamilton (Belfast) were umpires, and Mr. R.B. Walkington (Belfast), referee.

Mr. H.C. Kelly captained the Irish team.

The stillness was something intense, as Griffin and Nelson knelt for the ball. On the word "play" the latter made a rush, but the homes were all covered in an instant, and McWha being checked by Garvin, the latter's man being immediately attended to by McNaught, threw to Sinclair, who passed to his brother, but the latter lost in one of Watty's rushes, and down the field it flew. The spectators, as the ball flew toward the Canadian goal, having, in the meantime, broken out into an immense roar of applause. Struthers got under the ball and sent in a hot grounder which Dill warded, but Ross was after it, and coming round to the front, broke through all opposition, and scored inside one minute amid hearty applause.

The second game was started with the same result as before, but Griffin recovered himself and passed to Fraser. After several ineffectual attempts by Mackenzie and some little laziness and excitement in the Canadian field, J. Sinclair played exactly the same style of shot on Cleghorn as he did at the Oval, thus securing the game for the Irishmen.

The next game lasted only half a minute and was scored by Struthers with a beautiful bit of play.

The fourth game was a purely defensive one for the home team; after five minutes play Smith scored for the Canadians.

Again the Irishmen were on the defensive but played with great determination; after four minutes, a diagonal shot from Fraser passed Dill like a cannon ball.

The sixth, seventh and eighth games were taken by the visitors, Nicholson, Smith and Fraser being the successful men.

The ninth brought forth considerable play as the Belfast field captain called upon his men to beat the International score at the Oval, but they were unable to do so and Struthers scored another game for his side.

The time being scarcely up the Belfast men returned again to the charge and this time success rewarded their efforts, after about nine minutes' play. J. Sinclair again beat Cleghorn, a result which was received with every demonstration of delight.

After this exciting match, the
ONLY REAL MATCH
we have had since we left home, in which both spectators and players were into it with a will, reminding us of some of the good old fashioned ones at home, and at which, I am bound to say, both Belfast and Canadian were impartially and equally cheered.

An exhibition game with the Indians was played, resulting in a victory for the whites by 3 to 2....

Next morning we started for Portrush, which we reached at noon, had lunch, and, procuring two large traps (in the jaunting car style), started for the Giant's Causeway, some seven miles distant. A stop was made to visit the celebrated ruins of Dunluce Castle, and then the hostelry on top of the hill at the Causeway was reached. Boats were here taken and the two celebrated caves visited....

AT DERRY
Derry was reached the next afternoon; here, despite the wet weather, there was a very large attendance. The match was played with ten men a side and was won by the whites, eight games to four.

The famous walls of Derry having been visited, the train was taken to Enniskillen, in order to break the long journey to
DUBLIN,
which was reached about 10. After some sight-seeing, the match was commenced on the Lansdowne grounds. This was the last match of the tour, and both Indians and whites were equally determined to win. The ground is not of the smoothest, and there were plenty of obstacles in the shape of hurdles, blackboards, etc., so the play was just a little exciting. The first game was scored by the Indians, but the Canadians had their revenge by taking the following six.

The next morning we started for Belfast agian; Thursday was an off-day, and was spent chiefly in paying adieus.
THE LAST MATCH
The Canadians having offered Mr. H.C. Kelly, in acknowledgement of his kindness, to play a benefit for his club, which offer was accepted, we played one more match, the Indians against the ... Irish-Canadian team....

The game was won by the Indians in five straight.

The next morning we took the tender for the S.S. Dominion ...

Our Irish tour was an immense success, and none of us can ever forget the genuine Irish hospitality we met with on all hands and the deep debt of gratitude we owe to the many who showed us untold kindness....We travelled from Liverpool north as far as Aberdeen, back to London, then to the southwest coast of England, to the southeast, and up through the Midlands. After doing its manufacturing towns, we returned to Liverpool, then Manchester and the north of England, and as far East as Scarborough. From there we travelled, via the great shipping port, to Ireland, which we traversed pretty extensively, especially to the North of Dublin. Computing the distances by rail and water, which the team has travelled, when we shall have arrived,
ELEVEN THOUSAND LONG MILES
will be about the exact distance.... there were speeches made at the various bnaquets, such as the Imperial Club, the Birmingham, Manchester, London and Belfast, at which special attention was given to placing Canada well before the audience.... There is no

doubt a good work has been done in the cause of emigration, and that the country will
ere have long cause to remember with pleasure the trip of the Canadian Lacrosse Team
of 1883 to Europe....

Below is a resume of all the matches played:-

In Portland	2
" Scotland	7
" England	48
" Ireland	<u>5</u>
	62
Total played in Great Britain	60
Total number of matches, Indians vs. Canadians	58
Of these the Indians won	10
" " the Canadians	37
" " Drawn	<u>11</u>
	58
Majority for Canadians	27
Total number of games played Indians vs. Canadians	447
Of these Indians won	181
" " Canadians won	<u>266</u>
Majority for Canadians	85
Total number of International matches	4
Canadians won all.	
Number of games played	37
Of these Canadians won	32
Opponents	5
	37

These matches were played in 41 different cities and towns.

The number of matches played by each man is -

Struthers	62
Garvin	57
Mackenzie	54
Aird	52
Griffin	50
Fraser	49
Craven	49
Smith	47
Cleghorn	47
McNaught	46
Bonnell	45
Nicholson	3
Dwight	38
Bowie	17

The latter was a great deal of his time ahead, and frequently acted as captain.

The Montreal Lacrosse Club report of 1884 provides a sense of typical amateur competitions.

ANNUAL REPORT OF THE MONTREAL LACROSSE CLUB

MONTREAL, 1st April, 1885

GENTLEMEN:

This is the fourth occasion on which I have had the pleasure of presenting the Report of your Committee to the Annual Meeting of the Club.

At the Annual Convention of the National Amateur Lacrosse Association, held last April, Mr. Angus Grant, of ours, was elected President.

Desired changes in method of deciding the Championship by a majority of games won in a given time, were not carried at the convention; and owing to the protracted session, a proposition to allow 2nd Twelves of 1st class clubs to compete for Intermediate and Local Championships was not brought up....

After considerable correspondence an arrangement was made with the Toronto Club to fix a maximum of $250.00 for the expenses of each club when visiting the other; this was done with a view to encourage a reduction in the travelling expenses; as all over the $250.00 must be borne by the visiting club. It was intended to have a display of fireworks on the evening of the Queen's Birthday, but the weather was so unfavourable we had to postpone till the following Monday, which, no doubt, contributed to the non-success (financially) of the event.

The first match of the season was played on our grounds on the 17th May with the Caughnawaga Indians, whom we defeated by 4 games to 1....

On the 31st May we met the Toronto Club at Rosedale to play for the championship, which they had taken from the Shamrocks in the Fall of 1883.... Toronto took the first game ... Montreal the second ... Toronto the 3rd and 4th ..: the last game was accidentally taken by one of our own men....

On the 25th June (St. Jean Baptiste celebration,) we played an exhibition match with the Shamrocks, who took the 1st, 2nd, 3rd and 5th games in 5, 6, 7, and 28 minutes; A.E. McNaughton, for our side, taking the 4th in 25 minutes....

On the 28th June we played the Indians again ... Result:-Montreal, 1st, 3rd, 4th, and 5th games ...

On Dominion Day a mixed team of our boys visited the Metropolitan Club at Ottawa, and defeated them in 3 straight games at the Rideau Hall grounds ...

On 12th July we played the Shamrocks a practice match on our grounds, which resulted in a draw ...

On the same afternoon the Buffers and Duffers met, and the former inflicted a crushing defeat in 3 straight games on their unhappy opponents.

On the 19th July our representatives paid a second visit to Toronto to struggle for the pennant, which they captured and brought down to Montreal.... This was the first time for many years our club had held the championship, having played all round it and defeated the holders of it while we were outside the association, and was the signal for great rejoicing, and a number of the members went up to Cornwall to welcome the victors.

At the suggestion of Mr. Angus Grant, each player on the team and the Captain were presented by the club with a gold medal, which is to form a precedent for all future championship matches won; only one gold medal to be given, however, to each player, subsequent victories to be chronicled by a clasp.

The Shamrocks had a challenge in for a championship which we had to take up, and the 2nd August was fixed for playing it off on our grounds; as will be well remembered, and the match was played under protest against P. Green, one of the Shamrock team, and before, probably, the largest crowd of people ever assembled on any lacrosse field.... The match resulted in a most disastrous defeat in 3 straight games in 1, 14 and 13 minutes; and the Council of the National Association having decided the protest against us, the championship and pennant went to the Shamrocks.

On the 11th August the Metropolitans of Ottawa paid us a return visit, and we again defeated them in 3 straights with a mixed team ...

On the 2nd September, comparatively without practice, our team defeated the Caughnawagas 4 straight games in a complimentary match tendered to the British Association, at that time in session in the city....

On the 13th September our team was to have gone to Cornwall to play the local club; but of them picked only Messrs. Fraser and Paton went, with three second-twelve men, two juniors and 4 members of the Lancaster Club were picked up on the way.

Nothing more was ventured upon till the 11th October, when the Toronto Club visited us here, to play the first of a couple of home and home matches; and we defeated them by 3 games to one ...

On the 18th October our team met the Torontos on the Rosedale Grounds, and were defeated by 3 games to 1.... Our defeat was caused by the refusal of two players selected on the team to play at the last moment.

This closes the record of a very peculiar season, the salient points of which are winning the Championship, and the handsome balance of $1,318.66, which we carry to the funds of the Association ...

The Membership Roll now contains 937 names, including 78 life members; - an increase of 374 since this date last year; more than five times the increase during the previous 12 months.

> The whole respectfully submitted,
> T. L. PATON, *Hon.-Sec.*

The United States' complacency about lacrosse might be discerned by the Chicago Tribune's brief announcement of yet another title for the Shamrocks, despite the exhuberance of 15,000 spectators, on 16 October 1892, p. 4.

WON THE LACROSSE CHAMPIONSHIP
SHAMROCKS OF MONTREAL DEFEAT THE CAPITALS OF OTTAWA ON HOME GROUNDS

Montreal, Oct. 15 - Fifteen thousand people gathered on the Montreal Shamrock athletic grounds this afternoon to witness the final match between the Shamrocks of Montreal and the Capitals of Ottawa for the lacrosse championship of the world. The Shamrocks won three games out of five and carried off the championship amid the wildest cheers.

Despite the relatively sedate circumstances in the United States, lacrosse flourished in Canada as competition was organized across the country by 1890. An Outing article, October, 1892, pp. 76-80, detailed the rapid growth of the sport and its contribution to nationalistic spirit.

LACROSSE
by Ross Mackenzie

When, in 1763, the wily Objibway secured the possession of Fort Michilimackinac and massacred its British garrison, the game "Bagataway," through the medium of which he accomplished his purpose, was hardly as popular among the English-speaking nations as its lineal descendant, the Canadian national game, lacrosse, is at the present time.... up to the year 1860 lacrosse was a game comparatively unknown outside of a few Indian tribes in Canada, notably the Caughnawagas, a portion of the Iroquois nation whose reservation is on the bank of the St. Lawrence River, at the head of the famous Lachine Rapids. On account of the proximity of this village to Montreal, that city was the first to take notice of the game, and its grand possibilities were quickly recognized.

From a small beginning in Montreal the game of lacrosse has, in the last thirty years, spread to all quarters of the globe. Clubs are now flourishing in Australia and New Zealand. In England and Ireland the game is struggling with football for supremacy. In the United States, New York, Chicago, Baltimore, Boston, numerous other cities and various universities have their clubs, and a championship is competed for annually. Within the last few years it has been introduced into schools in France, and the govrernment has made a grant in order to foster and popularize it.

Canada still retains pre-eminence in the game, and from the Atlantic to the Pacific nearly every city, town and village turns out a fair percentage of its population as lacrosse players. In the two principal cities, Montreal and Toronto, centers perhaps the best lacrosse talent in the world, although in Cornwall, Ottawa, St. Catherines, Winnipeg, Vancouver, B.C., and New Westminster, B.C., many exponents of the game worthy of place in the first rank may be found.

The National Amateur Lacrosse Association, founded in 1867, has done good work in legislating for the game, and was, up to five years ago, the only organization of the kind in Canada, but the number of clubs increased so fast and the opening up of the Northwest Territories and connection with British Columbia made distances so great, that other associations became necessary. Now the National Association is composed principally of clubs in Eastern Canada. The Canadian Lacrosse Association looks after the interests of clubs in the western portion of the Province of Ontario. Manitoba has an association composed of clubs in the Northwest Territories, and the British Columbia Association takes charge of the Pacific Slope. Each of these associations regulates contests for championships - senior, intermediate, junior and district - and the majority of these are decided by a season's competition on a series basis, a schedule of the matches being arranged before the lacrosse season opens.

Besides keeping track of the various championships and settling club disputes ... the associations'chief duty is stamping out professionalism ... Outside of the Indians, who are now outclassed by the whites, there are no professional lacrosse players. There are many black-listed players, thanks to the work of the associations, but these men cannot take part in matches, and when the brand has been put upon them, they become pariahs of the lacrosse fraternity. In addition to these associations a league composed of the five leading clubs and styled the Canadian Lacrosse League, was formed two years ago. The members of this league were the Montreal and Shamrock clubs of Montreal, the Cornwall ... Ottawa ... and Toronto ... The winner of a series of matches between these clubs, it was conceded by the lacrosse public ... might well be hailed as champion, and they, finding that the associations were occupied in legislating for junior clubs whose interests were always made paramount to theirs, decided to cut loose and legislate for themselves....

Unfortunately difference of opinion in 1890 caused a split in the league. At its organization ... it was decided to limit the number of clubs to five ... The Capital Club of Ottawa, winner of the Intermediate Championship ... in 1889, was anxious to step into senior rank, and ... managed to persuade Cornwall, Ottawa and Shamrock clubs to agree to receive them ... thus violating the agreement.

The Montreal and Toronto clubs refused to vary ... and the consequence was disbandment.... The breech succeeded only in lessening the public interest ... and, the Capital Club, did not show itself fit for the company it aspired to. Early in '92 the six clubs met, and it was decided that the Ottawas and Capital clubs should amalgamate ... They ... have put on the field one of the strongest lacrosse aggregations seen in Canada for years....

The Canadian Lacrosse Association in Ontario had a very successful season in 1891, the St. Catherines Club coming out on top. This year the St. Catherines Club has been blacklisted...

In Manitoba lacrosse has languished ...

In British Columbia in 1891 a lively season was closed, with the New Westminster Club at the top, and this year a twelve match series is being fought ... The activity is, however, very unhealthy, as in their desire for supremacy they have awakened strong suspicions that the unwonted march of crack lacrosse players westward is not for the benefit of their health ...

The idea of giving the British public a practical illustration of the beauties of lacrosse originated in the mind of Dr. Beers of Montreal.... In 1867, having seen the game established as the national game of Canada, the doctor's ambition went further, and in 1869 he had almost completed arrangements toward taking a team of players over to the mother country, when a speculator ... scented a probable fortune in the enterprise and forestalled the project by taking over to England two teams selected from Caughnawaga Indians.... In 1875 Dr. Beers again took up the idea ... and as a result the first Canadian lacrosse team ... accompanied by a team of Caughnawaga Indians, went over in 1876 and made a tour through the United Kingdom.... and lacrosse has taken a firm hold in Great Britain. The crowning event of the trip was a command which the teams received to play before Her Majesty at Windsor Castle ... Financially the members of the team were heavy losers ... The teams returned to Canada in the fall of 1876, having been absent over two months ...from that time up to the spring of 1883 Dr. Beers worked steadily at the organization of another ... trip. The result ... was the tour of... 1883. The party traveled ... 10,646 miles -5,033 by rail and 5,613 by steamers.

As was the case in the previous tour, the expenses were largely in excess of the gate receipts, the traveling expenses and salaries of the Indians being a heavy item ... Royalty patronized the matches on three occasions.... A North of England and a South of England Lacrosse Association had been formed, as well as the Irish Lacrosse Union, with tributary associations; and matches, "England vs. Ireland" and "North vs. South," were of frequent occurrence....

Yielding to the repeated invitations of both Canadians and Americans, in 1886 the Irish Lacrosse Union sent over a team which made a tour through Canada and the United States.... They landed in New York in August, 1886, and on the day following their landing were beaten by the All America team. They then came on to Montreal, and ... they essayed three matches in one afternoon, viz., against the Shamrock Lacrosse Club, ... the Caughnawaga Indians and ... a Canadian team. The Shamrock team strained proverbial Irish hospitality and lost the match, the other two teams were not so polite, and the Montreal Club, which played them a much later on, also beat them.... the team went to Toronto, Niagara Falls, St. Catherines, Richmond Hill and Ottawa. In all of these places they ... were ... well beaten ... They also played at Brockville, and that town has the unenviable notoriety of being the only place where discourteous treatment was accorded the visitors. Owing to the liberal treatment given the Irishmen by players on this side of the water, the team was enabled to clear expenses...

The last trip of lacrosse players across the Atlantic was in 1888, when the Toronto Lacrosse Club sent a team over....

On this tour the Toronto's won all their matches ... The members were feted and entertained everywhere. In England ... was a special saloon carriage for all their journeys placed at their disposal, along with all transportation free of charge. In Ireland, the members of the team were put up at the residences of prominent citizens of Belfast...

Chapter 14

RACKET SPORTS

Racket sports experienced tremendous growth in the last two decades of the nineteenth century. Tennis, in particular, appealed to both the wealthy and the middle class, who found it a wholesome means of socialization between the sexes. More accessible than golf, tennis lent itself to the country club set or private urban sites. Restricted membership in such clubs allowed the growing middle class to set itself apart from those perceived as socially inferior. Despite the introduction of public courts in city parks by the 1880s, the masses were more interested in baseball, the preferred choice of the summer season.

By the 1890s middle class athletic clubs introduced an indoor alternative to tennis that could be practiced year-round. Outing provided an introduction and a brief history of badminton on 4 April 1891, p. 250

BADMINTON.

It is passing strange that a game of such antiquity, and one presenting possibilities of rare good sport, should have been so entirely overlooked in this country.... it is said to have flourished in India before the days of tennis in France ... Its name is of comparatively recent origin, said to have been given because the first game as now seen was played at Badminton, the Duke of Beaufort's country-seat, but as battledoor and shuttlecock there is no record of its first appearance. Certain it is that it flourished in England under various names before Major Wingfield in '74 patented his game of Sphairistike, which was nothing more than a revivial of tennis. It is known on pretty good authority that a game similar to tennis had been played in 1834; while between 1850 and 1864 there are a number of well-substantiated instances where it had been played regularly.

... In the past few years a small bit of interest has been awakening in badminton, until there are now a number of organized clubs abroad playing it regularly.... in America ... there are, so far as known, but two clubs which play the game ... It is possible to play it outdoors; in which case the shuttlecock, or "bird," as it is generally called, is weighted ... With even this precaution, however, it is not very satisfactory in open air, the slightest wind catching the feathers of the "bird," and rendering accurate playing wellnigh impossible.

But there is always some hall to be hired, but with the movement now making in athletics by women, and the success of a club devoted exclusively to the interests of their physical culture, it is high time some recognition was taken of this game and a club feature made of it.

... Why not a Cherry Diamond Badminton Club composed of the wives of Manhattan Athletic Club members? This is a suggestion that can be acted upon very generally throughout the country, and whether the game is improved or not is of small consequence compared to the great good it will do womankind in betraying them into some kind of physical exertion.... The greatest recommendation the game of badminton has is that the court can be laid out to suit the proportions of the space at hand, and made fast or slow as the players are disposed....

The game was introduced into this country in the early winter of '78-'79, by Mr. Bayard Clarke, who had seen it played in England, and believed it could be made successful here. He was joined by Mr. E. Langdon Wilks and Mr. Robert K. Richards, and together they organized the "Badminton Club of the City of New York." The first active membership of the club numbered about forty, and the meetings were held in the old armory building on Broadway and Thirty-fifth Street. The membership soon reached the limit of 200, and the demand for another club was created. The first club has always held its meetings in the afternoon, and as they had the tendency to make the attendance more feminine than masculine, the idea of a club holding evening sessions was favorably considered. Consequently, Mrs. Herman Clarke and Miss Rutherford organized the "Evening Badminton Club," which was an immediate success, and fairly outshone the elder organization ... there are six courts, forty-eight laughing, chattering, swiftly moving figures, and the air is filled with flying "birds."

The dimensions of the court ... may be one-third the size of a double tennis court, which is seventy-eight by thirty-six feet ... The courts should, if outdoors, be marked off by means of pegs and strings or a lawn-tennis marker; but better, and invariably indoors, by white chalk lines on the floor. In the centre are placed the posts, firmly planted in boxes of sand, which support the net. The net should be two feet to two feet six inches deep, suspended at a height of six feet from the ground, and firmly held by guy ropes attached to the posts.

The rackets should be similar to the ones used in the game of racquets, or of a very light tennis pattern. The shuttlecock may be large or small, as the players desire.... from one to four may play on a side, and .. the shuttlecock must be returned on the volley. The "bird" is served and returned under the same provisions, except that ... if it falls to the ground it is counted a miss to that player and to his side. The service shall be from the "service corner" the server and receiver each standing with both feet within their respective quadrants until the shuttlecock is struck. The divisions of the respective courts are only observed in the serve, or first hit; after that the partners may stand where they please on their side of the net. The "bird" must be served to clear the net and fall, without touching ropes or posts, inside the line of the service court, diagonally opposite from the server. If the net is touched in service, and the shuttlecock falls over, the stroke is considered as a "let," and does not count a "fault" against the person serving. In play, however, the touching of the net, so long as the "bird" falls over, is counted a stroke.

On the other hand, if the players touch the net or reach over it with their rackets, the stroke counts against them. In judging whether a player has reached over the net, the umpire should be careful to note if the "bird" is struck before it has crossed the net and not by the racket of the player, which is naturally carried forward by the impetus of the stroke, and which might arrive at a slight angle over the net, although the shuttlecock itself was struck fairly on the correct side. If however, the net is touched by the racket the stroke counts against the player, whether the shuttlecock was hit on the right side or not. Two "faults" put the "hand out." In all cases a shuttlecock falling on any of the boundary lines is regarded as a "fault," as if it had fallen outside of the boundary lines, both in service and play. Fifteen points consitiute the game, and in service no overhand stroke is permitted. The shuttlecock is judged by where it strikes, and not where it lies after falling. On club nights generally from ten to twelve games are played by each court, the first three counting toward a prize.... Finally as to costume there appears to be no rule....

HANDBALL

Like badminton, handball provided an alternative to tennis, and proved more accessible to the working class. Utilizing the hand as a racket, the game required no equipment other than a ball and a wall. Handball can be traced back to the ancient Egyptians; but it gained particular prominence in Ireland, where tournament play began in the early nineteenth century. Phil Casey, an Irish immigrant, introduced the game to America in 1882. Casey not only built courts, but he played the game. By 1887 he was recognized as the American champion, and conceded the world title when he defeated the Irish champion, John Lawler. When Casey retired, Michael Eagen rose to dominance of the sport, winning the AAU's first tournament in 1897. With AAU governance came modifications of the rules, court, and ball that accommodated greater participation by allowing one wall as well as the traditional four wall play. Hence, any schoolboy or street kid with a nearby building could enjoy an impromptu game. The street version of the game, already popular in New York by 1900, became acceptable in AAU tournament play thereafter, although both the AAU and the YMCA still fostered more customary three and four wall competition.

The Chicago Tribune announced Casey's title win, as well as the first AAU tournament; 30 November 1887, p. 2; and 8 January 1897, p. 8, respectively.

CASEY WINS THE HAND-BALL CHAMPIONSHIP

New York, Nov. 29. - The concluding games for the international hand-ball championship between Philip Casey of Brooklyn and John Lawler of Dublin, Ireland, were played in Brooklyn today. The match was for the first eleven in twenty-one games. Ten games were played in Dublin, of which Lawler won six and Casey four, so that he had to win seven of the remaining eleven in order to secure the trophy. He won them straight out of hand. In no game did Lawler score more than thirteen aces.

AMATEUR HANDBALL CHAMPIONSHIP

New York, Jan. 7.- The first amateur handball championship tournament in the United States began today at Jersey City. The Amateur Athletic Union offered three medals - gold, silver, and bronze - to the first three men at the finish. There were six entries, among them being Napoleon Lavoie of St. Roch, Que., and his entry gave the contest international tone.

The Canadian drew against J. Fitzpatrick of the Manhattanville Handball club, and defeated him.

Mike Eagen of the Jersey City Handball club defeated Dan McCarthy of the Harrison Handball club.

W. Schmidt of the Brooklyn Handball club defeated James J. Flaherty of the Jersey City Handball club. In the finals, tomorrow Lavoie and Eagen will play the first game. Schmidt will play off the tie with some well-known player and then meet the winner of the first game in a final.

TENNIS

A young American socialite, Mary Ewing Outerbridge, is generally credited with introducing tennis to the United States. She did so in the spring of 1874 at the Staten Island Cricket Club, where her brother was director, after learning the game from British military officers in Bermuda. Despite variations in rules the game spread rapidly throughout the East, South and Midwest. The formation of the United States Lawn Tennis Association in New York in 1881 assured the acceptance of the All-England rules by its 34 founding members. The first United States championships were conducted in August 1881 at the Casino Club in Newport, Rhode Island. Richard D. Sears held the singles title throughout the decade. The first intercollegiate match took place at Trinity College in Hartford, Connecticut in 1883, and the Intercollegiate Lawn Tennis Association, formed that same year, began sponsorship of a national tournament.

The Philadelphia Cricket Club offered a national championship for women by the late 1880s, with a women's doubles title awarded in 1889, when the USLTA won jurisdiction over female players. The Newport Casino hosted the first professional tournament in 1889, and a national mixed doubles championship appeared in 1891. The Canadian Lawn Tennis Association organized the first championships in 1894, and international team competition with England began in 1900 when Dwight Davis donated a challenge cup for annual competition.

The following, obtained from the Neighborhood History Collection at the Harold Washington Library in Chicago, illustrates the operations of a typical middle class tennis club, as well as its restrictive membership policies.

WOODLAWN TENNIS CLUB CONSTITUTION AND BY-LAWS

ARTICLE I.

Name

This organization shall be known as the "Woodlawn Tennis Club."

ARTICLE II.

Membership

Sec. 1. The active membership of the club shall be open only to young men of Wood Lawn Park, and shall not exceed thirty (30) in number.

Sec. 2. Any person may become an honorary member upon the payment of Ten dollars ($10.00). "see the By-Laws."

Sec. 3. Applications for membership, both active and honorary, shall be made in writing to the Secretary, who shall refer it to the Committee on Membership. Applications, upon receiving the sanction of the Membership Committee shall be posted for two weeks before being balloted upon the Club. Three negative votes shall constitute a bar to any applicant's admission.

Sec. 4. Any member of this Club may be expelled at any time for unbecoming conduct or failure to pay dues by a 5/7 vote of the Executive Committee.

ARTICLE III.

Officers

Sec. 1. The officers of the Club shall be:

a President, Vice President, Secretary, Treasurer and Captain. They shall be elected by ballot at the Annual meeting of the Club, to serve one year, or until their successors are elected.

Sec. 2. Committees

There shall be the following Committees:

a. Executive Committee, consisting of the Officers of the Club, and two active members, which shall have general control and supervision of the affairs of the Club, and the disposition of its fund.

b. Membership Committee, consisting of the Secretary and four active members.

c. Tournament Committee, consisting of the Captain and two active members, which shall have the management of all tournaments given by the Club.

d. Social Committee, consisting of the Vice President and two active members, which shall promote sociability among members of the Club.

The members serving on these Committees shall be elected in the same manner as the officers of the Club.

ARTICLE IV.

Duties of Officers

Sec. 1. The duties of the President, Vice President, Secretary and Treasurer shall be those usually pertaining to such offices.

Sec. 2. The duties of the Captain shall be to have the management and supervision of the grounds.

ARTICLE V.

Meetings

Sec. 1. The Annual Meeting of the Club shall be held at the Club grounds, or at a place to be designated by the President, on the first Monday in March.

Sec. 2. Regular meetings of the Club shall be held on the first Monday in each month.

Sec. 3. Special Meetings may be called at anytime by the Secretary upon the request of the President or any five active members.

ARTICLE VI.

Quorums

Sec. 1. Five active members shall constitute a quorum for the transaction of general business, at any regularly called meeting, except the Election of Officers and the amending of this Constitution.

Sec. 2. A majority of all the active members of the Club shall constitute a quorum for the election of officers.

Sec. 3. Five members of the Executive Committee shall constitute a quorum of that Committee for the transaction of all business.

ARTICLE VII.

Finances

Sec. 1. The initiation fee shall be Ten Dollars ($10.00).

Sec. 2. The Regular dues shall be Twelve Dollars ($12.00) per year, payable in monthly installments of One Dollar ($1.00) on the first day of each month.

Sec. 3. Members failing to pay dues within thirty days shall be considered as having forfeited their memberships.

ARTICLE VIII.

Amendments

This Constitution may be amended by a two-thirds vote of all active members, at a regularly called meting, ten (10) days notice of which has been given.

BY-LAWS

ARTICLE I.

Honorary Members

Sec. 1. No one can become an honorary member who is under 35 years of age.

Sec. 2. Honorary members shall have all the privileges of the grounds.

Sec. 3. The Lady members of their families shall have all the privileges which are accorded members of "The Ladies Auxiliary"

ARTICLE II.

Ladies Auxiliary

Sec. 1. The Ladies Auxiliary shall be composed of ladies named by active members of the Club and who shall be approved by the Executive Com.

Sec. 2. Each active member shall have the privileges of naming one lady as a member of this Auxiliary who shall enjoy the privileges of the Club for the Current year.

Sec. 3. The Executive Committee shall have the privilege of naming six additional members of the Ladies' Auxiliary.

Sec. 4. Members of the Ladies Auxiliary shall have the privileges of the grounds Mondays, Tuesdays, Wednesdays and Thursdays until 4 P.M. and Fridays all day, holidays excepted, providing that at no time shall they interfere with the playing of active members.

Sec. 5. Members failing to pay dues by the 20th day of the month shall have their names posted until same is paid.

Order of Business

to be used at all Regular meetings of the Club, in conducting the business of the meeting

1. Reading of minutes of previous meeting
2. Report of Officers
3. "   " Executive Com.
4. "   " Membership "
6. "   " Tournament "
7. "   " Social   "
8. "   " Other Coms.
9. Unfinished Business
10. New Business
11. Election of Officers
12. Adjournment

By the mid-1880s tennis players, as taxpayers, had won the right to practice in public parks. The construction of tennis courts and ballfields in the parks marked a distinct change from the landscaped, European model that encouraged more passive recreation.

The transition to active use of the parks by tennis players in New York was noted in Outing, May, 1884, p. 157.

LAWN TENNIS

LAWN-TENNIS clubs are not assigned courts or permitted to play in Central park, New York, and the tennis players of that city have at last been aroused to assert their rights in the matter, and have memorialized the Park Commissioners, claiming that, as the object of the parks is to promote rest and recreation, and as the game does not interfere with or trench the rights of the general public, it should be permitted, under proper regulations, in courts especially set apart.

On the other hand, the Brooklyn Park Commissioners have done their utmost for years to encourage healthful sports in Prospect park, affording special facilities for base-ball, lacrosse, bicycling, croquet, lawn-tennis, etc. This Year, Chief-Engineer John Y. Cuyler has sent out a circular which is commendable to the managers of all our public recreation grounds. From it we clip the following:-

At the smaller parks, viz., Washington park and Tompkins park, owing to the limited area available for tennis, preference will be given, first, to clubs of young ladies, and next to adult clubs, with membership of both sexes. Boys' clubs will be provided for at Prospect park. The courts will be laid out and maintained at all reasonable times. All employees are paid for their labor by the Park Commissioners, and no fee or remuneration of any kind for any service is expected or will be permitted, and any violation of this rule will subject the club to a withdrawal of its privileges and the employe' to discharge. The grounds will not be in condition for use until after the first of May, at which time arrangements may be made for play.

All players must provide themselves with tennis shoes, in order that the turf may not be unnecessarily damaged. Lockers and dressing-room accommodation will be provided to the extent of our resources, which are limited. Players are warned against making the rooms and lockers repositories for valuables....

Thomas Pettitt emerged as one of the top indoor court tennis players in America. In 1883 he traveled to England to challenge the best players in the world. Outing recounted his story in August, 1885, pp. 613-614, amidst nationalistic strains. Americans often measured their cultural progress in comparison to English standards.

PETTITT'S ENGLISH TOURS

...Since 1862 the professional championship of the world has been held in England, and the English amateurs of the first rank had for many years been able to concede odds to all the best players on the continent. Evidently Boston was the last place in the world to look for a rising star in the tennis world.... The recent performances in England of the "boy"... (Thomas Pettitt) are still fresh in the public mind....

MR. PETTITT first visited England in 1883, and his principal match there was the one in which he took from George Lambert the odds of fifteen for a bisque at Lord's.... Lambert won the first two sets, and Pettitt the last three ... In 1884 he again crossed the water, and played a much stronger game than in the previous year ... Perhaps his most noteworthy triumph of that season was his victory over the brothers John and Edmund Tompkins, whom he defeated at Brighton by eight games to four ... This year his most important game previous to the great match for the title was with C. Saunders, who is looked upon as the coming man among English professionals. Conceding the odds of half fifteen for a bisque, Pettitt won three sets to one. He also won a match with J. Harradine, to whom he gave fifteen to a bisque, and on April 29 he defeated Mr. J.M. Heathcote, the amateur champion of the world, in a practice game at Hampton court, giving fifteen for a bisque, and winning five straight sets, only one of which was close....

The grand contest for the championship has been fully reported in the English newspapers ... The impression derived ... has been that Pettitt was thoroughly outplayed ... and only gained the victory through his opponent's failing strength ... None of the critics gave any weight to the fact that Hampton court ... must have handicapped Pettitt ... Pettitt's difficulties ... arose entirely from being unable to find the length of the court, both for his service and return. Hampton court is two feet longer and eighteen inches wider than the Boston court ... It was undoubtedly the most remarkable struggle for supremacy in the entire history of the game, and another such contest is not likely to be winessed in this generation.... just previous to his departure for home Pettitt gave Lambert a bisque at the Manchester court, and defeated him without difficulty, the ex-champion scoring but four games in three sets....

Pettitt ... being only twenty-six should have a long career before him, perhaps equal to J. Edmond Barre, who won the championship in 1829 and held it for thirty-three years against all comers.... Challengers for the title will be obliged to come here... a natural consequence will be the building of more courts, and therefore a widening of the circle of interest....

Outing recorded the victories of James Dwight and Richard Sears in England, September, 1885, p. 757. Sears became a dominant player in American tennis by virtue of his talent and innovative technique.

LEAMINGTON TENNIS TOURNAMENT

At the Leamington Lawn-Tennis Club open tournament, on the Manor-House hotel grounds, Leamington, England, June 16, 17, and 18, Dr. James Dwight, of Boston, who for several years held, with R.D. Sears, the championship of America at doubles, won the challenge cup in the all-comers singles; and with J.C. Kay, the first prize in all-comers doubles. He had been for some time unfortunate in having trouble from a leg injury, but recovered in time for this tournament, which was one of the principal events of the year.

The latest stroke in lawn tennis is the English drive, played by Mr. Sears since his return from England. It is used in returning from near the base line, a low drive, and is executed by holding the handle of the racket perpendicular under the shoulder, and raising a bat by giving a half jump at the moment of striking. A violent forward rotation is imparted to the ball, which does not bound at all, but clings to the ground. If stopped at the net, the ball drops dead from the racket. No player in this country can use the stroke as yet with any certainty, excepting Mr. Sears, who scores many points with it.

The Chicago Tribune, in reporting the Western championship, 9 July 1887, p. 3, described the strategy of early play.

CHASE WINS THE CHAMPIONSHIP FOR THE WESTERN STATES

The match between A.C. Chase and B.F. Cummins for the championship of the Western States in the lawn tennis tournament yesterday was a very nice exhibition of tennis, but was not as interesting to look at as some other sets that have been played. The reason for this was that both played a back-line game, relying almost entirely on "cuts." It is the "volley" game, with its quick returns, that awakens the most enthusiasm. Cummins played best in the first set - at least, he was most effective then. He has a "cut" that is exceedingly deceptive, and which puzzled Chase not a little. However, after the first set Chase seemed to understand it better and won the other two sets with little difficulty. The score was 7-5, 6-3, 6-4.

...For doubles the first prize went to McClellan and Cummins of the Kenwood Tennis Club, and the second to the Chase brothers of Lake View....

Tennis spread rapidly from its eastern origins to the South and West. The developments were chronicled in Outing, March, 1889, pp. 496-504; and Overland Monthly, October, 1892, pp. 363-376.

LAWN TENNIS IN THE SOUTH

The remarkable interest displayed in lawn tennis throughout the North, and the increasing popularity of the game ... have been fully equaled in the South during the past two seasons.

... The Southern Lawn Tennis Association, which was organized in the fall of 1887, made it a part of its constitution that "no club which is situated north of Wilmington, Delaware, should be admitted to membership in the Association."... Winter visitors to the South find the game in full swing in every town from Wilmington, Delaware, to St. Augustine, Florida. Tournaments are held in the largest cities of the extreme South in the middle of winter ...

The enthusiasm of the extreme South has reached its highest point in St. August-ine, Florida, where a valuable challenge cup has been offered, to be played for in February or March of each year. The cup was last year ... won by Mr. H.G. Trevor, of New York City.... The St. Augustine Lawn Tennis Club has recently become a member of the United States Lawn Tennis Club, and the coming tournament will be held under its auspices.

... In Washington, particularly, the game has taken a long stride forward ... Turf courts can be used as late as December and as early as April ... Some years ago a few members of the Metropolitan Club built an asphalt court on I Street, and since that time there have been few winters when the court has not been in constant use.... Mr. W.V.R. Berry ... showed the value of his winter practice by capturing most of the rich prizes offered at Northern tournaments during the following summer, his rank among expert players being second only to the champion, Mr. R.D. Sears....

Prior to the sumer of 1887, tournaments for the championship of the South had been held on the grounds of the Delaware Field Club, at Wilmington, that club being a member of the United States National Lawn Tennis Association, and the tournaments being held under its auspices.

...Dr. F.P. MacLean conceived the idea of organizing an association, to be composed exclusively of clubs situated in the South ... active preparations were begun for the first tournament ... and on the 30th of October a meeting was held ... in Washington, at which delegates from the Baltimore Cricket Club ... the Delaware Field Club of Wilmington, and other smaller clubs scattered through Virginia and Maryland, met representatives at the prominent clubs of the District of Columbia. A permanent organization was effected, to be known as the Southern Lawn Tennis Association....

The first tournament of the Association was successful, far beyond the anticipation of its promoters. It was held on October 30 and the following days, at the United States Marine Barracks, The championship of the South, in singles, was won by Leigh Bonsal, of the Baltimore Cricket Club, and the same player, with L.V. LeMoyne as partner, secured the honor of the doubles championship for his club.... The prizes were donated to the Association by two prominent firms of New York City, A.G. Spalding & Bros. giving a challenge cup for the singles, to be won two years before it became the property of the holder, and Peck & Snyder presenting two silver cups to the winners of the doubles championship....

This tournament virtually ended the lawn tennis season of 1887 in the South. Its effect was noticeable, however, in the largely increased number of clubs and players in Washington and its vicinity.... It was determined that the next championship tournament should be held in the spring, and that the grounds of the Baltimore Cricket Club should be used ... Early in the month of May ... the most active players of Washington arranged a tournament for the championship of the District of Columbia ... on the courts of Kendall Green, the ably conducted Government college for deaf mutes, at the head of which is the well-known Dr. Gallaudet. Two tennis organizations ordinarily use these courts; the one composed mainly of college professors, and the other almost entirely of the students ...

Having secured these grounds, the committee made the tournament additionally attractive by adding two events for ladies, both a singles and a doubles competition. There are no ladies in the District whose skill rivals that of the seemingly invincible

Miss Robinson of Staten Island ... but there are many of considerable skill ... The championship of the District of Columbia, in ladies' singles, was won by Miss Bayard, a daughter of the Secretary of State, who had often demonstrated the strength of her game while a member of the Delaware Field Club of Wilmington. The contest in ladies' doubles was won by Miss Bayard and Miss Safford. The championship in men's singles was rather unexpectedly taken by Mr. John Pope, who had shown a considerable knowledge of the science of the game when representing Cornell University in the Intercollegiate tournament of the previous year. Mr. C.L. McCawley ... with Mr. Stevens as partner, succeeded in winning the final round of the doubles from Messrs. Woodward and Davidson, and thus carried off that championship.

The success of this tournament...did not ... affect... the next championship meeting of the Southern Association, held on the grounds of the Baltimore Cricket Club, on June 13 and following days.... Messrs. Bonsal and LeMoyne ... succeeded in winning the double event for the second time, and thus became the owners of the two cups presented by Peck & Snyder. A new champion made his appearance in the singles. Mr. A.H.S. Post ... won the championship without much trouble. Mr. Post is only seventeen years of age ...

There were about ten clubs in existence two years ago. There are now seventy, and the total number of players, as estimated by the "Capitol" newspaper, is two thousand....

Some few years ago a club ... was organized by several gentlemen of Washington, prominent among whom was John F. Waggeman. A clubhouse and grounds were secured on the Bladensburg road ... in the State of Maryland ... not more than three or four miles from the centre of the city of Washington. The club is known as the Country Club of the State of Maryland, or the Highland Country Club ... One of the earliest features added to the club was a tennis court ... it... occurred to ... Dr. F.P. McLean, who was a member and interested in the club, that this would be a grand place to hold a large tennis tournament...

...He felt that a tournament for the championship of the South, open to all comers, whether from the North or the South, would excite general interest...

As a first step, the Country Club of the State of Maryland applied for membership in the United States National Lawn Tennis Association, with the idea of holding the proposed tournament under the auspices of that Association....This action ... placed the National Association in an attitude of apparent rivalry to the Southern Association. The latter had already held a tournament in Baltimore ...and,... would not recognize any champion for the year except the winner of that tournament. The rivalry was more apparent than real, however, as Dr. McLean, the president of the Southern Association, was one of the originators... of the Country Club tournament....it is probable that the United States National Lawn Tennis Association ... will at the next annual meeting engraft into its constitution a clause under which other associations may be admitted to membership... thus making it a central and undisputed authority in lawn tennis throughout the United States....

The club had at this time but one lawn tennis court, and as soon as the tournament became an assured fact, it was at once decided to lay out four more....

The tournament was held on Tuesday, September 25 and the following days, and could hardly have been a greater success.... There were in all thirty-six contestants,

making it by far the largest tournament ever held in the South ... Dr. McLean had secured the presence of Thomas Pettitt, the professional champion of the world in court
tennis, and also remarkably expert in lawn tennis. Pettitt played two exhibition games
during the week ...

The play in the tournament proper demonstrated that Southern form is not yet up
to Northern, for ... the four men left to battle for the prize were all representatives of
the North....The final round was contested by Messrs. Mansfield and Miller, and was
won easliy by the former, who thus became the second champion of the South for
1888....

The double event was won by Messrs. Mansfield and Hoppin, but in the final round
Messrs. Davidson and Metcalf, the crack Washington team, gave a good exhibition of
double playing and won one set from the victors.... Northern players returned to their
homes with a very high opinion of Southern hospitality. A feature of the visit ... was
their call on the President of the United States. One morning about thirty of the players boarded a hay-cart, the property of that "same old negro" and drawn by two of his
mules, were taken to Washington, shown all points of interest, and, finally, invaded the
White House, where they were presented to President Cleveland.

...at Baltimore ... the lawn tennis interest is almost entirely centred in two clubs, the
Baltimore Cricket Club and the Towson Club of Towson, a suburb of Baltimore. Of
these two the Cricket Club is by far the more prominent. It is an old organization,
having been founded in 1874, but it was not until 1878 that the club, then quite small
in membership, leased grounds at Mount Washington, also a suburb of Baltimore ...

As the name signifies, the Baltimore Cricket Club was originally organized for
cricket purposes. But after lawn tennis was introduced as a club sport in the year 1879,
that game rapidly became so popular with the members that interest in cricket has
decreased, a fate somewhat similar to that which has befallen this scientific game in
our own St. George's Cricket Club of New York. The rapid rise of interest in lawn
tennis in popular interest could not be more plainly demonstrated than by the experience of the Baltimore Cricket Club. Its tennis courts were originally laid out on a part
of the cricket field, but the game became so widely played that it was found necessary,
in 1884, to grade an additional plot of ground, to be used for tennis alone, upon which
there are now ten excellent turf courts. This number was thought to be ample, but this
past season has shown the necessity for still larger accommodation, and the preparations are now being made for the construction of four dirt and four additional turf
courts....

... With a total membership of over two hundred, and a lively interest in sports of
every nature, the Baltimore Cricket Club is perhaps the most important athletic club
of the South. Next in importance is the Towson Club ... It has seven good turf courts,
and is particularly popular among ladies of the city.

At Wilmington, Delaware, is located one of the most flourishing clubs of the Southern section. The Delaware Field Club was organized in 1882, grounds were secured
and buildings erected in 1883, and the club was incorporated in 1885.... Lawn tennis
has always been the favorite sport of the members, and now it seems to be definitely
settled that the lawn tennis world is indebted to the Delaware Field Club for the introduction of "progressive tennis," a novelty founded on the once popular craze,
"progresssive euchre."

The club was one of the first to join the United States National Lawn Tennis Association, and in 1886 a tournament for the championship of the South, held on its grounds under the auspices of that association, was won by Mr. C.B. Davis, of Lehigh University. Mr. Davis was thus the first champion of the South, both in singles and doubles, for he also captured the latter event with Mr. R.H.E. Porter, of Lehigh, as a partner.... The grounds of the club will accommodate at least twenty-five courts, and as many as eighteen are in almost constant use. Out of a total membership of two hundred, about eighty are active lawn tennis players, and in this number are included several ladies, the most expert of whom is Miss Florence Bayard, a daughter of Mr. Cleveland's Secretary of State....

LAWN TENNIS IN CALIFORNIA

...It is really an astonishing fact that, as much as tennis is played throughout this country, so few people outside of the "society" set understand the intricacies of the game....

The enthusiasm of the spectators on the Coast is far greater, or, to say the least, more demonstrative, than that of the Eastern States. The tournaments in the West resemble Eastern college events in the fact that many different club "yells" are heard, and there is seldom a spectator who is not decked out in club colors.... Some twelve or fifteen members of the California Tennis Club joined forces and took a prominent station on the courts, to "help Will Taylor win the championship."...

The Pacific States Lawn Tennis Association was organized on July 3, 1890, and now has sixteen clubs upon its list of membership.

Unfortunately for the beauty of the game, it is impossible for the clubs of California to build turf courts on account of the long season in which no rain falls....The dirt court has been used to a great extent throughout the Pacific Coast, but during the winter season, when instead of snow comes the rain, the dirt court softens and is unfit for use for several days after a shower. It is for this reason that the principal clubs have adopted the use of asphaltum courts. These are a trifle more expensive to lay, but are less expensive to take care of afterward.

One of the most prominent of California clubs is the California Lawn Tennis Club, whose grounds are situated in the Western Addition of San Francisco. It has six courts and a very comfortable and commodious club house....

Joe Daly, the court keeper of the California Club, is the best professional player on the Coast, and in fact finds little difficulty in defeating the best players in practice.... Daly has taught the "chop stroke," which is used so effectively by a great number of the Pacific Coast players, to nearly all that use it. It is a stroke peculiar to him. He is rarely seen in public, except when he plays an exhibition match with some of the crack players.

The strongest rival of the California Club is the Oakland Tennis Club, which is a consolidation of the Lakeside and the East Oakland Clubs. It has four courts and a very pretty and artistic club-house....

The Alameda Tennis Club-house is a charming bit of rustic architecture surrounded by pine and live oak trees.... The club has two asphaltum courts, and has the best scoring stands of any of the clubs in the vicinity of San Francisco.

Tennis at the Leland Stanford Junior University has taken a good footing, and is now one of the most popular sports. Last year J.W. Thompson won the championship, beating the former champion, Campbell....

Within the last year a new club, known as the San Francisco Tennis Club has been organized in the city, and has on its membership roll the names of a number of good players who will undoubtedly take an active interest in the sport. There are a number of tennis clubs in Oakland, which, although they do not rank with the large and older clubs, are none the less important. These clubs are principally made up of younger players. The Madison Tennis Club and the Oakland High School Club are two very enterprising organizations, which have so far turned out some of the best players of the Coast.... The Madison Club has two asphaltum courts and are about to build a new club-house.

The University of California has taken a great interest in tennis, and has a regularly formed club which is a member of the association. S.S. Sanborn is the champion of the University, and is also a member of the Oakland Club; he is one of the foremost players of the Coast. His exhibition in the San Rafael tournament when he defeated Joe Tobin was one of the finest ever seen in the West....

Tennis in the Southern part of the State is a foremost sport. The tournament which was lately played at Santa Monica was the most successful ever held on Southern California. A.I. Alexander of Santa Barbara carried off the honors of the gentlemen's singles, beating Germain of Los Angeles. The Southern tennis players were treated to a great surprise in the doubles when the Carter Brothers, who were veteran English players, were defeated by the Chase Brothers of Riverside. The Chase brothers are very young players, and show remarkably good form in their games....

One could not hope to witness better tennis than was played throughout the tournament in San Rafael for the singles championship of the Pacific Coast, which ended July 4th. In the Championship round between William H. Taylor, Jr. of the California Lawn Tennis Club (holder of the championship) and Charles P. Hubbard of the Oakland Tennis Club (challenger and winner of the all-comers' tournament), the play was of a most scientific and highly exciting character.... Taylor's cool, slow play is simply perfect, and that was the means of his retaining the championship and gaining the beautiful cup as his personal property, having won it three times....

Hubbard's record in the East this summer has been a surprise to both Californians and Eastern people. It has long been a matter of conjecture as to how the players of the Pacific Coast would stand with the "cracks" of the East, and until this year no players of note from the West have entered Eastern tournaments. The rank of fifth at the end of the Nahant tournament is indeed most creditable. Of three men whom he defeated, two were ranked among the ten best players in this country last year, and the third in 1889 won the all-comers' at the national tournament at Newport. Hubbard was beaten at Newport in the second round by Clarence Hobart, the winner of the all-comers' at the same tournament a year ago, and ranked for the past year as second in the United States. There are a number of players on the Coast that play very close indeed to Hubbard, and it is gratifying to know that California tennis is not very much less advanced than the players in the Eastern States....

Tennis has had a great helper in C.R. Yates, of the California Club, and there are very few who have devoted more time to the interests of the charming game. He has been secretary of the Pacific States Association since the organization, and but recently resigned. Two years ago Yates won the all-comers' in the championship event at San Rafael, and is considered one of the experts of the Coast. He plays an aggressive net volley game when possible, and plays principally cut strokes.

Charles Bates of Oakland, is one of the most promising players on the Coast. Though quite young he is already champion of Alameda County, and has a remarkably good prospect of winning future championship events....

Sam Neel was for some time Bates's partner in doubles, when they were known as the "pony team" on account of their slight physiques....

H.H. Haight has played tennis for a number of years both in the Eastern States and upon the Coast. His tennis career started at Yale, where he played with the present cracks Huntington and Knapp. With Hubbard last year he won the championship in doubles of the Coast....

Joseph Tobin of the California Club is one of the few Californians who have entered any of the Eastern tournaments. His play in the doubles at Chicago with Hubbard was, according to all Eastern accounts, remarkably good. Tobin is one of the strongest men in doubles on the Coast, and ranks very well with the best in singles. In 1889 Tobin and McGavin held the double championship of the Coast....

Carr Neel is a very promising member of the Oakland Club, and plays one of the strongest games played on the Coast....

A.B. Wilberforce has played tennis for about thirteen years in England and in this country, and is very devoted to the game. Wilberforce is almost indispensable as a referee and scorer, and his success and willingness to help manage tournaments bring him upon nearly every tournament committee. His brother, H.W.W. Wilberforce, is the author of several books on tennis, and is considered one of the authorities in the tennis world....

A new feature in tournaments was introduced, in the lady scorers and umpires on the lines. There was not a complaint, and the ladies were a decided success as officials in the games. The interest in the ladies' play has greatly increased since last year, and consequently the play shows a decided improvement. The coveted championship for the singles was won this year by Miss Susan D. Morgan, of the California Club, and the prize was well earned, for Miss Morgan played a remarkably strong game. The finals between Miss Morgan and Miss Elizabeth Chew, of the Presidio, were very closely contested. Miss Chew plays a game that is without apparent exertion and places and drives in remarkable form. Miss Myra Lord, who has held championsship honors in Army circles in the East, plays one of the most pleasing games to witness of any of the ladies. Her service and back hand are particularly strong. Miss Mattie Gibbs is one of the strongest players of the Pacific States; she shows great judgment in her play and places exceedingly well. Miss Roberts, of San Lorenzo, Miss Capwell, and Miss McCoy, are among the lady players who rank well, and who have done very good work in the tournaments. Miss Ethyl Bates is the only player among the ladies who plays the net volley game, placing her strokes with great accuracy. The champion of last year, Miss Bertha Crouch, has not played this season in any of the tournaments, and was compelled to default the title on account of being in the East.

There was probably never a greater surprise in the tennis circles of the Pacific Coast than when Sam and Sumner Hardy defeated all comers and won the championship of the Pacific States. This was their first tournament, and consequently they were comparatively unknown. They have never played in a singles tournament of any note, and that is the reason why they have not been ranked with the best players of the Coast....

CANADA

The Montreal Athletic Asociation provided a brief report of its lawn tennis tournament in 1894.

LAWN TENNIS

GENTLEMEN:-

The Tennis Department formed last season was quite a success some 40 members enrolling their names as wishing to take an interest in this sport, and the courts were kept busy all the season.

To create an interest in Tennis your committee got up a Handicap Tournament. Some twenty members entered, the first match taking place in June, and it was well into August before the competition was over, Mr. P. Barton taking first place, and Mr. A.D. MacDonald second, and your committee would suggest getting up a Tournament this coming season to include single and double, and also to arrange matches with outside clubs. The game is increasing in popularity and more attention should be given to it.

A little more attention might be given to the care of the courts.

THOS. I. PATON,
Chairman.

Chapter 15

TRACK AND FIELD

Pedestrianism of the 1840s and 1850s fell moribund during the Civil War; but track and field events rebounded in the 1870s. Spurred by interest in the Scotch Caledonian games that featured money prizes for races and weight throwing contests, urban athletic clubs and colleges began to institute a wider scope of activities. The New York Athletic Club offered the first amateur track and field championships in 1876, that same year the Intercollegiate Association of Amateur Athletes of America began its annual competitions.

Training became more specialized as schools and athletic clubs hired professional coaches in the early 1880s. Performances in track and field were especially important to scientists who measured the improvement in human abilities. Some of the most prestigious universities set up labs for nutritional studies to find the most effective fuels to propel the human machine; while photographic studies enabled athletes to perfect their technique.

Lon Myers, a frail man, proved the most productive of track athletes, holding the records from 50 yards to a mile during the course of his career. Myers was charged with professionalism and the issue caused a split between simon pure traditionalists and their more liberal opponents. By 1888 a faction of New York athletic clubs split from the National Association of Amateur Athletes of America to form the Amateur Athletic Union. The latter evolved as the major governing body of amateur athletics in the United States.

Better technology, better techniques, and specialization brought an assault on the record books. Charles Sherrill, a Yale sprinter, began using the crouch start in 1888. Two years later, John Owen became the first person to run a hundred yards in less than ten seconds.

Nationalism fostered broader competition, and track became a highly commercialized spectator sport. When Lon Myers defeated Walter George, the English champion, in a series of three match races at Madison Square Garden in 1888, each netted $4,500. By 1894 college runners traveled to London to challenge their English counterparts and the New York Athletic Club defeated the London Athletic Club team in New York the next year. The inaugural modern Olympic games in 1896 engendered an interest in the marathon, and the first such race in the United States occurred in October of that year from Stamford, Connecticut to New York. The Boston Athletic Club initiated its famed classic on 19 April 1897.

The increasing nature of faculty control over students' athletic activities can be discerned in the following account of the University of California's track team for the 1895 season. The national scope of such activities became evident when the runners made their initial tour of the east with Professor George C. Edwards as faculty manager. The following was provided by the University of California Archives.

EXPENSE ACCOUNT OF THE TRACK TEAM OF 1895

Dear Sir:

I beg leave to submit to you my account as Manager of the Trans-Continental Track Tour of the University of California for 1895.

Receipts.

$ 1230.90	Cash Collected by A.W. North.
229.05	" " " F.W. Koch.
400.00	" " " Col. Edwards.
202.60	Gifts and Benefits Collected by A.W. North.
107.40	" " " " " F.W. Koch.
$ 2200.60	Total Collections, Repayable only from net Profits.
$ 75.00	Returns from Games at Princeton.
265.00	" " " " U. of P.
	" " " " I.A.A.A.A.
155.26	" " " " Union.
71.25	" " " " W.I.A.A.A.
150.00	" " " " U. of I.
393.56	" " " " C.A.A.
100.00	" " " " D.A.C.
$ 1210.07	Total Returns from Games.
$ 250.00	Special Loan, negotiated by Col. Edwards.

(Original Loan was $300.00 but $50.00 was returned.)

$3660.67 Total Receipts.

Expenditures.

Transportation:

11 Tickets to Chicago,	$ 577.50
" Berths " "	66.00
10 Tickets, Chicago to Newark	162.50
1 Ticket to Chicago	52.50
" Berth " "	6.00
1 Ticket, Chicago to Newark	16.25
6 Berths, " " "	30.00
11 Tickets, Newark to Jersey City	6.60
Jersey City to Princeton	25.80
Fare, Princeton to Philadelphia	18.34
" Philadelphia " New York	18.00
" " Games	7.50
12 Tickets to Chicago	195.00
8 Berths " "	36.00
11 Tickets, Chicago to Urbana and return,	56.65
1 Berth, Chicago to San Fran'sco	6.00
12 Tickets " " "	630.00

6 Berths, Chicago to Denver	36.00	
" " Denver to San Franc'sco	27.00	
Total transportation		$ 1973.64

Travelling expenses.

Of Manager before starting	22.50	
" on journey	47.85	
Of Captain before starting	2.00	
Of team on journey	126.65	
Expenses, part of team at Princeton	13.00	
Expenses balance of team	17.00	
Expenses of Manager to N.Y. City	12.50	
Meals to Chicago	19.65	
Expenses of Manager to Chicago	3.80	
" Team to "	5.25	
" of Bradley, Chicago to Oakland	10.00	
Expenses of Team, Chicago to Den.	21.25	
" " Denver to Oak.	35.00	
Total travelling expenses		$ 336.55

Hotel bills.

At quarters, prior to leaving	137.00	
At Princeton	197.00	
At Philadelphia	134.80	
At New York City	126.45	
At Schnectady and Albany	97.75	
At Chicago (1)	76.75	
At Urbana	114.00	
At Chicago (2)	86.50	
At Denver	93.00	
Total Hotel bills		$ 1063.25

Expressage

At Princeton	26.75	
At Philadelphia	2.00	
At New York City	5.50	
At Albany	7.10	
At Chicago (1)	3.08	
At Urbana	8.55	
At Chicago (2)	10.00	
At Denver	5.00	
Total expressage		$ 67.98
Total Telegraphing		$ 31.45

Entries to Games.

W.I.A.A.A.	5.00	
I.A.A.A.A.	6.00	
I.A.A.A.A.	16.00	
Total entries to games		$ 27.50

Stationary and postage.

Before starting	18.00	
During trip	11.70	
Total stationary and postage		$ 29.70
Total Incidentals		$ 130.34
TOTAL EXPENDITURES		$ 3660.41
BALANCE. $ .26		

Respectfully submitted.

A.W. North

Man'gr T.T.T. of the U.C.

Berkeley, Jan 24/96

I have reviewed the within statement and believe it to be correct.

Geo. C. Edwards

In Illinois, the state university not only organized its own intercollegiate programs, but took the lead in assuming governance of high school activities. The account of such an enterprise in the High School Weekly, 12 June 1893, p. 19, provides a hint of the meeting that later ensued, as Chicago area students, used to running their own programs, bristled at adult control.

AT CHAMPAIGN

It was hot, but it was fun. A pretty field, magnificent records, excited boys and beautiful girls - what more could the heart desire? Well, perhaps we would have enjoyed it better had our Chicago athletes taken off more prizes. To have a country school walk, or rather run and jump, in and calmly make more points than all the Cook county high schools put together was slightly humiliating. But they had to establish some fine records to do it, and there is no use crying over lost races. We can have one consolation, at the next field day (June 10th) no one will be "in it" aside from Cook county athletes.

The University of Illinois can not be too highly praised for the fine way in which the whole affair was managed.

As the contestants arrived they reported at headquarters and were assigned places of entertainment while remaining in Champaign. The boys of the university came forth readily and the committee had accommodations for 160 people offered for their use.

The evening preceding the games the delegates from the different schools were called together by Mr. Cleaves Bennent of the University of Illinois. A draft of a constitution for the Inter-Scholastic Athletic Association of Illinois was presented. Mr. White of Hyde Park, objected to clauses giving the University of Illinois a vote on the executive committee, but after being laughed at by the delegates and sat down upon by the chairman he sat down. A clause giving the presidency to the winning team and making graduates ineligible for office was incorporated and the constitution was adopted with only two votes in the negative -Hyde Park and Lake View. The games will be held each year at Champaign on the third Saturday in June.

The day of the games opened with dubious looking clouds, but Sol was propitious and soon everything looked happy, especially the games committee. This committee, consisting of Prof. Hall and Messrs. Arms, McNutt and Bennett, deserves to be congratulated on the splendid way in which the program was concluded. To run off sixteen events with over 200 entries in less than three hours was a great feat. The Peoria people had a crowd of about seventy seated in the middle of the grand stand; and, having plenty to yell for, they yelled.

GROWTH AND DEVELOPMENT

The evolution of track and field activities can be traced through newspaper accounts and magazine articles of the period. The Boston Globe, 27 August 1880, n.p., reported on the Caledonian Games, an ethnic festival featuring races and field events.

THE CALEDONIAN ANNUAL GAMES AT SPY-POND GROVE

The Caledonian club of Boston held its twenty-seventh annual picnic and games at Spy Pond grove, yesterday.... A finer day than yesterday they could not have had for their pastimes... From as early an hour as 9 a.m. the roads approaching the grounds were crowded with teams; in fact all sorts of conveyances carrying Scotland's bonnie lads and lasses in their native dress. The first sound which greeted the visitor was the bag-pipe, and the first sight was the peanut vendor with his Scotch peanuts papered up neatly. The wandering son of sunny Italy also had a chance to peddle his bananas, and the daughter of the Emerald Isle had a place for her basket of apples. Those inclined to try either their strength or lungs could also be accommodated, and those who wished to join in the light fantastic they had their places allotted to them in the pavilion. Higgins military band was in attendance and also the pipers of the club. At 11 o' clock those interested in athletic sports moved toward the arena and awaited the opening of the games, which were as follows:

Putting the heavy stone - in this contest there were nine entries, D.C. Ross taking first prize, having thrown 35 feet 8 inches...

Putting the light stone- This was won as follows: D.C. Ross, 43 feet 10 inches... There were nine entries in this contest.

Throwing the heavy hammer - The first prize was won by D.C. Ross, who covered 101 feet 4 inches. This is the best throw on record, and his feat caused no little applause from all present....In the above there were eight entries.

Tossing the caber - J. Melrose carried off first prize, 38 feet 10 inches ... Nine entries.

Short race - This race was for members only, and had but six contestants. T. Aitkin came in first ...

Boys' race - For members' sons under fifteen years of age, handicap, three yards to a year, had seven entries, and was won by C. Clark....

Throwing the light hammer - For members only, had nine entries and was won by A.D. McDonald, his score being 86 feet 7 inches ...

Old men's race - For members only over fifty years of age, was won as follows: J.C. McIntosh first ...

Sack race - This race caused no little merriment among the crowd, which, no doubt, helped the winners to victory. There were but four entries; J. Buchanan came in first ...

The three-legged race - This was won by Aitkin and Buchanan ...

Running high jump - In this contest there were eight entries, and it was won by E.W. Johnston, he making 5 feet 8 inches ...

Standing high jump - Six entries: E. W. Johnston first, 5 feet 2 inches ...

Pole vaulting - For the first place there was a tie between W. Robertson and T. Aitkin, both men having cleared nine feet ten inches ...

Hitch and kick - There was a tie between Donaldson and Reid for first and second place ...

Running long jump - This had six aspirants, A.C. Reid taking first place at 18 feet 3 inches...

One-mile race - This was quite a lively race, and the following records will show for themselves: J. Rain, 4 minutes 47 seconds ...

Three-mile walk - This had nine entries, and was won as follows: H. Armstrong, 22 minutes 20 1/2 seconds...

The hurdle race - This was a quarter of a mile, with eight hurdles, and it was won by E.W. Johnston in 1 minute 6 seconds...

Hop, step and Jump - This was won by H. McDonald, he covering 43 feet 1 inch ...

Highland fling - This was awarded as follows: First prize to W. Robertson ...

Broadsword dance - I. West first ...

Throwing the fifty-six pound weight - This was a very close contest, and was watched with an eagle eye by all on the grounds. The prizes were awarded as follows: D.C. Ross, 24 feet 10 inches ...

Throwing the heavy hammer - This was awarded to D.C. Ross for the score of 95 feet 10 inches ...

The five-mile race - There were thirteen entries for this contest, among whom were several well-known athletes, and the race was such as to create no little amount of excitement. Raine of Canada took first prize, having covered the five miles in 26 minutes 7 seconds ...

The ninety yard race - This was won by T. Aitkin in 9 1/4 seconds ...

The tug of war - This was won by the Scottish team. There were ten contestants on each side, and the excitement was intense, the general opinion being that the Irish team would win; but they lacked the experience of their opponents, who won the first tug in 1 minute 15 seconds, and the second in 4 minutes....

Notes of the Day

The prizes ... were paid to the winners at the conclusion of the day's sports.

The police force ... was admirably placed and order reigned supreme.

On the return of the club and its guests from the grove, Paine Memorial Hall was in order ... Speeches ... were indulged in up to the hour of 10 o'clock, when the seats were cleared away and dancing was in order until an early hour.

By the mid-1880s the Chicago Tribune reported on the highly commercialized and formal arangements of the Myers-George matchup in a series of articles: 12 February 1886, p. 3; 2 May 1886, p. 13; and 9 May 1886, p. 11.

MYERS AND GEORGE SIGN ARTICLES OF AGREEMENT

New York, Feb. 20. - Articles of agreement were signed today for a series of two or three running races between Lawrence E. Myers of this city and Walter S. George of London. This match makes Myers a professional athlete. It is to be a match for a trophy emblematic of the middle distance championship of the world and $2,000 in stakes. Besides, the gate money will be equally divided between the men. The first race is fixed for May 1, to be a 1,000 yard run, and the second a dash of three-quarters of a mile for May 8. Should each man win one of these events a 1,160 yard race, to be run a week later, will decide the match. W.B. Curtis of the *Spirit of the Times* has been chosen stakeholder and referee.

MYERS, THE AMERICAN RUNNER, EASILY DEFEATS GEORGE, THE ENGLISH CHAMPION

New York, May 1. - Lawrence E. Myers, the pedestrian wonder, who for eight years as an amateur runner delighted the people of the United States, Canada and England by his superb form and matchless speed, tonight opened his career as a professional by beating W.G. George, the English crack, in the first of a series of international races. The contest is to decide the middle distance championship of the world. The stakes are $2,000, and the best two out of three races will decide the result. The Madison Square Garden, where the contest took place, held an interested crowd of about 6,000 people. The starting point was on the backstretch on the southside of the garden, 120 yards from the finish line, and then four times around the 220 yard track. Myers won the toss and took the inside position. The first lap went by like a dream, and the second was just like it. Going up the backstretch on the third lap George for a moment seemed to be drawing away from Myers, but it was an illusion. He could not shake him off. The pace looked very hot to those who watched George. Myers was unquestionably jogging. In the last lap George sprang forward as if the bell had hit him. But Myers was still in the shadow's place. At the west end of the garden there was a flash of white beside George. The shadow had let himself loose. In a fraction of a second George was the shadow, a yard behind Myers. All the bad Indians west of the Mississippi could not have yelled as those 6,000 people did. The Englishman kept up his pace. Myers increased his. He flew around the lower turn and entered the home-stretch ten yard ahead. Then he eased up a little and entered home hands down and as fresh as a daisy, six yards in the lead. His time was 2:23 2/5. George finished two-fifths of a second later. Myers looked good for 200 yards more at the same pace. George could not have gone faster. The time was 10 2/5 seconds behind Myers' best record at the distance, made, however, outdoors.

MYERS WINS THE MANTLE

New York, May 8. - The mantle of the middle distance championship of the world ... this evening settled itself down gracefuully on the sinewy shoulders of Lawrence E. Myers at Madison Square Garden. The little American bundle of bone and muscle once more proved good ... by defeating W.G. George .. and finishing with an unknown quantity of "go" left in him.... most people were saying that the series of races betwen him and his plucky opponent would turn out to be a hippodrome. Myers was to win the first race at 1,000 yards, of course, because no one could beat him at that distance; George would capture the three-quarters of a mile ... and the third race, 1,160 yards, being a doubtful one, would draw a full house.... Today those knowing fellows, the bookmakers, were offering two to one on Myers for tonight's race.

...An intermission of fifteen minutes was given to get the track in order after the preliminary races. Then some one blew three shrill blasts on a whistle ... The band played "Hail to the Chief," and the crowd yelled like a thousand buzz-saws out on a picnic. Myers was seen advancing out of the west end of the garden ... He wore his customary Manhattan Athletic Club dress of white with a red diamond on the breast. The band changed its tune to "God Save the Queen" and George appeared. He wore a dark blue shirt and a pair of dark blue knee-breeches with pale blue trimmings. He was applauded and cheered heartily.

The track measures 220 yards and they had six laps to run. Myers had the inside track.... A flash, the report of a pistol, and they were off. The start was perfectly even, and the men ran side by side for half a dozen yards. Then Myers dropped behind George and began his usual practice of dogging the footsteps of his man.... George was four yards ahead....

The men maintained their relative positions through the first lap and entered the second the same way....They finished the second lap in the same positions. Going up the backstretch of the third lap Myers decreased George's lead to about three yards....

An officer of the course rang a bell as they entered the last lap. Down they went to the turn at the west end of the garden. They turned into the back-stretch with a straight run of seventy yards before the next turn. There was a wild yell that baffles description. Again came that marvelous flash of white, with the slim legs going like the driving-rods of an engine. Myers, in the fraction of a second had shot forward like a rifle-ball and passed the champion of England as if he were standing still. The men, the boys, the dudes and the girls all yelled. It was one universal outburst of boundless joy. It was all over. Myers was ten yards in front, and George's mouth was wide open, his face red, and his brow ruffled. Myers was still as calm as a mummy. He cantered around the turn, looked back once to see where George was, and ran home an easy winner by six good yards. The crowd went fairly mad, and the runners were followed out of the ring by a shrieking, howling, dancing crowd. The time was 3:15 8-15. Myers record at that distance made outdoors is 3:13. George's is 3:08 1/4.

In 1886 Myers recounted his career for Lippincott's Magazine, 38, pp. 220-224.

CONFESSIONS OF A CHAMPION ATHLETE

So you want to know how I became an athlete?

Well, in my mind it is a question whether I *am* an athlete, - that is, if broad shouldrs, well-developed muscles, etc., are characteristics of an athlete. At any rate, it is generally conceded that I am a runner; and if you want to know all about me in that capacity, here goes.

Just when I started to run I don't know. I guess it must have been when I was about two years old. Ever since I can remember I have been noted for my fleetness of foot. In early childhood my companions would pit me against the champion of some other "crowd," and I never failed to defeat my opponent. When about thirteen or fourteen years of age, I was a member of a baseball nine, all of the other members being grown men.... it was a common thing in those days for players to run for each other. This was what I was kept on the nine for; and many a game I've pulled out of the fire through my ability to run the bases in good style.

I was born in Richmond, Virginia, and after graduating from the Richmond High School, in 1875, I came north to live. My family first settled in Jersey City, where I joined a baseball nine, and where I attracted the attention of the boys by my ability to "cover ground." My mother having died of consumption when I was a baby, my father encouraged me in my fondness for out-door sports, thinking in this way to ward off the dread disease which was hereditary in my mother's family. Soon after my arrival in Jersey City, I secured a position with Schieffelin & Co., wholesale druggists, of New York. I stuck closely to business for four years, when my health began to fail. On consulting a physician I was told that unless I took more out-door exercise I would in all probability be troubled with some pulmonary complaint. About this time I was thrown in contact with a Canadian who had some reputation as an athlete. We worked at the same desk and our conversation would often turn upon athletic subjects.... I ventured one day to say I thought I could outrun and outjump him. He promptly accepted ... The next Sunday we visited Coney Island , where we had it out on the sandy beach. It was no trouble at all for me to defeat him at every game we tried. Much impressed by my ability ... he urged me to enter some of the athletic competitions given every Saturday afternoon by the different athletic clubs in and around New York. I finally consented, and on election day, 1878, I competed at the sports of the New York Athletic Club.... I easily won the quarter-mile run from the eighteen-yards mark, and could have won it from scratch....

Soon after my first race, I went to John Fraser, the well-known maker of running -, walking -, and other kinds of athletic shoes, for advice. Fraser had quite a reputation as a trainer, and was ever on the alert for a good man. He had heard favorable reports of me from my first race, but I was so delicate in appearance and was troubled with such a bad cough that it was with many misgivings he agreed to take me in hand. His wife, an English lady, entreated him not to have anything to do with me. "John," said she, "that boy has consumption; and if you undertake to train him it will kill him, and his people will blame you for it.".... I merely replied that I would take the chances ...

.... Nevertheless, I managed to beat everybody that opposed me; and in the fall of 1879 I began to lower records....The day I reduced the figures for the quarter-mile from fifty-two and one-fifth seconds to forty-nine and one-fifth seconds, and ran the last hundred and twenty yards without my right shoe, I never saw such a dumfounded crowd in my life. Why, the time-keepers at first refused to show their watches, each thinking that he had made an egregious error. Later in the same afternoon, when, with a pair of borrowed shoes much too large for me, I lowered the figures for a furlong, the excitement was intense. I think "my head was turned" from that moment ...

...All of the English authorities said it was just possible that the tracks were short or the people who held watches didn't know their duties. I now determined to go to England. So, in the spring of 1881, the Manhattan Athletic Club, of which I was and have always been a member, sent me across the big pond.... Mr. William Waddell, who was then secretary of the London Athletic Club, met us ... looked at me in a manner in which seemed to say, "I am sorry for you, young man, if you imagine you can beat our best men."...

I had never realized before how small in stature I was until I toed the mark for my first race on British soil. All of my opponents were great strapping fellows .... At the pistol's crack I was the first away, a position I held for about forty yards ... I heard just before the race that first one and then another of my opponents were to race me as hard as they could, so as to break me up in the interest of Phillips, who was to finish me.... and I fell back into third ... until half the distance had been covered, when I cut loose ... I won away off, and notwithstanding that the track was heavy, I broke the English record, doing the quarter in forty-nine and four-fifths seconds....

The papers had to give me credit, much against their will, and many excuses were made for Phillips. The following Saturday I made a new record for the half-mile, and, Saturday after that reduced the quarter to forty-nine seconds; and, to cap the climax, at the championship sports, July 16, I ran a quarter in forty-eight and three-fifths seconds, finishing in a walk.... and I dare say I am thought more highly of as a runner in England than in America. I have visited England three times ... won nearly a hundred prizes there, I have been beaten only once, and that was due to an unfortunate stumble at the start in a hundred-yard race.

How many prizes have I won? ... the number must be somewhere between three and four hundred. I think I must have given away over two hundred. The original cost of ny prizes could not have been far short of ten thousand dollars. One medal alone costs five hundred dollars, and a single cup nearly as much.

You want to know the best man I ever met? Now, that is a puzzler.... If I am to decide, I must give my vote to George and Phillips.... I beat George four times out of six we met, while Phillips had to put up with second place on the two occasions we came together. My best distances are from two hundred and twenty yards to three-quarters of a mile.

No, I never claimed to be the best hundred-yards runner in the world.... I am not heavy enough to ever become a veritable champion at this distance. I have long since given up distances of this length, for several reasons, first of which they are too uncertain. A bad start often causes a man to be beaten by an inferior.... I have run only one professional race, - i.e., one series; ... with George, this spring. You haven't seen the English papers ... some of the articles are very funny. They call the track a circus-ring, and say that ... George could not use his long stride to advantage. Mind you, I stride at least six inches longer than George ...

No wonder Englishmen make such good soldiers: they never know when they are beaten.

Yes, there are several challenges out for me ... I'll do very little running until late in the fall, when I may visit Australia. There is an Irishman there named Malone who has been doing some marvellous "times" at my distances. He will not come here, so I suppose I'll have to go to him. I met him in England in 1881, but reports say he is now a wonder.... You are going to publish what I've told you, are you not? I am afraid it will read very egotistical; but, then, it can't be helped, for it is impossible to talk about one's self without being so; at any rate, this has been my experience.

∞

Elite athletic clubs sought the best athletes to enhance their prestige. Myers was sponsored by the Manhattan Athletic Club, whose team embarked on a tour of Great Britain, covered by Outing, October, 1888, p. 76. Such competitions promoted both the club's reputation and nationalistic spirit.

MANHATTAN'S VICTORIOUS ATHLETES

THE Manhattan Club Team returned from England, August 12th, after an absence of ten weeks, during which time its members won a half dozen championships in the national games at Crewe and the international games in Dublin.... From Queenstown Conneff went to Belfast, and won the four-mile Irish championship run. From that time the team's career was a series of victories. The men went into training at the grounds of the London Athletic Club, and soon had themselves in excellent trim. Besides winning his four-mile race, Conneff won the English one-mile and the international one-mile championship races. He also beat Carter in a five-mile match race. Thomas Ray won the pole-vaulting championship, and Westing carried off the honors in the 100-yard race at Crewe, besides winning at the international races in Dublin at the same distance. Westing's time in the latter race was ten seconds. Clark, another member of the team, completed the list by winning the seven-mile walk at Crewe. Gold medals were awarded in each event. Westing has challenged Great Britain for the 100-yard championship of the world, the race to take place on the Manhattan Athletic Club grounds. Messrs. Ritchie and Woods have accepted the challenge. A similar challenge by Conneff for the mile championship has been accepted by Messrs. Hickman and Leaver. When these championship events come off they will excite great interest.

In June, 1890, Walter Camp contributed an article to Century magazine, pp. 203-212, reflecting upon the evolution, organization, specialization, and quantification of track and field events. Over the next two years Outing published articles on the performances and specialized techniques in each event by one of the star athletes of the period, Malcolm Ford.

TRACK ATHLETICS IN AMERICA

England has been in advance of us in track athletics, as in many other branches of sport ... But Americans are already realizing that the unfailing laws of nature demand more attention to the physical welfare of the body ... track athletics offer ... more individual endeavor, and demand nothing of that team work or united exercise which must always place something of a limit upon the universal enjoyment of and participation in the other sports.

The professional side offers but little of interest to us beyond the records. The reason for this is that, in America at least, professional running is ... under a heavy cloud of questionable practices in the way of buying and selling races....

The amateur ranks, however, offer a very different phase of the subject. Two classes may be at once selected ... These two classes are college athletes and other amateurs....

Of English universities Oxford was the first to possess an organized athletic club. This was forty years ago, and in a few years Cambridge followed ... Fourteen years later the first inter-university contests were held between these two at the cricket grounds of Christ Church. Ten years later American colleges held their first intercollegiate contest at Saratoga ... only a sort of side show to the inter-collegiate boat-racing of that date. The incentive of these contests, nevertheless, brought about the formation of athletic associations at both Harvard and Yale, Harvard's organization antedating Yale's by a few months. The Intercollegiate Association was not formed until college sports had been in progress for some three years. Then in 1876 the Intercollegiate Association of American Athletes of America was organized. The same year the New York Athletic Club gave an annual meeting for the decision of the amateur athletic championship of America. The year 1876, then, may be taken as the date when organization was first firmly established in both college and amateur clubs. The necessity for such organization was the rapid increase in interest and the number of the contesting clubs.... for in 1873 only three colleges competed, in 1874 eight, and in 1875 thirteen.... The number of events, which in 1873 was one, increased in the following year to five, and was twelve when the organization was formed.... the number at present is fifteen.

The various games which are generally classed under the term "track athletics" are walking, running, jumping, bicycling, pole vaulting, throwing of weights, and tog-of-war contests....

The fastest running thus far done by any amateur for one hundred yards from a standstill is ten seconds, and if one may believe ... sporting journals, amateur runners have been coming up to this limit occasionally ever since 1868, but not one has passed it.... some eight American amateurs and an equal number of Englishmen have dashed down the track in the even time of ten seconds ... This record was made first in London in 1868, and last in Detroit in 1889.... From a quarter of a mile down the races are run at the top of the man's speed, but the half-mile, mile, and above require the husbanding of strength ...

First the ground is accurately surveyed and measured, and the track so marked out that the required distance is given. The best tracks have straight sides, while the ends are upon moderate curves ... This distance is measured just eighteen inches from the inner edge, in order that the runner may have room to run freely and yet not be obliged to traverse more than the correct distance. When the track is thus mapped out the proposed space is excavated to the depth of six inches, and the curbings of seasoned lumber, an inch thick and eight inches wide ... Then the first layer, consisting of four inches of ordinary rough ashes ... is deposited for a foundation. This layer is carefully raked and leveled, and then covered with two inches of loam.... It is then rolled and watered frequently ... in order to have it thoroughly firm and hard. Finally the top layer, of cinders, is put on.... The object of all this is to give the runners a firm, dry, and elastic surface upon which to make their best efforts successfully.

One of the first things on entry to the grounds is a summary of records....

The English are partial to a single watch in the hands of an experienced timer; but to make a record in this country requires the presence of three timers or measurers, and two of these must agree or the intermediate one of the three be taken as the correct one... there is the referee, who decides all questions in dispute which are not otherwise covered by the rules, and who has the power to disqualify a competitor. Then there are two more assistants to the referee, who are called clerks, and who act as witnesses before him in case of fouls. There are three judges at the finish ... three other judges are called field judges; these measure and tally the trials of competitors in jumps, pole vaults and weight competition. There are three time-keepers, who take the time in the events requiring it. There is a clerk of the course, who notifies the contestants to appear at the starting time, and assigns them their positions. There is one starter, who assumes control of the competitors after the clerk has placed them in their positions, ... starts each race, and whose duty it also is to disqualify any contestant making a false start. There is a judge of walking ... There is one scorer, who records the order in which the contestants finish, as well as their time. Finally, there is one marshal, who has police charge of the inclosure. There is occasionally an official reporter ...

... In this 100-yard race one of the chief points to be mastered is the start.... for a fifth of a second means five feet of ground.... If an ordinary spectator were to watch the start of an experienced sprinter against a novice, he would almost invariably suspect collusion ... between the starter and the sprinter.... In all short races, those up to 300 yards, the penalty for a false start is to be put back one yard. Two yards is the penalty in races up to 600 yards, three yards in races up to 1000 yards, five yards in races up to a mile, and ten yards in those over a mile. In all races a third false start disqualifies the competitor ...

The 220-yard race is similar to the 100 in all respects. The contestants belong to the sprinter class ...

With the 440-yard, or quarter-mile, one sees the first signs of grief in those whose condition is not of the best, or who cannot hold out for the entire distance. It is at this instance that the runner shows that he is not a machine. The best illustration of this is shown in the records of the events. The speed of a runner at his best, as shown in the 100-yard race, is ten yards a second. This speed he holds with machine-like precision in the 220-yard race, the record being a bare fraction under 22 seconds. When the 440-yard race is reached, however, he cannot gather the power necessary to finish in 44 seconds, but at this distance we find the best man nearly 4 seconds behind time....

Hurdle racing is a sport which stands between running and jumping, being a combination of the two. It does not require a man of marked jumping ability, however, as the flights are only 3 feet 6 inches ... The point, in fact, at which the hurdler aims is to clear them just as little as possible ... The scientific hurdler now takes a certain number of steps between the flights, and ... actually clears them without a break in his stride ... The distance covered is 120 yards, and there are ten hurdles set ten yards apart with a 15-yard clear start and finish. Other distances are sometimes run, as 220 yards most commonly. In this caase the hurdles are a foot lower, and are set 20 yards apart. The amateur record for the 120-yard hurdle race is 16 seconds....

The walkers next attract our attention. To the ordinary pedestrian ... the gait is entirely unfamiliar.... Watch this man who walks a mile in seven minutes! It certainly seems as if he would twist his spinal column apart just above the hips.... The distinction between running and walking is, that in the latter the heel strikes the ground first, and some part of one foot is always touching the ground ... It requires the most expert of judges to see that the walking is fair, for there are a dozen tricks of gait ... Long-distance pedestrianism, such as six-day walking matches ... are now of the go-as-you-please class; that is, there is no restriction as to gait, the majority taking to a kind of jog-trot which yields the greatest results with the least fatigue.

To watch the jumping is rather a relief ... in the case of the long or broad jump the greatest distance covered in three attempts wins the event....

The high jump is made over a flat bar, which is supported on two uprights in such a position as to be easily dislodged. Competition begins at some height, selected by the measurers, which all the contestants can easily clear. The bar is then steadily lifted at he regulation of the measurers.... Three trials are allowed, and if on the third the jumper fails to clear the bar he drops out....

Pole vaulting is another species of jumping, in which the jumper aids himself by the use of a long pole which he plants in the ground ... and with which he lifts himself as he springs into the air. As the pole is reaching the perpendicular he swings himself over the bar... The same rule governs the pole vault as the running high jump ...

Putting the shot is a contest requiring not only the same amount of skill ... but also unusual muscular strength. The shot is an iron sphere weighing either 16 pounds or 24 pounds ... It must be put with one hand only, and in front of the shoulder. The competitor stands in a seven-foot square, and must not step out of this square in putting, nor until his put has been measured.... Three trials are allowed, and the contestants take turn as in the broad jump.

Throwing the hammer, like putting the shot, requires a combination of skill and muscular strength. The hammer is a metal sphere into which is set a handle, the projecting length of which ... is four feet, the combined weight ... being sixteen pounds. The throwing is done from a circle seven feet in diameter, and the competitor may not overstep the front of the circle until his throw is measured....

Bicycling has grown to be so common and widespread that it has a life, rules, and records quite apart from ordinary track athletics.

The tug of war is the only event in track athletics that necesitates any team work.... The limits for the aggregate weight for the four men constituting the team vary considerably, from 550 pounds up to 650.... although many heavy-weight teams are unlimited in regard to avoirdupois.... The time limit is five minutes, and the team having gained the most rope at the expiration of that time wins....

... In the 100 yards we stand on a level with the English amateurs, a few reaching ten seconds, but none going inside that limit. In the 220-yard run the English amateur has beaten our record. When we reach the quarter-mile, however, our men have not only won in records both here and on their own tracks, but have run away from all their champions in actual races. At the half-mile we have been recently overtaken by a fleet-footed Briton, while another of the race has shown us his heels in the mile. On the hurdle they have long surpassed us, but at the running high jump our champion has beaten their records ... The long jump we also hold, but the pole vault is theirs.

There is one feature ... known as handicapping.... As the term implies, handicapping is the taking away certain of the advantages of the superior men ... that they must not only do better than the rest in order to win, but do enough better to make it a fair struggle on both sides. Sometimes a time allowance is made to weaker men; more often ... competitors are placed at certain intervals... being proportioned to their relative ability ... The Amateur Athletic Union, which at present embraces the majority of prominent clubs, employs an official handicapper ... at a salary not to exceed $1500; he is expected to keep records and to handicap all entries ...

...The question of the age at which a man is fitted for his best athletic work has always ben a mooted one in all sports.... Hammer-throwing and weight-putting championships have been won by men over forty years of age, while boys of eighteen years have taken the 100 -yard, mile, jumping, and pole-vaulting championships ... The first annual championship meeting in 1876, had on its programme the following events: 100-yard, quarter-mile, half-mile, one-mile runs; 120-yard hurdle race; one, three, and seven mile walks; running high jump; running long jump; throwing hammer; and putting the shot. The present rules of the A.A.U. give events as follows: 100-yard, 220-yard, 440-yard, 880-yard, one-mile, and five-mile runs, one-mile and three-mile walks, two-mile bicycle race, pole vault, running high junp, running broad jump, throwing 16-

pound hammer, throwing 36-pound weight, putting 16-pound shot, 120-yard hurdle race, 220-yard hurdle race, individual tug of war, and team tug of war - a total of nine-teen....

Concerning the financial status of track athletics, while they do not, like base-ball, have an existence for the purpose of money-making, there is nevertheless a large amount of capital involved indirectly. Almost all of the clubs now prominent in this branch of sports have a winter existence, games, and habitat as well as an outdoor one. In most of the large cities there are athletic clubs which own desirable property.... The New York Athletic Club has a membership of twenty-five hundred abd property to the vlue of nearly $500,000. The Berkeley Athletic Club has only about five hundred men, but its property is valued at $400,000. The Athletic Club of the Schuylkill Navy, with a membership of over twelve hundred, is worth probably $75,000. The Detroit, the Manhattan, and the Staten Island Athletic Clubs are rich in membership and have a respectable amount of property.

One feature of these sports ... is the prizes. The first prizes given in English uni-versity sports were money prizes, but this practice was almost immediately altered, and there is now even a rule forbidding an athlete from pawning his medals or in any way converting them into money.... it has become the custom to have the prizes for record-breaking of more than merely nominal value....

The progress of track athletics in this country has been rapid.... The day has now come ... when they have an assured position at all the large universities and colleges, while in amateur athletic organizations track athletics have the first rank, and the other sports are of but minor interest....

A dispatch of the Chicago Tribune, 12 October 1890, p. 6, recounted the capture of one of the most coveted honors. Since 1868 sprinters had recorded marks of ten seconds for 100 yards; but John Owen was the first to break that barrier.

OWEN'S 100 YARD MARK

WASHINGTON, D.C., Oct. 11.- The greatest efforts of amateur running men have been set at naught by John Owen Jr. of Detroit. He ran 100 yards today in 9 4/5 sec-onds in sight of 5,000 people. Six watches in the hands of experts certified to the cor-rectness of the time. The starting was done by George D. Turner, the smartest pistol-firer in America. "Lon" Myers, Rene LaMontague, Wendell Baker, and all the other crack men whose names have become household words in sprinters' homes will now fall back into the dull dead ranks of "have beens."

The New York Times gave brief mention to Charles Curry's world record breaking performances in Canadian competition, 16 October 1892, p. 4.

BROKE THE SHOT-PUTTING RECORD

WINNIPEG, Man., Oct. 15. - Charles J. Curry the athlete broke three world's records today in putting the shot. He put the 24 pound shot 39 feet 9 3/4 inches, beating his previous record of 38 feet 11 inches. The 16-pound shot 43 feet 3 1/2 inches. Previous record 41 feet 9 1/2 inches, made by Gray at Travers Island in 1890. The 12 pound shot was put 54 feet 11 1/2 inches by Curry. The previous professional record was 50 feet 1/2 inch made by MacPherson in Brooklyn in 1887.

Some records resulted in great controversy, as indicated by a Harper's Weekly piece by Caspar Whitney on 25 April 1891, pp. 311-312. The advent of photography allowed for the resolution of such debates, engendered, in this case, by gambling and athletic club rivalry.

THE DOWNS QUARTER MILE RECORD CONTROVERSY

THE DOWNS record case will go down in posterity as the most remarkable piece of bungling in athletic history. The New York Athletic Club, of which Downs is a member, exhibited bad management at the trial last July, and since that time has shown an unprecedented indifference by its feeble attempts to have the grand performance recognized. Probably the most astonishing side of the matter, however, has been the ease with which a few significant seekers for cheap notoriety have been able to raise so much discussion....

On July 9, '90, Downs made an attempt on the Beacon Park race-track, Boston, to lower the quarter-mile record of 47 3/4 seconds, held by Wendell Baker. The trial was arranged by the New York Athletic Club, and three men of experience in such matters went down to Boston from here to take charge of the affair. There associated with them several other men of like experience in Boston. The track was measured by four of their number, and checked at each length of the tape. Timers were stationed at the 400-yard mark in 43 seconds, establishing the world's record for that distance, and breasting the tape at the 440-yard mark in 47 2/5 seconds.

Downs ran very strong, so strong that G.P. Cogswell, an old Harvard athlete, with a record under two minutes for the half-mile, who acted as pace maker from the 220 mark (which Downs reached in 23 1/4 seconds), although starting fresh, had all he could do to keep the lead. Mr. Cogswell declared himself astonished at the speed Downs showed in the last 220 yards. The spectators of the run included a number of Harvard and club men, and some of that professional element always to be found in the vicinity of race tracks. At the conclusion of the trial all of the officials agreed on the authenticity of the performance, and no dissenting voice was heard. Before Downs ran J.C. Hemment, who was on the grounds representing me, photographed him on his mark at the start.... Hemment then went down to the 440 yard mark, and caught an instantaneous photograph of Downs finishing and within about nine feet of the tape.... It may be stated, in order to throw further light on subsequent occurrences, that while the track was being measured, and, in fact, during the trial, the professional element among the spectators was very generous with advice and suggestions that were neither solicited, required, nor regarded.

The day following the event a sensation was created by a declaration from this source that the course Downs had run was short. Among equally trustworthy reasons put forth, was one that a workman had drawn a line across the track 20 feet back of the true finish, over which the tape had been held instead of at the 440- yard mark, and that another workman had cut a notch in the fence where Downs actually did finish, and that this was short of the prescribed distance. Now it was really remarkable that an ignorant laborer - a common everyday dirt-heaver - should have exhibited so great an interest in this event, and such preternatural discernment of future complication, as to first of all obliterate the 400-yard mark, and then, with an ingenuousness worthy of transcription, to draw a line across the track 20 feet back of the true finish line, making the arrow heads, etc., exactly like that at the finish. Next, with a flash of forethought positively bewildering, he cuts a notch in the fence where it is claimed Downs finished, and finally, this astonishing dirt-heaver, with a rare appreciation of the reward to come, surrounds his labors with Cimmerian darkness until the following day.

The cry of wolf having been raised, the trainer of one of Boston's athletic clubs and several members of the same club added their voices to the alarm, and have never lowered them since. I may dispose here of this trainer's testimony when I say that though he has proclaimed the loudest that Downs finished 20 feet short, he was about a quarter of a mile away when Downs breasted the tape. So much for him. Now for the other claims. At the beginning of the hubbub these sensation breeders declared that Downs could not have run the last 40 yards in the time which a comparison of the 400 and 440 yard figures shows must have been done. Downs finished strong, as the intantaneous photograph ... shows; and to cover 40 yards in that condition from a flying start in 4 2/5 seconds would be nothing remarkable. This disposed of, the detractors fell back on the 20-foot line drawn by the obligatory laborer, and dilated long and positively on this having been the place where Downs finished. When the instantaneous photograph of the finish was developed, lo and behold! there was the 20-foot line in the background showing clearly behind Downs ...

The wise men of the East, however, had followed their star too long to confess it a will-o'-wisp. A claim was at once made that the negative had been "doctored" - that the line had been drawn on the negative, the deluded contingent, in its ignorance, not knowing that a line drawn on the negative would show in front of Downs. To answer all claims, however, no matter how improbable, the negative was taken by Mr. W.B. Curtis, editor of *The Spirit of the Times*, and myself to photographic experts in this city, who made an affidavit, signed and sworn to before a notary, that the negative had not been doctored and that the line was taken simultaneously with the other objects in the picture.

The one remaining straw now was the notch in the fence. After its parentage had been put upon several, it ws finally acknowledged by John Graham, who said he cut it the day *after* the event. Graham held a watch at the 400 *yard mark*. Remember, the first claim was that a laborer standing at the *finish* cut the notch *immediately* after Downs finished. Notch, line, and theory gone, the chairman of the Boston contingent, known generally as the Latter Day Investigating Committee, launched into mathematics, and absolutely lost himself, his supporters, and his cause; the cultured Hub could no longer prove faithful to a standard raised on ignorance. From that day to this we have heard no more theories on the Downs record. Not one point raised by the opposition has been substantiated, while that instantaneous photograph remains intact.

I have entered into the details of this performance, that the entire country may have the absolute uncolored facts, and realize to what extremes the detractors of this record have gone to gain their point. One of the greatest athletic feats ever accomplished by man has been near being lost to him and the athletic world through the machination of a few soulless creatures....

Harper's Weekly reported on the national championships, 23 September 1893, p. 922, with less than enthusiasm, as the concern with punctuality, efficiency, and morality overshadowed record breaking performances.

THE NATIONAL ATHLETIC CHAMPIONSHIPS, 1893

THE NATIONAL ATHLETIC CHAMPIONSHIPS, held on the South Side Ball Grounds at Chicago, brought out four remarkably good performances and a lot of ordinary ones. With the exception of these four, and Puffer's fine work in the hurdles, the games were little above mediocrity. Added to this was the further fact that the events did not go off promptly, and the programme dragged out an hour longer than necessary. The 1/3 mile track was in fairly good condition, and as fast as the average, while there was abundant provision in the field events. The starting by H.S. Cornish was perfect, and there was nothing to mar the afternoon but the tedious way the events dawdled along and a bad mistake of the judges in picking the second and third in the 100-yards flat. Probably there were 1500 spectators, not more, and the day proved that track athletics have not yet reached the plane they should obtain in the West. The meeting showed also that the folly of the last few years in attracting the rag-tag and the bobtail has begun to make itself felt. The old element is fast disappearing, the old spirit dying out, and the spectators we used to see have already scattered, and unless athletic governors and managers shape their course between the amateur buoys, the only true and winning way, they will founder on the rocks of public opinion as sure as grass grows and water runs. The Chicago Club has an opportunity of doing great good or great harm to Western athletics, and there is no time like the present for beginning.

The track events hardly compare with last year's, when the 100 and 220 were done in 10 and 21 3/5 seconds, against 10 1/5 and 22 1/5 this year. The 440 and 880 in 50 and 1:58 3/5, against 50 2/5 and 2:01 4/5. Mile run last year 4:27 4/5; this, 4:32 4/5; 5 mile, 25:54 2/5 and 26:08 2/5; mile walk, 6:41 1/5 and 6:44 1/5; 3 mile walk, 22:27 1/5 and 23:44 4/5; 120-yards hurdles, 15 2/5 and 16 sec.; 220-yard hurdles, 25 2/5 last year and this; high jump, 6 ft. and 5.11; broad jump, 22 ft. 6 in., but this year 23. 4 1/2; pole vault, 11 ft. and 10 ft. 6 in.; shot, 43.3 1/4 and 47 ft.; hammer, 140 ft. 11 in., and this year 134 ft. 8 in. only; 56 lb., 34.8 3/4 and 34.5 1/2. In the standing high and broad jumps of the new events added to the programme the records were untouched, but in the running hop, step, and jump, E.B. Bloss made a world's record, 48 ft. 6 in.; in the pole vault for distance, A.H. Green, the old Harvard man, did 27 ft. 5 in., a world's record, and J.S. Mitchell also raised the record to 15 ft. 4 1/2 in. in throwing 56 lb. weight for height. These and George Gray's great put of the 16 lb. shot, 47 ft., constituted the records of the meeting, though Puffer's 25 2/5 over the low hurdles equalled his own record over a course with a turn. Of these, the distance pole vaulting and 56 lb. for height are games very little practised or the records would not be where they are.

There seems to be little interest and less improvement in the walks, and they ought to be taken off the programme as useles. The one and three mile records, 6:29 ... and 21:09 1/5, made by F.P. Murray in '83, have never been even approached. The English programme is more sensible than ours; it leaves off the one and three miles, but puts in a seven-mile walk. If we must cultivate that ungainly, artificial stride, let us have endurance with it. Maybe we can kill off the walkers and do away with the event....

THE SPRINTS brought out four men who are new to championship honors, though two of them have been running some time. Stage, Spence, Skillinger, and Buckholtz were the best of the lot, and the first is a good yard faster than any one of them, or any other sprinter on the track to-day.... Spence is an improving 10 1/5 man. Buckholtz fairly earned second place in the 100 yards, but the judges got mixed and left him out entirely. Neither Carr nor Walden, the Canadians, turned up. But Orton turned up a winner in the mile, and Conneff went to pieces broken up by his own disregard of training and other common-sense rules. This left Willie Day an easy thing in the five miles, quite as easy as had Puffer running in both high and low hurdles, Sweeney in the high jump, Gray in the shot, Mitchell in the 56 lb. hammer, and Schwaner in the standing high and broad jumps. The only contests of the day were in the quarter, which Allen pluckily won in crippled condition; the half, where Morris led half the way and was beaten out for even the place by Rowe, with Turner first; and in the mile walk, where Shearman won from Liebgold after a good struggle. Collis was outclassed in the 3 mile walk, and Liebgold won easily in slow time. Reber and Bloss fought out the running broad jump, but the latter could not get above 22.6, while Reber did 23.4 1/2, and would probably have broken his record if the wind had not been against him.

Despite the four world's records, it left the impression of being, on the whole, an uninteresting meeting.

Caspar W. Whitney

International challenges elicited a spirit of nationalism and full coverage in Outing, September, 1895, pp. 454-461.

INTERNATIONAL TRACK AND FIELD CONTESTS OF 1895

Not until the eighties had track athletics in America developed sufficiently for American amateur runners to pit themselves against English rivals with any hope of success. During the decade 1880-90 American performances on the track and field began to approach the English standard. The mother country was invaded by numbers of our athletes, both singly and in teams, who captured a few of the British records. The pioneers of them all were the great Myers and E.E. Merrill, in 1881, and they were followed by a stalwart host whose names will live long in the annals of American athletics....

In 1891 the Manhattan Athletic Club sent over a team of athletes which, after defeating most of the English and French cracks in everything save the distance runs, ended the season by taking four English championships - Cary winning the hundred-yard dash in 10 1/5 s.; Remington, the quarter mile in 51 s.; Queckberner, the hammer at 129 ft. 10 1/4 in. (he had previously established an English record at Manchester of 134 ft. 2 1/2 in.), while Ford tied with Bulger in the broad jump at 20 ft. 4 in.

For years it had been a cherished plan with certain Yale graduates to have an international meeting between Yale, as winner of the intercollegiate meeting here, and the winner in the meet between Oxford and Cambridge. In 1894, when Yale won at the intercollegiate meeting in May, a challenge was sent and promptly accepted by Oxford. In spite of her home victory, Yale was not well fitted to compete against Oxford, owing to the lack of a champion sprinter.... One crack sprinter would have sufficed to turn the scale for Yale in that dual meeting of 1894, as the Oxford sprinters that year were none of them better than second rate....The schedule of events included the hundred yard dash, the quarter-mile, half-mile and mile, the high hurdles, broad jump, high jump, shot and hammer. Of these Oxford won all the runs, the high hurdle, and tied in the high jump with Yale, losing only the weights and broad jump. The total score was Oxford - 5 1/2 points; Yale, 3 1/2 points, first place alone scoring. Below is appended a table showing the names of the winners and the times or distances of the different events:

EVENT	WINNER	SECOND	TIME OR DISTANCE
100-yd. dash,	Fry (Oxford),	Jordan (Oxford)	10 2/5 s.
16-lb. hammer,	Hickok (Yale),	Brown (Yale),	110 ft. 5 in.
120-yd. hurdle,	Oakley (Ox.),	Scott (Oxford),	16 3/5 s.
1 mile run,	Greenhow (Ox.)	Morgan (Yale),	4 m. 24 4/5 s.
Broad jump,	heldon (Yale),	Fry (Oxford),	22 ft. 11 in. *
440-yd. run,	Jordan (Ox.),	Sanford (Yale),	51 s.
16-lb. shot,	Hickok (Yale),	Brown (Yale),	41 ft. 7 1/2 in.
High jump,	Sheldon (Yale),	Cady (Yale)	5 ft. 8 3/4 in.
	Swanwick (Ox.),		
Half-mile run,	Greenhow (Ox.),	Rathbone (Ox.),	2m. 4/5 s.
Score	Oxford, 5 1/2 firsts; 4 seconds		
	Yale, 3 1/2 " 4 "		

*English measurement

... The deeds of these men and the athletic events of the years referred to were full of interest to athletes on both sides of the water, and it remains to be proved if this year will not demonstrate that a new era of international sport has commenced, and that six days of ocean travel is no more a bar to international athletics than to international business.

There have been this year three international challenges. The first in point of time and in importance was that from the New York Athletic Club to the London Athletic Club. The most important because it is in reality Great Britain against the United States, as by mutual agreement each club is at liberty to enroll any amateur athlete in its respective country as a member.

The challenge has been accepted by the London Athletic Club, and the following details have been agreed upon: The match is to take place on Manhattan Field, New York City, on September twenty-first. The London Athletic Club team will be guests of the New York Athletic Club, the latter bearing all expense. The schedule of events is as follows (first place only to count, dead heats to count one-half, and the number of competitors in each event to be limited to two from each club) - 100-yard dash, 220-yard dash, quarter-mile run, half-mile run, mile run, three-mile run, 120-yard hurdle, high jump, broad jump, hammer and shot.

... America appears to have the best chance of winning in September. Our men should take the hammer, the broad jump, the high hurdles and the shot. The Englishmen should take one, if not both, of the middle distances and the three-mile run. The chances in the sprints seem even, while the high jump and mile are uncertain events. As the London team is now made up, the chances favor England, but our climate and methods and a strange track may handicap the Englishmen considerably. That such affect performances was apparent in the Oxford-Yale games when Woodhull, who had a record of 1m. 59 4/5s., could not secure a place though the race was run in 2m. 04s.; Cady and Hatch were shut out in the hurdles in the poor time of 16 3/5s., and Pond and Sandford in the dash in 10 2/5s....

Since the championship meeting, Bradley and Downer have competed frequently, and in their last race, July 6th, they ran two dead heats at 100 yards, one of them in 9 4/5 seconds.

Beside the challenge from the New York Athletic Club to the London Athletic Club there have been three other challenges for international matches this summer. The first was from the executive committee of the Intercollegiate Association of Amateur Athletes of America to the Universities of Oxford and Cambridge, inviting a competition in track and field games, in England, between a team composed of the first and seconds in this year's intercollegiate championship games and a representative team of university athletes of Great Britain, selected by the authorities of Oxford and Cambridge.

Yale, Princeton, and Columbia voted against the challenge, while Harvard declined to vote. After some correspondence, Oxford and Cambridge declined the challenge, owing to the attitude of Yale and Harvard. The refusal of the Englishmen was accompanied by a formal challenge to Yale and Harvard for an athletic competition, to take place in America some time in the autumn. This attempt, too, fell through, as Harvard refused to accept the challenge.

Yale, after receiving notice of Harvard's decision, offered to meet the combined teams of Oxford and Cambridge Universities singly. If this was not deemed advisable by the English universities, Yale formally challenged the winner of the Oxford-Cambridge meet. Cambridge, the winner, has accepted the challenge, and the teams of the two universities will meet October 5th, on this side. The Yale team will, probably, be made up only from those men eligible to compete at the intercollegiate meeting this last June.

The list of events will include the following: 100-yard dash, 300-yard dash, 440-yard run, one-mile run, 120-yard hurdle, American style (i.e., light movable hurdles, set on cinder path), 120-yard hurdle, English style (*i.e.,* fixed hurdles on grass), high jump, broad jump, shot and hammer.

The Cambridge team will be composed of the first and second strings which competed for the light blue at the Oxford-Cambridge meet, on July 3d, and F.W. Jennings in the high jump....

In a comparison of these men by their past performances and present form, Yale, with the advantages of an American climate and track, should win.... Yale should win the 100-yard and possibly the 300-yard dash, both the hurdles, the broad jump, high jump, hammer and shot, while England should take the quarter, half and mile.

Whatever be the result, whether London or New York, Cambridge or Yale, England or America win, the year 1895 will always be remembered on both sides of the ocean as the year that made the representatives of American and English manliness acquainted with each other.

As teams sought to bring greater interest to competition they introduced relay races. Outing provided a history of its past utilitarian functions and the current state of development in November, 1893, pp. 151-153. The Penn Relays were introduced in the spring of 1893.

TEAM RACING

THE prototype of team racing, such as we see in our modern athletic contests, is to be found in the "torch race" of the Grecian games. This race was run either on foot or on horseback, and consisted in carrying lighted torches at full speed for a certain distance and then handing them, still lighted, to other runners, who in turn transferred them in the same state to a third pair, and in this manner they were passed on until the required distance was traversed, or until one of the torches was extinguished. In the latter case the race was given to the side whose torch was still burning; otherwise the party whose last representative reached the goal first was counted the winner....

The sending of the "fiery cross" - a light wooden cross dipped in blood and slightly singed by fire - among the Scotch clans in time of war, which Scott so powerfully described in the "Lady in the Lake," is a custom traceable to the same origin. All these events, whatever they may symbolize in the different religions, are but outgrowths of the relay or courier system of sending messages, a method which has existed from time immemorial in every country and which, in mountainous districts, was formerly the only method of communication....

At present the courier system is a thing of the past in all civilized countries, the King of Saxony being the last European ruler to give up his retinue of couriers, which, used to always precede his carriage. But in certain portions of India, where railroads have not yet penetrated, the mails are still carried by a system of relays, of which the night squad always goes out by twos, one runner carrying the mail and the other a blazing torch as a protection against snakes, tigers and other denizens of the jungles.

In America the system of relay running has never been at all prominent, except among the native tribes, whose performances are fully equal to any made in the Old World. The Mojave Indians have a religious race, which is almost identical with our modern team race; all the able-bodied males of the tribe, from novices of five to tottering veterans who were champions a half century back, take part in this great national relay race. The goals are one hundred and sixty yards apart, and the ceremony begins with a race between the boys of the tribe under sixteen years of age. These juvenile athletes are divided into two rival parties equal in number, who are stationed half at one goal and half at the other, and run two by two, the start always being made from the eastern goal; at the westward goal are two boys on their marks, neither of whom can start until the runner representing his side crosses the line. The race is won by the side which, by gaining nearly two laps on their rivals, enables one of its representatives to catch the runner ahead of him by the flying "chongo," or cue. The race may last for hours or even days before the necessary distance is gained by a side. After the boys' race comes that of the young men, and finally a race of veterans, while the climax of the whole is found in the race between the married and single men of the tribe, the losers to haul the wood for a great tribal scalp dance, where vanquished and victors alike drown their sorrows, or add to their triumphs by quaffing huge quantities of pulque, twixt the intervals of their terpsichorean diversion.

It is to the Fire Companies that the credit of perpetuating team racing in the United States must be given. A number of years ago it was the custom for all the rival fire companies from certain counties and districts to meet once a year at some appointed town and try each other's mettle at various athletic feats suited to their profession, such as horse races, "hook and ladder races," and the like, and among them all none was regarded with more interest than the "bean pot race," as it was then called. This was much like the team-racing of to-day, from four to six men being chosen who were to cover a certain distance bearing rival colors; but it differed in one important respect from the present team race in the fact that no man was forced to run a specified distance. For instance, in a mile race the first man might run half a mile and be succeeded by three sprinters, each running a little less than three hundred yards to complete the mile.... Worcester, Massachusetts, was the great headquarters of these meetings, and many a famous professional runner of to-day has begun his athletic career as a contestant in one of the far-famed "Worcester Bean-Pot Races." It was there that Mike Murphy, the famous ex-sprinter, one of the few professionals who has beaten even time in the hundred, first began his running. Andover and Exeter next made team running a permanent part of their athletic contests, and the excitement that has always attended these meetings fully attest their popularity.

Team racing, or relay racing as it now exists, is conducted as follows: Each contestant runs the same distance, has a standing start (formerly each man was allowed to run along with his predecessor, and thus obtain a flying start), and no competitor is allowed to start until touched by the team companion that precedes him. For example, a team race of a mile ... each man to run a quarter - the first two men are started from the mark by the pistol in the regulation method; as they approach the finish two fresh men take positions at the finish, each ready to start as soon as his team mate is near enough to touch his outstretched hand, and so on. The race is continued until the last two competitors start in for the last quarter; to the team of the one finishing ahead is given the race.

The secret of the immense excitement of a team race lies in the fact that there is continual running at full speed, for at every quarter fresh men are put in, who start off with a burst that keeps the excitement of the audience at a fever heat. In the assigning of the men to their various positions there is an opportunity for a great deal of judgment. As a usual thing the first starter should be the fastest man of the quartette, so as to obtain, if possible, a good lead for those following him, and the last man should be chosen especially with reference to his speed on the finish, that he may recover on the last part of the last lap any ground lost by his predecessors.

The system of training for team racing differs in one important respect from the training for an ordinary 440-yard dash, or whatever the selected distance may be. Instead of starting from the pistol, each man, with the exception of the leader, must become accustomed to starting the instant a team mate touches his extended hand, this involves several novel points in starting, which requires much practice to enable the runner to get off his mark with the same rapidity as by the regulation start. In the first place, the right hand, if the man uses the ordinary left foot start, must be extended as far back as possible, so as to minimize the distance his approaching team mate must cover. This bars out the familiar crouching start, which so many sprinters are now using. Again, the runner must watch his comrade over his shoulder, and begin to start a fraction of a second before he arrives, so that when the hands touch he may be already in motion. This last point requires the most assiduous practice, so as to obtain the golden mean between making a foul start and hanging on the mark after being touched. The fact, too, that the head must be slightly turned, so as to watch the approaching runner, increases the awkwardness and slowness which the novice always feels when starting in a team race, and requires much practice before it becomes easy. The best way to become accustomed to these details in starting is to let the team line up daily some twenty yards apart, and try some three or four relay starts, always taking care that each man be touched by the one who is to be his actual predecessor in the race.

Last winter there were a number of team races at different distances in many of our indoor meetings, and the applause which they have uniformly received seems to indicate that at no late date they will become a permanent part of all the large indoor meetings. Within the last year, too, intercollegiate team racing has been originated and with marked success....

The record of 3.25 1/5 for a mile team race is held by the Harvard team for this year, having been made at the N.J.A.C. games on May 30th. This supplants the previous record of 3.28 3/5 which was made by the Harvard Senior Class in the spring of 1892. The four men who constitute the record team are L. Sayer, N.W. Bingham, W.F. Garcelon and S.N. Merrill. The time by quarters was: first quarter, 51 4/5; half mile, 1.43 2/5; three-quarters, 2.34 1/5, and mile, 3.25 2/5.

By the 1890s women enjoyed more widespread participation in sport, and Vassar College decided to initiate a field day with track activities included, as reported by the Chicago Tribune, 10 November 1895, p. 5. The field day concept was meant to differ from male competition by deemphasizing winning and promoting community spirit and socialization among the participants. Industrial recreation programs began offering comprehensive track and field competition for women after the turn of the century.

GIRLS IN FIELD SPORTS
FIRST ANNUAL GAMES OF THE VASSAR COLLEGE ATHLETES

Poughkeepsie, N.Y., Nov. 9. - Rain did not interfere with the field day of the Vassar College Athletic Association. For two weeks the members had been preparing for today's contests in running, hurdle jumping and basket-ball. This was Vassar's first field day, and was looked upon as an experiment. Every effort was made to have the program carried through without publicity. The oval field is admirably adapted to secure the girls from undesired spectators, being surrounded by a thick evergreen hedge twelve feet high. Orders were given to exclude reporters, and the all masculine visitors. At 10 o'clock groups of excited girls were scattered over the oval. Each class selected a position and kept to itself.

The contestants were surrounded by the other members of their classes, and encouraged with pats on the back. The spectators were enveloped in mackintoshes or golf capes, and generally wore Tam O'Shanters. They had bows of class colors at their throats. The judges - Miss Welton, Miss Tiffany, and Miss Wentworth - occupied an open summer house, with Miss Banks, Chairman, and Misses Love, Thallon, Haight, and Vassar members of the Committee on Arrangements, Mrs. Kendrick, the principal; Prof. Ely, and other members of the faculty watched the preparations with some misgivings.

All girls who desired to compete were required to enter their names, and the list and was taken in hand by the principal, Mrs. Kendrick, Physical Director Dr. Thalberg, and Gymnasium Director Miss Ballentine. No girl in whom the slightest physical weakness was detected was allowed to compete.

Perfect Specimens of Girlhood.

The result was that no more perfect specimen of college girlhood could be found than the contestants. What is more, all the girls who excel in the games rank high in their classes, and from figures kept it is proved the greater the improvement in the physical condition of students during gymnasium season the greater their proportionate improvement in their class rank.

Misses Hotchkiss, Jones, Johnson, and Wilkinson lined up for the trial heats in the 100-yard dash. No uniform costume was worn. Some of the girls wore their gymnasium suits. Others wore divided skirts and blouse waists. Many wore short skirts over gymnasium suits, but the favorite outfit included white sweaters, just arrived in time for the games today. As the four girls took their positions the classes gave the college yell, "Rah, rah, rah, V-A-S-S-A-R!" each finishing with the class year.

The time-keepers, Miss Hart, Miss Platt, and Miss Skinner, took their positions with stop watches in their hands. The starter, Miss Love, stood just behind the girls. As she threw one hand up into the air everybody became breathless, waiting for the signal. The contestant, with foot advanced, hugged the line and crouched.

"Ping" went the starter's pistol. The audience, all women, jumped, and the contestants were away. With arms well to the side, shoulders, back, and heads thrown up, the four girls made a picture of grace. Artists would have found the runners worth studying. The turf was yielding and slippery. Miss Wilkinson, the winner, finished in 15 1/4 seconds - slow time, the girls said. In the second trial heat, Misses Reimer, Thallon, Fryon, and Vassar ran, and the last named won in 15 1/2 seconds.

Miss Baker Wins the Broad Jump.

For the running broad jump, Misses Baker, Harrison, Hero C. Johnson, Spaulding, Thallon, Ward, Wilkinson, and Love were entered, and each girl was credited with the best in three jumps. The winner, Miss Baker, made 11 feet 5 inches, and was quickly enveloped by her supporters in a heavy coat and mackintosh, and petted and rewarded with "Rah, rah, rah, V-a-s-s-a-r, Baker!"

In the 120-yard hurdle trial heats, the hurdles were only two feet high, but that was high enough, as the softness of the earth was equivalent to another six inches. Miss Spaulding made it in :25 3/4 and Miss Thallon in :24 3/4. These were only preparatory to the final.

The running high jump was one of the prettiest events of the day. Two girls held the ropes while Misses Baker, Borden; Brownell, Harrison, C. Johnson, Spaulding and Vassar did their best. Miss Brownell won, making a 48-inch jump. In this event the only accident of the games occurred. Miss Baker, who was second with a 46-inch jump, fell. When she got up there was a call for the doctor. Miss Baker had dislocated her thumb. Dr. Thalberg was on the field with rolls of bandages and simple remedies, and Miss Baker was able to play with the basket-ball team in the afternoon.

Only one 220-yard dash was run, and Miss Haight won it in :36 1/4.

Miss Vassar delighted the hearts of '98 by winning the final 100-yard dash in sixteen seconds. The last event of the morning ws the final heat in the 120-yard hurdle. The three competitors took the hurdles in as scientific a manner as if under the eye of the instructor in the gymnasium. Every hurdle was carefully calculated, and when Miss Thallon of Brooklyn won in twenty-five seconds it proved science had really told.

The professors were inclined to forbid the basket ball contests in the afternoon, but the plea of the students prevailed. The rain finally ceased and the fog lifted and the games ended pleasantly.

On the committee in charge of the games were: Miss Harriet Sketchley Banks of Englewood, N.J., who has been the Vassar tennis champion for three years; Miss Ella Louise Love of Chicago, Miss Ida Carleton Thallon of Brooklyn, Miss Helen Ive Haight of Auburn, N. Y., and Miss Elizabeth Forbes Vassar of Ballston Spa, N.Y.

Miss Love's Exciting Duty

Miss Ella L. Love of Chicago had, perhaps, the most exciting duty of the day. She was starter, and to her belonged the duty of firing the shot that gave the signal for each race to begin. Vassar girls, at least those that took part in the athletic games, are not given to the cultivation of nerves.

The evening of Vassar's first field day was celebrated by the first of four plays given during the year by the college's flourishing dramatic society, the Philalaetha. The play was the "Merchant of Venice."

After the game Mrs. Kendrick the principal said: "We want it distinctly understood this field day does not indicate the collefge has gone into 'sports,' as it is termed. Physical culture has always had a place at Vassar from the foundation of the college. The girls exercise and play games out of doors all of the time, but this is the first time the different kind of exercises and games have been brought together in one day. Formerly we received letters from parents requesting we excuse their daughters from exercise. Since the games have been introduced these letters are hardly ever received, and as the interest of the girls increases their parents' objections lessen.

"In many cases girls have given up eating candy because they found it interfered with their games. There are girls who have given up eating sweets altogether for the same reason. But Vassar will not allow a spirit of emulation to rule the students."

By 1900 competition moved beyond national challenges to the international sphere. In the inaugural modern Olympics of 1896 the Americans easily won the majority of the gold medals. The 1900 games, held in Paris in conjunction with the world's fair, were overshadowed by the larger spectacle. Nevertheless, the Chicago Tribune provided in depth coverage and pointed to a sabbatarian issue that would not be resolved until well into the twentieth century. The coverage is reprinted from 16-17 July 1900, p. 8 and 9, respectively.

AMERICANS WIN AT PARIS
TAKE EIGHT OF TEN EVENTS IN THJE FINALS

French Officials Decline to Permit Athletes Objecting to Sunday Competition to Try Again Today, Although Such an Agreement Was Understood ...

PARIS, July 15. - American athletes again swept the field in the international contests today, winning eight out of ten events in the finals. Bauer won the discus-throwing contest; Bennett won the 1500 meter race on the flat from Deloge; Baxter cleared 6 feet 2 1/4 inches in the high jump, and could have won with four inches less; Baxter took the pole vault at 10 feet 10 inches; Kraenzlein surpassed Prinstein's long jump of yesterday.

Prinstein thought he could jump again tomorrow, but the French authorities arbitrarily decided that the long jump, the pole vault, and the high jump concluded today. The Americans had been told they could finish tomorrow. A.G. Spalding entered a protest against the action of the officials.

The athletes of the Universities of Michigan and Syracuse staid out on account of Sunday.

The most remarkable contest of the day was the 2,500 meters race, which was won by Orton, who beat Robinson by three yards.

Americans Take Many Events

PARIS, July 15. - Although deprived of the service of some of her best athletes, who declined to contest in today's events of the world's amateur championships in the Bois de Boulogne, objecting to Sunday competition, America won eight out of ten of those decided, gaining five second positions and four thirds.

Weather conditions were perfect. The sun was just warm enough to make the muscles supple, and the sky was cloudless.

The management, taking a lesson from yesterday's confusion, had the course well policed, thus keeping spectators well within bounds and giving competitors unobstructed grounds on which to meet.

Unfair to Americans

The track and field events were run off quickly. One incident caused an unpleasant jar. The terms of the agreement were reached with the French officials at a joint meeting held in the rooms of the racing club on Wednesday night. At that time it was certainly understood by the Americans that the French had agreed that the field events in which they had entered, and in which it was proposed the finals should come off today, would be so arranged the Americans objecting to Sunday competition could contest alone on Monday, and that the record then made would be counted in reaching the final awards. Last night the French held a meeting and decided that events set for today must be concluded finally on grounds today, but that records made in the preliminary trials yesterday would stand.

This action was taken, it appears, on the ground that the other contestants objected to such an advantage being given to the Americans. Early in the day, some of the contestants, among whom were Bascom Johnson of the New York Athletic club and Charles Dvorack of the University of Michigan, the former of whom won the pole vault championship in London and the latter of whom is the intercollegiate champion, went to the grounds and were informed they could contest on Monday. On being so informed they went to their rooms. The decision also operated against Morris Prinstein of Syracuse University, who was prevented from competing today by the authorities of the college.

A.C Kraenzlein of the University of Pennsylvania, whom Prinstein beat yesterday, today jumped in the final for the broad jump and won over Prinstein's jump of yesterday by a small margin. Each had three jumps yesterday, but Kraenzlein had six more today, while Prinstein, although on the grounds, could not jump. He entered a protest after the games.

Penn Athletes Victorious

The representatives of the University of Pennsylvania had a large share in today's winnings, and their contesting caused some feeling among the other college men. Manager Ellis said:

"I have no authority to prevent the men taking part on my own responsibility and so told them, at the same time advising them that they should not contest. We have thirteen men in our team. Of these eight staid out today, but five decided they would remain in to the end."

In order to overcome the feeling caused by Johnson and Dvorack being out of the pole vault event the French officials have agreed to offer a special prize for a pole vault on Thursday.

American Team Enters Protest

On the initiative of Mr. Sherrill of Yale a protest, signed by all the American teams, has been presented to A.G. Spalding, director of sports at the exposition. It says:

We, the undersigned, beg to protest against the change in the agreed arrangements whereby our clubs are now unable to compete in field events on Monday, the records to count for the championships and to be filed as events. We do not agree to a substitution of a series of special field events to take the place of the above agreed arrangement.

As the Americans were so successful some of the bad feeling disappeared, but they might have had more seconds and thirds if the change had not been made at the last minute and scarcely without warning.

The number of spectators was much larger than yesterday's attendance, and the presence of a regimental band enlivened the occasion. Again the grand-stand was largely occupied by Americans, who cheered their champions, especially when George W. Orton of the University of Pennsylvania after seeming to be out of the long steeplechase made a magnificent spurt, beating an Englishman, who looked a certain winner as they came down the stretch. The enthusiasm at this point was intense.

Kraenzlein Wins Sixty Meters

The games began promptly at 2:30 p. m., but it was 7 o'clock before the last event was over. The first heat in the 60 meters flat went handily to Kraenzlein, with E.J. Minahan of Georgetown University second, and Pritchard of the English team third. Time, 7 seconds....

In the second heat Walter B. Tewkesbury managed to breast the tape just ahead of Rowley of New South Wales, with William J. Holland of the University of Georgetown third. Time, 7 1/5 seconds....

The final was a pretty contest, the men being breasts apart at the finish, with Kraenzlein first, Tewkesbury second, and Rowley third. Time, 7 seconds....

Sheldon Takes Shot Put

Richard Sheldon of the New York Athletic club was the only American to strip for the final in the shot-putting, as J.C. McCracken of the University of Pennsylvania and Robert Garrett of Princeton University refused to compete on Sunday. Crettier, Hungarian, and Paraskevopoulos, Greek, took their places. Neither of these could outstrip the puts made yesterday by McCracken and Garrett, and the final resulted with Sheldon first at 14 meters and 10 centimeters, which is said to beat the world's record; McCracken second, at 12 meters and 85 centimeters; and Garrett third, at 12 meters and 37 centimeters.

Long Captures 400-Meter Race

Only three started in the final of the 400 meters flat, as Lee, Frederick G. Moloney of the University of Michigan, and Dixon Boardman of the New York Athletic club, who had also qualified, refused to run today. This left Maxwell Long of the New York Athletic club, William J. Holland of the University of Georgetown, and Schulz, Dane. At the crack of the pistol Holland set a merry pace and held it well into the stretch, where Long caught him. The two had a heartbreaking run to the finish, which Long reached one yard in advance of Holland, Schulz being farthest to the rear. Time was 49 2-5 seconds, beating the French record of 50 3-5. Had the other American started America would undoubtedly have gained first, second, and third.

Had today's records alone decided the results of the discus throw Sheldon would have won, for today he outstripped his Hungarian competitors. But their records made in the preliminaries stood in the finals, and yesterday they did better, with the result that Bauer, Hungarian, was first at 36 meters and 4 centimeters, and Janda, Austrian, second, at 35 meters and 14 centimeters, with Sheldon third, at 34 meters and 60 centimeters. Soderstrom, Swede, and Paraskevopoulos also competed.

Englishman Beats Frenchman

The 1,500 meters flat race brought nine contestants to the tape, representing Denmark, England, France, Austria, and the United States. Messrs. David C. Hall of Brown University and John Bray of Williams College were the two American entries. Almost from the start the race seemed a contest between Bennett, English, and De Loge, French. These two raced around the turns close together, and, as they entered the stretch, they drew away from the others and had a hard tussle, which Bennett won by two yards, with De Loge second and Bray third. Time 4 minutes 6 seconds. Christensen, Dane; Kraschtil, Austrian; Louis, French; Rimmer, English; and Pukl, Austrian, also ran.

Although William P. Remington of the University of Pennsylvania and Carroll entered, I.K. Baxter of the University of Pennsylvania was the only American in the running high jump. He easily retained his reputation, winning first place with 190 centimeters. He made an effort to clear 197 centimeters, which would have given him the world's championship, but he failed.

In fact, the American victories were quite popular throughout the day with all present. The Europeans, representing the various countries, gave the Americans hearty welcome as they came to the scratch in every event. Leahy, Irish, was second in the high jump with 176 centimeters, and Goenzy, Hungarian, third, with 175 centimeters. Angersen, Norwegian; Steppin, German; Blom, Swede; and Monnier, French, also jumped.

Tewkesbury Beats French Champion

The Frenchmen were loud in their shouts as the contestants for the 400 meters hurdle came upon the track, as M. Tauzin, who has held the French record for years, was considered a sure winner. There were only three in the final. Tewkesbury went to the front as soon as the pistol was fired and was never headed. He jumped clearly, followed by Tauzin, Orton bringing up the rear. Thus they finished, although it was thought Orton would beat Tauzin, as he did so in the trials yesterday. Tewkesbury won rather easily, but Tauzin was only a yard ahead of Orton. Time 57 3/5 seconds.

Orton Wins Steeplechase

The 2,500 meters steeplechase handicap, which included stone fences, a water jump, hurdles, and other obstacles, created greater enthusiasm than all the other events of the day. Six men came to the scratch. With Alexander Grant and Edward R. Bushnell of the University of Pennsylvania declining to participate, the duty fell upon Orton or Newton to win the event for the Americans, and right well the former did it. England felt confident with Robinson, while France had Chastanie. Dunhoe represented Germany, and Kraschtil Austria. England and France made nearly all the running, with Orton resting at fourth place at the first take water. On the second round America, France, and England took the water jump abreast. On the third and fourth rounds England, France, and the two Americans were the only ones remaining in the race, so hot had been the pace. Orton was last, and as many thought, virtually out of it, but, on the turning home he woke up, passing Chastanie, and Robinson succumbed when about 100 yards from the tape, Orton crossing the tape five yards ahead of him, Robinson being about the same distance in front of Newton. The time was 7:34 2-5. Both Orton and Robinson fell after crossing the line, but they were soon about again.

Although Johnson and Dvorak were out of the pole vault, the Americans felt certain of winning there. The contest was long drawn out. Finally Baxter, Colkett, and Anderson, the Norwegian, alone remained. They tried several times, Baxter finally winning by 3 meters and 30 centimetrs, with Colkett second, 3 meters and 21 centimeters, and Anderon third, 3 meters and 20 centimeters. Kauser, Hungarian; Nilsson and Lemming, Swedes; and Gontier, French, also competed.

Kraenzlein Takes Broad Jump

The running broad jump brought the day to a close. Kraenzlein, in better form than yesterday, outjumped Prinstein's record and won with 7 meters and 18 1/2 centimeters, Prinstein coming second with 7 meters and 17 1/2 centimeters, and Leahy third, with 6 meters and 83 centimeters. Dellanoy, French, also jumped. Prinstein felt bad over the outcome and offered to jump against Kraenzlein to settle the question of superiority tomorrow, but the latter declined.

The contests will continue tomorrow, when there will be a 200-meter hurdle race, the hammer throwing event, the hop, step, and jump, the 4,000 meter steeplechase, the standing high and broad jumps,and the tug of war.

Arthur E. Duffy of Georgetown University, who fell yesterday in the final heat of the 100-meter dash, is quite lame and does not expect to be able to run for several months.

SEVEN MORE VICTORIES

PARIS, July 16.- Ray Ewry of the New York Athletic club won four events in the international games today. In the high jump he cleared 5 feet 4 1/2 inches, which is a fraction over the world's record. He won the three standing jumps with 34 feet 8 inches, the standing broad jump, and the hop, step, and jump.

Kraenzlein won the 200 meters hurdles by two yards.

Pennsylvania is severely blamed by the other colleges for competing on Sunday. It is alleged that Kraenzlein promised Prinstein not to compete on Sunday. Princeton and Michigan are incensed at Baxter and Colkett for competing on Sunday. Had the latter refrained Americans would not have won. Much jealousy is manifested.

Tysoe, an Englishman, won the 800 meters. Flanagan threw the hammer 167 feet 4 1/2 inches. The Swedish tug-of-war team made the French team look ridiculous. France has won nothing as yet.

Sixteen Firsts for America.

PARIS, July 16.- Twenty-one championship contests in connection with the exposition have been decided during the last three days, and America can boast of winning sixteen and of securing thirteen seconds and twelve thirds.

Ten events took place today, in which the Americans placed seven firsts, six seconds, and seven thirds to their credit. They captured the 200 meters hurdle race, the standing high jump, the three standing jumps, the long jump, the hop, step, and jump, the hammer throwing, and the standing long jump; and they did it easily.

In fact, the facility with which the American athletes carried off prizes finally grew monotonous. Three events were won by foreigners. The tug of war was not conrtested by the Americans. In the 800 meters flat race, which was won by an Englishman, Tysoe, the Americans took second and third places. In the remaining race, the 4,000 meters steeplechase, they failed to get a place, Englishmen taking all three. This result was somewhat of a disappointment for the American spectators, as they had hoped to see Orton repeat his splendid performance of yesterday. Rimmer took the lead at the outset and was never passed. McClain ran in close for two-thirds of the course, while Orton and Grant brought up the rear.

Orton a Disappointment.

Most of the spectators thought Orton was saving himself with the intention to spurt on the last round and to finish first at the tape, as he did yesterday, but the effort of yesterday proved too much for him. Although he ran gamely he was unable to secure a better place at the finish than fifth. His college comrades cheered him, endeavoring to encourage him with familiar yells, and when they found that, in spite of his pluck, he was beaten, they gave him a rousing ovation. The French champion was wildly spurred on by his compatriots and struggled with admirable grit, but he had to succumb to the superior trained English cross-country runners. Rimmer's time was half a minute better than the French record over the same course. A.C. Kraenzlein of Pennsylvania won the first heat of the 200 meters hurdle race easily in :27. Choisel, a Frenchman, was second, and George W. Orton of Pennsylvania was third. N.G. Pritchard, the champion 100-yard runner of India, defeated Walter R. Tewkesbury of Pennsylvania in the second heat in :26 2/5. T.B. McLain of

Pennsylvania was third.

The final heat was almost a walkover for Kraenzlein, who finished a yard ahead of his competitors. The race for place was vigorously contested, Pritchard again beating Tewkesbury, who finished third. Time :25 2/5. Rau, a German; Moloney of Chicago University, and W.P. Remington of Pennsylvania were among those who ran in the first trial heat; and Tausin, a Frenchman; Levis of Syracuse, and T.B. McClay of Pennsylvania contested in the second trial heat.

Clean Sweep in the Jumps

The three standing jumps events was easily an American victory, the athletes from the United States outjumping all the other competitors. The same can be said of the hop, step, and jump, which followed. Prinstein of Syracuse University, Connelly of Boston, and Richard Sheldon of the New York Athletic club qualified for the finals and jump off. Prinstein won, though Connelly pushed him hard.

The same entries competed in both these jumping contests, there being besides those already mentioned Jarvis of Pennsylvania, Horton of Princeton, John McClain of Michigan, Staff, a Swede; Steffen, a German, and Koppan, a Greek.

The 800 meters flat race brought six men to the tape for the final heat, Cregan of Princeton, David C. Hall of Brown, John Bray of Williams College, A.E. Tysoe, the English champion; Speidel, a Hungarian, and Deloge, a Frenchman.

One Event for England

It was a hard contest between Cregan, Deloge, and Tysoe until the stretch, where Deloge collapsed, leaving Cregan and Tysoe to fight it out. Tysoe had the advantage of the lead. Cregan ran gamely, but could not overcome the Britisher, who finished a yard in advance. Hall was third, some distance back.

The standing high jump was a contest for Americans. Ray Ewry of the New York Athletic club, who holds the record, won quickly. I.K. Baxter of Pennsylvania getting the place from Richard Sheldon of the New York Athletic club.

It was then announced that Ewry would attempt to surpass his own world's record of one meter sixty-three centimeters. This he did on the second attempt, clearing one meter sixty-four centimeters. The spectators cheered most heartily at this performance, and when, after a minute's rest, he cleared one meter sixty-five centimeters, there was much enthusiasm shown.

Hammer Throw a Walkover.

The Americans had the hammer throwing to themselves, their two Swedish rivals being utterly outclassed. The apparent unfamiliarity of the latter with the hammer caused some amusement among the spectators, not unmixed with a certain amount of apprehension, and once or twice the crowd behind scattered precipitately as the direction of the hammer showed a tendency to eccentricity. Flannagan was heartily cheered on his longest throw, as it was thought he had broken the record, but measurements show the throw to have been three inches short. Hare of Pennsylvania was second, with 151 feet 9 inches, and J.C. McCracken of Pennsylvania third, with 146 feet.

The tug-of-war proved more entertaining than scientific. The Scandinavian team was composed of much heavier men than the French. The Americans declined to enter the contest. This ended the day's program.

College men who were prevented from competing yesterday by the change in the agreed arrangements feel none too kindly toward the representatives of the University of Pennsylvania for contesting. The University of Michigan, with Dvorack; the University of Syracuse, with Prinstein; and Princeton, with two men in the pole vault and one in the high jump, were those suffering most. Some complain bitterly, declaring without equivocation that they have been unfairly treated.

Manager Jamison of Princeton says: "By the change our pole vaulters and high jumper were unable to compete, after traveling a great distance. Pennsylvania protested most strongly against Sunday games, but finally entered. I think her representative should have stood with those of the other colleges."

CANADA

Much like the United States, track and field competition in Canada developed through urban athletic clubs. The Montreal Athletic Association reported on its 1882 meets, which included participation by athletes from New York clubs; most notably Lon Myers, who would gain fame as a world champion.

MONTREAL AMATEUR ATHLETIC ASSOCIATION REPORT

MONTREAL, MAY 1883

To the Directors of the Montreal Amateur Athletic Association.

As suggested by your Committee last season, a cinder path 50 feet long ending in a patch seven feet square, and a level "shot" ground were built on the Lacrosse Grounds; whip handles for hammers, a round 56lb. weight and several other articles were procured, with which improvements, etc., we may consider ourselves fully equipped to carry on our athletic meetings.

The Pole high vault was added to the list of games, but did not provoke the competition looked for, we hope that next season will make it more interesting.

The Spring Handicap Games were held on Saturday, 3rd June, 1882, and wer very successfully carried out.

The following field officers were present:-

Referee - Lt. Col. E.A. Whitehead.

Judge of Walking - Wm. L. Maltby.

Judges at finish - Wm. L. Maltby, H.S. McDougall, A.W. Stevenson,

Time-keepers- H.W. Becket, Samuel Coulson, and R.B. Ross.

Starter - Thomas L. Paton.

Clerks of Course - Jas. D. Miller, and J.L. Gardner.

Measurers - Fred McIndoe, W. McNab.

Scorers - John W. Davis, Fred Cushing.

Sports Committee - H.W. Becket, *Chairman,* T.L. Paton, Geo. R. Starke, H.S. Tibbs.

Three Mile Walk.

Daniel Earle .... Montreal 1

T.P. Corcoran .... do 2

Time 26 min 40 sec. 5 competitors.

Putting the Shot

W.R. Thompson [4 ft.] .... Montreal A.A.A 1
Frank Lally, [3ft] .... Shamrock Lacrosse Club 2

Distance 33 feet. 3 competitors.

Long Throwing [Lacrosse.]

F. Lally .... Shamrock Lacrosse Club 1
W. Aird .... Montreal A.A.A. 2

Distance 403 feet. 3 competitors.

One Hundred Yards Run.

FIRST HEAT

A.F. Clerk [18 ft] .... Montreal A.A.A. 1
Lewis Skaife, [24 ft] .... do 2

Time 10 1/5 sec.

SECOND HEAT

F.A. Crowley, [21 ft] .... Montreal A.A.A 1
John Paterson, [15 ft] .... do 2

Time 10 1/5 sec.

THIRD HEAT

W.R. Thompson scratch .... Montreal A.A.A. 1
Gustave Delorme .... do 2

Time 10 1/4 sec.

SECOND TRIAL HEATS

FIRST HEAT

A.F. Clerk .... Montreal A.A.A 1
L. Skaife .... do 2

Time 10 1/4 sec.

SECOND HEAT

W.R. Thompson .... Montreal A.A.A. 1
E.A. Crowley .... do 2

Time 10 1/4 sec.

FINAL HEAT

A.F. Clerk .... Montreal A.A.A. 1
L. Skaife .... do .... } Tie.
W.R. Thompson .... do ....

Time 10 sec. 12 competitors

Bicycle Race 3 Miles.

Alan Arthur, [2 min] .... Montreal Bicycle Club 1
F.C. Holden, [scratch] .... do 2

Time 14 min., 28 sec. 6 competitors.

One Mile Run.

C.E. Gault, [125 yards] .... Montreal A.A.A. 1
R. Locke .... do Lacrosse Club 2

Time 4 min., 31 1/4 sec. 4 competitors

Throwing 56lb Weight.

H. Lawlor, [5 1/2 feet] 1
C.W. Trenholme [4 feet] 2

Distance 16 feet 8 inches. 3 competitors.

Four Hundred and Forty Yards Run.

J.J.Gethin, [40 yards] .... Montreal 1

L.C. Barron, [40 yards] .... " Lacrosse Club 2

Time 52 sec. 8 competitors.

Running High Jump.

Frank Lally, [2 in.] .... Shamrock Lacrosse Club 1

W.R. Thompson [scratch] .... Montreal A.A.A. 2

Height 5 feet 1 inch. 4 competitors

Half Mile Run.

N. Fletcher, [scratch.] .... Montreal A.A.A. 1

L.C. Barron, [60 yds] .... " Lacrosse Club 2

Time 2 min 11 sec. 6 competitors.

One Hundred and Twenty Yards Hurdle Race.

W.R. Thompson, [scratch] .... Montreal A.A.A. 1

L. Skaife, [9 feet] .... do 2

Time 21 1/4 sec. 4 competitors.

Pole High Leap

F. Lally .... Shamrock Lacrosse Club 1

W. Kerr .... Montreal A.A.A. 2

Height 8 feet 1 inch. 3 competitors.

Two Mile Race

Was scratched owing to lack of starters, but scratch race was made up.

D.D. McTaggart, [scratch] .... Montreal A.A.A. 1

James Baird, [60 yds] .... do 2

Time 10 min 25 sec. 4 competitors.

FALL CHAMPIONSHIP MEETING

The Fall Championship Meeting took place on Saturday afternoon October 7th 1882, and was a success in every way, save and except the fact that, as last season, the majority of the championships went to the United States. A strong delegation from New York was present, one of whom Mr. F.C. Lambrecht broke the record at "putting the shot."

Field Officers.

Referee - Lt. Col. E, A. Whitehead.

Judge of Walking - Wm, L. Maltby.

Time-keepers - Samuel Coulson, R.B. Ross, H.W. Becket.

Judges at finish - W.L. Maltby, A.W. Stevenson, H.S. MacDougall.

Starter - D.E. Bowie.

Clerk and assistant Clerks of Course - Thos. L. Paton, J.K. Whyte and J.L. Gardner.

Measurers - Geo. R. Starke, Wm. McNab.

Scorers - J.K. Reid, J.W. Davis, Fred Cushing.

Sports Committee - H.W. Becket, *Chairman,* Geo. R. Starke, Thos. L. Paton, Horace S. Tibbs and J. Keith Reid.

Three Mile Walk.

W.H. Parry .... Williamsburg N.Y. Athletic Club 1
W.G. Hart .... Manhattan N.Y. Athletic Club 2

Time 23 min. 12 sec. 5 competitors.

Throwing 56lb. Weight.

C.A.J. Queckberner, ... N.Y. Scottish American Club 1
F.L. Lambrecht, ... Pastime Athletic Club 2

Distance 23 feet 3 1/2 in. 4 competitors.

Pole Leap.

W.M. Phelan, ... Montreal 1
Wm. Kerr, ... Montreal Junior Lacrosse Club 2

Height 7 feet 4 in. 2 competitors

One Hundred Yards Run.

FIRST HEAT

J.B. White, ... Manhattan Athletic Club
S. Derrickson .... do do } Tie 1
W.R. Thompson, ... Montreal A.A.A. 2

SECOND HEAT

G.H. Wood, ... Shamrock Lacrosse Club 1
C.E. Schuyler, ... Manhattan Athletic Club 2

Time each heat 11 sec.

FINAL HEAT.

J.B. White, ... Manhattan Athletic Club 1
G.H. Wood, ... Shamrock Lacrosse Club 2

Time 10 sec.

One Mile Run.

A. Fredericks, ... Manhattan Athletic Club 1
Thomas Moffat, ... Montreal A.A.A. 2
C.E. Gault, ... do do 3

Time 4 min. 53 sec. 3 competitors.

Throwing the Hammer.

F.L. Lambecht, ... Pastime Athletic Club..................... 1
C.A.J. Queckberner, ... Scottish American Ath, Club 2
G.H. Wood, ... Shamrock Lacrosse Club 3

Distance 90 feet 7 inches. 3 competitors.

Four Hundred and Forty Yards Run.

L.E. Myers, ... Manhattan Athletic Club 1
N. Fletcher, ... Montreal A.A.A. 2
W.G. Robertson, ... do do 3

Time 52 sec. 3 competitors.

Bicycle Race, One Mile.

G.M. Smith, ... Montreal Bicycle Club 1
A.T. Lane, ... do do 2
H.S. Tibbs .... do do 3

Time 3 min. 44 sec. 3 competitors.

Running High Jump

A.L. Carroll,.............................. Staten Island Athletic Club 1
W.R. Thompson, ... Montreal A.A.A. 2

Height 5 feet 5 inches. 2 competitors.

Two Hundred and Twenty Yards Run.

FIRST HEAT.

S. Derrickson, ... Manhattan Athletic Club ....
G.H. Wood, ... Shamrock Lacrosse Club .....} .. Tie.

SECOND HEAT.

C.E. Schuyler, ... Manhattan Athletic Club ....
W.R. Thompson, ... Montreal A.A.A. ....} .... Tie.

FINAL HEAT.

G. H. Wood, ... Shamrock Athletic Club ....

Time 24 1/4 sec. 4 competitors.

Half Mile Run.

L.E. Myers, ... Manhattan Athletic Club 1
N. Fletcher, ... Montreal A.A.A. 2
W.G. Robertson, ...   do   do 3

Time 2 min. 14 sec.

Putting the Shot.

F.L. Lambrecht,.......................... Pastime Athletic Club................ 1
C.A.J. Queckberner,................... Scott. American Ath. Club 2

Distance 41 feet 4 1/4 in. Best on record. 2 competitors.

Running Broad Jump.

W. R. Thompson, ... Montreal A.A.A. 1
A.L. Carroll,.............................. Staten Island Athletic Club 2
C.E. Schuyler, ... Manhattan .... do do 3

Distance 19 feet 3 in. 3 competitors.

Two Mile Run.

D.D. McTaggart, ... Montreal A.A.A. 1
James Baird,............................   do   do 2
G. Ouimet, ... Montreal 3

Time 10 min. 51 sec. 3 competitors.

One Hundred and Twenty Yards Hurdle Race in heats.

W. R. Thompson .... Montreal A.A.A. 1
Lewis Skaife ....   do   do 2

Time 18 1/4 sec. 2 competitors.

Five Mile Bicycle Race.

F.C. Holden .... Montreal Bicycle Club 1
W.G. Ross ....   do   do 2
J.H. Low ....   do   do 2

Time 19 min. 55 sec. 3 competitors.

H.W. BECKET,

Chairman Sports Committee.

Chapter 16

WINTER SPORTS

CURLING

Before the advent of snow and ice making machines winter sports were largely confined to the northern climes. Played in Scotland, curling clubs were established in Canada as early as 1807. By the last quarter of the nineteenth century Winnipeg served as the curling center of the world. There the Manitoba chapter of the Royal Canadian Curling Club fostered new styles and techniques for the improvement of the sport. By that time the sport had become well-established in the United States as well.

James Hadley presented a brief history of curling in Outing, December 1889, p. 211, which follows; along with a more detailed account, also published by Outing, February 1895, pp. 422-426.

THE GAME OF CURLING

... The Montreal Curling Club is of older date, having been formed in 1807. Of the other clubs in Montreal ... the Thistle, which has the largest membership of all, dates from the year 1843. The Ottawa club was not formed till 1862. These, as well as the Three Rivers, the St. Johns and, I believe, the Sherbrooke clubs, are all iron players.

An old and honored organization is the Royal Caledonian Curling Club of Scotland, "The mither o' us a'," as runs the toast at many a curlers' dinner in the colonies. This body sends for competition each season in Canada a number of medals, which are allotted to certain districts, containing five or six clubs each. These clubs oppose each other during the season, and the surviving winner takes the medal, which is prized as coming from the curlers' fountain of honor. Betwen 1845 and 1873 many clubs in both Upper and Lower Canada affiliated with the R.C.C.C., and matters in dispute used to be referred to that body. This was found unsatisfactory ... and so, about 1860 a branch of the Royal Caledonian was established for the province of Quebec, a similar branch being instituted for Ontario in 1874, one for the Maritime Provinces still more lately, and now I understand there is one for Manitoba nad the Northwest. It is the duty of the branches to allocate the district medals and to regulate the playing of the clubs at large. There are ninety-eight active clubs and four "inactive" ones under the Ontario branch, with a total memberhip of about three thousand.

Bonspiels, or tournaments, where a large number of tournaments come together, are a great feature in curling. On such occasions the players make a day of it ... In this country people travel greater distances than ever Scotchmen did to take part in a bonspiel. The first large gathering of the sport, composed of United States and Canadian players, was at Black Rock, near Buffalo, in 1865, when twenty-seven rinks a side contended. The next was at Toronto, in 1887, when twenty-nine rinks, or one hundred and sixteen players on each side, took part. At a Montreal winter carnival not long ago points as far distant as New York, New Glasgow, N.S., and London, Ont., were represented by curling clubs. Central Park, New York; Paterson, N̊.J., and Milwaukee have been frequent rallying points for American curlers, when National Curling Club medals, the Mitchell gold medal, the Gordon champion rink medal and other trophies were to be competed for. And when the Ice Carnival was held at St. Paul, in February, 1886, the largest curling bonspiel thereabout was one of its features.... at bonspiels on Burlington Bay as many as one hundred and ten rinks, which means four hundred and forty players, from all parts of Ontario have taken part....

I learn from the annals of the Grand National Curling Club of America that in 1886-7 there were thirty-one clubs in the United States affiliated to that body. In 1887-8 there were thirty-nine. Their membership totaled seven hundred and eighty-three, in which I assume it right to include the Four-Brothers Club, which, though composed of Canadians, appears to be, like the rest, within the jurisdiction of the G.N.C.C. The Annual for 1889 gives forty-five clubs, with eight hundred and sixty members. There must be more clubs than this in the United States, however, and certainly no one can believe that the curlers of the Union are to be numbered by hundreds only.

In the Northwestern States the game is spreading fst, and fourteen out of the forty odd clubs whose names appear in the annual hail from Wisconsin, Minnesota and Illinois. New clubs are being formed, and it says a good deal for the prospecrts of the game in that quarter when we find one hundred and twenty contestants at one rink in Portage, Wis., last year in the match for the Morgan medal, a prize open to Chicago, Milwaukee and Illinois curlers. Ten new clubs came into the fold of the Grand National Curling Club during the season 1886-7, which is regarded by the secretary thereof in his report as " a sure sign that our organization is not losing, but gaining, as it gets more venerable." It is of interest to observe that the G.N.C.C., which has been established since 1867, distributed for competition in 1888-9 thirteen district medals, which were allotted to clubs in New York, New Jersey, Wisconsin, Minnesota and Illinois. Last year there were seventeen distributed, the area being apparently widened by the addition of the State of Pennsylvania. A meeting of the G.N.C.C. of America is to be held, I understand, at Toronto on July 9, next year. And it is expected that an international curling contest with fifty rinks a side will then be arranged for the winter of 1891-2....

CURLING IN THE NORTHWEST

... Originating in Norway and in Scotland, and adapted alone to countries where ice forms for a longer or a shorter period, it could not but be welcomed in a country whose people are so devoted to winter sports as the Canadians. It soon spread its sway over

Ontario and extended its influence westward, but it remained for Manitoba to be the scene of its greatest triumphs and the center of its highest development. This is due to the fact that there, from three to four months of good curling can be depended upon every season, and in the frosty northern atmosphere the ice is in that keen condition so dear to the heart of the veteran curler. From the beginning of December, when the rink is flooded with several successive layers of water to form, when frozen in turn, a smooth, level surface, until the final breakup toward the end of March, the ice is seldom out of condition. Its keen surface is further improved by sprinkling with warm water, which freezes in almost imperceptible nodules of ice, over which the stones rush with great celerity and with loud roar.

The game itself is deserving of all the commendation which its friends bestow upon it. A gentleman's game, it offers no opportunity for the cultivation of professionalism or crookednes; intensely democratic, it allows the statesman, the railway magnate and the mechanic to meet on an equality on the ice. It offers no opportunity whatever for rough play, but it gives plenty of exercise. It is a game of the exact sciences, too, for it inculcates a respect for the angle of incidence.

Age and youth are equally subject to its spell. It requires a concentration of thought that drives the problems of cankering business from the mind. It is a comparatively inexpensive game, and although played chiefly at night, it induces no bad habits of mind or body.

There is fascination in the gliding approach of the slowly-revolving stone; there is excitement in the onrush of a running shot as it dashes through the carefully laid guards, and in the collision as they fly before the impact of this stony messenger. There is inspiration in the cry of the skip - "sweep Her!" ("soop her up!") and how swiftly the brooms fly to polish the ice before the lagging stone.

Curling has been more or less in vogue in the Red River settlement since the early part of the century, and has been regularly played in Winnipeg since before the eighties. The first club organized was the Granite, of Winnipeg, in 1877. It was followed by Portage la Prairie in 1881, the Stony Mountain Club in '82, the Stonewall in '83, Carberry and Morden following in '87; and in the same year a second club, "The Thistles," was formed at Winnipeg.

In that year the Winnipeg clubs made the first move toward widening the sphere of curling, by the establishment of a Bonspiel to which neighboring rinks were invited. Portage la Prairie sent seven rinks, Carberry two, Stonewall two and Stony Mountain two.

The year 1888 first saw the international border line ignored in a truly sporstmanlike spirit at St. Paul, where nine Manitoba rinks were pitted against American rinks and in all but one contest were victors. The best skill of Portage, Wis.; of Milwaukee, Chicago, Fargo, Waupaca, St. Paul and Minneapolis failed to stay the swift advance of their northern invaders from over the imaginary line.

The success achieved at St. Paul inspired the Northwest with higher ambitions and led directly to the formation of the Manitoba Branch of the Royal Caledonian Curling Club, having for its territory a district larger than many a world-famous kingdom - from Port Arthur to Calgary, nearly fifteen hundred miles.

The result of the formation of the various clubs into an association was at once apparent. Within three months sixty-two rinks gathered at a Bonspiel in Winnipeg, where they competed on th fifth, sixth and seventh of March, 1889, for magnificent trophies and numerous gold and silver medals. Visitors and competing rinks were present from Eastern Canada and from the United States, some of them having the highest continental fame.

The first event was a Grand Challenge Cup, for which every one of the sixty-two rinks present competed. The contest, however, narrowed down to rinks skipped by Harstone (Granite), which was first; Sparling (Portage la Prairie), second; Fraser (Granite), third, and Paterson (Thistle), fourth.

The Tuckett Trophy eventually went to Rodgers (St. Paul).

The third event, the Grand International Trophy, was carried off by our American cousins, who played down among themselves until it was won by the famous Crusaders of Portage, Wis.

The Grand Points Competition brought out two hundred entries, the six highest scores being Mark Fortune, 28; Thomas Kelly, 27; C.W. Huffman, 26; M.C. Clarke, 26; J.C.McDoanld, 26; J.D. Flavelle, 26.

The Walkerville Tankard Competition was won by Fraser's rink, Sugden's rink being second.

The Bonspiel so auspiciously commenced became at once the annual event looked forward to by the curling fraternity, not only of the Northwest, but of all the provinces and of the curlers of St. Paul, who have been present on every subsequent occasion.

The next Bonspiel was held in Winnipeg, commencing on the eleventh of February, 1890. Over sixty rinks participated in the contests. In the Grand Challenge Cup the struggle soon lay in the fifth draw, between H.G. Wilson, S.G. Harstone, L.H. Erb (Winnipeg) rinks; W.H. Sparling (P. la P.), and J.D. Flavelle (Lindsay, Ont.) Erb and Flavelle went out, then the famous Harstone succumbed to Wilson, and on his beating Sparling by a score of 18 to 17, his rink became the possessor of the cup for that season.

In the second event the different districts competed as to which should send two clubs to Ottawa to compete for the Vice-Regal Tankard. This competition was not completed.

For the Grand International Trophy, five Canadian rinks ... defeated five American rinks... by a score of 131 to 71. In the subsequent competition between the Canadian rinks, it was won by D. Brown's Winnipeg rink.

The fourth event was the Tuckett Trophy. Nine districts of Manitoba and the Northwest entered two rinks each. In the second draw ... the Portage rinks, I.W. Thompson and W.H. Sparling, rose up and smote the two Winnipeg rinks utterly, by a score of 52 to 29.

The Royal Caledonia Tankard, the fifth event, Manitoba versus All-comers, was a fight ... in favor of the home rinks. By beating a famous Milwaukee rink by a score of 22 to 11, the most northerly club on the continent, the Saskatchewans of Prince Albert, Sask, proved their prowess.

In the Grand Point Competition there were one hundred and eighty entries. Dr. Jamieson, of the Thistles, took first prize ...

In the seventh event, Walkerville Tankard, sixty-two rinks entered.... Fortune won first place ...

The eighth event, the Watson prize, four pair of curling stones, had fourteen rinks entered.... Keewatin beat Calgary and won the stones.

The third annual Bonspiel of the Manitoba Branch of the R.C.C. was held in Winnipeg on th ethird, fourth, fifth, sixth and seventh of February, 1891. The attendance was larger this year than in former years, over three hundred curlers being present. The Ontario Branch of the Grand National Curling Club of the United States sent representatives. On the evening of the fourth, four hundred curlers and friends of curling assembled at a grand banquet in the Clarendon Hotel....

Fortune's Rink won the Grand Challenge Cup ... Two Canadian rinks, Flavelle of Lindsay and Fortune of Winnipeg, won the International Trophy in competition with Nettleton and Wm. Rogers St. Paul rinks. Score 43 to 30. Flavelle was the final winner of the trophy.

In the Tuckett Trophy Competition ... Fortune's and J. Paterson's Winnipeg rinks won the prize ... In the Royal Caledonia Tankard Competition ... Flavelle got the tankard at the final.

For the Walkerville Tankard sixty-four rinks entered. J. Paterson's Granite rink won it ... W.G. Fraser won the Points Competition Trophy ...

The Vice-Regal Tankard Competition narrowed down to a contest betwen two Portage la Prairie rinks ... and two Port Arthur rinks ... The Lake Superior men were too strong for their redoubtable Portage opponents, and beat them 27 to 25.

The Bagnall-Wyld system of drawing , to avoid byes, was adopted at this Bonspiel with satisfactory results.

The Bonspiel of 1892, which took place at Winnipeg on the ninth, tenth, eleventh and twelfth of February, was an era of splendid contests and great surprises. In spite of the skill of the old veterans, half a dozen famous rinks were defeated by new combinations, the provincial and western rinks showing up well ... The attendance of rinks (sixty-nine in all) and of curlers was larger than ever.

Winnipeg lost the Grand Challenge Cup....Flavelle won the trophy by beating Sparling, and it went to Ontario.

The Walkerville Tankard was won by Fortune after he had defeated W.A. Grant's Calgary rink....

In the International Contest ... the trophy was finally captured by Sparling.

The Tuckett Trophy was won by two Virden rinks, W. Cobb's and W.D. Craig's ... W.H. Grant, Calgary, won the Galt Trophy by a final victory over H. Barnes' Rat Portage rink.

Fraser's famous rink gathered in the Royal Caledonian Tankard after it was vainly fought for by McCullough's Stonewall rink to the last.... Fraser won first prize in Points Competition ...

The enthusiasm of the spectators who crowded the rinks was at white heat in many of the close contests between champions, so that at times it was a difficult matter to keep the ice clear. A skip required nerve to win.

The next two selections describe tournament play in Milwaukee and Chicago, two centers of curling activity in the United States. They are reprinted from the Chicago Tribune, 18 February 1886, p. 6; and 28 January 1894, p. 6, respectively.

CURLING AT MILWAUKEE

MILWAUKEE, Wis., Feb. 17. - The Milwaukee Curling Club's rink on Farwell avenue was the great centre of attraction this afternoon,, the contest of clubs in the National Curling Club for the Mitchell medal having been held there. At 1 o'clock the Milwaukee, Arlington, Portage, Chicago, Lincoln Park, Decorah, and Cambria Clubs reported at the rink to enter the contest.

Before 2 o'clock the several rinks had been drawn against each other, and the remainder of the afternoon put in very good work, considering the soft condition of the ice. The result was as follows:

Milwaukee Rink, No. 1, Hill, skip, 16, vs. Arlington Rink, No. 2, McMillan, skip, 15; Chicago Rink, No. 1, Wood, skip, 24, vs. Arlington, No. 1, Dunlop, skip, 23; Chicago, No. 2, Duncan, skip, 23, vs. Cambria, No. 1, 12; Lincoln Park, No. 1, Wilson, skip, 18, vs. Cambria, No. 2, Emsperger, skip, 17; Lincoln Park, No. 2, Forrest, skip, 27, vs. Portage, No. 1, Wells, skip, 13; Portage, No. 2, Jones, skip, 17, vs. Milwaukee, No. 2, Johnston, skip, 13.

The winning rinks in today's contest will resume the play tomorrow, the one rink from the Decorah also entering, to decide the possession of the Mitchell medal. This evening the visiting curlers were given a banquet by the Milwaukee Curling Club at the Plankinton House.

SOUTH PARKS BEATEN

The Chicago and South Park Curling clubs met yesterday afternoon at Lincoln Park for their second game in the Robert Clarke medal competition. Friday the Chicagos won by thirty points and yesterday they improved upon this to the extent of three, winning handily by thirty-three points. This heavy defeat was due to the poor work of two of the South Park rinks, who fell behind thirty points in their totals. Lindeman's rink made no showing at all against that skipped by J.B. Wood, and only twice in the twenty-one heads did they score more than a single point. On Rink 2 Kibbe had a Corbettlike victory, Rolthoefer's quartet playing miserably. Nelson versus Hill was a game worth looking at, and round this and Rink 4 all the interest of the game became centered. Both skips workied like Trojans. A big spurt by Nelson caused some dismay among Hill's men. Ten to three was the score at the tenth heat. Then Nelson's men failed to connect for four innings, and their opponents, coming up strongly, tied the score. From this on it was nip and tuck, and the nineteenth inning found them tied again. The two remaining heads yielded a point each to Hill, giving him the game. W. Nelson was the forlorn hope of the South Siders, and though he and his men made a gallant rally they came out one point to the bad. The Chicagos thus swept the ice, and should they win the next match, which will be played at South Park Tuesday, will capture the medal. In justice to the losers it must be said that they have been out of shape, and are quite capable of giving their victors a hard fight. While the match was on Dan Mackay thought he would have a go with Ralston at a single-handed game. He could only make a solitary point, while his opponent got tired rolling them up. The totals were: Ralston, 22; D. Mackay, 1. The ice was keen and in fine condition....

ICE HOCKEY

Primitive forms of hockey, such as shinny in Ireland or kolven in Holland, had been played in Europe for centuries; but Canadians most fully adapted the game to the ice. Informal rough and tumble games were played by soldiers garrisoned along frozen waterways in the 1840s and 1850s. Adopting rules from both rugby and lacrosse, students formulated their own version of the game, which they displayed in Montreal in 1875. McGill University students formed a club in 1877 and codified the rules in 1879. Hockey soon became a part of the program of the Montreal Winter Carnival, which hosted the first tournament in 1883.

Montreal established a city hockey league with four teams in 1885, and Ottawa soon followed with a league of its own. In 1886 Montreal, Quebec, and Ottawa united in the formation of the Amateur Hockey Association of Canada. Hockey first appeared in the United States at a winter carnival in Vermont that same year.

Several innovations changed the game during the early years of formalization. Reducing the number of players from nine to seven, and later, to six, sped up the game. in the late 1880s better sticks appeared and the puck was substituted in lieu of a ball. The use of goal nets originated in 1889.

In 1890 the Ontario Hockey Association formed in Toronto, and a club was organized in Winnipeg. The former established senior, junior, and intermediate championships by 1896 and became a powerful influence in amateur hockey circles. In 1892 Lord Stanley of Preston, Governor General of Canada, whose sons played for the top club in Ottawa, donated a challenge cup to be given annually to the most outstanding team.

Both Johns Hopkins and Yale Universities adopted the game in 1893, and four New York teams organized the United States Amateur Hockey League in 1896. A Baltimore league appeared the next year, and the Intercollegiate Hockey League was established in 1898.

With the introduction of prizes and tournament play the emphasis on winning led many clubs to coerce the best players with remuneration. Professionalism emerged as an issue throughout the 1890s and protestations regarding players' eligibility resulted in the formation of the Canadian Amateur Hockey League in 1899. A professional league started play in the United States in 1903.

The Montreal Hockey Club report for the 1884-85 season provides a sense of amateur play at that time.

ANNUAL REPORT OF THE MONTREAL HOCKEY CLUB

MONTREAL, 20th May, 1885.

GENTLEMEN, -

I have much pleasure in presenting the Report of your Committee on the first season's work.

A meeting of members of the Montreal Amateur Athletic Association was held at the Club House on Friday evening, 28th November, 1884; Mr. T.L. Paton took the chair, and explained that the meeting was called with a view of forming a Hockey Club in connection with the said Association; and it being the unanimous opinion of the members present that such a Club was advisable, the meeting proceeded to form a Constitution and Code of By-Laws, and to elect Officers for the year; which resulted as follows: -Mr. Thos. Fraser, President, Mr. W.D. Aird, Vice-President, Mr. F.W. Barlow, Hon. Sec. and Treasurer, with Messrs. J.G. Ross, F.M. Larmonth, Wm. Hodgson A.E. McNaughton and T.L. Paton as Committee.

The membership of the Club is only 19 - a small number - but I trust it will be largely increased next season.

The first season of the club has been a very successful one, and notwithstnding all the trouble and inconvenience the Club had to contend with - in the way of getting ice to practice on - I think we can show a very good record.

The season commenced with the Victoria Rink Tournament, and it fell to the lot of our team to play against the McGill Club on the Victoria Rink ice, on Tuesday evening, 20th January - play for two half-hours, - which resulted in our favor by two goals to none.

The following composed the team - T.L. Paton, F.M. Larmonth, W.D. Aird, Wm. Hodgson, D. McIntyre, R.A. Smith, and F.W. Barlow.

It was decided by the Carnival Out-Door Sports Committee to have a Carnival Hockey Club for a silver cup, to be presented to the Club winning the greatest number of games; and our Club entered a team to compete with the others. And on Wednesday, 28th January, our team played their first game in the Tournament with the Montreal Foot Ball Club, and gained a victory by 6 goals to 1.

The team was the same as played with McGill on the 20th January.

On Friday morning our same team played their second game in the Carnival Tournament with the Ottawa Club. Play two half hours, resulting in a draw of one goal each; play was resumed for an additional half hour, which resulted in another draw of one goal each: making two goals each in the hour-and-a-half; it was then decided that play should be stopped, and that the Carnival Committee should decide when the match should be played off. The Chairman of the Carnival Out-Door Sports Committee decided that the game should be played off on Saturday morning, at 8:30, and at about 9 o'clock the two teams faced each other again. Play to be two half-hours; and at the end of the two half-hours neither side had obtained any advantage of the other, and after a few minutes rest the teams were again called out to play an additional half-hour; and after twenty-eight minutes play, Aird put the puck through the Ottawa goals, and scored again for our team. The game was again started, and on time being called, no more games had been taken; thus our team won after a very hard fight.

On Saturday afternoon, by order of the Carnival Committee, our same team played the final game with the McGill Club. Play was for two half-hours; and was won by us by one goal to none, thus winning the Carnival Cup with the same team as played in the morning.

On Friday evening, 6th February, our team played the final game in the Victoria Rink Tournament with the Victoria Club. Play two half-hours; and was won by our team by one goal to none. The team was the same as played all along, in fact, the team was not changed during the season. After the above game both teams were entertained by the Directors of the Rink in their roooms; the mugs were presented to our team, viz: one to each player.

I trust the good record of the Club for last season will increase the membereship for next season, and induce some new players to come out. The greatest drawback last year to the team was getting the necessary practice with so limited a membership.

Respectfully submitted,

FRED W. BARLOW, *Hon. Sec.-Treas.*

Outing described the game, new to the United States, January, 1893, pp. 252-256. Goal nets were not yet widely used.

ICE HOCKEY

The sport-loving people of the United States and Canada are quick to appreciate and adopt any new game which demands skill and courage in its participants, and at the same time is attractive to spectators.... What the young men of to-day want is a game wherein such valuable manly qualities as pluck, strength, agility and good judgment can be shown to the best advantage; and what the spectator wants is a game that has dash, and excitement connected with it, is lively from start to finish, and does not necessitate a too great consumption of busy folks' time in watching it.

Such a game is what may be termed the national winter game of Canada - ice hockey - and it is quite safe to say that if climactic conditions allowed, it would speedily become the leading winter pastime in New York.

Hockey is a skating game, therefore few Americans, comparatively speaking, can indulge in it. Where mild winters prevail it cannot flourish, and except in the most northerly States of the Union, it could never attain such a popularity as it has already found in Canada. There every town of a size sufficient to maintain a skating-rink now possesses at least one club, while the larger cities and towns can number several. Montreal, the center of the game, and where the championship of Canada - for that matter, of the world as well - is now held, boasts the greater number. The members comprise as fine specimens of manhood as the athletic world can produce.

The name "hockey" is not an unfamiliar one, having been applied in England for years to a game somewhat resembling "shinny" ...

Unlike its namesake, the Canadian game requires truly skillful players as its exponents, and when properly played combines science, fast skating and grace. No game is stronger in fixing the attention of the onlookers. The kaleidoscopic changes of formation and glancing of varied colors are very pleasing as the gayly costumed players pass and repass the "puck" from end to end of the rink with the speed and accuracy of a lacrosse ball.

In Canada the championship matches are played, and clubs almost invariably practice in covered rinks.

The rink contains a sheet of ice about one hundred and eighty or two hundred feet in length by eighty or one hundred in width, no especial dimensions being stipulated in the rules of the Amateur Hockey Association of Canada.

Seven players constitute a side - their endeavor being, with the aid of regulation hockey sticks, to pass the puck through their adversaries' goal....

The puck is circular in shape, of vulcanized rubber, one inch in thickness, with a diameter of three inches.

The stick is made of hard wood - generally ash or hickory -steamed, and then bent to form the blade ... The blade ... is about one foot in length and an inch and a half in width. The handle, which is about three and a half feet in length, leaves the base at about an angle of forty-five degrees ... the only rule laid down by the association in reference to its manufacture being that the stick shall in no part be more than three inches wide.

The skate differs somewhat from the ordinary blade or figure skate, being slightly higher than either of these, that greater leverage may be obtained.... It is screwed to the boot, which is made especially strong to stand the strain.

The rules are somewhat similar to those laid down in football, the principal one being that a player must always be "on side," *i.e.*, never playing in advance of the puck; consequently he cannot take the puck on a pass from a player on his own side unless he be behind him when the pass is made ...

A player, if he happens to be out of play or offside, however, is put onside immediately upon a player of the opposing team touching the puck.

The goal-posts are placed six feet apart, at the ends of the rink, and are four feet high. They are held in position by being sunk in holes made in the ice.

A wooden wall, generally about two feet in height, borders the ice. From this the puck readily rebounds, and it becomes a material factor in the science of the game ...

The puck may be intercepted, but must not be carried or knocked forward by any part of the skate or person.

The team is made up as follows: four forwards - one on each wing and two center men - a cover-point, a point, and a goal-keeper....

It is the prime duty of the forwards to keep "on the puck" ... never alowing the opposing team to remain in undisputed possession for an instant.... working like bees to keep the puck near the goal in their opponents' territory, and to eventually score a game.

The position of cover-point is the most important on the ice and a difficult one to fill. The player is both on the offensive and the defensive, and must be ready at any time to check a player or return the puck; or ...dart through the line of opposing forwards in the hope of a shot at goal.

The point should be a tower of strength in both checking and lifting. He is purely a defensive player, and must allow no man to pass him ...

The goal-keeper takes position a few inches in advance of he goal-posts, and when the goal is threatened brings his feet together in the shape of a broad wedge, covring as much ground as possible between the posts. He is not allowed to kneel upon the ice. He must be exceedingly quick ... ward off the puck with his stick, catch it in his hands or intercept it with his skates.

The captain should be a man chosen through his experience as a player and for his quickness of judgment....

In a match the teams play two half-hours, changing ends at half-time after a rest of ten minutes. Umpires take a position behind each goal, and it is their duty to decide when a game has been scored.

A referee is chosen by mutual consent, or is appointed by the association. He sees that the rules governing the game are enforced, and carries a shrill whistle, which is blown when a foul has been made. Such a signal stops the game, and the puck must be "faced" where the foul occurred. The referee has power to rule off a player for persistent fouling or unnecessarily rough play. When the game is called the puck is "faced" by being placed between the center forward of each team, in the center of the ice, who simultaneously strike the ice, then each other's stick three times. After the sticks have met the third time, the puck is in play....

To witness a championship match is to at once appreciate hockey. The speed attained by the players, the clever dodging, the grace with which they elude their antagonists, the sharp checking, the long "lifts," the lightning "shoots" and the combined and clever team-play ... It is not without its dangers. The rapidity with which the players move ... the hard, close checking ... often inflict a nasty fall or bruise....

The "lift" and the "shoot" can only be acquired after many attempts ... In a "lift" the puck often attains the height of twenty or thirty feet, passing over the heads of the whole team.

It should never rise more than a foot above the ice in shooting, and accuracy in aim is a prime factor ...

Played in the home of the game, hockey never fails to draw large numbers of enthusiasts to important matches; and these spectators give the game their undivided attention, filling the air with cries of encouragement and applause as a player or team shows particularly brilliant pieces of play or strategy.

The matches are witnessed by crowds of enthusiastic spectators of both sexes and of all classes, from His Excellency the Governor-General and his household, down to the small boy on the rink's roof ...

Ladies have proved themselves ardent admirers of hockey. Large numbers of them attend every important match, and more than once teams composed of Canada's fairest buds have played the game, and played it well.

Hockey is not so fatiguing as a description of the game would lead one to suppose. A man playing carefully in his appointed position is seldom subject too prolonged attack....

The Canadian season of 1892 was a most successful one. The clubs are grouped in two unions, viz., the Ontario and Quebec, the latter the more prominent, inasmuch as the stronger clubs and the one at present holding the championship of Canada are affiliated with it. Its matches were played under the "challenge system," by the rules of which the holders of the championship are bound to accept any challenge from a club in the union within seven days of its receipt, otherwise they lose the game by default.

Early in the year the Montreal Amateur Athletic Association team, heretofore invincible, lost the title of champions to the Ottawas, but regained it at the end of the season, much to the disgust of the latter, who had defended the flags through many a contest.

The Quebec City Club is one of the foremost of the union, while Scott, one of its members, is claimed by many to be the cleverest player of to-day; but every leading club has its pet for whom they claim this especial distinction - the Ottawas, a Kirby or a Young, and in Montreal such names as Hodgson, Cameron and Low, become by-words in the athletic community, soon after the thermometer first registers the freezing-point.

The Ontario Union comprises clubs that have been organized within the last few years, and consequently is not as prominent as Quebec; but some of its clubs have already made a name for themselves, notably that of Osgoode Hall, Toronto, which promises to make a hard fight for first palce before another season passes.

The matches of this union were played in series.

One noticeable feature in the progress of the game is the number of junior clubs in existence and being organized, whose members are wonderfully clever on their skates, and whose greatest ambition is to take a place in the senior ranks as soon as strength and weight will permit. The players are purely amateur, and there is no instance of a charge of professionalism having been brought to the notice of the executive.

Cricket and curling are, I believe, the only two games over which Americans and Canadians struggle for international honors. Why should not Hockey make a third? There are many cities in the border States having sufficient ice during the winter months to make this scheme feasible.

St. Paul has already proved a rival to Montreal, with its carnival of winter festivities; but the game has not as yet been domiciled there.

The season of 1893 promises fair to surpass all previous ones, and it is to be hoped that the game which has become so popular in Canada may find admirers and participants across the line, and in the near future we will find American clubs competitors for the hockey championship of the world.

The Montreal Gazette reported on the proceedings of the Amateur Hockey Association, 15 December 1892, p. 8; and the first Stanley Cup challenge, 23 March 1894, p. 8.

THE HOCKEY ASSOCIATION

The annual meeting of the Canadian Hockey association took place last night in the M.A.A.A. rooms, when all the clubs were fully represented. Mr. Stewart, who has been president for four years, occupied the chair, and the delegates present were:-

Victorias - Messrs. Jack and Crathern.

M.A.A.A. - Messrs. Shaw, Cameron, and Irving.

Ottawa - Messrs. Russell, Kirby and Young.

Quebec - Messrs. Laurie, Powell and Scott.

Shamrocks - Messrs. Wall, Carpenter and McKenna.

Sherbrooke - Mr. Wilson.

McGill - Messrs. Costigan and Archibald.

Crystals - Messrs. Ritchie, McQuisten and Murray.

The Rebels, of Ottawa, were not represented.

After the reading of the minutes and the secretary and treasurer's reports, which were adopted, there were several communications received and read, the principal business being the applications of the Crystal hockey and Skating club and the McGill Hockey club. Both clubs were admitted, and the next business was the election of officers, which resulted as follows: - President - F.M. Jenkins, Ottawa.

First Vice-President - J. Crathern, Victorias.

Second vice-president - A. Laurie, Quebec.

Secretary-treasurer - J.A. Findley, Montreal.

Council - A. Ritchie, Crystal; Geo. Carpenter, Shamrock; M. Costigan, McGill; A.Z. Palmer, Ottawa Rebels; J. Farwell, Sherbrooke.

After some discussion it was decided that the council appoint a sub-committee to revise the constitution and by-laws, and report to the council at a future date.

Then the question of the evening was brought up, and that was deciding whether the series or the challenge system would hold good this year. A close vote decided on the series system.

Mr. Laurie, of Quebec, proposed that the next annual meeting of the association be held in Quebec. This was somewhat of a surprise, but when it came to a vote the combination of clubs outside the city carried the motion.

It had been said previous to the meeting that an effort would be made to freeze out the Crystal Hockey club from the senior series, and the effort showed itself in a motion to the effect that only the Montreal, Victoria, Shamrock, Ottawa and Quebec clubs be eligible to play for the senior championship. The Shamrock representative declined to enter the series, thus making room for the Crystals and the little scheme was spoiled, so that now the senior championship will be competed for by the Montreal, Victoria, Crystal, Ottawa and Quebec clubs....

Following is the secretary's report:-

MR. CHAIRMAN AND GENTLEMEN, - I have the pleasure to present the annual report of this association for the season of 1891 and 1892. The season was opened by the Ottawa and Montreal clubs in Montreal under date of January 8, the Ottawas being victors by a score of three goals to two. I believe that this is the first time since the formation of this association that the championship has been taken out of Montreal. The next match was on January 15, Shamrocks vs. Ottawa, and was won by Ottawa, eight goals to three. The Montreal club was next to be defeated by Ottawa on January 21 by a score of ten goals to two. On January 28 the Quebec club had a try for it, with the score at the end of the match in favor of Ottawa by three goals to none. On February 18 the Quebec club again visited Ottawa, but went away with a score of three to one against them. On March 7, the Montreal club again visited the Capital city and this time succeeded in bringing back the championship to Montreal by a score of one to none. This closed the season.

The intermediate championship was again held throughout the season by the second seven of the Montreal club. They defeated Brittania on January 13, Victoria on January 21, and the Shamrocks on February 17.

I would urge the adoption of the series system in place of the challenge, as a glance at the above will show the want of fairness, the Ottawa Hockey club having won all but the last match, still they are not champions.

... The trophy, to the value of $40, presented to the club winning the greatest number of championship matches, was won by the Ottawa club.

We regret to record the resignation of the Brittania club. The committee of this club find that the players they anticipated being able to procure werre divided amongst all the clubs now playing and decided it would be better not to attempt to weaken other clubs so as to build up their own....

We are still without any championship trophy, being short of funds, but the coming season ought to put this all right....

MONTREAL THE CHAMPION
THE OTTAWAS ARE DEFEATED AFTER A SPLENDID GAME.

The hockey season is over and the championship has been won. The season has been a long one, and perhaps the most brilliant in the history of the game....

... and now the M.H.C. again stand triumphant against the rest of the hockey world. At the beginning it seemed as if the last year's champions would not be in the game...

Not only the Canadian championship, but the Governor-General's cup depended on this match, and Montreal can fly its colors in the face of any hockey breeze that ever blew.

The Victoria rink last night held the largest crowd ever packed into the rink in its history....

It was a question of championship and Montreal had to win. There is one thing Montreal hates to do - that is to lose - and that settles it.

It may seem strange to anybody who knew the game to discover how the score came out as it did; but that fact is easily explained. Clever play and aquaintance with the rink accounted for it. In a match like this, where the championship of the whole country is in the balance, the players can afford to stand under more severe criticism than is usually meted out to amateur clubs, and in this connection it may be said that the referee was not nearly strict enough. The ice could not be expected to be good, and the conditions generally could be much improved upon if these great deciding games could be held earlier in the season. Nobody was ruled off, but James and Pulford ought to have been. Hockey is not necessarily synonymous with homicide.

Montreal won by three goals to one and the following were the men who put up the match: -

Ottawa	Position	Montreal
Morrell	Goal	Collins
Pulford	Point	Cameron
Young	Cover point	James
Kirby	Forwards	Routh
J. McDougall	"	Mussen
S. McDougall	"	A. Hodgson
Russel	"	Barlow

Referee - Mr. Scott, of Quebec
Umpires - Messrs. A. Anderson and W. Irwin.

SUMMARY.

Game	Club	Scorer	Time
First	Ottawa	Kirby	12 min.
Second	Montreal	Hodgson	10 min.
Third	Montreal	Barlow	9 min.
Fourth	Montreal	Hodgson	12 min.

In the first half Montreal had decidedly the best of the play. Their attack was almost perfect and their defence was invulnerable. McDougall and Russell seemed to be a whole team, but even their hard work was not equal to the resistance met with from Collins and James. The Montrealers had the best of the rushing game, a point in which they seemed to excel, for their combination seemed almost perfect up to the point of scoring. Then there was an obstruction in the way, and his name was Morrell. Shot after shot was religiously piled in the devoted fortress held by Ottawa, but none of them were absolutely straight. That little round bit of rubber seemed to have a magnetic attraction for the Ottawa flags, but somehow or other it could not get through. For eight minutes Montreal forced the visitors to a strictly defence game and nothing but the best sort of luck could prevent them from winning. It was Montreal first, last and all the time. Then the Ottawa men became aggressive and made things warm for Montreal. How warm it was may be judged from the fact that two hockey sticks were broken - one on each side; but this was merely accidental with a capital A. Then there was some trouble in the way of a scrimmage. There was a lot of chopping and it looked as if the Montrealers were going to win out on the start, but Pulford and Kirby got the rubber out of danger and the latter, following up his lead, passed to Cross, received it again from McDougall and then scored. Time, 12 minutes.

The second game was a beauty from a hockey point of view and one of the men who is deserving of particular credit is Hodgson, who played a magnificent game and made things particularly uncomfortable for the visitors. In fact, it was only the incomparable goal keeping of Morrell that saved Ottawa from a more decisive defeat. How it was that Montreal only scored one goal in the first half is one of those things that "no fellow can find out," for thier play certainly deserved better.

SECOND HALF

In the second half there was seen about as good hockey as could be wished for,. The visitors made great efforts and their attack was splendid, but the forwards could not pass Allan Cameron or James. The Montreal defence seemed impregnable, while Barlow, Hodgson and Mussen rushed that puck around in a way to make the Ottawa men nervous. In this half the visitors had a great many good chances, but they could not succeed in scoring. A short stoppage was made in this half on account of McDougall sustaining an injury to his leg. Another feature was the warning which the referee gave to Messrs. Pulford and James. The next goal, however, was scored by Barlow after nine minutes' play and it took twelve minutes more before Hodgson, after a splendid exhibition of hockey secured the third game for Montreal. No other goals were scored until time was called, and once again Montreal stands at the head of the hockey procession.

One of the pleasing features of the match was the display of ribbon. Every lady almost in the rink wore the favors of their particular club and never did belted knight in joust or tourney fight harder than the hockey men....

The proliferation of hockey teams, the competition for players, and the importance of success to civic pride are all evident in the Toronto Globe's account of the Ontario Hockey Association meeting, 9 December 1895, p. 8.

TOO MANY TEAMS

On Saturday afternoon when the annual parliament of the Ontario Hockey Association was convened at the Queen's Hotel nearly 50 delegates were present, representing about 20 clubs, an increase over the last yearly gathering of 30 delegates. Last year there was an appreciable decrease in the interest in the game taken in Toronto, which could be ascribed to the lack of a first-class representative city team, but legislation towards the formation of such a seven was enacted by the hockeyists on Saturday, both the local and outside delegates combining in furthering the scheme.

Many telling arguments were used by Vice-President McFadden in favor of establishing an intermediate series, which would embrace all the clubs that have proved themselves to be too strong for the junior and too weak for the senior, but it was thought by a goodly proportion of the members that the time was hardly ripe enough for so radical a change, and the matter was left in abeyance....

The first business transacted was the admittance of Norwood, Lindsay and the Victorias of Kingston to the full privileges of the association. The latter club takes the place vacated by the Athletics, but does not assume their liabilities. President Brown in opening the proceedings spoke glowingly of the progress of the association, which he though was largely due to the energetic efforts of the Secretary ... The large attendance he thought spoke well for the future of the game. The sub-committee's report ... expressed the opinion that the number of clubs in the senior series in Toronto and elsewhere was too great and the matches too many. It was pointed out that the Canadian Hockey Association is a five club league, and that a city the size of Ottawa was allowed only one team in the senior series.

Treasurer A.R. Creelman's statement ... showed that the affairs of the association financially were all that could be desired, there being a balance of $191.49....

McFadden wanted the rules altered so that a player could not play for more than one club during one season. This would shut out Bank League players from participation in the O.H.A. cup matches, and it seemed to be the general opinion that the league was the chief factor in the surfeit of hockey that Toronto had last year. After getting this expression McFadden withdrew his motion. An endeavor will be made to get the city clubs together for the organization of a representative Toronto team fit to hold its own with Queen's or any of the other eastern clubs....

The Executive Meeting

After the general meeting the Executive Committee met and discussed several matters which had been brought up at the meeting. The proposal to form a Toronto team composed of representatives from the big clubs, was accorded a great deal of attention, being dealt with from all points of view. It was argued that the Queen's seven was so far superior to any other of the teams in the senior series that they should be put in a class by themselves. It was suggested jocularly that Class B would suit them. President Brown thought that the Executive seemed to be really desirous of legislating against Queen's. The game, he said, was really in its infancy, and as years pass by Toronto will have a first-class team. Mr. McFadden thought that if things went on in Toronto as they did last year the final should be played in Stratford. A gate could be got there at least. Treasurer Creelman came forward with a suggestion that a sub-committee be appointed to interview the members of the different clubs to entertain their opinion as to the advisability of forming an all Toronto team. Messrs. W.A. Gilmour and A.R. Creelman were appointed for that purpose....

The matter of the intermediate series was pretty well threshed out, but nothing definite was done, and is not likely to be until next year. If adopted the clubs would be disposed like this: - Senior series - Queen's, Varsity, T.A.C., Intemediate -Victoria, Stratford, Trinity, London, Peterboro, Limestones, Granite Colts, Ayr, Berlin, Hamilton, Junior series - Petroles, Sarnia, Stratford II, London II, Guelph, Berlin, Wellington, Norwood, Lindsay, Victoria Colts, Volts, Peterboro, T.A.C. II, Victoria, Kingston. Secretary Tiffin is desirous that all clubs should forward their fees as soon as possible.

AFTER THE PUCK

The Banks of Ontario and Montreal have been admitted to the intermediate city series ... The combination team will not be out this winter.

The Fenelon Falls hockey team has been formed ...

Outing covered the expansion of hockey in Canada in an article published in January, 1896, pp. 242-247.

HOCKEY IN THE CANADIAN NORTH-WEST

... In the Canadian North-West hockey has lately become the leading winter sport. On the 3rd of Nov., 1890, a meeting was held in Winnipeg which resulted in the formation of the Victoria Hockey Club. Shortly after that, the Winnipeg Hockey Club was formed. After a number of matches had been played between the two teams the season ended in a draw, neither club having the advantage.

In 1891-92, it appeared as if the same result would be reached as each team had an equal number of victories to its credit. In the final match, at the end of the hour the tie was unbroken. In the lay to a finish, the Victorias scored first and won the championship of Manitoba. A club formed from the officers and men of "B" squadron Royal Canadian Dragoons, also took pat in the schedule of games. Many great struggles between these rivals - the Victorias and Winnipegs - have been witnessed in Winnipeg during the last few years, but the one that took place between them on the 16th of Dec., 1892, when they opened the season, was one of the finest exhibitions of hockey ever seen in the North-West. So evenly matched were they, that in spite of the most determined efforts on the part of each team, the match almost passed without either team scoring.

Hockey was viewed with some suspicion when first introduced into Winnipeg, and the players had to pay a good price for the privilege of securing a rink to hold their matches in, but it was not long before this state of affairs was changed, and the players were paid a good share of the door receipts.

The winter of 1892-3, was marked by a wave of hockey that rolled over the North-West like a flood. No town or village with any pretensions but had its hockey club. In Winnipeg the game basked in the popular and vice-regal favor, and spread and flourished until the city poured out its teams as did Thebes its armies from a hundred gates. At one time it was credited with some thirty clubs, great and small, but there were really less than half a dozen. These were sub-divided into teams until each profession or mercantile interest marshalled its men like a Scottish chieftain his feudatory vassals.

Gentle but heroic maidens bestowed their favor, like the Spartan maidens, upon those of distinguished prowess on the ice-field of fame, and more particularly upon those who, like their immortal protypes, earned the distinction of being carried home on a shie-shutter. A constant succession of matches of more or less interest were being carried on in the various rinks.

Toward the end of January, 1893, the suggestion was made that a picked team should be sent east to play for the honor of the province. It was due to the untiring energy of Capt. Evans, that the project eventually took shape, and it was largely due to his foresight and skilful generalship that the trip proved so successful. The public spirited merchants, business and professional men of Winnipeg readily provided the financial wherewithal....

Just before the combination left for the East, fire gutted the rink in which was kept the uniforms, skates and sticks of the Victorias, leaving them to commence their eastern trip with the inconvenience of everything new and strange.

The career of the Manitobans was watched with intense interest by the people of the city and province. Their reception in the East was one continued ovation. Everywhere they were recieved with open arms; their colors were worn in Toronto, Ottawa and elsewhere by an array of beauty and chivalry, that was an incentive to the western men to play hockey in a manner that surprised the trained eastern teams.

They left Winnipeg on Feb'y 6th. On the 8th they defeated the Victorias of Toronto, by a score of 8 to 2. In the same city, on the 10th, they knocked out the Osgoodes, by a score of 11 to 5. At Kingston on the 12th, after a hard fight on rough, bad ice, they beat their opponents 4 to 3. On the 13th, at the capital of the Dominion, they were overthrown by the famous Ottawas, the pride of Ontario's hockey, by a score of 1 to 4, but on the following day, they vanquished the Rebels of the same city 3 to 1.

At Montreal they met the finest team on the continent, and as a result lost by 4 to 7. In this match, they were plainly afraid of their redoubtable opponents at the beginning of play, and it was only toward the end that they really played at their best and turned the tide, crowding their opponents goal in a manner that led one observant person to remark to a Winnipeger: "If your team had half an hour longer, they would beat us." But the change came too late to save the battle.

While here, J.K. McCullough of the Victorias won the skating championship of Canada in all of the several events he entered for.

Turning back westward into Ontario again, the Manitobans gained a victory over Peterboro' on the 17th, by a score of 9 to 3, and on the 21st, utterly defeated a picked team of western clubs at London, by a score of 10 to 7. The last schedule game was played at Niagara Falls, and Winnipeg won by 10 to 4.

While in Toronto they were prevailed upon to play an exhibition match with a picked team of Toronto men. Fagged out by a succession of hard matches, and with the princely round of hospitality, they could not be roused to their best until the match was nearly over, and then they were clearly outplaying their opponents, but they had lost the match and the score stood 4 to 3 in favor of the Ontario men.

In this, their first campaign, they won 60 goals and lost 34, including the exhibition game at Toronto. On their return home they were accorded a warm reception, and several banquets were given them.

The success of Manitoba's representatives in the east, added to the strength of the hockey enthusiasm, and from that time until the break-up in spring, it hardly knew a competitor in public favor and in the columns of the city press.

In the same season, 1892-3, new clubs were formed at Portage la Prairie, Carberry and elsewhere. Some of these developed unexpected strength, notably, the one in Portage la Prairie. Not only did it defeat the Winnipeg teams sent against it, but it sent a team down to Winnipeg and inflicted a number of crushing defeats on the city intermediate teams, winning at the closeof the season the intermediate championship of the North-West. They lost 26 goals and won 52 during the season. Sheppard, the famous goal keeper, received his hockey education among the Portagers.

After a hard fight through the whole season, the Victorias won the senior championship. The Winnipegs, however, won a set of medals competed for in three matches with their victorious opponents, which tended to make honors nearly even.

The season of 1893-4 showed no flogging in the interest which hockey excited in the west, and its record is in every way one to be proud of locally. The senior teams were represented by the Victorias, the Winnipegs and the Dragoons. It was soon apparent that the cavalry were outclassed, and should have been enetered inn the intermediate series of matches... The intermediate teams were those of the Victorias, the Winnipegs, and the Portage la Prairie clubs.

Rat Portage sent a team up to explore the west, and although they were defeated in most of the places they visited - Portage la Prairie, Brandon, Carberry and Winnipeg - they profited enough in the end by their experience, as was shown by their record in 1894-5. The bankers of Winnipeg sent a team west which met with fair success. Carberry and Brandon had several severe contests on their fields. The bankers of Winnipeg were negotiating to send a team eastward, but nothing came of it.

At the last senior match, on the 7th of March, the Victorias won the provincial championship.... The Winnipeg intermediate team won the intermediate championship against the Victorias and Portage la Prairie. The hockey fever was spreading through the west, and numerous matches were played at Regina and other western centres.

The season of 1894-5 was a golden one for the game. Early in 1895 a team from the Victorias ... went east in search of glory, and they found plenty of it. Their opening match was played at the capital of the Dominion, and there, under the bright eyes of Canadian beauty, they defeated their opponents, the Ottawa team, by a score of five goals to two.

After this the western blizzard gained strength, and when it blew at Montreal, the storm cloud won by a score of five to one. It was at the ancient capital that the western men received their only check, and they lost by a score of two to three goals taken by the Quebec players. It is only fair to the Winnipegers to say that they did not receive fair treatment at the hands of several members of the crowd, who allowed personal feelings to overcome that spirit of fairness that should prevail when one of the contesting teams is from an outside point.

At Toronto the Manitobans redeemed themselves by winning a match there by the score of eleven to four. This series of matches, played with the finest eastern teams, demonstrated the right of the Victorias to be called the equals at least of the champion team of Canada.... On their way home, by appointment they, or a portion of the team, stayed a day or two at Minneapolis, and gave the Yankee players a few lessons in the game, winning an easy victory.

The Victoria senior team, almost identical with the one sent east, won the senior championship of the west. An intermediate team from the same club ... won the intermediate championship, after the usual schedule of games with the Winnipeg and Portage la Prairie teams and a team from the Stars, a new combination in the city which showed up well.

A team from Selkirk made a tour of most of the hockey towns, but were worsted in nearly every case....

A team of Rat Portage players made a starring tour of western towns, and their playing, although rather rough and heavy, was a surprise to all the teams they met. They played Brandon, Carberry and Portage la Prairie, and had a comparatively easy victory in most cases. In Winnipeg they defeated the Stars and the victorious Victorias (junior team), but were in turn beaten by the Winnipegs after a close struggle. This team will have to be reckoned with as a probable championship team in the intermediate series this season. They are powerful skaters and handle the stick well....

Although fishing nets had been improvised as goal nets before, their use drew widespread attention before being officially adopted. Previous to the decision a referee stood behind the open goal sticks to determine a score. Arbitrary decisions often evoked abuse by partisan fans. The Montreal Gazette announce the official testing on 30 December 1899, p. 2.

WITH THE NETS

The public trial of thre goal nets in hockey will take place at the Arena at 8:15 tonight in a match between the Victorias and the Shamrocks. Delegates from all the clubs in the C.A.H.L. will be in attendance, and the O.H.A. will send a strong representation to ascertain what effect the nets will have on the game.
WILL WATCH THE PLAY
Toronto, December 29. - Jos. Ross Robertson, Frank J. Nelson and A.H. Beaton, left for Montreal tonight to represent the Ontario Hockey executive at Montral tomorrow night when the new goal nets will be used for the first time in a match. They will report on the proposal to adop the new net in Ontario.
SOME FROM QUEBEC
Quebec, December 29.- The Quebec Hockey Club will send two or three representatives headed by Mr. Arthur Smith, captain of this year's team, to witness the trial of the hockey goal net at the Arena tomorrow evening, in the match between the Victorias and the Shamrocks.

The state of the game in the United States at the time can be ascertained by the brief announcement accorded to the championship in the New York Times, 24 May 1899, p. 4.

NEW YORK HOCKEY CLUB IS CHAMPION

The Hockey Club of New York and the New York Athletic Club played off a tie game at the St. Nicholas Rink last night, the Hockey Club team winning by a score of 5 to 0. The victory gives the Hockey Club second palce in the Amateur Hockey League, the Brooklyn Club having won the championship.

SKATING

FIGURE SKATING

Local figure skating contests transpired during the mid-eighteenth century; but standardized competitions began when the American Skating Congress agreed on a required program in 1868. Harper's Weekly provided a brief history of figure skating and the compulsory skills on 4 March 1893, p. 213. The National Amateur Skating Union, organized in 1886, eventually merged with the International Skating Union in 1907 to govern both figure and speed skating.

FIGURE SKATING

THERE is probably no recognized sport in which the fine points are so little understood by the general public as in figure skating. This is proven by the applause which frequently follows the exhibitions of showy skaters as compared to to finished and methodical competitors. In many of our amateur championship competitions this has been the case, and reporters of our daily papers have been the worst offenders, often putting their ideas in print when they have been in direct opposition to the judges' decisions.

This was noticeably so in the contest of 1886, when a Canadian skater was defeated directly on his merits, and under the very best judges in the country. It occurred way back in the early seventies, in Jersey City, and again last year....

Proficient judges are sometimes misled, as in the contest of 1867, when Frank Swift, the old-time champion, almost succeeded in getting the best of them. He was only able to make the one-foot 8's with his right foot, and in order to throw the judges off, he first skated the figure facing them, and turning around a few times, he started with his back to them, but on the same foot. The deception was not noticed at first; but when Mr. E.B. Cook, one of the judges, asked him to repeat the figure, it was discovered that he could not use his left foot.

Any one taking up figure skating will shortly discover that he has a very imperfect balance on one or the other of his feet, on the same principle that a man is right or left handed, and in order to overcome it, should learn at once to use both alike....

The first consideration is the outfit, namely, proper shoes and first-class skates....

The proper skate is largely a matter of opinion. In Canada most of the skaters take off the clamps and screw the skates to the bottom of their shoes.... The market is flooded with any number of skates that fasten with clamps, both heel and toe, but they are all too heavy, and weight is a large factor in figure skating. For figure skating it is necessary that the bearing be under the ball of the foot, which enables a sure and successful balance.

Annual figure skating contests take place in Russia, Norway, Sweden, Holland, Germany, England, Canada, and the United States, but tot his country alone belongs the honor of holding both the figure and speed championships.

Owing to the geographical situation, and consequent uncertainty of ice, the New York skaters are at a great disadvantage, but even so, they have succeeded in leading

the world for over twenty-five years. The figure skating contests abroad are very lim-
ited in character, and do not begin to demand such perfect control and balance as the
American championships. To better understand the requirements in the United States
I append a programme with full instructions.... There are twenty-three feats.

The object of this programme is set forth the movements of figure skating so as best
to test the proficiency of the skaters, and in an order that will economize the strength
of the contestants.... It is understood that, whenever practicable, all movements are to
be executed both forward and backward, on right foot and on left. It should be borne
in mind that grace is the most desirable attribute of artistic skating.

1. Plain forward and backward skating.
2. Lap Foot" - as field step and in cutting circle.
3. Outside edge roll, forward.
4. Outside edge roll, backward.
5. Inside edge roll. forward.
6. Inside edge roll, backward.
7. Figure 8 on one foot, forward.
8. Figure 8 on one foot, backward.
9. Cross roll, forward.
10. Cross roll, backward.
11. Change of edge roll, forward - commencing either on outside or inside edge.
12. Change of edge roll, backward - beginning either on outside or inside edge.
13. (a) "On to Richmond"; (b) reverse "On to Richmond."
14. (a) "Locomotives," forward, backward, sideways - single and double; (b) waltz
    step (not to be done on the point of the skate).
15. Spread-eagle, inside and outside edges.
16. Curvilinear angles: (a) single, double, chain, and flying threes, beginning on in-
    side or outside edge; (b) turns from outside edge to outside edge, or from inside
    edge to inside edge, forward and backward.
17. Grape-vines, including "Philadelphia twist," etc.
18. Toe and heel movements, embracing pivot circling, toe spins (pirouettes), and
    movements on both toes, etc.
19. Single flat-foot spins and double-foot whirls.
20. (a) Serpentines on one foot and on both feet; (b) change of edge, single and
    double.
21. Loops and ringlets on inside and outside edges, single and in combination.
22. Display of complex movements, at the option of the contestant.
23. Specialties embracing original peculiar movements.

The officials of a figure skating contest shall be three judges and one scorer. The
judging shall be done on a scale of points running from the number of contestants
down to 0. Experience has shown the following to be the most practicable method of
scoring: "The number to be given to the one standing first in any section shall be that
of the number of contestants. Should there be two or more of equal merit, they should
be marked the same number ... A total failure is marked zero." A fall does not necessarily constitute a failure. At the conclusion of each figure each judge shall, without
consultation with his associates, mark the number of points which he awards to each

competitor. These reports shall be compared and in case of disagreement the majority shall decide. The scorer ... shall not be permitted to inform any competitor of his standing until the close of the entire competition.

The event is open to amateur figure skaters of the world.

The programme was first adopted at a meeting of the American Skating Congress held in Pittsburg, Pennsylvania, February 3, 1868, and, with a very few alterations, has been in use ever since.

The first figure skating contest held in New York under the revised programme was at Mitchell's Pond, corner of Fifty-ninth Street and Fifth Avenue, during the winter of 1868.... The match was won by James Mead, of New York; Edward Martin second - there being in all five competitors.

The old Philadelphia Skating Club claim to have hald contests prior to that, and the writer also shows contests in Chicago as early as 1865, but the then existing programme was very limited.

The first principle of perfect skating is grace ...

It is a remarkable fact that the average figure skater is weak on what are termed the plain movements. Most of them devote their time and attention to the small figures, forgetting that a graceful skater on the rolls, etc., may obtain a lead in the score that is difficult to overcome.

The impetus necessary to execute the smaller or close movements is acquired almost entirely by the use of the disengaged or balance foot....

The loops, which are a series of disconnected rings, are made by the balance foot being carried out and away from the performing leg some fifteen inches, while in ringlets it is carried within about six inches. This is a very nice distinction, but produces very different results....

The first necessary balances for a successful skater are the changes of edge, commencing on outside and running to inside, as in making a letter S. When this is accomplished both forward and backward, on right and on left, the skater will have good control of himself, and can very easily pick up other movements.

Another important point is what is termed "skating to place," meaning the ability to run over the figure several times, always keeping on the original lines. This requires wonderful control, especially on one-foot and backward movements.

In the plain movements, rolls, etc., the same rule holds good, the skater being required to make his strokes of uniform length and equal curve.

In skating to place on the close movements we must give the palm to the Canadians, this being accounted for by the fact that they have so much practice, usually four months each year, in covered rinks.

Mr. Louis Rubinstein, of Montreal, certainly leads the world in this respect; the writer has seen him execute the double one-foot 8's and never vary but a few inches, and the figure will be as perfect on the ice as though drawn by a pair of compasses.

Probably the most showy figures sre the "grape vines," which give the skater a good chance for ingenuity, many of our best performers being able to execute from twelve to fifteen distinct and different vines.

In order to be successful in the spins and whirls, a strong stomach is necessary, otherwise dizziness is sure to follow. When you take into consideration that a skater will make fifteen revolutions on one foot and as many as thirty on two feet, at a very high rate of speed, it is a wonder that they are not seasick.

A successful figure skater must be very strong in the legs to stand the strain of competition. In the contest of 1891 there were four competitors, and it took over six hours to decide it; and of course difficult balances become much harder when the muscles tire. There is one great advantage of figure skating as a sport, and that is age is not a potent factor of success, as past history shows that many of our best-known experts were men well on to middle life.

It certainly is an enemy of dyspepsia and kindred troubles, and is most exhilarating though not the most violent sport known to this country.

The Montreal Gazette announced the formation of a Canadian Skating Association on 1 November 1887.

A CANADIAN ASSOCIATION

The following circular, which has been received, speaks for itself: -

You are hereby notified that a meeting will be held in the Victoria Skating rink, Montreal, on Wednesday, the 16th November next, at 8 o'clock p.m., for the purpose of forming an association to be called the Canadian Amateur Skating Association of Canada. To authorize the holding of championship meetings for speed and fancy skating during the winter. To draw up a universal code of rules and regulations for the governing of such meetings, as well as club meetings. Also for the purpose of furthering the interests of skating in Canada and forming a bond of union among the different skating clubs of the Dominion, and for the election of office bearers for the ensuing year.

F.C. Henshaw,
President Victoria Skating Club.
J.G. Ross,
President Montreal Hockey Club.
J.G. Muir,
President Victoria Hockey Club.
W.T. Virtue,
President Crystal Hockey Club.

The Montreal Gazette also proclaimed the Governor-General's reception for Louis Rubinstein on 23 February 1889, p. 8. Rubinstein, the Canadian figure skating champion since 1883, also won the United States' title in 1888-1889. He held the Canadian title until 1890 and reigned as one of Canada's first sports heroes.

CANADA'S KING OF THE ICE
LOUIS RUBINSTEIN DELIGHTS A DISTINGUISHED PARTY
MONTREAL'S KING OF THE ICE

Ottawa, February 22 - A few days ago Mr. Louis Rubinstein, the celebrated fancy skater, received a telegram from Captain Bagot saying that the Governor-General would be very glad to see him at Government House on Friday. The king of the ice arrived here this morning and had luncheon at Rideau Hall, after which he gave a fancy skating exhibition in the curling rink before Lord and Lady Stanley, Madame Albani, Sir James Grant, Sir George Baden-Powell and others. The skill of the skater delighted the viceregal party and led Mr. Gye to remark to his wife that Mr. Rubinstein could not sing but he could skate, and that she couldn't skate but she could sing, thus establishing as it were an equalization between Canada's championship skater and Canada's champion singer.

SPEED SKATING

Racing on ice skates took place in Holland in the sixteenth century; but the first formal competition occurred in Scotland in 1763, sponsored by the Edinburgh Skating Club. Competition began in other northern European countries a century later. Scottish immigrants brought the practice to America, where the first national championship took place in 1889. An International Skating Union was established in 1892 and world championship races initiated that winter in Amsterdam. Women's competition did not occur until the twentieth century.

The Montreal Gazette provided an account of a local race on 23 February 1889, p. 8.

THE FIVE MILE RACE AT THE DOMINION

As anticipated the race at the Dominion rink last night proved a splendid exhibition of power of endurance and speed. Unhappily Brown, who is training for the ten mile championship which takes place at the same rink on Monday next, did not start, his trainer advising him. The same excuse was made by Gordon ... Little Belleflur who has shown such good form in the late ten mile races during Carnival time, pluckily decided to compete against his two much bigger and renowned opponents though unluckily he fell in almost the start of the race and hurt himself against the rails, which surround the ice, which practically put him out of it. Only the three mentioned started, namely: W. Bellefleur and Wilfrid Latremouille of the Dominion Rink, and E. Irwin of the Victoria Club, and a grand race was the consequence.

The referee, Mr. Carter, got all the men off well together, but at the end of the first lap Bellefleur led with Latremouille next, while Irwin brought up the rear. This order was continued only for a few laps, when both the latter shot ahead and Bellefleur fell; he kept going however, but was too much rattled to keep on long, and he fell out when only half the distance had been covered. The race after this mishap became much quicker. First, Latremouille led, then Irwin got in front, and for four miles it was a see-saw, but after this Latremouille kept thelead no matter how hard Irwin tried to pass ... "Eight laps" shouted the scorers, meaning half the mile ... only eight more laps had to be skated. In the ninth lap Irwin ... Passed Latremouille amidst loud shouts and hur-rahs. Latremouille stuck close ... the speed now was tremendous, almost mile record time, and, although the track was new to Irwin, he kept ahead and stayed there, gradu-ally leaving the bigger man inch by inch only, and won by five yards. It was fine; no better race has ever taken place in Montreal ... The first mile was covered in 3 mins. 52 secs; 2 miles 7 mins. 30 secs; 3 miles, 11 mins; 4 miles, 15 mins. 3 secs; and 5 miles, 18 mins. 30 secs....

Outing congratulated Joseph Donoghue on his European success in February, 1891, p. 109.

SKATING

AMERICA has good reason to be proud of her athletic prowess, for our athletes in all branches have made enviable records. In skating ... they have attained the highest degree of excellence. This sport is practiced much more in countries situated further north than America, yet we are able to excel even the Norwegians at this, their most popular sport. Our American representative, Joseph Donoghue, of Newburgh, N.Y., has been skating in Europe for international honors, and has already suceeded almost be-yond the expectations of his friends. Donoghue issued a challenge to any skater in Norway or Sweden to skate him a 5-mile race, and it was accepted by Frederiksen, the Norwegian champion, and a race arranged for. It took place on December 12, and was easily won by Donoghue, in 16m. 28 3-5 s. At Harenveen, Friesland, on the 17th, he won the amateur mile race for the championship of Holland, easily defeating Vollmann and Pander, the champions of Friesland and Holland, in 3m. 9 4-5s., and the follow-ing day the 3-mile championship in 9m. 17s., beating the second man by about a minute. On the 24th he suceeded in winning the 1 1/2 mile international race at Lingay Fen, near Cambridge, England, in 4m. 46s., thus breaking the world's record of 4m. 52 1-5s,. made over the same course the day before by Smart, a professional skater.

At the international races at Amsterdam for the world's championship, on January 6 and 7, Donoghue succeeded in winning all four of the events. This is the most successful piece of skating on record. There has been a handsome cup offered for several years to the skater who would win three out of four, but it has never been won, and this year was withdrawn. Donoghue's time in each of the four championship events was as follows: The half mile in 1 minute and 25 seconds; the 2 miles in 6 minutes 10 4-5 seconds; the mile in 3 minutes and 2-5 of a second, and the 5 miles in 16 minutes 2 1-5 seconds. We congratulate Mr. Joseph Donoghue on his signal success!

John Johnson replaced Donoghue as the North American champion from 1893-1895. His 1894 title win is reprinted from the Chicago Tribune, 4 February 1894, p. 7.

JOHNSON HAS ALL THE BEST OF IT
THE MINNEAPOLIS SKATER WINS NEARLY ALL THE EVENTS AT MONTREAL.

MONTREAL, Que., Feb. 3. - The annual meet of the Canadian Amateur Skating Association, which took place this afternoon, was one of the greatest events of its kind ever witnessed in America. Nearly all of the great skaters in the world, including Joe Donoghue of Newburgh, N.Y., J.S. Johnson of Minneapolis, Norseng, the Norwwegian champion, Harry Davidson of St. Paul, Hulse of Toronto, and McCulloch of Winnipeg participated. Nearly 7,000 spectators were present. The ice was in splendid condition, and the general opinion expressed by all of the competitors was that the condition of the Montreal rinks should make this city the general skating center of the continent. The contestants did not seem to go in for record breaking, and the only record lowered was that of 220 yards, which was reduced by Johnson from 21 3-5 seconds to 20 seconds. The first race was 220 yards. Three trial heats were won by Davidson, Johnson, and Joe Donoghue. In the final heat Johnson got the start and kept the lead until the finish, although he was closely followed by Joe Donoghue. The half-mile was a pretty race. Johnson, Joe Donoghue, and Davidson were the starters in the final heat. Johnson again showed his marvelous powers and took the lead easily from the first. Donoghue made a determined effort to overtake him, but Johnson increased his speed and won easily in 1:31. In the one-mile race Johnson, Joe Donoghue, James Donoghue, Norseng, Davidson, McCulloch, and Hulse started. Norseng took the lead, followed by Johnson and McCulloch, with others behind. This order was kept up until the first lap, when Johnson amd Donoghue made a spurt and passed the others easily. Johnson again proved superior to Donoghue and passed the finish first, with Donoghue a good second. Time, 3:03. McCulloch made a plucky race. The five-mile race was the most exciting event of the day. Johson, Norseng, McCulloch, Joe Donoghue, and James Donoghue started. On the first lap Johnson took the lead, but evidently not preferring to face the wind for twenty laps, fell behind. In the second lap Norseng took the lead, followed by Johnson, McCulloch, and Joe Donoghue and Jim Donoghue. This order was maintained until the last lap. Norseng made a great effort to maintain his lead, but it was soon evident that he was not in it with either the Americans or the Canadians. Johnson and Joe Donoghue both passed him with a lightning gait and made for the finish almost neck and neck, with McCulloch close on their heels. They had almost reached the goal, Donoghue was increasing his speed, when Johnson, to the consternation of every one, fell within a few feet of the finish line. His body slid partly over the line, but both Donoghue and McCulloch had crossed the line and the judges gave them the race. Johnson's mishap was unfortunate, but those on the track generally expressed the opinion that the race in any event would have been Donoghue's, as at the time when Johnson fell Donoghue was passing him. Time, 16:11.

John Nilsson won the continental crown in 1896 and 1897, before turning professional. His subsequent world record performances appeared in the Chicago Tribune on 4 February 1900, p. 17, although his name was misspelled.

TWO NEW WORLD SKATING RECORDS
JOHN NEILSON LOWERS MARK FOR BOTH TWO MILES AND THREE MILES

Montreal, Feb. 3. - There was a large attendance at the Canadian Skating association championship races this afternoon and there was some fast racing. John Neilson of Minneapolis, the world's champion, established new world's records in the two miles and the three miles, professional, and James Drury, Montreal, won the one mile amateur. Summary of events:

220 yards - Frank Robison, Toronto, first; F.D. Gibb, Newburgh, N.Y., second. Time, :21.

One mile, professional - John Neilson, Minneapolis, first; Norval Baptie, Dakota, second. Time, 2:43 3-5.

50 yards, amateur - Robert Sonne, Montreal, first; E.A. Thomas, Newburgh, N.Y., second. Time, 1:25.

One mile, amateur - James Drury, Montreal, first; B. Sponner, Montreal, second; W. Thibeault, Montreal, third. Time, 3:00.

Two mile, professional - John Neilson, Minneapolis, first; Norval Baptie, Dakota, second. Time, 5:33 4-5 (world's record).

Three mile, amateur - E.A. Thomas, Newburgh, N.Y., first; James Drury, Montreal, second. Time, 9:22.

220 yard hurdle - R.T. Halcourt, Montreal, first; F.J. Robison, Toronto, second. Time, :27.

Three miles, professional - John Neilson, first; N. Baptie, second. Time, 8:41 1-5 (world's record).

Five miles, amateur - F.D. Gibb, Newburgh, N.Y., first; E.A. Thomas, Newburgh, N.Y., second; A.E. Pilkie, Montreal, third. Time, 16:17.

SNOWSHOEING AND SKIING

Snowshoeing in North America originated with the native Indian tribes, but Canadian urbanites adopted the pastime by the 1840s. The Montreal Snow Shoe Club was established in 1840, and that city remained the center of the activity over the next fifty years. While hiking with snowshoes, known as tramping, proved a popular social recreation for men throughout the period they also engaged in races, including steeplechases. The number of clubs and gambling on such races greatly increased after 1867. Within another fifteen years clubs spread across Canada, and snowshoeing became a major event on the Montreal Winter Carnival program. That city alone sustained 25 clubs. The exclusively male clubs served as a bastion of power and influence. In 1894 Quebec offered the first Canadian snowshoeing championship, but the sport had already encountered decline due to the widespread interest in ice skating.

Scandinavian immigrants brought skiing to North America, and the activity enjoyed particular favor in the northern states in which they settled. Although largely recreational, skiing served utilitarian and competitive endeavors in California, where mail carriers had to ski to Gold Rush mining camps. Both men and women engaged in competitive downhill racing. By the 1890s immigrant ski clubs began organizing competition in the Midwest. The United States Ski Club organized in 1891 and conducted its first tournament at Ishpeming, Michigan. The Aurora Ski Club of Red Wing, Minnesota used the same site for its ski jumping exhibit the next year.

The snowshoeing records are reprinted from Outing, March 1889, p. 510.

RECORDS OF SNOW-SHOE RACING

... For the various distances these are as follows:

	Min.	Sec.		Min.	Sec.
100 yards,		12	1 mile,	5	42 1/2
220 "		26	2 "	11	52 3/4
440 "	1	08	3 "	20	18 1/2
1/2 mile,	2	33	5 "	33	43

Mount Royal Steeplechase, distance about 2 miles, 500 yards, 17m. 20s.

The last record, as well as the others, is held by Mr. James G. Ross, perhaps the fastest all-round amateur who ever buckled on the "raquette."

It is not an uncommon thing, however, for clubs to traverse thirty, and even eighty, miles across country in a tramp. A tramp from Montreal to St. John's is a regular annual event with the Tuque Bleues....

The constitution and by-laws of the Aurora Ski Club of Red Wing, Minnesota, established in 1886, provides the organizational structure and workings of such groups.

1886
CONSTITUTION & BY LAWS OF AURORA SKI CLUB OF RED WING

I.
The name of the society shall be Aurora Ski Club of Red Wing; and to be to foster outdoor winter sport and especially the running on "Skis"
II.
The uniforms of the society shall consist of a red cap a white blouse blue knee breeches & red stockings and a blue belt.
III.
The officers of the society shall be a President Vice President Secretary Treasurer Captain & Lieutenant to be elected for the term of one year on the first Monday in January in each year -and which officers shall be Scandinavians or of Scan. descent and elected by balot.
IV.
The President shall at the beginning of each year appoint an executive Committee consisting of 5 members of the society together with the President and the Secretary thereof
V.
The President shall preside at all business meetings of the society and call extra meetings at the request of the executive Committee or 10 members of the society. In the absence of the President the Vice President shall perform the duties of the President.
VI.
The duties of the Secretary shall be to keep true and correct minutes of all the proceedings of said society and perform the necessary correspondence of the same.
VII.
The Treasurer shall receive and safely keep all money received on subscription dues and fees and pay all orders signed by the President and countersigned by the Secretary and also render an authorized account of all receipts and disbursements and submit the same to the society at its annual meeting each year.
VIII.
The Executive Committee shall have control of all the business of the society and shall have power to examine and decide all controversies that may arise within the same this

committee shall hold meetings as often as the business of the society may require it, the meetings to be called by the President.

IX.

At any regular or special meeting of this society ten members shall constitute a quorum.

X.

The order of business shall be
1. Reading Minuters
2. Roll call
3. Reception of new members
4. Report of committees
5. Miscellaneous and unfinished business

XI.

The membership shall be $1.00 for every person over 18 years and 50 cents under 18 years and annual dues of 50 cents per year which fee and annual dues shall accompany the application for admission. A Two thirds vote shall be required to admit new members.

XII.

The Captain or in his absence the Lieutenant may call the members together for drill and practice in Ski running.

XIII.

Members who fail to pay their annual dues shall after notification be dropped from the list of membership.

An Outing article, February, 1893, pp. 339-346, described the formation of a national association and its competitive tournaments.

SKI RUNNING

... It would be hard to say how far back we should look in history to find the first ski. Ski-running has been hundreds of years a sport, and longer still a means of locomotion. It is the national sport of both Norway and Sweden, though the particular home of ski-running is Thelemarken, a district or province in Norway, located about midway between the North Sea and the Baltic, the people of which are humble but very intelligent. From this mountainous district have come the most famous runners in the games at Christiana.

From the land of the North the Norsemen have brought to America the customs of their native home, amalgamating in customs and merging in habits as the years go by, but still preserving many of their distinctive national characteristics. When the earlier Norsemen came America-ward ... they brought with them a strong love for their national sport. But it was not until a single decade or so ago that any concerted action was taken toward preserving the sport among the sons of Scandinavia and popularizing it among the Americans.

The material necessary for ski-running is very simple, very durable, very inexpensive. The runners are plain affairs of hard pine or ash - pine generally, the springy, hard-fibered Norway pine making the best, though there is a kind of oak which gives smoothness and strength combined with the needful elasticity. The runners are from six to eight feet in length for adults, those of men being a little longer and wider than those used by women; for both sexes can and do use the skis.

There is a shallow groove in the middle of the ski, about an eighth of an inch deep and a half inch wide. This prevents slipping. Over the ski midway is a strap or laced thong, of rawhide in some cases; a strong withe made of some flexible twig or branch answers the purpose. It comes over the ball of the foot, and in most cases is the only fastening. Some runners prefer, in addition to this, a strap bound around the heel. This is found to be a rather dangerous thing, as there are cases where a runner's ankle has been broken by not being able to extricate his foot when thrown. The ski turns up slightly at the forward end. The propelling and steering stick, or "stav," as the Scandinavians call it, is of strong wood sharpened at one end. About six inches from the sharpened end in many cases there is a ball, so to call it, which keeps the stav from penetrating the snow too far.

The costume is as elaborate and expensive or modest as the wearer may wish. It is very similar to the costume worn by snowshoers of America and Canada. There is a long coat or frock reaching midwat to the knees, belted in at the waist. The feet are clad in whatever the wearer chooses, warmth without clumsiness being the essential. There are knee-breeches and high, coarse woolen stockings. The toque in this country is often similar to those of the tobogganers and snow-shoers: a close-fitting, knit visorless cap with long end and tassel - identical in shape with the Norwegian caps that mark the Southland fishermen. In color there is infinite variety ...

Ski-running may be roughly divided into two classes: First, that which is in a sense commercial - the using of the skis as a means of locomotion in portions of the country and at periods of the year when it is impossible to travel otherwise; second, that which pertains to the sport alone....

In a strict commercial sense, the ski has entered the new world, and several years ago the pioneer mail carrier in the fastnesses of the Rocky Mountains might occasionally be seen going his perilous journey on the safe, sure skis....

Those who are obliged to make long journeys on their skis through sparsely settled regions where food stations are far apart and lodging-houses unheard of luxuries, carry with them what are known as sleeping-bags. They are made of thick-furred skins, large enough to encase the whole body. Overtaken by night or storm, the ski-runner pulls on his sleeping-bag, draws in the head-part until he has just a breathing space, and sleeps snug in his warm nest ...

The second class of ski-runners, those who engage in the sport for the sake of the sport, are very numerous in Scandinavia. They are also rapidly growing in the northland region of America.

In the autumn of 1881 Mr. Carl Ilstrup, a prominent young Scandinavian interested in athletic sports, organized the first ski club in America. Mr. Ilstrup became the first

president of the club. It is called The Minnesota Ski Club," and has been in continuous organization since it was founded. It numbers about eighty members, all of whom
are enthusiasts. To Mr. Ilstrup it may be said, however, without any disparagement of
the efforts of others, belongs most credit fore the preservation and propagation of the
sport. He has worked hard to excite and maintain interest not only among his own
countrymen, but among Americans.

The sport has spread to other towns and cities in the Northwest, and there are now
clubs in St. Paul, Minn.; Stillwater, Minn.; Albert Lea, Minn.; Hudson, Wis.; Eau
Claire, Wis.; Red Wing, Minn.; Ishpeming, Mich., and at various other Northwestern
points. Two years ago it was decided to organize a national association. It was formed
in Minneapolis, and Mr. Ilstrup became its first president. It is called "The Ski Association of the Northwest." The officers of the association now are:

President, C.H. Boxrud, Red Wing, Minn.; vice-president, C.A. Dahl, Eau Claire,
Wis.; secretary and treasurer, Charles O. Huntress, Minneapolis.

Executive Committee: A. Backe, Stillwater, Minn.; John Nelson, Red Wing, Minn.;
Andrew Steraas, Eau Claire, Wis.; Christian Ilstrup, Minneapolis; Nels Clifton,
Ishpeming, Mich.

Tourneys are held at each national meeting. Sometimes the snow fails at the appointed
time, but a Northwest winter can generally be depended upon.... The winter of 1890-91
proved too warm in the Northwest for much active work by the national association....

There are two main events on the card for every ski tourney: the jump and the
long-distance run. This long-distance run is most interesting. An irregular course is
laid out for a given distance, say two or three miles, the more irregular and broken
the country the better. Each runner who enters in any one of the various classes
makes the long-distance run and awaits his competitors. Wonderful speed is shown.
Mikkel Hemmestvedt, the champion of Norway and America, in a long-distance run
covered eight English miles in 54m. 2s., while his brother, Torjus, covered the same
distance in 56m.

It being very hard to ascend a hill on skis until one has had the requisite training,
these long-distance runs include in their course as many steep hills as the topography
of the country will pemit. The practiced skiman shows great skill in going up these
hills; during part of the course tacking back and forth, like a yacht beating to windward.
Sometimes it is so arranged that the long-distance run includes a leap from the precipice with its attendant run, the runner continuing on his course after landing.

In the tournament other events are sometimes introduced. Two skimen will make
a given distance on one pair of skis, the one being directly behind the other. This, of
course, will be in competition with two others. Again, a course will be laid out down
a steep hill, where a man will traverse the distance against time, balancing himself most
deftly upon a single runner and traveling at a terrific pace. In deciding merit in jumping
competitions the skiman is credited not only on the distance he jumps but upon his
carriage, his tokens of daring, his appearance as he leaves the precipice, as he passes
swiftly through the air, and as he alights at the landing. The landing is upon an incline,
so that when the jumper touches the snow he may not receive the terrible jar which
would surely come to him if he struck upon a level surface.

Throughout the Northwest, while there are many hills, there are no mountains, so
that it becomes necessary at most tournaments to build a slide, a framework of stout

timbers projecting into the air far above the summit of the hill. This is coated with snow, thereby adding materially to the swiftness of the descent. Each contestant has three trials at the jump. The judges mark the contestant on these three jumps, the one having the highest average on thre distance jumped and on the character and the style shown while on his course being awarded the first place.

In a general way there are three classes for contestants. The first classs is fore the best of experts - all those who have won either first or second prizes at two tourneys; the second for all others who have reached mature years, and a third class composed of boys. Occasionally there will be a class devoted entirely to ladies, who frequently attain great proficiency. Each local ski association adopts its own rules, selects its own prizes, and while acting under the general rules of the national organization, forms particular rules to suit itself. The prizes given are usually in the form of medals, sometimes in money. The medals, as in most American sports, are held from year to year, until, after so many seasons holding, they become the property of the successful competitor.

When a man makes the long jump when competing with others in the tourney, he must alight on his feet and keep his feet until he reaches the bottom of the declivity. If he trips or falls it is marked against him. On the other hand, when the competitor is jumping against space, the distance to be jumped is the main thing - it makes no difference whether the jumper alights on his head or his feet. The unskillful skiman is likely to cut a most grotesque figure both in passing through the air and landing at the end of the jump, where his long skis are most curiously entangled with his legs, the man himself being buried in a mass of flying snow.

Another very interesting event in some tourneys is arranged in this manner: The steepest hill in the locality is selected, at the base of which the contestants and the crowd arrange themselves. The runner starts up the hill at a pace which is simply marvelous, when the angle of the declivity is taken into consideration, and as he goes, he throws off first his toque, then his toga or jacket, then his vest, then, mayhap his mittens, a pocket handkerchief, or any other article of light wearing apparel which he may have about him. This, of course, is all done while he is under swift motion. Turning at the crest of the hill, he sees far below, mayhap a half mile distant, his admiring friends and competitors. Swift as an eagle he starts on his downward course, his speed accelerating with every rod he travels. While going at this wonderful pace he must stoop down as he reaches each article of wearing apparel, snatch it from the snow, put it on, and arrive at the bottom as completely clad and equipped as when he started.

It is quite possible for a ski-runner on an ordinary trip to take a fair companion on his skis for a course up or down a hill. Many clubs are composed of both ladies and gentlemen, and pleasant jaunts are made through the country in threes and fours or it, may be with a score or two in the company.

In ski-running probably greater interest centers in the high jumping ... than any other one department of this splendid sport. It needs trained feet and a trained eye, care and experience and caution and, above all, nerve to be a successful jumper. Mounted upon the long, narrow pinewood skis, the runner pauses at the top of a high hill. His muscular form is sharply drawn upon the blue background of the sky. He poises himself, gives mayhap another tug at the fastenings of his slender runners. He is off down the hill at a terrific pace. Midway in the hill an embankment has been made, a snow-covered platform, which juts out from the hillside and forms the precipice from which he is to make the leap. Just as he reaches the brink he crouches low, holds his "stav" before him in two clenched hands and springs, bent, into the air, the marked curve he gives to his course propelling him all the further on his way. Quickly the resisting air must part before his great momentum - keen, wintry air that thrills like tingling wine....

There have been many famous recorded jumps, too, over seas, made by those who have contested for prizes in the great tournaments of Norway and Sweden; but it has remained for the American-Norwegian, Mikkel Hemmestvedt, a Thelemarken man, to break all official records by leaping, at the Red Wing, Minn., tourney, in 1890, a sheer 102 feet from precipice to landing. Mr. Hemmestvedt also holds the championship of Norway.

But fascinating and exhilarating as the jump is, it by no means comprises all there is in this remarkable sport.

The runs in the Northwest are seldom so long from start to precipice, as in Norway or Sweden, though here they give ample opportunity for acquiring great speed....

A word in closing about America's greatest ski-runner, Mikkel Hemmestvedt, who is now the champion of Norway and America. He was born in 1863, on a farm in Upper Thelemarken, Norway, and he lives at present in the little city of Red Wing, Minn., where he, with his brother Torjus, is engaged as a woodcarver. Torjus is also a remarkably fine skiman. Mikkel has been a ski-runner ever since he was old enough to mount a pair of the slender runners. In the local runs for boys in his native town he invariably carried off first honors. In 1881, at the age of eighteen, he took part in the great national tournament at Christiana, in company with his brother Torjus. The latter took the King's special prize, while Mikkel carried off the special prize of the Queen. Each received in addition to this a liberal purse. Mikkel took the King's prize in 1883, in 1885, and still again in 1886. On this last occasion he was awarded a magnificent gold medal. In the year 1885 Mikkel and his brother Torjus were participants in the national ski contest in Christiana. At this time they performed one of the most difficult as well as beautiful feats known to ski tourneys. Hand in hand from the top of the great hill they came with lightninglike velocity, their momentum increasing every second until at last they reached the precipice where, still hand in hand, they made a magnificent leap into the air, jumping a sheer sixty-five feet and striking the landing below without once breaking their hand-clasp.

In the spring of 1886 Mikkel came to America. He took part in the ski tournament held in connection with the ice-palace festivities held in St. Paul in 1887, his first appearance in this country, where he carried off first prize. Since then, in the different ski tournaments held throughout the Northwest, he has won eleven first and special prizes. On the 9th day of March, 1890, Mikkel was a contestant at Red Wing, Minn., for the local club's medal. In his third and last run he made the great effort of his life, a jump of 102 feet by actual measurement.

SELECTED BIBLIOGRAPHY

PRIMARY SOURCES

MANUSCRIPT COLLECTIONS

Allegheny Athletic Association, Ledger, Pro Football Hall of Fame, Canton, Ohio.

Aurora Ski Club, Constitution and By-laws, Minnesota Historical Society.

Senda Berenson Papers, Smith College Archives.

Chicago Golf Club, Charter, Constituion and By-laws, Chicago Historical Society.

Richard Dott Papers, University of Michigan Archives.

Montreal Amateur Athletic Union, Records, Meeting Minutes, Yearbooks, National Archives of Canada.

Neighborhood History Collection, Club records, game accounts, Harold Washington Library, Chicago.

Washington Park Club, Rules, Booklet, Programs, Yearbooks, Manuscript, Chicago Historical Society.

Works Progress Administration, Foreign Language Press Survey, University of Chicago and Harold Washington Library, Chicago.

University of California, Berkeley, Archives, Track team accounts.

Josephine Wilkin Papers, Smith College Archives.

NEWSPAPERS AND MAGAZINES

American Bicycler, 1880.

American Journal of Social Science, 1884.

Andover Review, 1888.

Atlanta Constitution (1895).

Atlantic Monthly, 1889-1890.

Bicycling World, 1880.

Boston Globe (1880, 1883, 1894).

Brooklyn Eagle (1892).

Century, 1887, 1890, 1894, 1896-1897.

Chautaquan, 1888.

Cheyenne Daily Sun-Leader (1897).

Cheyenne Leader (1900).

Chicago Times-Herald (1895).

Chicago Tribune (1880-1900).

Clark's Horse Review, 1892.

Cosmopolitan, 1888-1889.

Dziennik Chicagoski (1890, 1896-1897).

Education, 1892.

Fortnightly Review, 1894.

Forum, 1896.

Harper's Weekly, 1883, 1887, 1889-1897.

High School Journal, 1888, 1890-1891.

High School Weekly (1893).

Horse Review, 1896.

Knowledge, 1887.

Lippincott's, 1886-1887, 1892.

Louisville Courier-Journal (1891).

Medill High School Echo, Chicago (1897-1898).

Mind and Body, 1900.

Montreal Gazette (1883-1884, 1887, 1889, 1892, 1894, 1897, 1899).

New England Magazine, 1890.

New Orleans Times-Democrat (1892).

New York Herald Tribune (1893).

New York Times (1889-1893, 1895, 1897, 1899-1900).

North American Review, 1891, 1895.

Outing, 1884-1896.

Outlook, 1893, 1895-1897, 1899.

Overland Monthly, 1891-1892.

Popular Science Monthly, 1888, 1894, 1897.

Review of Reviews, 1890.

Saturday Review, 1882.

Science, 1899.

Scientific American, 1891-1893, 1895-1897, 1899-1900.

Scribner's Magazine, 1889, 1891.

Sewanee Review, 1897.

Sporting and Theatrical Journal (1884-1885, 1887).

Sporting Life (1882-1883).

Sporting News (1886).

Svornost (1883-1884, 1890-1892).

The Canadian Magazine, 1896.

The Horseman, 1892.

The Nation, 1890, 1892-1894.

Toronto Globe (1895, 1897).

Zgoda (1892-1893).

BOOKS AND GENERAL WORKS
Athletic Sports (New York, 1897).

Elizabeth C. Barney, "The True American Sportswoman," *Fortnightly Review* (August 1894), 263-277.

E.L. Godkin, "The Glorification of Athletes," *The Nation* (1 December 1892), 406-407.

A.B. Hart, "The Status of Athletics in American Colleges," *Atlantic Monthly* (July 1890), 63-71.

Sophia Foster Richardson, "Tendencies in Athletics for Women in Colleges and Universities," *Popular Science Monthly* (February 1897), 517-526.

N.S. Shaler, "The Amateur Problem in Education," *Atlantic Monthly* (January 1889), 79-88.

AQUATIC SPORTS
W.A. Brooks, "Winter Work of the Harvard Crew," *Harper's Weekly* (4 March 1893), 213.

Edwards Roberts, "Yachts and Yacht Clubs of California," *Outing* (April 1896), 16-21.

Caspar Whitney, "Harvard-Yale Boat Race," *Harper's Weekly* (2 July 1892), 634-635, and by the same author, "Annual Meet of the American Canoe Club," *Harper's Weekly* (3 September 1893), 849.

Charles G. Yale, "Yachting in California," *Overland Monthly* (June 1891), 561-583.

BASEBALL
Walter Camp, "Baseball for the Spectator," *Outing*, 16 (1890), 831.

Henry Chadwick, "Art of Pitching. New Rules for 1889," *Outing* (May 1889), 119-121.

Richard Dott Papers, University of Michigan, 1882 baseball tour.

Joe J. Ellick, "Experiences of a Baseball Umpire," *Lippincott's*, 38 (1886), 444-448.

W.F. Hopkinson, "The Theory of the Curve Ball," *Outing* (May 1887), 98.

J.A. Tyng, "The Evolution of the Amateur Pitcher," *Harper's Weekly* (11 May 1895), 444-446.

J.M. Ward, "Base-ball Player. Is he a Chattel?," *Lippincott's* (August 1887), 310-319.

R.W. Wood, "Demonstrating the Curve of the Baseball in the Classroom," *Science* (8 December 1899), 851.

BASKETBALL
James Naismith, *Basket Ball for 1893.*

Elizbeth F. Read, "Basketball at Smith College," *Outlook* (26 September 1896), 557-558.

Smith College Monthly (April 1894).

BICYCLING
A.L. Benedict, "Dangers and Benefits of the Bicycle," *Century* (July 1897), 471-473.

Chicago Cycler's Guide, 1893.

R.L. Dickinson, "Bicycling for Women. The Puzzling Question of Costume," *Outlook* (25 April 1896), 751-752.

Henry J. Garrigues, "Women and the Bicycle," *Forum* (January 1896), 177-186.

George D. Gideon, "A Defence of the Two Class System in Bicycle Racing," *Harper's Weekly* (23 March 1896), 286.

Hermes Bicycle Club, *By-Laws* (Chicago, 1883).

Edward Howland, "A Bicycle Era," *Harper's Monthly*, 63, 281-286.

P.H. Jacobsen, "The Detroit Wheelmen," *Outing* (July 1891), 355-341.

Marguerite Merington, "Women and the Bicycle," in *Athletic Sports*, 209-218.

Albert Mott, "The Racing Side of Bicycling," *Harper's Weekly* (11 April 1896), 366.

Charles E. Pratt, *The American Bicycler. A Manual for the Observer, the Learner, and the Expert* (Boston, 1880), and by the same author,"Legislation as to Bicycles in Highways," *Outing* (May 1887), 157-161.

Dr. B.W. Richardson, "How Cycling Injures Health," *Review of Reviews* (April 1890), 287-288.

Benjamin W. Richardson, "What to Avoid in Cycling," *North American Review* (August 1895), 177-186.

J. West Roosevelt, "A Doctor's View of Bicycling," in *Athletic Sports*, 221-233.

Minna Caroline Smith, "The Tricycle for American Women," *Outing* (March 1885), 423-426.

BOWLING

American Bowling Congress, *Constitution, By-Laws, Rules and Regulations* (Chicago, 1903).

John G. Hemmer and W.J. Kenna, eds., *The Western Bowlers' Journal Bowling Encyclopedia. A History of Bowling* (Chicago, 1904).

J.B. Paret, "Bowling for Spares," *Outing* (December 1890), 233.

Augustus E. Vogell, "Form in Bowling," *Harper's Weekly* (25 March 1893), 291.

EQUESTRIANISM

Francis Trevelyan, "The American Turf. The Race-Courses of the East," *Outing* (May 1892), 129-131.

Caspar Whitney, "Polo in America," *Harper's Weekly* (1 August 1891), 569-572, 582.

FOOTBALL

Walter Camp, "The Game and Laws of American Football," *Outing* (October 1887), 68-76, and by the same author, "Detail of a Defensive Play," *Outing* (December 1890), 209-211; "Interference in Football," *Harper's Weekly* (19 November 1892), 1115; "Football of 1893. Its Lessons and Results," *Harper's Weekly* (3 February 1894),

117-118; The New Rules and the Forwards," *Harper's Weekly* (3 November 1894), 1053-1054; *Football Facts and Figures* (New York, 1894).

Alexander Johnston, "The American Game of Football," *Century*, 12 (1887), 888-898.

Spalding Guide, 1894.

Spalding's Official Football Guide, 1895.

GOLF

Chicago Golf Club, *Charter and By-Laws*, 1909.

James P. Lee, *Golf in America* (New York, 1895).

H.J. Whigham, *How to Play Golf* (Chicago, 1897).

GYMNASTICS

Isabel Barrows, ed., *Physical Training, A Full Report of the Papers and Discussions of the Conference Held in Boston in November, 1889* (Boston, 1890).

Edward Hitchcock, "The Gymnastic Era and the Athletic Era of Our Country," *Outlook* (18 May 1895), 816-818.

Hartvig Nissen, "Gymnastic Systems," *Education*, 13 (November 1892), 150-159.

RACKET SPORTS

James Dwight, "Form in Lawn Tennis," *Scribner's Magazine* (August 1889), 131-144.

Idem., "Court Tennis," *Scribner's Magazine* (January 1891), 99-106.

R.B. Metcalf, "About Tennis," *Outing* (November 1884), 104-106.

Richard Sears, "Drive Stroke," *Outing* (September 1885), 757.

C.R. Yates, "Lawn Tennis on the Pacific Coast," *Outing* (July 1890), 271-279.

TRACK AND FIELD

E.H. Baynes, "The History of Cross Country Running in America," *Outing* (March 1894), 484-490.

John Corbin, "Foot Racing," *Outing* (December 1893), 220-224.

Malcolm Ford, "Hop, Step, and Jump," *Harper's Weekly* (14 March 1891), 19, and by the same author, "Sprinters," *Outing* (May 1891), 83-89; "Distance Running," *Outing* (June 1891), 205-210; "Hurdling," *Outing* (July 1891), 322-329; "Running High Jumping," *Outing* (August 1891), 371-375; "Pole Vaulting," *Outing* (April 1892), 42-48; "Shot-Putting," *Outing* (July 1892), 280-287.

Philip Weaver, "Track Athletics in California," *Overland Monthly* (June 1892), 609-624

WINTER SPORTS

James C. Allen, "Snowshoeing in Canuckia," *Outing* (March 1889), 505-510.

John C. Martin, "Snow Shoeing in Canada," *Outing* (February 1885), 373-376.

C. Bowyer Vaux, "Figure Skating," *Outing* (January 1890), 250-251.

Caspar Whitney, "Canadian Ice Carnival," *Harper's Weekly* (10 February 1894), 126-127.

SECONDARY SOURCES

GENERAL WORKS

R. Brasch, *How Did Sports Begin?* (New York, 1974).

John Durant and Otto Bettmann, *Pictorial History of American Sports* (New York, 1952).

Elliott J. Gorn and Warren Goldstein, *A Brief History of American Sports* (New York, 1993).

Kathryn Grover, ed., *Hard at Play. Leisure in America*, 1840-1940 (Amherst, 1992).

Ralph Hickok, *The Encyclopedia of North American Sports* (New York, 1992).

Robert J. Higgs, *Sports. A Reference Guide* (Westport, Conn., 1982).

James Mangan and Roberta Park, eds., *From Fair Sex to Feminism* (Totowa, N.J., 1987).

J.A. Mangan and James Walvin, eds., *Manliness and Morality. Middle Class Masculinity in Britain and America, 1880-1940* (New York, 1987).

Alan Metcalfe, *Canada Learns to Play* (Toronto, 1987).

Don Morrow et. al., *A Concise History of Sport in Canada* (Toronto, 1989).

Donald J. Mrozek, *Sport and American Mentality, 1880-1910* (Knoxville, 1983).

Benjamin G. Rader, *American Sports. From the Age of Folk Games to the Age of Spectators* (Englewood Cliffs, N.J., 1983).

Steven A. Riess, *City Games. The Evolution of American Urban Society and the Rise of Sports* (Urbana, 1989).

Ronald A. Smith, *Sports and Freedom. The Rise of Big-Time College Athletics* (New York, 1988).

J.E. Sullivan, "The Growth of American Athletics," *Spalding Guide, 1908*, 60-72.

Roy Winnick, ed., *ABC Sports Complete Book of Sportsfests* (Princeton, 1981).

Larzer Ziff, *The American 1890s. Life and Times of a Lost Generation* (New York, 1966).

AUTOMOBILE RACING

Albert R. Bochroch, *American Automobile Racing. An Illustrated History* (New York, 1974).

BASEBALL

Nancy B. Bouchier and Robert Knight Barney, "A Critical Examination of a Source on Early Ontario Baseball. The Reminiscence of Adam E. Ford," *Journal of Sport History*, 15:1 (Spring 1988), 75-87.

Bill James, *Bill James' Historical Baseball Abstract* (New York, 1986).

Peter Levine, *A.G. Spalding and the Rise of Baseball. The Promise of American Sport*

Daniel M. Pearson, *Baseball in 1889. Players vs. Owners* (Bowling Green, Ohio, 1993).

Robert Peterson, *Only the Ball Was White* (New York, 1984).

Harold Seymour, *Baseball. The Early Years* (New York, 1960), and by the same author, *Baseball. The People's Game* (New York, 1990).

David Q. Voigt, *American Baseball. From Gentleman's Sport to the Commissioner System* (Norman, Okla., 1966).

BASKETBALL

Joan Hult and Marianna Trekell, eds., *A Century of Women's Basketball. From Frailty to Final Four* (Reston, Va., 1991).

Robert W. Peterson, *Cages to Jump Shots. Pro Basketball's Early Years* (New York, 1990).

BICYCLING

Richard Hammond, "Progress and Flight. An Interpretation of the American Cycle Craze of the 1890s," *Journal of Social History*, 5 (Winter 1971), 235-257.

Robert Smith, *A Social History of the Bicycle* (New York, 1972).

Marshall W. Taylor, *The Fastest Bicycle Rider in the World* (Brattleboro, Vt., 1972, reprint).

BOWLING

American Bowling Congress, *First Fifty Years, 1895-1945* (n.p., 1945).

BOXING

Michael T. Isenberg, *John L. Sullivan and His America* (Urbana, 1988).

Jeffrey T. Sammons, *Beyond the Ring. The Role of Boxing in American Society* (Urbana, 1988).

EQUESTRIANISM

Mary Lou LeCompte, *Cowgirls of the Rodeo. Pioneer Professional Athletes* (Urbana, 1993).

Philip A. Pines, *The Complete Book of Harness Racing* (New York, 1982).

FOOTBALL

Thomas Bergin, *The Game. The Harvard-Yale Football Rivalry, 1875-1983* (New Haven, 1984).

Bob Braunwart and Bob Carroll, *The Alphabet Wars. The Birth of Professional Football* (n.p., 1981).

Walter Camp, *The Book of Football* (New York, 1910).

Walter Camp, *The Book of Football* (New York, 1910).

Richard M. Cohen et. al., *The Scrapbook History of Pro Football* (Indianapolis, 1977).

Parke H. Davis, *Football. The American Intercollegiate Game* (New York, 1911).

J. Thomas Jable, "The Birth of Professional Football. Pittsburgh Athletic Clubs Ring in Professionals in 1892," *Western Pennsylvania Historical Magazine*, 62 (April 1979), 131-147.

J. Hammond Moore, "Football's Ugly Decades, 1893-1913," *Smithsonian Journal of History* (Fall 1967), 49-68.

Ronald A. Smith, *Sports and Freedom. The Rise of Big-Time College Athletics* (New York, 1988).

Alexander M. Weyand, *The Saga of American Football* (New York, 1955).

GOLF

Editors of Golf Magazine, *America's Golf Book* (New York, 1970).

GYMNASTICS

Jarka Jelinek and Jaroslav Zmrhal, *Sokol Educational and Physical Culture Association* (Chicago, 1944).

Henry Metzner, *History of the American Turners*, revised ed. (Louisville, 1989).

RACKET SPORTS

John W. Reznick, ed., *Championship Handball* (West Point, N.Y., 1976).

TRACK AND FIELD

Gerald Redmond, *The Caledonian Games in Nineteenth Century America* (Cranbury, N.J., 1976).

WINTER SPORTS

E. John B. Allen, *From Skisport to Skiing. One Hundred Years of an American Sport, 1840-1940* (Amherst, 1993).

Alan Metcalfe, "Power. A Case Study of the Ontario Hockey Association, 1890-1936," *Journal of Sport History,* 19:1 (Spring 1992), 5-25.

Don Morrow, "The Knights of the Snowshoe. A Study of the Evolution of Sport in Nineteenth Century Montreal," *Journal of Sport History*, 15:1 (Spring 1988), 5-40.

INDEXES

INDEX OF NAMES

INDEX OF SUBJECTS

INDEX OF INSTITUTIONS

INDEX OF GEOGRAPHIC AND PLACE NAMES

FROM ACADEMIC INTERNATIONAL PRESS*

THE RUSSIAN SERIES Volumes in Print

2   **The Nicky-Sunny Letters, Correspondence of Nicholas and Alexandra, 1914-1917**

7   Robert J. Kerner **Bohemia in the Eighteenth Century**

14 A. Leroy-Beaulieu **Un Homme d'Etat Russe (Nicholas Miliutine)...**

15 Nicolas Berdyaev **Leontiev** (In English)

17 **Tehran Yalta Potsdam. The Soviet Protocols**

18 **The Chronicle of Novgorod**

19 Paul N. Miliukov **Outlines of Russian Culture Vol. III** Pt. 1. The Origins of Ideology

20 P.A. Zaionchkovskii **The Abolition of Serfdom in Russia**

21 V.V. Vinogradov **Russkii iazyk. Grammaticheskoe uchenie o slove**

22 P.A. Zaionchkovsky **The Russian Autocracy under Alexander III**

23 A.E. Presniakov **Emperor Nicholas I of Russia. The Apogee of Autocracy**

25 S.S. Oldenburg **Last Tsar! Nicholas II, His Reign and His Russia** (OP)

28 S.F. Platonov **Ivan the Terrible** Paper

30 A.E. Presniakov **The Tsardom of Muscovy**

32 R.G. Skrynnikov **Ivan the Terrible**

33 P.A. Zaionchkovsky **The Russian Autocracy in Crisis, 1878-1882**

34 Joseph T. Fuhrmann **Tsar Alexis. His Reign and His Russia**

36 R.G. Skrynnikov **The Time of Troubles. Russia in Crisis, 1604–1618**

38 V.V. Shulgin **Days of the Russian Revolutions. Memoirs From the Right, 1905–1907.** Cloth and Paper

40 J.L. Black **"Into the Dustbin of History"! The USSR From August Coup to Commonwealth, 1991. A Documentary Narrative**

41 E.V. Anisimov **Empress Elizabeth. Her Reign and Her Russia, 1741–1761**

44 Paul N. Miliukov **The Russian Revolution** 3 vols.

THE CENTRAL AND EAST EUROPEAN SERIES

1   Louis Eisenmann **Le Compromis Austro-Hongrois de 1867**

3   Francis Dvornik **The Making of Central and Eastern Europe** 2nd edition

4   Feodor F. Zigel **Lectures on Slavonic Law**

THE ACADEMIC INTERNATIONAL REFERENCE SERIES

The Modern Encyclopedia of Russian and Soviet History 58 vols.

The Modern Encyclopedia of Russian and Soviet Literatures 50 vols.

The Modern Encyclopedia of Religions in Russia and the Soviet Union 30 vols

Soviet Armed Forces Review Annual

Russia & Eurasia Facts & Figures Annual

Russia & Eurasia Documents Annual

USSR Calendar of Events (1987- 1991) 5 vol. set

USSR Congress of Peoples's Deputies 1989. The Stenographic Record

Documents of Soviet History 12 vols.

Documents of Soviet-American Relations

Gorbachev's Reforms. An Annotated Bibliography of Soviet Writings. Part 1 1985–1987

Military Encyclopedia of Russia and Eurasia 50 vols.

China Facts & Figures Annual

China Documents Annual

Sino-Soviet Documents Annual

Encyclopedia USA. The Encyclopedia of the United States of America Past & Present 50 vols.

Sports Encyclopedia North America 50 vols.

Sports in North America. A Documentary History

Religious Documents North America Annual

The International Military Encyclopedia 50 vols.

SPECIAL WORKS
S.M. Soloviev **History of Russia** 50 vols.
SAFRA Papers 1985-

*Request catalogs